CHRISTOLOGY IN DIALOGUE

CHRISTOLOGY IN DIALOGUE

EDITED BY

ROBERT F. BERKEY

AND

SARAH A. EDWARDS

THE PILGRIM PRESS

CLEVELAND, OHIO

The Pilgrim Press, Cleveland, Ohio 44115
© 1993 by The Pilgrim Press

Unless otherwise noted, biblical quotations are from the New Revised Standard
Version of the Bible, © 1989 by the Division of Christian Education of the National
Council of the Churches of Christ in the U.S.A., or the Revised Standard Version of
the Bible, © 1946, 1952, and 1971 by the Division of Christian Education of the
National Council of the Churches of Christ in the U.S.A., and are used by
permission

98 97 96 95 94 93   5 4 3 2 1

Library of Congress Cataloging-in-Publication Data
Christology in dialogue / [edited by Robert F. Berkey and Sarah A. Edwards].
p. cm.
Includes bibliographical references.
ISBN 0–8298–0956–2
1. Jesus Christ—History of doctrines—Early church, ca. 30–600.
2. Jesus Christ—History of doctrines—20th century.
3. Christianity and culture. 4. Christianity and other religions.
I. Berkey, Robert F.   II. Edwards, Sarah A., 1921–
BT198.C455   1993
232—dc20   92–47004
CIP

CONTENTS

PREFACE

Christology is the study of the meaning of Christ. In these essays the terms "Christology" and "Christological" are used not only in the narrow sense to describe Jesus as the Christ-Messiah, but also in the broadest sense to include the historic roots of messianic thought in Judaism, the age-long hope for a savior in many faiths, and above all to express the mystery and meaning of Jesus Christ as Lord for the Christian community.

Christological interpretations emerge in a constant dialogue between Christian affirmation and the worldviews in which they have taken shape. The purpose of these essays is to offer the reader some windows through which to observe the shaping of this dialogue both in its beginnings and in the contemporary world.

We are delighted and grateful that many distinguished students of the New Testament have graciously contributed to this project. We are likewise gratified to be able to include essays from those whose theological and scholarly interests reside outside of the New Testament, colleagues who have been willing to draw upon the tools and content of their respective disciplines in order to articulate a fuller understanding of New Testament Christology. Finally, we are especially pleased to be able to include comments from those who, while not sharing this Christological faith, have been willing to join us in this dialogue. We trust that the essays collected here will provide readers with new insight into the nature of this central core of Christian faith and guide them into their own dialogue with Christology.

As editors, we would like to thank the staff of The Pilgrim Press, particularly James J. Heaney, Richard E. Brown, Marjorie M. Pon, and David M. Perkins for their patient assistance in the publication of this book.

We would further like to express our appreciation to Harvey K. McArthur for his support and encouragement in the development of this project, and beyond that, for his writings and teaching, which have so profoundly influenced our own understanding of Christology in dialogue. Our affectionate thanks also go to their respective spouses, Carolyn M. Berkey and Robert L. Edwards, for their patience and support across the years and especially in the preparation of this book.

Robert F. Berkey

Sarah A. Edwards

PART ONE

SHAPING THE DIALOGUE

CHAPTER ONE

THE CONTEXT OF THE CURRENT DIALOGUE

ROBERT F. BERKEY

There is no question about the importance of Christological affirmations in the New Testament and their significance for the theological stream that has continued to flow from those twenty-seven books that emerged in late antiquity. Surely no issues of Christian thought have gone through more thorough analyses in this century than the problems pertaining to the New Testament affirmations of the unique, unprecedented, once-for-all character of the person of Jesus, affirmations appropriately designated under the general rubric of Christology. Any pilgrimage into the subject will carry the traveler back through the decades of twentieth-century New Testament criticism, as well as out into the broader fields of contemporary New Testament interpretation.

Raising Christological issues invariably confronts the inquirer with some of the most probing historical and literary questions relating to Christian beginnings and leads with equal deliberation into the complicated and variegated world of Christian theology in all its cultural, social, and ecumenical relationships. The essays in this collection trace Christological affirmations and formulations in that important period during which they were taking shape, both during and immediately following the life, death, and resurrection of Jesus. But of course those Christological formulations did not emerge in a literary and intellectual vacuum, nor were their definitions and implications finalized solely within what were to become the canonical confines of the New Testament. Those who would understand Christology, whether in its historical development or in its contemporary significance, must always be willing—indeed, eager—to stay with that dialogue all the way from the thought world of the first century through the interfacing of Christological claims with the complex theological and secular contexts in which those affirmations are still being hammered out in the contemporary world. This collection can in no way guide the reader through that entire spectrum, but the essays that follow offer some important places to stop and ponder, to reflect and question, and to confront and engage with that stream whose waters began in the early decades of the first century of our common era.

The purpose of this introductory chapter is to set forth in broad terms the general context in which modern New Testament scholars have engaged in their critical and historical dialogue with New Testament Christological claims, and consequently the context in which the historical, exegetical, and interpretative essays in this collection have taken shape. If one were to return to the mainstream of liberal Protestant biblical and theological interpretation existing at the beginning of this century, one might find it difficult to understand how Christology could have survived in serious discussion through this final decade, at least in any form close to its two-nature Chalcedonian dress. Recalling the work of so important a historian/theologian as Adolph von Harnack will be sufficient to recover what was a dominant mood among critical scholars when he gave his now famous lectures in Berlin, published in 1900 under the title *Das Wesen des Christentums*. For Harnack, historical criticism had clearly established a picture of Jesus not so much in transcendent Christological terms but as a kind of spiritual genius: "Jesus is convinced that he knows God in a way in which no one else ever knew him before, and he knows that it is his vocation to communicate that knowledge of God to others by word and deed—and with it the knowledge that men are God's children."[1] One also recalls the statement frequently cited as expressive of Harnack's antiChristological bias: "The Gospel as Jesus proclaimed it has to do with the Father only and not with the Son."[2] Although Harnack eventually credited Paul's theologizing for happily releasing the historic message of Jesus from the limitations of its Jewish setting, he nonetheless saw Christology always as a kind of threat to the "majesty and simplicity of the Gospel," indeed, as a "perverse proceeding to make Christology a fundamental substance of the Gospel."[3]

Harnack's reconstruction of the "essence" of Christianity carried with it the general outlook that "enlightened" theology of the nineteenth century had embraced so enthusiastically, namely, the conviction that the Pauline and subsequent interpretations *about* Jesus, especially as these were eventually defined and articulated in a non-Jewish, Hellenistic environment, distorted the earlier, simpler, and more acceptable (rationally more understandable?) ethical and spiritual *message* of the historical Jesus. In one sense, attempts thus to redefine Christianity in terms of Jesus' own inner spiritual consciousness, historically demonstrated and proven, might well have placed an even stronger emphasis on the *person* of Jesus (Christology?). However, such interpretations *about* the person gave way finally to an emphasis on ethical and spiritual truths generally affirmed and appropriated, while traditional messianic, universal, transcendent, incarnational declarations were either radically redefined or set aside entirely. What was then universalized was the *message* rather than the *person*, all of which served as a fundamental denial of Christology as it had been biblically and then dogmatically defined.

Even a cursory glance at the world of New Testament interpretation makes it clear that the Harnackian model did not prevail and that the more traditional and transcendent Christology did not collapse in the face of historical criticism. When the World Council of Churches was organized in 1948 in Amsterdam, its member churches declared their common acceptance of Jesus as God and Savior. Here were Christian communions, representing in some ways the very fruits of Enlightenment theology, less than half a century removed from Harnack's Berlin lectures, affirming for the twentieth century an explicitly Christological claim that Harnack and those of his persuasion could only have rejected outright. From the vantage point of the last decade of the twentieth century, it is clear that the whole theological climate, Christologically speaking, has undergone dramatic and continuing changes. While Roman Catholic theology never embraced the same radical redefinition that is represented in Harnack's reconstruction of Protestant Christianity's essence, Catholic thought also has experienced a significant revival of Christological interest and affirmation.[4] Diversity continues to dominate exegetical, theological, and dogmatic discussions, whether in Protestant or Catholic circles, but the point to be pondered here is the survival of Christological interest as it has withstood the onslaught of nineteenth-century attempts to spiritualize or ethicize New Testament Christological affirmations.

Das Wesen des Christentums is surely not the context in which Christological discussions now take place. Even as Harnack was addressing his Berlin audience, new Christological breezes were beginning to blow across the field of New Testament investigation and interpretation, although only the most sensitive and well-informed observer might have noticed. What were some of the parameters of this fledgling revolution? To answer that question fully would require a more detailed discussion than can be attempted here, but a few observations about the context in which Christological reflection continues are important.

At the center of this shift away from Harnack's "de-Christologizing" was the dilemma posed by Johannes Weiss in *Die Predigt Jesu vom Reiche Gottes*, a book written in 1892, although only recently made available in English.[5] Weiss's conclusions, later expanded and popularized in the work of Albert Schweitzer,[6] called attention to what was viewed as the somewhat embarrassing result of modern critical and historical analyses of the New Testament, namely, that the figure of Jesus ultimately exposed by critical investigation was an apocalyptic fanatic declaring the end of the age, the beginning of the Kingdom of God. Gone from the Weiss/Schweitzer reconstruction was Harnack's underlying assumption that the Jesus of history must or can by definition be found compatible with Enlightenment spirituality. And while these notions of Weiss and Schweitzer seemed devastating in certain respects, the loss of Harnack's spiritual paradigm had the opposite effect of forcing New Testament critics to turn with renewed vigor to the *person* of Jesus, which from the earliest layers of Christian tradition had occupied the center of all theological/Christological affirmation. In short, although the Weiss/Schweitzer conclusions about the figure of Jesus were destructive of the assumptions imposed by "enlightened" criticism, they also carried the seeds of a revived interest in Christology. Indeed, anyone who read Weiss's *Die Predigt* found ample reason to question the historical validity of Harnack's spiritualized, non-Christological picture of Jesus, and it is that line of questioning that has been pursued with utmost seriousness during the twentieth century.

Other factors began to emerge at the same time. A fundamental and still unanswered question was raised in 1901 with the publication of William Wrede's *Das Messiasgeheimnis in den Evangelien.*[7] Wrede pointedly raised the issue of the "messianic secret" inherent in Mark's reconstruction of the life of Jesus, a motif frequently adhered to in the other Synoptic Gospels as well. That in turn raised again a series of questions about what, if any, Christological affirmations were made by Jesus himself. Martin Kähler's earlier work, *Der sogennante historische Jesus und der geschichtliche biblische Christus*,[8] defined the underlying question of whether the "real" Jesus could be recovered from the Christologically controlled Gospels, a central problem that was to be dealt with by the later form critics.[9] As a result, the assumption that critical investigation could make available an accurate reconstruction of the historical Jesus was beginning to erode dramatically, which redirected attention to the essentially Christological framework and substance of the New Testament.

By the 1920s the entire theological mood was changing as European Protestants in particular were introduced to Karl Barth's "strange new world within the Bible."[10] In that new world we were confronted with Jesus not so much as a spiritual teacher but as the Word made flesh, as revelation and judgment, as reconciliation and salvation. In addition to all this was the form-critical dilemma suggesting that the Gospels themselves were ultimately determined and shaped by that Word of salvation (kerygma). C. H. Dodd's *Apostolic Preaching and Its Development*, published in 1936, made the case for a consistently unified kerygma (Christological raw materials!) running through the entire New Testament: Acts, Gospels, Epistles.[11] Theological and exegetical discussions were adding up to a new and revitalized awareness of the Christological character of the New Testament, and it is within that same strange new world that the contemporary dialogue has developed. Such a climate would have been only vaguely apparent when Harnack was describing his "essence" of Christianity in 1900.

Readers can benefit from the many systematic surveys of recent Christological studies.[12] Here we focus instead on areas that constitute some of the major stress points within the entire range of New Testament Christological discussion, whether approached historically and exegetically or interpretatively and theologically. Surely all would agree that one of the major and still unresolved issues in this debate is the fundamental question, "Where did it all begin?" Is Christology essentially a product of the postresurrection Christian community? Or did

Christology have its birth in Jesus' historic self-awareness? The remainder of this essay examines this question of Christological origins, both because of its widespread importance in recent discussions and because the major issues of Christological inquiry and interpretation ultimately carry us back to that fundamental problem.

The contemporary phase of this debate proceeds from the important and well-known conclusions of the late Rudolf Bultmann. His point of view can be summed up in the opening line of his *Theology of the New Testament*: "The message of Jesus is a presupposition for the theology of the New Testament rather than a part of that theology itself."[13] For Bultmann, Christology is wholly a product of the postresurrection Christian community, a position he reached only after a rigorously and consistently applied form-critical analysis of the gospel records.[14] This left him with continuing and fundamental reservations about what can be known with certainty of the historical Jesus. In his introductory comments to *Jesus and the Word*, Bultmann reminded his readers that only through a critical analysis of the many-layered Synoptic tradition is "an oldest layer determined," although even there "we have no absolute assurance that the exact words of this oldest layer were really spoken by Jesus."[15] Bultmann's refusal to locate Christology within Jesus' self-disclosure is rooted both in his reservations about the historical validity of the gospel traditions and in his insistence that the nature of the kerygma is confirmed not in historical proof but in the faith created by the resurrection.[16] Bultmann's emphasis on the fundamental distinction between the proclamation *of* Jesus and the proclamation *about* Jesus was never compromised even in his later works. His stance is well known and still fundamentally accepted among many contemporary New Testament scholars, although their numbers are declining. R. H. Fuller, one of the contributors to this book, has worked out his Christological studies from that very form-critical framework.[17] Harvey K. McArthur, also a contributor, remains essentially a Bultmannian when he sums up the position in the following statement from a 1969 essay:

> *In the historical area I reject as largely unprofitable the theories that the Gospels contain substantial quantities of eyewitness material or that they are the end product of a professionally controlled oral tradition. On the other hand, I stand on the boundary between the more*

radical form critics and those who hold that by the eclectic use of a variety of criteria a relatively substantial sketch of the teaching of Jesus, and perhaps of his ministry, may be made probable. In my judgment there is, unfortunately, no reason to believe that these sketches will ever be sufficiently stable to serve as a foundation for the construction of a traditional Christology.[18]

There has been some tendency for certain Bultmannians to ground Christological claims in what *can* be recovered of the historical Jesus. Sometimes labeled the "post-Bultmannians," this group has presumably modified Bultmann's insistence on the fundamental break between the historical Jesus and the proclaimed Christ. The movement is said to have begun with a 1953 Marburg lecture given by Ernst Käsemann, "The Problem of the Historical Jesus,"[19] and James M. Robinson sympathetically reviewed the so-called "new questers" at an early stage of this development.[20] Perhaps best known among the original post-Bultmannians, at least in the English-speaking world, is Günther Bornkamm, whose full-length life of Jesus has been available in translation for a little more than thirty years.[21] But this group has not resorted to the older attempt to probe the inner consciousness for clues to Jesus' Christological awareness, nor has it parted company in any decisive way from the methods and fundamental presuppositions of Bultmannian form-criticism. In fact, the sum of what these post-Bultmannians have isolated as historical is not much greater than what Bultmann himself consistently accepted as historically highly probable. The difference is more subtle, with these modified Bultmannians emphasizing lines of continuity they see between the historical Jesus and the proclamation about Jesus in the kerygma, a stress that carries important Christological implications. Yet when the differences are assembled, the distinction between Bultmann and these followers is insignificant, at least in terms of Christological origins. Indeed, Bultmann always held to the position that there is an implied Christology in Jesus' historic message, especially in his call to decision with respect to the Kingdom of God:

{Jesus} gave no teaching about his own person, but he said that the fact of his work was the ultimate decisive fact for men. . . . What is decisive is not what he proclaims but that he is proclaiming it. . . .

But his call to decision certainly implies a Christology—not as metaphysical speculation about a heavenly being nor as a character-ization of his personality somehow endowed with a messianic con-sciousness, but a Christology which is proclamation, summons.[22]

Emphasizing the messianic character of Jesus' "activity" (Born-kamm),[23] or what Ernst Fuchs refers to as "language event,"[24] does not undo the fundamental agreement between the post-Bultmannians and Bultmann himself. This is not to minimize the importance of the contributions of "new questers," but to suggest that in Christological terms that school continues to locate the fundamental beginnings of Christology within the post-Easter community of faith and not in the claims of the historical Jesus. The impact of Bultmannian form-criticism remains an important factor in the context of contemporary Christological dialogue.

One study that falls within the Bultmannian framework has opened up new directions and deserves more attention than it has received. We refer to Willi Marxsen's *The Beginnings of Christology: A Study in Its Problems.*[25] Though Marxsen, like Bultmann, assigns specific Christological titles only to the post-Easter community, he takes the position that the pre-Easter/post-Easter distinction is in fact a misleading way of getting at the issue of Christological origins. In one sense Marxsen is even more skeptical than Bultmann when he says of historical analysis in the Gospels: "I am not able to differentiate between historical and tendentious traditions. The historical element has been screened by the tendency."[26] This suggests that Marxsen is challenging form-criticism's criterion of dissimilarity as a test of historical validity,[27] for in his view one cannot draw a clear line between the pre-Easter proclamation of Jesus and the explicit Christology that blossoms only in the postresurrection era. Rather, Christology appears "where the *relationship* between Jesus and the believer becomes visible for the first time."[28] That relationship, Marxsen maintains, is visible in both the pre-Easter and post-Easter communities, and he uses it as his primary criterion for examining such historical Christological data. For one example of how this operates, Marxsen points to Mark 8:38: "For whoever is ashamed of me and of my words in this adulterous and sinful generation, of him will the Son of man also be ashamed, when he comes in the glory of his Father with the holy angels." Surely, Marxsen insists, the early Christians understood this saying in a Christological manner, even though in transmitting the words of Jesus they did not transform them into an explicit messianic pronouncement. The uniquely defined relationship between Jesus and his listeners establishes Christology— in this instance a relationship that is messianically qualified by the coming of the Son of Man. Wherever that relationship appears, one confronts a Christology just as clearly as if the designation were made either by Jesus or by the community. In fact, Marxsen argues that a saying such as Mark 8:38 is sometimes more profoundly Christological than more explicit messianic claims where the person of Jesus is isolated from the dynamic of his relationship to his followers, a dynamic that for Marxsen is the crucial test, whether in the pre- or postresurrection contexts.[29]

We could address important questions to Marxsen's suggestions, but we will point out only that this is an intriguing alternative to the standard and more rigid form-critical procedure of allowing explicit Christology to be determined by the use of certain designations or titles. Marxsen is aware that there is a conceptual distinction between less direct Christological identifications (e.g., Mark 8:38) and the more precise titular affirmations that occur with increased frequency in the later strata of the tradition. Yet working within the form-critical procedures for isolating the earlier, more historic layers in the Gospels, Marxsen has posed a new and promising criterion that may offer some means of avoiding the pre- and post-Easter cul-de-sac that has characterized both Bultmannian and post-Bultmannian analyses of Christological origins, a challenge that has been taken up by more recent discussions.

In general, however, form-critical presuppositions and approaches have tenaciously and consistently insisted Christology be viewed as a product of the community of resurrection faith, at best allowing only for implicit Christological affirmations by Jesus himself. The post-Bultmannians stirred up renewed interest in the less direct messianic hints found in the words and activities of Jesus. Even this positive trend is offset by prevailing attempts among other form/redaction critics to eliminate *all* Son-of-Man sayings from the earliest layers, thus further widening the gap between Jesus' proclamations and the Christological claims of the later church. Though we must in this essay avoid any detailed discussion of the various titles used in New Testament Christological discourse, the Son-of-Man problem is so crucially related to historical Jesus claims that it is necessary to offer a few comments in this regard.

The way in which one understands the Son-of-Man sayings has a profound effect on one's view of Jesus' messianic self-awareness. Even the casual reader of the New Testament will notice that this title (if a title it is) has been handled in a prescribed and limited manner. It is surprising that the phrase is the only presumed messianic designation that the Synoptic writers have placed directly on the lips of Jesus and that, where it is so used, it is consistently set forth in the third person, so as to suggest the possibility that Jesus could have been referring to someone other than himself. In the one Markan incident where Jesus admits to the *Christos* title (Mark 14:62), his words immediately shift to a third-person saying about the coming of this Son of Man. Add to this the oft-observed fact that the title in the Synoptics is never used by anyone other than Jesus and that with one exception (Acts 7:56) it disappears entirely in the New Testament literature outside the Gospels.

This has aroused a great deal of curiosity among critics, and for the present context it is important to point out that even Bultmann included some Son-of-Man sayings within the earliest tradition, insisting, of course, that Jesus used the title to designate the one who was to come at the end of the age and that the church only later identified that apocalyptic figure with the resurrected Christ. Accordingly, Bultmann found this title simply an expression used by Jesus to state his confidence that the Kingdom of God was about to supplant the present age.[30] Of course, many non-Bultmannian critics have not only accepted the use of this title in the tradition, but have characteristically understood its meaning in connection with Jesus' own messianic proclamation.[31] The point is that the Son-of-Man sayings have had strong and widespread support as being in some sense authentic, and that such support has come even from those critics deemed to be the most negative in terms of what they accept and reject as historical tradition.

A number of studies have picked up on a segment of a position defended long ago by H. B. Sharman that the Son-of-Man sayings and the Kingdom-of-God statements are not linked in the Gospels.[32] Philipp Vielhauer, for example, understood all the Son-of-Man sayings as secondary,[33] and his position has been essentially maintained by Hans Conzelmann.[34] Norman Perrin, pointing out that the Son-of-Man title is virtually nonexistent in Jewish apocalyptic tradition, has likewise insisted that these sayings are absent from the genuine Jesus tradition in the Gospels.[35] But the issue remains unsettled, and M. de Jonge in his recent Christological study is among an emerging number of interpreters who have reasserted the importance of Jesus' unique use of the phrase as a way of defining the eschatological importance of his ministry.[36] While not arguing that Jesus employed Son of Man as a messianic title, James Dunn has supported the notion that Jesus may have used the terminology derived from Dan. 7 to underline confidence in his eschatological function "as the one who would be vindicated beyond his anticipated suffering and death and play the decisive role in the final judgment."[37] Whether as a messianic title or not, Jesus' use of the phrase carries important implications for his ministry's messianic/eschatological significance. The consequences for the discussion of Christological origins are enormous, and again, this must be seen as a part of the diverse context of the current dialogue.

The entire form-critical approach has provided some stumbling blocks that cannot be avoided in any serious attempts to probe the origins of Christology. This should not blind us to the fact that there remain a substantial number of New Testament scholars who have not bowed to Bultmannian form-criticism and whose refusal to do so provides us with a more positive assessment of the Christological character of Jesus' historic ministry. For example, some have in one way or another rejected the underlying claims of form-criticism, thereby avoiding a serious threat to the reliability of the Gospels. One example of this is offered by certain modern Scandinavian scholars who have argued that the oral tradition was transmitted in a rabbinic-like manner and that material thus preserved contains a more or less reliable picture of the historical Jesus.[38] For them, oral tradition was preserved substantially intact and then later incorporated into the written Gospels, a view that challenges the Bultmannian notion that the preliterary tradition was constantly changing. With similar conclusions, certain British New Testament critics, while dealing positively with methods of form-critical analysis, have rejected the principle that whatever reflects the thinking of the early church must be considered inauthentic.[39] Joachim Jeremias' conclusions that Jesus' unique sense of sonship (hence, Christological self-awareness) is reflected in his use of the Aramaic *Abba* when making references to God are well known among New Testament students,[40] and Oscar Cullmann has valiantly defended the use of "Son" as a self-designation of Jesus.[41] Others, without resorting to any explicit claims on Jesus' part, argue that the messianic title is in some sense demanded by the fact that Jesus was tried and convicted on that presumed claim.[42] If accepted, this makes more feasible a Christological awareness in the person of Jesus.

C. F. D. Moule's *The Origin of Christology* is an example of specific efforts to locate Christological origins well within the message of the historical Jesus.[43] Moule focuses on the contrast between those who view Christology as the result of an "evolutionary" process and those who prefer to understand it in terms of "development." Moule's overall analysis is clear, even though there is some overlap between what can be described as development and what can be defined as evolution. The evolutionist sees a fundamental break between the historic claim *of* Jesus and later claims *about* his person; in Moule's terms, the evolutionary understanding corresponds to the form-critical conclusion that Christology is at most implicit in the message of Jesus. The developmentalist sees Christological patterns growing directly and materially out of the self-affirmations of Jesus; this position, while recognizing that certain changes did take place in Christological formulations, insists that there is a material continuity between pre- and postresurrection patterns. Moule adheres to the second pattern, insisting that the combination of continuity and change suggests development rather than evolution in the formulation of New Testament Christology.[44] Moule is aware of the many differences among the New Testament Christologies, and he knows that the gospel records reflect a certain Christological reshaping brought about by the later Christian communities. But his position is clear when he says, "My main point is not that all Christological expressions in the New Testament are adequate for modern statements of Christology, but that they are all more successfully accounted for as insights, of varying depth, into what was there in Jesus, than as a result of increasing distance from him."[45] Moule then goes on to test his development hypothesis in relation to the four main titles: Son of Man, Son of God, Christ, and *Kyrios*. In each instance, Moule finds the Christological substance already present in the mind and thought of Jesus. And what is even more surprising in the light of the modern dialogue, Moule understands these designations in ontological, not merely functional, terms. He hesitantly suggests that preexistence itself falls within the framework of the developmental, so that even the high Christological dimension has a place within Jesus' self-awareness.[46]

Moule's Christological conclusions are important not only because they locate Christology within the self-affirmation of Jesus, but also because they reflect a movement among New Testament interpreters away from the hiatus created by the Bultmannian methodology. In another survey I. H. Marshall draws similar Christological conclusions.[47] Although Marshall is an avowed evangelical by theological persuasion, he too brings to his study an acceptance of mainstream critical methods. The Tübingen scholar Martin Hengel, known for his extensive work in the backgrounds of New Testament thought,[48] similarly supports the notion that Christology had explicit beginnings within the pre-Easter message of Jesus.[49] Though more cautious than Moule or Marshall, Hengel also emphatically locates the idea of divine sonship within the realm of the historic proclamation of Jesus. If Hengel is hesitant to attribute the notion of preexistent sonship to Jesus himself, he nevertheless finds that idea present in the earliest layers of the Synoptic tradition and thus in close proximity to the historical Jesus. Hengel recognizes the distinction between explicit titles and more implicitly articulated claims. However, in line with the conclusions of Moule and Marshall, he does not finally see any material break between the claims of Jesus and the later, post-Easter proclamation.[50] Finally, while making it clear that Jesus' own sense of sonship stopped short of any preexistent or incarnational Christology, James Dunn forcefully argues that Jesus "understood and expressed his relationship to God in terms of *sonship*," that he understood "that his sonship was something *unique*," constituting even a "metaphysical otherness," though not as a "pre-existent Son of God."[51] Perhaps most significant, these scholars are unanimous in the opinion that ontological perspectives on Christology do not depend on any direct interaction between the kerygma and the more remote Hellenistic world.

This brings into focus what remains the fundamental issue in the contemporary dialogue over Christological origins. Though the Bultmannian position remains intact among an impressive number of New Testament critics, including those commonly designated as post-Bultmannians, there remains a substantial wing of critical opinion in support of the traditional notion that Christology began with Jesus. These issues are still unresolved, and any responsible Christological discussion, whether biblically or theologically pursued, must make its way through such a maze of conflicting opinion: on critical grounds, one may dismiss the notion of a pre-Easter Christology, or, using the same critical tools, one may support the opposite conclusion that Christology did begin with Jesus of Nazareth. But one cannot fail to recognize that the two starting points make a difference. One can move with Bultmann along the form-critical, existentializing pathway,[52] one that has led some (though not Bultmann) to question entirely the New Testament's "once for all" claim for the person of Jesus.[53] Or, by insisting that the New Testament's Christology grew directly from the One for whom that claim was made, one can proceed to the Johannine assumption that Jesus' transcendence comes ultimately from his own "I am." Christological dialogue must finally wrestle with this issue, even if ambiguity plagues us to the very end. For purposes of this essay, it must be said that such ambiguity has played a consistent and important role in modern Christological discussions.

A related problem, and one that has also played a central role in attitudes about Christological origins, centers on the formative environment by which New Testament thought was shaped. The crucial issue concerns the formulation of Jesus' divinity, as expressed in the designations Son of God and *Kyrios*. Was this mode of Christological affirmation appropriate to, compatible with, a Jewish monotheistic tradition? Or was Hellenistic thought the more likely vehicle behind the formulation and transmission of these concepts? Does incarnational Christology find its religious home in the Greek mysteries, in an incipient Gnosticism already beginning to appear at the time of the rise of Christian affirmations about Jesus, in Hellenistic Judaism, or in some self-styled combination of these? Understanding the nature of these settings and relating Christological origins to these various options continues to be a prominent part of modern New Testament investigation.

Wilhelm Bousset's monumental *Kyrios Christos* marked the beginnings of the contemporary phase of this discussion.[54] In that work Bousset made his now well-known case for the Hellenistic mysteries as the cradle of New Testament Christological formulations, especially as they became explicit in the work of the apostle Paul. That segment of the so-called history-of-religions school held sway through a substantial portion of the critical discussion that was to ensue, and the substance of that position was, with some modifications, reaffirmed in more recent times in the work of Bultmann.[55] Bultmann was no doubt better informed than Bousset about the Palestinian thought-world in which the earliest phase of Christian expression took shape, but he nevertheless remained convinced that the primary locus of Christian soteriological and Christological formulations was the Hellenistic, Gentile world of thought and belief. Bultmann agreed with Bousset that Jewish messianic and apocalyptic interpretations soon were overshadowed by the Hellenistic *Sitz im Leben*, and that a "divine nature" Christology supplanted the earlier apocalyptic setting in such a way that *Christos* itself lost that original eschatological function as a title.[56] Hence the earliest community's anticipated deliverer, the one who was expected to return on the clouds in judgment, soon was transformed, via Gentile categories of thought and expression, into the *Theios Aner*. Given the strong affinities between these two scholars, it is no surprise to discover that the preface to the fifth German edition of Bousset's *Kyrios Christos* was written by none other than Bultmann. In that preface, his sympathies are clearly allied with the main lines of Bousset's interpretation, even though Bultmann incorporated the progress research had made in the meantime.[57]

The issue of the environment of Christological origins has also met with much controversy, and it moves today in a direction quite different from that of Bousset and Bultmann. The need to reexamine old assumptions has become evident, partly due to important textual discoveries (especially the Qumran documents and the Gnostic materials from Nag Hammadi) resulting in new assessments of both Christianity and Judaism in this formative period. Recent scholarship has turned its attention especially to the Jewish context out of which Christianity emerged. It is not simply a matter of turning from Hellenism to Judaism as the more legitimate context in which to view early Christology; there has emerged in recent studies a profound recognition of the variegated character of both Judaism and Hellenism, and of even further complications that confront us in the merging of these two traditions well before the rise of Christianity. More than forty years ago, W. D. Davies provided a powerful reminder that rabbinic thought itself was a reflection of an involved process of the interweaving of these traditions.[58] For Davies, even Paul's most ontologically phrased Christological statement in Col. 1:15 was to be understood in the context of rabbinic thought and expression, and he shunned the notion that it is necessary to link such passages directly to the philosophical and religious outlook of the Gentile world.[59] Davies' insistence upon Jewish traditions as a (the?) primary context of Pauline thought has carried over in recent years to a more generalized tendency to emphasize the Judaic or Hellenistic/Judaic side of New Testament backgrounds as a whole. In the light of this, some modern interpreters have raised questions about several basic conclusions in New Testament scholarship. Some have questioned even the notion so cherished among Protestants that justification by faith in Christ is *the* glass through which Paul's thinking must finally be seen.[60] Martin Hengel[61] has argued that at the time of the Maccabean crisis, Judaism had already undergone a significant transformation wrought by its encounter with Hellenism, and E. P. Sanders' work on the thought of Paul continues with this conclusion that Palestinian Judaism in its Hellenized dress was the formative setting for Pauline thought.[62] The notion of a clearer distinction between Palestinian Judaism (at least in its Judean form) and Hellenistic Judaism, together with the conclusion that Christian thought is better explained by the latter, continues to have significant support.[63] But more pertinent is the fact that there is an increasing tendency among New Testament authorities to relate even such titles as Lord and Son of God to that rich and varied background of thought that marked both Palestinian and Diaspora Judaism, and that the existence of such titles does not necessarily depend on direct contacts with the Gentile world. That alone, of course, does not affirm their use by the historical Jesus.

These developments are apparent in the many ways in which recent Christological analyses have proceeded. For example, Ferdinand Hahn suggests that between Palestinian (Jewish) Christianity and Hellenistic Christianity per se there existed a Hellenistic Jewish-Christianity whose *Sitz im Leben* is located in that Hellenized Judaism found both in Palestine and in the Diaspora, and that it was precisely within the Hellenistic Jewish-Christianity that the title Lord (*Kyrios*) assumed its divine connotations.[64] While Hahn agrees that the earliest layer of Palestinian Christian tradition reserved the *Kyrios* title essentially for the One who was to return in glory,[65] he insists that such affirmations about Jesus' divine authority *and* substance do not await ultimate contact with the Hellenistic/Gentile world.

This does betray a sometimes subtle change taking place within the perspective of New Testament scholarship, a change in which the locus of Christological expression is being viewed increasingly in connection with its Judaic and Jewish-Christian setting. The Bousset/Bultmann history-of-religions tendency to locate ontologically defined Christologies exclusively within the nexus of Gentile tradition has had to face serious challenges in recent studies. Some scholars whose form-critical methods are in substantial agreement with those used by Bultmann are nevertheless taking a significantly different view of the underlying character and substance of the *Sitz im Leben* out of which Christian traditions emerged. And this has a way of moving Christological expressions into closer contact with the historical Jesus. Even Bultmann saw that the earliest Palestinian material was probably associated with the historical Jesus.[66] If those earliest layers encompass even the possibility of a divine nature Christology, then it is not possible to dismiss those higher Christological affirmations from the historical Jesus himself. The rediscovery of Jewish roots of New Testament thought is of tremendous significance in the search for the origins of Christology.

Thus far we have concentrated on the broad framework of Christological discussions from the perspective of New Testament critical scholarship. One further matter is pivotal to everything said about Christology, and that is the affirmation of the resurrection. Whether one argues that Christology began within the consciousness of Jesus or later, somewhere within the life and faith of the early Christian community, the substance of Christology is always shaped by, created by, and understood through the New Testament's resounding affirmation, "He is risen!" The resurrection may be seen as mere confirmation of Jesus' own work and words, or it may be understood as the very atmosphere in which Christology was born. The importance of the resurrection in the New Testament's story is such that specific comments are necessary to round out this discussion.

The form-critical school again isolated the resurrection as the dividing line between the historical Jesus and the kerygma in the early church. For Bultmann, the implicit Christology in Jesus' call to decision in the light of the inbreaking Kingdom of God was made explicit by that resurrection faith. In that context, the crucified Jesus came to be viewed as the Christ, the exalted Son of Man who would soon return to consummate the kingdom he had announced in his historic ministry. Yet when Bultmann spoke thus of the resurrection, he was not articulating the existence of an empty tomb or the presence of a *soma* that could be defined in normal historical terms as an "event." The event, rather, was the proclamation of the risenness as it was aroused in the faith of the earliest Christian community. The resurrection was for him not that which occurred in Jerusalem (Luke) or Galilee (Mark/Matthew) or both (John), but in the affirmation itself: "The real Easter faith is faith in the word of preaching which brings illumination. If the event of Easter Day is in any sense an historical event additional to the event of the cross, it is nothing else than the rise of faith in the risen Lord."[67] This means that the resurrection as the raw material of Christology is inseparable from affirmations *about* the historical Jesus. As Bultmann understood it, the confirmation of the resurrection is to be isolated not in an empty tomb nor in material manifestations, but in the proclamation of the Word and the response of the believer to that Word.

A large number of modern discussions of the resurrection have followed the Bultmannian model, especially those of interpreters who are identified with Bultmannian form-critical analysis. Conzelmann reflects the same approach when he says, "History cannot establish the facticity of the resurrection."[68] Willi Marxsen, though attempting to answer objections regarding the subjectivity of his interpretation of the resurrection, insists that the *extra nos* implied in the New Testament narratives of the resurrection is in fact the same reality attested to by the various symbols of exaltation. For Marxsen, the *extra nos* is not to be identified or confirmed in an empty-tomb/appearance tradition. What is resurrected is the reality (transcendent) that gave Christological meaning and significance to the life and, especially, the death of Jesus, and by which is affirmed his continuous reign and anticipated return in glory as the Son of Man.[69] This is a repetition of the Bultmann dictum, "The faith of Easter is just this—faith in the *Word* of preaching."[70]

A substantial wing of New Testament interpretation has consistently and emphatically defined resurrection not in terms of its historical manifestations but in terms of revelation and response. For these, the truth of the resurrection is found not in what happened on the third day but in the proclamation of the ultimate significance of Jesus: Paul's "word of the cross." While the Bultmann school has not reduced the resurrection to a mere psychic phenomenon,[71] it has defined the event more specifically in relation to its ongoing proclamation and reception, and not to any event of history. It was in that context that Bultmann understood the beginnings of Christology, a Christology that therefore is defined in functional, existential terms rather than in more objective, ontological formulations characteristic of traditional Christian theology. Not only does the resurrection establish a Christology, but, for Bultmann and his followers, the way in which the resurrection is understood and articulated determines that Christology's form.

This existentialized, demythologized understanding of the resurrection has drawn criticism from many corners, especially from those whose theologies (Christologies) are more traditionally and evangelically defined. But in recent years a renewed emphasis on the historical character of the resurrection has emerged, most notably in the exegetical and theological work of Wolfhart Pannenberg.[72] Pannenberg, who operates both as a critical exegete and systematic theologian while not resorting to a traditional or orthodox historicism, has restated in bold terms the objective, historical dimension he understands to be inherent in the resurrection. He recognizes the serious problems in thus articulating the character of the resurrection. The claims that are made for this event place it in a category that is *sui generis*, and there can be no adequate analogies to articulate its character and meaning. The resurrection, Pannenberg argues, is an eschatological event that has revealed Jesus as history's own end. Pannenberg's terminology sometimes seems reminiscent of Bultmannian language, especially when he characterizes Jesus as an eschatological event. But an important distinction is that Pannenberg will not allow an understanding of Jesus' resurrection that turns out to be merely a proclamation about the meaning of the past. Rather, the resurrection is itself an event, and contrary to the stream of modern thought described above, Pannenberg articulates the objectivity of the resurrection by references both to the empty-tomb narratives and the witnesses to Jesus' appearances.[73] There is some overlapping with traditional form-criticism, for Pannenberg agrees that Jesus' nonmessianic ministry was transformed into Christology only in the light of the resurrection. But it is in the understanding of the resurrection that Pannenberg's approach displays its distinctive character, for what he says divides the nonmessianic historical Jesus from the Christ of faith is not an affirmation but an event.

One confronts here a creative Christological study—one, among others, that has renewed an emphasis on the resurrection in bluntly nonexistential terms. Where that will lead over the next decades cannot be determined. However, Pannenberg's emphasis on the event character of the resurrection significantly challenged Bultmannian orthodoxy, and it provides an important context in which Christological questions can be historically and theologically raised. Pannenberg's understanding of the resurrection has led to his own extensive analysis of Christology in the thought of the church, and this more historicized view of the resurrection has made its way into the thinking of both New Testament exegetes and systematic theologians attempting to articulate Christian faith in the modern world. Hans Küng, for example, although still reflecting Bultmannian affinities, insists that the resurrection event is real and not just "a way of expressing the significance of Jesus' death."[74] He emphasizes his stance further when he says: "Easter there is not a happening *merely* for the disciples and their faith. Jesus does not live *through* their faith. The Easter event is not a function of the disciples' faith. . . . But Easter is an event primarily for Jesus himself. Jesus lives again *through God—for their faith*."[75] Reaffirming the resurrection as an event rather than as a myth redefines the entire character of Christological discussions. Pheme Perkins likewise views resurrection as an event (albeit eschatological as opposed to historical), an event that she sees as creative of Christian universality and Christian praxis.[76] An existentialized or functionalized understanding of Christology "from below" continues to be a prominent factor in the current debate, as is evident in John Hick's collection of essays *The Myth of God Incarnate*,[77] and in the discussions that have proceeded from that collection for more than a decade. Hick's preface makes clear the stance of the book's contributors when it calls for a theology that recognizes that Jesus' identity as "God incarnate, the Second Person of the Holy Trinity living a human life, is a mythological or poetic way of expressing his significance for us."[78] Surely much of the liberal, critical stream of modern Christian thought remains at home with Christologies in which the resurrection is mythologically rather than historically interpreted, and where divinity is existentially rather than ontologically understood.[79] For some, this process has led more radically to a Christology void of any necessary connection with the historical Jesus,[80] while others have attempted to locate the authority of Jesus somewhere within the boundaries of his historic person, especially in his word of liberation.[81] But once the resurrection is viewed with both its historical and ontological concreteness, Christology assumes a historical and existential character—and perplexing problems as well. Christological understanding must in no small measure be linked to the outcome of the historical and theological inquiry into the nature of the resurrection.

Contemporary views of Christology continue to display widely variant patterns, but within that diversity New Testament critics and theologians share a consensus affirming Christology in one form or another as the mainspring of the literature and of the community of faith out of which it emerged. At the beginning of this century there was no clear consensus in support of this singular, once-for-all significance of the person of Jesus, but the climate has changed significantly. The Harnackian notion that the essence of the New Testament and of early Christianity is to be defined through a set of superior, unique, spiritual and moral values enunciated by Jesus does, if true, take on a kind of "Christological" character or flavor—a Christology "from below." That may appear attractive to some, but such uniqueness does not hold up under rigorous historical, especially form-critical, scrutiny. The consensus today about the affinities of the message of Jesus is that Jesus' outlook must be located within the broad range of first-century Palestinian Judaism, and that what differences there are still place Jesus at least marginally within Jewish categories.[82] So it is Christology, whether originating with Jesus or with his followers, that the New Testament marks as the center of Christian faith, even though those claims do not present a consistent pattern. At the same time, Jesus is set forth as the One who taught "with authority"; the One "conceived by the Holy Spirit"; the One whom God made "Lord and Christ"; the "Son" through whom God has spoken in these latter days; the Son of Man who will come in "great power and glory"; and perhaps the most cosmic of all, the "Logos made flesh."

The chapters that follow examine such issues. Those in part 1 explore facets of the dialogue between New Testament Christologies and the world in which such reflections about Jesus first emerged. Very importantly, we have included in this section Reginald Fuller's discussion that succinctly articulates form criticism's "criterion of dissimilarity" as the means for sorting out the "uniquely" historical in the Jesus tradition. That criterion, still hotly debated, continues as one means for isolating those unique fragments of the Jesus tradition as distinguished from his Jewishness, on the one hand, and his "Christness" imposed by what form critics insist to be the postresurrection tradition. This is an important tool because it provides common ground for maximalist and minimalist historians to begin their explorations into the person of Jesus. Part 2 moves the Christological dialogue to the writings of the New Testament witnesses, beginning with the question of a Jesus Christology and concluding with Pheme Perkins' essay on the Christological significance of the resurrection. These seminal formulations were to become canonical, and as such, they constitute the parameters of subsequent Christological discussion. The dialogue did not conclude with these canonical trajectories but has continued into our modern world. Accordingly, in the last two sections of this collection we have solicited discussions of Christologies that have been shaped by interaction with other faith traditions (part 3) and with the varied intellectual and social views of the contemporary world (part 4).

"Dialogue" is the key word, and it carries our conviction that Christology loses its vitality when it is not so engaged. Whether in their first-century or in their Chalcedonian or Enlightenment clothing, Christological formulations have always fallen short of finality. The Bultmannian analysis in particular has become a warning that Christology is never final but always in dialogue: with the early church, with the religious and mythological presuppositions and commitments of the Jewish and Hellenistic world, and perhaps most important, with the worldviews of our own age and time. Christology may be a quest for such finality, but that finality is always perceived only in part. To put it another way, Christology is defined not so much by the empty tomb as by the encounter that unleashed that resounding summons for the disciples to move on to Galilee. Christological finality is not to be evoked through historic demonstration, whether Saint Paul's "He appeared to me" or the bishops' unanimous assent at Chalcedon or, for that matter, the diverse claims of modern scholarship. Christologies, be they ancient or modern, are evoked first and always by dialogue, beginning perhaps with Jesus' question to the disciples: "Who do others say that I am?" The essays in part 3, then, deal with Christology as it is still being forged in the confrontation of Christians with those who do not share the Christological claim for Jesus. We believe that such a confrontation requires a two-way street, and we are delighted with the Küng-Segal and the Kerr-Ayoub dialogues in this section. Here we have in modern modes a reliving of ancient dialogues. And in part 4, we move into that emerging struggle to speak of Christology in the midst of some of the major philosophical, social, and cultural struggles of our modern world, culminating with Karl-Joseph Kuschel's examination of the broader issue of Christology in dialogue with pluralism itself. We present these essays to reflect primarily on the continuing dialogue—whether that which erupted in the ancient Roman world or that which even now establishes and defines the many contours of Christological dialogue. Above all, we trust that the essays collected in this book will not only provide readers with new insight into this core of Christian faith, but that they will guide those same readers into their own dialogues with Christology.

NOTES

A version of this essay first appeared as "Christological Perspectives: The Context of Current Discussions" in *Christological Perspectives*, ed. Robert F. Berkey and Sarah A. Edwards (New York: The Pilgrim Press, 1982), 3–23. Used by permission.

1. Adolf von Harnack, *What is Christianity?* trans. Thomas Bailey Saunders (New York: Harper & Bros., 1957), 128.

2. Ibid., 144.

3. Ibid., 184.

4. E.g., Jon Sobrino, *Christology at the Crossroads: A Latin American Approach*, trans. John Drury (Maryknoll, NY: Orbis Books, 1978); or Hans Küng, *On Being a Christian*, trans. Edward Quinn (Garden City, NY: Doubleday, 1976). For a review especially of some of these recent liberation Christologies, see John Parr's "Liberating Jesus" in part 4 of this collection.

5. Richard Hiers and David Holland, eds., *Jesus' Proclamation of the Kingdom of God* (Philadelphia: Fortress Press, 1971).

6. See *The Mystery of the Kingdom of God*, trans. Walter Lowrie (New York: Macmillan, 1950); and *The Quest of the Historical Jesus*, trans. F. C. Burkitt (New York: Macmillan, 1968), chaps. 19, 20.

7. William Wrede, *Das Messiasgeheimnis in den Evangelien* (Göttingen: Vandenhoeck & Ruprecht, 1901).

8. Martin Kähler, *The So-Called Historical Jesus and the Historic Biblical Christ*, trans. and ed. Carl E. Braaten (Philadelphia: Fortress Press, 1964).

9. Still the most thorough form-critical analysis is Rudolf Bultmann's *History of the Synoptic Tradition*, trans. John Marsh (New York: Harper & Row, 1976).

10. See, e.g., Karl Barth's "The Strange New World Within the Bible," in *The Word of God and the Word of Man*, trans. Douglas Horton (London: Hodder & Stoughton, 1928), 28–50. It was that "strange new world" that lay at the center of Barth's then "new theology," still frequently labeled as neoorthodoxy.

11. This small book has now gone through many printings; it was first published in 1936 by Hodder & Stoughton (London).

12. Recent studies include C. F. D. Moule, *The Origin of Christology* (Cambridge: Cambridge University Press, 1977); James Dunn's comprehensive study, *Christology in the Making* (London: SCM Press, 1990); Marinus de Jonge, *Christology in Context* (Philadelphia: Westminster Press, 1988); Walter Kasper, *Jesus the Christ*, trans. V. Green (New York: Paulist Press, 1976); and the recently collected essays of Nils Dahl, *Jesus the Christ*, ed. Donald Juel (Minneapolis: Fortress Press, 1991). Three earlier studies offer important information regarding Christological titles: Reginald Fuller, *The Foundations of New Testament Christology* (New York: Charles Scribner's Sons, 1965); Ferdinand Hahn, *The Titles of Jesus in Christology*, trans. Harold Knight and George Ogg (New York: World, 1969); and Oscar Cullmann, *The Christology of the New Testament*, trans. Shirley C. Guthrie and Charles A. M. Hall (Philadelphia: Westminster Press, 1964).

13. Rudolf Bultmann, *Theology of the New Testament*, trans. Kendrick Grobel (New York: Charles Scribner's Sons, 1951), 1:3.

14. See Bultmann, *History*.

15. Rudolf Bultmann, *Jesus and the Word*, trans. Louise Pettibone Smith (New York: Charles Scribner's Sons, 1958), 12.

16. See Rudolf Bultmann, "Christology of the New Testament," in *Faith and Understanding*, ed. R. Funk (New York: Harper & Row, 1969), 262–85.

17. See Fuller, "The Criterion of Dissimilarity: The Wrong Tool?" (in part 1 of this book) and *Foundations*; Hahn, *Titles*.

18. Harvey K. McArthur, "From the Historical Jesus to Christology," *Interpretation* 23, no. 2 (1969): 190–206.

19. Originally published under the German title "Das Problem des historischen Jesus," in *Zeitschrift für Theologie und Kirche* 51 (1954): 125–33; English trans. in *Essays on New Testament Themes*, trans. W. J. Montague (Naperville, IL: Alec R. Allenson, 1964), 15–47.

20. James M. Robinson, *A New Quest of the Historical Jesus* (Naperville, IL: Alec R. Allenson, 1959).

21. Günther Bornkamm, *Jesus of Nazareth*, trans. Irene and Fraser McLuskey, with J. M. Robinson (New York: Harper & Bros., 1960).

22. Bultmann, "Christology," 283.

23. Bornkamm, *Jesus*, esp. 25–26, 171ff.

24. Ernst Fuchs, "Jesus' Understanding of Time," in *Studies of the Historical Jesus*, trans. A. Scobie (London: SCM Press, 1964), 104–65.

25. Willi Marxsen, *The Beginnings of Christology: A Study in Its Problems*, trans. Paul J. Achtemeier (Philadelphia: Fortress Press, 1969).

26. Ibid., 19.

27. See Hans Conzelmann, *Jesus*, trans. J. Raymond Lord (Philadelphia: Fortress Press, 1973); Reginald Fuller, *The New Testament in Current Study* (New York: Charles Scribner's Sons, 1962), 33; Ferdinand Hahn, "The Quest of the Historical Jesus and the Special Character of the Sources Available to Us," in *What Can We Know of Jesus?* trans. Grover Foley (Philadelphia: Fortress Press, 1969), 44–48; Norman Perrin, *Rediscovering the Teaching of Jesus* (New York: Harper & Row, 1967), 15–49. That same principle of dissimilarity provides the chief criterion for Herbert Braun's reconstruction of the ministry of Jesus in *Jesus of Nazareth*, trans. Everett Kahlen (Philadelphia: Fortress Press, 1919).

28. Marxsen, *Beginnings*, 21 (emphasis added).

29. Ibid., 32–33.

30. Bultmann, *Theology*, 1:30ff. See, e.g., Mark 8:38 and other Synoptic passages where the apocalyptic use of the title appears always as a third-person reference.

31. See, e.g., Moule, *Origin*, 11ff.

32. H. B. Sharman, *Son of Man and Kingdom of God* (New York: Harper & Bros., 1943).

33. Philipp Vielhauer, "Gottersreich und Menschensohn in der Verkündigung Jesu," in *Aufsätze zum Neuen Testament* (Munich: Chr. Kaiser Verlag, 1965), 55–91.

34. Hans Conzelmann, *An Outline of the Theology of the New Testament*, trans. John Bowden (New York: Harper & Row, 1969), 6; see also Conzelmann, *Jesus*, 43ff.

35. See especially Norman Perrin, "The Son of Man in Ancient Judaism and Primitive Christianity: A Suggestion," in his *A Modern Pilgrimage in New Testament Christology* (Philadelphia: Fortress Press, 1974), 23ff.

36. de Jonge, *Christology*, 171–72; also Ben Witherington III, *The Christology of Jesus* (Minneapolis: Fortress Press, 1990), 261–62.

37. Dunn, *Christology*, 253; also 87f.

38. H. Riesenfeld, *The Gospel Tradition and Its Beginning* (London: A. R. Mowbray, 1957); see also Birger Gerhardsson's more detailed study, *Memory and Manuscript*, trans. Eric J. Sharpe (Lund: G. W. K. Gleerup, 1961). An even earlier suggestion of this approach can be seen in Nils Dahl, "*Anamnesis*: Memory and Commemoration in Early Christianity," originally a lecture given at Oslo in 1946 and now published in a collection of Dahl's essays, *Jesus in the Memory of the Early Church* (Minneapolis: Augsburg, 1976), 11–29.

39. See especially Vincent Taylor, *The Life and Ministry of Jesus* (Nashville: Abingdon Press, 1955), 13–50; see also T. W. Manson, *Studies in the Gospels and Epistles* (Philadelphia: Westminster Press, 1962), esp. 3–12, 20–27, 40–45.

40. The overall results of Joachim Jeremias' studies are apparent in his *New Testament Theology*, trans. John Bowden (New York: Charles Scribner's Sons, 1971), 61ff.

41. Cullmann, *Christology*, 283ff.

42. Werner Georg Kümmel, *The Theology of the New Testament*, trans. John E. Steely (Nashville: Abingdon Press, 1973), 71–73.

43. Moule, *Origin*.

44. Ibid., 1–10.

45. Ibid., 5.

46. Ibid., 138–41.

47. I. H. Marshall, *The Origins of New Testament Christology* (Downers Grove, IL: InterVarsity Press, 1976).

48. Martin Hengel, *Judaism and Hellenism*, trans. John Bowden (Philadelphia: Fortress Press, 1974).

49. Martin Hengel, *The Son of God*, trans. John Bowden (Philadelphia: Fortress Press, 1976).

50. Ibid., 63–66.

51. Dunn, *Christology*, 32; see also James Dunn, *The Evidence for Jesus* (Philadelphia: Westminster, 1985), 30ff.

52. Rudolf Bultmann, *Jesus Christ and Mythology* (New York: Charles Scribner's Sons, 1958).

53. Van Harvey, *The Historian and the Believer* (New York: Macmillan, 1966),

esp. chap. 8, where Harvey discusses the issue of "once-for-all-ness" with respect to the event of Jesus. See also Schubert Ogden, *Christ Without Myth* (New York: Harper & Bros., 1961), in which the author argues that Bultmann was inconsistent in not carrying his demythologizing program through to the historical Jesus.

54. Wilhelm Bousset, *Kyrios Christos*, trans. John E. Steely (Nashville: Abingdon Press, 1970).

55. See Rudolf Bultmann, *Primitive Christianity in Its Contemporary Setting*, trans. R. H. Fuller (Cleveland: World, 1956). See also his *Theology*, in which his discussion of pre-Pauline and Pauline Christianity assumes the presence of this formative Hellenistic background; see esp. 1:63, the opening paragraph.

56. Bultmann, *Primitive Christianity*, 176–77.

57. Bousset, *Kyrios*, 8–9.

58. W. D. Davies, *Paul and Rabbinic Judaism* (1948; New York: Harper & Bros., 1967).

59. Ibid., 150ff.

60. See Krister Stendahl, *Paul Among Jews and Gentiles* (Philadelphia: Fortress Press, 1976). This collection of essays includes his now famous article "The Apostle Paul and the Introspective Conscience of the West," originally published in *Harvard Theological Review* 56 (1963): 199–215.

61. Hengel, *Son of God*.

62. E. P. Sanders, *Paul and Palestinian Judaism* (Philadelphia: Fortress Press, 1977); that same interpretation continues in Sanders' brief study, *Paul* (New York: Oxford University Press, 1991).

63. That view was essentially affirmed in Samuel Sandmel, *Judaism and Christian Beginnings* (New York: Oxford University Press, 1978).

64. Hahn, *Titles*, 103ff.

65. Ibid., 89ff.

66. Bultmann, *Jesus*, 12ff.

67. Rudolf Bultmann, *Kerygma and Myth*, ed. H. W. Bartsch (New York: Harper & Bros., 1961), 42.

68. Conzelmann, *Jesus*, 94–95.

69. Willi Marxsen, *The Resurrection of Jesus of Nazareth*, trans. Margaret Kohl (Philadelphia: Fortress Press, 1970), 138–48.

70. Bultmann, *Kerygma*, 41 (emphasis added).

71. See, e.g., Conzelmann, *Jesus*, 94–95.

72. Wolfhart Pannenberg, *Jesus-God and Man*, trans. Lewis Wilkins and Duane Priebe (Philadelphia: Westminster Press, 1968).

73. Ibid., 108–14.

74. Küng, *On Being a Christian*, 351; Küng's emphasis.

75. Ibid., 352.

76. See her *Resurrection* (Garden City, NY: Doubleday, 1984), esp. 29ff. and 401–13.

77. John Hick, ed., *The Myth of God Incarnate* (Philadelphia: Westminster Press, 1977).

78. Ibid., ix.

79. See the chapter by John Macquarrie in part 4 of this collection; contrast Lester Muray's discussion of process theology and Christology, which follows Macquarrie's discussion.

80. See n. 53, above.

81. See John Parr's chapter in part 4 of this collection.

82. See John Meier's recent book on Jesus, *A Marginal Jew: Rethinking the Historical Jesus* (New York: Doubleday, 1991).

CHAPTER TWO

MESSIANIC EXPECTATIONS IN THE CONTEXT OF FIRST-CENTURY JUDAISM

OTTO BETZ

EDITED BY SARAH A. EDWARDS

Messianic expectations are unique to and characteristic of the religion of Israel. They flourished when the people of God suffered under the rule of a foreign power such as Babylon or Rome or under the yoke of a half-Jewish tyrant such as Herod the Great. Then a descendent of David whose government would be characterized by righteousness, wisdom, and fear of the Lord was expected to be chosen and raised up by God as king. Such a Messiah of Israel was promised and described in the Scriptures. The foundation of the messianic hope in ancient Israel was laid by God's promise, announced by the prophet Nathan, that someone of the house of David would reign forever (2 Sam. 7:12–15). The importance of this promise becomes evident from Psalms 89 and 132 and from the prophecy of Isaiah (9:5f.; 11:1–5). This messianic tradition was actualized for the Jews in New Testament times and for Jesus and the early Christians. They all hoped for the messianic fulfillment of the promise that God would raise up the offspring of David and establish the throne of the kingdom forever. God would be to the Anointed One like a parent to a child, chastening the child when necessary but never completely withdrawing grace. A second type of final savior is a prophet such as Moses, announced in Deut. 18:15–22: for the last redeemer will be like the first, Moses.

MESSIANIC EXPECTATIONS UNDER THE HASMONEANS: QUMRAN

The Qumran community had established its hope for a savior of Israel upon Nathan's oracle. They had compiled the authentic writings of the so-called Essenes and deposited them in the caves around Qumran near the Dead Sea. We find a rich form of messianism in these texts. In 2 Sam. 7[1] the Qumran exegetes emphasized the fact that God would build a house for David. They understood it spiritually as "a sanctuary [consisting] of men" in which "works of the Law" were offered to God. God has already begun to establish this temple, which actually is the eschatological community of Qumran.

In this community two savior figures were expected. At the end of days, the "Shoot of David" would rise together with the "Interpreter of the Law." The latter was called the Messiah of Aaron and ranked before the Messiah of Israel.[2] This messiah would be the ideal representative of the priests and serve the members of the New Covenant as an expert on the Law.

The Messiah of Israel is the traditional Son of David, the "Star arising from Jacob" and the "Scepter standing up from Israel." He was expected to crush their enemies.[3] Note the parallelism in the passage. "Star-Scepter" supported the belief in two messiahs: the "Star from Jacob" as the "Interpreter of the Law" is the Messiah of Aaron; the "Scepter from Israel" as "Prince of the whole Community" is the Davidic Messiah of Israel.

The basic biblical text for the Messiah of Aaron was found in the prophecy of Moses on the priestly tribe of Levi (Deut. 33:8–11, see 4 Q Testimonia 14–20): Levi was to "teach the statutes of God for Jacob and the Law to Israel." A remarkable description of the enlightening priestly task is offered in another fragmentary text: "He will make atonement for all the sons of his generation and will be sent to all the sons of [his time?]. His word will be like a word from Heaven, and his teaching as the will of God. As the sun of the world he will shine, and his fire will be seen in all the ends of the earth."[4]

The task of the Messiah of Israel was illustrated especially clearly in Isa. 11: He would judge the poor with righteousness and defeat the nations with the strength of his mouth.[5] The Essenes of Qumran were opposed to the Hasmonean high priests because they were not Zadokites and were therefore illegitimate. Moreover, Aristobulus I and his followers had usurped the title "king" without being descendants of David. They had also become high priests and kings through the support of the Gentile Seleucid government. But the genuine ruler of

Israel must be raised up by God, anointed with the Holy Spirit, and given an everlasting kingdom.[6] The Qumranites even believed that the two messiahs would rise from their midst. Their community represented the true covenant and the holy plantation that would produce the shoot of Jesse.[7]

We also find this dual messiahship in the Testaments of the Twelve Patriarchs, where their offices are described more explicitly and extended to the Gentiles. To the tribe of Judah is given the kingdom, which, however, is second to the priesthood of Levi.[8] The passages in Num. 24:17 and Isa. 11 depict the messianic king: he will rise as the star from Jacob and shine like the Sun of Righteousness. He will be anointed by the Spirit and the blessing from heaven and mediate this spirit of grace to Israel. The shoot from the root of Judah shall be a righteous ruler for the Gentiles, too; he will judge and save all those who call upon the name of the Lord.[9]

Even more beautiful is the description of the final high priest, to be raised by God.[10] He, too, will shine like a star in the sky and be the light of wisdom like the sun.[11] He will receive the glory of God and transfer it to his sons. In his richness the Gentiles will be illuminated by the grace of God.[12] Finally, he will open the gates of Paradise and give the fruit of the tree of life to the holy ones to eat.[13] The rise of the two messiahs can be preceded by the coming of a prophet such as Moses, as promised in Deuteronomy.[14]

At Qumran the turning point of the ages will be marked by a revolution in heaven. Michael, the angel of Israel (Dan. 10:21; 12:1), will be raised up among the divine beings and become Milki-Sedeq, the King of Righteousness.[15] Then Milki-Resha, Belial, the angelic prince over the evil spirits and adversary of the children of light—will be defeated decisively.

MESSIANIC EXPECTATIONS UNDER THE HERODIANS: THE PSALMS OF SOLOMON

After Jerusalem had been conquered by the Romans under Pompey in 63 B.C.E., the so-called Psalms of Solomon expressed the despair of the Jews and their messianic hope: "A man alien of our race" stood up against the sinful rulers in Israel; his victory is understood as God's judgment on the Hasmoneans, who had dishonored the throne of David (Sol. 17:6–9). God has chosen David as king over Israel and sworn to him that "never should his kingdom fail" (Sol. 17:5). Therefore God was asked to raise up "unto them their king, the son of David, at the time foreseen by Him" (Sol. 17:23). The oracle of Nathan justifies this expectation: the Messiah must be a descendant from David. His divine sonship is not mentioned as such, but he is called "the Anointed of the Lord" (Sol. 17:36). Isa. 11 reveals the liberating rule of this Davidic king: he will judge the tribes of Israel with righteousness and wisdom and sanctify them (Sol. 17:28–31, 35f., 48; see Isa. 11:2, 4); he will smite the earth with the rod of his mouth (Sol. 17:39; see Isa. 11:4). His basic virtue is the fear of the Lord (Sol. 17:44, see Isa. 11:3). On the other hand, God is the real sovereign, ruler, and savior of Israel (Sol. 17:1–4, 51) and the owner of the land who will protect and help God's people (Sol. 18:1, 10–14). Thus the Messiah is God's instrument and the mediator of God's Spirit.

The messianic hopes of the psalmist were not fulfilled during his lifetime. The Idumean Herod conquered Jerusalem with the help of the Roman legions and became king of Israel for a long period (37–4 B.C.E.). The Jews considered him a usurper of the throne and a tyrant who economically exploited Israel for his own glorification. Herod was made king by the grace of the first Roman emperor, Octavianus, who to Herod was a savior and guardian of peace and public welfare, a blessing for all the nations subject to him. In the countries of the East, those benefactors (*euergetai*) were believed to be superhuman beings and were honored with a special cult. Herod considered himself a worthy representative of the emperor and a benefactor for Israel in this Hellenistic sense.[16] Therefore, he expected that the Jews might flatter him with statues and honors that he might offer his personal protectors.[17]

On the other hand, Herod wanted to comply with Israel's idea of divine kingship. In this case, his rule and achievements had to be in basic agreement with those of David and Solomon and with the messianic expectations according to 2 Sam. 7 and Isa. 11. Unlike the Hasmoneans, Herod never wanted to officiate as high priest. His achievements as king of Israel were impressive and in his opinion should have satisfied the Jews. He had acquired a kingdom as large as that of David; he had increased its wealth and culture and adorned the cities with beautiful buildings, as did Solomon. Therefore, messianic ambitions were not alien to him. That is why he tried to prove Davidic descent for himself. He claimed that his ancestors had been Jewish exiles of David's house in Babylon.[18] According to the church father Epiphanius, the Herodians mentioned in the Gospels (Mark 3:6; 12:13//) were Jews who believed that Herod the Great would come again as the messianic king.[19]

Josephus seems to have pointed to Herod's messianic claims in an indirect way. In his *Antiquities*, the report on Herod's decision to rebuild the temple of Jerusalem[20] is preceded by the legendary story about the Essene prophet Menachem (Manaemos).[21] This prophet greeted Herod, when he was still a boy going to school, as "King of the Jews."[22] When young Herod reminded him that he was only a private citizen, Menachem "slapped him on his backside" and told him that "he had been found worthy of this by God."[23] If he would love justice and show piety toward God and mildness to the citizens, he would reach eternal glory. Actually, he would forget those virtues.

In the light of 2 Sam. 7, the composition and details of these two events in Herod's life are quite significant. David had been planning to build a temple in order to express his gratitude to God after he had completed a palace for himself in Jerusalem (2 Sam. 7:1f.). Herod established his palace in the Upper City, whereby foreign craftsmen had assisted him.[24] But then he occupied himself with rebuilding the temple,[25] "for making a full return to God for the gift of his kingdom,"[26] and for assuring "his eternal remembrance."[27] According to 2 Sam. 7 this was the task of David's son: "He shall build a house for my name and I establish the throne of his kingdom forever" (v. 13). If 2 Sam. 7 was related to the Messiah, the endeavor of rebuilding the temple could reveal the claim to messiahship (see Mark 14:58–62).

Josephus told the story of the Essene prophet Menachem because he wanted to explain Herod's sympathy for the Essenes. This may have messianic connotations as well. Menachem greeted the young man Herod, slapped him on his backside, and told him that he would have good fortune and eternal glory.[28] Herod wanted to actualize the oracle of Nathan. The reign of the messianic son of David would be characterized by the mark of eternity and by the steadfast love of God (2 Sam. 7:13, 15). When he committed iniquity, God would chasten him with the rod of men and with the stripes of the sons of men (v. 14b).

Menachem "chastened" young Herod "with the stripes of men" in order to show him symbolically that "one's fortune can change."[29] Later on, Herod must have understood this prophecy as election for messianic kingship. Josephus also writes that "when Herod was at the height of his power, he sent for Menachem and questioned him about the length of time he would reign."[30] Then he began to rebuild the temple, using the temple of Solomon as a model. According to Herod, the second temple was lacking sixty cubits in height when compared with that of Solomon. Because Cyrus and Darius had prescribed these dimensions,[31] he did away with those limitations.

But the Jews rejected these ambitions. They hated Herod. After his death they complained before Octavianus that he had been a transgressor of the Law and worked for the destruction of the Jews.[32] The hope for a Davidic messiah was upheld. This we see from the 14th and 15th Benedictions of the prayer *Shmone Esre*:

> *Return in mercy to your city, Jerusalem, and dwell in it, as Thou hast said. Build it soon in our days as an eternal building and in it establish the throne of David quickly. Be blessed, O Lord, who buildest Jerusalem. May the shoot of David, your servant, sprout quickly. Praise his horn through your help. Be blessed, Lord, who lettest sprout the horn of salvation.*

THE ROMAN PREFECTS IN JUDEA
AND THE FAILURE OF THE MESSIANIC PROPHETS

Herod the Great was succeeded by his son Archelaos, a king whom the Jews also hated. They sent a delegation to Rome to complain about Archelaos and to ask for Jewish autonomy. Octavianus divided Herod's realm into three ethnarchies under the sons of Herod, but added Samaria, Judea, and Jerusalem to the Roman province of Syria. Archelaos was removed and sent into exile by the emperor.[33] An Essene prophet had interpreted one of the king's dreams as meaning that the king's reign would end soon. As in the case of Herod, time was

Archelaos's great concern: would the Herodian dynasty last forever, as had been promised for the house and throne of David, or would God bring it to a sudden end, as with the kingship of Saul? This question was answered when Octavianus dismissed Archelaos.[34]

However, the Roman prefects, sent by the emperor as his representatives, were even worse than Herod and his sons. They wanted to extort as much money as possible during their brief administration. They did not understand the religious feelings of the Jews, to whom the defilement of the Holy Land and of the sacred city was highly offensive. The census, ordered by Quirinius in 6 C.E., caused the rise of a fourth party that developed into the Zealots and the Sicarii. They wanted to fight for the honor of God and for the freedom of Israel. Josephus holds them responsible for the Jewish revolt in 66–70 C.E. that resulted in the conquest of Jerusalem and the destruction of the temple.[35]

The messianic expectations grew stronger during the time of Roman occupation. Josephus says that the attempt to realize these hopes was made by false prophets. Some of them, like Theudas or the Egyptian Jew, are mentioned in the New Testament (Acts 5:36; 21:38). According to Matt. 24:11, 24, Jesus announced the appearance of false prophets and pseudo-messiahs; this prediction came true. Josephus gives a summary report on the activities of impostors and deceivers "who called upon the crowd to follow" them into the desert. There they would show unmistakable "signs and wonders," to be accomplished in harmony with "the design of God," i.e., in agreement with the holy Scriptures.[36] Pilate eliminated the movement of a Samaritan prophet who had commanded his compatriots to follow him to Mount Gerizim; there he wanted to rediscover the holy vessels that had been hidden since the time of Moses. Before the masses could go up the mountain, Roman troops stopped them. Many were taken prisoner and their leaders were killed.[37] Under Cuspius Fadus (45–46 C.E.), Theudas had persuaded many Jews to follow him to the river Jordan. He promised to split the river and so provide an easy passage to the other side. But the Roman cavalry attacked the crowd, killed many of them, and captured Theudas, who was executed.[38] Under the procurator Felix (59–60 C.E.), a Jew coming from Egypt appeared with his adherents on the Mount of Olives. There he promised that the walls of Jerusalem would collapse at his command and provide free access to the city.

Again, Roman soldiers dispersed the crowd; the Jewish prophet became "invisible."[39]

Here we have a new type of messianic savior. These saviors did not follow the ideal of David, probably because they could not claim to be his descendants. Rather, they wanted to be prophets like Moses, as promised in Deut. 18:15–22. They tried to prove the truth of their divine commission through signs similar to those done by Joshua, who split the Jordan (see Josh. 3:14–17) and brought down the walls of Jericho (Josh. 6:20). Such signs could reveal that God was with those prophets. To Josephus, the failure of such a demonstration revealed a false prophet "who presumed to speak a word in My name which I have not commanded him to speak . . . that same prophet shall die" (Deut. 18:20). This judgment held true for the great rabbi Gamaliel. In his famous council given to the Jerusalem Sanhedrin he said with regard to the Jesus movement: "If this plan or this undertaking is of man, it will fail; but if it is from God, you will not be able to overthrow them" (Acts 5:38f.).

Luke lets Gamaliel say about Theudas: "He rose before these days claiming he was someone" (*einai tina*; Acts 5:36). This is a strange way of describing a commission given by God, but it may be more correct than the direct self-proclamation "to be a prophet" that Josephus insinuates of those patriots.[40] The vague word "someone" indicates to me that these men were not simply self-made messiahs and impostors. They believed in their call, but waited for the final decision of God, who was supposed to determine their exact role and eschatological task, whether to serve as prophet or as messiah. Theudas may well have spoken of himself as "Son of Man" (*bar anash*), which is the Aramaic equivalent of the Greek pronoun *tis* (someone). Those Jews who knew their Bible may have understood the significance of such an indefinite expression; they may have linked it with Dan. 7:13f. We must remember that Gamaliel compared the movement of Theudas and of the Egyptian with that of Jesus (Acts 5:33–39). Jesus did not proclaim himself directly as Messiah and Son of God, but spoke of the "Son of Man" and indicated that he was chosen by God.

Flavius Josephus believed that messianic prophecy was fulfilled with the Flavian emperor Vespasianus.[41] In this connection he speaks of an "ambiguous oracle" mentioned also by Tacitus[42] and by Suetonius[43] that says: "At that time someone [*tis*] of them will become ruler over the world." Josephus says that it was erroneous to relate this oracle to a man of the Jewish people. Clearly, Vespasianus, who was hailed as emperor by his legions in Judea,[44] was meant. Prior to that, Josephus had proclaimed the same prophecy.[45]

FULFILLMENT OF THE MESSIANIC EXPECTATIONS: JESUS THE MESSIAH OF ISRAEL

Jesus of Nazareth was crucified as "the King of the Jews" (Mark 15:26). This is a fundamental historical fact. In Jewish terms, Jesus was believed to be the Messiah of Israel. Messiah (Christ) is central among the titles given to Jesus in the New Testament; it appears about 250 times. For Paul, the confession "Jesus is the Christ" became a kind of name: "Jesus Christ." Even the non-Christians Josephus,[46] Tacitus,[47] Suetonius,[48] and Pliny[49] used the name Christ (*Christos*, *Christus*, *Chrestus*) when they spoke of Jesus.

2 Sam. 7 was the basic text for the messianic self-understanding of Jesus. Mark's report on the trial of Jesus must be interpreted from this point of view. The witnesses who spoke against Jesus in the nocturnal hearing before the Sanhedrin said: "We heard him say: I will destroy this temple that is made with hands, and in three days I will build another not made with hands" (Mark 14:58). They must have understood this temple saying of Jesus in the light of 2 Sam. 7: it indicated the claim for messiahship, for the Son of David shall build a house for the Lord (v. 13). But the witnesses were wrong with regard to the first half of their testimony. Jesus did not intend to destroy the sanctuary in Jerusalem (see Mark 13:2). The new temple, to be built by him, was to be the community of the repentant Israelites, the church of the Messiah (Matt. 16:18; see Hos. 6:2). After the witnesses had failed to prove their point, the high priest could turn to Jesus and ask the decisive question: "Are you the Christ, the son of the Blessed?" (Mark 14:61; see 2 Sam. 7:14). Jesus affirmed it; his claim to be the Messiah and Son of God was declared blasphemy that deserved death (v. 63f.).

In Mark 12:37 the use of 2 Sam. 7 provides the answer for this disturbing question of Jesus: "David calls him Lord [the enthroned messiah] so how then is he his son?" The Messiah is the Son of David indeed (2 Sam. 7:12). His true dignity is his divine sonship (v. 14). This makes him superior to David, his father according to the flesh.

The dual sonship of Jesus was confessed in the earliest Christian creeds, such as Rom. 1:3f.: Jesus "was descended from David according to the flesh and designated Son of God in power according to the Spirit of holiness by his resurrection from the dead." Luke shows how Peter, the apostle to the Jews, and Paul, the apostle to the Gentiles, unfolded the good news of the dual sonship of Christ in their great speeches (Acts 2 and 13). Peter declared on Pentecost that David was a prophet of Jesus Christ. The king himself had understood the oracle of Nathan messianically: "God had sworn with an oath to him that He would set one of his descendants upon his throne" (Acts 2:30; see 2 Sam. 7:12; Ps. 132:11). Therefore he could speak of the "resurrection," the "raising up" (*anastasis*) of Jesus Christ: he foretold in Ps. 16:8–11 that the Messiah would not be abandoned to Hades, his flesh would not see corruption (Acts 2:25–28, 31). This was fulfilled in Jesus' resurrection from the dead (Acts 2:32). Moreover, David foresaw Jesus' resurrection as his exaltation at the right hand of God; he was "raised up" to the throne (Acts 2:33). This second aspect of the *anastasis* was foretold by David in Ps. 110:1: "The Lord said to my Lord, sit at my right hand, till I make thy enemies a stool for thy feet." Through the resurrection God has made the crucified Jesus "both Lord and Christ" (Acts 2:36); thus the Son of David became the Son of God (Rom. 1:4).

Paul proclaimed the gospel of the twofold resurrection of Christ and of his dual sonship in the synagogue of Pisidian Antioch (Acts 13): God raised Jesus from the dead (v. 30, 34–37, according to Ps. 16:10) and raised him up, exalted, and enthroned him to become Son of God (v. 33, according to Ps. 2:7, functioning in the way of Ps. 110:1). Moreover, 2 Sam. 7:12–14 was reiterated on an eschatological level by the angel Gabriel. He had to announce to Mary that her child "would be called Son of the Most High, and the Lord God would give him the throne of his father David; he would reign over the house of Jacob forever" (Luke 1:31–33; see 2 Sam. 7:13f.).

The main Christological titles of the New Testament are prepared and offered by these predictions of David: the Christ was the Son of David and the Son of God (2 Sam. 7:12–14; Ps. 2:7); he became Lord (*Kyrios*) through his exaltation and enthronement (Ps. 110:1). But the titles were grounded in the ministry of the earthly Jesus, who understood himself as Messiah, Christ. The cross of Golgotha became a saving event through the fact that "Christ [the Messiah] died for our sins in accordance with the scriptures," that he was buried and raised on the third day (1 Cor. 15:3f.). The death of a nonmessianic Jew would have had no such eschatological meaning.

The scriptural prophecy that confirmed the necessity of the suffering and resurrection of the Christ (see Acts 17:3; Luke 24:26, 45f.) was especially Isaiah's song about the Servant of the Lord (52:13–53:12). In the *Targum Jonathan*, the Aramaic rendering of the prophets, the Servant of the Lord was identified with the Messiah. But the suffering was attributed either to Israel or to the enemies. The Servant is depicted as the savior who will be successful and highly exalted.[50] This means that he will liberate the Israelites from exile and humiliation and make many of them obedient observants of the Law. Jesus and the early Christians, however, emphasized that the Messiah has to suffer according to the Scriptures and that he will save the people of God through his voluntary and vicarious death (Mark 10:45; 14:22–24). This constitutes the peculiarity and uniqueness of the messianic faith of the New Testament over against the expectations of the Jews.

Because of the emphasis on the atoning suffering of the Messiah, other "messianic" prophecies of the Hebrew Bible were moved to the background or reinterpreted. Thus the Davidic texts that suggested the triumph of the Messiah in wars and his political rule over the nations came to be understood differently (Gen. 49:10f.; Num. 24:17; Dan. 7:13f.). For example, the "Star from Jacob" was for Matthew a real star, which rose in the east and led the Magi to Bethlehem (chap. 2). But the ministry of Jesus is sometimes described in accordance with Isa. 11: it is performed in the power and wisdom of the Spirit of God (Mark 6:2). Jesus called his disciples by virtue of a superhuman insight (Mark 1:16–20; John 1:42–51, see Isa. 11:3) and he judged the poor with righteousness (Matt. 5:3–12, see Isa. 11:4).

We also find the messianic interpretation of the Moses tradition in the New Testament. Jesus was the prophet like Moses (Acts 3:22; 7:37; Luke 9:35); he too did signs and wonders that proved his divine commission (Acts 2:22). Miracles such as the stilling of the storm or the feeding of the five thousand remind us strongly of the salvation of Israel at the Red Sea and of the bread from heaven in the wilderness (Mark 4:35–41; 6:30–44; see John 6:1–21). But Jesus rejected the demand to do "signs from Heaven" (Mark 9:11f.; see Matt. 4:1–11). He was obedient to the thoughts and ways of God, which are very different from our expectations of a divine Savior.

NOTES

1. Fragment 4 Q *Florilegium*.
2. 1 QS 9:11; 1 QS A 2:11.
3. 4 Q *Testimonia* 9–13 according to Num. 24:15–17.
4. 4 Q *Aharonique* (ed. J. Starcky).
5. V. 4; cf. 1 QS b V 24f.
6. 1 QS b V 21.
7. 1 QH 8:10f.
8. T Judah 21:2–4; T Levi 8:11–15.
9. T Judah 24, see Isa. 11:1, 4, 10.
10. T Levi 18.
11. T Levi 18:3f.
12. T Levi 18:7–10.
13. T Levi 18:11.
14. Cf. 1 QS 9:11; 4 Q *Testimonia* 5–8.
15. 11 Q *Melch*; 1 QM 17:6, see Ps. 82; 110:1, 4.
16. *Antiquities* 15:383.
17. *Ant.* 16:157f.
18. *Ant.* 14:9.
19. *Panarion* XX 1.
20. *Ant.* 15:380–402.
21. *Ant.* 15:373–79.
22. *Ant.* 15:373, 375f.
23. *Ant.* 15:374.
24. *Ant.* 15:318.
25. *Ant.* 15:380–402.
26. *Ant.* 15:387.
27. *Ant.* 15:380.
28. *Ant.* 15:373–76.
29. *Ant.* 15:374.
30. *Ant.* 15:377.

31. S 385f.
32. *Ant.* 17:304ff.
33. *Ant.* 17:344.
34. *Ant.* 17:344–48; 2 Sam. 7:13, 15.
35. *Ant.* 18:1–10.
36. *Jewish Wars* 2:258–60; *Ant.* 20:167f.
37. *Ant.* 18:85–87.
38. *Ant.* 20:97–99.
39. *Ant.* 20:169–72.
40. *Ant.* 20, 169; *War* 2:261.
41. *War* 6:312.
42. *Historiae* V 18.
43. *Vespasianus* c.4.
44. *War* 6:313.
45. *War* 3:352, 400.
46. *Ant.* 18:63f.; 20:200.
47. *Annales* 15:44.
48. *Claudius* 25.
49. *Epistulae* 10:26.
50. See Tg 52:13.

CHAPTER THREE

THE CRITERION OF DISSIMILARITY: THE WRONG TOOL?

REGINALD H. FULLER

Quite independently of each other, the late Norman Perrin and the present writer formulated in a systematic way a number of criteria of authenticity that were being used especially in Germany to enable the critical reconstruction of the Jesus tradition in the Gospels.[1] One criterion in particular has proved to be highly controversial. This is what I originally called the criterion of distinctiveness. The definition of it was taken from Bultmann's discussion of the similitudes: "(1) the similitude is authentic where its content is opposed to Jewish morality and piety; (2) where it reflects the eschatological temper characteristic of Jesus' proclamation; (3) where such teaching exhibits no specifically Christian traits." And I drew from Bultmann the conclusion that "traditio-historical criticism eliminates from the authentic sayings of Jesus those which are paralleled in the Jewish tradition (apocalyptic and rabbinic) and those which reflect the faith, practice and situations of the Post-Easter Church as we know them outside the gospels."[2] Norman Perrin designated this criterion as the "criterion of dissimilarity" and took his formulation of it from Hans Conzelmann's celebrated essay "Jesus Christus." Conzelmann presented it this way: "So far as the reconstruction of the teaching is concerned the following methodological basis is valid: we may accept as authentic material which fits in with neither Jewish thinking nor the conceptions of the later [Christian] community."[3]

This criterion has been vigorously attacked, especially in Great Britain.[4] The most thorough critique has been offered by Morna Hooker, now Lady Margaret Professor of Divinity at the University of Cambridge, in the last of her three discussions of the subject.[5] There she

44

marshals no less than nine arguments against this criterion. To my knowledge, only one voice has been raised in Britain in defense of the criterion, and that is David Mealand's.[6]

The most important criticisms can be summarized as follows. The remainder of this essay will be devoted to answering each point in succession.

1. Our knowledge of first-century Judaism and of early Christianity is limited. Hence what we take to be dissimilar may not in fact have been so. Further knowledge may wipe out all that passes the criterion of dissimilarity and leave us nothing.[7]

2. Since Jesus was a first-century Jew, he must have agreed with first-century Judaism, and his followers must have agreed with him in many things.[8]

3. The criterion is circular. The same materials (viz., the Gospels) are used to establish both what the early church taught and what Jesus taught. There is no way of breaking out of the circle.[9]

4. The criterion does not give us what we want. We want to know what is *characteristic* of Jesus; the criterion instead gives us only what is *unique*.[10]

5. Several object to the skepticism involved in the use of the criterion. It leaves a distorted picture of Jesus because it may throw away much that is genuine.

6. The criterion is subjective in its application. This objection is expressed in different ways. Some contend that it is a faith assumption to presume that there was something unique about the historical Jesus. Hooker makes two points in this connection: (a) its decision on what is dissimilar is subjective and (b) its decision on Jesus' unique eschatological stance is subjective as is shown by the various interpretations scholars of Jesus' eschatology offered.[11]

7. Some critics of the criterion have argued that it is safe so long as it is used positively, that is, if used not to eliminate material as unauthentic but to establish it as authentic.[12]

As far as I know, Norman Perrin never published any reply (although he did have a vigorous argument with Hooker at the SNTS [Society of New Testament Studies] meeting in 1971). And the Germans who use the criterion tend to ignore any criticism unless they are uttered in German. It therefore behooves me, as one who has been the object of attack, to reply. I will try to answer each point in turn.

1. It is true that our knowledge both of first-century Palestinian Judaism and Christianity is deficient, but in regard to Judaism the situation has considerably improved since the discovery of the Qumran materials. We now have some knowledge of the eschatological stance of certain groups who stood nearest to the origins of the Christian movement, and so we are able to see the difference between them and the message of Jesus. It is theoretically possible that another discovery similar to the Qumran finds would turn up evidence for a community holding precisely the same eschatological stance Jesus did. But we need not fear this, for one would expect that such figures would have provoked so much opposition that they would have been crucified or otherwise disposed of, and perhaps have launched a movement marking a radical shift from Judaism, although in the case of Jesus the Easter event must also be factored in. Meanwhile we have to work with the evidence we have, remembering always that all historical reconstructions can never claim more than a high degree of probability, never absolute certainty. Users of the criterion of dissimilarity have sometimes been guilty of claiming such certainty. (Norman Perrin, who could be very dogmatic about his conclusions, was probably guilty of that at times.) Still, we have to work with what we have.

It is equally true that our knowledge of the early Christian community is limited. But the evidence that we do have is there, and where it is applied in the use of the criterion of dissimilarity its use is not likely to be undermined by the discovery of fresh data. We do know that the earliest community proclaimed that Jesus entered upon his messianic office at his exaltation (Rom. 1:3; Acts 2:36) and that a development occurred in which his messianic office was dated backward first to his baptism (or possibly to his transfiguration and then to his baptism) and finally to the moment of conception/birth.[13] This justifies our suspicion that Jesus material in which messiahship is attributed to him in the post-Easter sense is either the creation or the adaptation of the post-Easter community.[14] Such material should be laid aside, at least provisionally, in any reconstruction of the Jesus tradition.

2. It is certainly true that Jesus agreed with Judaism on many points and that his followers would have agreed with him. I pointed

this out in one of my discussions of the criterion of dissimilarity, and the critics have duly noted it, although they have usually complained that this was only a grudging concession.[15] And it is true that neither Norman Perrin nor the Germans have shown much awareness of this obvious fact. We have to define the sort of questions on which agreement is to be expected if Jesus was a first-century Palestinian Jew and the disciples followers of Jesus, and the sort of things on which there are differences for very good reason. On the Jewish side, Jesus obviously agreed with Judaism that God was Creator, that God was active in history, particularly in Israel's salvation-history, that God demanded righteous conduct through the law and spoke through the prophets, and so on. These matters are generally accepted truths of the Jewish religion, without which no one, including Jesus, would be a true member of the Jewish community. Where Jesus can be shown to differ, and therefore where he exhibits himself as most characteristic, is the *way* (recognized by the application of the criterion of dissimilarity) in which he held these truths. Jesus offers in his word an immediate experience of God as creator. He enunciates the immediate demand of God. He confronts men and women with the immediate eschatological presence of God.[16]

As for his agreement with the early church, we can for instance establish that he and they agreed that God could be addressed as *Abba*. This is sometimes taken by the objectors as a demonstration of the inconsistency with which the criterion of dissimilarity is applied. But there is a difference. Paul says that for the believer to call God "Abba" is something that can be done only in the Holy Spirit, through whom the believer has been adopted into a relationship with God. Jesus' use of Abba, on the contrary, does not depend on a relationship into which he has been brought by the hearing of the apostolic proclamation or by baptism into the name of Jesus. For him that relationship expressed in the use of Abba is primal and unmediated. As he does not teach as an abstract truth that men and women can call God "Father." He invites them through his word into the privilege of calling God "Abba," so that they are dependent upon him in doing so. Thus there is both similarity and dissimilarity between Jesus' use of Abba and Paul's use— similarity in that the same word is used, dissimilarity in that in Jesus' proclamation it is made possible for others by response to his eschatological message, while for Paul it is made possible by response to the apostolic kerygma and reception of the Holy Spirit. The criterion of dissimilarity here points not to absolute difference but to continuity amid discontinuity.

3. Circularity of argument is always a danger when sources are limited. What is needed is a *dos moi pou stō* outside the gospel materials. The authentic Pauline letters, and especially the pre-Pauline materials within those letters, provide the best starting point.[17] The next best bet is the primitive Christological material enshrined in the kerygmatic speeches in Acts.[18] The use of this material gives an entrée into the different levels of tradition within the Gospels and enables us (with other methods, such as the distinction between connecting links and the bodies of pericopes) to reconstruct painstakingly the three levels of the gospel traditions: the Jesus level, the community level in oral tradition, and the redactional level of the evangelists. Unless we are prepared to take the risk of distinguishing between these three levels, we reduce the whole of the Gospels to one level. This is then assigned indiscriminately to the Jesus level,[19] or equally indiscriminately to the redaction level. The first results in uncritical incredulity, the second in skepticism far more thoroughgoing than that of which the critics of the criterion of dissimilarity complain.

4. There is a logical distinction between what is characteristic and what is unique, but I would argue that when applied to Jesus the two turn out to be largely identical. It might be objected that this is a faith assumption rather than an objective application of the dissimilarity test. But Jesus' crucifixion points to a radical difference between his stance and Judaism, and given the shift that took place between the early first-century Judaism and the earliest post-Easter community, it is surely reasonable to assume on purely historical grounds that the primary cause of this shift was the appearance of the earthly Jesus. Consequently, there must have been elements in his teaching and activity that distinguished him from the Judaism in which he was reared. This assumption is legitimately made in the case of all figures who altered the course of history, for example, Socrates. In the historical Jesus the major feature that satisfies our criterion in this regard is of course his eschatological stance.

5. Does the criterion of dissimilarity unduly narrow reconstruc-

tion of the earthly Jesus, his message and ministry? It all depends on what motivates the interest in the early Jesus. If one is an old-fashioned Ritschlian liberal Protestant like Harnack, or an equally old-fashioned orthodox conservative like H. P. Liddon, for both of whom the earthly Jesus was the direct object of faith, one will not be satisfied with the historical Jesus of Bultmann, or with that of Bornkamm and Conzelmann. But if the reason for inquiry into the historical Jesus is to provide a legitimate basis for the post-Easter kerygma, then I would submit with Leander E. Keck that "the thorough criticism [in which I would include the use of the dissimilarity test] of the Gospels does provide us with sufficient data about Jesus that the contour of his life as a whole can come into view, and that this can be the core of Christian preaching and the dominant *datum* with which theology works."[20] These data may be summarized under six headings: (1) Jesus' eschatological message, (2) his radical demand, (3) his teaching on God, (4) the authoritative call to follow him, (5) his voluntary self-exposure to rejection and martyrdom in his commitment to his message, and (6) the radical questioning of the Jesus cause by his followers as a result of his rejection and martyrdom and the reinstatement of their faith in him through the Easter event. These six data—and there are doubtless others—comprising as they do a critically assured minimum, provide an adequate basis for the kerygma of the post-Easter community, which interpreted Jesus' career, viewed in the light of Easter, as the eschatological act of God.

6. Is the criterion of dissimilarity subjective in its application? The first form of this charge, namely, that it is a faith assumption to suppose that there was something unique about the historical Jesus, has been dealt with under objection 4 (above) in connection with the relation of what is unique to Jesus to what is characteristic of him. The second form of this charge deals specifically with the question of Jesus' eschatological stance. It is alleged that the disagreement among scholars as to what this stance was renders all decisions on that score subjective.[21] First I would contend that this should not impede us from endeavoring to reconstruct Jesus' eschatological proclamation to the best of our critical ability and from submitting our results on this subject to the judgment of our peers. Morna Hooker does the same when she accepts the parables as likely to go back to Jesus, despite the

fact that their eschatological message is variously interpreted.[22] And Hooker exaggerates the degree of scholarly disagreement in Jesus' eschatological stance. If on Hegelian lines we regard Schweitzer's thoroughgoing (future) eschatology as the thesis, and Dodd's realized eschatology as the antithesis, we may discern the emergence of a synthetic consensus in such scholars as Jeremias, Cullmann, and Kümmel, all of whom in various ways combine present and future elements in their reconstruction of Jesus' eschatology. The Bultmannian existential interpretation should be seen precisely as a modern hermeneutical restatement of Jesus' eschatological message rather than as an exegesis of it. It is a statement of what that message may *mean* for today (in the German context, no doubt) rather than what it *meant*. Basically, it operates with the same synthesis of future and present eschatology.

7. It is attractive to restrict the criterion of dissimilarity to a positive function, that of discovering what can reasonably be attributed to the pre-Easter Jesus rather than to the post-Easter *Kyrios*. For our concern is precisely to find out what that Jesus did say and do. In practice, however, it generally tends to be used both positively and negatively. It is used positively when, for example, it is argued that Jesus' radical demand is authentic on the ground that it differs both from contemporary Judaism and from the post-Easter church. It is used negatively when it is decided that any saying which reflects the explicit Christology of the post-Easter community is not authentic to Jesus. Actually, the critics of the criterion of dissimilarity sometimes object that its users do not apply it radically enough—as when, for example, it is objected that passages adduced for an indirect or implicit Christology in the pre-Easter Jesus should be rejected. This objection seems quite unwarranted, for there is a real difference between implicit and explicit Christology,[23] and the implicit Christology can be eliminated only if it is interpreted in an explicit sense. There is a real difference between a Jesus who confronts men and women with eschatological presence (in word and deed) of the living God, and one who overtly adopts messianic titles as self-designations. The first challenges his hearers to a response, the other answers the questions before they are asked. We would agree that especially the negative use of its dissimilarity should be conducted with great caution and with a consciousness of the tentative character of its results. Its practitioners,

myself included,[24] have tended to be too dogmatic about our elimina-
tions from the authentic Jesus material.

In conclusion, it can be said that the criticisms of the criterion of
dissimilarity are valuable insofar as they challenge its users to be more
tentative about their results. But I still believe it to be the best tool we
have if what we want is a critically assured minimum, rather than a
maximum that appears excessively vulnerable to skepticism and doubt.

NOTES

Reprinted from *Christological Perspectives*, ed. Robert F. Berkey and Sarah A.
Edwards (New York: The Pilgrim Press, 1982), 42–48. Used by permission.

1. Reginald H. Fuller, *A Critical Introduction to the New Testament* (London:
Duckworth, 1966), 94–98; Norman Perrin, *Rediscovering the Teaching of Jesus* (New
York: Harper & Row, 1967), 39–47.

2. Rudolf Bultmann, *History of the Synoptic Tradition* (Oxford: Blackwell, 1972),
205.

3. Hans Conzelmann, *Jesus*, trans. J. Raymond Lord (Philadelphia: Fortress
Press, 1973), 16.

4. Morna D. Hooker, *The Son of Man in Mark* (Montreal: McGill University,
1967), 6–7; F. Gerald Downing, *The Church and Jesus*, Studies in Biblical Theology
2/10 (London: SCM Press, 1968), 111–30; Morna D. Hooker, "Christology and
Methodology," *New Testament Studies* 17 (1970/71): 480–87; R. S. Barbour, *Traditio-
Historical Criticism of the Gospels: Some Comments on Current Methods* (London: SPCK,
1972), 1–27; D. G. A. Calvert, "An Examination of the Criteria for Distinguishing
the Authentic Words of Jesus," *New Testament Studies* 18 (1971/72): 209–19 Morna
D. Hooker, "On Using the Wrong Tool," *Theology* 75 (1972): 570–81; R. T. France,
in *History, Criticism, and Faith*, ed. C. Brown (Downers Grove, IL: InterVarsity Press,
1976), 108–17; Eric Mascall, *Theology and the Gospel of Christ* (London: SPCK, 1977),
87–97; I. Howard Marshall, *I Believe in the Historical Jesus* (London: Hodder &
Stoughton, 1977), 201–3.

5. "On Using the Wrong Tool." Mascall merely repeats Hooker's arguments in
this article. Marshall repeats some of them.

6. "The Dissimilarity Test," *Scottish Journal of Theology* 31 (1978): 41–50. I am
greatly indebted to this article.

7. E.g., Hooker, "On Using the Wrong Tool," 575.

8. E.g., Ibid., 576.

9. E.g., Calvert, "Examination," 212, 214; France, in *History*, 112.

10. Hooker, "Christology and Methodology," 481; "On Using the Wrong Tool," 574.

11. Hooker, "On Using the Wrong Tool," 576.

12. Calvert, "Examination," 219; Hooker, "Christology and Methodology," 486; France, in *History*, 114. Already Oscar Cullmann had made the same point in "Unzeitmässige Bermerkungen zum 'historischen Jesus' der Bultmannschule," in *Der historische Jesus und der kerygmatische Christus*, ed. Helmut Ristow and Karl Matthias (Berlin: Evangelische Verlagsanstalt, 1961), 266–80, esp. 277; also Oscar Cullmann, *Salvation in History* (New York: Harper & Row, 1967), 18.

13. Raymond E. Brown, *The Birth of the Messiah: A Commentary on the Infancy Narratives in Matthew and Luke* (New York: Doubleday, 1977), 29–32 and elsewhere.

14. I would argue in general for adaptation rather than creation. Nearly all the principal synoptic messianic titles, *Christos, Kyrios*, Son of God, Son of David, Son of Man, have *some* roots in the authentic Jesus material, even though none of them was used directly as a self-designation by Jesus himself.

15. E.g., France, in *History*, 110.

16. These statements summarize the findings of various participants in the New Quest (Käsemann, Fuchs, Bornkamm, Conzelmann). It is gratifying that John A. T. Robinson, after a period in which he one-sidedly (although in the British situation understandably) emphasized the human side of Jesus, has most recently taken up this God-sidedness of Jesus from Fuchs and others; see J. A. T. Robinson, *Can We Trust the New Testament?* (Grand Rapids, MI: Eerdmans, 1977), 104–7.

17. See, e.g., A. M. Hunter, *Paul and His Predecessors* (London: SCM Press, 1961).

18. The debate on pre-Lukan elements in the kerygmatic speeches of Acts continues. A reasonable position is that of Eduard Schweizer, "Concerning the Speeches in Acts," in *Studies in Acts*, ed. Leander E. Keck and L. Louis Martyn (Nashville: Abingdon, 1966), 208–16. As they stand, the Acts speeches are Lukan compositions, but they enshrine pre-Lukan and primitive Christological materials.

19. As happens in Hooker's treatment of the Son-of-Man materials in *The Son of Man in Mark*.

20. Leander E. Keck, *A Future for the Historical Jesus* (Nashville: Abingdon Press, 1971), 262.

21. It is incorrect to say that Bultmann sees the eschatological emphasis as "wholly future" (ibid.). It is a future that decisively qualifies the present. The kingdom is "schon im Anbruch" (Rudolf Bultmann, *Theology of the New Testament* [London: SCM Press, 1952], 1:7).

22. E.g., Hooker, "Christology and Methodology," 486.

23. As far as I am aware, the only critic to eliminate implicit 1:7 as well as

explicit Christology from the authentic Jesus material is Howard M. Teeple, "The Origin of the Son of Man Christology," *Journal of Biblical Literature* 84 (1965): 211–50, esp. 227.

24. As when I overconfidently eliminated the logion Matt. 5:17 from the Jesus material, in *A Critical Introduction to the New Testament*, 96.

CHAPTER FOUR

THE GRECO-ROMAN BACKGROUND
OF NEW TESTAMENT CHRISTOLOGY

THOMAS SCHMELLER

TRANSLATED BY IRMGARD DÖRING KLEE

"*Sotēr tou kosmou*," savior of the world—that is what Christians around
the end of the first century called their Lord Jesus (John 4:42; 1 John
4:14). In a synonymous phrase, Julius Caesar was called "*sotēr tou
oikoumenē.*" The famous inscription of Priene celebrates Augustus as the
"Savior," sent by providence, because he "ended war and arranged
peace." Saviors can be gods, particularly Zeus as guarantor of world
order and Asklepios as healer, but also human beings such as doctors,
philosophers, generals, and, of course, rulers. The sources[1] indicate
that a savior resides close to the boundary between the divine and the
human. There *was* such a borderline in the Hellenistic realm, but it was
obscured. The limbo was populated by demons, heroes, and divine
humans, because "relative to man, the deity is not simply a different
being, but the perfect form of the same being."[2]

The following is an overview of specific beings and types in this
limbo as far as they are relevant to New Testament Christology. Rele-
vancy in that sense is not measured by the influence that these beings
might have had in the formation of New Testament Christology. Such
influence can only rarely be substantiated. The point is rather to sketch
the cognitive horizon under which Greco-Roman audiences of the
Gospel would have had access to the person and function of Jesus
Christ. This cognitive horizon was made up of mythical and historical
figures, and making the distinction is difficult.

THE HUMAN GOD

With few exceptions, it was self-evident in the Greco-Roman world that gods are close to people, at least in the sense that they intervene in the human world. Gods observe what is happening, get involved, help, hinder, reward, punish, make history. The manner in which their involvement was perceived was manifold. In Homer's anthropomorphic mythology gods think and act just like humans, sire children, participate in human wars. This view lasted, especially in folklore, into the era of the Roman emperors. In educated circles such myths were interpreted philosophically. To the Stoics, for example, the various myths of gods were allegories for the one divine logos, whom they also called Zeus, who gives life and works in all things, who puts forth the best order.

The intervention of the gods becomes particularly interesting for us when it involves the taking on of human form.[3] One of Homer's verses, much debated in antiquity, runs like this:

Gods, after all, are walking through the cities too, in many forms;
They come and look as aliens from foreign lands,
Examining meanwhile men's pride and righteousness.

(*Odyssey* 17.485–87)

In many stories gods move around the earth in human form. Often the motivation for this metamorphosis is an attempt to test people, as, for example, with Apollon and Poseidon, who "assumed the likeness of men [*eikasthentes anthrōpois*]" (Ps-Apollodor, Bibliotheca 2, 5, 9)[4] and entered the service of King Laomedon in order to learn if he was as unreliable as reputed.

The possibility of encountering gods in human form, not only in the past but in the present, was taken for granted during New Testament times. In Acts 14:8–18 Paul heals a lame person. The reaction of the masses was this:

They shouted in the Lycaonian language: "The gods have come down to us in human form!" Barnabas they called Zeus, and Paul they called

Hermes, because he was the chief speaker. The priest of Zeus, whose temple was just outside the city, brought oxen and garlands to the gates; he and the crowds wanted to offer sacrifice. (Acts 14:11–13)

Similarly, in Acts 28:6, Paul is taken for a god because the bite of a snake does not affect him. In both cases the power of a miracle arouses in the spectators the idea of divinity.

Certainly the above passages are no real parallels to the New Testament concept of the incarnation of the Son of God: always there is a rather short period of human likeness, never a true transformation into a human being. The differentiation is not so much the human birth, but the human death. Eternity, not as a condition without beginning but as an existence without end, is so characteristic of the Greek gods that they often are called "the undying." This, however, is not so certain for gods at the center of ancient mystery cults. It was, and often still is, said of those gods that they would experience death and resurrection, and that within the cult the mystic could share in this death and resurrection. This view in such generality can no longer be supported today. A distinction must be made between the death and the revival of the cult god. The idea of resurrection is rarely approximated except in the myth of Adonis. However, Adonis' periodic shuttling between the world of the dead and the world of the gods demonstrates that he is a deity of vegetation who lives and dies in rhythm with nature. Furthermore, worshipers of this god are not known to participate in his fate. Therefore, the proximity to the belief in the resurrection of Jesus is remote. On the whole, the idea of a deity's revival is untypical for mystery cults.[5]

A different situation exists with the death of a deity. Elements of suffering and dying are farther spread in myths and cults. Burkert,[6] however, calls attention to the fact that such elements are not necessary parts of a mystery cult (compare the Mithras cult, which does not contain any). They can be found not only in mystery cults but also, for example, in the Herakles cult. The inclusion of the cult participants in the death of the deity, therefore, is not a central issue. In view of the New Testament witness to the death of Jesus, it is important that the dying of the mystery deity is neither voluntary nor does it have a proxy character.

We meet another kind of human god when gods appear as carriers of culture for humankind. Thus Zeus sends Hermes to teach people the rules of coexistence under a code of justice, or he sends Dionysus to introduce viticulture.[7] This appearance of gods among people is different from the kind mentioned above in three respects: it does not involve a test, but a helping hand; the assistance requires a protracted presence; and we find here the element of one god being sent by another. The close proximity to New Testament Christology is obvious.

The extreme case of a human god in the Greco-Roman world, and, concurrently, the most Christlike deity, is Asklepios. The mythological representations of this figure are in conflict with one another and can best be explained by assuming the following historic development:[8] Asklepios originally was a pre-Greek earth god in Thessalia. In Greek mythology he was demoted to a hero: Apollon became his father (and thus gained superiority over his former rival Asklepios), a mortal became his mother. The child Asklepios was raised by the wise centaur Chiron and was taught medicine. When Asklepios himself raised the dead, he was—due to Hades' complaint—killed by the lightning of Zeus. Here occurs a change that transforms Asklepios into a genuine god again: because of his achievements for humankind (particularly the founding of medicine) and because of his martyrdom for them, Asklepios earned the heretofore doubtful state of divinity. For the people who searched and found healing in his sanctuaries, this status of deity was without question. Thus a personal and almost pietistic relationship to a god developed.

Such an emotion is invoked by the words with which Aelius Aristides, the second-century B.C.E. orator and admirer of Asklepios, describes how he received therapeutic instructions from the god:

> *The revelation was devoid of any doubt, just as one could feel the appearance of the god with all certainty in a thousand other instances. One sensed his touching, and felt his coming, in a state between sleep and wakefulness. . . . What person could describe this state with mere words?* (Orbis Antiquus 48, 32)

Since the fifth century B.C.E., the sanctuaries at which such revelations took place, along with miracle and dream healings, psychosomatic cures, and medical treatments in our modern sense, spread from the central cult location in Epidauros.

Asklepios, the kind god who understood and soothed human suffering, had, in cult and in skill, traits that were similar to those of Christ. Thus, according to the Paians of Epidauros, the thrice-repeated appeal to Asklepios was: "Hail, Lord, great Savior, Savior of the World [*oikoumenēs sotēr*]." In art, the image of Asklepios probably had an influence on the image of Christ. How strongly Asklepios was taken as a rival to Christ in Christian circles can be seen in the eager, at times polemic, disputations in the old Christian Apologists. With Asklepios, however, there is no real equivalent to the forgiveness of sins as bestowed by Christ.

We turn now to the "godly human." The figure of Herakles shows how difficult it is to separate the two. Like Asklepios, Herakles is the son of a divine father and a mortal mother. Like him, he gains deification through his efforts and achievements. But in Herakles the heroic, and thus the solely human, aspect is much more dominant than in Asklepios, either because of the different background of the Asklepios myth, as presented above, or because of the different nature of this god's achievements.

THE DIVINE MAN

The question of whether the *theios anēr* (divine man) actually existed as a type during Greco-Roman times seemed to be resolved in the negative around the end of the 1970s. The entire concept, most extensively developed by Ludwig Bieler,[9] therefore apparently had died. Since then, however, published studies have given a cautiously more positive opinion.[10] According to this recent trend, the *theios anēr* is not a clearly defined type, but a concept that serves well as an ideal. One can compose a list of phenomena that are related more or less to the *theios anēr* (inasmuch as they show superhuman aptitudes and effects) without ever having been attributes of a single historic figure.

D. Tiede[11] distinguished between two types. One would be the Miracle Charismatic who would prove divinity by miraculous works that surpass human capacities; the other would be the Sage whose godliness would rest in particularly great insight and virtue. Tiede himself limits his classification by confining it to the period up to the middle of the second century C.E., and even then only to educated circles.

This goes well with the kind of development assumed by G. Theissen.[12] According to him, the *theioi andres* of the archaic and classical period were shamanlike miracle charismatics and seers who at times also acted as philosophical-religious teachers. During the period of Hellenism, historically active great personages were looked upon as divine: astounding achievements of poets, philosophers, athletes, and rulers demonstrated the *theios anēr*. Since the beginning of the Christian era, a new irrationalism can be recognized that manifests itself, aside from the growth of astrology and magic, in a return of the miracle charismatics as *theioi andres*. Therefore, during the period of the Roman emperors, several types coexisted at first. In educated circles the "rational" view of Hellenism may have persisted longer. Even there the popular, undifferentiated image of the *theios anēr* that does not distinguish between philosopher, miracle charismatic, and magician finally prevailed.

> *The "divine man" was, in some cases even from birth, possessor of that "theion ti" which gave him the wisdom (sophia or philosophia) to unravel the secrets of the controlling powers of the universe, thus himself becoming a power, and giving proof of that power by actualizing it in miracles.*[13]

A few examples will clarify these developments and the various types.

The two biographies from antiquity about Pythagoras (sixth century B.C.E.) originated with Porphyrius (third century C.E.) and Jamblichus (fourth century C.E.). Both portray Pythagoras as a *theios anēr* in the broader sense, i.e., as a miracle worker and a philosopher or scientist. There are reports about Pythagoras healing through music and song; having power over animals, wind, and waves; and effecting miraculous changes of locale. Jamblichus describes the contemporary reaction to Pythagoras:

> *Some took him for the Pythic god, others for Apollon from the land of the Hyperboreans, some for Paian, again others for one of the*

daemons living on the moon: Everyone declared him to be a different Olympian who had appeared to those then living in human form in order to help the lives destined for death, to righten them.
(Pythagoras 30)

W. Fauth delineated the parallels and differences between Pythagoras and Jesus.[14] The most important are: Pythagoras is seen as the son of a god; however, the determination of the divine father vacillates, so that unlike Jesus, he is not the "Son of (sc., the one) God." Pythagoras combines "common knowledge (astronomy, mathematics, music, natural philosophy) with secret knowledge (mysticism, magic). . . . The revelation knowledge of the Son-Logos is missing."[15] Because of a trip to Hades, Pythagoras has a certain connection with death, but this has nothing to do with redemptive dying and resurrection. Although his miracles demonstrate some analogy to the work of Jesus, they merely reveal the superiority of the soul, not the beneficial breaking-in of the Kingdom of God through the Son of God.

Another philosopher, comparable to Pythagoras but living at the time of Jesus, was Apollonius of Tyana, who also combined miracle charisma with salvation doctrine. In his biography by Philostrat (about 170–249 C.E.) we find an idealized description of a perfect Pythagorean philosopher and religious reformer whose life-style is ascetic and vegetarian, who propounds correct (bloodless) worshiping of the one God, and who is a great counselor because of his special insight and knowledge of people. Apollonius was also thought to be the son of a god (Proteus or Zeus), and he performed exorcisms and natural and healing miracles on lame and blind persons. The biography contains further parallels with Jesus: both men's births are accompanied by miraculous events, both are accused by their opponents of sorcery, both gather apostles about them who safeguard and transmit information about their master, and both are accepted into heaven. However, the limitations presented for Pythagoras relative to Jesus also apply here.

Among the *theioi andres* also are some who were famous as miracle workers or as sages. Of special interest is the divine sage who can be found in the Cynic and Stoic realm (though not only there: Epicurus also was considered divine). Diogenes, for example, was praised by Kerkidas as "son of Zeus" (Diog. L VI, 77). Dion of Prusa calls him an "overseer" (*episkopos*) of people (or. 9.1); Epictetus describes him as a messenger and "spy" (*kataskopos*) who served people by investigating alleged evils (Discourses 1, 24, 6). He was a servant of Zeus, "so gentle and kind-hearted that he gladly took upon himself all those troubles and physical hardships for the sake of the common weal" (Discourses 3, 24, 64–65).

While the Cynics saw in the sage an attainable model, the Stoics lifted him to such heights that it was doubtful he could exist in reality. Nevertheless, for the Stoics he was also a model to be imitated. His divinity manifests itself in the perfection of his virtue, but its source is the logos that dwells in him and guides him. Seneca especially develops the image of this divine sage: he is closer to God than to people and only his mortality differentiates him from the Divine (epistles 41, 4–5; 53, 11; 73, 14–16).

The last phenomenon of a divine man we will consider is the Hellenistic ruler cult, particularly its extension into the imperial cult during the New Testament era. As we have already seen, the boundary between the human and the divine realms was fluid insofar as a deity was perceived to possess the highest imaginable realization of qualities that to a lesser degree also applied to people. Now, the quality that related the ruler to the gods was power. A Greek maxim states it concisely:

> *What is a God? That which is strong.*
> *What is a king? He who is equal to the divine.*[16]

In the Hellenistic world the ruler cult began with Alexander the Great. He was greeted by the priest of the oracle of Ammon in Egypt as "Son of Re"; after that he at times had himself surrounded with divine adoration. The Ptolemaic and Seleucid rulers also were treated as gods. One peculiarity of the Hellenistic versus the later Roman ruler cult was that the Greek was founded on specific and concrete deeds of power and charity, while the Roman emperor was entitled to divinity through the enormous powers of his office, powers that otherwise would only be possessed by a deity.[17]

We will not explore the history of the imperial cult here, but it is worth mentioning two characteristics that date back to Augustus and (with some exceptions) survived into the second century. One is the restraint of the *ruling* emperor regarding divine veneration. Augustus did not present himself as a god, but as "divi filius," i.e., a son of Julius Caesar, who was deified after his murder. Like Julius Caesar, Augustus was only accepted as one of the state gods by a ruling of the Senate after his death. The second characteristic limits the first: there were marked differences in the west and east empires with respect to attitudes toward the living emperor. In the west, Augustus did not permit a cult of his person; in the east, he tolerated the building of temples for a unison cult of him and the goddess Roma. In the east the cult was meant mainly for the living emperor, and at times ended after his death.

These differences give rise to different functions of the imperial cult. In the west, it had less to do with the person of the emperor than with his office, which embodied the unity of the empire and ensured its preservation. The recognition of the need for such a power carrier led to his veneration within the framework of Roman religiosity. In the east, the experience of the power of an emperor led to the cult; the integration of this power into the traditional, symbolic system was one way to explain and render familiar an otherwise inexplicable and threatening invasion of might, first during Hellenism and then during the Roman empire.[18]

Which religious position did the deified emperor really hold? This is not a qualitative leap, but more the devoted recognition of a leader by the assigning of a higher status to him. This assumption is confirmed in the Roman arena by the choice of the appellation "*divus*" rather than "*deus*": a *divus* is more than a human, but not a *deus* in the true sense. In the Greek arena such differentiation in terminology did not exist. But even here it is clear that there was a distinction between rulers and gods: the cult could be terminated after the death of the ruler; the ruler cult was described as *isotheio timai*, "honors equivalent to those paid to the god,"[19] thus comparing the ruler cult to the cult of gods, but also distinguishing them one from another; sacrifices were made to the gods *for* the emperor, while those *to* the emperor generally were made only under a unison cult together with gods or his ancestors.

The Christians did not participate in the imperial cult, although it was distinct from the cult of gods. John, in Revelation, shows how this could become a problem:

Then I saw another beast that rose out of the earth; it had two horns
like a lamb and it spoke like a dragon. It exercises all the authority
of the first beast on its behalf, and it makes the earth and its inhab-
itants worship the first beast, whose mortal wound has been healed.
(Rev. 13:11−12)

The first beast usually is interpreted to mean Emperor Domitian (81−96 C.E.), who had himself addressed as "Lord and God"—an exception in the first century. The second beast possibly is a person or institution having to do with the implementation of the imperial cult in Asia Minor. The Christians, to whom Revelation is addressed, were harassed because of their refusal to participate in the imperial cult, although it was not a systematic persecution by any means.

This refusal is an expression of the side-by-side orientation of the Christian and the pagan savior that we mentioned at the beginning. Because Augustus appears as "savior," as we have seen in the inscription of Priene, his date of birth is called the beginning of the "good news," and his great achievement is "peace." The scene of the shepherds in Luke 2:1−20 is often read with this background in mind. The "good news" of the angel about the birth of the Savior in the city of David, and the hymn of the angels singing about peace on earth, was understood to be either a derivation from the imperial cult or a conscious opposition to it. Nonetheless, A. D. Nock showed that not even the combination of these concepts in Luke 2 necessarily suggests imperial cult language.[20] But it is certain that for pagan Christians the deified emperor, and in a broader sense the other godlike humans and humanlike gods, had a peculiar relationship to Jesus Christ: a mixture of competition and noncompetition. Competition, insofar as they furnished models for interpretation of Christology[21] and were then defeated by Christ on their own grounds. Noncompetition, because the turning toward the Christian form of monotheism removed all superhuman beings from the divine sphere, except for Christ. Paul surely has this ambivalence in mind when he writes:

We know that "no idol in the world really exists," and that "there
is no God but one." Indeed, even though there may be so-called gods

in heaven or on earth—as in fact there are many gods and many lords—yet for us there is one God, the Father, from whom are all things and for whom we exist, and on Lord, Jesus Christ, through whom are all things and through whom we exist. (1 Cor. 8:4–6)

NOTES

Abbreviations for works from antiquity are according to the *Theological Dictionary of the New Testament*, vols. 1–4, ed. G. Kittel; vols. 5–9, ed. G. Friedrich (Grand Rapids: Eerdmans, 1964). Abbreviations for modern works are according to the *Abkürzungsverzeichnis der Theologischen Realenzyklopädie* (Berlin: de Gruyter, 1976).

1. Cf. W. Foerster, "sotēr A," *TDNT* 7:1004–12.

2. H. D. Betz, "Gottmensch," 2, *RAC* 12:234–312.

3. Cf. D. Zeller, *Die Menschwerdung des Sohnes Gottes im Neuen Testament und die antike Religionsgeschichte*; D. Zeller, ed., "Menschwerdung Gottes—Vergöttlichung von Menschen," *Novum Testamentum et Orbis Antiquus* 7 (Fribourg: University Press, 1988), 141–76, here 160–62.

4. This and other places in Zeller, *Menschwerdung*.

5. W. Burkert in *Ancient Mystery Cults* (Cambridge: Harvard University Press, 1987), 75, does not even count the Adonis cult as one of the true mystery cults.

6. Burkert, *Ancient Mystery Cults*, 75–76.

7. References in Zeller, *Menschwerdung*, 163–64.

8. Compare W. Fauth, "Asklepios," *KP* 1:644–48; R. Herzog, *Asklepios*, *RAC* 1:795–99; similarly L. Bieler, "THEIOS ANĒR. Das Bild des 'göttlichen Menschen,'" in *Spätantike und Frühchristentum*, 12 vols., vol. 2 (Wien: Oskar Höfels, 1935/36), 105–7.

9. Ibid.

10. G. P. Corrington, *The "Divine Man": His Origin and Function in Hellenistic Popular Religion*, American University Studies 7/17 (New York: Lang 1986), esp. 43–45; B. Blackburn, *THEIOS ANĒR and the Marcan Miracle Traditions: A Critique of the THEIOS ANĒR Concept as an Interpretative Background of the Miracle Traditions Used by Mark* (Tübingen: Mohr-Siebeck, 1991), esp. 96; Betz, "Gottmensch," 235. On the problem of claiming the *theios anēr* concept for Jesus, cf. M. Smith, "Prolegomena to a Discussion of Aretalogies. Divine Men, the Gospels, and Jesus," *JBL* 90 (1971): 174–99, esp. 188–95.

11. *The Charismatic Figure as Miracle Worker*, SBL diss. ser. 1 (Missoula: SBL, 1972).

12. *Urchristliche Wundergeschichten. Ein Beitrag zur formgeschichtlichen Erforschung der synoptischen Evangelien* (Gütersloh: Mohn, 1987), 263–72.

13. Corrington, "Divine Man," 145.

14. *Pythagoras, Jesus von Nazareth und der Helios-Apollon des Julianus Apostate.* Zu einigen Eigenheiten der spatantiken Pythagoras-Aretalogie im Vergleich mit der thaumasiologischen Tradition der Evangelien. "With regard to some peculiarities of the Pythagoras Aretalogy in late antiquity, in comparison to the thaumasiological tradition of the gospels," *ZNW* 78 (1987): 26–48, here 47–48.

15. Ibid., 47.

16. Cited per E. Ferguson, *Backgrounds of Early Christianity* (Grand Rapids: Eerdmans, 1989), 159.

17. Cf. P. Herz, "Der römische Kaiser und der Kaiserkult," in Zeller, *Menschwerdung*, 115–40, here 131–33.

18. Thus the main thesis of S. R. F. Price, *Rituals and Power: The Roman Imperial Cult in Asia Minor* (Cambridge: Cambridge University Press, 1984), esp. 247–48.

19. S. R. F. Price, "Gods and Emperors: The Greek Language of the Roman Imperial Cult," *Journal of Hellenic Studies* 104 (1984): 79–95, here 88.

20. A. D. Nock, "Early Gentile Christianity and Its Hellenistic Background," in *Essays on Religion and the Ancient World*, ed. Z. Stewart, 2 vols., vol. 1 (Oxford: Clarendon, 1972), 41–133, here 78–83.

21. Cf., e.g., Justin, Apol. 21:1–2: "And when we say also that the Word, who is the first-born of God, Jesus Christ, our teacher, was produced without sexual union, and that He was crucified and died, and rose again, and ascended into heaven, we propound nothing new and different from what you believe regarding those whom you esteem sons of Jupiter."

CHAPTER FIVE

CHRISTOLOGY IN DIALOGUE
WITH GNOSTICISM

ELAINE H. PAGELS

EDITED BY SARAH A. EDWARDS

A focal point of this dialogue is the differing Gnostic and Orthodox views of Christ's passion. Gnostic Christians "deny the reality of the incarnation of Christ," says Lebreton in his *History of the Primitive Church*,[1] stating what most historians have taken for granted as a fundamental characteristic of Gnostic heresy. For many, Gnosticism is virtually synonymous with Docetism: the teaching that Christ did not actually take on a human body, but only appeared to do so; that while he seemed to ignorant bystanders to be suffering and dying on the cross, his inner, spiritual nature remained untouched by such human vulnerability. Yet evidence from Valentinian texts discovered at Nag Hammadi challenges this assumption. The author of the *Gospel of Truth* acknowledges Jesus' passion and death: "nailed to a tree,"[2] he was "slain."[3] For the sake of redemption, "the merciful one, the faithful one, Jesus, was patient in accepting sufferings . . . since he knows that his death is life for many."[4] The author gives a moving account of Jesus' death: "He was nailed to a tree. . . . He draws himself down to death though life eternal clothes him. Having stripped himself of the perishable rags, he put on imperishability."[5]

The *Tripartite Tractate* introduces the Savior as "the one who will be begotten and who will suffer."[6] Moved by compassion for those who existed in mortality, he willingly became "what they were. So, for their sake, he became manifest in an involuntary suffering. . . . Not only did he take upon himself the death of those whom he intended to save," but he also accepted their "smallness." Furthermore, the author describes his incarnation: "He let himself be conceived and born as an infant in body and soul."[7]

Yet the *Tripartite Tractate* expounds this teaching as a paradox. The one who is born and who suffers is the Savior foreseen by the Hebrew prophets; what they were unable to recognize was "that which he was before, and what he is eternally, an unbegotten, impassible Word, who came into being flesh."[8] Similarly, the *Gospel of Truth* described Jesus' suffering and death. It goes on to say that "the Word of the Father goes forth into the all . . . purifying and bringing it back into the Father, into the Mother, Jesus of the infinite gentleness."[9] The *Interpretation of Knowledge* articulates the same paradox. "On the one hand, the Savior becomes vulnerable to suffering and death; on the other, he is the Word, full of divine power."[10]

So "he was crucified and he died"—yet because the death he died was that of sinful humanity, it was, in this sense, "not his own death, for he did not deserve to be killed for the sake of the human church."[11] Yet through his voluntary suffering, "we receive forgiveness of sins," as the "one who was disgraced" is revealed to be "the one who redeemed."[12]

A third Valentinian text, the *Epistle to Rheginos* (*Treatise on Resurrection*), approvingly cites Paul's declaration that the Savior suffered,[13] but adds, referring to 1 Cor. 15:55, that he "swallowed up death."[14] To clarify the paradox, Valentinus explains that "the Son of God, Rheginos, was Son of Man. He embraced them both, possessing the humanity and the divinity, so that on the one hand he might vanquish death through his being Son of God, and that on the other through the Son of Man the restoration to the *Pleroma* might occur."[15]

Not one of these sources denies that Jesus actually suffered and died; all, apparently, assume it. Yet all are concerned to show how, in his incarnation, Christ transcends human nature, so that in his passion and death he prevails over death by divine power. The evidence from Nag Hammadi confirms what Harnack, more perceptive than later interpreters, observed: "The characteristic of Gnostic Christology is not *docetism*, but the doctrine of the *two natures*."[16] The Valentinians, he adds, were the first to take up this problem, which was to become the center of patristic Christology two centuries later.

Even Irenaeus specifically distinguishes the Valentinian position from that of Docetism.[17] But, Irenaeus adds, they insist on distinguishing between different "persons" in Christ, "claiming that one being suffered and was born, and that this was Jesus, but that there was another who descended upon him, and this was Christ . . . and they argue that he who came from the demiurge, he who was from the dispensation, he who sprang from Joseph, was the being subject to suffering."[18]

In other words, "the psychic Christ suffered, together with the body that had been formed in the dispensation." However, the divine spirit that descended upon him "remained apart from suffering; for it was not suspectable to suffering, being both incomprehensible and invisible."[19] The Valentinians explain, therefore, that this spirit departed when Christ was brought before Pilate; it was his human nature, the psychic nature, together with his body, that experienced passion and death.

Yet, while he admits that the Valentinians join with other members of the church in confessing that the Savior suffered and died, Irenaeus insists on expelling them from the church as apostates and heretics.

Clearly their theology differs from his: they maintain that the divine spirit remains apart from suffering. But what is so heretical, so dangerous, so blasphemous about this interpretation of Christian doctrine? We cannot find the answer to this question as long as we consider controversies between orthodoxy and heresy exclusively in terms of the history of dogma, as scholars traditionally have done. When we investigate the writings of the "fathers of the church" and of their Gnostic contemporaries to see how Christology actually functions in each type of literature, we may see that it involves specific practical issues—often social and political ones as well. For Christians of the first and second centuries, controversy over the interpretation of Christ's passion and death involves an urgent practical question: how are believers to respond to persecution, which raises the imminent possibility of their own suffering and death?

Irenaeus' defense of martyrdom is precisely the context of his attack on Gnostic views of Christ's passion.[20] In this he is not unique. Every one of the anti-Gnostic writers—Ignatius, Justin, Tertullian, Hippolytus, Irenaeus—endorses martyrdom as a "sacrifice acceptable to God" and praises the martyr as a heroic athlete, a warrior for Christ who gains the crown of victory through death. Above all, martyrdom offers to the Christian the opportunity to "imitate the passion of Christ."

All of them, on the other hand, attest that those they call "heretics" tend to oppose any enthusiasm for martyrdom. Some consider it foolish, wasteful of human life, and therefore contrary to God's will. They argue that "Christ, having died for us, was killed so that we might not be killed."[21]

Now we can see the relevance of the theological argument: only if Christ suffered and died in the same way that we ourselves do can our suffering and death imitate his. But if—as the Valentinians and others suggest—Christ's experience essentially differs from ours, in that the divine Savior could not suffer, then our experience cannot be equivalent to his. The believer's suffering could be analogous only to the passion of the *psychic* Christ or of his body. Consequently, the experience of Christian martyrs could not be a true "imitation of Christ's passion."

Those who express the greatest concern to refute heretical interpretations of Christ's passion are, without exception, persons who know from firsthand experience the dangers to which Christians are exposed: arbitrary accusation, arrest, torture, and execution. The great opponent of heresy, Bishop Ignatius, for example, arrested and condemned, accepted the death sentence with joyful exultation as his opportunity to "imitate the passion of my God!" (Rom. 6:3). What does his Christology mean to him? Ignatius says:

> *Jesus Christ was truly prosecuted under Pontius Pilate, was truly crucified, and died. . . . But if, as some say (who are atheists, that is unbelievers) that his suffering was only an appearance,* then why am I a prisoner, and why do I long to fight with the wild beasts? In that case, I am dying in vain. . . . In that case, why have I given myself up to death?[22]

Justin Martyr, protesting the persecutions in his second *Apology*, cites specific accounts of believers falsely accused and executed.[23] He admits that he himself is in continual danger: "I, too, therefore, expect

to be plotted against and crucified."[24] Justin says that when he personally witnessed Christians enduring public torture and execution, he
became convinced of their divine inspiration.[25] Justin notes persecution
of Christians worldwide: mentioning Christians pursued in Palestine in
the time of Bar Kochba, he declares to Trypho:

> *It is clear that no one can terrify or subdue us who believe in Jesus
> Christ throughout the whole world. For it is plain that, though be-
> headed, and crucified, and thrown to the wild beasts, in chains, in
> fire, and all other kinds of torture, we do not give up our confession;
> but the more such things happen, the more do others, in larger num-
> bers, become believers.*[26]

Consistent with his personal convictions concerning martyrdom
and his courageous acceptance of his own death sentence is Justin's view
that "Jesus Christ, our teacher, who was born for this purpose, was
crucified under Pontius Pilate, and died, and rose again"[27]—the sole
purpose of refuting "wicked and deceitful" Gnostic doctrines.[28] Elsewhere he attacks those "called Christians," followers of Simon, Mar-
cion, and Valentinus: "We do not know," he admits, whether they
indulge in promiscuity or cannibalism, but "we do know" one of their
crimes: namely, that "they are neither persecuted nor put to death" as
martyrs.[29]

Like his predecessors, Irenaeus, the great opponent of the Valentinians, is a man whose life is marked by persecution. He mentions
many who were martyred in Rome. He knew from personal experience
the loss of his beloved teacher, Polycarp, who was caught in mob
violence, condemned, and burned alive among his enemies. Twelve
years later, in the summer of 177, Irenaeus witnessed growing hostility
to Christians in his own city. First they were prohibited from entering
public places; then, when the provincial governor was out of the city,
"the mob broke loose. Christians were hounded and attacked openly.
They were treated as public enemies, assaulted, beaten, and stoned.
Finally they were dragged into the forum, . . . were accused, and, after
confessing to being Christians, they were flung into prison."[30]

In spite of all this, Irenaeus expresses no hostility toward his fellow townsmen—but plenty against the Gnostic "heretics." Like Justin, he attacks them as "false brethren" who "have reached such a pitch of audacity that *they even pour contempt upon the martyrs, and vituperate those who are killed on account of confessing the Lord, and who . . . thereby strive to follow in the footsteps of the Lord's passion,* themselves bearing witness to the one who suffered."[31]

Tertullian, another fierce opponent of heresy, describes how the sight of martyrs tortured and dying initiated his own conversion. Tertullian, like Irenaeus, connects the teaching of Christ's suffering and death with his own enthusiasm for martyrdom: "You must take up your cross and bear it after your Master. . . . The sole key to unlock Paradise is your own life's blood."[32] Tertullian directly traces the rise of heresy to the outbreak of persecution. This, he says, impels terrified believers to look for theological means to justify their cowardice.

> *This among Christians is a time of persecution. When, therefore, the faith is greatly agitated and the church on fire . . . then the Gnostics break out: then the Valentinians creep forth; then all the opponents of martyrdom bubble up . . . for they know that many Christians are simple and inexperienced, and weak, and . . . they perceive that they are never to be applauded more than when fear has opened the entries of the soul, especially when some terrorism has already arrayed with a crown the faith of martyrs.*[33]

Like Tertullian, Hippolytus had witnessed the terror of the Severan persecution of 202. Hippolytus's zeal for martyrdom also is matched by his hatred of heresy. He concludes his massive *Refutation of all Heresies* by insisting that only orthodox doctrine concerning Christ's incarnation and passion enables the believer to endure persecution.

> *If he were not of the same nature with ourselves, he commands in vain that we should imitate the teacher. . . . He did not protest against his passion, but became obedient unto death . . . now in all these acts he offered up, as the first fruits, his own humanity, in order that you, when you are in tribulation, may not be discouraged,*

but, confessing yourself to be one like the Redeemer, may dwell in ex-
pectation of receiving what the Father has granted to the Son.[34]

In his mid-seventies, Hippolytus fulfilled his own exhortation: arrested on Maximin's orders in 235, he was deported and exiled to Sardinia, where he died.

What pattern, then, do we observe? The opponents of heresy in the second century—Ignatius, Polycarp, Justin, Irenaeus, Tertullian, Hippolytus—are unanimous in proclaiming Christ's passion and death and in affirming martyrdom. Simultaneously, they all accuse the heretics both of teaching false Christology and of "opposing martyrdom." Irenaeus declares:

> *The church in every place, because of the love which she cherishes to-*
> *ward God, sends forth, throughout all time, a multitude of martyrs*
> *to the Father; while all others not only have nothing of this kind to*
> *point to among themselves, but even maintain that bearing witness*
> *(*martyrium*) is not at all necessary . . . with the exception, per-*
> *haps, of one or two among them . . . who have occasionally, along*
> *with our martyrs, borne the reproach of the name, as if they too had*
> *obtained mercy, and have been led forth with them, being, as it*
> *were, a sort of retinue granted to them. For the church alone sustains*
> *with purity the reproach of those who suffer persecution for righteous-*
> *ness' sake and endure all sorts of punishments, and are put to death*
> *because of the love which they bear toward God, and their confession*
> *of his Son.*[35]

What attitude do Gnostics take toward martyrdom, and on what grounds? Evidence from Nag Hammadi shows that their views are surprisingly diverse. Some affirm it; others repudiate it. By contrast with other Gnostic Christians, the Valentinians take a mediating position. One thing, however, is strikingly clear: in every case, the interpretation of Christ's passion corresponds to the attitude toward martyrdom.

One group of Gnostic texts insists, no less than the orthodox, on the reality of Christ's suffering and death. The *Apocryphon of James*, like the *Second Apocalypse of James* and the *Apocalypse of Peter*, raises the question of Christ's passion in the context of the disciples' anxiety as they anticipate persecution. The Lord responds that their suffering must become identical with his:

> *If you are oppressed by Satan and persecuted and you do his {God's}*
> *will, I say that he will love you, and make you equal with*
> *me. . . . Do you not know that you have yet to be shut up in prison,*
> *and condemned unlawfully, and crucified without reason, and buried*
> *{shamefully} as {was} I myself? . . . Verily I say unto you, none*
> *will be saved unless they believe in my cross. But those who have be-*
> *lieve in my cross, theirs is the kingdom of God. . . . Verily I say*
> *unto you, none of those who fear death will be saved; for the king-*
> *dom of death belongs to those who put themselves to death.*[36]

This Gnostic author not only insists that Christ really suffered and died, but also encourages the believer to choose suffering and death in order to become "better than I: make yourselves like the Son of the Holy Spirit!"[37]

Heracleon articulates a wholly different attitude from his orthodox contemporaries. He expresses none of their enthusiasm for martyrdom, none of their acclamation of the martyr's "glorious victory." Above all, he never suggests that the believers' suffering and death imitate those of Christ. To Irenaeus, Hippolytus, or Tertullian, who argue for martyrdom on the grounds that the believer, in suffering, becomes identified with the suffering Christ, the Valentinian could reply that the *psychic* believer's experience is, indeed, analogous to that of the *psychic* Christ; but the experience of one who is pneumatic is analogous to that of the *pneumatic* Christ, whose nature transcends suffering. Such a view could well prompt Irenaeus's angry response that these Gnostics "show contempt" for the martyrs and devalue their sacrifice as if it were evidence of merely *psychic* faith, and that the heretics claim that true witness (*martyrium*) "is *their* system of beliefs."[38]

Valentinian Christology involves a second major problem: the constitution of Christ's body. This controversy proved so critical that it divided the Valentinians into two different schools. The Eastern school, including such teachers as Theodotus, maintains that Christ's body is purely *spiritual*. On the contrary, theologians of the Italic school, including Heracleon and Ptolemy, insist that Christ's body is woven from the psychic element.[39] What makes this issue so significant that it could split the Valentinians into different camps? What does it mean, and how does it relate to the interpretation of Christ's passion?

This element of Valentinian Christology will remain obscure until we recognize that its function is essentially *ecclesiological*. The passages concerning this debate focus less on Christ's passion than on his church. Both Eastern and Western Valentinian teachers characteristically interpret Christ's body as "his body, for the church." For example, the first of Theodotus' teaching that Clement records declares that Jesus is clothed with the "pneumatic seed," that is, with "the elect."[40]

The Valentinian sources from Nag Hammadi apparently accept the Western version of Christology and its corresponding ecclesiology. The *Interpretation of Knowledge* explains how the Savior took on the "flesh of condemnation" and participated in the condition of those "condemned in Adam," conjoining in himself "the one who was disgraced" and "the one who was redeemed."[41] Consequently, as Klaus Koschorke shows, "his body," the church, consists of both those who have received gnosis and those who have yet to receive it.[42] The *Tripartite Tractate*, which describes the "unbegotten and impassible Logos" who came in flesh and took on a body and soul, a human birth, and human suffering, teaches a corresponding ecclesiology. The author acknowledges that "the spiritual race immediately became a body of its head" when he appeared, because "the election shares body and essence with the Saviour." But the other "members" hesitated to join themselves with the Savior as members of his body: they "needed a place of instruction" in the present age.[43]

Is the church—the "body of Christ"—to remain "split,"[44] divided between the "lesser" and the "greater" members, between "members that are still dead"[45] and those who are spiritually "alive"? The author of the *Interpretation of Knowledge* pleads with all members of the church to join together in the loving union appropriate to the body of Christ, who "loves his members with his whole heart."[46]

While the *Interpretation of Knowledge* encourages unity in the present time, the *Tripartite Tractate* offers an eschatological vision of the entire body restored to its original unity. The elect who have received gnosis already are joined with the Savior and share his body; but the "calling" must await the bridechamber that will celebrate the union of Christ and his "body," the church, in the eschatological future.[47] "All the members of the body of the church are in a single place and receive the restoration at one time, when they have been manifested as the sound body—the restoration into the pleroma."[48]

Then "those [who are] mixed" and "those [who are] unmixed" will "join with one another."[49] For "when we confessed the kingdom which is in Christ, we escaped from the whole *multiplicity of forms* and from *inequality and change*"—conditions that characterize the present age. "For the end will receive a unitary existence just as the beginning": those who now are separate, the *elect* and the *called*, now divided as "male and female," "slave and free," shall all become one, restored to a state "where there is no male nor female, nor slave and free . . . but Christ is all in all."[50]

Valentinian theologians describe this eschatological reunion as the resurrection of the body, in which "Jesus Christ the great champion . . . receives to himself . . . the church, that is, the *elect* and the *called*, the pneumatic from the Mother, and the psychic from the dispensation, and he saved and raised what he had received and what, through them, was consubstantial."[51]

The Savior, having taken upon himself the pneumatic element, then assumed "the psychic church, which . . . he took on and blended with himself."[52]

Since the Savior came into the cosmos to reveal himself to psychics, whose perception is limited to their physical senses, he took upon himself, besides the pneumatic and psychic elements, "a body, having a psychic nature, yet prepared with indescribable skill, in order to become visible and tangible and capable of suffering."[53] Harvey misreads Valentinus, as regards the human nature of Christ, as essentially Docetic. It was *animal* (psychic) but not *material* (hylic)." On the contrary, the Valentinians insist that Christ had to become incarnate in order to become accessible to those "who needed education through the senses."[54] They further declare that it was precisely his human *nature* that experienced suffering.

Why did the orthodox interpretation of church unity—and of martyrdom—prevail? We have observed a close connection between outbreaks of persecution and zeal for orthodoxy. This may suggest that when violence increasingly menaced small provincial Christian groups, they attempted to ensure survival through solidarity with Christians throughout the known world. They moved toward increased communication with other groups, especially with well-established churches. So Irenaeus, bringing news of the martyrs in Lyons, traveled to Rome.

In the process of increased communication, the diversified earlier communities were pressed by their common danger to reach agreement—indeed, unanimity—on matters of holy days, a canon of scripture, and a creedal confession of faith. Increasingly stratified orders of institutional hierarchy were established to consolidate the communities internally and to authorize communication with Catholic churches throughout the world. Those who followed this growing consensus in doctrine and church politics also belong to the churches that—confessing the crucified Christ—became conspicuous for their martyrs. On the other hand, groups of Gnostic Christians who resisted such doctrinal conformity, questioned the value of martyrdom, and often opposed the increase of hierarchical church office were scattered and lost.

NOTES

This essay originally appeared as "Gnostic and Orthodox Views of Christ's Passion" in *The Rediscovery of Gnosticism: Proceedings of the International Conference on Gnosticism at Yale, New Haven, Connecticut, March 28–31, 1978*, ed. Bentley Layton, *The School of Valentinus*, vol. 1 (Leiden: E. J. Brill, 1980–81). Used by permission of Elaine H. Pagels and E. J. Brill.

1. Jules Lebreton and Jacques Zeiller, *History of the Primitive Church*, 2d ed., trans. E. Messenger (London: Burns, Oates, Washbourne, 1949), 299, 355–357.

2. *Gospel Truth* 18:24; 20:25 (hereafter *G Tr*).

3. Ibid. 20:5.

4. Ibid. 20:10–14.

5. Ibid. 20:25–32.

6. *Tripartite Tractate* 113:32–4 (hereafter *Tri Trac*).

7. Ibid. 114:33–115:11.

8. Ibid. 113:35–38.

9. *G Tr* 23:33–24:9.

10. *Interpretation of Knowledge* 17:35–38 (hereafter *Interp Kn*).

11. Ibid. 4:30–33.

12. Ibid. 12:25–13:20.

13. *On Resurrection* 45:26 (hereafter *On Res*).

14. Ibid. 45:14–15; cf. 1 Cor. 15:55.

15. *On Res* 44:21–34.

16. Adolf von Harnack, *History of Dogma*, trans. N. Buchanan (Boston: Roberts, 1897), 1:258.

17. Irenaeus, *Adversus omnes Haereses*, 3.18.6 (hereafter *Haer*); cf. Tertullian, *Adversus Valentinianos*, 26.

18. *Haer* 3.16.6.

19. Ibid. 1.7.2.

20. Ibid. 3.16.6.

21. Tertullian, *Scorpiace* 1 (hereafter *Scorp*).

22. *To the Church of Tralles*, 10.1 (hereafter *Trall*); *To the Church of Smyrna*, 4.2 (emphasis added).

23. *2 Apology* 2 (hereafter *Apol*).

24. Ibid. 3.

25. Ibid. 12.

26. *Dialagoue with Trypho* 110.4.

27. *1 Apol* 13.

28. *2 Apol* 15.

29. *1 Apol* 26.

30. Frend, *Martyrdom*, 5.

31. *Haer* 3.18.5 (emphasis added).

32. *De Anima* 55.

33. *Scorp* 1.

34. *Haer* 10.13.17.

35. Ibid. 4.33.9.

36. *Apocryphon of James* (hereafter *Apocry Jas*).

37. Ibid. 4:38–6:18.

38. Ibid. 6:19–20.

39. Hippolytus, *Refutation of All Heresies*, 6.35.5–7.

40. Excerpta ex Theodota 1.1–2.

41. *Interp Kn* 11:36–13:20.

42. K. Koschorke, "Gnostic Instructions on the Organization of the Congregation." The tractate "The Interpretation of Knowledge" from CGXI in vol. 2 of this work, especially Sec. 2 and 4.

43. *Tri Trac* 122:12f.

44. *Interp Kn* 6:39.

45. Ibid. 17:23–29.

46. Ibid. 15:18–19.

47. *Tri Trac* 122:19–27f.

48. Ibid. 123:16–23.

49. Ibid. 132:3–12.

50. Ibid. 132:16–18 (emphasis added).

51. *Exc Thdot* 58.1.

52. Ibid.

53. *Haer* 1.8.3.

54. Ibid. 1.6.1 (emphasis added); cf. Origen, *Commentary on Jo* 13.60; *Exc Thdot* 23.1.

PART TWO

CHRISTOLOGY IN THE MAKING
THE NEW TESTAMENT DIALOGUE

CHAPTER SIX

DID JESUS HAVE A CHRISTOLOGY?

ROBERT F. BERKEY

The question raised in this chapter's title has been answered both positively and negatively. It is answered in the affirmative by those New Testament scholars who remain persuaded that within our present Greek Gospels, originating no earlier than 65 to 70 C.E. are authentic traditions that recall at least portions of the historic life and message of Jesus. These same scholars believe such recollections can be recovered with reasonable certainty through the use of modern critical tools and thereby can provide us with important historical data that may even convey something of Jesus' convictions about his messianic role and function.

The question is answered negatively by those who, applying similar tools to the same gospel records, conclude that the chronological, linguistic, cultural, and above all, theological gulfs between the Gospels and the historical Jesus make the uncovering of any reliable Jesus tradition extremely tenuous, an especially problematic uncertainty where the issue of Jesus' messianic awareness is at stake. Those who come down heavily on the negative side of the question insist that all "bits and pieces" contained within the gospel tradition were from the start viewed through the prism of belief *about* Jesus, which prism then transformed those records into "gospels" used to promulgate faith in Jesus as the Messiah/Son of God. For this more skeptical group, Christological beliefs set in motion a continuous recasting of Jesus as the divine Messiah of God, an ongoing process that in the New Testament found its ultimate fulfillment in the Fourth Gospel's Jesus as a self-conscious, self-proclaiming "Word made flesh."[1]

It is clear that the task of reconstructing Jesus' historic ministry is more complicated than any simple reassembling of the "bits and pieces"

81

pulled piecemeal from the Gospels. Modern critical studies of the Gospels incorporate historical tools that the seeker must be willing to use without reservation in the difficult process of distinguishing the authentic (i.e., historical) fragments from the more elaborate narrative and discourse structures preserved by those convinced of Jesus' messianic, once-for-all character and mission. Confronting such formidable historical barriers, some may be persuaded that critical analysis itself must be abandoned in order to preserve the sacred integrity of the texts together with the Christ therein portrayed. But in addressing this question, we are intentionally and emphatically adopting the alternative stance taken by scholars who refuse to be so intimidated but who persist in the notion that the search for a Jesus Christology constitutes a legitimate historical inquiry that must be addressed in open and critical discussion.

Such criticism clearly poses a dilemma for those inquirers who remain committed to a belief in Jesus' messianic, transcendent significance. Anyone convinced that Jesus is God's Messiah (whether or not it is assumed that such belief began with Jesus) will surely experience a kind of scholarly schizophrenia when forced to discuss Christological convictions in the context of radical historical skepticism with respect to Jesus in his first-century setting. Christological affirmations are by nature marked with the assurance of faith claims, whereas historical affirmations are "opinions" that can be debated only within relative degrees of certainty. The question inevitably arises: Does not such critical investigation place the search for Christological beginnings on the same shifting ground as the search for, say, the outlook of a George Washington, an Abraham Lincoln, or a Winston Churchill? To associate such uncertainty with the search for a historical Jesus believed by many Christians to be the ultimate manifestation of God constitutes a problem of no mean significance. Theological instincts, whether those of ancient gospel writers convinced of Jesus' messianic transcendence, or of contemporary historian/ theologians who happen to share those same beliefs, are bound to arouse expectations of certainty that are not possible within the province of modern critical and historical methods. So, however one approaches this precarious search, it seems undeniable and unavoidable that confidence in the declaration that Jesus is the Messiah/Son of God is bound to be somewhat shaken under the scrutiny of historical analysis. Simply to question the historicity of, shall we say, the Matthean and Lucan birth accounts (which presume to narrate Jesus' divine sonship) is to question the integrity of the narrator as well as of the tradition itself. Such criticism becomes even more unsettling once our specific question is introduced: Did Jesus' self-awareness include a Christological dimension? Did Jesus believe himself to be that same messiah affirmed and promulgated by the gospel narrators and, by extension, the remainder of the New Testament witnesses? And if Jesus did understand his purpose and mission in such lofty, transcendent terms, did he then so declare himself to his disciples?

The Synoptic Gospels, following Mark's lead, seem to have assumed with some consistency (1) that they were telling the Jesus story in order to promulgate their central and continuing belief that Jesus was/is the Messiah (Mark 1:1); (2) that this messianic faith was in fact the gospel accepted and declared by the original disciples (and no doubt by other followers as well), beginning at the time when they were directly involved with Jesus' historic ministry (Mark 8:29); and (3), though here with considerably less clarity, that those same disciples derived their messianic faith from Jesus' assumptions about himself (Mark 8:30).

It is in connection with the third of these assumptions that the question of a Jesus Christology emerges most explicitly, and where the most serious and controversial issues arise. If one concludes that the disciples did derive such messianic faith from the historical Jesus, then the answer to the question raised in the title of this chapter is affirmative. That would still leave open the possibility of ongoing Christological elaborations, especially in the post-Easter era, elaborations such as those visible in any comparison between, say, Mark's and John's versions of Jesus' Christological declarations. But should it be decided that the Gospels do not provide ample evidence for Jesus' Christological awareness, then serious doubts will ultimately fall on the second of these assumptions as well. It would be difficult to understand how the disciples during Jesus' lifetime could have reached such extraordinary Christological conclusions apart from any such proclamation on the part of Jesus. Indeed, to deny that messianic convictions were at least implicitly drawn from the historic interactions between Jesus and the disciples ultimately supports the radical alternative: that Christology arose only with the early Christian community in the wake of the Easter event, and that Christological assumptions were then anachronistically attached to the gospel narratives of Jesus' life and ministry.

All historical queries about Jesus must necessarily proceed directly to these Gospels; with so little information about the historical Jesus in the remainder of the New Testament writings, there is no place else for the search to turn. But again, even in those theologically controlled and reworked Synoptic narratives, the assumption that Christology originated with Jesus is at best ambiguously preserved. The portrait of Jesus in the Fourth Gospel leaves us with the clearest unequivocal support for Jesus' messianic convictions, convictions that in this case include not only his divine origins but the assumption that such divinity actually preexisted creation itself.[2] If the Synoptics recount Jesus' self-proclaimed messiahship at all, they do so with considerably less clarity. Mark, considered by most New Testament scholars to be the pattern more or less followed by the other two Synoptic narratives,[3] provides but a single, explicit messianic self-claim, where Jesus, responding to the high priest's "Are you the Christ?" answers with a resounding "I am" (Mark 14:61–62). Even here, any comparison of Jesus' extraordinarily blunt response with the more equivocal reply preserved in the Synoptic parallels immediately reveals puzzling ambiguity. Mark's direct and forthright claim is mitigated by Matthew's substitute, "You have said so" (see Matt. 26:64; cf. Luke 22:67–68).

The picture becomes even murkier once one ponders the element of secrecy that the Synoptics frequently attach to such messianically related declarations. In response to Peter's "You are the Christ" comes Mark's somewhat surprising summation: "And he [Jesus] charged them to tell no one about him" (Mark 8:30). Why should such an important and determinative affirmation be held back? This so-called "messianic secret" has remained a puzzle within Markan studies, a problem isolated and emphasized in the work of William Wrede at the beginning of the present century.[4] Wrede argued that Mark incorporated this secret motif to explain the assumption that Jesus' messiahship became a matter of *public* announcement only after the resurrection, when the full implications of that covert messiahship were unveiled for the first time. Heikki Raisanen's recent reexamination of Wrede's classic study, while in many ways critical of Wrede's conclusions, points out that Wrede's analysis of the secret presumes that earlier Christological traditions had already connected Jesus' messianic status with the resurrection.[5] In any case, Wrede's isolation of the secrecy motif contributed substantially to subsequent twentieth-century assumptions about the fundamental gap between the Jesus of history and the Christ of the Gospels.

Starting then with the assumption of that gap's significance, a large sector of twentieth-century New Testament interpretation has broadly rejected a Jesus Christology. Such rejection has been especially associated with the work of Rudolf Bultmann, whose methods and conclusions are summarized in more detail in the introductory chapter to this collection.[6] Bultmann focused particularly on resurrection faith as the formative context that effectively Christologized an otherwise non-Christological Jesus of history. This conviction was reinforced through the development of his form-critical analysis, which was constructed on the presumed connection between Christology and resurrection faith. Bultmannians generally have insisted that where Christological designations are explicitly articulated by disciples (Peter's "You are the Christ"), by the gospel writers (Mark's "The beginning of the gospel of Jesus Christ"), or, for that matter, by Jesus himself ("I am," in response to the high priest's question), these are always the result of the interweaving of Jesus' pre-Easter announcement of the coming kingdom with the church's post-Easter proclamation of Jesus as the embodiment of that kingdom.[7] Bultmann's classic and categorical denial of a Jesus Christology is worth repeating: "He [Jesus] gave no teaching about his own person."[8] It is almost impossible to overemphasize the impact of Bultmann's historical and theological analysis of the Gospels, and the results of that analysis with respect to a Jesus Christology.

From Bultmann's form criticism evolved a set of working assumptions and principles that with varying intensity have governed a broad spectrum of modern gospel studies. These assumptions have been characterized by that same fundamental skepticism regarding the historical reliability of the gospel texts in general and of a Jesus Christology in particular. The prevalence of such skepticism has had the practical and reductionist effect of placing the burden of proof on the shoulders of all who would affirm any Jesus Christology within the gospel portraits,[9] an assumption that is the reverse of what one might expect. "Enlightenment" (liberal) New Testament studies from the turn of the century on had long since redefined and restated Christology in ethical/moral, spiritualized/existentialized, and very importantly, nontranscendent terms—a Christology sometimes depicted as a Christology "from below." But Bultmannian analysis broke even more radically with traditional Christology by shattering all reasonable hopes for recovering any form of a historical Jesus Christology within the church's biased and highly Christologized Gospels. In spite of his emphasis on the hyperboles marking Jesus' announcement of the inbreaking kingdom (its call for decision now in the face of God's eschatological warnings, its demand for radical obedience, etc.), Bultmann always maintained his conviction that it was only as the proclaimer of God's inbreaking eschatological power that Jesus spoke, never as any self-affirmed Messiah whom God had sent "in the fulness of time." And while the so-called post-Bultmannians presumably allowed for the plausibility of a Christology implicitly encapsulated in those radical pronouncements and activities of Jesus, for them explicit Christology always awaited its final unveiling in the Easter proclamation.[10]

The historical skepticism associated so closely with the Bultmann school is the result of what finally sifted down into form criticism's so-called "criterion of dissimilarity," which methodologically limits historical authenticity to those sayings and narrations that do *not* reflect the Easter faith.[11] With that criterion as a beginning, any explicit Christological claims in the Gospels, whether from Jesus or his followers, are by definition set apart from any Jesus Christology. Theoretically, this criterion functions more in epistemological than in substantial terms: i.e., it challenges the ability to ascertain a Jesus Christology rather than to affirm or deny the actuality of Jesus' messianic identity. But for all practical purposes, with the criterion of dissimilarity in full use, the search for any significant Jesus Christology seems bound to fail. Even the post-Bultmannians—while presumably giving limited credence to implicit rather than explicit messianic affirmations, to commensurability rather than continuity between Jesus and the gospel tradition—have characteristically preserved that same gulf between the Jesus of the Gospels and any working Jesus Christology.

The question of a Jesus Christology was not to be left exclusively in the hands of Bultmannian form critics. Using form critical methods more as a window of access than as a barrier to the historical Jesus, many

British and, to a lesser degree, American New Testament scholars have reached more positive conclusions in the search for a Jesus Christology. Even among German scholars, where radical form criticism maintained its greatest stronghold, Bultmannian skepticism never gained universal support. Criticisms of Bultmannian procedures are now sufficiently widespread to signal that the Bultmann era is no longer at center stage. Bultmann's rigorously defined methods remain a vital legacy for all New Testament scholars attempting to reach even a minimal consensus on what can be considered historical. But at the same time, serious questions need to be addressed especially to form criticism's built-in assumption that Easter faith was always the final context in which Christological affirmations were shaped. If such a "line in the sand" must finally differentiate "the proclaimer from the proclaimed," to use Bultmann's terminology, then the search for a Jesus Christology must remain in limbo.

Many discussions of alternative methodological and historical issues with respect to a Jesus Christology are now readily available. A very thoughtful and nontechnical analysis of overall historical Jesus issues is James Dunn's *The Evidence for Jesus*, where the reader will find a clear discussion of the issues relating particularly to the Son of God question.[12] There is much to be learned by continuing the search for a Jesus Christology through analyzing those Christological parallels derived from first-century Jewish and Hellenistic contexts of Christological development,[13] exploring the distinctive Christological titles such as Son of Man and Son of God, or even examining Jesus' use of distinctive words such as *Abba* when addressing the Deity.[14] Moreover, there are materials in the Gospels that, although not Christological in its narrower understanding, do offer important reflections of that broader transcendence so characteristically attached to the gospel portraits of Jesus. Some of these can surely meet the most critical standards of historicity, even those that are imposed by the criterion of dissimilarity. To assume that all such intimations of transcendence attached to the work and words of Jesus must derive their substance from Easter faith seems to be based on preconceived notions rather than on the evidence at hand.

The Easter faith clearly interacted in a variety of important ways with emerging Christological affirmations, whether those of Jesus or of his followers.[15] In the Gospels, for example, where Jesus refers predictively and quite specifically to his own forthcoming resurrection (e.g., Mark 8:31), one suspects that the narrators, informed by their knowledge of the story's outcome, were using a certain anachronistic license in their pre-Easter narrations. There remain also those more subtle cases where preresurrection incidents within the ministry of Jesus seem framed in literary, stylistic, and theological forms strikingly similar to those that surface in narratives of the resurrection itself (e.g., cf. the so-called transfiguration scene in Mark 9:2–8 with Luke's description of the Emmaus Road encounter between the resurrected Christ and the disciples in Luke 24:13ff.). But to view resurrection faith as the sole prism that shaped pre-Easter claims to transcendence (whether Jesus-proclaimed or disciple-proclaimed) is unwarranted. For the New Testament theologian/historian arbitrarily to exclude the historical Jesus from this larger arena of transcendence is to fail to take seriously the portrait of Jesus that the gospel writers have so carefully and intentionally presented.[16]

What we are suggesting is simply this: that any serious examination of the Gospels confronts the reader with an intriguing and persistent "flow of transcendence" expressed through widely varying narrative forms and verbal expressions, and which transcendence is bound to the person of Jesus: sometimes in affirmations made about Jesus' authority (Mark 1:22); elsewhere in the fulfillment Jesus associates with his exorcisms and healings (Matt. 12:28; Luke 11:20); and especially in the more overt declarations of messiahship, whether from Jesus, as in Mark 14:62, or from others who declare him to be the Messiah/Son of God (Mark 8:29). Even if it seems necessary to cast aside those more specifically Christological declarations because they reflect the Easter context, there is no reason to treat such broader expressions of transcendence as automatically post-Easter, or as something less than Christology. The later Bultmannians in particular resolved this dilemma by distinguishing between explicit and implicit Christological claims, but that separation seems contrived.[17]

Expressions of transcendence are powerfully reflected in the unprecedented eschatological proclamation attached so persistently to the words and actions of Jesus in the Gospels, and which expressions are to be categorized as Christological. Profound Christological meaning can be gleaned from what C. H. Dodd long ago isolated and designated as "realized eschatology" in the sayings and activities of Jesus. Dodd used that phrase to articulate what he understood as Jesus' unique claims for eschatological fulfillment declared within the context of his historic ministry. The unprecedented thrust of Jesus' pronouncements, Dodd argued, was not the more familiar promise of future life and happiness in God's new age, but rather the assurance that God's eschatological intrusion was already actualized in Jesus' Galilean ministry of teaching and healing. As is familiar to New Testament scholars, Dodd based his argument particularly on those texts he considered among the most authentic Jesus traditions, included in which was Jesus' declaration that in his exorcisms "the kingdom of God has come" (Matt. 12:28; Luke 11:20).[18] And while the precise meaning of this text may still be debatable, few New Testament scholars would assign its origins to any postresurrection context.[19] Even Bultmann insisted that this saying "is full of that eschatological power which must have characterized the activity of Jesus."[20] That Dodd proceeded to eliminate and/or recon-strue all traces of apocalyptic in Jesus' kingdom sayings suggests that he was using realized eschatology as simply another kind of prism, in this case to filter out all apocalyptic eschatology from the legitimate sayings of Jesus.[21]

Our point is that one need not accept Dodd's anti-apocalyptic biases, nor even the full implications of realized eschatology, in order to recognize and appreciate the significant Christological implications of Jesus' kingdom sayings. Even if actual entrance into the kingdom remained always a future hope in the thought of Jesus, as a recent scholar has once again pointed out,[22] that does not cancel what we would see as the Christological substance inherent in Jesus' declaration that his presence marked the division of the ages (Matt. 11:12–13; Luke 16:16), as well as the beginning of the kingdom itself. Both resurrection and Parousia remained in the future, but that does not thereby limit Christology to the future! To put it another way, Jesus' understanding of his mission was identified as eschatological realiza-tion, and that translates into a transcendence that fits our broader understanding of Christology. Bultmann, of course, always insisted that Jesus' "word" was promise rather than fulfillment, a kingdom still to come rather than a kingdom already realized. But he also insisted that the eschatological warnings had placed the destinies of Jesus' hearers in the balance, that their place in God's eschatological scheme was already settled on the basis of their acceptance or rejection of those warnings.[23] More striking still is the fact that when Bultmann addressed those same eschatological texts hermeneutically (i.e., existentially), he found a radical (eschatological) and unprecedented demand for decision *now* in the face of the inbreaking power of God.[24]

This seems remarkably close to the meaning that Dodd found expressed in Jesus' self-proclaimed manifestation of the kingdom. When Bultmannians—even later post-Bultmannians—rejected "realized eschatology" by confining Jesus' ministry only to an announcement of the kingdom's imminence,[25] they were unnecessarily separating Christological implications from Christology. It is not necessary to resolve all the issues of realized eschatology in order to uncover the transcendence so broadly reflected in the work and words of Jesus. Metaphors of transcendence abound in the language of Jesus' parables concerning the kingdom. Along these lines readers will profit from the late Norman Perrin's summary of some important recent work that has been done in studies dealing with parabolic language and symbols.[26]

Outside the Gospels this transcendence may be associated with specific messianic titles and/or functions that are often tied to the resurrection. Moreover, apart from the Gospels, messianic status is only rarely linked in any direct way to the actual content of Jesus' historic work and/or words (e.g., see again Acts 2:22), an omission that remains problematic. Nevertheless, in what is surely our earliest Pauline writing (1 Thessalonians), the apostle reminded Christians in Thessalonica that their future salvation already began with Jesus' crucifixion, although even here crucifixion was itself connected with resurrection: "For since we believe that Jesus died and rose again, so, through Jesus, God will bring with him those who have fallen asleep" (1 Thess. 4:14). It is worth observing that Paul may even have connected that last statement to what he immediately declared as "the word of the Lord" (see 1 Thess. 4:15). Elsewhere in articulating his "received gospel" Paul claims that "Christ died," that he "was buried," and then that "he was raised on the third day" (1 Cor. 15:3–4). It seems impossible to imagine a Pauline image of the historical Jesus apart from some Christological implications.

Except for the Fourth Gospel, direct evidence for the existence of an explicitly defined preresurrection Jesus Christology remains either absent or, at the very least, vague. In what may be a very early Christology preserved in Acts 3:20, one might even argue some were in fact reserving Jesus' full and explicit messiahship for its ultimate declaration in the Parousia itself. Notwithstanding, there remains a profound sense of eschatological newness affirmed well within the range of Jesus' historic ministry, which, as we have argued, should not be discounted when searching for a Jesus Christology. According to an important Q tradition (generally agreed to be the earliest layer of the Synoptic tradition), Jesus' declaration of such newness is powerfully articulated in his response to the Baptist's envoys, who had been sent to determine whether this Jesus of Nazareth was a bona fide messiah: "Go and tell John what you have seen and heard: the blind receive their sight, the lame walk, lepers are cleansed, the dead are raised up, and the poor have the good news preached to them" (Matt. 11:2–6; Luke 7:18–23). The same aura of transcendent authority is preserved when, following Peter's "You are the Christ," Jesus appears not only to accept all that Peter intended by that confession, but goes on to interpret precisely how that messiahship is already functioning in his own gathering of the righteous in preparation for the final judgment: "Whoever is ashamed of me and my words in this adulterous and sinful generation, of him will the Son of Man also be ashamed when he comes in the glory of his Father with the holy angels" (Mark 8:38). With even more dramatic transcendence comes that Christological bolt from the blue whereby sonship is presumably conveyed by Jesus himself in a text whose origins have been increasingly assigned to a very early level of gospel tradition (Q?): "All things have been delivered to me by my Father, and no one knows the Son except the Father, and no one knows the Father except the Son and anyone to whom the Son wishes to reveal him" (Matt. 11:25ff.; Luke 10:21–22).[27]

Arguing that resurrection exclusively is what gave rise to Jesus' Christological identity, and thereby ruling out any substantive Jesus Christology, is a fallacy too long perpetrated by form criticism's influence in New Testament interpretation. That the Synoptic Gospels are reluctant to attach explicit Christological claims to Jesus' proclamation is clear. Undoubtedly, resurrection faith played some decisive—even creative—role in establishing and ultimately articulating the proclamation of Jesus through Christological titles, a process of elaboration that began with the New Testament and continued through and even beyond the creedal formulations that culminated at the Council of Chalcedon in 451.

So then, once again, the question: Did Jesus have a Christology? If an affirmative answer means a return to some precritical orthodoxy armed with an essentially Johannine set of claims about Jesus' sense of purpose and mission, then a negative response is more compatible with the truth. That Jesus anticipated the elaborated incarnational Christologies that developed through the first four centuries is not a real option. But surely there are alternatives to that Johannine syndrome! It is indeed difficult to imagine the Jesus of the Fourth Gospel in any believable historical setting—whether in the first century or our own. The more subtle, secretive, covert, even silent Jesus who emerges in the Synoptics seems a more viable option, although one that does not exclude a broadly defined Christological awareness on the part of Jesus. Forced to choose, most scholars certainly would take their stand on the side of the synoptics. Jesus' inner convictions probably can never be fully and satisfactorily recovered from the church's Gospels, a powerful warning put before us many decades ago by Bultmann himself. Indeed, it was his uncompromising criticism and theological integrity that forced New Testament interpreters to face these historical questions with a seriousness unprecedented in modern New Testament criticism. The question cannot be evaded by anyone who takes the historical *and* Christological claims in the Gospels seriously.

But in answering that question here, and in terms of all that has been said above, we want to restate in the strongest terms that the Gospels are remarkably persistent in presenting Jesus as the One who himself conveyed that sense of uniqueness (transcendence) that we cannot clearly distinguish from Christology. We find that sense of mission especially clear in the eschatological convictions attributed to Jesus in what are commonly regarded as the earliest Synoptic sources (Mark and Q). Those of Bultmannian persuasion will underscore what they have always argued, namely, that such pre-Easter transcendence it is at most an *implicit* Christology that became explicit only in the wake of the resurrection. We must disagree, if for no other reason than the arbitrariness attached to their conclusion. The New Testament witnesses combined Jesus' sense of mission with resurrection faith to produce Christological formulations marked by such notions as preexistence, even Godness. And it seems worth noting that such emerging Christologies came to serve political, social, and ecclesiastical purposes, as well as theological ones, in the ongoing New Testament dialogue with Christology. Segments of that dialogue continue in the remaining chapters in this section.

NOTES

1. For a discussion of "messiahship" as defined by and limited to its essentially Jewish context, see Otto Betz's "Messianic Expectations in the Context of First-Century Judaism," in part 1 of this collection. For purposes of the present essay, "Christology" is intentionally used in the broader sense to include not only historic messianic terminology drawn from Jewish literature and thought, but also the adaptations of that of such terminology in "Christian" Christological interpretation in which notions of divinity were applied. Those more incarnational uses found in the New Testament are normally deemed to have been influenced by the broader Hellenistic world in which Christianity was to move, dimensions of which are discussed in the Pagels and Schmeller essays also in part 1. The application of the latter in Christian usage are more fully treated in several chapters in part 2.

2. See Harvey K. McArthur, "Christology in the Predicates of the Johannine *Egō Eimi* Sayings," later in this same section. Because the Gospel of John is normally thought to be farther removed from the historical tradition, that material will not play any significant role in our comments.

3. The classic statement of Markan priority among the Synoptics and the so-called "two-document" hypothesis with respect to the Synoptic Gospels remains B. H. Streeter's *The Four Gospels* (London: Macmillan, 1924). That position has been challenged by a number of contemporary scholars; see especially W. R. Farmer, *The Synoptic Problem*, 2d ed. (Macon, GA: Mercer University Press, 1981). An excellent collection of essays/articles for and against the priority of Mark is available in Arthur J. Bellinzoni, Jr., *The Two-Source Hypothesis: A Critical Appraisal* (Macon, GA: Mercer University Press, 1985). A much briefer earlier summary of arguments for and against the priority of Mark can be found in William A. Beardsley, *Literary Criticism of the New Testament* (Philadelphia: Fortress Press, 1970), 64–74. In any case, this present discussion presumes that the earliest Synoptic sources are most probably in Mark and Q.

4. See the brief discussion of Wrede in chapter 1 of this collection.

5. See *The "Messianic Secret" in Mark's Gospel*, trans. Christopher Tuckett (Edinburgh: T. and T. Clark, 1990), esp. 38–75; see also Tuckett's edited collection of recent essays on issues arising from the "messianic secret" in *The Messianic Secret* (Philadelphia: Fortress Press, 1983).

6. See chapter 1 in this collection.

7. The classic statement of Bultmannian form criticism is in Bultmann's *History of the Synoptic Tradition*, trans. John Marsh (New York: Harper & Row, 1976). For a nontechnical summary and assessment of this method of gospel analysis, see Edgar V. McKnight, *What is Form Criticism?* (Philadelphia: Fortress Press, 1969), esp. 57–78.

8. See Rudolf Bultmann, "Christology of the New Testament," in *Faith and Understanding*, ed. R. Funk (New York: Harper & Row, 1969), 283.

9. For a clearly presented defense of that burden of proof, see Harvey K. McArthur, "The Burden of Proof in Historical Jesus Research," *Expository Times* 82, no. 4 (January 1971): 116–19.

10. See chapter 1 in this collection.

11. See Reginald Fuller's article in part 1, "The Criterion of Dissimilarity: The Wrong Tool?"

12. London: SCM Press, 1985, esp. 30–52; a larger and more recent study is Ben Witherington III's *The Christology of Jesus* (Minneapolis: Fortress Press, 1990). Witherington's conclusions clearly support the possibility of uncovering a Jesus Christology, although he is not always as convincing as one might hope in dealing with the pivotal issues raised by Bultmannian form criticism; see, e.g., his rather easy dismissal of the criterion of dissimilarity, p. 28. A recent and comprehensive discussion of historical Jesus issues is John Meier's *A Marginal Jew: Rethinking the Historical Jesus* (New York: Doubleday, 1991).

13. See articles in part 1 of this book.

14. For a recent discussion of the Son-of-Man problem see Witherington, *Christology*, 233ff.

15. For a brief discussion of the relationship between resurrection and Christology, see Pheme Perkins' essay later in this same section; also, her earlier and full-length study, *Resurrection: New Testament Witness and Contemporary Reflection* esp. 78–84, 215–46, and 391–408.

16. Along such lines, we would strongly commend the suggestions of C. F. D. Moule, who argues for a developmental rather than an evolutionist approach to the relationship between a Jesus Christology and that of the post-Easter tradition; see the introductory discussion in chapter 1 in this collection.

17. Willi Marxsen was moving along such lines, at least in part, in the article referred to earlier in chapter 1. There, it will be recalled, Marxsen locates Christology in the dynamic of the interaction between Jesus and the disciples, a dynamic that Marxsen describes as implicitly messianic. Our only question is whether there is in

such cases any substantive difference between what is explicit and implicit, what is postresurrection or preresurrection.

18. The first edition of *The Parables of the Kingdom* was published in 1935 (London: Nisbet and Co., Ltd.). The most recent America edition was published by Charles Scribner's Sons (New York, 1961).

19. See N. Perrin, *Rediscovering the Teaching of Jesus* (New York: Harper & Row, 1967), 63–67.

20. *History of the Synoptic Tradition*, 162.

21. See W. G. Kümmel's "Eschatological Expectations in the Proclamation of Jesus," in *The Kingdom of God*, ed. Bruce Chilton (Philadelphia: Fortress Press, 1984), 36ff.

22. See Witherington, *Christology*, 206.

23. See his *Theology of the New Testament*, trans. Kendrick Grobel (New York: Charles Scribner's Sons, 1951), 1:9f., 19–22.

24. See especially Bultmann's *Jesus Christ and Mythology* (New York: Charles Scribner's Sons, 1958), 22ff.

25. See Robert F. Berkey, "Realized Eschatology and the Post-Bultmannians," *Expository Times* 84, no. 3 (1972): 72–77.

26. *Jesus and the Language of the Kingdom* (Philadelphia: Fortress, 1983).

27. See James Dunn, *Christology in the Making* (London: SCM Press, 1989), 24f., where Dunn points to the growing acceptance of such texts among a broad spectrum of New Testament scholars.

CHAPTER SEVEN

PAULINE CHRISTOLOGY
SHAPING THE FUNDAMENTAL STRUCTURES

JAMES D. G. DUNN

In an influential monograph, Martin Hengel maintained that more developments in Christology happened within the period of Paul's ministry than in the whole of the next seven centuries.[1] Hengel's claims may be exaggerated,[2] but they are truthful enough to underline the importance of Paul's treatment of Christology and the extent to which subsequent Christian understanding of Christ has been dependent on Paul's formulations, like it or not.

How should we characterize and sum up Paul's contribution to this theme so crucial to Christian theology? What are the central emphases in this Pauline Christological thought that has had such an important role in shaping Christian thinking?

The answer cannot be found in what Paul tells us about Jesus' ministry prior to Good Friday and Easter. It is well known that Paul says next to nothing about Jesus' life, apart from its final suffering. And although it is possible to detect in Paul's ethical exhortations an influence of the Jesus-tradition—both Jesus' example and his own teaching, which is stronger than is usually acknowledged[3]—Paul makes no attempt to focus his Christology on the pre-Good Friday Christ.

What then of Christ's death? One thinks immediately of key texts such as Rom. 3:24–26 and 2 Cor. 5:21. While such texts lie close to the heart of any Christian doctrine of atonement, a notable feature of Paul's treatment of Christ's death is the extent to which he relies on what are generally agreed to be earlier formulations (e.g., Rom. 3:24–25; 4:25; 8:34; Gal. 1:4; 2:20).[4] Paul did not seem to have much new to say about the death of Christ. For example, in Romans, after the lengthy indictment of 1:18–3:20, the response of 3:21–26 seems very brief, and presumably could be so brief because the understanding of the death of Christ encapsulated there could be taken as common ground between Paul and even those churches he had never visited before. Of course he preached "Christ crucified" and recognized that a crucified Messiah constituted a scandal for most of his Jewish peers (1 Cor. 1:23; 2:2; Gal. 3:1), but already the issue seems to be an echo of an older, intra-Jewish debate, with Paul able to take the messiahship of Jesus so much for granted that "Christ" functions for the most part as a quasipersonal name throughout his letters. This is not to deny that the cross was very much at the center of Paul's gospel, but if we are looking for the points at which Paul made his own contribution to Christological thought, we probably will have to search elsewhere.

What then of Christ's resurrection and exaltation? One thinks at once of the fact that "Lord" is Paul's favorite title for Christ precisely because Christ's resurrection and exaltation are the vital presuppositions of his lordship. Yet here too the most relevant word may be "presuppositions," because, once again, the key statements that "explain" Christ's lordship seem to be pre-Pauline formulas that Paul inherited (Rom. 1:3–4; 10:9–10; Phil. 2:9–11).[5] And even where resurrection is at the heart of the discussion (1 Cor. 15), it is not the resurrection of Jesus, either its facticity or its nature, that is at issue (15:3–8, 12–19). In other words, Christ's resurrection and exaltation can hardly be ignored as essential starting points of Paul's Christology, but they themselves do not provide its central thrust. Essential foundations, no doubt, but for the Pauline superstructure we have to inquire further.

These considerations should not be perceived as polemical or unduly radical. I am not denying the central importance of Christ's death and resurrection behind and within Paul's theology. But if we focus our attention on them we run the risk of stopping short at where Paul started. The traditional emphasis on these undeniably foundational elements of all Christian theology may obscure Paul's further contribution, which was to integrate the already established axioms of Christ's atoning death and eschatological resurrection into an overarching Christological schema, and thus to secure the significance of these individual elements within a larger theological framework.

CHRIST AND ADAM

We start with what Paul clearly sees as the Adamic significance of Christ, a significance for the history and salvation of humankind equivalent to that of the (mythical) Adam. *Adam* began the history of humankind and thus sums it up. In particular, in accordance with a doctrine of human fallenness that Paul can again assume (e.g., Wisd. of Sol. 2:23–24), Adam sums up humankind in its mortality and submissiveness to human appetite and selfish desire. In Adam, all die; death is the end for all who share human traits and family likenesses. *Christ*, in contrast, opens up the possibility of a new beginning—a humanity no longer enslaved by its animal nature, no longer subservient to selfish desire, and no longer fearful of death. In Christ, all shall be made alive (1 Cor. 15:22).

At first this seems a thin strand indeed out of which to construct one of the principal load-bearing beams in the superstructure of Pauline Christology. The Adam/Christ parallel comes to clear expression in only two passages in the Pauline letters, Rom. 5:12–21 and 1 Cor. 15:20–22, 44–49. But these passages are more significant than at first appears and make explicit what is more frequently implicit elsewhere.

For one thing, the passages constitute two of the most distinctive Pauline elaborations of his two foundational axioms—Christ's death and resurrection. He characterizes the death of Christ in a sequence of striking, epigrammatically concise antitheses as the counterbalance (and more than counterbalance) of Adam's sin—the death that was an act of obedience outweighing the death that was the punishment of disobedience (Rom. 5:15–19). The resurrection of Christ he characterizes in the epigram already cited as the definitive answer to the last enemy, death: Christ's resurrection does not make any difference to the fact that all die, but it does give hope of life beyond death. The last Adam who became life-giving Spirit is a more powerful representative figure than the Adam who became a living soul (1 Cor. 15:22, 45).

Thus it also becomes clear that it is precisely as last Adam that Christ has undone the damage wrought by Adam, that in a figure equivalent in significance to Adam the remedy to the cancer of human sin is presented. Paul repeatedly reverts to the language and imagery of Gen. 2–3 in what is his most sustained indictment and description of the human condition: a humanity that has refused to rely on God and give God due glory (Rom. 1:19–25); a humanity that has lost out on the glory initially given to Adam (3:23); a humanity that has fallen victim to the enticing deception of sin (7:7–12); a humanity that shares in the consequent futility and subjection to decay (the opposite of glory) of the cosmos as a whole (8:19–23). The significance of this Christ is that he has made possible the restoration of that same glory to humanity by himself receiving a glory that he seeks to share with others (Rom. 8:29–30; 2 Cor. 3:18–4:6; Phil. 3:21).[6]

In a series of insightful studies, Morna Hooker has shown how far the Adam/Christ parallel extends in Paul in terms of what she calls "interchange in Christ."[7] Adam exchanged his share in divine glory for slavery to sin and death. Christ changed places with this Adam, sharing Adam's subjection to sin and death in order that Adam might experience Christ's victory over sin and death. The pattern of interchange is most obvious in passages referring to Christ's death (Rom. 8:3; 2 Cor. 5:21; 8:9; Gal. 3:13; 4:4; Phil. 2:6–8). But it embraces the whole of Jesus' life: it was because his life had a representative character that his death could have the same character (Rom. 8:3; Gal. 4:4; Phil. 2:6–8). Because of this Adamic character of Christ's entire ministry, Paul thinks of the process of salvation as a sharing in Christ's sufferings, a becoming like him in his death (as in Rom. 8:17; 2 Cor. 1:5; 4:10–12, 16–18; Phil. 3:10–11). Hooker shows how the pattern of interchange extends even into ethical exhortation (e.g., Rom. 13:14; 15:1–3).[8] At all events, an ethical dimension in Adam Christology is very clear in Col. 3:9–11 (and also Eph. 4:22–24).

To an extent not usually appreciated, Adam Christology also embraces the thought of Christ's resurrection and exaltation. More striking still, it includes the affirmation of the lordship of Christ. This becomes clear in the way Paul and his contemporaries freely ran together Ps. 110:1 (the key text validating Christ's lordship) and Ps. 8:4–6 (the key text for Adam Christology): in appointing Christ as Lord (Ps. 110:1), God had put all things under his feet (Ps. 8:6; 1 Cor. 15:25–27; Phil. 3:21; Eph. 1:20–22; also Heb. 1:13–2:8; 1 Pet. 3:22). In other words, the exaltation of Christ as Lord was also the fulfillment of the divine purpose in creating humanity; the lordship of Christ is the completion of the lordship of Adam. The Creator's program, which broke down in Adam, has been "run through" again in Christ and achieved its original goal. Those "in Adam" share in the tensions of a fractured creation; those "in Christ" (will) share in the fulfillment and completion of God's purpose for creation as a whole.[9]

This last thought links us into one of the most pervasive (it occurs more than eighty times) and characteristic motifs in Paul's writings—the understanding of believers as "in Christ." A frequent variant is "in the Lord," and correlated phrases include "into Christ" (e.g., Gal. 3:26–28), "through Christ" (e.g., Rom. 5:1), "with Christ" (e.g., 2 Cor. 4:14), and "the body of Christ" (e.g., 1 Cor. 12:27). It is no accident that there is a cluster of such phrases in Rom. 6:1–11—that is, immediately following the exposition of Christ in Adam terms in Rom. 5:12–21—because the "in Christ" language is a natural outworking of Adam Christology. The idea of Christ as in some sense a "corporate" person[10] is part and parcel of Adam Christology. So too is the thought of Christ as the eldest of a new family of God, the firstborn of (the new) creation (Rom. 8:29; Col. 1:18). In his parallel to and contrast with Adam, Christ provides an alternative template for humanity.

Adam Christology can thus be seen to form an extensive feature in Paul's theology. More important, it provides an integrating framework both for Paul's Christology and for his entire gospel. In expressing the significance of Christ, more than any other Christological motif, Adam Christology embraces Christ's entire life and ministry: Christ as sharing with the Adamic fallenness of humanity; Christ as exchanging the death of sin for the death of obedience leading to life; Christ as fulfilling the divine purpose for humanity through his resurrection and exaltation to lordship. In broader terms, Adam Christology embraces the entire scope of salvation: the eschatological significance of Christ's actions as introducing a new and final epoch in God's dealings with humanity, which sees the final goal in terms of the fulfillment of the original purpose; an individual salvation, which is a conformity to the last Adam's suffering and death with a view to the future full conformity to his resurrection; a corporate salvation, which sees the embodiment of the divine ideal of humanity only in a community of faith; a cosmic salvation, which does not seek to escape the material and bodily but looks for the salvation of humanity as part of a redeemed creation.

Not all these themes are unique to Paul. The Philippians hymn is probably pre-Pauline (Phil. 2:6–11), and one of the clearest expositions of Adam Christology is to be found outside Paul (Heb. 2:5–18). Nevertheless, several of the extended features outlined above are both characteristic of and distinctive to Paul. And the use of Adam Christology to provide such an overarching and integrating framework is certainly to be attributed to Paul. As such, Adam Christology must be counted as one of the central emphases in Pauline Christological thought, an essential part of Paul's contribution to Christian theology.

CHRIST AND WISDOM

The theme of Christ and Wisdom is even less evident in Paul than that of Christ and Adam. It is explicit in only one passage, 1 Cor. 1:24 and 30: "Christ the power of God and the wisdom of God"; "Christ Jesus, whom God made our wisdom." But to anyone familiar with the Jewish wisdom tradition, it is also evident in 1 Cor. 8:6 and Col. 1:15–17. In both passages Paul speaks of Christ's role in and relation to creation in terms that, in Jewish thought, were most characteristically used for the personification of divine wisdom (as in Prov. 3:19; 8:22, 25; Sir. 24:9; Wisd. of Sol. 7:26).[11] And anyone who was aware of the way in which Deut. 30:12–13 was related to divine wisdom in Jewish reflection (as in Bar. 3:29–30) would recognize that Paul was playing with an identification of Christ and Wisdom in Rom. 10:6–8. Even so, the theme, explicit or immediately implicit, is brief. Why then single it out as one of the leading edges of Pauline Christology? The answer lies not only in the fact that the ramifications of the Christ-Wisdom association are far-reaching in Paul's own theology, but, still more, in the fact that Paul's identification of Christ and Wisdom constitute the first statement of a motif that was to become the principal focus in the burgeoning Christology of the next two centuries.

The female figure of divine wisdom was familiar in religious thought of the ancient Middle East as one of the chief ways of expressing belief in the divine care and fruitful provision for creation. Particularly in the myth of Isis the ancients expressed their convictions about the cycle of life and death and their dependence on the natural cycle of fertility. The wisdom writers of Israel had domesticated this widespread belief in divine wisdom, the key to success in life but hidden from human eyes, by identifying her with the Torah (Sir. 24:23; Bar. 3:9–4:4). In passages such as 1 Cor. 8:6 and Col. 1:15–17, the first Christians in effect were doing the same thing; identifying this divine wisdom with Christ. Where Jewish wisdom writers said to the wider world, "Here in the Torah is the divine wisdom on which you depend and which you seek," Paul and the first Christians could express the significance of their gospel in similar terms: "Here in Christ is the sum and epitome of the divine wisdom by which the world was created and is sustained." In making this identification between Christ and Wisdom, Paul and the first Christians were using a theme that constituted a major element in the ancient Mediterranean world's search for meaning and a major element in Jewish diaspora apologetic.

Note the specific twist that Paul gave to this line of Christian apologetic: his initial and, as we have seen, only explicit identification of Christ and Wisdom comes in 1 Cor. 1. Here Paul shows that he was well aware of the ancient world's thirst for wisdom, whether in terms of human cleverness and rhetorical sophistication, or in terms of human perception of what is a fitting outworking of the divine purpose of salvation. Such human estimates of how divine wisdom comes to expression within human society Paul challenges boldly and bluntly with the cross. Christ is the measure of divine wisdom; and by that Paul means not the Christ of creation or the Christ of exaltation, but Christ crucified (1 Cor. 1:22–24). The significance of this Wisdom-Christ spans all of time, from creation (1 Cor. 8:6) to new creation (Col. 1:15, 18); but the cross is the midpoint that symbolizes the character of the whole. Thus Paul anchors this major theme in the religious self-understanding of the ancient world firmly in Christ, and stamps the whole with the gospel of the cross.

At the same time, the identification of Christ and Wisdom provides a crucial vehicle for expressing the divine, or more than human (more than Adamic, we may say) significance of Christ that was a feature of Christology from the beginning. Because Wisdom, in Jewish thinking at least, was a way of speaking of the one *God's* care and provision for God's creation, the identification of Christ with this Wisdom becomes a powerful way of expressing *God's* care for God's people and provision for their salvation (most clearly in Wisd. of Sol. 10–11). Hence it provides an even more potent description of Christ's significance than speaking of God's putting forward Christ as a means of atonement (Rom. 3:25), or even of God in Christ as "reconciling the world to himself" (2 Cor. 5:19), which could be interpreted simply in terms of divine inspiration rather than pushing toward the thought of incarnation (as becomes clear later in John 1:14). So, too, the affirmation of Christ as divine wisdom can be seen as an alternative to speaking of Christ as proof of the divine faithfulness to all God's promises (2 Cor. 1:20), and thus plugs into one of the central themes of Romans—God's faithfulness to God's promises to Abraham and Israel (1:17, 25; 3:3–7, 25; 4; 9:6; 15:7–13).[12]

The Wisdom-Christ identification also gives us the clue to how Paul can speak so boldly about the divine significance of Christ in language that seems at first to threaten the Jewish axiom of monotheism that he shared. Jewish talk of Wisdom could be almost as bold, but it was clearly understood as simply a way of expressing the one God's care for creation and provision for God's people (as Wisd. of Sol. 10–19 shows). Although the exalted Christ shares in God's lordship as object of devotion and source of divine blessing (as in Rom. 1:7 and Phil. 2:9–11), Paul does not understand this as any sort of compromise with or even redefinition of his faith in God as one (e.g., Rom. 3:30; 1 Cor. 8:6); Christ as divine wisdom is the Wisdom of the one God and in no way an alternative, far less competing source of authority (1 Cor. 3:23; 11:3; 15:24, 28). Even in the later Titus 2:13, Jesus Christ is thought of as the glory of God, that is, the visible manifestation of God's majesty, rather than as (another) God alongside the one God. By formulating the divine significance of Christ in wisdom language, Paul was able to retain the already burgeoning Christology within the constraints of the Jewish monotheism that remains axiomatic for Christian theology.[13]

Paul's Wisdom Christology thus serves as a fundamental and integrating structure in Pauline theology similar to that afforded by Adam Christology. It secures the continuity of the Christian epoch not only with creation (as does the Adam theme) but also with Israel (both Jewish and Christian wisdom writers are speaking of the same Wisdom). It provides an apologetic theme of tremendous power in the ancient world indicating the universal significance of Christ. In Paul in particular it becomes stamped with the theology of the cross, preventing any Docetic divorce between the human and the divine in Christ. And it holds together the strongest assessments of the divine significance of Christ and his work within the framework of the common Jewish/Christian conviction that God is one. It is precisely for these reasons that Wisdom (or equivalently expressed, Logos-Word) Christology became the mainstream of classic Christological reflection leading up to the third and fourth century creeds.[14] The character of Christology stamped on it by Paul's development of Wisdom Christology determined its future.

Here too we cannot speak of exclusively Pauline contributions. With Col. 1:15–20, as with Phil. 2:6–11, we are probably dealing with a pre-Pauline formulation; and Heb. 1:1–3 is as manifestly a wisdom formulation as anything in Paul. Nevertheless, as with Adam Christology, our clearest and earliest expressions of Wisdom Christology come from Paul: several of the emphases are distinctive of Pauline theology; and the range of his theological writings enable us to see how widespread are the ramifications of Wisdom Christology. Here too Wisdom Christology must be counted as one of the major emphases in Pauline Christological thought, and his reworking of it an essential part of Paul's contribution to Christian theology.

ADAM-CHRIST-WISDOM

All that remains is to point out the importance of the fact that Paul called in not just the (mythical) figure of Adam to illuminate the significance of Jesus and his work, but also the (mythical) figure of divine Wisdom. He found it necessary to use *both* integrating frameworks, not simply one or the other.

We can talk of the *complementarity* of the two themes and frameworks. At this earliest stage, we may say, both the character of the Christ event and the theological traditions available to fill out its significance pushed Christology, as expressed by Paul, in a double direction. One highlighted what might be summarized as the humanity of Christ, the other the divinity of Christ. But it was not the significance of Christ as such, or of Christ in himself, that was perceived to be at stake, but the significance of Christ in relation to humankind and to God. In Adam Christology we are speaking about *humanity*, not about the humanity of Christ; and in Wisdom Christology we are speaking about deity, not about the *deity* of Christ.

This doubly representative significance of Christ comes to expression in these Christologies. Christ as Adam shows us what God intended humanity to be. Christ as Wisdom shows us what God is like in God's creating, sustaining, and saving concern for all creation. The recognition that *both* are integral to Christology, as Paul clearly demonstrates, prevents Christology from degenerating either into an idealist or exemplarist Christology or into a Docetic or Gnostic Christology. Holding *both* together, in the terms that Paul was already providing, ensured that classic Christology always had the shape of an ellipse, held in place by its twin foci, rather than a circle spinning off into a Christocentric humanism (Christ only as ideal humanity) or a Christocentric theism (Christ alone as God for us).

On the other hand, we have to talk of the *overlapping* character of the two emphases. In Paul's theology this comes out both in the conception of Christ as the image of God and, once again, in the thought of Christ as *Lord*. The latter, we have noted, can be referred both to Christ's Adamic role as crown and head of creation (1 Cor. 15:25–27) and to Christ as the one Lord in his wisdom role as divine agent in creation (1 Cor. 8:6). Christ as Lord thus represents both God's purpose for the humankind God created and the lordship of God in that act of creation. Paul does not allow the thought of Christ's lordship to spin free from the lordship of God (as 1 Cor. 15:28 makes abundantly clear). In the concept of Christ as Lord Paul is able to hold together the divine significance of Christ, particularly in view of his resurrection, and the oneness of the creator God.

Similarly, in the Pauline letters we find that the *image of God* is referred both to Christ's Adamic role and to Christ's wisdom role. As to the former, we may think of Rom. 8:29: the son is the image to which, as "firstborn among many brothers," Christians are being conformed. Or 1 Cor. 15:49: as believers have borne the image of the first, earthly Adam, so they will bear the image of the last, resurrected Adam. As to the latter, the most obvious example is Col. 1:15: "He is the image of the invisible God" through whom all things were created. In 2 Cor. 3:18–4:4 the thought is both of believers being transformed into God's image and of Christ as embodying the image of God; is this Adam or

Wisdom? In Col. 3:10, is Christ the image of God as Adam or Wisdom?

The point is that the concept of the image of God can be used both for Adam *and* for Wisdom. It can denote both the image on the rubber stamp and the image that the stamp puts on the page; it can be used both for the agency used in creation and for that which is created. It is in this overlapping role that it is referred to Christ. Christ as bearing the divine image is the One who bridges the gap between creator and creation. In this supreme mediatorial role the two central strands of Pauline Christology overlap and intertwine. Christ as the image of God, even more than Christ as Lord, is the nodal point at which the two great arcs of Pauline Christology intersect and that thus prevents them from falling apart into a mutually destructive dichotomy.

In Christ as Adam and Christ as Wisdom we find the two major integrating themes of Pauline Christology, themes that integrate the other emphases of Pauline Christology and complement and overlap with each other in such a way as to provide the basic framework for all future Christology.

NOTES

1. M. Hengel, *The Son of God* (London: SCM Press, 1976), esp. 2 and 77.

2. See my *Christology in the Making* (London: SCM Press, 1980, 1989), 351 n. 1; also *The Partings of the Ways* (London: SCM Press, 1991), chaps. 9–11. I apologize for referring so often in what follows to my own work, but in a summary treatment it seems to be the simplest way to document both the detailed exegesis on which claims are based and the other secondary literature with which I dialogue.

3. See, e.g., discussion in A. J. M. Wedderburn, ed., *Paul and Jesus: Collected Essays* (*Journal for the Study of the New Testament* Supp. 37; Sheffield: *Journal for the Study of the Old Testament*, 1989), and M. B. Thompson, *Clothed with Christ: The Example and Teaching of Jesus in Romans 12.1–15.13* (*Journal for the Study of the New Testament* Supp. 59; Sheffield: *Journal for the Study of the Old Testament*, 1991).

4. See particularly part 1 in W. Kramer, *Christ, Lord, Son of God* (London: SCM Press, 1966); K. Wengst, *Christologische Formeln und Lieder des Urchristentums* (Gütersloh: Gütersloher, 1972).

5. See those cited in n. 4.

6. On these passages, and Rom. 5:12–21 above, see my *Romans*, Word Biblical Commentary 38 (Dallas: Word, 1988).

7. Collected in M. D. Hooker, *From Adam to Christ: Essays on Paul* (Cambridge: Cambridge University Press, 1990).

8. "Interchange in Christ and Ethics," *Journal for the Study of the New Testament* 25 (1985); also in *Adam to Christ*, chap. 4.

9. See more fully my *Christology*, chap. 4.

10. See particularly C. F. D. Moule, *The Origin of Christology* (Cambridge: Cambridge University Press, 1977), chap. 2.

11. For this and the supporting data for what follows, see my *Christology*, chaps. 6 and 7.

12. The point is more obscure for us than it would be for readers familiar with Old Testament and LXX thought, because in Romans the single theme of divine faithfulness is spread between the several variations of the same theme—God's faithfulness, God's truth, and God's righteousness; see, e.g., my *Romans*, 41, 44, 63, 132–33, 135–36, etc.

13. See my *Partings*, chaps. 10–12.

14. See, e.g., J. N. D. Kelly, *Early Christian Doctrines* (London: Black, 1960), chaps. 4 and 5.

CHAPTER EIGHT

JESUS AND THE NEW PEOPLE OF GOD: CHRIST AND COMMUNITY IN THE GOSPEL TRADITION

HOWARD CLARK KEE

The traditional approach to Christology in the Gospels has concentrated on messianic titles: Son of Man, Son of God, Son of David, Suffering Servant, etc. After scholars examine the background of these terms in the Jewish scriptures, they analyze their use by the New Testament writers and note comparisons and differences. Then they examine the ethical demands of Jesus as portrayed in the Gospels. This approach almost completely misses the dynamic of the New Testament writings.

The role of Jesus as seen in the setting of Judaism at the turn of the eras should be central in the analysis of the New Testament. There were two primary questions for Jews in this period of despair of achieving national autonomy and disillusionment with the secularization of the priesthood: What are the qualifications for participation in the covenant people of God, and who is (or are) the agent(s) through whom God is going to reconstitute them? In first-century Judaism there was no single answer to these questions, as recent studies of the Dead Sea community and of the Pharisees[1] have shown. Not until the Mishnah and Talmud took shape in the period from the second to the sixth centuries C.E. did the shift from what Neusner has aptly termed "formative Judaism" to "normative"[2] or orthodox Judaism occur.

In the first-century setting of Judaism, with its complex of variety and change, Jesus must be seen as the agent of God called and empowered to challenge those who claim to be the covenant people and to invite them to share in the new community that God is constituting through him. There was in the first century C.E. no single paradigm for the renewed covenant people or for the role of God's agent to accomplish this renewal. Given the diverse social and cultural dimensions of the Jews in this period, the range of images for both the community of God's people and the divinely endowed instrument(s) of renewal was wide. To use the traditional Christian theological terms with Christology must be understood in direct relationship with ecclesiology. What is called for, however, are less traditional terms, for which the basic questions are: What is the role of Jesus as God's agent for reconstituting God's people? And how do God's people understand themselves as qualified for participation, and as responsible for life and action, within the new community?

Analysis of the New Testament writings from this perspective leads to the conclusion that, as in Judaism, there was for the early Christian no single model for the community nor for the agency of Jesus as its founder. It is essential to see that there is in every book of the New Testament a dynamic relationship between how the community is seen as constituted and what the role of Jesus is as God's agent to establish this new people. At least six different models of community may be discerned in the New Testament. These models are not to be confused with categories or fixed patterns that can be imposed on the biblical material. Rather, they are heuristic tools that can bring into focus certain characteristic features, although these are conceptual and structural variations in some details among those visions of community that on the whole may be associated with one model. One should be aware of the influence of the sociocultural setting implicit in these various models that affects the depiction of both the community and the divine agent through whom it is seen as being brought into being.[3]

The models that serve this mode of sociocultural analysis and the New Testament writings akin to each may be designated as follows:[4]

1. The Community of the New Age[5]
   The Q Source
   Paul's Authentic Letters
   Gospel of Mark
   1 Peter
2. The True Community of Israel
   Gospel of Matthew

THE COMMUNITY OF THE NEW AGE: THE APOCALYPTIC MODEL

Despair about the present order and the incumbent religious and political leadership is typical of apocalyptic communities. This despair is most vividly represented in the book of Daniel. There the crisis resulting from enforced Hellenization under Antiochus Epiphanes had led some Jews to look beyond even the Maccabean attempt to resolve the difficulties through the establishment of a royal-priestly dynasty as the agency for reconstituting the people of God. Instead of accepting the Maccabean regime as God's solution to the needs of the people, the community behind Daniel expected direct divine intervention to establish such rule. In this view, the solution for God's people is not gradual improvement or incremental reform, but radical change through a chosen agent of God. The transformation is already in process and will be brought to fruition by God in the near future.

Insight into this divine purpose has been revealed to an elect community, whose members are to regard themselves as significantly different from their traditional kindred and therefore to behave by different norms. They are to expect opposition from the religious and political authorities, and they are warned that they will experience hostility and even martyrdom as they remain faithful to what God has disclosed concerning the divine purpose and the norms by which they are to live in the interim before the present order comes to an end. The agent through whom this expected renewal will occur is a human being ("one like a son of man"; Dan. 7:13–14) whose values and mode of life stand in sharpest contrast to the successive world rulers of history. He is both the true representative and the divinely chosen deliverer of the faithful community that God has called and is establishing.

In this essay, the analysis of the apocalyptic model is limited to one of its manifestations: the Q source. (Q is here taken to be the non-Markan material common to Matthew and Luke. References are to the Lukan version of Q, which seems to be closer to the original.) Variant examples of the apocalyptic model are to be found in the Gospel of Mark, the letters of Paul, and, with important differences, in the late first-century First Epistle of Peter. Only the Q version of this model will be detailed here.

The Q Source

God's Purpose at Work in Human History through Jesus

In the Q material,[6] Jesus' proclamation of the coming of the Kingdom of God is placed in the context of preparatory activity through the epochs of the "law and the prophets," culminating in the coming of John the Baptist (16:16). With the appearance of Jesus and the launching of his ministry of the Goods News in word and act there has also come a time of conflict, so that those who "enter" the Kingdom of God do so in a situation of violence. Dramatic evidence of this struggle is present in Jesus' exorcisms, which are seen as manifestations of the cosmic conflict between the purpose of God and the opposition of the powers of evil, here symbolized by Beelzebul (11:14–20). Jesus' expulsion of the demons is a public sign of the impending defeat of Satan and the establishment of God's rule in the earth. The onlookers are called by Jesus to choose sides: for Jesus and the work of God that he has begun among them, or for Satan, God's adversary. Meanwhile, Jesus' followers are to live in constant hope and expectation of the establishment of God's rule in the earth (11:2–4), asking only for supply of their daily needs and forgiveness of their sins. They live in confidence that God's purpose will soon be revealed and achieved, and that what they now discuss in the privacy of their meetings will be publicly proclaimed (12:2–3).

Jesus' Role as Agent of the Renewal of God's People

The preparatory role of John the Baptist in the Q source pictures him as not only the climax and conclusion of the era of the law and the prophets (16:16), but also as the crucial transitional figure who prepares for the coming of Jesus and for the redefining of the people of God. The latter theme is evident in John the Baptist's declaration that physical descent from Abraham is not to be regarded as an adequate criterion for identity as one of God's children (3:7–8). This insight is spelled out in greater detail in the interchange between Jesus and the questioners who come from the imprisoned John (7:18–35).

In response to these inquirers, Jesus' public activity in healing and inviting the outsiders ("the poor") to share in the new people of God is justified by an appeal to the prophetic promises that are paraphrased in answer to John's question: Are you "the one who is to come"? Jesus replies, "Go and tell John what you have seen and heard: the blind receive their sight, the lame walk, lepers are cleansed, and the deaf hear, the dead are raised up, and the poor have good news preached to them" (Luke 7:22; cf. Isa. 29:18–19; 35:5–6; 61:1). The importance of John's preparatory role in the purpose of God is affirmed emphatically with appeal to scripture (7:26–27; Mal. 3:1), but John is pictured as the end of the old era and a nonparticipant in the new community of the Kingdom of God. Jesus' criticism of his contemporaries is that they have not responded positively to either John's asceticism or to the freedom and joy that Jesus embodies and proclaims in his role as "friend of tax-collectors and sinners." Instead, the religious leaders denounce him as a "glutton and a drunkard," using the terms from Deut. 21:20 by which a family repudiated its nonconforming son, calling for his execution by the community through stoning.

Jesus' call to his role as agent of covenant renewal is seen in Q as involving his personal struggle with the temptation to exploit his extraordinary powers for selfish ends; that is, to try to gain a wide popular following. Though differing in important details from its Old Testament counterparts, the Q version of the struggle with the devil recalls the stories of inner conflicts and challenges connected with the divine calls to leadership of God's people experienced by Moses, Isaiah, and Jeremiah. At stake in each case is the destiny of God's people and the communication *to them* of the divine message for them as the covenant community. Those who respond to that message through Jesus will include not only people with a Jewish birthright, but also outsiders who are open to hear the word from God, as exemplified by the non-Israelite "queen of the south" who came to hear the wisdom of Solomon and by the penitent people of Ninevah who responded to the message of Jonah (11:29–32).

The Elect Community to Whom the Revelation is Given

Qualifications for participation in the new community are vividly indicated in the parable of the great supper (14:15–24). Those initially invited to share in the feast decline to attend because they are preoccupied with day-to-day affairs, while the "poor and maimed and blind and lame" from the city are called and join the feast, as do those from outside the city in the "highways and hedges." The former represent those who have been ritually and socially rejected from within Israel, and the latter symbolize the complete outsiders. Criteria for participation in the new age by the people of the New Covenant are radically redefined in terms of need and willingness to have God meet those needs, as contrasted with the people who traditionally identify themselves as the true heirs of God's people on ethnic and ritual grounds. The essential qualification for sharing in the new community is trust in God, through which the human situation can be transformed, as symbolized by the uprooted and transplanted tree (17:5–6). But the powers of the new age are already operating invisibly and unnoticed by many, like leaven hidden in some measures of meal (13:20–21).

The special insight that has been granted to those in the new community is indicated in Jesus' prayer of gratitude to God for having revealed the divine purpose "to babes" rather than to those who consider themselves to be "wise and understanding" (10:21–24). Perception as to who Jesus is and who God is has been reserved for those to whom "the Son chooses to reveal him." Those who share in these divinely granted insights are pronounced "blessed" and contrasted with the earlier generations of Israel whose prophets and kings were unable to discern God's purpose for and through these people—a purpose that has now been disclosed by Jesus. The cities of Galilee, which have on the whole rejected Jesus and refused to repent in response to the message he proclaimed, are contrasted with the Gentile cities, Tyre and Sidon, which are here pictured as ready to repent. The crucial factor is the response—either trust or rejection—to Jesus as messenger and agent of God's plan for renewal of the covenant.

The Values and Behavior of the Traditional Covenant People Contrasted with Those of Jesus and His Followers

The benefits that the members of the new community enjoy as a consequence of their trust in Jesus and his message are described in terms of the contrast between their present condition, humanly perceived, and what God has in store for them in the age to come (6:20–23). Now they are "poor"; then they will share in the life of God's Kingdom. Now they are hungry; then their needs will be fully satisfied. Now they are sorrowful; then they will be filled with joy. Now they are hated and rejected by their contemporaries because of their identification with Jesus and his message; then they will be filled with joy and showered with rewards. They may take comfort in the fact that earlier God's prophetic messengers also met with hostility and martyrdom.

In the present, however, their attitudes toward their opponents are to be utterly different from standard human reactions to those regarded as enemies (6:27–33). Instead of replying in kind to hostility and hatred and avarice, they are to react with love, blessing, and forgiveness. By their response in love, they demonstrate that they are indeed children of God, who is "kind to the ungrateful and the selfish" and, above all, "merciful." By adopting this manner of life, the community is sharing in the laying of the foundation of the new people of God, which even the streams and floods of hostility cannot undermine or destroy (6:47–49).

Warnings of Opposition and Conflict that the Community Will Experience

Jesus' solemn warnings (9:57–60) to those who declare their intention to follow him include notice that commitment to him and the new community may result in homelessness (like the Son of Man who has nowhere to lay his head) and in priorities that will override even family obligations ("let the dead bury the dead"). To align oneself with Jesus is to arouse conflict and divisions within one's own family (12:51–53), which is expressed in hyperbolic form as hating one's parents, children, and siblings (14:26). Jesus declares that to become his follower one must accept the prospect of martyrdom—taking up the cross (14:27)—and he warns (11:49–51) that he and those who join his movement will experience martyrdom such as that suffered over the centuries by God's special messengers and prophets—from Abel in the first book of the Hebrew canon (Gen. 4:8) to Zechariah in the last book (2 Chron. 24:20–21). They will be among the "prophets and apostles" who will be persecuted and killed. On the other hand, there may be situations in which shrewd compromise with the civil authorities may be appropriate and necessary if the work of the Gospel is to be carried forward (12:58–59).

The invitation is now open to join the community in preparation for the coming of the Kingdom of God, but the opportunity is not open-ended. When it ceases, those who belatedly declare their desire to participate will find that it is too late, and they are excluded. In the coming reign will be the great figures of ancient Israel—Abraham, Isaac, and Jacob—as well as people from every corner of the earth. All of them will be joined in the communal meal that symbolizes and celebrates the fulfillment of God's rule in the creation (13:22–30). Yet there is also in the Q tradition (13:34–35) a recurrent note of lament for "Jerusalem," symbolizing the traditional people of God who have refused to heed the invitation to share in the new age that Jesus is bringing. As a consequence, their "house is forsaken" (Ps. 118:26) and they will not recognize who Jesus is until they are ready to affirm him as the "blessed one who comes in the name of the Lord" (13:34–35; Ps. 118:26). Meanwhile, the traditional people of God will be preoccupied with daily routines and unprepared for the ultimate vindication of the Son of Man, who has been rejected by this generation (17:22–37). Only the faithful will be ready for his Parousia and will experience vindication by him, while the decay and debris of a fallen civilization will attract the vultures.

The Promise of Vindication of the Elect Community

The basic criterion for participation in the life of the new people of God is public acknowledgment of Jesus as the "Son of Man," and hence as agent for establishing God's rule on the earth (12:8–10). Conversely, to fail to discern the Spirit of God at work in Jesus' message and activities and to reject him is a blasphemy for which God offers no forgiveness. The members of the community are to be free of anxiety about the ordinary needs of life, relying instead on God's grace and providence. Their foremost objective must be to share in the coming of the kingdom, which is God's gift rather than an earned benefit. In preparation, they must be willing to give up earthly possessions, sharing what they have with others and assigning the highest value to the kingdom and its coming.

That Jesus is now absent from the community is explained in the Q tradition by the parable of the pounds (19:11–27). Although Luke has added allegorical details that explain the delay in the Parousia and the rejection of Jesus by the Jewish officials (vv. 11, 12, 14, 15a, 26, 27), the basic theme of the original parable remains that the members of the community have been assigned responsibilities in the present situation for which they will one day be called to account. In view of that future day of reckoning, they must now be faithful in discharging their tasks. But at the same time, there is promise of reward and vindication for them when the Kingdom of God is fully and finally established (22:28–30). Those who have remained faithful to Jesus, sharing in the hostility, persecution, and even martyrdom that was his experience, will participate in the consummation of the New Covenant when God's Kingdom comes. They will take part in the eschatological meal (which resembles the one described in the appendix to the Scroll of the Rule in the Dead Sea Scrolls from Qur'an) when the Messiah is enthroned. They will also see the judgment that will fall on the twelve tribes of Israel who have failed to recognize Jesus as God's agent for renewal of the covenant. Clearly, the eucharistic meal is seen as an anticipation of the fulfillment of God's purpose in the world, which will be accomplished by Jesus.

THE TRUE COMMUNITY OF ISRAEL:
THE GOSPEL OF MATTHEW

A dramatic shift in the presentation of the Jesus tradition is evident when one compares the Q material with the Gospel of Matthew. Here a clear correlation is presented between the role of Jesus and the model of community that is operative in this gospel. The overarching aim of the portrait of Jesus, beginning with the account of his birth and early life, is the fulfillment of God's intention as set forth in the scriptures. This image is sustained throughout Matthew to the closing account of Jesus' postresurrection appearance to his followers.

Matthew's Portrait of Jesus

The origins of Jesus and the launching of his ministry are grounded in the history of Israel by the genealogy that opens the book. The central figures there are the founders of the covenant people: Abraham and Israel's model king, David. The tragic decline of the people is exemplified by the exile in Babylon, although this also serves as the implicit prelude to the renewal that is to take place through Jesus. The firm hand of God in these historical developments is apparent in that the fourteen generations between each of these crucial phases of Israel's history represent a doubling of the sacred number of seven. Joseph, Jesus' legal father, is descended from David and resides in his city, Bethlehem. God communicates the divine purpose through dreams, as God did to Jacob (Gen. 31), to Joseph (Gen. 37–42), to Solomon (1 Kings 3:5), and even to Nebuchadnezzar (Dan. 2). In fulfillment of scripture are the birth of the son (Isa. 7:14; 8:8–10), its occurrence in Bethlehem (Matt. 2:6; Mic. 5:1; 2 Sam. 7:12), the visit and gifts of the Magi (Ps. 72:10f.; Isa. 60:6), the flight to Egypt (as in Exodus), and the return (Hos. 11:1), the new residence in Nazareth (2:23, probably referring to Judg. 13:5 or Isa. 11:1), the extent of the period of Jesus' testing (Matt. 4:2; Exod. 24:18ff. for Moses; 2 Kings 19:9 for Elijah), the use of scripture in the testing process itself (Matt. 4:4; quoted from Deut. 8:3), and Jesus' move to Capernaum in a Gentile-dominated area (Matt. 4:14; Isa. 8:23; 9:1; Ps. 107:10).

Jesus as Messenger to God's People: The New Moses

The potential for a geographically and culturally wide response to Jesus is indicated in the summary statement in Matt. 4:23–25: Jesus' fame spreads throughout "all Syria," and those brought to him include people with every kind of ailment, as well as crowds drawn from the Gentile cities of the Decapolis and from Galilee, Jerusalem, and Judea. Yet the style and strategy of the gospel as a whole builds on the prototype of Moses as God's agent to constitute and organize the covenant people. The structure of this gospel consists of the framing introduction (birth stories, Matt. 1–3) and a concluding section (Passion and commissioning of the disciples; Matt. 26–28), with the main body of material presented in a fivefold division, each part of which consists of an account of Jesus' activity and a block of his teaching. The end of each of these five sections is marked by a variant of the phrase, "When Jesus had finished" (7:28; 11:1; 13:53–58; 19:1; 26:1). The parallel with the fivefold law of Moses is clear. Violating this symmetry is Matt. 23, with its bitter attack on what was emerging at the end of the first century as rabbinic Judaism. Almost certainly this is a later addition to Matthew's gospel arising out of the conflict between the two parallel movements, each of which claimed to be the true heir of the covenant tradition as embodies in the Pentateuch. This tension is explicit in the antitheses of Matt. 5–7, where Jesus' interpretation of the Law is set over against that of the traditional Jewish understandings of Moses, and it reaches its climax in the claim that Jesus taught with *exousia*, as contrasted with the scribes (7:28–29).

The Community of the True Covenant

The conflict between traditional Israel as perceived by the developing rabbinic tradition and the new community—now called the *ekklesia*—is pointed up throughout the Gospel of Matthew. Israel is described as a leaderless people (9:36), in terms drawn from the time of the Exodus (Num. 27:17) and in Micaiah's warning to Ahab (2 Chron. 18:16). This theme is repeated by Matthew alone in 10:6 and 15:24. The direct competition between the Jewish gatherings and those of Jesus' followers is made explicit in the repeated references to "*their* synagogues" in Matt. 4:23; 9:35; 10:17; 12:9; 13:54; 23:34, and in the challenges to synagogal practices in 6:2, 5; 23:6. There is a comparable challenge to their interpretations of scripture in Matt. 23, where rabbinic legal piety is broadly and bitterly denounced.

The climax to this conflict comes in Matthew's version of Jesus' encounters with the authorities in Jerusalem and the trial scenes. Building on the debates described in Mark 11:27, Matthew intensifies the criticisms of Israel's leaders: tax-collectors and sinners will go before the religious leaders into the Kingdom of God, because the former believed the message of John the Baptist and repented (Matt. 21:31). Employing the prophetic image of Israel as God's vineyard (Isa. 5), Matthew reports Jesus as declaring that the Kingdom of God will be taken from these leaders and given to another nation (*ethnos*) that will produce the appropriate fruits. The leaders are said to respond to this charge by recognizing that the parable is being told against them (21:33–46). Similarly, Matthew adapts and allegorizes the parable of the great supper in Luke 14:15–24: the supper has become a marriage feast (Israel as God's bride); the central character in the wedding is the king's son (the messianic king); the response of those invited is not preoccupation with routine business (as in Luke) but the killing of the messengers sent by the king (God); consequently, the king sends troops and destroys the city (an obvious reference to the destruction of Jerusalem by the Romans under Titus in 67–70).

Similarly, in Matthew's version of the Passion story responsibility for Jesus' death is placed directly on the religious leaders and the people (27:25), while Jesus is declared innocent by Judas (27:3–5) and by Pilate and his wife (27:18–19, 23–24). Accordingly, Jesus is reported as predicting that the hostility and persecution that his followers will experience will be at the hands of the Jewish leaders (10:17–23).

Historically, the community represented by Matthew's gospel, with its claims to be the true heirs and interpreters of God's covenant with Israel, was living in an atmosphere of mounting conflict as Judaism reorganized itself in the decades following the destruction of the temple and the resultant end of the priesthood and the cultic system as the avenue of access to God and the means of maintaining covenantal identity. The detailed critique of emergent rabbinic Judaism in Matt. 23 expands, supplements, and intensifies the debates reported in Mark

11–12. Significantly, this chapter opens with a reference to "Moses' seat" (23:2) as the locus for communicating the divine purpose to God's true people—a role that is now being discharged by Jesus.

THE MODELS FOR THE OTHER GOSPELS

The Gospel of Luke builds on the theme in Q of Jesus' reaching out to the excluded and the Gentiles. In the second volume of his work, the Acts of the Apostles, Luke shows how this operates when the gospel reaches across ethnic, cultural, and geographical limits.[7] I have called Luke's model "The Community That Transcends and Transforms Ethnic and Cultural Boundaries."

By contrast, the Gospel of John, while preserving the theme of the inclusiveness of the new community, emphasizes the direct experience of new life that is opened for the members. Both the organic images of the community (shared meal, vine and branches, sheep and shepherd) and the content of Jesus' addresses to them point up the mutuality and renewal of life within the group. Many details have their parallels in the accounts of the mystery cults of the Greco-Roman period. The model for John's gospel is "The Community of Mystical Participation."

Discernment of these models does not require forcing the evidence into a preconceived mold, but enables the interpreter to recognize the basic pattern in terms of which the gospel tradition has been appropriated and transmitted. Useful analogies and differences may be discerned by this method among the New Testament writings and between them and other Jewish and pagan materials. For the Gospels, this approach helps to bring into focus the twin themes of the early Christian tradition: How is the community of the covenant to be defined? And how does Jesus function as God's agent to effect this renewal?

NOTES

1. The voluminous writings of Jacob Neusner have pointed up these issues, beginning with his earliest work, *From Politics to Piety: The Emergence of Pharisaic Judaism* (Englewood Cliffs, NJ: Prentice-Hall, 1973), and continuing with his major study, *The Pharisees: Rabbinic Perspectives* (Hoboken, NJ: KTAV, 1985), and the essays

in *Major Trends in Formative Judaism*, Brown University Judaic Studies (Atlanta: Scholars Press, 1983, 1984). A similar reconstruction of these developments is offered by Shaye J. D. Cohen in *From the Maccabees to the Mishnah* (Philadelphia: Westminster Press, 1987).

2. This term was coined by G. F. Moore in his classic study, *Judaism in the First Three Centuries* (Cambridge: Harvard University Press, 1927–30).

3. The epistemological and hermeneutical principles on which this analysis of the gospel material rests has been set forth in my theoretical study, *Knowing the Truth: A Sociological Approach to New Testament Interpretation* (Minneapolis: Fortress Press, 1989). There I built on the insights of T. S. Kuhn concerning the powerful effect of accepted paradigms on scientific theory in his *Structure of Scientific Revolutions* (Chicago: University of Chicago Press, 1970), and on the sociology of knowledge insights of Peter Berger and Thomas Luckmann in *The Social Construction of Reality* (Garden City, NY: Doubleday, 1967).

4. Analysis of all these models and of the New Testament writings grouped under each model will be undertaken in my forthcoming book, *Who Are the People of God? Models in Judaism and Early Christianity.* Here examples of only two models are expounded.

5. This term is taken from the title of my analysis of the Gospel of Mark, *Community of the New Age: Studies in Mark's Gospel*, reprinted with corrections by Mercer University Press, Macon, GA, 1983.

6. Here I have used a modified version of my reconstruction of Q as set out in my *Jesus in History* (New York: Harcourt Brace Jovanovich, 1977). An early theological analysis of Q is that of Richard A. Edwards, *A Theology of Q* (Philadelphia: Fortress Press, 1975).

7. This theme is developed in my *Good News to the Ends of the Earth: The Theology of Acts* (Philadelphia: Trinity Press International, 1990).

CHAPTER NINE

CHRISTOLOGY IN THE PREDICATES
OF THE JOHANNINE *EGŌ EIMI* SAYINGS

HARVEY K. MCARTHUR

A distinctive feature of the Gospel of John is the repeated occurrence of *egō eimi* ("I am") phrases. This phenomenon is more striking in Greek than in English, since in classical and Koine Greek the first-person singular is indicated by the form of the verb, and the *egō* is unnecessary unless some special emphasis is intended. Admittedly there are occurrences of *egō* in Greek literature where only the most doctrinaire interpreter could insist that some special emphasis is intended. But even when allowance has been made for these deviations from the rule, the frequency of the *egō eimi* combination in John as over against Greek literature in general and the other Gospels in particular constitutes a notable phenomenon.[1] The distinctiveness of the Johannine usage is clearly demonstrated by the statistics. Passages where the word order is reversed or words intervene between the *egō* and the *eimi* are not included in the following figures:[2]

Total N. T.	*4th Gospel*	*Apocalypse*	*John Epistle*	*Matthew*
47	24	4	0	5
Mark	*Luke*	*Acts*	*Rest of New Testament*	
3	4	7	0	

The truly significant occurrences of *egō eimi* phrases fall into two categories:[3] (a) Those without any expressed predicates: 6:20; 8:24, 28, 58; 13:19; 18:5, 6, 8; and (b) those with expressed predicates: 6:35, 41, 48, 51; 8:12; 10:7, 9, 11, 14; 11:25; 14:6; 15:1, 5.

There are three major theories concerning the occurrences of *egō eimi* without expressed predicates. (1) Some scholars hold that they reflect a colloquial Greek idiom in which *egō eimi* is the equivalent of "It is I" or "I am he" or the like. Clearly this is an appropriate interpretation in John 9:9, where the man formerly blind insists that he is indeed that person, saying *egō eimi*, "I am he." Some of the occurrences of this same phrase on the lips of the Johannine Jesus are obvious parallels to this usage, for example, 6:20 and 18:5, 6, 8. But those who take this position affirm that all occurrences of *egō eimi* without expressed predicates fall into this category and that in every case a predicate is implied by either the immediate or the general context.[4] (2) Many modern scholars are not satisfied with this solution and, while conceding that some passages without expressed predicates are correctly interpreted as involving implied predicates, insist that in at least some instances these passages follow a pattern derived from the Hebrew scriptures, their translation into Greek, and the continuing Jewish usage. According to this view, some of these passages—most frequently at least John 8:58 and 13:19—constitute a divine self-revelation on the part of Jesus. (There continues to be a dispute as to which passages in the Hebrew scriptures gave rise to this theophanic usage.)[5] (3) A third position is that some of these passages may intend to reflect a divine self-revelation on the part of Jesus, but that this usage is derived not specifically from Hebrew-Jewish models but rather from a more widespread Eastern and Hellenistic style.[6]

I am personally persuaded by the arguments advanced in support of the theory that some of the *egō eimi* passages without predicates do indeed reflect Hebrew-Jewish usage, and that in these passages the evangelist understands the statements to imply a self-revelation of deity on the part of Jesus. Certainly some of the passages may reflect the colloquial usage and equal "I am he" or the like, for example, 6:20 and 18:5, 6, 8. The situation is complicated by the possibility that the Johannine author, with his demonstrated love for double meanings, may sometimes be deliberately ambiguous.[7] Thus, in chapter 18, when the soldiers come asking for Jesus of Nazareth, he says to them "*egō eimi*." In the context the initial meaning must be simply "I am he." But when the evangelist reports that the soldiers then fell to the ground before him, it is legitimate to ask whether the phrase does not carry some more impressive force. For me the decisive considerations supporting the thesis that some of the absolute *egō eimi* passages are theophanic following a Hebrew-Jewish pattern are: the absence of clear examples of the absolute *egō eimi* in Hellenistic or Gnostic literature (although these literatures include *egō eimi* sayings with predicates); and the evidence of the Hebrew scriptures, the Septuagint, and later rabbinic literature that Yahweh was identified in this code language.[8]

A decision concerning the background of the absolute *egō eimi* in John does not automatically resolve the more complex issue of the provenance of the phrases with *egō eimi* plus predicate. This latter question involves the larger problem of the provenance of the Johannine discourses. This issue and others connected with the *egō eimi* plus predicate phrases will be considered in the subsequent sections as follows:

1. *Provenance: The background of the Johannine discourses and the* egō eimi *phrases with predicates.*

2. *Historicity: Are the* egō eimi *sayings with predicates actual sayings of Jesus?*

3. *The actual texts: What observations may be made about the seven (thirteen) texts taken as a group?*

4. *Contemporary appropriation: What is the continuing significance of these passages for the contemporary Christian community?*

PROVENANCE

In 1925 Rudolf Bultmann published an epochal article in which he argued that John's gospel is fully intelligible only when it is recognized that behind its thought-world and terminology stands the mythology of Gnosticism, more specifically the Mandaean form of Gnosticism.[9] He was building on the research and translations of earlier scholars, but his article was the boldest and most massive argument for the Mandaean hypothesis,[10] and critics referred to what developed as the "Mandaean fever." Bultmann cited twenty-eight points at which there is an apparent parallel between Johannine and Mandaean passages. In each of these twenty-eight cases, he cited first verses from John's gospel and then a series of statements from the Mandaean literature. In most cases these parallels were accompanied by still further parallels from the Odes of Solomon, the Acts of Thomas, or the Acts of John, and occasionally passages from other literature out of the early Christian period. The extant Mandaean literature is centuries later than John's gospel, but Bultmann insisted that the gospel had been dependent on an earlier form of that literature. He argued that the Johannine thought-world presupposed a mythological background but that the evangelist had moved out of and away from that mythology. In other words, the evangelist—or his community?—demythologized the myth and so must come after the myth. The eleventh of Bultmann's twenty-eight points dealt specifically with the *egō eimi* phrases with predicates, and there are Mandaean parallels such as "I am a shepherd," "I am a fisherman," "I am the ambassador of light," "I am the word of the first life," "I am the son of God whom the father has sent here." It should be added that while Bultmann stressed the Mandaean background of the Fourth Gospel he was quite aware that the evangelist utilized the terminology of that conceptual world for purposes in conflict with Mandaean thought.[11]

Almost anyone reading carefully through Bultmann's article will agree that there are numerous and striking parallels between John's gospel and the Mandaean and related literature that Bultmann quotes. (However, if one reads the Mandaean literature itself, the overall impression is that its thought-world is strange and bizarre to one nurtured on the language of the Fourth Gospel.) It is much more complicated to attempt an explanation of the observed similarities. The most obvious problem in Bultmann's theory is that of chronology. The extant documents of the Mandaeans are from the sixteenth century, and while they clearly originated at some earlier period, they cannot have reached roughly their present form until the seventh or eighth century. This is demonstrated by the various allusions to the emergence and dominance of Islam. At that time the movement was concentrated in the Mesopotamian valley, where it continues to the present day as a small sect south of Baghdad. Yet the existence of the group may be traced back to the third and fourth centuries C.E. by coins and tablets. Furthermore, linguistic and other evidence indicates that while the group spent most of its time in the Mesopotamian valley, its origin was west of there in Syria, Palestine, and Transjordan. And K. Rudolph, in his major study of the Mandaeans (1960–61), concluded that Mandaeanism had its origin in the pre-Christian Syrian gnosis of West Aramaic culture.[12]

Over more recent decades substantial attacks have been launched against the position represented by Bultmann. In 1939 Ernst Percy published *Untersuchungen über den Ursprung der Johanneischen Theologie*,[13] in which he argued that the Fourth Gospel was not dependent on Mandaean or Gnostic concepts, since the Johannine views on dualism, the Redeemer, and redemption are significantly different from those in Mandaeanism and Gnosticism. He argued further that Gnosticism developed out of early Christianity and that Mandaeanism was a late form of Gnosticism. Subsequent discoveries and research have made it more difficult to argue that Gnosticism developed out of Christianity. Furthermore, while there are clear differences between Johannine and Gnostic emphases, scholars are divided as to whether to stress the differences or the similarities. It is well known that a half-filled glass of water may be described either as half full or half empty.

C. H. Dodd's magisterial study *The Interpretation of the Fourth Gospel* (1953) discussed Mandaeanism, concluding that "alleged parallels drawn from this medieval body of literature have no value for the study of the Fourth Gospel unless they can be supported by earlier evidence."[14] Dodd specifically rejected Bultmann's argument that the developed mythology evident in Mandaean literature must have preceded the simpler allusions in the Fourth Gospel, though this did not entirely dispose of Bultmann's contention that some references in the Fourth Gospel are not fully intelligible unless one presupposes an unexpressed mythology similar to that in Mandaean literature. Dodd was not so explicit in the rejection of Gnosticism as a possible background for the gospel, but it is clear that he preferred to interpret the Fourth Gospel out of the Hebrew scriptures, the Septuagint, Plato, and the Hermetic literature rather than out of the Gnostic world of thought.

In 1961, C. Colpe published *Die Religiongeschichtliche Schule*, which was in effect an attack on the attempt to interpret John out of Mandaean or Gnostic categories. He argued that one cannot retroject back into the first century of the Common Era, or still earlier, the full-fledged systems known to us from the second century. Single motifs from the later systems *can* be found in the earlier period, but the presence of these isolated motifs does not justify the assumption that developed systems existed. More specifically, Colpe argued against the existence of the *Urmensch-Erlöser* myth in the earlier period, contending that it did not develop until the Manichaean movement.

Of particular interest was the second edition of Eduard Schweizer's *Egō Eimi* (1965).[15] In the 1939 original edition, he had accepted in general the position of Bultmann concerning Johannine dependence on Mandaeanism (though skeptical about the possibility of identifying a written *Vorlage* used by the evangelist). However, in the introduction to the 1965 edition, Schweizer stated that while he still believed in a pre-Christian origin for Mandaeanism in the vicinity of Palestine, he was no longer prepared to argue for direct dependence by the evangelist on that Mandaean tradition. In fact, somewhat earlier he had indicated that the discussion by C. H. Dodd had convinced him more stress should be laid on the Old Testament background of Johannine thought, that is, as over against a Mandaean or Gnostic background.[16]

Jan-A. Bühner's *Der Gesandte und Sein Weg im 4. Evangelium* (1977)[17] is the most recent and substantial attempt to demonstrate that the Johannine motif of the Messiah as one sent from God was based on the Old Testament and rabbinic concept of the *schaliach*. Bühner recognizes that throughout the eastern Mediterranean world there was a common pattern of the legal messenger and his responsibilities, but he contends that the precise form that this takes in the Fourth Gospel reflects the nuances of Judaism rather than those of Gnosticism. There is need for much further discussion of Bühner's contentions, but it is not clear that they will be universally persuasive. For example, he cites a number of *egō eimi* sayings with predicates from later Jewish and rabbinic materials.[18] But a comparison of the dozen or so passages with the Johannine materials underlines two points: the comparative paucity of these occurrences alongside their concentration in the Fourth Gospel, and the contrast in form between the Jewish passages listed and the Johannine. Those from Jewish literature simply follow the pattern already found in the Hebrew scriptures, for example, "I am Raphael," "I am Michael," "I am Metathron," "I am the angel of death." But it is immediately clear that these differ from the Johannine "I am the bread of life," "I am the light of the world," "I am the true vine," and so on, which are closer to the Mandaean parallels than to the Jewish (though this does not settle the issue of dependence).

Edwin Yamauchi in the 1983 revision of *Pre-Christian Gnosticism* adds a concluding chapter that updates and supports his original conclusion that the various Gnostic movements did not include the concept of a preexistent Heavenly Redeemer until after the encounter with the Christian community. His work contains a compendium of the various views and arguments on the question of Gnostic influence on the Fourth Gospel. [19]

In addition to these efforts to assuage the "Mandaean fever," mention needs to be made of the major recent commentaries by C. K. Barrett, R. E. Brown, and R. Schnackenburg. All reject or at least minimize the dependence of the gospel on Mandaean or Gnostic thought. [20]

Since the experts have not yet achieved unanimity in their views about the origins of Gnosticism or Mandaeanism, other New Testament scholars are compelled to make their own decisions on the basis of their feel for the course of the debate. My own tentative conclusions, which are somewhat against the stream of current criticism, are as follows:

First: In view of the widespread and diversified forms of Gnosticism that existed in the second century, it is highly probably that there were Gnostic groups in the first century. I accept Rudolph's conclusion that an early type of Mandaeanism was present in the first century.

Second: Assuming the existence of such first-century movements, it is plausible to assume that the evangelist and his community borrowed—directly or indirectly—from such movements, specifically in the *ego eimi* sayings with predicates. This may have been encouraged by the existence of the somewhat different Jewish "I am" sayings.

HISTORICITY

Are the *ego eimi* sayings with predicates the actual sayings of Jesus, or are they more naturally understood as sayings produced by some segment of the later Christian community? The informed reader of the previous section will have recognized that my acceptance of an early Gnostic background for the Johannine discourses leads almost inevitably to a negative verdict with respect to the historicity of these sayings. But the fundamental objections to the historicity of these sayings are not dependent on theories about Gnostic motifs in the Johannine material.

The real difficulty in regarding the *ego eimi* sayings as the actual sayings of Jesus is created by the contrast between the teachings of Jesus as described in the Synoptics and the presentation in the Fourth Gospel.

The difference is one both of content and of style. Certainly it has been argued that Jesus may have had more than one teaching style and content, and these may have varied depending on the audience. Thus it has been suggested that the Synoptics reflect his public teaching, while the Fourth Gospel reflects his more intimate conversations with his disciples.[21] But there are difficulties in this hypothesis. For one thing, John 18:20 reports Jesus as saying to the high priest that the latter should have no difficulty in determining his teaching, since he had taught nothing privately that he had not also said openly. At the very least this must express the understanding of the evangelist, who assumes the identity of Jesus' public and private teaching. More decisive for the present purpose is the fact that the elements in the Johannine account of Jesus' teaching that contrast with Synoptic portrayal appear in his public addresses as well as in his private conversations with his disciples.

As far as content is concerned, the central contrast is in the open and high Christology of the Fourth Gospel. The authority with which the Jesus of the Synoptics spoke and acted did give rise to such questions as "Who then is this, that even wind and sea obey him?" (Mark 4:41 and parallels) and "Why does this man speak thus? It is blasphemy! Who can forgive sins but God alone?" (Mark 2:7). But the disciples are reported not to have recognized his Christological role until Caesarea Philippi, and even then there is no suggestion of his preexistence or his oneness with God. Certainly the Synoptic Jesus did not use such language about himself. In John's gospel the high Christology is explicit from the very beginning in the language of the evangelist (the prologue) and in the statements by his earliest followers. In chapter 4 he explicitly identifies himself to the Samaritan woman as the Messiah, and makes high Christological claims both in public pronouncements and in statements to his disciples. The *egō eimi* sayings with predicates are simply a continuation of this open proclamation of his own person. Those in chapters 6, 8, 10, and 11 are addressed to a general public, while those in chapters 14 and 15 are addressed to the inner circle. The contrast is not absolute, since the Synoptics contain the so-called "bolt from the Johannine blue" in Matthew 11:25–27 (Luke 10:21–22), and there are *egō* sayings attributed to Jesus in these Gospels.[22] But the contrast is unmistakable, and it is underlined by the nature of the controversies reported respectively in the Synoptics and in John. In the latter the controversies center around the claims made by Jesus for himself, as would certainly have happened had he made such claims.

If the content of the *egō eimi* passages indicates an openly declared high Christology in John that contrasts with the teaching recorded in the Synoptics, it is equally true that the style of the proclamation is a contrast. While there are a limited number of *egō eimi* passages in the Synoptics without predicates, there are no occurrences of *egō eimi* with predicates like those in John. The contrast remains clear whether one regards the *egō eimi* sayings with predicates as developments out of early Gnosticism or a reflection of Jewish or rabbinic terminology. In either case, few would regard these Johannine sayings as historical.

If these sayings originated in the language of the Johannine community and not on the lips of Jesus, how are we to understand the thought process by which this modification of the tradition took place? A partial answer begins with the recognition that the evangelist was not a Ph.D. candidate working in a seminar on historiography. This is not to belittle his achievement; it may be an almost unmixed blessing that he was not a modern researcher of that type. He was a believer who had heard and appropriated the Christian message. As he appropriated it, his conceptual world was transformed by the new faith, but the new faith also underwent change as it worked like leaven in this conceptual world. To some extent the new faith had to be expressed in the categories the evangelist was already using. This type of change is easily demonstrated from Christian history. Presumably the earliest Palestinian Christians found the title Messiah or Christ entirely adequate to express their concept of Jesus. But when the message moved into the outside Gentile world, the affirmation that Jesus was the Christ would have been intelligible to listeners only after a preliminary lecture on Jewish messianic expectations. Even then the title might not have been religiously satisfying to them. Thus the title Messiah soon lost its special significance and was replaced by terms that were religiously more satisfying, for example, Lord, Son of God, and Savior. William Barclay, with his gift for putting positively what might appear to some to be negative, observes concerning the Johannine discourses:

We can be fairly certain that Jesus did not make these claims for himself, at least not in the way in which the discourses make them. What we have here is not the precise words which Jesus spoke, but that which the Christian church discovered and knew {about} him, under the guidance of the Spirit, to be.[23]

Volume 2 of the firmly conservative *International Standard Bible Encyclopedia* (1982) contains two articles on John's gospel: "The Gospel According to John" by Leon Morris and "Johannine Theology" by I. H. Marshall. Morris concedes that the evangelist has translated what Jesus said so that "the final choice of words is his and not that of the Master . . . [and] we must allow for John's preference for various idioms and expressions." However, he insists that all is a faithful reproduction of Jesus' intention.[24] Marshall makes a similar statement but speaks of John's language as a "legitimate development" from the teaching of Jesus.[25]

Only the most resolutely conservative scholars would insist that Johannine *egō eimi* sayings are the literal words of Jesus. Most others would agree broadly with the quotation from Barclay, but some might seek a further clarification of the language. Does it assume that the Johannine language identified Jesus as he was objectively and permanently, or does it express instead what he was for a given group in a given cultural situation.[26]

THE ACTUAL SEVEN (THIRTEEN) TEXTS

It is not feasible to discuss each of the seven (thirteen) predicates that appear in the *egō eimi* passages, but a few observations may be made about the group as a whole. Perhaps the most important observation is that each of the predicates is a way of identifying Jesus as the bearer of "life." This is immediately clear in four of the seven statements:

I am the bread of life. (6:35, 48)

I am the light of the world; he who follows me will not walk in darkness, but will have the light of life. (8:12)

I am the resurrection and the life. (11:25)[27]

I am the way, and the truth, and the life. (14:6)

Furthermore, in the remaining three passages the motif of life is present explicitly or implicitly in the immediate context. Thus 10:7 ("I am the door of the sheep") is followed in 10:10 by the statement "I came that they may have life, and have it abundantly." In the good shepherd passage (10:11, 14) it is affirmed that the good shepherd lays down his life for his sheep, and though it is not explicitly stated, the point is that he lays down his life so they may have life. Finally, in the "I am the true vine" passage (15:1–10) the thrust of the argument is that believers have fruit-bearing life only insofar as they remain in vital connection with the "true vine." So it is no exaggeration to affirm that all occurrences of *egō eimi* with predicates are affirmations that Jesus is the life-bearer and life-giver.[28]

The identification of Jesus as the life-giver is scarcely surprising, since the focus of the proclamation in the Fourth Gospel is on (eternal) life. The term *life* (*zoē*) occurs thirty-six times in this gospel, and in seventeen of these occurrences it is further defined as "eternal life." A comparison of the passages with and without the adjective "eternal" makes it clear that the two forms are used interchangeably; that is, the same concept is intended even if "eternal" is not included. "Eternal life" is not a standard Greek term; it appears to have emerged in Jewish Greek with the literal meaning of "life of the age," that is, "life of the age to come." In the Synoptics, with or without "eternal," it appears to refer to existence beyond death, though in John's gospel it is an experience entered into at the moment of positive response to Jesus (cf. 3:36; 5:24, et al.). It is correct to say that "eternal life" is what the gospel is all about, and for the evangelist Jesus is the bearer of that eternal life.

A second observation about the *egō eimi* passages with predicates is best expressed in the form of a question: Is it accidental or deliberate that there are precisely seven different images used in these passages?[29] Unfortunately this tantalizing question does not have a clear-cut answer. For much of the eastern Mediterranean world seven was a mysterious and significant number. Furthermore, the Apocalypse of John, which belongs somehow to the Johannine literature even though not written by the evangelist, used patterns of seven so extensively that some believe it is the key to the overall structure of that book. But one cannot interpret the Gospel of John in the light of the Apocalypse, and the term *seven* never actually occurs in the gospel. However, many have speculated that the gospel deliberately cited seven miracles in the ministry of Jesus, specifically identifying the turning of water into wine as the "first of his signs" and the healing of the nobleman's son as the "second sign" (2:11 and 4:54). It is somewhat curious that the count is not continued beyond this point, and the reader is left to wonder whether the evangelist had precisely seven miracles in mind. Some have noted that the gospel has no "I am the water of life," which might have been anticipated along with "I am the bread of life," "I am the light of the world," and so on. Such an *egō eimi* saying would have been particularly appropriate in 4:1–42 (the Samaritan woman) or 7:37–39 (Jesus' words on the last day of the feast). It could be argued that the tradition already contained seven such sayings and that there was no room for an "I am the water of life" sayings. Such speculation is only that and cannot provide a basis for insisting that the evangelist deliberately reported seven and only seven *egō eimi* plus predicate saying. If one believes that the evangelist was concerned with a sevenfold pattern in this connection, one must probably argue that the gospel was an "in-house" document, that is, a document to which the original readers brought information no longer available to others. This is a genuine possibility, but it cannot be demonstrated on the basis of present evidence.

Another observation concerns the relation of these passages to the cluster of terms referring to "truth" or "true" (*alētheia*, *alēthēs*, *alēthinos*). The statistics indicate the prominence of these terms in comparison with the rest of the New Testament.

	Total N.T.	Fourth Gospel	Three Epistles	The Apocalypse	Rest of N.T.
alētheia	109	25	20	0	64
alēthēs	26	14	3	0	9
alēthinos	28	9	4	10	5
Totals	163	48	27	10	78

Three of the seven passages use one or the other of these terms, either in the passage itself or in the immediate context:

6:32–35   *Truly, truly, I say to you, it was not Moses who gave you
           the bread from heaven; my Father gives you the true* (ton
           alētheinon) *bread from heaven. For the bread of God is
           that which comes down from heaven, and gives life to the
           world. . . . I am the bread of life; he who comes to me
           shall not hunger, and he who believes in me shall never
           thirst.*

14:6   *I am the way, and the truth* (hē alētheia), *and the life; no
           one comes to the Father, but by me.*

15:1   *I am the true* (hē alēthinē) *vine, and my Father is the vine-
           dresser.*

There has been extensive discussion about the precise nuance
intended by the evangelist in the uses of these terms.[30] For the present
purpose there is one central question: Is Jesus identified as the true life-
bearer over against false earthly claimants, or, alternatively, is this
language the expression of a heavenly versus earthly dualism—either
the dualism of a popular Platonism or that of early Gnosticism? Thus in
10:7, 9 ("I am the door") there appears to be a contrast between Jesus
and other historical persons who might claim the same role (cf. 10:8:
"All who came before me are thieves and robbers"). Scholars differ about
the identity of these thieves and robbers, but presumably they were
historical leaders. The same thrust is apparent in 10:11, 14 ("I am the
good shepherd"), where other would-be shepherds are called "hire-
lings." In the bread discourse of chapter 6, however, there is an explicit
contrast between heavenly bread and earthly bread. Yet the apparent
put-down of Moses (6:32) suggests that Jesus is here contrasted with
Moses and the Exodus manna. In John 15:1, 5 ("I am the true [*alēthinē*]
vine") there is no explicit reference to the earthly-heavenly contrast, but
it is likely that Jesus is the heavenly vine over against mere earthly ones.
In fact, the widespread use of "vine" for Israel may well mean that the
evangelist had in mind also the contrast between Judaism and Christianity.[31] Thus in some passages the heavenly-earthly contrast may be
intended; in others the contrast is between Jesus and rival historical
figures; and in some cases both contrasts may be involved.

CONTEMPORARY APPROPRIATION

Before dealing directly with the possibilities of contemporary appropriation, there are—at least in the minds of some—two obstacles that must be removed. These issues were touched on in the above section on historicity, but they require more direct confrontation. The first obstacle is essentially theological and is hinted at by the phrase "contemporary appropriation." The phrase itself suggests that there is, or may be, some difference in the way the first-century Christian community "appropriated" the Johannine language and the way that same language should be appropriated today. This suggestion is understandably resisted by any who hold that theological language not only points toward a truth or reality but actually articulates that truth or reality is an absolute and permanent form. This issue affects not just Johannine language but all theological language, whether that of the Bible itself or of subsequent generations. I would argue that theological language is essentially "pointing language"; that is, it points toward a perceived truth or reality. The language of the pointer is substantially conditioned by the particular time and place in which the pointing occurs. Thus the cultural context in which the pointer lives will affect the language of the pointing. I contend that it is impossible for a modern Western person to think and feel in the categories of the first century, whether those of the Palestine world or the larger Hellenistic world. Individuals may claim to repeat the first-century words and to believe them in precisely the same sense as did the evangelist behind the Fourth Gospel. In actual fact the words may be the same, but the tune is not! No matter how faithfully first-century Greek sentences are translated into English, they do not convey the same undertones and overtones for the modern reader that they did for the reader of the first century. (And this is true whether one regards the first-century world-view as superior or inferior to that of the present.) This issue could be discussed at greater length, but it is adequate here simply to underline the presuppositions behind this section, namely, that the conceptual world of the Johannine community was radically different from ours and that it is therefore necessary to find other language to convey the truth and reality to which it sought to point. The difference between the language of the Synoptics and John is itself evidence of the appropriateness of a language change when a given truth is transferred from one cultural context to another. In the same fashion, we are called upon to seek, or at least to consider, new language in view of our cultural differences with the world of the Johannine community.

A second obstacle is of a different kind and will be an obstacle to a quite different group of people. It is the argument that the "I am" sayings are not necessarily the actual words of Jesus. It was suggested earlier that the evangelist attributed to Jesus words that he, and presumably his community, found most adequate to express the significance Jesus had for them and their religious experience. They could have written a theological treatise, as was done in the case of 1 John, and then the reader conditioned by nineteenth-century historiography would not have been disturbed by this process. To use an old illustration, those early Christians were working out for themselves the meaning of the words that the earlier tradition had brought them in the same way that the Platonic dialogues worked out the meaning of Socrates' teaching as seen from the perspective of subsequent years. Some of the words of Jesus, or words assumed to be his, undoubtedly initiated this process, and they carried it further in the ongoing life of the community. In the Fourth Gospel there is a trivial illustration of how this development of the words of Jesus may have begun. All readers of the Synoptics will have noted the frequent occurrence of Jesus *logia* beginning with the formula, "Truly, I say to you." This introductory formula occurs some fifty times in the Synoptics. And the same formula occurs some twenty-five times in John's formulation of the words of Jesus. But in the Johannine formula the "truly" is always doubled, for example, in John 1:51: "Truly, truly, I say to you, you will see heaven opened, and the angels of God ascending and descending upon the Son of man." Surely only the most resolute literalist would insist that Jesus sometimes used one "truly" and sometimes two, and that the Synoptists selected only the one group of sayings while John selected only those with two occurrences of "truly"![32] While in this instance the evangelist made only a minor stylistic variation from the earlier tradition, it demonstrates that he did not feel obliged to retain precisely the words received in the tradition, but was prepared to amplify them so as to bring out more clearly their intent *as he understood it*. The rewriting in the Johannine discourses may have gone far beyond this innocuous stylistic change, but in principle the procedure was simply an extension of the same process. The significant question for the modern reader should not be, Are these the literal words of Jesus? but rather, How can we express in today's terminology the meaning that the Johannine community found in Jesus and conveyed through the words they attributed to him?

It was pointed out that all the *egō eimi* sayings with predicates were ways of identifying Jesus as the bearer and giver of life. But the life referred to was not ordinary physical life, nor was it primarily life after death (though the evangelist undoubtedly anticipated some form of existence after death). Rather, the evangelist was speaking of a particular kind or quality of life, more specifically a life in which this earthly existence is linked with the eternal source of all life. In fact, this is the central thrust of the gospel as a whole, as expressed in the concluding statement of chapter 20 ("and that believing you may have life in his name"). No doubt there are many ways this central affirmation might be reexpressed in different terminology, but one of the simplest reformulations would be to affirm that Jesus in his ministry emerged as the bearer of and witness to the meaning of human existence.

It will be remembered that Paul Tillich in *The Courage to Be* (1952) classified human anxiety in three forms and suggested that one of these predominated in various ages of history. Thus the Hellenistic world displayed anxiety in the face of fate and death; at the end of the Middle Ages the dominant anxiety was that created by a sense of guilt and condemnation, while in the modern world emptiness and meaninglessness predominate as the source of anxiety. Whatever quarrels some may have with Tillich's schematization, it does seem true that in the Western world the dominant anxiety is that induced by emptiness and meaninglessness. The average modern-day person is not obsessed by the question of what happens after death and does not seem to experience Luther's "pangs of an awakened conscience." But modern-day people are haunted by emptiness and meaninglessness, and much of their lives are frenetic efforts to fill the void. This malaise cannot be made to disappear simply by stating that the drama of Jesus' career witnesses to the meaning of human existence! But this kind of language may serve as a bridge to the questions that stir people deeply and the answers proclaimed in the Christian tradition.

Certainly I am not suggesting that the classic "I am" sayings in John should be replaced for liturgical or devotional purposes by such phrases as "I am the meaning of human existence"! This would be to replace powerful symbolic language with a prosaic phrase. But some such understanding of the symbols may help to refill them with the vitality and significance they once carried.

NOTES

A version of this essay first appeared as "Christological Perspectives in the Predicates of the Johannine *Egō Eimi* Sayings" in *Christological Perspectives*, ed. Robert F. Berkey and Sarah A. Edwards (New York: The Pilgrim Press, 1982), 79–94. Used by permission.

1. See Virgil P. Howard, *Das Ego Jesu in den Synoptischen Evangelien* (Marburg: Alwert Verlag, 1975). Pages 10–27 discuss the occurrences of "I" in Greek, Hebrew, Aramaic, and the Septuagint; pages 28–75 discuss the use of "I" in the history of religions, with special reference to the *egō eimi* phrase.

2. I have included only passages in which *egō eimi* occurs in that order and without any intervening words. Other lists differ slightly: e.g., Rudolf Schnackenburg, *Das Johannesevangelium*, 3 vols. (Freiburg: Herder, 1965ff.), 2:59 (vol. 1 in English [New York: Herder & Herder, 1968]), and Moulton and Geden, *A Concordance to the Greek Testament*, 2d ed. (Edinburgh: T. & T. Clark, 1899), ad loc.

3. Three of the passages in John's gospel are not regarded as "significant": 4:26; 8:18; 9:9.

4. On these passages, see Dean Alford, *The Greek Testament*, 4 vols., new ed. (Boston: Lee & Shepard, 1877); and Marcus Dods, *The Expositor's Greek Testament* (New York: Dodd, 1905), vol. 1. This appears to be the view also of Chrysostom (see *Homilies on St. John*, Nicene and Post-Nicene Fathers, First Series, vol. 14 [New York: Christian Literature Co., 1890]), although his comment on 8:58 may be an exception ("As the Father uses the expression 'I am,' so also does Christ").

5. This position has been developed especially by D. Daube ("The 'I Am' of the Messianic Presence," in his *The New Testament and Rabbinic Judaism* [London: Athlone, 1956], 325–29), E. Stauffer (*Jesus and His Story* [New York: Knopf, 1960]), H. Zimmermann ("Das Absolute *Egō Eimi* als die neutestamentliche Offenbarungs-

formel," *Biblische Zeitschrift* 4 [1960]: 54–69, 266–76), and Philip B. Harner (*The "I Am" of the Fourth Gospel* [Philadelphia: Fortress Press, 1970]). It appears in the commentaries of W. Bauer (*Das Johannesevangelium*, 2d ed. [Tübingen: J. C. B. Mohr, 1977]), R. H. Strachen (*The Fourth Gospel*, 3d ed. [London: SCM Press, 1941]), C. K. Barrett (*The Gospel According to St. John* [London: SPCK, 1955]), R. H. Lightfoot (*St. John's Gospel* [Oxford: Clarendon Press, 1956]), Raymond E. Brown (*The Gospel According to John*, Anchor Bible 29, 29A [New York: Doubleday, 1966, 1970]), and John Marsh (*Saint John*, Pelican New Testament Commentaries [Harmondsworth: Penguin, 1968]). They do not all agree on precisely which occurrences of the absolute phrase carry this special force. This position had been taken earlier: e.g., H. J. Holtzmann on John 8:24 (see his *Evangelium, Briefe und Offenbarung des Johannes*, 2d ed. [Freiburg: J. C. B. Mohr, 1893]).

6. I believe this is the position of Rudolf Bultmann, *The Gospel of John* (Philadelphia: Westminster Press, 1971). On 8:58 he explicitly rejects the suggestion that the *egō eimi* equals "I am God" or that it reflects Old Testament usage. But on 6:20 he says the phrase is "the traditional formula of greeting by the deity." On 13:19 he says that "the Revealer" is to be supplied as predicate. In the extended note on 6:35 he states that a sacred formula is not intended in 4:26; 1:18, 23; 18:5, 6, 8.

7. Oscar Cullmann, "Der johanneische Gebrauch doppeldeutiger Ausdrücke als Schlüssel zum Verständnis des vierten Evengeliums," *Theologische Zeitschrift* 4 (1948): 360–72.

8. See n. 5.

9. See Rudolf Bultmann, "Die Bedeutung der neuerschlossenen mandäischen und manichäischen Quellen für das Verständnis des Johannesevangeliums," *Zeitschrift für die neutestamentliche Wissenschaft* 24 (1925): 100–146. See also Rudolf Bultmann, "Der religiongeschichtliche Hintergrund des Prologs zum Johannesevangelium," *Eucharisterion*, Studien zur Religion und Literatur des Alten und Neuen Testaments, n.s. 19 (Göttingen: Vandenhoeck & Ruprecht, 1923), pt. 2, 1–26; and Bultmann, *The Gospel of John*.

10. See the translations of M. Lidzbarski (*Ginza: Der Schatz oder das grosse Buch der Mandäer* [Göttingen: Vandenhoeck & Ruprecht, 1925]; *Das Johannesbuch der Mandäer* [Giessen: Töpelmann, 1915]; *Mandäische Liturgien*, Abhandlungen der Königliche Gesellschaft der Wissenschaften zu Göttingen, new series 17/1 [1920]), and Ethel S. Drower, ed. (*The Canonical Prayerbook of the Mandaeans* [Atlantic Highlands, NJ: Humanities Press, 1959]).

11. While Bultmann has been the leader in defense of the Mandaean theory, he has been supported by other scholars, e.g., W. Bauer. H. Becker, who was a student of Bultmann's, goes so far as to reconstruct a hypothetical Gnostic *Vorlage* that was utilized by the evangelist (see H. Becker, *Die Reden des Johannesevangeliums und der Still*

der gnostischen Offenbarungsrede [Göttingen: Vandenhoeck & Ruprecht, 1956; actually completed in 1941], 129–36). Hans Conzelmann appears to provide some agreement with Bultmann (see Hans Conzelmann, *An Outline of the Theology of the New Testament* [New York: Harper & Row, 1969], 330f.), but his statement is too brief and cautious for a clear judgment.

12. K. Rudolph's presentation (*Die Manaeer*, Forschungen zur Religion und Literatur des Alten und Neuen Testaments, 92, 93 [Göttingen: Vandenhoeck & Ruprecht, 1960, 1961]) is still the nearest approach to a definitive study of the Mandaeans available. The critics of Bultmann insist that there is need for a major critical study of Mandaean literature indicating the various chronological layers. This would be of enormous value, but it may be an impossible task until new sources are discovered.

13. Ernst Percy, *Untersuchungen über den Ursprung der Johanneische Theologie* (Lund: Gleerup, 1939). See the comments of Jan-A. Bühner, *Der Gesandte und sein Weg im 4. Evangelium* (Tübingen: J. C. B. Mohr, 1977), 29–30.

14. C. H. Dodd, *The Interpretation of the Fourth Gospel* (Cambridge: Cambridge University Press, 1953), 115–30. See the comments of Bühner, *4. Evangelium*, 49–51, and Bühner's criticism of Dodd's *Tendenz*.

15. Eduard Schweizer, *Egō Eimi*, 2d ed. (Göttingen: Vandenhoeck & Ruprecht, 1965). Schweizer's position is of special interest, since he had been a student of Bultmann's and the first edition of *Egō Eimi* was in many respects a continuation of Bultmann's analysis.

16. Eduard Schweizer, *Church Order in the New Testament* (Naperville: Allenson, 1961), esp. 118 and nn. 445, 447.

17. See the summary of Bühner's study, *4. Evangelium*, 422–33. It is hoped that the near future will see major discussion of the views Bühner has supported.

18. Ibid., 156–57.

19. Edwin Yamauchi, *Pre-Christian Gnosticism*, rev. ed. (1973; Grand Rapids, MI: Baker, 1983), chap. 12, "Pre-Christian Gnosticism Reconsidered a Decade Later," 187–249.

20. In fact, the current tendency is away from stress on Gnostic sources for the Johannine tradition.

21. L. Morris, *The Gospel According to John*, New International Commentary on the New Testament (Grand Rapids: Eerdmans, 1971), 47, appears to support this view.

22. Howard, *Das Ego Jesu*, 1–9, presents the evidence.

23. See William Barclay, *The Gospels and Acts* (London: SCM Press, 1976), 118. For other discussions of the "historicity" issue, see E. C. Hoskyns, *The Fourth Gospel*, rev. ed. (London: Faber & Faber, 1947), 58–85 ("The Historical Tension of the Fourth Gospel"); Dodd, *Fourth Gospel*, 444–52 ("Appendix: Some Considerations upon the

Historical Aspect of the Fourth Gospel"); Strachen, *The Fourth Gospel*; Morris, *John*, 40–49 ("History and Theology"); Schnackenburg, *Das Johannesevangelium*, 2:67–70; Brown, *John*, 1:xli-li; and V. Taylor, *The Names of Jesus* (New York: St. Martin's Press, 1953), 132f.

24. Leon Morris in *International Standard Bible Encyclopedia* 2 (Grand Rapids: Eerdmans, 1982), 1098, col. 2.

25. I. H. Marshall in ibid., 1081, col. 2.

26. This is a major theological watershed, and consciously or unconsciously, those who deal seriously with the Christian tradition must make their own decisions before they can proceed.

27. On the variant reading at John 11:25, see B. M. Metzger, *A Textual Commentary on the Greek New Testament* (London: United Bible Societies, 1971), 234.

28. See S. S. Smalley, *John: Evangelist and Interpreter* (Exeter: Paternoster Press, 1978); and Schnackenburg, *Das Johannesevangelium*, 2:60–61.

29. See Schnackenburg, *Das Johannesevangelium*, 2:60.

30. See Brown, *John*, 1:499–501 and the bibliography noted there. See also Dodd, *Fourth Gospel*, 170–78.

31. See Brown, *John*, 2:674–79; and Barrett, *St. John*, 392ff. An extended discussion of the "Vine" as Israel appears in the Midrash Rabbah on Lev. 26:42 (section 36/2, which is on pp. 457–59 of the Socino translation). Similar but more abbreviated comments are frequent in rabbinic thought.

32. Although Morris, *John*, 170, says, "No satisfying explanation of this has been put forward," speaking of the double "truly" in the Fourth Gospel. This may mean that he does not accept what most would regard as the obvious explanation.

CHAPTER TEN

LOGOS AFFILIATIONS IN
JOHANNINE THOUGHT

PAUL S. MINEAR

Contemporary students of the Gospel of John agree that it is impossible to understand its Christology without dealing with the idea of the logos.[1] I am equally convinced that it is impossible to understand any major accent in John's thinking without dealing with the same concept. The logos thought pattern pervades the later chapters as clearly as it dominates the prologue.[2] And in these later chapters it is a major star in the constellation of ideas—the ideas of God, the world, the church, salvation. I will explore the affiliations of the logos idea with these other ideas in the belief that such an analysis will add to our understanding of logos Christology.

We should first recognize the intricate subtlety and baffling complexity of John's symbolic language. It is no simple matter to adapt one's own linguistic habits to his elusive vocabulary or to restructure one's mental processes into some degree of conformity to his. Virtually every word in his lexicon carries a range of foreign reverberations; our ears must therefore be very sensitive.[3] John's unit of thought was not separate words but entire sentences, indeed often entire clusters of symbols. Each verbal image evoked many antonyms and synonyms.[4] The affiliation of one idiom with its neighbors provides better clues to the structure of thought than do fixed definitions of the separate words.[5] This means that we must explore each cluster of concepts as a whole, taking soundings of the deeper levels rather than samplings of the surface. When we are confused by the movement of John's thought, we must remember that he remains the best judge of what he was trying to say. We must be able to move out of the habitat of our own familiar ideas and into the habitat of his unfamiliar thinking.[6] Thus we will take six soundings from passages in which the logos concept is affiliated with other concepts in illuminating patterns.

FIRST SOUNDING: JOHN 5:19–38

When we examine this text in the fifth chapter with a view to tracing the affiliations of logos, we may first notice several virtually synonymous expressions. Although the noun *logos* appears only twice, the verb *legō* appears five times, three of which are introduced by Jesus' prophetic exclamations, *amēn, amēn*. Three times the term *voice* is used, and each time with emphasis on the power of this *phonē* to give life to the dead. Four times this voice announces a final judgment (*krisis, krinō*). On nine other occasions speech takes the form of witnessing (*martyria, martyreō*) both on the part of God and of Jesus. In some instances the image of speaking merges into that of doing redemptive works; the word becomes a deed, and the deed a word. Throughout the passage, verbs are as strategic as nouns, actions as significant as speech. Although the thought focuses upon this combination of speaking-acting by God and Jesus,[7] the horizons that come into view are the widest that can be conceived.

Now we should examine the two explicit uses of logos, two verses that, although separate, provide a carefully constructed antithesis.

> *Very truly I tell you, anyone who hears my logos and believes him who sent me has eternal life, and does not come under judgment but has passed from death to life. (v. 24)*

> *The Father who sent me has himself testified on my behalf. You have never heard his voice {phonē} or seen his form. And you do not have his logos abiding in you, because you do not believe him whom he has sent. (vv. 37–38)*

From the construction of these statements, and from their intended contrasts, we can draw several inferences:

- *There is a one-to-one correlation between hearing the logos, believing in God who sent Jesus, and having the abiding presence of the logos.*[8]

- *Speaking/hearing Jesus' logos (v. 24) is equivalent to speaking/hearing God's logos (v. 38).*
- *The difference between hearing/believing and not hearing/not believing is the difference between being freed from God's condemnation and being bound over to final judgment.*
- *There is a one-to-one correlation between condemnation and death, between freedom and life.*
- *The transition from death to life takes places simultaneously with hearing the logos, along with its coordinate actions of believing, witnessing, etc.*
- *This transition creates a strong bonding between God as sender, Christ as the one sent, and the hearers as believers.*
- *The same transition creates a communal habitat for the logos; the community that hears becomes the antithesis of the community that does not hear.*

This body of inferences shows that in tracing the correlations of the logos we have entered a distinctive universe within which thinking takes place. The logos has served to establish an ultimate *inclusio*. In being spoken by Jesus, God's logos is as primal as God's first word on the day of creation; linkage to that day is never far from John's thinking, as 1:1–4 demonstrates with its clear echo of Gen. 1:1–3. Similarly, God's logos is as final as the day of judgment, with its implicit reference to the curse of death and separation from the tree of life in Gen. 3.[9] Whenever the logos is spoken by Jesus, it forces hearers to situate themselves between those ultimate boundaries, which can no longer be viewed as distant possibilities but must be respected as immediate actualities. The choice between life and death remains the same as the choice made by Eve and Adam; the consequences of that choice are measured by the image of the final judgment. This explains why the thought of God's voice is fused with the thought of God's works "from the foundation of the world." All this gives to the simple word *logos* many dimensions: protological and eschatological, theological and Christological, ecclesiological and soteriological.

SECOND SOUNDING: JOHN 6:48–71

Chapter 6 represents one of the major pivots in the narrative, a pivot in which the conflict between Jesus and the leaders of Israel reaches a climax and in which many disciples, on learning what discipleship demands, are so offended by the difficulties that they turn away.[10] The debate with the leaders centers in understanding how Jesus could be "the bread of life.

> *I am the bread of life. Your ancestors ate the manna in the wilderness, and they died. This is the bread that comes down from heaven, so that one may eat of it and not die. I am the living bread that came down from heaven. Whoever eats of this bread will live forever; and the bread that I will give for the life of the world is my flesh.*
> *(6:48–51)*

That declaration appears to result in complete incomprehension among the adversaries: "How can this man give us his flesh to eat?" (v. 52). The disciples understood a bit more; they understood enough to be so offended, shocked, in fact, as to reject their leader.

It is easy to miss the reason for their rejection. "This logos is difficult; who can accept (*akoueiv*) it" (v. 60). It may help us to grasp the force of this response if we interpret both this logos and the word for accepting it in consonance with the thrust of 5:24 that we analyzed in the first sounding. What did this logos refer to that made it so difficult, so impossible, for these disciples to accept (the verb *akouein* in this context means hear, obey, believe, abide in)? Only two things can fully explain their apostasy. First, the identification of the "bread of life" with Jesus' "flesh and blood" made it clear, at least to John's readers, that this bread was nothing less than Jesus' death for the life of the world. Second, the acceptance of this logos was a commitment to join him in that voluntary dying. The conjunction of those two things (the messianic Passion to be shared by the disciples) made this logos offensive; yet that same double truth made Jesus' words the channel of "spirit and life" (v. 63). The word was simultaneously death-demanding and life-giving. So difficult was this logos that, as Jesus rightly said, "No one can come to me unless it is granted by my Father" (v. 65). Judas' betrayal was a good index of this difficulty, one that the devil was quick to exploit (v. 71).

Here, then, is another mysterious cluster of interlocking images. John's thought passes smoothly from the single word *logos* to the plural *hrēmata*, and as smoothly from hearing to seeing, from bread to flesh and blood, from drinking blood to abiding in Christ.[11] The cluster of symbols points to an enduring complex system of associations that constitutes the habitat of John's thought. Each metaphor retains its own distinctive affiliations, yet the meaning of each figure is directly contingent on those affiliations. The total stream of consciousness is much greater than the sum of its parts. This is surely due in part to the fact that the entire stream is dominated by Christian memories of the Passion story. As a consequence, when a congregation, in celebrating the eucharist, reads this text, each of these metaphors calls into play a rich symbolic resonance. And whenever the congregation joins in the Lord's Prayer, the petition for daily (the translation "daily" has very weak justification) bread may be enriched by the Johannine version: "Lord, give us this bread always" (v. 34). The bread is the logos of life that is spoken through voluntary dying.

THIRD SOUNDING: JOHN 8:31–47

In the eighth chapter the debate between Jesus and the Jews continues with even greater intensity. It is in the midst of this debate that Jesus declares, "I am the light of the world" (8:12), a manifesto that reminded readers of the first command in creation, "Let there be light." Now, as then, the creation of the light dispersed the darkness. In this case the light impelled a division of the Jews into two communities, believers and unbelievers. Only one of these two could be the true family of Abraham, the community in which the logos dwelt:[12] "Then Jesus said to the Jews who had believed in him, 'If you abide in my logos, you are truly my disciples, and you will know the truth, and the truth will make you free' " (vv. 31–32).

These are Abraham's descendants. And what of their adversaries? "Why do you not understand what I say? It is because you cannot accept [*akouein*] my logos. You are from your father the devil, and you choose to do your father's desires. He was a murderer from the beginning" (vv. 43–44).

In both of these citations "you" is plural; Jesus separated two communities by using the logos. Where the logos dwells, a family bond is formed; members of this community are at once children of Abraham and of God. The logos liberates this community from slavery, makes it immune to death, commissions it to continue Jesus' mission. The symbol of an indwelling logos carries this entire panoply of implications; they will become clear, of course, only after the Son of Man has been lifted up from the earth (v. 29).

Conversely, there is nothing bland about the dereliction of the community in which the logos finds no home, a community of slaves believing they are free and of fornicators persuaded of their own purity. No children of Abraham, these, but rather children of the devil, that archetypal progenitor of lies and murder. The reference to this "murderer from the beginning" summons up memories of the first human murder, when one son of Eve killed the other in a religious dispute (Gen. 4:1–5; also 1 John 3:4–17). The polemic is fierce indeed. But it is not merely the animosity between two religious communities, each claiming to be superior to the other. This is a polemic between their two progenitors. On one community had rested God's curse because of its complicity in the serpent's deceit and its participation in fratricidal violence. That shedding of blood could be remedied only by the giving of blood; that darkness could be overcome only by light. Only a savior from the beginning could defeat a murderer from the beginning, by giving his flesh for the life of the world.[13] So the appearance of the logos disclosed a chain of being that reached from Eden to the present, revealing the inner definition of every community, its freedom or slavery, its truth or illusion, its participation in life-taking or life-giving. One community lifted Jesus up from the earth, i.e., crucified him; the other testified that the logos of Jesus had been the logos of light and life from the first day of creation.

FOURTH SOUNDING: JOHN 12:44–50

This passage in the twelfth chapter is the final appeal that Jesus made to the authorities, an appeal that clarified the results of receiving or rejecting the logos. The chain of being that we noted earlier becomes here a closely linked chain of sending and, in fact, a chain of eternal life.

> *I have come as light into the world, so that everyone who believes in me should not remain in darkness. I do not judge anyone who hears my words and does not keep them, for I came not to judge the world but to save the world. The one who . . . does not receive my word has a judge; on the last day the logos that I have spoken will serve as judge. . . . The Father who sent me has himself given me a commandment about what to say. . . . His commandment is eternal life.* (12:46–50)

Here Jesus identified the logos with God's commandment. To obey this word is to obey the commandment.[14] But the commandment is rather unusual. Does the word refer to the commands in the Decalogue or to the commandment to love, with all its implications? No, here the command is eternal life, a life that comes in the form of light. A strange correlation this: logos = command = life = light.[15] But it is not so strange when we notice the same correlation in the prologue (John 1:1–3) and in the Genesis saga of creation (Gen. 1:1–3). In Genesis, too, the command was obeyed and as a result light was separated from darkness. That is the command that John identified with eternal life. Logos thus forges a bond among believers in Christ that also binds them to the primal action of God in creation, before human sin had corrupted God's design—that is, before God had said to Adam, "You are the earth and to the earth you shall return," cutting off access to the tree of life (Gen. 3:19–23). The curse was a command; its remedy was a command.

This command also specifies the other half of the cosmic *inclusio*, the eschatological function of the logos to match its protological function. In the last day the same logos will judge everyone who rejects the commandment of light and life. It could hardly be otherwise, if what Jesus said was faithful to what God commanded him to say. It could hardly be otherwise, if the logos had the function of revealing the descendants of Adam, Eve, and Cain. The use of this *inclusio* reflects a universal range of thinking, orienting each response to the logos within the farthest horizons, the first day of creation, and the last day of judgment—both days lying far beyond the reach of human tinkering. Yet those far horizons lose their distance at the moment when the logos is spoken afresh by those whom God sends. The commandment "*is* eternal life" and is not a gift to be postponed until after death. The logos brings the command nearer than either yesterday or tomorrow. Likewise, the salvation of the world that comes with the logos is not some future Utopia or El Dorado, some peace for which today's war is fought.[16] This light is something that believers can already see!

FIFTH SOUNDING: JOHN 17:6–26

Both old and new affiliations come to the surface in the prayer of Jesus in the seventeenth chapter. Here the logos is seen as the bond between God, Jesus, and Jesus' messengers. To God Jesus says, "I have given them *your* logos" (v. 14). In this process Jesus is essential as an intermediary: "the words that you gave to *me*, *I* have given to them" (v. 8). The reception of this logos creates a continuing vocation on the part of these messengers: "They have kept *your* logos" (v. 6; all emphases added). The logos forms both the source and strength of their vocation, thus uniting Christology and missiology. Just as Jesus' mission enfleshed the logos of God (1:14), so their mission enfleshed the logos of Jesus and of God. "As you have sent me into the world, so I have sent them into the world" (v. 18). The gift to them of the logos entails hatred by the world to which they are sent (v. 14), but this hatred cements the bond of self-giving between sender and sent: "They are yours . . . mine are yours . . . yours are mine" (vv. 9–10).

These messengers "keep" God's logos by achieving and maintaining unity among themselves that matches the unity between God and Jesus. To keep the logos is to accept with joy their dangerous work in the world and to be guarded from the deceptive attacks of the devil. In fulfilling their assignment they will be sanctified in the truth. How does John think of this sanctification, this "being made holy"? The norm of holiness is, of course, provided by Jesus' self-sacrifice. His path to the glorification of God is theirs as well. As God is glorified in Jesus, so, too, will Jesus be glorified in them (vv. 1, 10). These corollaries may be added to our list: logos = sanctification = glorification = crucifixion.

The concluding petitions in the prayer bring into view an extension of the chain of life, a fourth link to be added to the earlier links: God, Jesus, his apostles. Now appears the generation of those who believe through the work of Jesus' messengers. All who believe through their logos learn that God has loved them "as you have loved me," a love, it must be noted, that existed before the creation of the world and that is designed for the salvation of the world (v. 24). Where the logos is, there God is, there love is—a love linked to the action when God founded the world.

SIXTH SOUNDING: JOHN 1:1−18

That action, of course, is the point at which John began his story.

> *In the beginning was the logos*
> *the logos was with God*
> *the logos was God . . .*
> *All things came into being through the logos . . .*
> *What came into being was life. (vv. 1−4 paraphrased)*

These words can be read as a prelude to the entire gospel, but they can as easily be read as a summary. In our various soundings we have noted echoes of these opening words, indicating that these verses were written by someone who knew what was to follow. The basic accents are obvious, though precise interpretations have baffled exegetes for centuries. Readers are confronted first of all with a logos-*theology*: "The logos was God." Readers are also confronted with a logos-zoology; in this symbolic universe where all things are made through the logos, life (*zoē*) is defined for the children of God by their birth from above. This is a very different zoology, to be sure, but its importance to John cannot be denied.

> *The life was the light of all people,*
> *the light shines in darkness,*
> *and the darkness did not overcome it. (1:4−5)*

As we have seen, the entire gospel recounts this struggle between the light and the darkness. Victory was won by the light when the logos, rejected by way of crucifixion, disclosed the truth that this logos-God was the parent of Jesus and of Jesus' logos-born siblings (20:17).

The prologue was carefully structured to accentuate the antithetical relationship of two communities (a logos sociology, if you wish). One was defined as those who accepted the light, received the logos, believed in the name of the logos, and became children of God through its power. The other community was defined as the darkness that unsuccessfully tried to overcome the light, as the *kosmos* that did not know the light, as the people who did not accept the light, and as those who had a contrary birth and parentage. The entire gospel spelled out in detail the conflict between these two communities and thus disclosed who belonged to which family.

In our third sounding we discussed the shape of that conflict in chapter 8. By announcing himself as "the light of the world," Jesus incited a division among "his own" into two communities, only one of which accepted the logos. The opposing family was composed of children not of Abraham but of the devil, who "from the beginning" had been a liar, a deceiver, and a murderer (8:43–44). Their parentage was determined by their decision to act in accordance with the devil's desires.

"A murderer from the beginning"—that is the decisive clue to the identity of this parent and of this family. The reference to those who acted in accordance with such desires takes us back to the opening chapters of Genesis. The prologue is not only an appeal to the primal word of God that created light and life, it also echoes the account in Gen. 3 and 4 of the emergence of sin and death. Here appeared the first murder, the action of Cain that was instigated by the "demon" crouching at the door, whose "desire" was for Cain (4:7). That murder, in turn, was the first sequel of the curse on the serpent: enmity between its seed and that of the woman.

It is this link to Gen. 3 and 4 that explains the enigmatic and redundant verse in the gospel that reads: "who were born not of blood or of the will of the flesh or of the will of man, but of God" (1:13). If this negative statement applies to the children of God, its positive antithesis applies logically to their opponents, the children of the devil. Their birth is indicated in three different phrases:

Who were born of bloodshed. The Greek word for blood (*haima*) appears here in the plural, which in Hebrew usage often meant blood-shed and often is so translated.[17] In the light of John's identification of the devil as a murderer from the beginning of the devil's children as adversaries of the light, we detect here an echo of the curse on Cain, the first murderer,[18] and of the earlier curse on the serpent in which God promised continuing enmity between its seed and that of the woman. In this idiom, successors to the serpent and to Cain were born of bloodshed (here the prologue anticipates Jesus' own death).

Who were born of the will of the flesh. Here we detect another subtle reference to the Genesis curses and a reason for the apparent redundancy. If we are justified in hearing an echo of God's curse on the serpent and on Cain, we may be justified in hearing an echo of the curse on Eve: "Your desire [*apostrophē*] shall be for your husband" (Gen. 3:16; cf. also Gen. 4:7). In writing "the will of the flesh" John may have had this curse in mind. He may have understood Eve's bondage to sexual passion as punishment for her disobedience to God's command, a bondage from which the children of God have been freed.

Who were born of the will of a husband (andros). The second part of the curse on Eve was: "Your husband shall rule over you" (Gen. 3:16). That part encapsulates the long human story of male domination, with all the brutalities, conscious and unconscious, of which males have been guilty. It is from such a legacy that the logos-born children of God have been freed.

The ultimate punishment of the first human parents had been exclusion from the garden and the tree of life and a return to the earth, "dust to dust" (Gen. 3:19, 22). In this regard the prologue celebrates a total reversal, in that those who are born of God enter the realm of life and light. They are now heirs of the truth; they are, by implication, no longer the dupes of the crafty serpent's lies (1:14). They receive "grace upon grace" by implication, not the curse. Their reliance is not on the law but on the knowledge of God, the vision of God, and the fullness of divine glory. In this conception of life and light, Genesis may have shaped the basic vocabulary, but the story of Jesus determined the understanding of what happened when the logos came to the logos' own and was rejected. The logos' crucifixion and glorification won the victory for all who were "born of God" (1:13): "The word became flesh and dwelt among us . . . and we have seen his glory" (1:14).

Here for the first time in the gospel we encounter the personal pronouns *we* and *us*. This is an important signal that indicates how readers should interpret what follows. The gospel is more than the product of a single author's mind; it is the result and the substance of conversations among the logos-born, containing their meditations about their own genesis as children of God. It is neither a biography, nor a history, nor a collection of doctrines, nor a segment of Scripture—and it is clearly not a theological essay on Christology. It is a series of conversations among those who have received God's grace and seen God's glory.[19]

These conversational partners have been made aware of the frontiers that separate three contiguous worlds of thought and that illustrate three different sets of children/parent relations. One of these is the empirical, visible world where children can simply identify their parents as John and Mary Doe. In a second world, equally empirical yet invisible, the children think and act in accordance with the desires of their parent, the serpent or devil. In a third world, always new and yet always the primal creation of God, the thought and action of God's children are empowered and directed by the love disclosed in the first-born Son.[20]

We should now summarize the basic functions of the logos in Johannine protology. Logos is *group-binding* in the sense that it constitutes the cohesive element in this third realm where all children are one in the same sense that God and Jesus are one (17:21). This binds the present community with both its ancestors and its successors, all those who have received Jesus' "fullness" (1:16). Within this realm no generation can be superior to any other generation, because the very term *generation* is defined genetically and not chronologically.

The logos is *time-binding* in that all children receive a sense of time that links them to the beginning and end of God's work of creation and redemption. Those who live in this realm find that what happened in the beginning and what will happen at the end are more decisive than what happened yesterday or what will happen tomorrow in the realm of John and Mary Doe. This sense of time relativizes the significance of sacred calendars with the annual repetition of holy days and holy seasons. Logos measured and punctuated time in a very different way.[21]

By living "among us," the logos created a different sense of space; it was genuinely *space-binding*. Jesus prayed that all who accepted the logos would be with him "where I am" (17:24). After his death, one of the most agonizing confessions was that of Mary: "We don't know where . . ." (20:13). But the disciples came to know the truth of his promise: "I will come again and will take you to myself, so that where I am, there you may be also" (14:3).[22] This transcendence of geographical space relativized the holiness of holy places[23] as well as the importance of living in a selected city or nation.

So when John wrote "we have seen . . . ," he and his readers entered a realm of space and time, of birth and death, of conflict and victory that was the antithesis of the serpent's realm of deceit and death. Here the verbal symbol of logos fused their memories and duties and hopes. It strengthened their will to accept persecution, but discouraged any martyr-complex by giving absolute priority to the power and demands of love. By the birth it shared with God's first-born, this community received a sense of its distinctive identity and vocation. "In the beginning was the word."

NOTES

1. Following the precedent of the Greek I will not capitalize the term *word* or *logos*. The NRSV has used capitals in the prologue but not elsewhere in the gospel, but this creates a misleading separation in thought where none exists.

2. In this conviction I differ from much recent scholarship. R. Schnackenburg, for example, believes that the contrasts between prologue and gospel are so great as to show that originally the prologue was a hymn that has been transformed into a literary preface (*The Gospel According to St. John* [New York: Herder & Herder, 1968], 224–49).

3. An example of this foreignness is the Johannine concept of peace. Cf. my essay "The Peace of God: Conceptions of Peace in the New Testament," in *Celebrating Peace*, ed. L. S. Rouner (Notre Dame: Notre Dame Press, 1990), 118ff.

4. For the many expressions that are synonymous with the Father/Son image, cf. my essay "Inclusive Language and Biblical Authority," in *Faith and History*, ed. J. T. Carroll, E. E. Johnson, and C. H. Cosgrove (Atlanta: Scholars Press, 1991), 347–51; also "The Idea of Incarnation in First John," *Interpretation* 24 (1970): 293–97.

5. The significance of an image may be measured by the number of associations and allusions it arouses in the mind. Cf. H. Meyerhoff, *Time in Literature* (Berkeley and Los Angeles: University of California Press, 1955), 23–24; also my *John, The Martyr's Gospel* (New York: The Pilgrim Press, 1984), 92–102.

6. Scholars who are unwilling to do this are guilty of an insidious attack upon the text itself; cf. S. Sontag, *Against Interpretation* (New York: Farrar, Straus & Giroux, 1966), 5–7.

7. John's reliance on this paternal/filial image can easily be misconstrued; cf. *Faith and History*, 340ff.

8. In this passage the word *logos* is sometimes translated as "teaching." It is much more than teaching; it is "the very person of Jesus as the manifestation of the Father" (J. F. Forestall, *The Word of the Cross* [Rome: Biblical Institute, 1974], 192).

9. In 5:24, lines 3 and 4 seem to be redundant: "does not come under judgment, but has passed from death to life." That redundancy is relieved if we take line 3 as canceling the curse of God in Gen. 3:14–18 and line 4 as canceling the death that climaxed that curse.

10. The function of this narrative in John is comparable to the "recognition scene" in Mark 8:22–9:1, where the accent falls on the linkage between the identity of the Messiah, the necessity for suffering on the part of the disciples, and the offense caused by such linkage.

11. This image of mutual indwelling, conveyed by the Greek *menein*, was vital in Johannine thought. Cf. R. E. Brown, *The Gospel According to John* (New York: Doubleday, 1966), 1:511–512; also my *John, The Martyr's Gospel*, 92–93. Because of the archaic character of the English *abide*, the NRSV has often rendered *menein* as "continue" or "remain"; this virtually excludes the rich associations of the traditional *abide*.

12. This strain in John's thought has for centuries been used to fan the flames of anti-Semitism, a tragic betrayal of the Jew whose love for his people led to his death. The fact that John traced the violence back to Cain, acting under the instigation of the serpent, shows that his concern was with all such violence, with a universal human guilt. Cf. my *John, The Martyr's Gospel*, 24–36.

13. This grounding of thought in the Genesis story of creation-and-fall establishes a perspective that transcends later ethnic and religious conflicts. Adam, Eve, and Cain were neither Jews nor Gentiles but archetypal representatives of all races and religions. For the more immediate relevance of this passage to the historical situation faced by Jesus, cf. my essay "Writing on the Ground: The Puzzle in John 8:1–11," *Horizons in Biblical Theology* 24 (1991): 23–37.

14. Cf. S. Pancaro, *The Law in the Fourth Gospel* (Leiden: E. J. Brill, 1975), 403–51.

15. This use of logos illustrates a point made by G. Vann: "The prophetic vision is many-levelled, mingling past or present with future, the temporal with the eternal, the literal and the metaphorical, history with symbol" (*The Eagle's Word* [London: Collins, 1961], 12).

16. Cf. Rouner, *Celebrating Peace*, 126–30.

17. Cf. Brown, *John*, 1:12.

18. The episode of Cain and Abel left other important impressions on early Christian thinking. Matt. 23:35; Luke 11:51; Heb. 12:24; 1 John 3:12.

19. For a discussion of this ability to see, cf. W. A. Meeks, "Equal to God," in *The Conversation Continues: Studies in Paul and John*, ed. R. T. Fortna and B. F. Gaventa (Nashville: Abingdon Press, 1990), 317–19.

20. The complexity of this thought is well described by W. A. Meeks: "What we see in the Fourth Gospel . . . is . . . an exegetical and interpretive process by which a new religious movement interpreted Scripture, interpreted Jesus, interpreted its own history, and interpreted the world in one complex dialectic" ("Equal to God," 311).

21. Cf. my *To Die and To Live* (New York: Seabury Press, 1977), 107–22.

22. Cf. my *John, The Martyr's Gospel*, 123–31.

23. Cf. my essay "The Holy and the Sacred," *Theology Today* 47 (1990): 7–10; also, "Holy People, Holy Land, Holy City," *Interpretation* 37 (1983): 18–31.

CHAPTER ELEVEN

CHRISTOLOGY AND THE CROSS

SARAH A. EDWARDS

Cross and resurrection—Christology was born of the need to reconcile these paradoxical realities. "Without the cross," said Martin Kähler, "there would be no Christology."[1] Conversely, without the resurrection there would be no need to probe deeply into the meaning of Christ.

Jesus died "the most cruel, repulsive, the most horrible form of death."[2] He was executed by the Romans in a degrading torture reserved for the most despicable criminals. If he had quietly passed away, been thrown off that cliff in Nazareth, or even stoned by the Jews for blasphemy, the theological task of the early church would have been far less urgent. As it was, any affirmation splintered against the cross. "When Christians hailed as Messiah and worshipped as Lord one who had died on the cross, a central theological problem was raised."[3]

On the other hand, the resurrection broke open all previous perceptions. From beyond the boundaries of time and space, out of the mysterious tremendousness of God, the startled apostles beheld the glorious reality of the living Lord. "While they still disbelieved for joy" (Luke 24:41). They realized the curse of the cross had been taken away. To the people at Pentecost Peter proclaimed, "God has made him both Lord and Christ, this Jesus whom you crucified!" (Acts 2:36).

I will explore here the Christological transformation in the understanding of the cross in the canonical Gospels and in the letters of Paul.

JESUS' UNDERSTANDING OF HIS OWN DEATH

What do the Gospels show us about Jesus' understanding of his death? Beneath the sheen of resurrection it is difficult to grasp his thinking. So much depends upon our understanding of the horizons of his humanity. If the Lord were fully human, his consciousness must have been congruent with the healthy self-image of a mature and sensitive person. When he became incarnate, he surely "emptied himself, taking the form of a servant, being born in the likeness of men" (Phil. 2:7).[4] This is contrary to much Christian doctrine, especially that of the Roman Catholic church, where Jesus is considered to have had full knowledge of his divinity throughout his earthly life. Nevertheless, radical self-emptying, κένωσις, is the only way to avoid making a mockery of the suffering of the Lord.

Almost from the beginning of his ministry, Jesus apparently understood that his death would be violent. Through his profound awareness of God working through his life, his power to teach and to heal, and his charismatic appeal to the people of the land, he enraged the leaders of the Jews. It was not long before the Pharisees "held counsel with the Herodians, how to destroy him."[5] None of this growing hostility deflected him from his course. He presently began to share his certainty of a violent demise with his disciples. This is clearly the origin of the Passion predictions, although they have been encrusted with specific details added after the event.[6] Finally Jesus set his face steadfastly to go up to Jerusalem,[7] sensing what awaited him there.

The most profound indication of Jesus' understanding of his death was given in the acted parable of the last supper. In presiding over the meal, as was the Jewish custom, the Lord took bread and blessed and broke it and gave to all those seated at the table. But he interrupted this time-honored sequence to lift up the fractured loaf and said, "This is my body, broken ἔκλασεν ὑπέρ, for you" (1 Cor. 11:24). The preposition ὑπέρ essentially means "for the sake of" and follows words of sacrifice.[8] In Paul's account it is used only with the bread, and this is clearly closest to the Lord's authentic words. The Jewish table ceremony also included the blessing and sharing of a cup; in words that may or may not go back to Jesus, Paul writes, "This cup is the new covenant in my blood" (1 Cor. 11:25), thus referring to the ratifying of the Mosaic covenant in the blood of bulls and so honoring the Hebraic taboo against drinking blood.[9]

Because the evangelists were either Gentiles or at home in Gentile culture, they were more comfortable with the idea of imbibing blood. John pushes this to the limit when he writes, "[The one who] drinks my blood has eternal life . . . for . . . my blood is drink indeed" (John

6:54–55). The other evangelists are less radical, although they also go beyond the parameters of Jesus' authentic words. Mark uses ὑπέρ only with the cup and strengthens its sacrificial meaning by adding ἐκλυννόμεν, poured out, softening it by keeping "of the covenant" (Mark 14:24). Matthew follows Mark but changes ὑπέρ to the gentler πέρι, for, adding the new phrase, "for the forgiveness of sins" (Matt. 26:28). Luke uniquely begins his account of the Last Supper with an additional cup, so linking it with the Passover Seder.[10] He underlines the sacrificial significance of Jesus' death by using ὑπέρ with both elements (the only evangelist to do so), adding διδόμενον, given, to the bread words, and keeping ἐκλυννόμεν with the cup: "This is my body given sacrificially for you. . . . This is my blood . . . poured out in sacrifice for your sake" (Luke 22:19–20).[11] Thus even within the formalized pericope of the Last Supper, the Lord's words about his death have been expanded and deepened in meaning. Within this context the Christological interpretation of the cross has already begun.

PRIMITIVE CHRISTOLOGICAL TRADITIONS ABOUT THE CROSS

Primitive Christological traditions about the cross take two forms, narrative and kerygmatic. It is impossible to ascertain with any certainty which form is earlier. Both reach back deep into the life of the apostolic church and reflect its imperative to evangelize.

The kerygma proclaims God's astounding act of salvation in the life and death and resurrection of Jesus Christ.[12] A comparatively short and pithy sermon, it seems to have originated as a missionary tool. A note in Kittel's *Wörterbuch* states: "The kerygma is the mode in which the divine logos came to us."[13] Although it is Christologically more correct to say that the divine Logos initially came to us in the Incarnation (John 1:14), this was indeed the experience of the new convert who first knew the coming of the Logos in the word of preaching. Paul writes to the Corinthians: "For since in the wisdom of God the world did not know God through wisdom, it pleased God through the folly of what we preach to save those who believe" (1 Cor. 2:21). The missionary purpose of the kerygma is made clear by the appeals to accept Jesus as Lord and Savior that frequently follow these statements. After Peter heals the lame man begging beside the Gate Beautiful, he proclaims Christ to the "people of Israel" and invites them to "repent and turn again, that your sins may be blotted out, that times of refreshing may come from the presence of the Lord" (Acts 3:19).[14] Similarly, Paul follows the kerygmatic Christ hymn in Philippians with the exhortation to "work out your own salvation with fear and trembling, for God is at work in you both to will and to work his good pleasure" (Phil. 2:12–13).[15]

Although there are few explicitly kerygmatic statements in the Gospels, the missionary appeal is everywhere implicit. Each pericope is shaped to win a faith response. In the words of Günther Bornkamm, it is the reader's task to find "the history in the kerygma and the kerygma in the history."[16] The original conclusion of the Fourth Gospel maintains that "these [signs] are written that you may believe that Jesus is the Christ, the Son of God, and that believing you may have life in his name" (John 20:31).[17]

The primitive kerygmatic tradition about the cross is significant because of its unequivocal affirmation of the crucifixion as an integral event in the work of salvation. Paul writes to the church at Corinth:

> *For I delivered unto you as of first importance what I also received, that Christ died for our sins in accordance with the scriptures, that he was buried, that he was raised on the third day in accordance with the scriptures, and that he appeared to Cephas, then to the twelve, . . . then to the apostles . . . and to me. (1 Cor. 15:3–8)*

Martin Hengel considers this the "most important confessional statement in the Pauline epistles and at the same time in the primitive Christian tradition."[18] Thus the kerygma witnesses to the crucifixion of the Christ and to his resurrection.

The second primitive Christological tradition about the cross is the Passion narrative. It enriches the kerygma by portraying the aching depth of suffering and the magnificent faith of the One through whom salvation was wrought. Like the kerygma it is ultimately based upon the testimony of eyewitnesses.

"The early passion story probably developed soon after the resurrection."[19] Many scholars concur.[20] As Martin Kähler observed, "The gospels are passion narratives with an extended introduction."[21]

The oral witness that underlies the Gospels was probably first recorded in small units, perhaps centered around a special theme. A good example is the "Handbook of the Way," called Q.[22] Before the invention of printing, the time and expense involved in copying a manuscript (literally by hand) were so great that once a text was incorporated into a longer work, the original was no longer reproduced.[23] Consequently, there are no extant copies of the primitive Passion story. A possible exception is the brief original stratum of the Gnostic Gospel of Peter. In *The Cross That Speaks*, John Dominic Crossan suggests that it is "the one passion and resurrection narrative from which all the canonical versions derive."[24] While the case is far from proven, a review in the *Journal of the American Academy of Religion* concludes that "the Gospel of Peter contains primitive elements of the passion . . . [that] may attest to a complex tradition that had a variety of readings."[25]

The complexity of the canonical Passion narrative raises questions about its cohesiveness as a document. There is a surprising discrepancy in the placement of several passages: Matthew uses them in his Passion story, while Luke cites them earlier in his gospel:

Parable of the great supper	*Matt. 22:1–14*	*Luke 14:15–24*
Lament over Jerusalem	*Matt. 23:37–39*	*Luke 13:34–35*
Parable of the flood	*Matt. 24:37–44*	*Luke 12:39–40;*
		17:22–36
Parable of the good and wicked servants	*Matt. 2:45–51*	*Luke 12:41–46*

A similar change in setting occurs with the cursing of the fig tree, the parable of the talents, and the judgment by the word.[26] In placing these teachings within the last days of Jesus' life, Matthew was perhaps trying to give them a deathbed significance. It is therefore surprising that, unlike Matthew, Luke does not follow Mark in setting the giving of the Great Commandment at this time, but locates it during the Galilean ministry.[27] The discrepancy in dating the cleansing of the temple is almost certainly chronological rather than theological. All four evangelists know it was Jesus' first act upon entering Jerusalem. Because the Synoptics only record one visit, they set this event in Holy Week. John notes that the Lord came to Jerusalem three times, and he places the event very early in his gospel.[28] Finally, although the farewell discourses in John provide a profound Christological understanding of the cross, there is a general consensus that they were not added to the Passion narrative until the final editing of this gospel.[29]

How then did the Passion narrative develop? Joseph Fitzmyer postulates its origin in a kerygma, although this is unlikely because the two traditions developed early and were shaped by different concerns. Probably both traditions grew out of the apostles' experience of cross and resurrection. The second stage in the development of the Passion story as Fitzmyer sees it is a short account beginning with Jesus' arrest, Mark 14:43. The next stage is a longer version opening with Palm Sunday.[30] Edward Best modifies this schema by starting the short account at Mark 14:1 with "Jesus' Death Premeditated."[31] Perhaps no scholar has made a closer textual study of the Passion story than Kurt Aland in his *Synopsis of the Four Gospels*.[32]

To test these hypotheses I charted the Passion narrative using Aland's *Synopsis* and beginning with Palm Sunday. I set the material in parallel columns to show where the four Gospels read together. Only the Synoptics agree; Luke and Matthew incorporate pericopes of Q and individual readings of L, M, and John. Space does not permit the chart to be included here, but I will summarize its findings:

Aland includes 58 pericopes in the Passion narrative beginning with Palm Sunday. Here the four Gospels read together 29X = 50%. The Synoptics are parallel to each other 10X = 17%. Mark and Matthew are together 4X = 7%; Mark and Luke 2X = 2%; and Luke and John 3X = 4%. There are 7 readings from Q, 12%; 19 from L, 33%; 10 from M, 17%; and 14 from John alone, 26%.

Following Best's hypothesis that the short precanonical account begins at Mark 14:1, "Jesus' Death Premeditated," produces a version with 33 pericopes. Here the four Gospels read together 23X = 69%. The Synoptics are parallel 2X = 6%. Mark and Matthew are together 3X = 9%; Luke and John 2X = 6%; and Mark and Luke do not share any readings. There are no readings from Q; 13 from L, 39%; 5 from M, 15%; and 12 unique readings in John, 36%.

Beginning with Jesus' arrest in Mark 14:43 cuts the precanonical story to 21 pericopes. In this segment the four Gospels read together 7X = 33%. The Synoptics are parallel 3X = 14%. Mark and Matthew are together 3X = 14%. Neither Mark and Luke nor Luke and John share any readings. There are no readings from Q; 10 from L, 47%; 5 from M, 24%; and 8 unique readings in John, 38%.

Several findings from this chart seem to support the hypothesis that the precanonical Passion narrative began at Mark 14:1. Most striking is the rise in the congruence of the four Gospels to a high of 69%. This is also close to the point where Q drops out. When Fitzmyer comments on the congruence of Luke and John in the Passion story,[33] he must be looking at Mark 14:1–43 because this is where most of their agreements lie. Finally, this hypothesis has the further advantage of including the Last Supper in the primitive Passion narrative.

In *Passion Narratives and Gospel Theologies* Frank Matera examines "each passion narrative in terms of the particular [Synoptic] evangelist's theology."[34] This is a splendid way to deal with the canonical material, and in Matera's hands it yields some significant insights. Approaching the matter of Christology and the cross through a precanonical Passion narrative that took shape soon after the resurrection turns the study around. This primitive tradition then becomes the foundation upon which the theologies of the Gospels depend. It is also highly probable that Paul gained his understanding from this or a similar document while in Jerusalem with Cephas.[35]

CHRISTOLOGY AND THE CROSS IN THE LIGHT OF THE PRIMITIVE PASSION NARRATIVE

When the early Christian community began to shape the Passion narrative, one of its first priorities was to show that Jesus, although crucified, was worthy to be affirmed as Lord and Christ. Although the glorious sheen of Easter lies over all, it is seldom explicitly mentioned save in the Johannine discourses, which, as noted above, were added later. That wonderful act of God is witnessed in the closing chapters of the Gospels.

Jesus was worthy to be proclaimed as Lord because he was not a criminal, despite dying a criminal's death. Even in the eyes of his principal judge, he was guiltless:

Pilate then called together the chief priests and the rulers and the people and said to them, "You brought me this man . . . and after examining him . . . behold, I did not find this man guilty of any of your charges against him, neither did Herod, for he sent him back to us. Behold, nothing deserving death has been done by him." (Luke 23:13–17)

The Fourth Gospel concurs. Three times Pilate says, "I find no crime in this man!" (John 18:38; 19:4). In Mark he asks, "What evil has he done?" (Mark 15:14). In Matthew, Pilate's wife warns him to "have nothing to do with that righteous man!" (Matt. 27:19). The mob becomes violent, perhaps further aroused by some priestly *baksheesh*.[36] They cry out, "Crucify him! Crucify him!"[37] Pilate timidly accedes to their demands. Jesus goes to Calvary. When it is over, the Roman soldier who presided over his execution declares, "Certainly this man was innocent!" (Luke 23:47).[38]

Second, Jesus was worthy to be proclaimed both Lord and Christ because of the depth of his character and his unusual response to suffering. This is a major theme in the primitive Passion narrative. In Gethsemane Jesus reveals his hard-won acceptance of God's will.[39] Through his arrest, trials, and crucifixion, Jesus displays a quiet, steady patience.[40] His tenderness toward the woman who anoints him[41] and the widow who gives her last penny[42] and his yearning over Jerusalem[43] reflect a sensitive and compassionate nature. The boundary between human and divine stretches very thin when on the cross Jesus prays for those who have just nailed him there: "Father, forgive them!" (Luke 23:34).[44] The words echo down the centuries and stand inscribed on the ruined wall of Coventry Cathedral above the charred cross, "Father, forgive!"

Jesus is worthy to be both Lord and Christ. This is the first important Christological witness of the primitive Passion narrative. The second important witness is that his death was a sacrifice. As we have seen, the Lord himself understood his dying in this way. On the night in which he was betrayed, over the shared and broken bread, he said, "This is my body given in sacrifice for you."

A sacrifice is "a gift to God to induce [divine] aid," a means of obtaining blessing or forgiveness.[45] It was the principal act in the cult of ancient Israel. The victim of such a ritual was usually a male animal without spot or blemish.[46] When, like Mary and Joseph, those making the offering were poor, they could give the priest "a pair of turtledoves or two young pigeons" (Luke 2:24). Although a sacrifice generally involved the death of a living creature, the practice was occasionally used metaphorically. In Ps. 51 it is written: "The sacrifice acceptable to God is a broken spirit; a broken and a contrite heart, O God, thou wilt not despise."

During the time when the early Christian traditions were being shaped, several competitive cults arose. While their views were not systematically articulated until later, the evidence of Galatians, Colossians, and even the Gospel of John shows that they were to be reckoned with throughout this period. The early church opposed them on many grounds, especially where they threatened to undermine the reality of Jesus' sacrifice. Docetism taught that "the Savior did not operate in the realm of flesh at all, but only in the appearance of a body." To Docetists, Jesus' death upon the cross was an illusion.[47] In her article "Christology in Dialogue with Gnosticism," Elaine Pagels argues that the Gnostics were not Docetists. They held a Christology based upon an early form of the classical doctrine of the two natures of Christ. While accepting the reality of Jesus' death,[48] they maintained that only his human nature suffered on the cross while his divine nature stood apart.[49]

The primitive Passion narrative portrays the death of Christ with no metaphors, no evasions, no halfway participation. Unless he was *wholly* involved upon the cross, he could not have made what the *Book of Common Prayer* calls a "full, perfect and sufficient sacrifice."[50] Despite claims to the contrary, there is no question that Jesus himself made this sacrifice. Throughout his last hours he is either in full view of the disciples or closely guarded by Roman soldiers. His full humanity is stressed again and again. In Gethsemane Jesus is sorrowful and troubled as he struggles in a very human way to accept God's will.[51] After he is sentenced to death, he is brutally scourged.[52] On the way to Calvary he is too exhausted to carry the heavy cross, and it is laid on the shoulders of Simon of Cyrene.[53] In John's gospel, however, he is able to bear it himself.[54] Perhaps this is intended as a subtle sign of his divine strength. While on the cross Jesus cries out in anguish, "My God! My God! Why hast thou forsaken me?" (Matt. 27:46; Mark 15:34). He then sips wine from a sponge.[55] After his body is taken down it is wrapped in a clean shroud for burial.[56] Thus the Passion narrative leaves no doubt it was truly Jesus who made this sacrifice.

But in the Easter narratives that follow, the situation is reversed. There the emphasis is on Jesus' divinity, while his humanity is only lightly indicated. The folded grave cloths in the empty tomb show that the body once was there.[57] When Jesus appears to his disciples in the upper room, he invites Thomas, who had doubted the reality of his resurrection, to "put your finger here and see my hands, and put out your hand and place it in my side" (John 20:27).

While the Lord's humanity is made clear in this early account of his passion, his divine nature is sketched in with only a few quick strokes. Yet the godlike dimension of Jesus shines through the words from the cross, "Father, forgive!" Other indications occur in the Fourth Gospel. As Christian Beker puts it: "John fuses cross and resurrection in such a way that the cross is no longer a scandal but the gateway to glory."[58]

When Jesus was arrested, as John tells it, he came forward and said to Judas and the soldiers, " 'Whom do you seek?' They answered him, 'Jesus of Nazareth.' Jesus said to them, 'I am he!' . . . When he said to them, 'I am he,' they drew back and fell to the ground" (John 18:4–6). In his article on the Johannine *egō eimi* sayings, Harvey McArthur comments that these phrases are "more striking in Greek than in English, since in classical and Koine Greek the first-person singular is indicated by the form of the verb, and the [pronoun] egō is unnecessary unless some special emphasis is intended."[59] McArthur goes on to say that when Jesus answers the soldiers in this way, "the initial meaning must be simply 'I am he.' But when the evangelist reports that the soldiers fell to the ground before him, it is legitimate to ask whether the phrase does not carry some more impressive force."[60] Raymond Brown feels "there can be little doubt that John intends 'I am!' as a divine name."[61] When the soldiers fall to the ground at Jesus' words, are they prostrating themselves in the appropriate position for worship? Or are they fainting in awe before this unexpected encounter with the numinous? Either action would be appropriate in the presence of a theophany.

As John records it, at the moment of his death Jesus did not merely slip away. Rather he said, "It is finished!" (John 19:30). The Greek verb τετέλεσται means "it is perfected, completed, accomplished." It is echoed in one of the later discourses, "Father, the hour has come. . . . I glorified thee on earth, having accomplished the work which thou gavest me to do" (John 17:1, 4). Then, with divine control, "he bowed his head and gave up his spirit" (John 19:30).

Paul stands on our side of Easter. Unlike the other apostles, he neither knew Jesus during his earthly life nor witnessed his crucifixion. Therefore he did not tell the stories of Jesus, but tried always in a pastoral way to bring his grace to bear upon the lives of his people. "For I decided to know nothing among you," writes Paul to the church in Corinth, "nothing . . . except Jesus Christ and him crucified" (1 Cor. 2:2). He taught his churches about the sacrifice the Lord had made for them. "Christ died for our sins" (1 Cor. 15:13).[62] He "redeemed us from the curse of the law" (Gal. 13:4). We are now "justified by his blood" (Rom. 5:9). We are "justified by his grace as a gift through the redemption which is in Christ Jesus, whom God put forward as an expiation by his blood, to be received by faith" (Rom. 3:24–25). Then Paul sums it all up: "Christ our Passover lamb has been sacrificed for us" (1 Cor. 5:6).

Christ our Passover: this powerful metaphor runs through the primitive Passion narrative. The Passover was and is "Israel's cherished feast of national liberation."[63] Christ our Passover sacrifice liberates us from sin and suffering and death. Luke finds this concept so significant that he, alone among the Synoptics, introduces it into his account of the Transfiguration. When Moses and Elijah appear to Jesus in glory, they speak of τὴν ἔξοδον αὐτοῦ that he is to accomplish in Jerusalem" (Luke 9:31).[64] Unfortunately, the newer translations have them speak of his "departure,"[65] the King James Version says "decease," and the Good News Bible has the prophets tell Jesus that he will "soon fulfill God's purpose by dying." Thus they lose the rich overtones of "exodus," the Greek title of the second book of Torah, the story of that amazing journey begun at Passover, taking the Israelites from Egyptian bondage to freedom as God's children in the promised land. Leaving the Mount of Transfiguration, Jesus begins his own exodus from the constraints of sin and death through his paschal sacrifice to the glorious liberty of life in love and joy and peace. This journey begins in Luke 9:51 when Jesus "sets his face steadfastly to go to Jerusalem" and ends in 19:40 on Palm Sunday: ten chapters, 42 percent of this book.

All four Gospels make much of the timing of Jesus' death. In the Synoptics the Last Supper coincides with the first and most important night of the Passover Seder.[66] In Egypt, after the Israelites had eaten their meal of unleavened bread and all but their own firstborn had been slain, Pharaoh hastily exiled the people. So began their Exodus (Exod. 12:21–34). In the same way, after his last meal with the disciples, Jesus began his final journey to the cross. John, however, does not interpret the Last Supper as a Passover celebration. Instead, he understands Good Friday as the Day of Preparation.[67] The Lord was crucified at the same time that all over Jerusalem lambs were being slain in preparation for the feast. Thus in this gospel he was indeed "the Lamb of God who takes away the sins of the world" (John 1:29, 36).

CONCLUSION

The Christology of the primitive Passion narrative and of Paul was not articulated in the polished phrases of a Nicene Creed, but it was vibrant with the vitality of faith. The early Christians affirmed two truths: Jesus was worthy to be both Lord and Christ; Jesus was their Passover, sacrificed for them and for us all. They saw "in the dark mystery of the cross the grace and love of God."[68]

NOTES

1. Martin Kähler as quoted by Jürgen Moltmann in *The Crucified God*, 2d ed. (New York: Harper & Row, 1973), 114. Cf. F. F. Bruce, *Paul: Apostle of the Heart Set Free* (Grand Rapids: Eerdmans, 1980), 253; Marinus de Jonge, *Christology in Context* (Philadelphia: Westminster Press, 1988), 173; John Knox, *The Death of Christ* (New York: Abingdon Press, 1958).

2. Hans Küng, *On Being A Christian*, trans. Edward Quinn (Garden City, NY: Doubleday, 1976), 396. For detailed descriptions of crucifixion in all its brutality, see Jouette M. Bassler, "Cross," *Harper's Bible Dictionary*, ed., Paul J. Achtemeier (San Francisco: Harper & Row, 1985), 194–95; J. F. Strange, "Crucifixion, Method of," *Interpreter's Dictionary of the Bible*, supp. vol., ed. Keith Crimm et al. (Nashville: Abingdon Press, 1976), 199–200; Edward N. West, *Outward Signs* (New York: Walker, 1989), 21–22.

3. *Harper's Dictionary*, 195.

4. Cf. Knox, *Death*, 112, and throughout his writings, where radical κενῶσις is a significant part of his critical apparatus.

5. Mark 3:6//Luke 6:1 ("What to do about Jesus"). Also Mark 14:1–2//Matt. 26:3–5//Luke 22:22 and Mark 14:2//Matt. 26:24//Luke 22:15–20.

6. Mark 8:31–33//Matt. 16:2–3//Luke 9:22; Mark 9:31//Matt. 17:22–23//Luke 9:44; Mark 10:33–34//Matt. 20:17//Luke 18:43.

7. Mark 10:32//Matt. 20:17–19//Luke 18:31–4. Cf. John 11:6–16.

8. *A Greek-English Lexicon*, 4th ed. rev., ed. Arndt and Gingrich (Chicago: University of Chicago Press, 1952), 838–39. Martin Hengel, in *The Atonement*, trans. John Bowden (Philadelphia: Fortress Press, 1983), 37, reads too much into περι, translating it "for the forgiveness."

9. Exod. 24:4–8; Deut. 15:23; Lev. 17:10–14.

10. Luke 22:15; Exod. 12:1–13:6. Although the Old Testament accounts do not specifically mention cups, both Jeremias and Achtemeier note that a first-century Passover meal in Palestine began with the Kiddush cup, which is apparently what Luke had in mind here. Joseph A. Fitzmyer, *The Gospel According to Luke*, Anchor Bible, vol. 28A (Garden City, NY: Doubleday, 1985), 1390–91.

11. My translation. Cf. Knox, 48.

12. *Interpreter's Dictionary of the Bible*, vol. 2, ed. George Buttrick et al. (New York: Abingdon Press, 1962), 444; *Harper's Dictionary*, 524.

13. *Theological Dictionary of the New Testament*, vol. 3, ed. Gerhard Kittel, trans. Geoffrey W. Bromiley (Grand Rapids: Eerdmans, 1979), 716 n. 16.

14. A similar invitation follows Peter's Pentecostal preaching, Acts 2:38–39. Other kerygma in Acts 4:8–12 and 5:30–32 are not followed by an invitation.

15. Other kerygmatic statements in Paul include Rom. 5:8–11; 6:1–4.

16. Günther Bornkamm, *Jesus of Nazareth*, trans. Irene and Fraser McLuskey with James M. Robinson (San Francisco: Harper & Bros., 1959), 21. One of the few kerygmatic statements in the Gospels is Luke 24:15–23.

17. My conclusion; cf. Raymond E. Brown, *The Gospel According to John*, Anchor Bible, vol. 29A (Garden City, NY: Doubleday, 1970).

18. Hengel, *Atonement*, 37.

19. Ms. note by the late John F. Whealon, archbishop of Hartford. See also R. H. Fuller and Pheme Perkins, *Who Is This Christ?* (Philadelphia: Fortress Press, 1983), 15–17.

20. Brown, *John*, vol. 29A, 786, and *Interpreter's Dictionary*, supp., 644; Bornkamm, *Jesus*, 155; de Jonge, *Context*, 177; Dibelius as cited by Frank J. Matera, *Passion Narratives and Gospel Theologies* (Mahwah, NJ: Paulist Press, 1986), 9; Fitzmyer, *Luke*, vol. 28A, 1360, where he also notes Jeremias and V. Taylor agree; W. G.

Kümmel, *Introduction to the New Testament*, trans. Howard Clark Kee (Nashville: Abingdon Press, 1975), 51–52 and 77 n. 81.

21. Martin Kähler, as quoted, e.g., by Bornkamm in *Jesus*, 17. J. R. Donahue, *Interpreter's Dictionary*, supp., 644, notes that the Passion story occupies 20 percent of Mark's Gospel.

22. Frederick C. Grant, *The Gospels: Their Origin and Their Growth* (New York: Harper & Bros., 1957), 61. Another example is Mark 1:21–2:12, which Harvey McArthur once called "a day in the life of Jesus in and around Capernaum." Similarly, Luke 4:31–41.

23. Bruce Metzger, *The Text of the New Testament* (Oxford: Clarendon Press, 1964), 14–18.

24. John Dominic Crossan, *The Cross That Speaks* (San Francisco: Harper & Row, 1988), 17.

25. George W. E. Nickelsburg, Review of *The Cross That Speaks* by Crosson, *Journal of the American Academy of Religion* 59, no. 1 (Spring 1990): 162.

26. Matt. 21:18–28//Mark 13:34–37//Luke 19:11–27; Matt. 25:14–30//Mark 13:34–37//Luke 19:11–27; Matt. 10:40–41, 18:5//Mark 9:37//Luke 9:48, 10:16//John 11:47–53.

27. Matt. 22:34–40//Mark 12:23–34//Luke 13:6–9.

28. Matt. 10:40–41, 18:5//Mark 9:37//Luke 9:48, 10:16//John 11:47–53.

29. Brown, *John*, vol. 29A, 586.

30. Fitzmyer, *Luke*, vol. 28A, 1361–62.

31. Edward Best, *The Temptation and the Passion*, 2d ed. (Cambridge: Cambridge University Press, 1990), 89–90; Grant, *Gospels*, 78–79; Kurt Aland, *Synopsis Quattuor Evangeliorum*, 4th ed. rev. (Stüttgart: Württembergische Bibelanstalt, 1967), 425.

32. Aland, *Synopsis*, 276ff.

33. Fitzmyer, *Luke*, vol. 28A, 1365.

34. Matera, *Theologies*, 6.

35. Gal. 1:18. Acts 9:10–19 notes that Paul was baptized by Ananias, thus implying that he also received instruction from him about the traditions of the church. He already knew about the resurrection from his vision on the Damascus Road, Acts 9:3–6. Cf. 2 Cor. 12:2–6.

36. "Now the chief priests and elders persuaded the people. . . ." Matt. 27:20.

37. Matt. 27:23//Mark 15:13//Luke 23:21//John 19:6.

38. In Matt. 27:54 and Mark 15:39 he says, "Truly, this was the Son of God!"

39. Matt. 26:36–46//Mark 14:32–40//Luke 22:39–46. John 12:27–28 is also a close parallel. It now stands at the beginning of the "Book of Glory" so that his Gethsemane pericope reflects not Jesus' agony but his majesty.

40. Matt. 26–27//Mark 14–15//Luke 22–23//John 18–19 passim.

41. Matt. 26:6–13//Mark 14:3–9. Neither //Luke 7:36–50 nor //John 12:1–8 are in the primitive Passion narrative.

42. Mark 12:41–44//Luke 21:1–4.

43. Matt. 23:37–39. Luke 13:34–35 is not in the Passion narrative.

44. Cf. John Knox, *The Man Christ Jesus* (Chicago: Willett, Clark, 1942), 63–64.

45. *Interpreter's Dictionary*, supp., 764. For a longer but similar definition, cf. *Webster's Ninth Collegiate Dictionary* (Springfield, MA: Merriam-Webster, 1988), 1035.

46. Roland de Vaux, *Ancient Israel*, trans. John McHugh (New York: McGraw-Hill, 1961), 415–19. The sacrifices made in the Second Temple are detailed in Lev. 1–7.

47. Williston Walker, *A History of the Christian Church*, 4th ed. (New York: Charles Scribner's Sons, 1985), 66. Cf. Elaine Pagels's "Christology in Dialogue with Gnosticism" in part 1 of this collection.

48. Pagels, "Gnosticism"; John Knox, "Docetism," in *Interpreter's Dictionary*, vol. 1, 860.

49. Pagels, "Gnosticism."

50. *Book of Common Prayer* (New York: Seabury Press, 1953), "Holy Communion," 80.

51. Matt. 26:38–39//Mark 14:34–37//Luke 22:41–45.

52. Matt. 27:28–29//Mark 15:17–20//Luke 23:26//John 19:1–2 has this done to Jesus before Herod, apparently with less physical abuse.

53. Matt. 27:32//Mark 15:21//Luke 23:26.

54. John 19:17.

55. Matt. 27:34, 48//Mark 15:36//John 19:29–30. In Luke 23:36 he is offered wine (vinegar) but seems not to have drunk any.

56. Matt. 27:59//Mark 15:46//Luke 23:53//John 19:40.

57. John 20:7. In Matt. 28:6//Mark 16:6 they see where the body of Jesus lay. In Luke 24:3 "when they went in they did not find the body."

58. J. Christian Beker, *Paul the Apostle* (Philadelphia: Fortress Press, 1989), 201.

59. See Harvey K. McArthur's "Christology in the Predicates of the Johannine *Egō Eimi* Sayings" in part 2 of this book.

60. McArthur, "Egō Eimi."

61. Brown, *John*, vol. 29A, 818.

62. Perhaps echoed in Mark 10:45//Matt. 20:28—"to give his life a ransom for many."

63. Matera, *Theologies*, 156; F. L. Cross and E. A. Livingston, eds., *Oxford Dictionary of the Christian Church*, 2d ed. rev. (New York: Oxford University Press, 1990), 753.

64. Cf. Fitzmyer, *Luke*, vol. 28A, 794–800.

65. RSV, NRSV, NEB, NREB.

66. Mark 14:12//Matt. 26:17//Luke 22:7. Note Luke 22:15, where Jesus says to his disciples: "I have earnestly desired to eat this Passover with you before I suffer."

67. John 19:14, 31, 42. John, alone of the evangelists, strengthens the Day of Preparation significance of Jesus' death by having the people place "the sponge full of vinegar on hyssop," John 19:29. In Exod. 12:22, Moses tells the people to "take a bunch of hyssop and dip it in the blood [of the slain Passover lamb] and touch the lintel and two doorposts" so the angel of death will pass over that house. Cf. Brown, *John*, vol. 29A, 930.

68. Küng, *Christian*, 401.

CHAPTER TWELVE

CHRISTOLOGY AND THE RESURRECTION

PHEME PERKINS

When Paul wrote to the Corinthians, "If Christ has not been raised, then our preaching [kerygma] is empty, and your faith is empty" (1 Cor. 15:14), was he referring to soteriology or Christology? Did he mean that we could not affirm that the cross had reconciled us with God (e.g., Rom. 4:24–25)? Or did he mean that we could not speak of Christ as exalted Son of God (e.g., Rom. 1:3–4)? Of course, soteriology and Christology are not neatly separated in the New Testament.[1] But, the distinction is not unimportant. When statements about the resurrection appear in early kerygmatic formulas, are they dependent upon a soteriology grounded in the cross, in Jesus' death "for us"? This conviction is crucial to Rudolf Bultmann's famous claim that Jesus rose into the kerygma, as well as to other interpretations of the resurrection that insist that it refers to what happened in the experience of Jesus' disciples.[2]

If Christology is not purely "functional," a symbolic variant of soteriological claims, then a necessary connection between resurrection and Christology implies that claims about the person of Jesus are at stake. Resurrection grounds statements about Jesus that we otherwise would be unable to make. In this context, Christological titles such as Lord and Son of God, as well as the hymnic affirmations that Christ is exalted to God's right hand (e.g., Phil. 2:6–11; Col. 1:15–20), come into play.[3] We should recognize at the outset that these early formulas are not concerned with the fate of Jesus' body,[4] but with his exaltation to the right hand of God. Exaltation language appears to be more primitive in this context than resurrection terminology because it separates Jesus from the other pious faithful in a way that resurrection imagery does not.[5]

Rom. 1:3–4 embodies a pre-Pauline kerygmatic formula that suggests a two-stage Christology. The one who had enjoyed the dignity of "Son of David" during his earthly life is designated Son of God as a consequence of the resurrection.[6] The expression "designated Son of God in power according to the spirit of holiness from resurrection of the dead" (v. 4) contains several ambiguities. If "in power" refers to the mode of Jesus' being Son of God, then the change that results from the resurrection does not take one who was once not Son of God and make him such. Rather, Jesus, exalted with God, now participates in God's salvific power. For Paul, himself, that participation is referred to elsewhere as having the power to give life to believers (Phil. 3:10; 1 Cor. 15:45).[7]

The phrase "from [his] resurrection from the dead" might be temporal, designating the point at which Christ is invested with this power. Or it might be causal, indicating that Jesus' new activity is in some way a consequence of the resurrection. In either case, this pre-Pauline formula suggests that the Christological designation Son of God is associated with the resurrection. The most plausible background to the imagery of Jesus as "installed" as God's Son at the resurrection is the early Christian use of Ps. 2:7.[8] But we should be careful not to presume that titles such as Lord or Son of God can be derived merely from the claim that God had raised the crucified. Vindication of the righteous sufferer does not endow him or her with God's own power.[9] The title and the imagery of resurrection are not associated in pre-Christian sources. Some prior Christological or soteriological conviction about Jesus led the earliest Christians to associate the messianic imagery of the Davidic king with Jesus. However, the formula clearly speaks of Jesus as being installed as Son of God in power. It implies that the resurrection marked a crucial juncture in Jesus' divine sonship.[10]

What does Jesus' exaltation to sonship with power imply? For the earliest kerygmatic formulas, the reference is probably eschatological.[11] Other pre-Pauline formulas speak of salvation as rescue from divine judgment (1 Thess. 1:9–10). Jesus' earthly ministry and the subsequent preaching of the apostles gathers the community of the elect. But the emergence of that community is not the end of the story. It still anticipates salvation at the judgment. The kerygmatic formula of Acts

3:19–21 links Jesus' designation as the Messiah who fulfills the prophecies of restoration with that second coming.[12]

Resurrection as exaltation to divine power is a presupposition in those traditions that apply the Son of Man imagery from Dan. 7:13–22 to Jesus. Daniel sees a human being ascend to God's throne and receive dominion over the nations of the earth. This vision indicates that the powers that now rule the world will be defeated and the righteous will inherit an everlasting rule. The New Testament uses this collective imagery of the exalted Jesus (cf. Acts 7:56; Rev. 1:13; 14:14).[13] Whereas the ascent of the Son of Man in Daniel had signaled the end of the dominion of evil rulers over the righteous, the exaltation of Jesus in the New Testament judgment sayings implies that Jesus is the one who executes God's judgment (cf. also John 5:27; Mark 8:38; 14:62; Luke 11:30; 17:26–30; 21:36; Matt. 13:41; 19:28; 24:30; 25:31). This authority cannot be derived from the Danielic text itself, in which dominion is conferred on the righteous who have endured the rule of those evil powers destroyed by God.[14] Consequently, it would appear that while resurrection as exaltation to God's presence is a necessary condition for the Christological confession that Jesus is the one who will come as Son of Man/judge, it is not a sufficient condition for the emergence of that belief.

We have been examining early Christological formulas in which the resurrection of Jesus is a necessary link between two stages, the earthly life of Jesus and his future coming with God's power. In these examples the Christological or soteriological significance attached to the life of Jesus is specified less clearly than his postresurrection investiture with God's power. That the latter is in some sense a function of the former becomes evident in the pre-Pauline hymn preserved in Phil. 2:6–11.[15] The selfless obedience of the one who accepted the worst human degradation has been matched by God's vindication of the sufferer. God has bestowed the divine name Lord on Jesus so that he is worthy of worship. The eschatological dimension of this worship is evident in the fact that it serves as a manifestation of God's own sovereignty and glory.[16]

The righteous not only endure a world whose rulers are hostile to God, they also suffer "for righteousness' sake" at the hands of the wicked. The martyrs of 2 Macc. 7 anticipate God's vindication, when the bodies that suffer physical torture are raised up by their creator. The suffering righteous of Wisd. of Sol. 2 live eternally in God's presence. The wicked who thought that killing the righteous negated Jesus' claim to be God's son learn too late that only the righteous are immortal (Wisd. of Sol. 5:1–16).[17] The two-membered formulas that associate Christ's death "for us" and his resurrection (e.g., Rom. 4:25; 8:34) employ this imagery. Consequently, Paul can speak of our justification as a result of Christ's resurrection (4:25; 8:34).

Resurrection as vindication of the one who suffered on the cross also plays an important role in the Passion/resurrection predictions of the Gospels (e.g., Mark 8:31; 9:31; 10:33–34). The primary function of the Passion/resurrection "contrast schema" (cf. also Acts 2:23–24; 3:13–15; 4:10; 5:30–31) is soteriological.[18] Jesus is the source of God's salvation. God has turned the human evil of killing the Righteous One into an occasion of redemption for those who believe. A pattern of verbal allusions to Daniel in the Passion/resurrection predictions makes it possible to identify Jesus with the suffering righteous and with the heavenly figure who comes on the clouds to receive the final kingdom. Jesus' destiny is also shared by those who follow him, because their suffering discipleship will be matched by participation in his rule (Mark 8:38).[19]

The association between resurrection and Christology in the traditions that we have been considering points toward Jesus' eschatological role. The risen Lord will be God's agent in judgment and in establishing the kingdom of the righteous that is the ultimate manifestation of God's sovereignty. The various images and titles associated with the risen Jesus are evidence of the unique relationship to God that is presupposed by the gospel message of salvation through faith in Jesus.[20] However, redemption is not limited to future expectation even in the early formulations.

The risen Lord also has a present relationship to the community of believers through the Spirit. Jesus is endowed with the "spirit of holiness" (Rom. 1:4). Consequently he was also felt to be the source of that Spirit in the ongoing experience of the community (e.g., Rom. 8:11; John 7:37–39). The Fourth Gospel turns the gift of the Spirit to the community into an event that occurs on Easter (John 20:22). For the

Johannine community, Jesus is the source of the Spirit that confers eternal life on the believer.[21] This soteriological claim is also a Christological affirmation of Jesus' identity with the Father.

Matt 28:16–20 also understands the resurrection/exaltation of Jesus as the foundation for his ongoing presence in the community. The divine authority that has been conferred on Jesus through his resurrection also grounds the mission conferred on the disciples to convert the nations to what Jesus has taught. The Christological claims in this passage remind the Matthean reader of the name by which the child fulfills Isaiah's prophecy, "Emmanuel, God with us" (Matt. 1:23). Jesus' presence is invoked within the community (Matt. 18:20) as well as in its claim to embark on a mission that goes beyond the limits of his earthly ministry (Matt. 10:5) to address the nations.[22] The trinitarian baptismal formula makes the Christological development behind this section of Matthew clear. The risen/exalted Jesus is identified with God's glory or presence with the people.

While atonement formulas presented Jesus' death as a sacrifice that reconciled a sinful humanity with God (e.g., Rom. 3:24–26), forgiveness was not fixed in the past. Christ's presence in the community also mediated forgiveness through his role as intercessor (e.g., Rom. 8:34; 1 John 2:1–2). Hebrews has developed this tradition into a unique Christology of Christ as the eternal, heavenly high priest whose obedient death was the perfect sacrifice (Heb. 4:14–5:10). Hebrews combined the tradition of Christ as high priest with that of Jesus as preexistent, divine Son (cf. Heb. 1:3–5).[23] In both cases, Hebrews demonstrates a tension between older traditions for which the resurrection as exaltation is the moment at which Jesus enters the full reality of his divine glory and the understanding of Jesus as eternally Son. Insofar as the obedient death of the Son is the concrete action of a human person (Heb. 5:7–10), Jesus appears to "become" heavenly high priest through the complex event that is both crucifixion and exaltation. Heb. 5:9 suggests that Christ was perfected through suffering in the sense of being adapted for the office of intercessor that he would assume.[24]

The ambiguities in the Christology of Hebrews point toward the need for Christological reflection that grounds the affirmations about Jesus that tradition had associated with his status as risen and exalted. Other chapters in this book treat the specific details of these Christological options. We have already indicated that merely coming to believe that God had vindicated Jesus' righteousness by taking him from death into the divine presence, as anticipated in Jewish sources, would not require the Christological and soteriological claims attached to the risen Jesus. Consequently, it was inevitable that Christians would seek to formulate Christologies that locate the relationship between Jesus and God in a unique relationship that existed prior to the resurrection.

The infancy narratives depict Jesus as uniquely "son" of God because of the special creative act in the birth of the child. God's relationship to Jesus is different from the divine relationship with any other human person. Preexistence traditions represented in early hymnic materials (Col. 1:15–20; Heb. 1:3–4; John 1:1–18) identify Jesus with God's image, Wisdom, or Word. God's Wisdom has been active in creation since the beginning. However, Jesus renders Wisdom present among humankind in a new way.[25] How God's Wisdom/Word is embodied in Jesus was not specified. But Jesus' relationship to God as Son could be seen as the consequence of the indwelling Wisdom or Word of God. Jesus is seen to be Savior not because God's saving power is active in Jesus' ministry, death, and resurrection but because Jesus is one with God.

The recognition that in Jesus a human person is uniquely identified with God created its own metaphorical and logical dilemmas. For some, as in most Gnostic Christologies, Jesus can only be the expression of the primordial heavenly Savior. The bodily elements of Jesus (or any other human person) were felt to have no place with the divine. The story of salvation becomes the tale of a lost divine wisdom that must be gathered from this world of darkness through the activities of heavenly revealers: the divine mother, Wisdom; the heavenly Adam; and the redeemer Christ.

Traditional Christology tended to emphasize the reality of Jesus' identification with God; contemporary thinkers often seek to find a Christology that is free of the apparent mythology of preexistence and incarnation. The human person of Jesus, identified with God's liberating compassion for the poor, becomes the center of Christologies "from below." The tradition of resurrection as vindication of the suffering righteous reemerges as God's promise to the victims of injustice that history will not belong to the powerful. God's cause embodied in Jesus continues. In this context resurrection expresses a soteriological claim about God. The resurrection of Jesus reflects the culmination of a human life lived as the perfect embodiment of God's involvement with suffering humanity.[26]

NOTES

1. See Reginald H. Fuller and Pheme Perkins, *Who Is This Christ?* (Philadelphia: Fortress Press, 1983), 1–11. Paul's remarks could be read as references only to the activities of preaching and believing, but the logic of the passage suggests that he does intend to allude to the content of preaching and faith (see Gordon D. Fee, *The First Epistle to the Corinthians* [Grand Rapids: Eerdmans, 1987], 738–45).

2. Fuller and Perkins, *Christ*, 36, 41–43; J. Galvin, "Jesus Christ," in *Systematic Theology: Roman Catholic Perspectives*, vol. 1, ed. F. Schüssler-Fiorenza and J. Galvin (Minneapolis: Fortress Press, 1991), 302–3.

3. Fuller and Perkins, *Christ*, 41–49; P. Perkins, *Resurrection* (Garden City, NY: Doubleday, 1984), 215–46.

4. Although it seems unlikely that any first-century Jew would think of Jesus being exalted into heavenly glory while his body remained in the tomb (cf. A. J. M. Wedderburn, "The Problem of the Denial of the Resurrection in I Corinthians XV," *Novum Testamentum* 23 [1981]: 236), the amorphous character of Jewish language about the destiny of the righteous, which often involves astral immortality or communion with the angels (cf. M. Hengel, *Judaism and Hellenism*, vol. 1 [Philadelphia: Fortress Press, 1974], 196–99), could support an eschatology that looked to a personal, spiritual life in God's presence irrespective of what happens to the physical body.

5. This is so unless one uses a temporal marker, "first fruits of the dead" (1 Cor. 15:23), or the corporate person, "new Adam" (1 Cor. 15:22), to separate Jesus' resurrection from that of the believer, which is deferred until the end-time (1 Cor. 15:24–27). The awkwardness of an individual resurrection that somehow anticipates the awakening of all the pious is evident in the legend that some of the righteous had been raised with Jesus (Matt. 27:52–53; apparently based on the prophecy of Ezekiel, cf. Perkins, *Resurrection*, 125).

6. Whether or not Paul presupposes the preexistence of the Son cannot be determined on the basis of this formula alone. However, the heavily weighted second clause does suggest that Christ's postresurrection state is "higher" or "greater" than that enjoyed during his earthly life (cf. J. A. Fitzmyer, "Romans," in *New Jerome Biblical Commentary*, ed. R. E. Brown, J. A. Fitzmyer, and R. Murphy [Englewood Cliffs, NJ: Prentice Hall, 1990], 833).

7. Ibid.

8. Cf. Acts 13:33 (J. D. G. Dunn, *Christology in the Making* [Philadelphia: Westminster Press, 1980], 35–36).

9. See D. Juel, *Messianic Exegesis: Christological Interpretation of the Old Testament in Early Christianity* (Philadelphia: Fortress Press, 1988), 25.

10. One should be careful not to speak of the resurrection as revealing or initiating that status, because the first part of the formula speaks of Davidic descent. It suggests a sense in which Davidic texts (e.g., 2 Sam. 7:10–14; see Juel, *Messianic Exegesis*, 61–66) were applied to Jesus during his lifetime. See J. A. Fitzmyer, *The Gospel According to Luke*, Anchor Bible, vol. 28 (Garden City, NY: Doubleday, 1981), 208.

11. Cf. Dunn, *Christology*, 35. Dunn speaks of the eschatological reference in the pre-Pauline formula as the beginning of the resurrection of the dead. Because the latter is a subtheme in the broader scenario of eschatological judgment (Perkins, *Resurrection*, 39–50), Jesus' role as the agent of divine judgment seems more appropriate to the pre-Pauline formula. Dunn's proposal is influenced by the Pauline reformulation of the tradition in 1 Cor. 15:20.

12. Cf. G. W. MacRae, "Whom Heaven Must Receive Until the Time: Reflections on the Christology of Acts," *Interpretation* 27 (1973): 151–65.

13. There is no clear evidence for use of the expression "Son of Man" as the title for an individual prior to the New Testament period, although the parables of Enoch do describe a heavenly figure identified with Enoch as "Son of Man" (e.g., 46:2–4; 48:2; 62:5–7, 13–14; 69:27–29; cf. Fitzmyer, *Luke I–IX*, 209).

14. Cf. Rudolf Schnackenburg, *The Gospel According to John*, vol. 2 (New York: Crossroad, 1980), 113.

15. For a retroversion of this hymn into first-century C.E. Palestinian Aramaic see J. Fitzmyer, "The Aramaic Background of Philippians 2:6–11," *Catholic Biblical Quarterly* 50 (1988): 470–83.

16. Cf. B. Byrne, "Philippians," in *New Jerome Biblical Commentary*, 795–95.

17. Cf. Perkins, *Resurrection*, 44–46.

18. Rudolf Pesch, *Das Markusevangelium II. Teil Kommentar zu Kap. 8,27–16,20* (*Herder's theologischer kommentar zum Neuen Testament* 2.2; Freiburg: Herder, 1977), 53.

19. Cf. Jane Schaberg, "Daniel 7, 12 and the New Testament Passion-Resurrection Predictions," *New Testament Studies* 33 (1985): 209–17.

20. Cf. the reformulation of New Testament Christology from the perspective of soteriology by Arland J. Hultgren, *Christ and His Benefits* (Philadelphia: Fortress Press, 1987), 11–23.

21. Schnackenburg, *John*, 157.

22. Cf. Perkins, *Resurrection*, 133–36. B. Viviano treats Matt. 28:20 as an adaptation of the covenant promise of divine fidelity ("Matthew," in *New Jerome Biblical Commentary*, 674).

23. Cf. H. Attridge, *Hebrews* (Philadelphia: Fortress Press, 1989), 146–47.

24. Cf. Attridge, *Hebrews*, 153.

25. Fuller and Perkins, *Christ*, 58–62; Dunn, *Christology*, 187–209.

26. Cf. Jürgen Moltmann, *The Way of Jesus Christ* (San Francisco: Harper Collins, 1990), 236–73. Moltmann broadens the perspective of resurrection hope from human solidarity to include the natural world as well.

PART THREE

CHRISTOLOGY IN DIALOGUE
WITH OTHER FAITHS

CHAPTER THIRTEEN

THE SINGER AND THE SONG: CHRISTOLOGY IN THE CONTEXT OF WORLD RELIGIONS

KENNETH CRAGG

Christology set to music? the heading seems to ask. If so, then we must go to Handel and to Bach's Chorales. But—musicians apart and intending theologians—the phrase about the singer and the song serves well to set the transition from the two preceding sections to this, the third, namely, "Christology in Dialogue with Other Faiths."

Can Christology accord with dialogue? To the Buddhist it would seem to limit it unwarrantably. Christology involves so many Christian presuppositions. It is firmly within theology, as we will argue below—and theology is not an agreed-upon starting point between faiths. Theisms only very tenuously accommodate with Asian faiths—if at all—in view of concepts of *anatta*, the not-self, and of *maya*, or "illusion," that seem incompatible with the purposiveness that theisms read in life and history. If, to underwrite some notion of compatibility, we opt for Asian doctrines of a transcendental unity within which disparity of doctrinal, ritual forms is of no account, we are still far from the instincts of Semitic theology that find their forms real and vital. Reconciliation of opposites excites an opposition that does not reconcile. Christology is close to the center of the tension here; it purports to be the clue to what is real, the clue given from within the real itself.

Faith in Jesus as the Christ, then, would seem to be ready for dialogue only on its own terms and from its own point of departure. Let us meet, it seems to say, on territory we Christians choose. Let ours be the privilege of hospitality; you can be our guests. But if there are to be "host-faiths," must not dialogue mean that we also will meet away from home? Will it suit the enterprise if we insist on staying inside the familiar comforts of race, language, culture, memory, and society? Will it serve to mediate between disparities if, with Raimundo Panikkar, we seek to find "the Christic" in any and every register of the transcendent simply using Christology because it can carry more than Christian meanings?[1]

If not, and if we truly seek dialogue holding a Christian Christology, we must reckon honestly with what is being asked of other parties. We must forgo the advantages of our own familiarities by reaching more carefully into theirs. We may even let the advantage be reversed by moving within their rubrics. Dialogue must equalize occasions so that all are grappling with the uncongenial as part of the art of elucidating what is cherished.

This returns us to our musical metaphor. Jesus being the Christ has much to do with "the still, sad music of humanity." It is crucial from the outset to insist that Christology has to do with Jesus being the Christ. Christology as a term and a discipline has been so much in the Greek vein of inquiry, of formulas and abstract definition. Almost like a clinical science, it can theorize, occupying itself with status, rank, and dignity, with terms like *physis* and *ousia*. These belong with the Greek mind and are *ex eventu*. They ponder a personality, a history, an achievement, a life lived and a death died—the Christ event. The Christhood in all these belongs squarely with the Hebraic tradition. The Christ was *Mashiah*, a theme long in the nation's soul, a heritage of expectancy and hope.

The hope theme reached back into the entire doctrine of creation, of divine responsibility about humankind. It is in the very being of God that we have to locate the messianic wellspring. "One in deed with the Father" must have precedence over "one substance with the Father." The metaphysical Christology (if we may so speak), the Christology of definition and creed, lives only because of the actuality of the living, dying Jesus in the history. If we define our Christology at Chalcedon it is only because we learn it in Gethsemane. There is first the song of Jesus the singer before philosophy undertook to tell, in its own language, what it heard.

"How shall we sing the Lord's song in a strange land?" (Ps. 137:4) was the bitter question of the exiles in Babylon. "We" meant "the Lord's people," burdened with "the strange song" they had sung in "the Lord's land," a song of disloyalty and wrong, which had been divinely requited with the misery and pain of exile. Were the captors merely tormentors, or were they curious when they inquired about "the songs of Zion"? Query or taunt, it touched the raw nerve of Jewish anxiety.

We will not explore here the veiled process by which Jews arrived at their version of themselves and of their history, or the mysteries that lie behind patriarchal narratives, the saga of Moses and the Exodus and the reading of the land, the memory, and the promise. We realize that the history is told as through a prism of theology having to do with tribal self-awareness. We appreciate that the history is written in a retrospect of conviction, so that what happened *is* what "what happened" meant within the realm of belief about it. There is no escape from the implicit circularity. Whatever the "bare facts," it is the "clothed facts" that signify. The former are irrecoverable. Their interpretation had to do with elemental things that belong to all peoples, places, and prides, the who and where and whence and whither of human communities, identity, territory, and time. What is significant about the Hebraic is the intensity with which their self-awareness was felt and the legacies it left to all humankind.

At its heart was this vital sense of divine lordship, of a creating intention behind all things. "By the word of the Lord were the heavens made." Intentionality, rather than mere "beginning," is the meaning of creation, containing any question as to "how" within the answer "why." That answer was the delegacy of humankind, the entrustment to a divine proxy of the estate of the good earth, the dominion that Islam, identically, calls the *khilāfah*, in which all things constitute a sublime trust via a mundane nature responsive to the brain and brawn of the human creaturehood. This reading of history accords well with the current climate of technology if the latter is read in responsible terms and is not hailed as a perquisite of users turned usurpers.

The Hebraic sees this human imperium as being exceptionally possessed, educated, and exemplified by Jews. Hence the conviction about Moses and the land, about David and the kingdom, about Solomon and the temple, and the celebration of the psalmist about "the walls of Zion." Then came exile and the seeming failure of the possession, the education, and the example. The once "enlandized" had become "disenlandized." Physical exile was the tragic symbol of apparent divine defeat entailed by the compromises of the human proxy. But could such defeat be final without disqualifying the entire scheme of things heavenly and earthly on which divine lordship itself was staked?

The messianic hope derived from the pain and anguish of this question. It had to do with the very fidelity of God, with the intentionality of the world, and—because of these—with the destiny of Israel. Without some vindication of history and of God, futility must envelop all. This is the crucial theme of the messianic thought. Lesser strands are no doubt woven into its fabric. But it is here that its meaning must be found—in the loyalty of God to creation as a faithful Creator and in the dependent redemption of humanity via the credible renewal of God's people.

Because it lay at the heart of these inclusive dimensions, the messianic hope became the focus of the very bewilderments that required it. Would the Davidic monarchy be the proper clue, established anew of a "throne of wisdom and justice forever"? Or, if priesthood was the touchstone of a holy people, would a high-priestly Messiah be the Lord's anointed? Perhaps an entire nation keeping authentically just one true Sabbath could constitute the messianic fact. Given that all these had already been discredited, was there any point in asking history somehow to redeem itself? Or given that realistic measure of despair, should Christians await the Messiah who comes "on clouds of power," descending in apocalyptic finality to inaugurate the reign of God? In that event was the true posture of human hope a withdrawal into the wilderness to merit in piety the great intervention or simply to await it?

Perhaps a different clue was emerging from the travail of the prophets. While priests could be secure in the assurance of their rituals, the great prophets could only wrestle with the register of evil and incur, through their vocation to accuse, the enmity of a society restive under accusation. In such an incurring of what their mission cost, they could be seen as standing proxy for the righteousness of God in an obdurate and unrighteous world. In that inevitable suffering they served to uphold the true intentionality within God's creation against travesties of it in the popular will. In that sense they vindicated God. They kept open the option of good by refusing to concede that it was no longer on stage. In "not being overcome of evil" they held open a future that might "overcome evil with good." Such was their servant vocation—costly, lonely, and precarious. But perhaps it held the clue to where the Messiah would learn. It is the clue where history encounters Jesus of Nazareth.

Before we reach him in Christian Christology, we should notice within the Jewish community how long disillusion about the messianic hope has led to a marked downplaying of Messianism as a dimension of things Judaic. A recent example is Jacob Neusner's view that although Judaism has indeed given the world messianic thoughts, it has "left them like rubble after a building has been completed." Certainly after the loss of the temple and the fall of Jerusalem, rabbinic Judaism in the Palestinian and Babylonian Talmuds embraced the idea of corporate sanctification of the people of the Torah, the Mishnaic notion of the holy community around the synagogue. Neusner castigates his colleagues Joseph Klausner and Gershom Scholem for having provided "constructs that in fact never existed in any one book, time or place or in the imagination of any one social group." The Messiah can only be "what Israel is."[2]

This reading no doubt owes much to the will to dissociate the Jewish community from the alleged realization of the Messiah made by Christianity. Other writers, Gershom Scholem among them, see the Messiah as simply the principle of hope, in which Jews are involved in perpetual futurism. The Messiah never comes in order that the Messiah may always be awaited. To identify hope is to betray hope. There is always the fear that wrong may postdate the supposed messianic action and thereby disprove it. We will return to this point as part of the urgent dialogue of the Judaic with the Christian view.[3]

Meanwhile, it is a useful angle from which to take up the New Testament theme of a messiahship identified and realized in and by Jesus of Nazareth. We have already outlined the diversity of messianic anticipation, and it is within the bosom of that diversity that Jesus' ministry lay. Neusner claims that—in the strict sense of the word—the Messiah is a myth, that myth presupposes a story, and "there is no story."[4] That the story is truly there in Jesus as the Christ is the Christian witness.

We face in the New Testament something of the same situation we noted earlier about Hebraic self-documentation. We used the words "a prism of understanding," a history told in the retrospect to which it is believed to have led. If we speak of the Christ event, we must acknowledge it as comprising what happened and what "what happened" meant. The experience of the disciples was inseparable from the historicizing of Jesus. We do not have impartial witnesses. But we realize that, in the very nature of the witness, impartiality would be improper, indeed the silencing of witness itself. We are handling a history of the sort to generate the faith by which, and by which alone, it could itself be told. Only second to what Jesus was to his disciples was what he caused them to be to him, themselves the proofs of his significance.

Keeping this clear in our thoughts, we situate the ministry of Jesus within the messianic scene. If we are to know who the messianic person is we must know the messianic pattern. The who and the how will have to identify each other. To know either is to know the other. That mutuality has to be read within the self-consciousness of Jesus, about which we will be wise to be duly reticent and tentative. There are mysteries here, and theology must be disciplined about history. "Who do people say that I am? Who do you say that I am?" (Matt. 16:13–15) are not idle questions meant to elicit mere credence. Jesus' ministry up to that point has generated deep questions as to truth and what is proper to it in the face of enmity and wrong. Jesus' actual encounter with human "establishment," via his preaching and compassion, is certainly messianically existential. It concerns what hope has to be about—the kingdom, righteousness, and the way to the future. Those issues cannot fail to shape questions about himself, who he is, and where he is going. Is Jesus at Caesarea Philippi not communing with his disciples about destiny, comparing his own reading of the shaping future with theirs? To be sure, they fail him in their response, for they are walking in familiar ways of "Israel's kingdom" and the end of Roman power.

Jesus, it seems from the exchange, is acting according to other criteria, reading in the actualities of his reception in the world a vocation to suffering. He seems to draw upon the precedents present in the Suffering Servant. His conversation holds clear echoes of the themes of the servant songs of Isaiah.[5] His will to obedience as the stuff of sonship to God leads him to contemplate "the cup which my Father has given me." It is clear from agony and travail that this is no macabre death wish. Nor is it remotely consistent with the Jesus we know to ascribe it to some dark conspiracy to precipitate divine intervention by presenting "the majesty on high" with a crisis that might make it imperative. Only Judas, we may conjecture, may have harbored such thoughts. So Jesus comes to Gethsemane and beyond in conscious awareness of what the messianic meaning is and how the task is to be fulfilled.

That we are right to think so may be proven through the experience of the disciples in the immediacy of the climax—which is where we also learn it. But we do not do so blindly. Rather, we penetrate within their records to the impulse by which they made them. Out of the bereavement of their false hopes they came to the recognition of their true one, in Jesus crucified and risen. The resurrection is that recognition evoked, wondered at, and told. "God has made this same Jesus . . . Lord and Christ." What could be seen and known as the sin of the world—present in the will to crucify—could be also seen as borne away in the meaning of the cross. Here the wrongness of creation and of humanity, the wrongness that challenged the sovereignty of God and the destiny of creaturehood, received, in the love that suffers, the answer that was truly commensurate with the perversity of the human and the majestic of the divine. To stand in awe and joy before this fact is the being of Christology. Here the singer, here the song.

But what of dialogue? How shall we hear the singer and the song with Jewish, Muslim, Asian ears? The surprising thing about the Jewish decision of those first disciples is that they quickly assumed it was a song for all the world. Oddly, they soon broke out of the privacy of Judaic vocation. They thought of what they had in trust as being not only about the sin of the world, of which no one race was unilaterally guilty, but also about a savior of the world, in whom Judaic messianic meaning had become the prize of all, because "whosoever would might come." Also, significantly, the later puzzlement about the nonarrival of the Parousia they awaited did not diminish the confidence about the reality of what had been achieved. It simply adjourned the future tense of it without forfeiting the present fact.

Historians have to reckon with many teasing problems about the shape of Christian development in the early centuries. We need to keep always in mind that perhaps we only hear from the dominant parties in a tangled story. But historical circumspection leaves the central logic of Jesus' messiahship intact. Judeo-Christian dialogue has to wrestle with the Judaic conviction that it is nonmessianic and with the Christian assurance of its reality. There is first the problem, already noted, of evil postdating the alleged messianic event. It was a long Jewish assumption of messianic thinking that the wrong of the world would have to reach a zenith; otherwise, the Messiah would not have dealt with its ultimate reaches. Hence the notion of the messianic woes preceding the ultimate apogee, and the prayer: "May Messiah indeed come but may I not live to see the day!"

This, however, is to think only chronologically. Need the ultimate in evil be a point on a calendar? Or could it be an epitome in life? Is the measure of evil quantitative or qualitative? Does it make sense to refer to "the sin of the world" and yet find it in an event that antedates much subsequent wrong? Why not, if we have in mind an inclusive symbol of the *quality* of what is wrong with humanity? It is this that the Christian mind found in the will to Jesus' crucifixion. It saw there a conspiracy of compromise political, of prejudice ecclesiastical, of callousness popular, and of expediency communal—each necessary to the other as factors in the climax—hence the verdict about the sin of the world, where that which represents our wrongness as human is seen to be taken up into a transaction of forgiveness in which we can cognize, or recognize, the reality of our own forgiveness. We do not then need to forgo a past and present fact in order to have a future hope—as must be the case if messiahship is perpetual futurism.

Instead, the nature of this past determines and demands a future in accordance with its meaning—the reproduction, in the forgiven community of faith, of the saving principle of its own forgiveness. The ongoing redemption is via the faith of it, in consistency with its now-disclosed secret. The singer and the song have entered history. "What is lacking in the sufferings of Christ" (Col. 1:24) in the time that follows them is supplied in the reproduction of the principle within them, but only by virtue of their having been, once and for all, what inclusively they were.

Such is the Christian understanding of the place and relevance of the cross of Jesus in the economy of God. It incurs, however, another charge that, for profound reasons, the Jewish mind is moved to make.

This relates to what is seen as gross "overloadedness." How can one event epitomize human sinfulness? Were not crosses numerous on many hills in Rome? What of the Holocaust, with its threat to all belief in a God of integrity? Or it is observed that there was something more accidental than deeply malicious about the verdict against Jesus—a sad victimization, an unhappy travesty of justice—rather than some ultimate mystery of wickedness. The Christian reading of the cross needs to be more modest, less decisive, if it is to do right by that event in particular and by history at large.

The point deserves attention, though it would not "mean" the same for the disciples, from within whose own tragedy of failure the cross had to be read. Yet how could they but fail a master who seemed not to want to be aided, much less rescued, in the only terms they could thus far understand.[6] Easter was in them before it was in the world. The church saw in their apostolic knowledge of it the key to its meaning. Within them the messianic issue—"we trusted that it was he who was to redeem Israel" (Luke 24:21)—was actually lived, in perplexity, in disaster, and in fulfillment. The drama was sufficient within itself with an inclusiveness that both explains and warrants the conviction about it to which it gave rise. All other sin and tragedy *can* be read in its light. Christian dialogue claims neither more nor less, and every other wider, later mystery of evil may be mirrored there.

Seeing within in "the only Name by which we must be saved" (Acts 4:12—itself a messianic discourse) does not have to do with singular or plural in the arithmetic sense, but with inclusiveness. Here is "the Name," the mark—in the love that suffers—of that by which all evil is redeemed. Wrong is not encountered in theory, only in fact. The deed, either way, is the thing. When wrong is taken for what it is, all turns on the *how* of the taking. Resentment perpetuates the enmity, may even "justify" the evil. Stoic indifference restores no relationship. Vengeance retaliates. The only name, rubric, principle, within which evil is borne away is the one where it is borne with forgiveness. And forgiveness always costs. But the name, the rubric, the principle— these are eminently reproducible in redeeming community. When they are, it is still "the only name," the name of the Messiah, Jesus. This is why messianic meanings persist, beyond the messianic achievement and because of it. It is a sad misreading of this "once-for-all" and "now-ever-so" to write, as Jacob Neusner does, that "the ahistorical Christ of Paul, lacking all biography, because the Jesus of Q, of Matthew, Mark and Luke, and ended up as the Jesus Christ of John and of everyone beyond."[7]

The Muslim's problems with the Christian's Christology are almost legion. The Qur'ān firmly withdraws Jesus from all Christological dimensions as the Creeds express them, although it uses throughout the title *Al-Masīh*. It comprehends Jesus solely under the rubric of prophethood, albeit a prophet virgin-born. We must here think within that rubric and locate ourselves firmly on Islamic ground. For, as Islam sees it, there is nothing more than, other than, prophethood in the economy of God with humankind. Messengers are sent and, it is hoped, messengers suffice. Ignorance, forgetfulness, sloth, and inattention must be addressed. These the words of the warners, guides, messengers from God can suffice to overcome, to correct and amend. Prophets may differ in the range of their audiences or the wealth of their meanings, though all essentially agree. "More than a prophet" there is not. Hence the final veto on the thought of Jesus as incarnate—a notion that is also utterly derogatory to the nature and exaltedness of God.

Dialogue can begin from this point, letting Islam be the host on its own terms. Divine "sending" (a word all Semites share) implies a divine stake in the human response. Prophets associate God with the world, at least in terms of the obedience they enjoin. There is that which God seeks that we are meant to render. The possibility that render we may not makes prophets, who are not sent to puppets, necessary.

We realize further that when obedience is withheld, the messengers bear the price. Their summons to the human world is precisely what evokes—if such it be—the disobedience. Their presence is the test case of humanity. Without them and the "law" they bring, we would still be wrong, but not deliberately so. They act to bring out our implicit obduracy to what they require, the will-not-to power that we have within us. The sequel makes for the pain of the prophets. It was emphatically so in the experience of Muhammad, for whom the hostility of the Quraish was a grievous burden "breaking down his back" (Surah 94:3).[8] It was agonizingly so for Jeremiah, hence his passionate "Confessions."

It is important to reckon with this phenomenon of prophetic suffering; it is entailed on God's behalf. The hostility that shapes the persecution is meant for the divine message. We may conclude that the prophets suffer by proxy on behalf of God. We may ask, then, seeing that God is in them in the sending, is God in them in the suffering? That the divine name is staked in them cannot be qur'anically doubted, given the steady insistence on the divine vindication of them that is also the vindication of God in them. Hence the "manifest victory" of Muhammad; hence the heavenly rapture of Jesus, seeing that he was not granted outward earthly success. All qur'anic prophets are finally justified in the sequel to their bearing of the task of prophethood. But at least we have the thought, present in all this, of a human participation in divine purposes and a divine involvement in their human entail, an entail that may be costly suffering. There seems here to be something congenial to New Testament faith.

The case goes further. Just as any song implies a singer, so every message engages a messenger. Muslims usually understand "sentness" as a matter of words only, of verbal deliverance later to be inscribed in scriptures, recited by the faithful. But does it not also involve a personality? How the "sent" relates to the "sent-to" will become part of the significance. Controversy, as for Muhammad, will develop between prophet and people. The argument may well enter, as it does in the Qur'ān, into the very fabric of the gathering text being uttered. "They are saying" so "you say" is the Qur'ān's refrain in the period where such encounter dominates the scene.

What avails then is not only the "what" of the verbal but the "how" of the human. We pass from truth in speech to something like truth through personality. This happens in the origins of Islam, though the "personal" is thought to be confined only to tradition, outside the actual Qur'ān. Muhammad nevertheless becomes, in the revelatory situation, a paragon of what Islam must be. He is an index to the interpretation of what he says. How the prophet takes the experience of suffering to which we earlier referred is central in revelatory significance for any prophethood. For that may be the touchstone of his import.

We are in no way proposing here to read incarnation into Islam. But it cannot be excluded from what prophethood may entail. No "word is made book" without being in some sense "made flesh" in the human sentness that "carried" it. In the long Hebraic tradition, prophets such as Amos, Hosea, and Jeremiah signified not only by what they said, but more by what they were. The sense of what was written in them, rather than merely said by them, comes to its deepest pathos in the Suffering Servant, where it is a portrait that reveals because it is only a portrait that suffices. The divine portraiture in the human is what we mean by "the light of the knowledge of the glory of God in the face of Jesus Christ" (2 Cor. 4:6). Christology in debate with Islam can be seen to be the Christian corollary of prophethood. This sense of things fits readily into any reading of the inner consciousness of Jesus, moving, as we have seen, into his discerning the messianic vocation that the actualities of his ministry as "prophet of Nazareth of Galilee" presented to him. Jesus only suffered as he did because he taught as he did, and in suffering he did not cease to teach.

It follows that the significance of any prophethood is not arbitrarily imposed like a text upon a page or a saddle on a back. There is always a singer in the song, a persona in the theme, truth via personality, so that life becomes a sacrament of meaning, save perhaps in the most rudimentary forms of divine afflatus.

But can the sense of the human on behalf of the divine that is central to prophethood be taken into that distinctive measure that Christians understand as the Incarnation? Will it be unworthy of God, improper to humankind? Can it include that dimension of suffering in which, for Christian faith, incarnation and atonement are one, belonging together in that for which Jesus understood himself born (John 18:37)?

The redemptive quality of suffering is not totally excluded by or from Islam. But the cross, as history, as gospel, is certainly denied. Divine forgiveness is thought of as within the effortless will of God, who in a majesty of mercy has no need of saviors. Moreover, to think of Jesus suffering for us, in any sense, offends against the law of no burden-bearer bearing any burden but his or her own. This frequent qur'anic dictum, together with the insistence that God only calls souls to account for what is their own, makes any Christian theme about redemption impossible. Yet this truth that guilt is inalienable need not be taken to preclude that evident burden-bearing, one for another, that is always with us in "the bundle of life," where the consequences of wrong cannot be confined to the wrongdoers but extend across society. Then *how* injury, calumny, wrongs of every kind are taken will decide *whether* they are forgiven, and the forgiving will always be costly. That life is vicarious in this way is a fact of daily experience. Whether we can think of it as being so with the divine compassion, vis à vis the human perversity, and whether we can well identify that double issue in the wounds of Jesus, will always be the theme at stake in Christian/Muslim dialogue. The one finds it compellingly true, the other disconcertingly improper in the divine sovereignty.

At least we are together in letting the question pass into what we earlier called the economy of God. God is always the question of questions. As noted, Christology is within theology. Christians believe in God via Jesus as the Christ, but only because in the meaning of Jesus as the Christ they have the self-expression of God. The saying of John 14:1, "You believe in God, believe in me," is reversible, and the verb may be either indicative or imperative. Having the Christ whom Jesus is believed to be, we believe we have God willing and devising so to be known. God's devising is seen to be altogether congenial to the divine nature it discloses and to be entirely related to the wrongness about us that, in the cross, figures so centrally in what the disclosure reveals. Those necessary dimensions are its great credentials: this singer, this song. Christology, we might say, is the music of God in the key of humankind.

Christology, then, allows us to be theists in that without it, as the cynic said, we might find it difficult to approve of God. Theism without theodicy defaults on its own meaning. The Christ event, the messianic action, substantiates the very nature of God. Perhaps this is the best meaning we can give to the Latin, through the Greek, of the creedal phrase about "being of one substance with the Father." That of, and from, God who "embodies" what faith and hope awaited from God underwrites and authenticates who God truly is. This, in the Greek idiom of classical Christology, was what creedal language was at pains to say. What transcends eternally and what transpired in time and place are one in being, the Father and the Son. But Christian dialogue needs to take this affirmation into the thought-world of other theisms, not primarily in the abstractions of Greek ontology but in the living history by which "Christ was God's" (Paul in 1 Cor. 3:23)—God's deed, God's action, God's policy, God's answer, or—in our analogy—God's music. Let Chalcedon be interpreted in Gethsemane, the two natures in one achievement.

But how, bound thus into history, does the Christian Christology relate to faiths in Asia that see themselves transcending Semitic forms? Is there only the Christian Christ or can the Christ, whom Paul insisted was "not divided," in fact be multiplied?

A seminal thinker who thinks the answer to the last question could be yes is Raimundo Panikkar. His thought is often elusive. But he invites his readers to distinguish between an identity and any act of identification of it. In Panikkar's term, "the Christic" is "the identity," "identification" of which is made by Christians when they acknowledge the Christic Jesus. But other acknowledgments of the Christic may be made elsewhere with equal warrant.

An immediate perplexity arises, namely, whether or how that sense of the Christic that is rightly identified as such in Jesus as Christ (in the way we have studied) can extend and define outside the particulars that belong with it in him. Those particulars have to do with divine love, with human wrong, with significant history, with ultimacy present in time, with "faithful creation," and much more. If these are truly retained, will they not necessarily condition and control what can be identified as Christic alongside them? So much would seem to be implied by opting for a Christ-related term in the first place (a usage that Panikkar justifies simply as being a term familiar to Christians).

There is indeed for Christians an extension of the Christic into the redeeming community, of love incarnate into the sacramental community of love's endeavor in the world.[9] But these are understood to belong inseparably with the one Christ event. "We love because he first loved us" (1 John 4:19). Will the disinterest of karmic conformity, the nonhistorical awe of Krishna, the transience that enjoins the nonself accommodate or allow what the Christ-referent of the Christic requires? Perhaps so, in the mystery to which Panikkar appeals and by assigning to forms alone these Christian particulars—forms that only point to the transcendent, which, while employing them, always eludes them.

There is much more to the work and mind of this complex thinker, with his fascination for the significance of rivers—Jordan,

Ganges, Tiber—rivers with ghats for purity, rivers with waters for frontiers, rivers with bridges for crossing. And—where we chose to begin—there are the waters of Babylon, where the burdened spirits of exiles yearn for their songs. As a Hispanic-Indian, Panikkar seeks to make the Ganges the truly universal river, which he sees not as "the Jordan of Hinduism" but as the inclusive stream that symbolizes the true catholicism, or wholeness, of religion meaning, "the crossroads of reality where all realms meet." He stands for "that about which one should not believe that it is here or there," which cannot be anywhere monopolized. All that is, is for him "Christophanic."

He would wish us to leave all things open-ended. "Trust the God who trusts men," he suggests.[10] It is, as we have seen, a very biblical dictum. It describes creation and dominion. But it also pays the price of risk. It vulnerabilizes God. It seems to point into Gethsemane. For that reason the Christian conscience will always believe itself in trust with the risk of God as the very meaning of humankind. Therein is the meaning—and the music—of Christological faith.

NOTES

1. Raimundo Panikkar (b. 1918) is a figure of world renown in the mutual bearing of Buddhist, Hindu, and Christian discipleships. See *The Unknown Christ of Hinduism* (London, 1964; Maryknoll, NY: Orbis, 1981). Also, *Myth, Faith and Hermeneutics* (Maryknoll, NY: Orbis, 1970). And see below, n. 10.

2. Jacob Neusner, *Messiah in Context: Israel's History and Destiny in Formative Judaism* (Philadelphia: Fortress Press, 1984), 227. Gershom Scholem published his *The Messianic Idea in Israel and Other Essays* with Shocken Books in New York in 1971. Joseph Klausner wrote *The Messianic Ideal in Israel from the Beginning to the Completion of the Mishna*, trans. W. F. Stinespring (New York: Macmillan, 1955).

3. It is conspicuous both in Scholem and in Martin Buber. See the latter's *Two Types of Faith: A Study of the Inter-Penetration of Judaism and Christianity*, trans. N. P. Goldhawk (New York: Harper & Row, 1961).

4. Neusner, *Messiah*, preface and conclusion.

5. E.g., themes of "ransom," the servant "being despised," the given "cup," "the covenant in the blood." There is also an intimate relation between vocation as "servant" and as "son."

6. This aspect of the trauma of Jesus' disciples was studied significantly from within Islam by Muhammad Kamil Husain in the fifties. See his *City of Wrong: A Friday in Jerusalem*, English trans. by this writer (New York: Seabury, 1966).

7. Neusner, *Messiah*, 228.

8. The reference, seeing that the surah is early, may be to Muhammad's "burden" of anxiety about the genuineness of what he was receiving when it was new or about its continuity during agonizing pauses in its recipience. But the other meaning of a burdensome vocation throughout is real and deep.

9. Borrowing W. H. Vanstone's word is *Love's Endeavor, Love's Expense* (London: Darton, Longman and Todd, 1977), a rich exploration of faith in incarnate Word. Note especially the concluding poem, "Omnipotence."

10. In Jacob Neusner, ed., *Christian Revelation and World Religions* (London: Burns and Oates, 1967), 153. On the "rivers," see *The Myth of Christian Uniqueness*, ed. John Hick and Paul Knitter (Maryknoll, NY: Orbis Books, 1987), ix.

CHAPTER FOURTEEN

CHRISTOLOGY IN
CHRISTIAN-MUSLIM DIALOGUE

DAVID A. KERR

BRIDGE OR BARRIER?

Is Christology a fit subject for Christian-Muslim dialogue? The long history of Christian-Muslim encounter has seen Christology as a primary issue of controversy, often the subject of acrimonious debate, rarely productive of interreligious understanding. The problematic can be traced to the texts of Christian and Muslim sacred scriptures, the New Testament and the Qur'an. Their respective testimonies to Jesus' prophethood entail differentiated witness of his relationship to God and his place in the history of divine guidance/salvation.

The Qur'an upholds Jesus Son of Mary (*īsā ibn mariam*) as a true prophet and messenger of God, bearer of the gospel (*al-injīl*) that brought guidance and admonition to the children of Israel (*banū isrā'īl*). His life is said to have been confirmed by the Holy Spirit, as evidenced in the miracles of his birth and healing ministry. He is acknowledged, with his mother, as a sign (*aya*; 23:50) of God's peace (*salām*) and mercy (*rahma*), and is ennobled with several names of honor—the most important among them being the Messiah (*al-masīh*), God's "word [*kalima*] which He bestowed on Mary, and a spirit [*rūh*] proceeding from Him" (4:171).[1] As Jesus is said to have confirmed "the Law [*al-tawrā*] which came before me," so the Qur'an testifies that he gave "glad tidings of an apostle to come after me, whose name shall be Ahmad" (61:6).[2] To his enemies' claim to have killed him by crucifixion, the Qur'an retorts with the charge of disbelief (*kufr*), denying their boast with the proclamation that "God raised him up unto Himself" (4:159). Looking beyond the end of Jesus' earthly ministry, the Qur'an affirms that "on the Day of Judgment he will be a witness [*shahīd*] against them" (4:159)—i.e., against "the People of the Book" (*ahl al-kitāb*) who indulge in the conjectures of human doubt (4:157) in preference to "the statement of truth" (19:34) with which the Qur'an confirms Jesus as prophet in historical and eschatological perspectives: "Peace be upon me the day I was born, the day I die, and the day that I shall be raised up to life." (19:33).

The Qur'an's affirmation in these terms of Jesus' prophethood continues with a rebuke of Christians for some of the claims they make of him. The New Testament acclamation of his being "yea . . . much more than a prophet" (Matt. 11:9; Luke 7:26) is met by the qur'anic declaration that "the Messiah, Jesus Son of Mary, was [no more than] an apostle of God" (4:171). The doctrine of incarnation finds no haven in qur'anic scripture, which interprets Jesus' miraculous birth (without fatherly participation) as an analogue of the creation of Adam—in each case the power of God's creative command "be and it is" (*kun fa yakun*) being evidenced in human lives (3:59), as it manifests itself in the myriad signs of nature.[3] Though Jesus and his mother were untouched by sin,[4] the Qur'an insists that they were fully human: "They had both to eat their [daily] food" (5:78).

Appealing to Christians, therefore, the Qur'an urges that they "say not 'three' " (4:171). "Will ye worship besides God something which hath no power either to harm or benefit you? . . . Exceed not in your religion the bounds [of what is proper], trespassing beyond the truth, nor follow the vain desires of people who went wrong in times gone by—who misled many, and strayed [themselves] from the even Way" (5:79–80). At times this question is pressed polemically, as the Christians are identified with disbelievers, particularly in their refusal to recognize the validity of Muḥammad's prophethood (5:84). Yet the Qur'an also addresses itself in charity to Christians, seeing them as "nearest in love to the believers" (5:85). As "People of the Book," they are to be invited "to the way of the Lord with wisdom and beautiful preaching," to be argued with "in ways that are best and most gracious" (16:125).

The Qur'an adopts a sort of dialectical approach to Christianity (a term it never uses) around the antitheses of affirmation and negation. By holding these polarities in tension the Qur'an establishes a dialogue with Christians, the theological significance of which is not bound by considerations of historical context. Although the word *dialogue* nowhere occurs in the Qur'an, the dialogical spirit of its attitude to Christians is expressed in the verse much quoted by Muslim proponents of the art: "Say: 'O People of the Book! Come to common terms as between us and you: that we worship none but God; that we associate no partners with Him; that we erect not for ourselves lords and patrons other than God.' If they turn back, say ye: 'Bear witness that we are Muslims [bowing to God's Will]' " (3:64).

Modern Christian studies of this qur'anic material have largely been undertaken by Western scholars, who have mainly adopted a historical or historical-critical approach to issues of exegesis that is taken as a precondition of scholarly dialogue.[5] Other Western Christian studies attempt to interpret the qur'anic material by dialogical hermeneutics that aspire to what has been termed a "community of truth."[6] Reference to some of these works will be made later.

It is important to give attention to the less well-known attempts by modern Muslim writers to interpret the life of Jesus by scholarly disciplines, through the medium of the Arabic language. A recently published annotated guide, *Works about Christianity by Egyptian Muslim Authors (1940–1980)*, includes information about several interesting biographical studies of Jesus.[7] Comparison of four of the most important of these studies will reveal the range of Muslim approaches to the interpretation of Jesus' life and ministry.

ʿAbd al-Ḥamīd Gūdah al-Saḥḥār's 1951 account, *The Messiah, Jesus the Son of Mary*,[8] shows an empathy with the New Testament record of Jesus' moral and spiritual teaching and seeks to harmonize the historical events of Jesus' life with the qur'anic data. Al-Saḥḥār thus denies that Jesus died at the crucifixion and, as with much of post-qur'anic Islamic tradition, has Judas Iscariot die in his stead.

More famous is the work of one of Egypt's leading novelists, ʿAbbās Maḥmūd al-ʿAqqād. His *The Genius of Christ*,[9] first published in 1953, incorporates archeological and other historical evidence and includes, in its second edition (1958), material from the Dead Sea Scrolls. On this basis he offers a penetrating contextualization of Jesus' moral teaching, especially as communicated through parables. However, he sets his discussion of the crucifixion in the context not of history but of Muslim faith, leaving ambiguous the historicity of the event.

The same is true of Muḥammad Kāmil Ḥusayn's *City of Wrong: A Friday in Jerusalem* (1954),[10] which explores reflectively what may have gone through the minds of those who witnessed the mystery of the end of Jesus' earthly ministry: Jewry, the disciples, and the Romans. Although this work is about the human conscience more than the life of Jesus, it brilliantly illustrates how the subject matter of Jesus' ministry—particularly the Sermon on the Mount—can provoke Muslim reflection into the moral and psychological condition of humankind.

A more recent study is that of Fatḥī ʿUthmān, *With the Messiah in the Four Gospels* (1961),[11] which deals positively with Jesus as a moral teacher and guide, using much of the New Testament material as evidence. Here again is a firm rejection of the historicity of the crucifixion, and with it of Christian understandings of incarnation and redemption. ʿUthmān also emphasizes the problem of Christian nonrecognition of Muḥammad's prophethood as an issue that needs to be addressed in dialogue; in Muslim perspective, he argues, it is an inalienable part of the meaning of Jesus' message and ministry.

These scholarly writings about Jesus—Christian studies of the Qur'an and Muslim reflections on biblical witness—point to Christology as a subject that invites Christian-Muslim dialogue. The writings may even serve as bridges for dialogue. But important evidence warns that they do not necessarily make for easier dialogue on the topic than in the past. The 1977 Islamo-Christian Congress in Cordoba, Spain, brought together a group of Spanish Christians and North African Muslims for discussion about Jesus and Muḥammad, only to find that their dialogue was seriously impeded by the different theological perspectives that they brought to the founders of their two religions. This was a reminder of the degree to which Christian-Muslim dialogue may be an "opposition of similarities"[12]—i.e., concepts or persons that Christians and Muslims appear to share may actually mean very different things in the distinct integrities of two religions that have evolved in historical, social, and cultural competition with one another.

Aware of this, the Austrian Muslim intellectual Smail Balic, himself an advocate of Muslim-Christian dialogue with "common ethico-social and religious objectives," argues that Christology should be put aside because Islamic meanings of Christ are quite different from those of Christian theological confession. There can be nothing theological about Jesus, he argues, because "Islam rules out any incursion of the human into the sphere of the divine." While the Qur'an elevates Jesus above other mortals, he remains no more than "a subject of the history of prophets" by which God guided humankind until revelation was sealed by the final prophet, Muḥammad. Balic sees the stories of previous prophets, including Jesus, containing much that is of value for ethical emulation; but, he argues, "they have no direct function in the active faith of Muslims." All this he contrasts to what he regards as Christian theology's concern for "a personal union between God and man," particularly in Jesus, and concludes: "No practical results are likely to come from Muslim-Christian dialogue in regard to Christ."[13]

The Second Vatican Council recognized Islamic reverence for Jesus and his mother as one of the reasons why "the Church also has a high regard for the Muslims," and therefore urged that "a sincere effort be made to achieve mutual understanding . . . to preserve and promote peace, liberty, social justice and moral values." However, the postconciliar *Guidelines for Dialogue between Christians and Muslims*, issued by the Pontifical Council for Interreligious Dialogue, is cautious when it addresses the subject of Christology: it recognizes with "joy" the "position of greatness and privilege granted to Jesus by the Qur'an," while drawing attention to what are judged to be "fundamental differences which separate Muslim belief from Christian belief in Jesus as Son of God and God Himself."[14]

FOUR MUSLIM WRITERS IN THE WEST

We examine now the writings of four Muslims living in the West, each of whom has written about Jesus out of his experience of Muslim-Christian dialogue.

Isma'īl al-Fārūqī

The work of Isma'īl Rājī al-Fārūqī (d. 1986), Palestinian emigré to the United States, includes a serious attempt to construct a systematic evaluation of Christianity in relation to Islam.[15] Approaching his topic through historical-critical analysis, he seeks to distinguish the Jesus of the essence of Christianity from the variety of cultural Christianizations of his life and ministry that have evolved in the history of Western (i.e., non-Semitic) Christianity. Jesus is axiomatically a preacher of monotheism and of universal ethical values. His person and message are inseparable, for he modeled in life what he preached. The essence of both comprises the highest moral values of truthfulness, chastity and charity, which together make for peace in the spiritual sense that Jesus intended when he spoke of the kingdom of God: not a political goal nor an eschatological hope, but a life attuned to God's will here and now. His lived message was world-denying only in the conditional sense of opposition to the tragic human temptation to espouse the lower values of transient creation. Creation, al-Fārūqī argues, is not inherently evil, nor human nature sinful. The possibility of peace is demonstrated in the life Jesus lived, showing others how to conduct themselves in relation to the world. This, according to al-Fārūqī, is the meaning of redemption: not something achieved vicariously by a single act in Jesus' life, be it his coming into the world or his death, but his message, which, as he lived it, provided a method of redemption by which human beings are able to realize the grace God has invested in them. "The holy of holies of Christianity," al-Fārūqī writes, "namely, the ethical teaching of Jesus, his world view, his realization of the tragic nature of human existence, that is to say, of the conflict between values which is innate in the very nature of reality, and his attempt at solving that conflict in an exemplary manner in his own life, which is what constitutes his redemptiveness—all this is substantially there, already given in the few genuine statements, anecdotes, and deeds of his life, in the purified Christianity we have described."[16]

These redemptive principles, al-Fārūqī argues, were "transvalued" in the process of Christianity's Western Christianization, with the result that serious cultural distortions obscured the essence of Jesus' message and meaning. At the level of ethics, extreme asceticism robbed Christianity of its balanced relationship with nature, and the vacuum was filled by an institutional exclusivism that tied religious values to citizenship of the Christian empire and the established church. The essential rationalism of Jesus' message was obfuscated by Greco-Roman mysticism that turned Jesus into a divinity and invented a "saviorism" that is tantamount to a moral disqualification of humanity ("peccatism"). "Western Christianity," al-Fārūqī concludes, "deprives man of his freedom, of his responsibility, of his self-respect."[17]

Al-Fārūqī contrasts the Western transvaluation of Christianity against what he calls "the Arab spirit," which had no moral or spiritual difficulty in accepting "the grace of Jesus' teaching." This spirit he identifies with the earliest Palestinian Arab Christians, known in later church history as Ebionites—"from a Hebrew word which means poor; and 'poor' was a name applied to the early Christians, especially in the land of Jesus . . . to point to their social status as well as to their dedication, since a good number of these first converts chose poverty as a moral purification enjoined by Jesus himself."[18] These were the exemplaries of the Arab spirit of pure Christianity, al-Fārūqī opines; he applauds their resistance to Western Christianization as the sole means by which the legacy of Jesus was preserved until the advent of Islam, which "welcomed to its bosom the fairest flowers of Christianity . . . [who] dedicate[d] to it [i.e., Islam] the whole fruit of their genius."[19]

Al-Fārūqī's criticism of Western Christianity is reminiscent of the argument of the tenth-century Persian rationalist, ethicist, and philosopher ʿAbd al-Jabbār, who argued that Christianity had been Romanized rather than Rome Christianized.[20] Al-Fārūqī thus stands in an identifiable tradition of Islamic analysis of Christianity, and it is important to note how closely his ideas echo elements of early twentieth-century German historical criticism, notably the work of Adolf von Harnack and later of Adolf Schlatter. Both Harnack and Schlatter drew attention to the significance of possible Jewish-Christian influence on Muḥammad and the Qur'an and suggested that Islam may be seen as the historical transformation of Jewish Christianity.[21] Though al-Fārūqī's writing does not admit direct connection with this school of German criticism, the notes to the chapter of his work summarized here indicate the extent of his reading in Christian dogmatic history and evidence the fact that his views were formed in close intellectual dialogue with currents of modern Christian thought.

ʿAlī Merad

A very different study of Jesus comes to us through the pen of ʿAlī Merad, an Algerian scholar living in France, where, in his student days, he fell within the intellectual circle of Louis Massignon (d. 1962). Massignon's contribution to Islamic study and the intellectual-spiritual underpinning of Christian-Muslim dialogue cannot be overestimated.[22] Shortly after the Second Vatican Council declared its respect for Muslims, Merad was invited to address the Pontifical Institute of Arabic and Islamic Studies on the subject of Christ according to the Qur'an.[23]

In contrast to both Balic and al-Fārūqī, he offers us a remarkable analysis of the qur'anic portrait of Jesus as a theomorphic being—neither God nor angel (qur'anic negations that Merad treats as literal and categoric), nor yet an ordinary mortal. He notes that the Qur'an nowhere applies to Jesus the Arabic term *bashar*, meaning "earthly, mortal being," and insists that the term *'abd*—by which the Qur'an introduces Jesus' life and ministry in his miraculous cradle speech[24]—"expresses not the notion of 'humanity' but of service to God."

Within this perspective of obedience, Merad explores the qur'anic meaning of two of the terms by which Jesus is ennobled among the prophets—as God's word (*kalima*) and spirit (*rūḥ*). These he interprets as actual attributes of Jesus, not merely reminders of the efficacy of God's command (*amr*) in Jesus' birth and miracles. "The *kalima* should be understood in the sense of the object itself of the good tidings"; while the term *rūḥ*, if obscure of meaning, as applied to Jesus suggests "a spiritual nature infinitely more eminent than ordinary natures," indicating "a special relation to the person of God."

On qur'anic grounds, therefore, Merad does not hesitate to recognize in Jesus "an exceptional nature" or to speak of him as a prophet of "surpassing dignity." Although this remains short of "a sharing in the divine essence, something which is incompatible with the Muslim conception of pure unitarianism (*tawḥīd*)," Merad nevertheless insists on his judgment that "this Qur'anic exaltation of Christ can . . . be interpreted as a form of glorification of the whole human race."

Merad does not explain how Jesus' glorification comprehends humanity as a whole. The ambiguity between what is exceptional of Jesus and general of humankind seems to be resolved solely in the belief that the "supreme grace of God," which is explicitly evident in Jesus, is inherent, or at least potential, in every human being. This supposition is strengthened by Merad's interpretation of the crucifixion. Denial of Jesus' death he takes to be both the literal and logical meaning of the

Qur'an. "The elevation of Christ to heaven is a gratuitous act of the Almighty, who is free to act as he wills in his creation." This is but one way, argues Merad, in which the prophets as a whole "affirm a sort of 'custom of God' (*sunnat allāh*), that of the final triumph of faith over the forces of evil and adversity." The Christian understanding of the Passion implies to Merad that God had failed, whereas he interprets the Qur'an to mean that "God does not abandon his own." God's victory therefore is not won by an act of redemption, either in the general Christian sense or in the sense suggested by al-Fārūqī. Rather, it comes about through the hope in God that Jesus' earthly end invokes. Human sharing in this hope, exemplified in Jesus, is what makes possible humanity's "supreme dignity, its consummation."

Maḥmoud Ayoub

A Lebanese scholar of North American citizenship, Maḥmoud Ayoub follows a line of thought comparable to Merad's. In an interesting pair of articles he provides a scholarly review of Islamic Christology based on the history of Qur'an commentary among both Shīʻī and Sunnī exegetes.[25] He agrees with Merad in interpreting the qur'anic portrait of Jesus as one that "denies the divinity of Christ, but without denying his special humanity." In contrast to Merad, he does not interpret the Qur'an as categorically denying the historicity of Jesus' death by crucifixion, though with Merad he sees the focus of the Qur'an as pointing to something other than the event itself. The Qur'an, Ayoub suggests, is denying the ability of the Jews, representing humanity as a whole, to defeat God's will, which was embodied in the person of Jesus as God's *kalima* and *ruḥ*. "The claim of humanity (here exemplified in the Jewish society of Christ's earthly existence) to have this power against God can only be an illusion." The Qur'an, he concludes, passes "an accusation or judgment against the human sin of pride and ignorance."

Ayoub goes beyond Merad in accepting the concept of redemption, perhaps because there is in the Shīʻī interpretation of Islam an understanding of the purposive value of human suffering. This is what Ayoub means by redemption, which he sees as a motif running throughout the history of religions, evidencing a profound "religiousness . . . both ancient and universal."[26] He explains it as "the affirmation of life in the face of death," which takes many different forms from ancient Mesopotamia (Tammuz), through the Hebrew prophets (the servant of the Lord), to the "crucified Christ," and on to suffering of Ḥusayn's martyrdom at Karbala. The suffering of these persons of faith finds redemptive efficacy as they are remembered by later generations of faithful and their struggles are emulated in the lives of others who strive for justice and peace. In this analysis Jesus is not the unique means of redemption, but a convincing demonstration of its universal reality.

ḤASAN ASKARI

A fourth example of contemporary Muslim Christological reflection, born of dialogue with Christians, is found in the writing of Ḥasan Askari, an Indian by birth who has resided for many years in England. His attachment to Jesus is both qur'anic and biblical, in the latter case centering upon the Sermon on the Mount.[27] Askari's guiding thought about the meaning of Jesus, however, is taken from the qur'anic specification of his being a sign (*aya*).[28] Yet, as Askari observes, Jesus is unlike any other sign of which the Qur'an speaks:

> *The heavens and the earth, the day and night, the sun and moon, thunder and lightening, life and death, the different stages of man's life, his mating and his food, his cattle and his children, the early hours of the morning, the dead and still nights, the winter and summer, the dry and dusty earth, the refreshing and life-giving rain, the ships sailing amidst vast waters, the storm and the safe approach to the shore.*

Jesus, Askari emphasizes, is a sign of a different order to those of nature; he signifies the relationship between God and humanity.

Askari speaks in voice similar to Merad's and Ayoub's, but his reflection on the efficacy of Christ's sign is differently nuanced. "The Sign refers to how ambiguous and how difficult is the sphere of this relationship, how deeply man can deceive himself in the name of God, how truth could be used to destroy truth, how the most elaborate and confident theologies could become a wall between God and man."

One might be excused the thought that Askari's critique of religion, theology, and doctrine owes something to his acquaintance with the reformation tradition of Christian thought and modern secularism. More direct, however, is his debt to mysticism, both Islamic and Christian, with its radical awareness of the unknowableness and hiddenness of God, before which reality humankind can only bow in humility and silence. Askari's mistrust of doctrine expresses itself in a preference for the symbolic, and in Jesus he sees the symbolization of the dialogical way in which God communicates with humanity. God is hidden and manifest, silent and listening, equally as God acts and speaks. Human speech should reciprocally be infused with silence and prayer. In this way the Word of God and the human word maintain their "dialogical character," symbolized in Jesus, in whom "the Person is the Word."

Jesus symbolizes the dialogical character of divine-human relationship; Askari also sees this symbol as one that "liberates man from the dead circle of monological religion and restores unto him his genuine dialogical existence." In this regard Askari directs his argument against secularism as much as religion, interpreting the symbol of Jesus as a judgment against the tyranny of modern communication, which, in the age of cybernetics, speaks in "an imperative mood." The cure against the resultant human despair that marks the twentieth-century lies, Askari argues, in "inter-religious dialogue [that] is therefore urgent and imperative."

In this regard he sees Muslims and Christians as bearing a responsibility second to none, because the Qur'an binds them "fundamentally [in] a dialogical relationship." Once again Jesus is the common sign of this relationship, present to Christians and Muslims not in creed, but as the effective sign of the Word of God that "stands between." Askari interprets this as a dialectic between Christianity's controlling concept of the Word as Person and Islam's prevailing perception of the Word as Book. "Their separateness," he contends, "does not denote two areas of conflicting truths, but a dialogical necessity." They function within a single complexity of faith as mutual correctives: "When the Qur'an rejects the incarnation of God in Christ, it corrects the idolatry of the Person as Word of God, and this it does by establishing the supremacy of Speech [kalām] as Revelation. But when the Qur'an narrates the events of the life of Jesus, and refers to the manner in which the Jews had flouted the revealed truth of God, it invokes the supremacy of the Person of Christ as Word [*kalima*] of God."

PATTERNS OF CHRISTIAN-MUSLIM DIALOGUE ABOUT CHRIST

This survey of four contemporary Western examples of Muslim thought suggests that Christology has already become a fitting subject for Christian-Muslim dialogue. It would be wrong to imply that the work of individual scholars, often exploratory in nature and tentative in conclusion, immediately changes the mind-set of religious communities. Scholars who choose interreligious dialogue as the intellectual, moral, and spiritual context of their work are still relatively few in an age that gives so much lip service to interfaith communication. The influence of the Muslim scholars we have examined must not be overstated. But the fact that their Christological reflection arises from the context of Muslim-Christian dialogue must offset the pessimism of Smail Balic, for example, and balance his remark that "it is primarily Christian missionaries, or certain Orientalists who are either themselves theologians, or who are well disposed to Christian theology, who overestimate the role of Jesus in the Koran."[29] Possibilities for Christian-Muslim dialogue about Christological issues are available, and should not be avoided if they can be taken up in a manner that advances common Muslim-Christian reflection on the divine-human relationship.

For dialogue to be useful, however, its meaning must be clear. The literal meaning of the word *dialogue* is "talking through." Applied to religions, it challenges them to talk through barriers that are as much social, cultural, and political as they are theological. It searches for a new way of conceiving the relationship between religions: not to construe them only as rivals in a mundane, social understanding of religious history, but to envision the history of religions as facets of an inclusive movement of "human religiousness."[30] Within this vision, which is worldwide and history-long, it is possible to identify an Islamo-Christian history of complex interrelationship in which Christians and Muslims have struggled to express their common sense of divine-human relationship in diverse ways that reflect the cultural and social complexities in which they live. Dialogue has no interest in eradicating or syncretizing these differences, but seeks rather to relate them creatively to a larger complex, the recognition of which requires the dynamic interaction of its parts. To facilitate this goal dialogue tries to articulate new questions, and even if answers may not be forthcoming, it encourages shared reflection by people of faith from within the common human experience of what transcends or inheres their sense of existence and moral purpose.

Applied to Christological discussion between Muslims and Christians, Merad expresses this vision in the conclusion of his lecture to the Pontifical Institute of Arabic and Islamic Studies: "It would be presumptuous of a Muslim to believe that he possesses the whole truth with regard to Jesus, and to refuse to take the road opened to him by the Qur'an of seeking other testimonies." Merad's vision of mutual witness is inherent in each of the Muslim writers we have examined: al-Fārūqī gives priority to considerations of cultural history as it has affected Islamic and Christian testimonies of Jesus; Merad's own exegesis of the qur'anic verses on Jesus raises the issue of Muslim and Christian understanding of humanity, and of how God's Word can be said to be present in a person; Ayoub calls Christians and Muslims to think together about redemption as a category of "human religiousness," evident in the universal history of all religion; Askari posits a dialectical relationship between Islam and Christianity, the refusal of which seriously impairs both religions.

Christian respondents to these invitations to dialogue are not lacking, although they are relatively few in relation to the sum of Christian theologians. However, four areas of Christian engagement around Christological issues can be identified.

In the perspective of cultural analysis, Wilfred Cantwell Smith and Hans Küng are both interested in the Semitic character of the Islamic witness of Jesus as a dialogical balance to the Hellenistic and Latin molds of classical Christian Christologies. Küng, in his major exploration into interfaith dialogue, *Christianity and the World Religions*, relates this to Harnack's interest in Jewish-Christianity, which, he suggests in a piece of historical reconstruction not dissimilar to that of al-Fārūqī, was "renewed" through the emergence of Islam in the seventh century after having been suppressed during the formative period of Christian theology in Greco-Roman culture. Not to disqualify the latter (in the manner of al-Fārūqī), Küng nonetheless sees Islam as a necessary "corrective" that serves to remind Christianity of its own past and to enrich its future as, in dialogue with Islam, both religions challenge one another to "mutual transformation."[31] Smith's comparable analysis concludes with the provocative question: "Is it conceivable (theoretically conceivable) that if Jesus came back to earth today, he might perhaps say, 'The Muslims have understood me better than the Christians'?"[32]

To such a question Kenneth Cragg probably would answer no, on the evidence of his book *Jesus and the Muslim: An Exploration*.[33] Much as he is concerned to take the qur'anic witness of Jesus in all seriousness and to set Christological discussion within "a mutual theology," he treats the New Testament witness as normative, against which he cannot but see the qur'anic portrait of Jesus as somehow "attenuated." Yet his methodology for dialogue is not to add what he deems to be missing from the Muslim understanding, far less to coerce Muslim agreement with Christian beliefs; rather, he seeks to deepen mutual understanding of Jesus by encouraging Christians and Muslims to search more deeply into the heart of the matter—the meaning of God's presence in history, in persons, in suffering, which is inalienably the theme of both scriptures. Cragg believes the divinely revealed answers to shared human issues of faith are to be found as prophecy is deepened into messiahship, but he accepts that if this is indeed true, Muslims must find their qur'anic way of discerning it. This is not a counsel of scriptural isolation, however. While each religion has its proper autonomy, he argues, the autonomies of religions have but one humanity. Dialogue is a means of bringing our common humanity to bear on the hermeneutical responsibilities we have in relation to our respective scriptures, helping us to interpret them in loyalty to what Cragg terms "a community of truth."

ISSUES FOR THE FUTURE

If progress in Christian-Muslim dialogue around Christology is to be continued within this vision of a community of truth, what issues need to be addressed?

It is often observed that interreligious dialogue is best advanced where, as a "dialogue of life" or a "dialogue of deeds," priority is given to ethics. This is repeatedly the stance of Muslims themselves, as we are reminded by Smail Balic's negativism about Christological discussion, partly on grounds that it is unlikely to produce ethico-social results. We have seen that twentieth-century Egyptian Muslim writing about Jesus has focused on the ethical content of his ministry. This suggests that an ethical approach to Christology should be the first priority in Christian-Muslim dialogue, both to understand the core of Jesus' prophetic teaching as contained in, for example, the Sermon on the Mount, and to apply his ethical standards to issues of human life and society with which qur'anic ethics are also deeply concerned.

This could offer an alternative approach in Christian-Muslim dialogue to the issue that has caused so much misunderstanding and controversy in the past, namely, the personhood of Jesus himself. "Whom do you say that I am?" is a question that can only be addressed in the context of the character of Jesus' life and teaching, and their impact upon those who lived with him. This is one of the insights of Muḥammad Kāmil Ḥusayn's study *City of Wrong: A Friday in Jerusalem*. Ḥusayn leaves the question unanswered, but ʿAlī Merad's qur'anic reflections point us to "Christ's surpassing greatness." The challenge of wrestling with this question in dialogue raises three major issues: the need for mutual redefinition of terms such as "Word," "Spirit," "Son of Man," "Son of God," and "Messiah," bearing in mind the historical-cultural considerations raised by al-Fārūqī, Küng, and others; the need for mutual consideration of how these terms, applied to Jesus, help us understand the nature of his and all humanity in relation to ways in which the one God acts in and through human history; and by no means least, the need for further mutual discussion about hermeneutical methodologies for the interpretation of our scriptures in dialogue.[34]

The historicity of the crucifixion will expectedly remain an issue of differing opinions among Muslims themselves and between Muslims and Christians. This need not deter us from dialogue, however, since the process of dialogue is one of talking through, without presumption of eventual agreement. The reasons why Muslims deny the crucifixion perhaps have less to do with an historical event as such than with divine intention within and beyond the historical process. The reasons why

Christians affirm this particular event have less to do with a dead prophet than with the renewal of existence in this life and beyond death. Since neither of these themes is inimical to the other, it is possible that Christians and Muslims will come to understand more deeply the complementarity of their underlying convictions as they continue to wrestle with the divisive issue of the crucifixion in dialogue.

Christian and Muslim meanings of suffering perhaps bring us to the most profound concern of all religions. The struggle to find purposive value in the most wretched of human experiences, and to refuse to isolate it from the nature of divine-human relationship, is existential to the lives of Muslims and Christians as human beings. Answers to this mystery cannot be contained in mere doctrinal formulas that at best serve as repositories of earlier generations' tentative conclusions. For Christians and Muslims to remain open to each other as they wrestle with this issue may not resolve the philosophical, moral, and spiritual dilemmas of our human uncertainties, but it can help us to a self-critical reconsideration of our respective histories, without which the dialogical vision of a shared future would be irredeemably triumphalistic.

Dialogical discussion of these issues cannot be pursued within Christological parameters drawn solely by the Christian tradition. While this essay has drawn attention to the degree to which these are inclusive of some contemporary Muslim thought about Jesus, we must not neglect Fatḥī ʿUthmān's reminder that, in Muslim perspective, Jesus is inseparable from Muḥammad in a continuum of prophethood. "What say you of Muhammad?" is a question which is only beginning to surface in Christian-Muslim dialogue. The complex issues of history, ethics, and revelation that the question raises compel us to widen the framework of Christological reference.[35]

This inventory of issues for continuing Christological dialogue between Christians and Muslims sounds oppressively intellectualist. A dialogue of words needs neither defense nor apology. It finds legitimacy and empowerment, however, within a prior ethical commitment to a dialogue of deeds expressed in a dialogue of life. To challenge history is an act of revolution. It is as Muslims and Christians commit themselves to enacting this revolution in the lives they live, as witnesses of Jesus and Muḥammad, that the vision of an Islamo-Christian history becomes the reality within which their intellectual task can be sustained.

Human speech, Askari reminds us, should begin in the silent listening of prayer. In a brief excursus into the Hesychast (Christian Orthodox) and Ṣūfī traditions, Seyyid Hossein Naṣr commends prayer as the deepest type of dialogue, a "dialogue of the spirit." He reflects on the significance of what is known in the Christian tradition as the Jesus Prayer, which find its equivalent in the Ṣūfi prayer of the heart. "More than ever before what matters is the prayer of the heart which has been miraculously preserved to this day in the Orthodox tradition while it continues as the central practice of Sufis throughout the Islamic world. To understand the significance of this prayer . . . is to grasp the profound inner resemblances between Christian and Islamic spirituality."[36]

Christology raises profound and hopeful issues for Muslim and Christians alike. If hopes are to be realized, and dialogical relationships deepened, it will be primarily through the power of prayer that Christian-Muslim Christological discussion may befit God's service and glory.

NOTES

1. Qur'anic quotations are taken from A. Yusuf Ali, *The Holy Qur'an: Text, Translation and Commentary* (Islamic Foundation in cooperation with the Muslim Students' Association of the United States and Canada, 1975).

2. This is interpreted in Muslim commentary to refer to Muḥammad, in fulfillment of the New Testament Paraclete prophecy (John 14:16; 15:26; 16:7). Y. Ali notes: "Our doctors contend that Paracletos is a corrupt reading for Periclytos, and that in their original saying of Jesus there was a prophecy of our holy Prophet *Aḥmad* by name" (ibid., 1540). For further discussion of this issue, see W. Watt, "His name is Ahmad," *Early Islam: Collected Articles* (Edinburgh: University Press, 1990), 43–50.

3. See "Hasan Askari," below.

4. This belief may be inferred from the Qur'an (3:42), but is explicit in the *ḥadīth* (Traditions of the Prophet), where it is said: "There is none born among the offspring of Adam but Satan touches it. A child therefore cries loudly at the time of birth because of the touch of Satan, except Mary and her child." M. Khan, *The Translation of the Meanings of Ṣaḥīḥ al-Bukhārī* (Medina al-Munawwara: Islamic University, 1979).

5. The most important among these are: H. Michaud, *Jesus selon le Coran* (Neuchatel: Delachaux et Niestle, 1960); G. Parrinder, *Jesus in the Qur'an* (London:

Faber and Faber, 1965); H. Raisänen, *Das Koranische Jesusbild* (Helsinki: Finnische Gesellschaft fur Missiologie und Okumenik, 1971); N. Robinson, *Christ in Islam and Christianity: The Representation of Jesus in the Qur'an and the Classical Muslim Commentaries* (London: Macmillan, 1991); O. Schmann, *Der Christus die Muslime* (Gütersloh: Gerd Mohn, 1975); C. Schedl, *Muḥammad und Jesus* (Vienna: Herder, 1978).

6. This phrase is taken from A. K. Cragg, *Muḥammad and the Christian: A Question of Response* (London: Darton, Longman and Todd; Maryknoll, NY: Orbis Books, 1984). Cragg applies this vision in *Jesus and the Muslim: An Exploration* (London: George Allen and Unwin, 1985). Cf. M. Hayek, *Le Christ de l'Islam* (Paris: Seuil, 1959).

7. H. Goddard in *The Muslim World: A Journal Devoted to the Study of Islam and of Christian-Muslim Relationships in Past and Present* (Duncan Black Macdonald Center at Hartford Seminary) 70, no. 2 (April 1980): 251–77.

8. ʿAbd al-Ḥamīd Gūdah al-Saḥḥār, *Al-Masīḥ ʿĪsā ibn Mariam* (Cairo: Dar al-Misr li'l-Tiba'a, 1951).

9. ʿAbbās Maḥmūd al-ʿAqqād, *ʿAbqariyya al-Masīḥ*, 1st ed. (Cairo: Matba'a Dar Akhbar al-Yawm, 1953); *Ḥayāt al-Masīḥ*, 2d ed. (Cairo: Dar al-Hilal, 1958).

10. Muḥammad Kamil Husayn, *Qarya Zalīma* (Cairo: Maktaba al-Nahda al-Misriyya, 1954). Trans. A. K. Cragg as *City of Wrong: A Friday in Jerusalem* (Amsterdam: Djambatan, 1959; New York: Seabury Press, 1966).

11. Fatḥī ʿUthmān, *Ma'a al-Masīḥ fi'l-Anājīl al-Arba'a* (Cairo: Maktaba Waḥba, 1961; al-Dār al-Qawmiyya li'l-Tiba'a wa'l-Nashr, 1966).

12. This phrase is borrowed from C. Adams, "Islam and Christianity: The Opposition of Similarities," in *Logos Islamikos*, ed. A. Savory and D. Agius (Toronto: Pontifical Institute of Medieval Studies, 1984), 287–306.

13. S. Balic, "The image of Jesus in contemporary Islamic Theology," in *We Believe in One God*, ed. A. Schimmel and A. Falaturi (New York: Seabury Press, 1979), 1–8.

14. M. Borrmans, *Guidelines for Dialogue between Christians and Muslims*, trans. R. Speight (New York: Paulist Press, 1990), 54.

15. The following summary is based on chap. 3 of *On Arabism: Urubah and Religion: A Study of the Fundamental Ideas of Arabism and of Islam as Its Highest Moment of Consciousness* (Amsterdam: Djambatan, 1962), 58–120.

16. Ibid., 69.

17. Ibid., 99.

18. Ibid., 101–2.

19. Ibid., 110.

20. S. Stern, "ʿAbd al-Jabbār's Account of How Christ's Religion was Falsified by the Adoption of Roman Customs," *Journal of Theological Studies* 19 (1968): 128–85.

21. A. von Harnack, *History of Dogma*, trans. from the 3d ed. by Neil Buchanan

(New York: Dover Publications, 1961), 287–317; N.B. 310: "Islam, as a religious system, is based partly on syncretistic Judaism (i.e., Jewish Christianity) . . . and without questioning Moḥammed's originality, can only be historically understood by taking this into account." A. Schlatter, "The Evolution of Jewish Christianity into Islam," *Evangelisches Missionsmagazin* (1918): 251–64. These sources are both quoted in H. Küng, *Christianity and the World Religions*, trans. P. Heinegg (London: Collins, 1987), 123–24.

22. Y. Moubarac, *Recherches sur la Pensée Chrétienne et l'Islam* (Beyrouth: Universite St. Joseph, 1977).

23. First published in French in *Revue de l'Occident Musulman et de la Mediterannee* 5 (1968): 79–94. Published in English in *Encounter: Documents for Muslim-Christian Understanding* (Rome) 69 (November 1980): 1–17.

24. "He said: 'I am indeed a servant ['*abd*] of God: He hath given me revelation and made me a prophet" (19:30).

25. "Towards an Islamic Christology, I: An image of Jesus in Early Shi'i Muslim Literature," *Muslim World* 66 (1976): 163–88; "Towards an Islamic Christology, II: The Death of Jesus, Reality or Delusion," *Muslim World* 70 (1980): 91–121.

26. M. Ayoub, *Redemptive Suffering in Islam: A Study of the Devotional Aspects of 'Ashura' in Twelver Shi'ism* (The Hague: Mouton, 1978), 231.

27. See "Sermon on the Mount" in H. Askari, *Spiritual Quest: An Inter-Religious Dimension* (Pudsey, West Yorkshire: Seven Mirrors, 1991), 89–97.

28. H. Askari, "Dialogical Relationship between Christianity and Islam," *Journal of Ecumenical Studies* (Philadelphia) 9, no. 3 (1972). See also H. Askari, *Inter-Religion: A Collection of Essays* (Aligarh: Printwell, 1977), 62–71.

29. Balic, "Image of Jesus," 3. A candidate for Balic's criticism would be Robert C. Zaehner, one-time Spalding Professor of Eastern Religions and Ethics, All Souls College, Oxford (d. 1974), whose audacious essay on Christ in the Qur'an (*At Sundry Times* [London: Faber and Faber, 1958], 195–217) reinterprets the grammatical syntax of qur'anic statements about Jesus to harmonize them with orthodox (Catholic) doctrine in criticism of orthodox Muslim interpretation.

30. My argument at this point is indebted to the thought of Wilfred Cantwell Smith, particularly his essay "Muslim-Christian Interrelations Historically: An Interpretation," in his *On Understanding Islam: Selected Studies* (The Hague: Mouton, 1981), 247–64.

31. Küng, *Christianity*, 122–30.

32. Smith, "Understanding Islam," 260.

33. See n. 4.

34. Important work has begun in this regard, as recorded in the Muslim-Christian Research Group, *The Challenge of the Scriptures: The Bible and the Qur'an*, trans. S. Brown (Maryknoll, NY: Orbis Books, 1989).

CHAPTER FIFTEEN

THE MIRACLE OF JESUS: MUSLIM REFLECTIONS ON THE DIVINE WORD

MAHMOUD AYOUB

The human spirit in all its richness, its faith and hope, its love and creativity, is mirrored and indeed celebrated in the life of Jesus, who is "high honored in this and the next world" (Q. 3:45). [1] He was born in a lowly and lonely spot of God's earth, far from the power centers of this world and its empires. [2] Yet his miraculous birth was celebrated in heaven, announced by angels, and made the focus of human history. As we, Muslims and Christians, reflect on the life of Jesus and its meaning for our faith and history, we can now more than ever before strive together to hear the voice of God challenging us through our scriptures to a greater understanding of God's will for human creation.

Some of what I will say in these reflections will be controversial, at least to Muslim readers. However, I am motivated not by controversy for its own sake, but by two qur'anic challenges. The first calls us all, the people of the Book, to come together to a common resolve that we worship God alone. The challenge is for us to achieve a consensus of faith and to remind ourselves, our nations, and our societies that our loyalty must be to God alone and not to any human-made institutions: "Say, 'O people of the Book, come to common terms as between us and you: that we worship none but God; that we associate no partners with him; that we erect not for ourselves Lords and patrons other than God' " (Q. 3:64). [3]

The second qur'anic challenge is that of the infinity and openness of God's Word, which transcends human comprehension and yet demands that it be interiorized and understood anew by the people of faith in every age. The Qur'an declares: "Were all the trees of the earth pens and the ocean (ink) supplemented by yet seven oceans like it, the words of God would not be exhausted" (Q. 31:27).

Before reflecting on the miracle of Jesus in our two faith traditions, clarification of the meaning of the word for "miracle" in the Qur'an and the qur'anic view of miracles may be helpful. "Miracle" in the Qur'an is *ayah*, that is, a divine sign. A miracle may therefore be a universal divine sign in the creation, such as the day and night and the creation of heaven and earth, the winds that carry rain clouds by means of which God revives the earth, after its death, and the seas that carry ships laden with goods for the benefit of humankind (Q. 2:164).[4] Another more inclusive meaning of the word *ayah* or sign is the Word of God itself. It is either the Word revealed to humankind with a challenge that it be accepted and lived by, or the creative word of command (*amr*). This is the great miracle of creation and revelation.

Early in Muslim history the concept of miracle took on important theological and political significance. Then the burden of proof of God's election of some faithful servants to be favored with the gift of prophethood or nearness to God fell not only on God, where it ought to be, but on human logic and rationality. Thus Muslims took it upon themselves to explain God's purposes. A miracle came to mean not a sign of God's infinite mercy and power, but an act or occurrence that violates the norms of the natural order and of which none but God and God's prophets are capable.

I argue that the qur'anic concept of miracle is far closer to the spirit of Islam, as an attitude of absolute surrender to God, than that which was evolved later by Muslim theologians. The Qur'an makes frequent reference to miracles. But a miracle must have a purpose. Never in the Qur'an do we see a miracle simply as a show of power, even spiritual power; rather a miracle must speak to the situation of the people. When, for example, Abraham confronted a tyrannical king who thought of himself as God, Abraham manifested God's will and power by being thrown into a fire that God made "coolness and peace" for him (Q. 21:69). The purpose of the miracle is to show that God has power over nature as well as over human folly and arrogance.

The miracles ascribed to Moses in the Qur'an have a similar purpose and message. There again, a ruler of an admittedly great nation and home of an equally great civilization saw himself as God. The miracles of Moses were designed to show that God is Lord. Thus neither the magic nor the great civilization of Egypt would count for much before God. Indeed, the Qur'an states clearly that Moses was not sent expressly to free the children of Israel from Egypt, but primarily to call an arrogant king, Pharaoh, and his people to God.[5] This, moreover, was the mission of all the prophets of God according to the Qur'an.

Jesus lived at a time when science began to grow into a systematized discipline. He lived after the rise of Greek medicine and the development of scientific thinking through Greek philosophy, culminating in Plato, Aristotle, and their successors. He, furthermore, lived among a people who were struggling to formulate a universal eschatological worldview. Some, taking the early books of their scriptures literally, denied the hereafter and the resurrection. Hence, the miracles of Jesus were miracles having to do with life—its fullness, meaning, and purpose.

Jesus is himself a divine sign, one to be celebrated with joy, marvel, and faith. In the Qur'an as in the Gospel, the angels bring to Mary the glad tidings of a great miracle—the unique birth of a unique child, the "Word of God," the "son of the Most High" (Q. 3:45; Luke 1:32–33).

Both the Gospel of Luke and the Qur'an begin their account of Jesus' nativity with a genealogical narrative followed by a glorious annunciation to Mary of a miraculous child with a unique mission. In the Gospel of Luke, the angel says to her: "The Holy Spirit will come upon you, and the power of the Most High will overshadow you; therefore the child to be born will be called holy, the Son of God" (1:35). I will return to the significance of the epithet "Son of God" later.

In the qur'anic narrative the angel who appeared to Mary was sent to her by God. He was the angel of revelation. The same angel who brought the Word of God, the Qur'an, to Muhammad brought the Word of God, Jesus Christ, to Mary: "I am the messenger of your Lord," he said, "come to bestow upon you a pure child" (19:19).

We cannot fully appreciate the meaning of Jesus' birth without studying it in the context of the sanctified life of his mother. Mary was, according to the Qur'an, purified and chosen by God for God's special favor: "Remember when the angels said, 'O Mary, God has surely chosen you and purified you; He has chosen you above the women of humankind' " (3:42).[6] Only as an unblemished virgin could she serve as a receptacle of the divine Word. The parallel of Mary's sanctity and election with Muhammad's status as the recipient of the Word of God in Muslim piety deserves further study.

The Qur'an first came to Muhammad not in the humdrum of Mecca and Medina, but in the cave of Mount Hira', where the prophet was in seclusion, preparing his mind and soul for the awesome task of receiving and transmitting the Word of God to the world.[7] It was in the same solitude, in the "easterly place" where Mary secluded herself from her people, that the angel encountered her in a good, one might say handsome, human form.[8] According to tradition the angel Gabriel often appeared to Muhammad as a handsome man.[9] As the prophet in the cave of Hira' was bewildered, so was Mary. She was afraid. But the angel reassured her. The language in both the Gospel and Qur'an is one not of pure narrative, but of celebration. Surah 19, which recounts the birth of Jesus, has been one of the most popular and beloved surahs of the Qur'an.

The miracle of life that is Jesus unfolds further as a lifegiving and sanctifying divine force. When Mary conceived him, the Qur'an relates, she withdrew from her people. Was it only from a sense of embarrassment, bewilderment, or shame that she shunned human society? Might it also have been from a sense of gratitude for God's special favor that she wished for solitude to try to fathom the great mystery that enveloped her? The beautiful hymn of divine magnification (Luke 1:46–55) that Mary proclaimed in answer to the angel's annunciation expresses exultation and gratitude to God.

There in the place of her seclusion, according to commentators, the labors of childbirth brought her to a dried-up stump of a palm tree, which God revived to bear fruit; commentators tell us that fruit was the best food for women suffering the pangs of childbirth.[10] As Mary struggled alone with her emotions and the travails of childbirth, a voice from beneath her called out, consoling and encouraging her. This voice is said by commentators to have been that of Jesus. He comforted his mother, saying, "Do not grieve for your Lord has made a brook pleasantly to run beneath you. Shake the palm tree, and it will drop ripe fruit down to you. Eat and drink and be consoled."[11]

The miracles that the Qur'an attributes to Jesus during his ministry are miracles of life and healing. Some are paralleled in nonbiblical traditions contemporary with the gospel records of Jesus' birth and infancy. Among these is the miracle of fashioning birds of clay and breathing life into them by God's permission. In the infancy Gospels this miracle is given as one of the child Jesus trying to impress his playmates.[12] In the Qur'an it is intended to show God's power as the Creator through the agency of the divine Word, Jesus. The Qur'an credits Jesus alone among the prophets with raising the dead, giving sight to those born blind (as the Arabic word *akmah* indicates), and healing the lepers and the sick.[13]

I do not advocate that we accept the theology of one tradition and reject that of the other. Rather, I wish to understand the meaning for our life of faith of the Qur'an's insistence that it confirms the scriptures that came before it, the Torah and the Gospel. This claim is based on the transcendent and timeless unity of the Word of God, as all scriptures come from one source: God.

"God brings you glad tidings of a word from Him whose name is Jesus Christ," the angels said to Mary (Q. 3:45). It is worth noting that the word *kalimah* is a feminine noun. The Qur'an is here speaking not of a name but of an actual being, of the Word of God manifested in human life and history. Is all this merely metaphorical, or even metaphysical? Or is there not a mystery far greater than we have been able to fathom for the last fourteen hundred years?

The verses describing Jesus in the Qur'an are not without mystery. They continue to challenge both Muslims and Christians to understand, however imperfectly, God's will for us as people of faith. They challenge us to affirm, or at least not to lose sight of, the humanity of Christ. "I am the worshipful servant of God. He gave me the Book, and made me a prophet." In fact, was not Christ's humanity and his servantship one of the greatest challenges to the church? The humanity of Christ was one of the original doctrines of the Christology of the church. It was frequently invoked against Gnostic, Docetic, and other heresies that threatened the integrity of the Christian faith. This doctrine, moreover, has continued to be the focus of the Christological debate, not only within the church but also between the church and the Muslim community. Muslims often remind Christians of the words of

Jesus according to the Fourth Gospel: "Go to my brethren and say to them, I am ascending to my Father and your Father, to my God and your God" (John 20:17).

Who then is Jesus, the miracle of life, of love, and of healing? He is the Word of God and the servant of God and the messenger of God. He is the Savior of us all, for what is salvation but healing? A savior is not simply one who dies for the sins of others, but also one who heals the sickness of the human soul; one who infuses life into dead spirits by his own life and spirit. The original meaning of salvation is to be healed, to be made wholesome, to be truly restored to life. This, according to the Qur'an, was the mission of Jesus.

Jesus' close proximity or nearness (*qurb*) to God is affirmed in the qur'anic insistence that Jesus did not die but was taken up to God and remains with God.[14] Hence, Jesus, who came to humanity as the Word of God, to heal and to save, to carry the process of divine revelation in human history further—to make things easy, to make things that were unlawful lawful (Q. 3:50)—subsists with God, awaiting a cosmic mission of healing and salvation. According to Islamic tradition, Jesus will come again and exercise his power of healing. He will forever destroy falsehood, as embodied in the Dajjal, the great falsifier, the anti-Christ. Then will God reign forever.

To return to the qur'anic objection to calling Jesus the "Son of God": the Qur'an criticizes Christians who attribute an offspring (*walad*) to God. Only once, to my knowledge, does the Qur'an use the word *ibn* (son), and there it uses it to chastise both the Jews and Christians—the Jews for saying, "Uzayr is the Son of God," and the Christians for saying, "Jesus is the Son of God."[15] *Ibn* has several meanings and connotations. A youth whom the Prophet brought up, Zayd B. Harithah, was called "the son, *ibn*, of the Messenger of God." The word son is generally used to express a relationship of love or care and not necessarily a physical or blood relationship.

Christians would certainly agree with Muslims that Jesus is not an offspring by generation, *walad*, of God, but that he is our brother, and the older son in the family of God of which we are all members. In this human family are individuals and progenies chosen by God for a special mission.

The Qur'an presents us with the great challenge of seeing Jesus in this wider context of humanity's relationship with God. It states: "God chose Adam, Noah, the House of Abraham, and the House of Imran above all beings. They are of one progeny, following one another" (Q. 3:33–34). Jesus and his mother, as special members of this blessed progeny, symbolize the unity of the human family around the prophetic model. If all prophets are one family, then are we, their followers, not members of this family that God has favored and blessed?

If we celebrate with joy God's miracle in Jesus Christ, the Word of God, the words of the angels, "Peace on earth, and good will towards humankind," have a special meaning and relevance to our troubled world today. The miracle of Jesus, like the miracle of the Qur'an, is not a once-only event, but an everlasting source of blessing, guidance, and salvation.

NOTES

1. In this verse Jesus is described as *wajih*, meaning high-honored, notable, being in the forefront, in this context, among the peoples of this world and the denizens of the world to come. He is also one of the *muqarrabin*, meaning brought near both in intimacy and proximity to God.

2. While the Gospels stress the poor and humble circumstances of Jesus' birth, the Qur'an emphasizes Mary's loneliness and total dependence on God's succor. The nativity story in both scriptures, however, is one of celebration of a unique event of God's intervention in human history. If read carefully, the qur'anic and gospel accounts may be seen to complete and complement, rather than oppose or contradict, one another. See Matt. 1:18–2:11, Luke 1:26–2:20, and Q. 19:16–34.

3. This is one of several verses in the Qur'an where God directly enjoins the Prophet as well as the Muslim community to deal with the people of the Book on the basis of unity of faith in the one God and in the revealed books; see Q. 3:113–15 and especially Q. 29:46.

4. God's omnipotence and wisdom is a frequently recurring theme in the Qur'an.

5. See for example Q. 79:15–26.

6. For the significance of Mary's election, see my commentary on this verse in *The Qur'an and Its Interpreters*, vol. 2 (Albany: State University of New York Press, 1992).

7. In two of the three of the earliest surahs of the Qur'an the Prophet is

commanded to "recite," that is, publicly proclaim, and "warn." (See Q. 96:1–5 and Q. 74:1–2.) For the intensity of the experience of the encounter with the angel Gabriel, see *Mishkat al-Masabih*, translation with explanatory notes by James Robson, (Lahore: Sh. Muhammad Ashraf, 1975), 1252–53.

8. See Q. 19:16–17.

9. The angel Gabriel is said to have appeared at times to the Prophet in the guise of Dahya al-Kalbi, the most handsome young man of Makkah.

10. For example, see Ismai'il Ibn Umar Kathir's comments in *Tafsir al-Qur'an*, 6 vols., vol. 4 (Beirut: Dar al-Andalus, 1977), 449–51.

11. Ibid. See also Q. 19:24–26.

12. See the *Gospel of the Infancy of Jesus Christ* 15:1–6, in *The Lost Books of the Bible and the Forgotten Books of Eden* (New York: Meridian Books, 1974), 52–53.

13. See Q. 3:49 and Q. 5:113.

14. See Q. 3:54 and 4:157. For a detailed discussion of Muslim views of the death and ascension of Jesus to heaven, see my "Towards an Islamic Christology, II: The Death of Jesus, Reality or Delusion," *Muslim World* 70, no. 2 (April 1980): 91–121.

15. For a study of the terms *ibn* and *walad* see my "Jesus the Son of God: A Study of the Terms *Ibn* and *Walad* in the Qur'an and Exegetical Tradition," in a *Festschrift* in honor of Willem Bijlefeld (Gainesville: University of Florida Press, 1992).

CHAPTER SIXTEEN

CHRISTIAN SELF-CRITICISM IN THE LIGHT OF JUDAISM

HANS KÜNG

TRANSLATED BY KENNETH BREWER AND STEFFEN LÖSEL

David Flusser contends that Jews and Christians can meet one another comfortably and learn from one another in the discussion of the teachings of Jesus—but not in the discussion of Christology. Without underestimating the diverse traditions about Jesus within Christianity that are based on the Synoptic Gospels, he adds: "For many Christians, however, such discussion does not directly touch their central Christian experience and concern, even though it may prove helpful and strengthen their own belief. For them knowledge of the 'historical' Jewish Jesus is but a necessary frame for the center of their belief, namely, the metahistorical drama of Christianity."[1] By this metahistorical drama, Flusser means such concepts as the preexistence of Christ, his resurrection, his return to God, and his future second coming.

In fact, the preexistence and incarnation of Christ, as well as the doctrine of the Trinity, are considered to be the central dogmas of Christianity. We cannot evade these questions of Christian dogmatics, especially after the distinction made by Gotthold Ephraim Lessing between the "religion of Jesus" and the "Christian religion," as well as that by Martin Buber between the "faith of Jesus" and the "faith in Jesus." Indeed, many Jews approach the dialogue with Christians with the slogan, The faith *of* Jesus unites us; the faith *in* Jesus divides us.

CHRISTIAN SELF-CRITICISM

Admittedly, an ecumenical path toward peace with the other prophetic religions will be truly feasible only when it is linked with

Christian self-criticism—and that on the basis of the New Testament itself. Happily, signs of such self-criticism are evident in the life of the Christian churches.

We recall the 1980 statement of the German Catholic bishops that "certain Christian faith affirmations such as the 'same essence of the Son of God' [with God's self] appear to Jews as radically un-Jewish" because they seem "to contradict strict Monotheism absolutely." Previously, the guidelines and directives for carrying out the council's declaration (*Nostra aetate*, 1974) had urged understanding specifically on the issue of the incarnation: "In the same way, they [the Catholics] will strive to understand the difficulties the Jewish soul finds in connection with the mystery of the Incarnation precisely because of the Jewish stress on a high and pure concept of the divine transcendence."[2] Moreover, the 1990 European Protestant document *Declaration or the Encounter between Lutheran Christians and Jews*[3] underscores that the relationship between Christians and Jews is rooted "in the witness of the one God and his fidelity to his covenant, as it is handed down in the books of Holy Scripture (our Old Testament) which we share together."[4] Although the document does not deal directly with the issue of the Trinity, it stresses the following demand: "the indispensable requirement for our encounter is the readiness of Christians to listen to the witness of the Jews, to learn from their faith and life experience, and thereby to become aware of new aspects of the biblical tradition."[5]

In this matter one must strongly support all efforts aimed at something like a "Christian theology of Judaism." Clemens Thoma, one of the foremost Christian interpreters of the Jewish tradition, asserts:

> *A Christian theology of Judaism approaches and interprets with radical seriousness Judaism's functions as the origin of, contradiction to, and partnership with, the Christian churches. . . . It is a theology critical of the Church because and to the extent that it wishes to remind the Christian churches of Christianity's Jewish heritage and the Christian elements in Judaism, it must point out that ignorance of these facts has been partly responsible for superficial attitudes, confusion, and errors, today as in the past.*[6]

It is no secret that the classical Christian doctrine of the Trinity, with its distinctions within the Deity (three persons but one nature), is not intelligible either to Jew or to Muslim. Why, they ask, don't Christians simply abandon the claim to believe in the one God—a belief affirmed by Abraham as well as by Moses and Jesus—since they add to that unitary concept a second person and, indeed, three persons within the Godhead?

To brush aside this challenge as blindness or stubbornness, as has been done for centuries, is to overlook our own Christian problems. At least since the Enlightenment, the rise of historical-critical exegesis, and the subsequent development of critical analysis of Christian dogma, thoughtful Christians have raised similar issues. They recognize, along with Jews and Muslims, that the traditional Christian doctrine of God developed using concepts borrowed from the contemporary Syrian, Greek, and Latin culture. But in the present age these conceptual tools are often more misleading than illuminating. The Christian teaching about God, as classically formulated in the doctrine of the Trinity, is very complicated. It is a confusing word game with three "hypostases," "persons," or "*prosopa*"; two "processions" or "comings forth"; and four "relations" or "connections." And Christian theologians since Augustine have needed hundreds of pages to explain matters that seemed so simple to Paul and John.

Jews have said all along what Christian theologians prefer not to hear and still less to answer: What shall we do with all such dialectical, theological tricks with regard to the one God? Why and for what purpose is a distinction made between nature and person in the Godhead? Is not the God of the New Testament totally a unity, not divided this way or that: the One and Only? What actual differentiation can be made between Father, Son, and Spirit within the One-and-Only God that does not destroy the unity of God? Why claim any distinction between God as "Father" and God's nature, a distinction allegedly grounded in the subject itself? Is that still the New Testament message? Why add anything to the unity and uniqueness of God—anything that could only reduce or eliminate that unity and uniqueness?

Naturally the Jewish dialogue partners will want to know: What compelled such a complicated development of dogma in Christianity? Here I intend to sketch briefly—on the basis of my earlier presentations[7] and the recently researched materials in our institute[8]—how from the New Testament, i.e., the original Christian message, those "central Christian dogmas" can be made intelligible. At least I trust that these concepts may cease to appear to Jews as completely absurd or even blasphemous. In conversations with brothers and sisters from other religions everything depends on avoiding false confrontations.

It would be absurd from the Christian side to demand particularly from Jews, who are the preservers of the belief in one God, something radically un-Jewish or absolutely contradictory to strict monotheism. Have not Christians inherited from their Jewish leader the belief in the one and only God? An understanding of the Jewish soul and a listening ear for the witness of the Jews can become fruitful only if it leads Christians to reconsider their Jewish origins. In this respect the Christian theology of Judaism can be redefined along the lines of Clemens Thoma: "It is a theological attempt by Christians to point to and to present the consequences which result for Christianity from the fact that Jesus, his first disciples and the evangelists, were Jews and lived in Jewish surroundings."[9]

It is not possible here to present a detailed statement of the way in which Christian theology developed over the centuries in response to the conceptual worlds through which it passed. However, we will consider self-critically the issues of divine sonship, incarnation, and the Trinity—with special reference to the Jewish roots.

WHAT DOES IT MEAN TO SAY THAT GOD HAS A SON?

It is often not widely known among Jews, as well as among Muslims and sometimes even among Christians, that the word *Father* is used for God both in Judaism and in the Hebrew Bible.[10] Also in the Hebrew Bible the phrase "Son of God" is used for human beings, sometimes for the people of Israel[11] or for the Israelites as "Children of God"[12] and as "Sons of the living God."[13] But above all it is used for the king of Israel.[14]

The question now is, Did the Jew, Jesus of Nazareth, ever designate himself "Son of God"? Before answering this question it is important to remember that Jesus of Nazareth, like his Jewish contemporaries, was not committed to formulas and dogmas. One needs only to read the Synoptic Gospels to realize that Jesus neither engaged in deep speculations, as the Greek philosophers and the mystics did, nor did he deal with the complicated casuistry of debates about the Halakoth. He spoke in aphorisms, short stories, and parables from everyday life—all of which were normally intelligible and easy to remember. Generally he did not present his own person, his role, or status. His proclamation centered on God: "May his name be hallowed," "May his kingdom come," "May his will be done." Every person should fulfill God's will through the service of others. There were no secret revelations, no profound allegorical teachings with mysterious meanings. Jesus did not interrogate his contemporaries about true belief, orthodox confession, or the injunctions of the Halakah. What he hoped for was not theoretical reflection, but the practical decision to discipleship and orthopraxis in the radical sense of active love and concern.

Such preaching about God is certainly not unacceptable to Jews; it is not "radically un-Jewish." But how can it be made intelligible to Jews that this proclaimer of the Kingdom of God came to be called Son of God and even God? In the light of these circumstances is it any wonder that Jesus did not speak in the concepts of later theology and did not proclaim as a great mystery that God is one in nature but at the same time manifest in three persons, or that Jesus was the second divine person and had taken on a human nature? But now we must ask the constructive question: How is the relation of Jesus to God to be understood according to the New Testament? This is the basic Christological question (and in essence the trinitarian question).

On three points the sources are perfectly clear. First, Jesus himself spoke, prayed, struggled, and suffered out of an ultimately inexplicable experience of God, a sense of God's presence, yes, even a sense of unity with God as his father. Second, he did not, however, actually use the title Son of God himself. On this point historical-critical scholarship, whether Jewish or Christian, is in agreement. Third, his actual claims for himself exceeded those made for a prophet. Here is where the dispute between Jew and Christian begins. Jesus claimed for himself authority against the teaching and practice of the religious establishment; in effect, he claimed divine authority. One may judge this positively or negatively, but he claimed to be "more than Moses," "more than the prophets." He placed in question the absolutized temple as well as the absolutized Law, the holy traditions and regulations, the distinction between clean and unclean and between the righteous and the unrighteous. And he proclaimed this not for some day or some future, but for here and now. From this perspective it becomes understandable why he was executed.

But how is it to be explained that, despite his shameful death, there developed a Jesus movement, a faith in Jesus as God's Son? It must be remembered that it was only after his death and resurrection that the believing community used the title Son and Son of God for him. These experiences gave rise to the faith that he had not been left in death but that instead God had raised him into God's own eternal life. And this development should still be comprehensible for a contemporary Jew.

First of all, these events gave to Jews who had followed Jesus a practical reason and an inner logic why he who had called God his father without timidity would then also be called the Son by his believing followers. The proclamation about this God was now inseparably bound with the person Jesus. And the Father was no longer accessible without the Son. It was no longer the king of Israel who was God's son par excellence, but Jesus the Messiah. Second, it was easy for the followers of Jesus, as Jews, to think of his exaltation to God as analogous to the enthronement of the Israelite kings. According to Jewish tradition, the king was appointed Son of God at the moment of his accession to the throne. Similarly, the Crucified One was now appointed Son of God by his resurrection and exaltation. Ps. 2 reported such an enthronement ritual with the words, "You are my Son, today I have begotten you" (v. 2). Here "begetting" is a synonym for exaltation. There is no thought in this expression of a physical-sexual (or metaphysical) begetting in the sense of the Hellenistic sons of God anywhere in the New Testament!

Therefore, in one of the oldest and probably pre-Pauline faith confessions, found in the introductory verses of the letter to the Romans, it can be said that Jesus Christ was "designated Son of God in power according to the Spirit of holiness by his resurrection from the dead." Consequently Ps. 2, which denotes the accession to the throne, can be picked up in the New Testament and applied to Jesus: "He [God] said to me [according to Ps. 2:7, to the king, the anointed; according to Acts 13:33, however, to Jesus], 'you are my Son, today I have begotten you.' " And how did this transference take place? Because here in the New Testament traditional Jewish thinking is manifest: Jesus is begotten as king, begotten as Anointed One (= Messiah = Christ), begotten as representative and Son, and this event happens "today," i.e., in the present. Clearly by this passage Acts does not refer to the Christmas story, but rather to Easter; not the Feast of the Incarnation is meant, but rather the resurrection and exaltation of Jesus. In the same way Ps. 110:1 was transferred in the New Testament from the priestly king of Israel to Jesus exalted to God in order to manifest him as Son of God: "The Lord said to my Lord, 'Sit at my right hand.' "[15]

What then is meant by the divine sonship in the original Jewish sense and, hence, also in the New Testament? Without question it is not a descent, but the appointment to a position of authority and power in the Hebraic sense found in the Old Testament. It is not a physical divine sonship, as many Jews suppose today and rightfully reject, but an election and empowerment of Jesus by God entirely in the sense of the Hebrew Bible. Against such an understanding of divine sonship hardly any objection can be raised from the standpoint of Jewish belief in one God: the original Jewish followers of Jesus could very well have held such a belief. In fact there is no fundamental clash here with modern Jewish monotheism.

But this understanding was not the end of the story. The original dispute between Jews and Christians about Jesus of Nazareth was followed later among Gentile Christians with Hellenistic thought patterns by the dogmatic elevation of Jesus as Son of God into full equality with God, so that even his formal adoration by Christians became possible. The fourth-century dogmatic developments at the Council of Nicea and Chalcedon produced the classic trinitarian formulations: Jesus was "of the same nature as the Father" and "one God in three persons." To Jews of that day this appeared flatly to contradict the basic commandment, "No God beside the one true God." And the Muslims, who emerged in the seventh century, had exactly the same reaction. Would the Aramaic-speaking Jewish-Christians of Jerusalem even have understood such doctrines?

After the first century, the Jewish-Christians, who had moved away to the east, ceased being a corrective against the Western-

Hellenistic speculation and the Roman organizing tendency in the church. Further developments made it all the easier for the church to view itself as the only legitimate people of God, the ones who had inherited the promises to Israel. Among those developments were the reduction of the Jewish people themselves to an insignificant group (at least in the West) after the total destruction of Jerusalem (135) and their expulsion from Palestine. At the same time the church of the Gentiles, despite oppression, constantly gained power during the third century. So with Constantine's change in attitude at the beginning of the fourth century, the church became and empire church. Increasingly it understood itself as the only "true" Israel, the "new" Israel, the "spiritual" Israel, the group that believed itself to have preserved the great intentions of Israel's prophets. This, it believed, gave it the right to despise the "old" Israel, the Israel of the "flesh," the ultimately "untrue" Israel. In order to go further into the difficult Christological question it is necessary to deal first with the question of the incarnation.

WHAT DOES INCARNATION MEAN?

God's Word is seen in Judaism as mediator between God and humanity. The first modern Jewish systematic theologian, Kaufman Kohler, drew attention to the fact that the creation of the world was mediated through God's created word:

> *The Word appears . . . as the first created messenger, who has acted and continues to act as mediator between the world-spirit and the visible world order. Even more significant than in the realm of the visible creation, the word of God has become the mediator of the intellectual-moral world order in God's revelation to prehistoric humanity as well as the bearer of the divine teaching to Israel. For along time, therefore, the 'Word' (Hebrew:* maamar; *Aramaic:* memra; *Greek:* logos) *was called in the older Haggada the medium of God's revelation along with the* Shechinah.*"[16]*

But the church's proclamation of Christ as the Incarnate Word led to the suppression of these motifs. According to Kohler, it gradually happened that *one attributed a personality to this word of God, or logos, as "the first created Son of God." This occurred in Hellenistic circles under the influence of platonic and Stoic philosophy as in the thought of Philo of Alexandria. This, in turn, raised the logos to a kind of representative of God. And from there it was only a short step to elevate this figure still further to a rival of God as occurred on the part of the church with its concept of the Word made flesh in Christ.*[17]

So also in Judaism it was understood that the infinite God can become very close to humanity, and humanity close to the infinite God. The high and lofty one can bend down to humankind, can descend, can be with and accompany humanity. "I dwell in the high and holy place, and also with him who is of a humble and contrite spirit" (Isa. 57:15). After all, Israel's God is the very God of Israel, who remains near as the gracious and merciful one even in their darkest hour. "For what great nation is there that has a god so near to it as the Lord our God is to us, whenever we call upon him" (Deut. 4:7).

But as close as God and humanity may come to one another, in Jewish thought they always remain sharply distinct. Therefore, to claim that at some time in history God became human is considered blasphemous by Jews to the present day. For many Jews this cannot be correct, because the Christian claim of an incarnation of God has, as a matter of fact, produced exceedingly "bad fruit" for the people of God (Israel). On the contrary, as Clemens Thoma correctly points out, a doctrine for Jews "cannot be true or genuine if it is focused hostilely and pejoratively against God's people, the Jews, and the Sinai revelation which was witnessed by this people."[18] But the basic objection is that with the incarnation (as happened already with the Israelites worshiping the golden calf) there occurs *shittuf*, a Hebrew term indicating a blasphemous commingling, connecting, or joining of something created with God. Indeed, Christians must face this question: Is not a similar thing taking place in the Christian worship of Jesus as God?

Not at all! Such a mingling is not affirmed by Christians, and there is no talk about a "rival of God." Admittedly, as we have already indicated, with the spread of Christianity in the world of Hellenistic thought, and with the transformation of apocalyptic-Jewish-Christian thought patterns into those of Hellenistic-Gentile-Christians, Jesus was increasingly presented as the Son of God in the sense of being of the same nature as God. This inevitably led to increasing theological difficulties. The more theologians attempted to define this relation between God and Son in the categories of Hellenistic thought, the more problems they had in harmonizing faith in the one God with belief in the divine sonship. And all the more problems they had in distinguishing the Son of God from God while at the same time affirming the oneness of God.

With the passing of time the relationship of Father, Son, and Spirit became increasingly a *myserium logicum* in which the contradiction between unity and multiplicity appeared to the close observer to be overcome only verbally, only with ever new conceptual distinctions (ultimately between nature and person). Is God one divine nature and three divine persons? Is Jesus Christ one divine person with two natures, one divine and one human? In the light of such theological distinctions it is scarcely strange that the gospel of this God (Israel's) and of this (Jewish) Jesus as the Anointed One, Messiah, Christ, could not be made believable to the Jews and then later to the Muslims. Conversions from Judaism (and later from Islam) became increasingly rare. Among the Jews in the Christian empire the name of Jesus was vigorously suppressed.

Have we arrived at a dead end with respect to Christian dialogue with Jews? Not necessarily. For when we turn from the history of dogma to the New Testament, the decisive question is not, How are three persons in the Godhead related in the one divine nature? Or, how do the two natures in Christ function in one person? Such questions present themselves more or less inevitably when we attempt to think in terms of Hellenistic-nature categories. In the language of the New Testament the question is rather, How is the unity of God and Jesus, of Father and Son (and then also of the Spirit), to be conceived and affirmed—and in such a way that the unity and uniqueness of God are preserved, as well as the identity of the person Jesus Christ?

The New Testament speaks about a "sending" of God's Son[19] or about a "becoming flesh" of God's Word,[20] not a "sending" of God's self or a "becoming flesh" of God, but rather of God's Word. How must these expressions be understood? Are all the bridges to Judaism broken by such language, as Kaufmann Kohler and many other Jewish theologians assume? In his significant study of the Christology of preexistence, Karl-Josef Kuschel has demonstrated persuasively that the Pauline statements about the sending of the Son do not presuppose the preexistence of Christ as a mythological heavenly being. Instead they are to be understood in terms of the Jewish concept of the sending of prophets. "The metaphor of 'sending' (borrowed from the prophetic tradition) expresses the conviction that the person and the work of Jesus were due to God's initiative and not merely an inner-historical development."[21] Appealing to Catholic exegetes, Kuschel concludes that there is "nothing in the letters of Paul about the pre-existence of the Son or about his being of the same essence with the Father. On the contrary, the same essence hypothesis stands in conflict with the statement that Jesus is the 'image' or 'likeness' of God."[22]

The same is true in the Gospel of John. At least in this gospel one cannot speak of a "metahistorical drama of Christ," as has often been suggested from the Jewish side.[23] In the Fourth Gospel—the latest in the canon—it is still formulated in this way: "And this is eternal life, that they know thee the only true God, and Jesus Christ whom thou hast sent" (John 17:3). Then again, "I am ascending to my Father and your Father, to my God and your God" (John 20:17). God and Jesus Christ are here clearly distinguished. So this gospel contains no speculative metaphysical Christology torn away from the Jewish roots. Rather, it proclaims a sending and revelation Christology based on the world of Jewish Christianity. Though it contains and stresses preexistence sayings, they are nonmythological.

John does not ask about the metaphysical essence and being of the preexistent Christ. He is not concerned with the knowledge that before the incarnation there were two pre-existent divine persons who are bound together in one divine nature. This conception is foreign to him. Foreign to him also is the notion of an "inner divine begetting": "I and the Father are one." This phrase has nothing to do with dogmatic speculative expressions about the relationship of essences within the Godhead.[24]

What then was John's positive intention with these phrases?

> *The confessional expression is in the foreground: the man Jesus of Nazareth is, in person, the logos of God. He is the logos precisely as a mortal man; however he is that only for those who are prepared to believe trustingly that God's Word is in his word, that God's activity is present in his activity, that his way is the way of God, and that in his cross God's compassion was manifest.* [25]

What then is to be said about the incarnation of the Son of God? Certainly this concept is foreign to Jewish thinking; it is borrowed from the Hellenistic world. But this term may be understood correctly from the Jewish context. It would be completely wrong for Christians to focus on the *punctum mathematicum* or *mysticum* of the conception or birth of Jesus. [26] The Greek model of incarnation must be understood and interpreted out of the context of the history of Jesus the Jew. When this is done correctly, the concept refers to the total earthly life and death and new life of Jesus. For in all his speaking and preaching, in his total behavior and destiny, in his entire person, the man Jesus acted not as God's rival or competitor, but instead preached, manifested, and revealed God's word and will. Therefore we can say that in Jesus God's word and will took on human form. Even in the Jewish context the following statement could be ventured: He, in whom word and deed, teaching and life, being and acting fully coincided, he is God's Word, Will, and Son in human form. Here the concern is with a unity of Jesus with God. But even according to the Christological councils, the concern is not with a mixing or joining; rather—as in the New Testament—it is about a unity of understanding, of intent, of actions. In brief, it is about the revelation of God through Jesus.

THE TRINITY—AN INSTRUMENTAL OBSTACLE?

If there is a single fundamental trust of the Jewish faith that the tradition holds unshakably, it is the "Shema, Israel," i.e., "Hear, O Israel: The Lord our God is one Lord" (Deut. 6:4). Throughout the centuries this insight was continuously interpreted as the Jewish systematic theologian Louis Jacobs explains in a brief summary. [27] This confession of the unity, uniqueness, and singleness of God demonstrates once again the radical rejection not only of any dualism but also of any trinitarianism. Admittedly some Jewish critics have reproached the Kabbalists with a tendency toward trinitarianism, but the Kabbalists emphatically rejected all such accusations. The Jewish martyrs would have given up their lives rather than concede any form of trinitarianism.

In later centuries the Jewish community felt itself to be strongly supported by the strict monotheism of Islam, which had emerged as a world power threatening Christendom. The triumph of Islam over Christianity in many areas looked to Jews like the triumph of the God of Abraham over the triune God of the Christians. In the theological debates of Middle Ages—especially in Spain—the trinitarian question played a major role from both sides. Those on the Christian side, however, too often argued by using problematic analogies that could be easily refuted instead of arguing directly from the New Testament.

On the other hand, well-informed Jews have always known that, in principle at least, the Christian tradition has held fast to the unity of God. According to common Christian understanding the talk about Father, Son, and Spirit must never under any circumstances be turned into a doctrine of two or three gods (that is, into anything like the Egyptian concept of Osiris, Isis, and Horus, or the Indian trilogy of Brahman, Shiva, and Vishnu). For Jesus and for Christians in all times God has remained as the One and only One. There is—according to the Hebrew Bible—no other god apart from the eternal God. In addition to monotheism and polytheism, there is no third option. This is true also for the New Testament, despite the flourishing theological specula-tion. Again, in the New Testament there is no simple identity between God and Jesus, even though such tendencies were present in heterodox movements of the early centuries. The Son is not God the Father, and God the Father is not the Son: "Son" is not simply another name for God.

Is the transcendent God present in the immanence? This is not blasphemy, this is in no way an un-Jewish concept. Judaism too recognizes the divine descending and condescending that does not in any way annul but rather confirms the deity of God. The presence, the existence, the immanent activity of God, who was, is, and will forever be, is expressed in rabbinic Judaism with terms such as *Shechinah* (from "to dwell"), i.e, God's "dwelling," but also the "glory" (*kavod*) and "splendor" (*hod*). And God's dwelling is among the human beings on earth. The rabbis made clear that God's special presence was to be found not just in the sanctuary, the tend of the covenant, or the temple, but that God can dwell also in the community of the people—even in the exile: "*Im-manu-El*" ("God is with us").

And why should God's presence, *Shechinah*, now dwell in a single person instead of in the temple, so that God's hidden glory should shine forth? A division, a splitting apart, or a disunity in the one and only God cannot possibly be meant by this. Admittedly the *Shechinah*, the indwelling and the revelation of the one and only God, is experienced only through faith. God's wisdom (*logos*) is hidden in human flesh, manifest only to believers. "And the Word became flesh and dwelt among us, full of grace and truth; we have beheld his glory, glory as of the only Son from the Father" (John 1:14). Thus it states in the prologue to John's gospel. Thus it is affirmed in the Pauline tradition: "For in him the whole fullness of deity dwells bodily" (Col. 2:9). It is only from the Jewish perspective, therefore, that it is possible to understand correctly what twenty centuries of Christianity and all the churches unanimously affirm. In Christianity the foundation and center of faith is not a sacred book or law. Instead, it is God (theocentrism), but God—as experienced by the earliest Jewish-Christians—as manifested in the historical person Jesus Christ, where God was definitively revealed, made explicit and concrete through Christocentrism. It is essential to recognize that it is this person—not a book or a law—that establishes the definitive measure of the Christian understanding of God and of humankind.

I know what we Christians expect on this point from our Jewish (and Muslim) dialogue partners. I hope with all my heart that the dialogue may continue on this issue, not in order to demonstrate who is in the right but to deepen trust in God. One thing must be conceded to the Jewish dialogue partner in order to establish a common basis in advance: the principle of God's unity attested to in the New Testament is clearly *not* that of a single divine nature shared by several entities or beings (as has been widely held since the development of the post-Nicene theology of the fourth century). Instead, the principle of unity is the one God from whom all things come and toward whom all things are oriented. It follows that the New Testament is not interested in metaphysical-ontological statements about God, or about the static, serenely self-contained essence of a triune deity. The New Testament is far more concerned with soteriological-Christological statements about the way and manner in which God's revelation through Christ functions in this world. It is concerned about God's dynamic activity in history— about God's relation to and with humanity. Given these presuppositions from the New Testament, and in the light of the Jewish perspective, how is the faith in Father, Son, and Spirit to be understood and articulated? This is a test for any Christian theology. I attempt here a brief summary:

> To believe in God the Father means, according to the New Testament, to believe in the one God. Judaism, Christianity, and Islam have this belief in common.
>
> To believe in the Holy Spirit means to believe in God's effective power and strength in humankind and in the world. Again, Jews, Christians, and Muslims have this belief in common.
>
> To believe in the Son of God means to believe in God's revelation in the man Jesus of Nazareth. This is the area of decisive difference among the three prophetic religions.

DOES GOD REQUIRE THE SACRIFICE OF GOD'S OWN SON?

Too easily Christians, and especially Christian theologians, assume that the execution of Jesus was a sacrificial death and that it was the highest demonstration of God's love: "For God so loved the world that he gave his only Son, that whoever believes in him should not perish but have everlasting life" (John 3:16). In support of such a view, this passage from John is too readily cited without careful reflection.

Entirely in line with Jewish tradition, Pinchas Lapide speaks critically of this concept: "That God requires a human sacrifice in order to reconcile his own creation with himself; that He, the Lord of the world is unable to justify anyone without a blood offering is for Jews both unintelligible and contrary to the Bible."[28] Human sacrifice is an abomination to God. Lapide then raises the following question:

What kind of God is it who can say "Yes" to the sadistic death agony of his child? Indeed, who even inflicts the strictly heathen torture of the crucifixion as a vicarious atonement? Or as an appeasement for God's anger, according to Roman custom as Augustine describes it? Or as a tricky ransom deal between God and the devil as Origen has it? Or, as Anselm of Canterbury sought to prove in his satisfaction theory, as a feudal compensation and payment for guilt?[29]

What can be said from the perspective of the Christian tradition in response to such comments? Several traditional Christian concepts, some partly rooted in the New Testament itself, require correction. Certain elementary statements need to be made. The death of Jesus was brought about by human beings; it must not be explained, despite post-Easter exuberance, as the decision and saving will of God, so that the crucifixion is understood as divine intention and action. What God allowed to happen God did not explicitly will, much less plan and initiate. The God of the New Testament is no other than the God of the Old Testament, to whom human sacrifices are an abomination. It is not as if God rejected the sacrifice of Isaac in the Old Testament only in order to inflict it horribly on Jesus in the New Testament.

To avoid the impression that Christian theology became aware of this problem only through Jewish objection, I will quote what I wrote many years ago on the basis of modern research, especially in the field of New Testament exegesis: "Can it be disputed that specifically the concept of *expiatory sacrifice*, at least in popular expositions, has frequently led to distressing misunderstandings? Is God so cruel, even sadistic, that his wrath can be appeased only by the blood of his own Son? Is it possible that an innocent person must serve as scapegoat, or whipping boy and substitute, in place of the actual sinners?"[30]

In response to such questions I made several points clear:

1. According to the New Testament, the first Jewish followers of Jesus faced a monstrously difficult question: How in the light of their faith that Jesus had entered a new life with God were they to understand his painful, repulsive, and shameful death? If it was to be viewed as a totally evil event, then what does this say about the will of God; if it was a saving event, then why this horrible death? The concept of an atoning death plays at best a marginal role in the Synoptic Gospels.

2. In the New Testament, and also in the Patristic literature, there is no single, exclusive, normative model of interpretation for the death of Jesus. There are instead various multifaceted interpretations of meanings that mingle with each other: the juridical (Jesus' death as justification for the sinner); the cultic (Jesus' death as substitution, sacrifice, sanctification); the commercial (Jesus' death as payment of ransom); and, finally, the military (Jesus' death as battle, and victory, over evil powers).

3. Jesus himself was seen in many different roles but, because of his earthly death, ultimately as a paradox. He was seen as the Teacher—but abandoned; as the Prophet—but unrecognized; as the Witness—but betrayed; as the Judge—but condemned; as the High Priest—but sacrificed; as the King—but crowned with thorns; as the Victor—but crucified.

4. The significance of the crucifixion was, therefore, described in correspondingly diverse ways: as example, as redemption, as liberation, as the forgiveness of sins, as purification, as sanctification, as reconciliation, and as justification.

One must ask: Is it really surprising that not all of these conceptions and metaphors, which were intended to express in various ways the salvific significance of Jesus' death, are fully intelligible today? Some of the thought patterns are foreign to us. A few could be directly misleading.[31]

The necessary critique of the "Satisfaction Theory" developed by Saint Anselm of Canterbury cannot be developed here (it is correctly viewed as a "metahistorical drama of Christ"). But this much needs to be stated: The "feudal" doctrine of redemption must be understood against the background of the jurisprudence system developing in the early Middle Ages. It seemed plausible from that perspective to attempt a totally rational demonstration of the necessity for the Incarnation and, above all, of the necessity of redemption by means of the death on the cross. Already Thomas Aquinas questioned the logical persuasiveness of this theory. Certainly it cannot be accepted when we evaluate it on the basis of the New Testament. Neither is it possible to accept the theory of the ontological transformation of the world either on Good Friday or Easter Sunday.

This must suffice to indicate the direction in which a dialogue between Christians and Jews (and then also Muslims) concerning the difficult questions pertaining to the teaching about God, Christ, and redemption.

As difficult as this may be for the Jewish and Muslim partners to accept, the following must be stated unequivocally and clearly from the Christian side, if only to avoid insincere discussion: The test for being a Christian is not the church tradition that developed centuries later about the Trinity, the Incarnation, the Satisfaction Theory—otherwise the earlier Christians could not be regarded as actually "Christian." Rather, the test is the faith in the one and only God, the actual following of Jesus Christ in trust and in the power of the Holy Spirit. And this Spirit, I am fully convinced, works in the dialogue with Jewish (and Muslim) brothers and sisters, works where the Spirit wills, and leads us wherever the Spirit will.

NOTES

This essay originally appeared as "Christliche Selbstkritik im Lichte des Judentums" in Hans Küng's *Die religiöse Situation der Zeit: Das Judentum* (Munich: Piper Verlag, 1991). A different English translation appears in *Judaism: Between Yesterday and Tomorrow*, trans. John Bowden (New York: Crossroad, 1992). Used by permission of the author.

1. D. Flusser, "Christianity," in *Contemporary Jewish Religious Thought: Original Essays on Critical Concepts, Movements, and Beliefs*, ed. Arthur A. Cohen and Paul Mendes-Flohr (New York: Charles Scribner's Sons, 1987), 63.

2. "Richtlinien und Hinweise für die Durchführung der Konzilserklärung 'Nostra Aetate,' Artikle 4 vom 1. Dezember 1974," ed. by the Vatican Commission for the Religious Relations to Judaism, in *Die Kirchen und das Judentum. Dokumente von 1945 bis 1985*, ed. R. Rendtorff and H. H. Henrix (Paderborn: Verlag Bonifatius, 1988), 48–53. Citation from p. 49.

3. Cf. "Erklärung zur Begegnung zwischen lutherischen Christen und Juden," released by der Jahrestagung der Lutherischen Europäischen Kommission Kirche und Judentum (LEKKJ), Driebergen/Neiderlande on May 8, 1990.

4. Ibid., 1.2.

5. Ibid., 3.2.

6. C. Thoma, *Christliche Theologie des Judentums* (Aschaffenburg: Pattloch, 1978), 43.

7. Ibid. Cf. H. Küng, *On Being a Christian*, (trans. Edward Quinn [Garden City, NY: Doubleday, 1976), especially the main section; *Does God Exist?* chap. G III;

"Christianity and the World Religions," chaps. A IV, 3; B IV, 2; C I, 2; "Christianity and Chinese Religions," chap. 2, p. 2.

8. Cf. Karl-Josef Kuschel's comprehensive study on preexistence Christology, *Geboren vor aller Zeit? Der Streit um Christi Ursprung* (Munich: Piper, 1990).

9. Thoma, *Christliche Theologie des Judentums*, 43.

10. Cf. Deut. 32:6, 18; Jer. 3:4; Isa. 64:8; Mal. 2:10.

11. Cf. Exod. 4:22f.; Hos. 11:1; Jer. 31:9.

12. Cf. Deut. 14:1.

13. Cf. Hos. 1:10.

14. Cf. 2 Sam. 7:14; Ps. 2:7; 89:7f.

15. Cf. Mark 12:36; Matt. 22:44; Luke 20:42; Acts 2:34; Heb. 1:13.

16. K. Kohler, *Grundriß einer systematischen Theologie des Judentums auf geschichtlicher Grundlage* (Leipzig: Fock, 1910), 148f.

17. Cf. ibid., 149. This thought is further expanded in the newer American edition of the book *Jewish Theology Systematically and Historically Considered* (New York: Macmillan, 1918), chap. 32.

18. C. Thoma, *Theologische Beziehungen zwischen Christentum und Judentum* (Darmstadt: Wissenschaftliche Buchgesellschaft, 1989), 112.

19. Cf. Gal. 4:4; Rom 8:3.

20. Cf. John 1.

21. Cf. Kuschel, *Geboren vor aller Zeit?* 393.

22. Cited by Kuschel, ibid., 390. The quotation that Kuschel cites stems from B. v. Iersel, "Sohn Gottes im Neuen Testament," in *Concilium* 18 (1982): 190.

23. Cf. Flusser, "Christianity," 64.

24. As Kuschel convincingly summarized the findings of the newer Catholic and Protestant exegetes in *Geboren vor aller Zeit?* 502. The quotation cited by Kuschel stems from H. Strathmann, *Das Evangelium nach Johannes* (Göttingen: Vandenhoeck und Ruprecht, 1951), 170.

25. Kuschel, *Geboren vor aller Zeit?* 502.

26. On the problem of the virgin birth, cf. Küng, *On Being a Christian*, chap. C VI, 3.

27. Cf. an extensive survey concerning the Jewish commentary by Louis Jacobs, *Principles of the Jewish Faith: An Analytical Study* (London: Vallentine-Mitchell, 1964), 95–117.

28. Pinchas Lapide, *Warum kommt er nicht? Jüdische Evangelienauslegung* (Gütersloh: Gütersloh Verlagshaus Gerd Mohn, 1988), 59.

29. Ibid.

30. Küng, *On Being a Christian*, 424.

31. Cf. ibid., chap. C VI, 2, "Interpretations of Death."

CHAPTER SEVENTEEN

DIALOGUE WITH PROFESSOR HANS KÜNG

ALAN F. SEGAL

As Hans Küng says, Jesus has always been easier for Jews to appropriate than the Christ or the proclaimers of Christ. After all, Jesus lived and died a Jew. His idiom was Jewish; his followers were Jewish; his enemies were Jewish. Many scholars have gone so far as to think (wrongly in my estimation) that Jesus was a Pharisee. His opinions on resurrection certainly appear to be Pharisaic, and some of his legal statements are similar to Pharisaic preaching. Some opinions, like his position on divorce, even appear to support one or another of the early rabbinic positions, although in the case of divorce he supported the Shammaite position, which is not how the law inclines. He also seems to have had the same interest in freeing the people from their psychological dependency on Roman rule, if not from Rome itself. His message of repentance, love, and the coming Kingdom of God are in the same tradition as those of both the rabbis and the prophets. Jesus' faith seems much easier to understand within Judaism than the faith of his followers in him.

On the other hand, Paul and his high Christology have always seemed very strange to Jews (even though, unlike Jesus, Paul actually was a Pharisee, hence in the same tradition that preceded and anticipated the rabbis). John's discussion of Jesus' divine prehistory, descent into the flesh, ascent back to God, and the transformation of people who believe in him has seemed strange to Jews familiar with rabbinic traditions. Paul, although he does not spell out such rarified doctrines, also has a very high Christology. And for Paul transformation is everything, the very essence of Christian experience. Thus, the greatest Jewish scholars of early Christianity have almost all been united in their disjunction of Jesus from Paul. Graetz, Dubnov, Klausner, Sandmel, even Rubenstein have seen in Paul a Hellenistic Jew at best, removed from the soil of Palestine, a man with a Gentile spirit who understood how to market Jesus' teaching but not the environment in which Jesus lived and died. This line of scholarship has culminated in the recent work of Hyam Maccoby, who unlike most of his predecessors is not a scholar in this field. For Maccoby, Paul is not even a Jew but an imposter who pretended to be Jewish so as to import Gnosticism and the mystery religions into Christianity. This interpretation of Paul and his variety of Christianity, though it is a polemical caricature fed by outrage at the Christian mistreatment of Judaism, only serves to under-line the predisposition of Jews to seek out the Jewishness of Jesus while characterizing Paul as an apostate and inauthentic Jew. In fact, both Jesus and Paul were Jews, however different they may have been, and it is Paul who tells us most about the sources of Christology, which is also a product of Jewish experience.

David Flusser is correct in saying that the easiest place for Jews and Christians to meet is in the person of Jesus and not in the more rarified claims that the church has made about him. For Jews, the preexistent Messiah and resurrection are partly troublesome (although not entirely), while the incarnation and the title of Son of God seem positively un-Jewish. Yet it is Professor Flusser himself, when speaking in his capacity as historian, who pointed out the close relationship between Christology and rather abstruse Jewish mystical documents of the first century, documents that in the end tell us much about how the early Christians understood the career of Jesus after they had experi-enced his resurrection. When the issue is the actual historical relation-ships between Judaism and Christianity the poles reverse; it is Paul and Christology that have the easiest background to trace in Judaism.

The reason is, first of all, because Jesus is such a mystery to us as historians. So few aspects of his life actually pass the "criterion of dissimilarity," the academic test we set up for ourselves to assure us that our sources, entirely Christian in nature, are giving us an accurate picture. The criterion of dissimilarity tells us that we may not be fully sure of any account of Jesus in the Gospels unless it is not in the interest of the church to tell us these details. It is an outlandish and difficult criterion. But it is necessary to prove to us that indeed there was a Jesus, an important affirmation against the culture despisers of Christianity who claim that the entire document is a fraud. The criterion of dissimilarity is the kind of historical tool necessary to prove the actual existence of Jesus when every report about him comes from people who have previously accepted him as their personal Savior. And it does its job well—it shows us that there was a man named Jesus and that he died on a cross. It also shows us that his life was immensely important to those who knew him.

While the Gospels are not likely to be frauds, they are not easy to use as historical documents. Any biographer of Jesus must take a number of chances and play a game of percentages in accepting evidence from the New Testament, because not enough information from the Gospels actually passes the criterion of dissimilarity to formulate a portrait, much less a life. Most of the material that Jesus preaches that sounds like Pharisaism or Jewish wisdom does not pass. What does pass it the apocalyptic core of Jesus' message. And this brings us into a realm that Pharisaism never attempted, with its quietistic view of authority. Thus, the Jesus who is presented in such a lively fashion in the Gospels recedes into the mists as a historical figure when we apply the canons of historical method.

As Professor Küng says, "He actually called into question not only the absolutized temple, as well as the absolutized law, but also the borders between clean and unclean, the just and the unjust." These are reasonable guesses: Jesus did seem to be actively antagonistic to the temple, certainly much less interested in the issue of ritual purity than the Pharisees, and he had a different opinion in specific instances about where the line between the just and the unjust ought to be drawn. Of all these characteristics only his opposition to the temple, with its political function, is likely to have gotten him in enough trouble to force his execution at the hands of the Romans. Whatever else Jesus may have been—and there is no reason why he could not have both spoken wisdom, given Torah, and also preached apocalypticism—he surely preached the immediate approach of the kingdom and acted strongly against the temple, the symbol of political rule. After this, most of the man Jesus recedes into darkness.

Instead, it is Paul and the strange and unfamiliar concepts of his Christology that give the historian, Jew or Christian, the easiest access. This accords in a particularly exciting way with Professor Küng's insistence that we encounter both the man Jesus and the Christ of faith. Indeed, it is my opinion that both the man and the Christology were entirely at home within the Jewish milieu and that, ironically, it is the Christology to which we have most access.

To be sure, the Judaism that Paul represents and that serves as a background for his Christology is a Judaism that was not overtly embraced by the rabbinic movement. But it was not entirely ignored by Judaism, either; instead, it became part of the vast mystical heritage of Judaism, existing under the rabbinic surface and being disciplined by it. On the face of it, Judaism and Christianity look very different, as Professor Küng says. The key to understanding the relationship between them is to look at the apocalyptic/mystical parts of Judaism in which the doctrine of God's many manifestations crops up.

It is from esoteric Bible interpretations that Christology emerges. In the Bible, God was sometimes described in human form. In other places, such as Exod. 23:21f., an angel is mentioned who has the form of a man and who carried within him or represents "the name of God." The human figure on the divine throne described in different ways in Ezek. 1, Dan. 7, and Exod. 24, among other places, was blended into a consistent picture of a principal mediator figure who, like the angel of the Lord in Exod. 23, embodied, personified, or carried the name of God, YHWH, the tetragrammaton. We shall see that this figure, greatly elaborated by Jewish tradition, becomes a central metaphor for the Christ in Christianity. To see how, we must trace its history in Judaism.

Several Jewish traditions discuss the *eikon* or image of God as Adam's prelapsarian appearance, an especially glorious and splendid form that humanity lost when Adam sinned; in Gen. 1:26 humanity is described as being made in "the image and form of God." The same image and form of God is thereafter associated with God's human appearance in the Bible or the description of the principal angel of God who carried God's name. Most significantly, the human figure on the Merkabah that Ezekiel describes is called "the appearance of the likeness of the glory of the Lord." Thus, God's glory or *Kavod* can become a technical term for God's human appearances.

It seems likely that this enigmatic human appearance of God, discussed with appropriate self-consciousness in the Bible, is related to the so-called "Son of man," which is not a proper name. The heavenly Son of Man appears in the vision in Dan. 7:13 in which an Ancient of Days appoints a human figure ("one like a son of man") to execute justice in the destruction of the evil ones. This human figure is best understood as an angel.[1] Later on in Daniel, resurrection is promised both for the faithful dead and for the most heinous villains, who will be resurrected so that they may be sentenced to eternal perdition. *Hamaskilim*, or "those who are wise," apparently the elite of the apocalyptic group, will then shine as the stars in heaven (Dan. 12:3). This scripture essentially states that the leaders will be transformed into angels, because the stars were identified with angels in biblical tradition (Job 38:7).

The preeminence of this angel is due primarily to the description of the angel of the Lord in Exodus. Exod. 23:20–21 states: "Behold, I send an angel before you, to guard you on the way and to bring you to the place which I have prepared. Give heed to him and hearken to his voice, do not rebel against him, for he will not pardon your transgression; for my name is in him." The Bible expresses the unique status of this angel by means of its participation in the divine name.[2] Thereafter, in Exod. 33:18–23, Moses asks to see the glory of God. In answer, God makes "his goodness" pass in front of Moses but cautions, "You cannot see my face; for man shall not see me and live. . . . Behold, there is a place by me where you shall stand upon the rock; and while my glory passes by I will put you in a cleft of the rock, and I will cover you with my hand until I have passed by; then I will take away my hand and you shall see my back; but my face shall not be seen." Yahweh, the angel of God, and God's glory are melded in a peculiar way, which suggests to the passage's readers a deep secret about the ways God manifested God's self to humanity.

The relationship between these traditions and the Christian title "Son of God" is not intuitively clear. But Son of God is one of the terms that Hebrew uses regularly to designate angels (e.g., Dan. 3:25; Joseph and Aseneth 23:10).[3] Furthermore, it suggested messianic status, because it was often used by God to describe the ruler, the Messiah. It was also a term understandable to the Greek environment: the sons of gods were heroes such as Hercules and Achilles. It seems clear that these titles were applied to Jesus by his immediate disciples in an attempt to understand what he was. As a result, we find in Paul the clearest examples of the combination of meanings for this term: "Who was descended from the seed of David according to the flesh and designated Son of God in power according to the Spirit of holiness by his resurrection from the dead" (Rom. 1:3f.). This sentence relies on an ancient confession of faith within the church. It is Jesus' resurrection that begins the welding of his human character as the seed of David together with the divine status as the Son of God, as indeed angelic status is divine. Paul also believed that the transformation Jesus underwent is the beginning of the transformation of all who believe in him. Thus, his Christology and his eschatology go together in perfect harmony.

The synthesis that we see for the first time in Paul is underlined by the Gospels, which work more fully with apocalyptic literature and especially Daniel. Indeed, the most common Hebrew scripture used by the New Testament to demonstrate Jesus' special status is not a traditional messianic prophecy. No traditional prophecy would have solved the problem that history had given to the Christians, to find a prophecy of messianic suffering.

Ps. 110, however, contains the perplexing line: "The Lord said to my Lord, sit at my right hand until I make your enemies my footstool." Ps. 110 is an important Old Testament text in early Christianity, although the actual number of quotations is fairly small. The opening verse is quoted by Jesus in a discussion about the son of David recorded in each of the Synoptic Gospels (Matt. 22:41–46; Mark 12:25–37a; Luke 20:41–44). The wording of the verse is identical in the three versions. The verse is quoted in Peter's Pentecost speech (Acts 2:34), and the opening verse of Ps. 110 is included among the string of biblical verses cited in Heb. 1. Hebrews also quotes Ps. 110:4 three times (Heb. 5:6; 7:17, 21). The actual quotations of the opening psalm verse are identical, and all agree word for word with the Septuagint (except for the consistent omission of a definite article that appears before the first "Lord" in Ps. 110:1a LXX). Even so, these few direct quotations are enough to place Ps. 110 as the most often quoted Old Testament text in the New Testament; the New Testament rarely actually quotes directly from the Old Testament, preferring to make allusions.

Significantly, the number of allusions to Ps. 110 in the New

Testament are very high. Nestle's chart lists eight New Testament allusions to v. 1, not counting the Synoptic parallels, and six allusions to v. 4. In his book on the subject David Hay lists thirteen more. Furthermore, the verses were rarely quoted in post-biblical Jewish tradition.[4]

The New Testament uses this verse for several reasons. It appears to be part of the very central Christian intuition about the identity of Jesus. To see it, one must analyze the passage. The passage has two "Lords" in it: "The Lord said to my Lord." The first Lord is God, as even the Hebrew made clear. But the second Lord in Hebrew appears to be the king, or David. In the Greek version the word used is *Kyrios*, which is a usual and traditional way for Greek-speaking Jews to refer to God, even though in Greek it may also mean a human lord. Christianity apparently identified one Lord as God and the second as the person who was raised to sit by God. This person was Jesus, on the basis of his resurrection. And because he receives the title Lord, he is also divine. Furthermore, the New Testament appears to connect this fairly obscure Ps. 110 passage with another obscure passage in Dan. 7:13, where a figure known literally as the Son of Man (a term that means something like "human being, mortal" in the Hebrew, or actually, in this case, the Aramaic idiom, Barnasha).

> *I saw in the night visions, and behold with the clouds of heaven*
> *there came one like a son of man, and he came to the Ancient of*
> *Days and was presented before him. And to him was given dominion*
> *and glory and kingdom, that all peoples, nations, and languages*
> *should serve him; his dominion is an everlasting dominion, which*
> *shall not pass away and his kingdom one that shall not be destroyed.*

The New Testament conflates two unrelated biblical passages because of the central event of Jesus' existence, his resurrection on Easter morning, an event that was completely real to the earliest Christians but that, because of its uniqueness, is beyond our ability to verify. On the other hand, note that nothing in the two passages is messianic. Ps. 110 is a psalm of David, and David may be the second

Lord of the psalm in its original version. This is stated directly by Acts in discussing the passage at Peter's speech: "David did not ascend into the heavens," but Jesus did—the conclusion is that he was exalted to God's right hand. But there is no real evidence that before Christianity a person exalted to the right hand of God would be understood as the Messiah. In other words, there was no tradition that the Son of Man in Dan. 7:13 was a messianic reference. In the context of that prophecy, it seems clear that the Son of Man is some kind of angelic creature or hypostasis of God.

Where does the messianic reference come from? Not from previous biblical exegesis in Judaism, that seems clear. Judaism may have occasionally fixed its gaze on these verses, but nothing of similar interest was adduced from them. This messianic claim that Christianity makes about Jesus is in some way the most difficult of all claims to account for on the basis of exegetical traditions or even popular expectations. To find out where the messianic claim comes from, one has to look to the events of Jesus' life.

The inscription on the cross, and not any particular tradition about scripture before Jesus, is what most clarifies the issue. Unlike Paul, who left us his personal thoughts, we have no records of what Jesus thought he was doing during his earthly mission. The Gospels were not written by him or his immediate successors, but by the second generation of Christians, most of whom had no immediate knowledge of their Savior. Furthermore, Jesus himself seems reluctant in the stories to accept this title of Messiah when some of his followers suggest it. The Jews too are portrayed as being skeptical. The only people who take the claim at face value are the Romans. They arrest Jesus on a charge of sedition, and as the inscription over the cross, "Jesus of Nazareth, the King of the Jews," shows, they execute him as a pretender to the independent throne of Judah. Whatever Jesus intended for his mission, the Romans understand him as a potential political threat. The Jews are depicted as horrified at the inscription—let it read instead that "he said he was king of the Jews." The Gospel of Mark is careful to show that that is one thing that he never said about himself. Jesus never claimed to be king of the Jews. Luke and Matthew appear to fabricate a messianic genealogy for him.[5]

The reader will find more detailed discussions of this phenomenon in my essay "Paul's Ecstasy," in *Paul the Convert*.[6] What needs only to be clarified here is the necessity for Jewish historiography to follow Professor Küng's advice as well. The relationship between Judaism and Christianity seems strange from the point of view of rabbinic Judaism. Yet once one looks at the peculiar and esoteric traditions about the angels of the Lord and the various intermediary figures that inhabited the Hellenistic Jewish heavens, the rise of Christology seems just as Jewish as the man Jesus.

In the end, it is not the inherent Jewishness of the Christian tradition that makes dialogue between Jews and Christians possible, but the good will on both sides to bracket differences and talk to each other as equal dialogue partners. A conciliar spirit of discussion seems to be able to overcome any differences and to be more important than the interesting historical facts of whether certain ideas within Christianity have a Jewish or Hellenistic background. These are of great historical importance, but they begin to serve polemical purposes when put into the service of dialogue. I would hope rather that Christianity and Judaism, and indeed the Abrahamic religion, Islam, can serve as important dialogue partners for each other, meeting on a common ground and working together to encounter humans of good will of any religious persuasion.

NOTES

1. Matthew Black, "The Throne-Theophany Prophetic Commission and the 'Son of Man': A Study in Tradition-History," in *Jews, Greeks, and Christians: Religious Cultures in Late Antiquity*, ed. Robert Hamerton-Kelly and Robbin Scroggs (Leiden: E. J. Brill, 1976), 57–73; Christopher Rowland, "The Vision of the Risen Christ in Rev. 1:13ff.: The Debt of an Early Christology to an Aspect of Jewish Angelology," *Journal of Theological Studies* 31 (1980): 1–11; and Jarl Fossum, "Jewish Christian Christology and Jewish Mysticism," *Vigiliae Christianae* 37 (1983): 260–87.

2. See on a related theme James Charlesworth, "The Jewish Roots of Christology: The Discovery of the Hypostatic Voice," *Scottish Journal of Theology* 39: 19–41.

3. See for example Martin Hengel's important book, *The Son of God: The Origin of Christology and the History of Jewish-Hellenistic Religion* (Philadelphia: Fortress Press, 1976).

4. See the important book by Donald Juel, *Messianic Exegesis* (Philadelphia: Fortress Press, 1988), especially his chapter on Ps. 110.

5. See N. A. Dahl, *The Crucified Messiah* (Minneapolis: Augsburg Fortress Press, 1991).

6. Alan F. Segal, *Paul the Convert: The Apostolate and Apostasy of Saul the Pharisee* (New Haven: Yale University Press, 1990).

CHAPTER EIGHTEEN

CHRISTOLOGY: THE DIALOGUE OF EAST AND WEST

JOHN DYKSTRA EUSDEN

THE NEED AND THE PROBLEM

Several years ago, at one of the first Buddhist-Christian conferences in Japan, held in the Center for the Study of Japanese Religions in Kyoto, a Buddhist scholar leaned over the table and said to me, "Do you know who Saint Paul is talking about in Gal. 2:20 when he says, 'It is no longer I who live, but Christ who lives in me'?" I thought I knew, but I was wrong. The answer came forcefully: "Buddha!" Later in the course of the meeting, a Christian colleague, also leaning across the table somewhat defiantly, declared, " 'No one can come to me unless the Father who sent him draws him. . . . I am the living bread which came down from heaven' " (John 6). In the midst of such forcefully uttered biblical quotations and subsequent elaborations, there was not much dialogue that day.

Matters have changed and now dialogue is running wild. Conferences abound on both sides of the Pacific, and the list of those of us who have written books and articles of a comparative nature is constantly growing. This is particularly true in the case of Buddhism and Christianity, and often with special reference to Christology itself. *Buddhist-Christian Studies* is one of the leading journals in the field, offering articles on comparative approaches in Buddhism and Christianity and on the salvific roles of Gautama Buddha and Jesus Christ. One major contributor, Masao Abe, who has had personal and professional influence on me over the years, in 1984 in Honolulu delivered a crucial paper entitled "Kenotic God and Dynamic Sunyata." His statement has called for many responses, criticisms, and elaborations and has been reissued in several forms.[1]

258

Buddhists have shown in conferences and dialogues with Christian theologians an increased interest in the person of Jesus Christ—who is Christ, what did and does he do, what are his similarities with Buddha, what is the meaning of incarnation? This essay will concentrate on Buddhist interest in Christology, which comes from Pure Land, Zen, and even Nichiren practitioners and thinkers.

THE CASE OF HINDUISM, BRIEFLY CONSIDERED

Most Hindu thinkers would assert that Jesus Christ is an avatar, one of many periodic appearances of divine reality on earth. Because there is no claim of exclusiveness or once-for-all-ness about any appearance in Hinduism, the idea and even the teachings of Jesus Christ are welcomed into a family of avatars. Hindus would venerate and celebrate the particular form of Brahman, the supreme source of all life and energy, which would be known to them in their own culture and traditions. But it is possible in most Hindu constructs to meld Jesus into the plethora of other forms. Krishna, the divine, vibrant, energetic incarnation (one of many) of the great god Vishnu is often quoted:

In every age I come back
to deliver the holy,
to destroy the sins of the sinner,
to establish righteousness.

Jesus could be thought to be one such avatar who has "come back" from God to accomplish the same tasks, but in a different setting and culture. Therefore there is little attempt in Hinduism to mark the singleness or the uniqueness of the Christological event—and not much necessity to find a way through the stormy crosscurrents of comparison and dialogue.

Mahatma Gandhi (1869–1948) represented this compassionate openness to Christianity and its central figure with grace and reconciling hope. To him, it was more important to assert that "all gods are good and all people are brothers and sisters" than to enter into the intricacies and subsequent judgments of comparative attempts. Gandhi devoted energy and study to the New Testament and found parallels with his beloved Bhagavad-Gita, the Song of the Divine One. He spoke of the figure Jesus and Christian teachings, especially as they related to *satyagraha*, the proclamation that truth as understood in one's heart should be translated directly into nonviolent social action. This inner truth, according to Gandhi, could only be such if it was based on love—God in any tradition and in any form could only be truth because of love. Such assertions brought Gandhi close to the teaching of Jesus and Christological formulations. Gandhi's openness and imaginative overlapping are found in many other modern Hindu thinkers and practitioners, for example, Radhakrishnan, Rabindranath Tagore, and Vinoba Bhave.[2]

An attempt to speak of Christology as seen through the eyes of other traditions is fraught with difficulties. Jesus Christ is viewed from different starting points by a Hindu, a Buddhist, a Jain, a Muslim. Any discussion moves in what Van der Leeuw called the "borderlands" of comparative hermeneutics, where lines of analysis and even tentative conclusions are difficult to sort out. It is an intricate task to find the "inner consistency" of a particular tradition before one begins the task of comparison with other perspectives. It may be true that in the diversity of gifts there is one spirit, as Saint Paul asserts, but every tradition has an as-yet-ness and a still-to-be-ness about its central affirmations. Assuming, however, that one could see in broad brush-strokes a consistency or pattern in the Vedic tradition, philosophical and popular Hinduism makes little response to the Christological affirmations of the West. It is more likely to incorporate where possible and to live and let live.[3]

On one point, however, Hinduism would raise a major question. Christians often present Jesus Christ as having a definite, clearly de-fined role in salvation and in the larger metaphysical understanding of the world. Where is the *maya* in Christ? This bewitching term can mean power and wisdom on the one hand, but, on the equally impor-tant other hand, obstacle, mystery, mirage-like character, even re-sistance. *Maya* represents the phenomenal, fleeting nature of all exis-tence, whether earthly or divine. Christology in its proclamations appears to be too clean-cut, structured, linear. Paul's typical, assured, time-dividing statement in Rom. 8:21–22 would be strange to most Hindus. "The whole creation itself will be set free from its bondage to decay and attain the glorious liberty of the children of God. We know that the whole creation has been groaning in travail together until now."

SOME COMMON ASSERTIONS OF
BUDDHISM AND CHRISTIANITY

Were Buddha and Christ similar teachers? Yes and no. Each used startling, puzzling statements to instruct their disciples—and, they hoped, to lead them to a new kind of wisdom and action. When a saddened mother came to the Buddha carrying a dead child in her arms, she was hoping for a miracle. The Buddha did not say to her that he could bring back the dead. Rather, he suggested that she search for a single mustard seed that came from a household in which there had never been a death. He offered no sermon on the nature of good and evil, but rather a directive that she discover for herself that others, too, had suffered loss and that in some kind of compassionate sharing she might find a lessening of her grief. Jesus' use of parables contains much of the same thrust—no lecturing, but an enigmatic stress on experience and confrontation. When speaking about allegiance to Caesar or God, he said, " 'Bring me a coin, and let me look at it.' And they brought one. And he said to them, 'Whose likeness and inscription is this?' They said to him, 'Caesar's.' Jesus said to them, 'Render to Caesar the things that are Caesar's, and to God the things that God's.' And they were amazed at him" (Mark 12:15–17).

In both traditions there are many examples of jolting questions and assertions that involve non sequiturs and reversals. In Zen Buddhism, following the general Buddhist insistence upon ultimate separation from a teacher in order to find one's true self, the chant "Kill the Buddha, kill the Buddha" is repeated over and over. Jesus denies his mother and family in a blunt statement. "While he was still speaking to the people, behold, his mother and his brothers stood outside, asking to speak to him. But he replied to the man who told him, 'Who is my mother and who are my brothers?' " (Matt. 12:46–48). Indeed, Zen people often say that Jesus can be understood as Zen master, using *koan*, or puzzling, reversing sayings in order to send a disciple in another direction both psychologically and intellectually.

But the differences in teaching abound. The "true self" emphasis in Buddhism, particularly in Mahayana Buddhism, stands apart from the basic orientation of the gospel teachings. The consistent teaching of repentance, the insistence that a believer align herself or himself with the second Adam, or Christ, rather than the first Adam of the Garden of Eden, the stress on the covenant of grace rather than a covenant of works, the repetition of the judgment to be administered in the eschaton, or the final end, as found in Matt. 25 and elsewhere—these are part of Jesus' *didache*, or teaching. These elements, if found in Buddhism even in their most general extension, are presented with different referents and implications.

The similarity does continue, however, in Pure Land Buddhism, where the stress is on *tariki*, or other power, as opposed to *jiriki*, or self-power. Still, the teachings of Honen and Shinran, the great formulators of Pure Land, do not contain the strong identification of human sinfulness and brokenness. In Christianity, something has to be "broken through" by the grace of God. The saying of the *Nembutsu*, the chanting of a declaration that one need only depend on the saving grace of Amida Buddha in a strong, faith-centered perspective, is close to gospel proclamations. But the Synoptic Gospels have a more elaborate and extensive (but not necessarily better) set of requirements for faithful living.

Both Buddha and Christ had a forest or a desert experience during which they sequestered themselves for spiritual concentration, a time in which they confronted temptations and searched for a direction in their ministry and teaching. Each "returned to the world," eschewing a search for personal salvation alone and a practice of solitary meditation. Each founded a *sangha*, a spiritual community of followers, and worked intently with their disciples, not asking whether or not their movement would succeed in the world. Each was concerned with the acorn motif, believing in a small, intense beginning from which might come growth. Even Buddha's four noble truths and eightfold path were offered first to immediate followers and not proclaimed as a broadside. The New Testament words fitted both: "He who has ears to hear, let him hear" (Luke 8:8).

A favorite biblical text among Buddhists, especially those who are Rinzai or Soto Zen in Japan, is Phil. 2:5–11:

Have this mind among yourselves, which you have in Christ Jesus, who, though he was in the form of God, did not count equality with God a thing to be grasped, but emptied himself, taking the form of a servant, being born in the likeness of men. And being found in human form he humbled himself and became obedient unto death, even death on a cross. Therefore God has highly exalted him and bestowed upon him the name which is above every name, that in the name of Jesus every knee should bow, in heaven and on earth and under the earth, and every tongue confess that Jesus is Lord, to the glory of God the Father.

Masao Abe and other Buddhist commentators on this text understandably stress the *kenosis*, or "emptying," of Christ. This *kenosis* is an example of Jesus' true self-realization and becomes a model action for his followers. Christ emptied himself not only in order to find himself, but also to become a true servant for all people. The motif is similar to the concept of the Boddhisatva or heroic being in Buddhism, a term standing even for the Buddha himself, who out of compassion gave himself for others. This giving is not something static or assigned, but results from a dynamic action, discipline, decision. Abe calls it dynamic *sunyata*—a vibrant openness, receptivity, an embracing blankness, emptiness. Interpreting this passage and others in the New Testament, Buddhist philosophers will argue, from understandable Mahayana perspectives, that such *kenosis* is also *plerosis*, or fullness, making the point that emptiness alone has the power of leading to completion and well-being. When Zen practitioners chant and shout *mu* or "nothing" at the end of *zazen*, they are pushing away distractions and rational constructions. But they also engage in this practice because of the belief that it will lead to *u*, or fullness and completion. The *u* produces a connection with all things and parts of the world—which is Buddha himself. But there can be no fullness without emptiness first.

The self-emptying Christ interpretation leads to further insistences in some Buddhist thought. God acting in and through Christ also empties God's self, leaving behind divine will and, out of compassion, relating God in love to all creation. As Buddhists think about

Christology, they find that this imaginative, provocative emptying motif is the strongest assertion of parallelism.

The occasions of questioning and doubt in the Gospels, found dramatically in the temptations and the dialogue in the Garden of Gethsemane, are strikingly similar to vexing questions that Buddhist teachers ask of themselves. The eighteenth-century Zen master Hakuin, often called a revitalizer and the greatest leader of a half-century of the Rinzai sect in Japan, spoke often about the "Great Doubt." This doubt could be so overpowering that it could lead to *daishi*, the "Great Death," in the bonds of which one was spiritually immobilized, residing in a kind of Kierkegaardian deep despair. Paul Tillich resonated with this form of Buddhist thought, finding parallels with his elaboration of existential despair as it related to religious experience and Christological formulations.[4]

Buddhists speak convincingly of the parallels between the perspectives, freely discussing the meaning, or lack of it, in the designation of a "gap," an abyss, a wrestling. More than in Christian thought, there is a celebration of these doubts, uncertainties, and unanswerables. They may be all that one can have at certain times, whether thinking about spiritual experience or Christology. Christ plunged into his doubt and questioning—it was all that he could do at certain times. This Buddhist insistence is connected strongly with postmodernist philosophy and deconstructionist thought, in which the pieces and "grams," no matter how scattered and incomplete, are to be sought after and accepted as the reality of the moment. Do not look for a complete picture or a systematic presentation of Christ (or of any idea or concept). Contemporary poets, novelists, and nature writers have added to this understanding with indirect references to the subject of Christology. Annie Dillard writes of "going into the gaps," for these are back parts of God that we alone will be able to see. She urges us to "spend an afternoon" with the small, incomplete things in order that we may have a perspective and a connection that is nonassuming and genuine.[5]

A PARTING OF THE WAY

Buddhists have understandable difficulty in accepting the full force of incarnational statements. Either the Buddha is that true self that dwells within each practitioner, as many Zen people would say, or the Buddha is a divine being who awaits the practitioner and can be called upon, as many Pure Land people would say. Other divisions would offer variations, but seldom does one discover a Buddhist resonance with the assertion that Jesus is fully God and fully human, or a positive response, say, to the prologue of John. Hindus have far less struggle with incarnational theology, particularly those who worship Krishna. But in either of those broad traditions, the concept of the separateness of the two strands—the rabbinic teacher-prophet and the divine Word—is difficult to understand, let alone maintain. And perhaps in Christianity they can only be held together in faith.

The prophetic declarations of Jesus are not to be viewed in a parallel sense. The defense of the poor who own the realm of God, as Luke puts it; the blatant criticism of power, ecclesiastical and otherwise; the criticism of hypocrisy in high and low places; the call for nonviolence, expressed to immediate followers and to the world—some of these may be understood in part, but not with the urgency and unity as expressed particularly in the Synoptic Gospels. The close connection with the prophets of the Jewish Bible places Jesus in a relationship to a determining culture that is vastly different from the antecedents of Hinduism and Buddhism.

The eucharistic event in Christian worship becomes not only a way of remembering, but a liturgy of confession and an act of partaking in the multifaceted meaning of the person of the incarnate Lord. There are some connections, especially in Hinduism, but the parallelism is fragile. The messianic dimension of Jesus Christ, inherited from the teachings of the Jewish Bible and elaborated on his own, makes for an uneasy association with Hinduism and Buddhism. "Are you he, or are we to wait for another?" Jesus gives ambiguous answers, or rather puzzling ones, but increasingly it becomes clear in the Gospels, Synoptic and Johannine, that he is part of a tradition to rule and save—in a different way, to be sure, but clearly as part of ancient messianic hope. The Jewishness of Jesus Christ is part of the Christological uniqueness.

PERSONS IN DIALOGUE

We are, we hope, at a point where we can listen, respond with respect and thankfulness, and in the process amplify our spiritual connection with a world larger than we have ever conceived. Perhaps we can do this without staking out our claims or even our starting points—without saying at the outset, for example, "I am a Christian" or "I am a Buddhist." Perhaps we should just begin to speak about things that matter to us in the hope that our brother and sister believers of whatever perspective will discover that we all have much in common in God's world. That can be done without giving up our history and our practices. In fact, in true dialogue, our own way can become clearer without becoming oppressive to sisters and brothers who sit across some imaginary table.

There is both an outside or objective dialogue and an inner or silent one. The outside one is what we say with compassion and in hope of useful comparison for the life of the Spirit. The inner one is what happens to us in the process of saying and listening. How have we been amplified in thinking about new dimensions of divine presence? What have we learned about aesthetics and liturgy in worship? What have we learned about compassion and love?

To close with a personal note, from one who is an ordained Christian minister/teacher *and* a member of two Buddhist temples in Kyoto: Different ways can be put together. But only if one listens genuinely to the parts, honoring them as different and rejoicing in their presence as together they contribute to life in the Spirit.

NOTES

1. See summary of reactions in Masao Abe, "The Impact of Dialogue with Christianity on My Self-Understanding as a Buddhist," *Buddhist-Christian Studies* 9 (1989): 64–70.

2. See especially Radhakrishnan, *The Hindu View of Life* (New York: Macmillan, 1968). Also, Heinrich Zimmer, *Philosophies of India*, ed. Joseph Campbell (New York: Meredin Books, 1956); *Myths and Symbols in Indian Art and Civilization* (Princeton: Princeton University Press, 1974). For an account of a Westerner turned Hindu, see Agehananda Bharati, *The Ochre Robe: An Autobiography* (Garden City, NY: Doubleday, 1970).

3. See the helpful account by Michael Pye, "Skillful Means and the Interpretation of Christianity," *Buddhist-Christian Studies* 10 (1990): 17–22, and attendant articles in this volume.

4. See Carl Olson, "The Existential Doubt of Tillich and the Great Doubt of Hakuin," *Buddhist-Christian Studies* 9 (1989): 5–12.

5. Annie Dillard, *Pilgrim at Tinker Creek* (New York: Bantam, 1974), 276–77.

PART FOUR

CHRISTOLOGY IN DIALOGUE WITH CONTEMPORARY CULTURE

CHAPTER NINETEEN

CHRISTOLOGY
IN DIALOGUE WITH EXISTENTIALISM

JOHN MACQUARRIE

When I speak of existentialist Christology, I have in mind the teaching about the person of Jesus Christ that one finds in such writers of recent times as Rudolf Bultmann, Fritz Buri, and Friedrich Gogarten. It could be claimed, however, that the sophisticated views of these scholars are no more than a modern counterpart to the oldest Christology of all, for what did the earliest disciples mean when they hailed Jesus as "Christ" or "Lord" or even "God"? Surely such language was, to begin with, confessional, situational, even emotive, rather than descriptive. The disciples were declaring their own attitude to Jesus. They were trying to express what he had come to mean for their own existence. This is especially obvious in the use of the title *Lord*. It is true that this word had many connotations, in the first instance from Old Testament usage and then as time went on from Hellenistic religion as well. But essentially the word *Lord* is a rank word, not a descriptive word. To call someone "Lord" is not to describe him but to indicate the relation that subsists between him and the speaker or the group to whom the speaker belongs. "The '*kyrios*' christology," writes Graham Stanton, "expresses the authority of the Lord over the individual and the Christian community and is often related to ethical statements."[1]

One might agree that these earliest acknowledgments of Jesus as Lord or Christ were not yet Christology in the strict sense. No doubt they were first used in the heat of the moment, so to speak—the moment of perception or conversion or recognition. Later they passed into liturgy, which recaptures and brings to life again the creative moment of faith. The confessions attributed to Peter (Mark 8:29) and Thomas (John 20:28) may or may not be accurately reported, but there certainly were such moments. The Christ hymn of Phil. 2:5–11 is from a later stage, when the confession of lordship has been stylized for liturgical use.

But Christology, as part of the theological enterprise, always needs something more—it needs reflection. That reflection is not yet present at the moment of the original confession of faith, but it is beginning to appear in liturgy, so far as this has a meditative character. Nevertheless, confession and liturgy provide the raw material for Christology and do not yet constitute Christology itself. Thus, I do not want to claim too much when I say that modern existentialist Christologies are a counterpart to the very earliest Christologies. It might be more accurate to say that existentialist Christology goes far toward recapturing the strongly personal, evaluative, confessional character of the earliest Christian responses to the person of Jesus Christ, and this is important when one remembers how quickly Christology took a metaphysical turn.

To be sure, the confessional and personal strains were never quite lost. One cannot explain the passion that went into the early Christological controversies unless it is acknowledged that behind the disputes about metaphysical terminology there was the deeper issue of a "right" personal relationship to Jesus Christ. Yet that became more and more obscured. To say that Jesus is Christ or Lord or God was increasingly understood as descriptive language, to be explicated in terms of substance, nature, person, subsistence, and the like.

The existential strain in Christology was strongly reasserted for a time at the Reformation. Luther defined God in the Large Catechism in existential rather than metaphysical terms: "That to which your heart clings and entrusts itself is, I say, really your God."[2] The same approach colored his treatment of Christ, but it was Melanchthon who gave the almost classic statement:

> The mysteries of the Godhead are not so much to be investigated as adored. It is useless to labor long on the high doctrines of God, his unity and trinity, the mystery of creation, the mode of the incarnation. . . . To know Christ is to know his benefits, not to contemplate his natures and the modes of his incarnation.[3]

Both Luther and Melanchthon modified their early existential emphases, but they seem at this point to have injected into the Lutheran tradition an existential concern that has kept reappearing. Thus in the nineteenth century one finds Albrecht Ritschl condemning metaphysics and any theology that consists of a mixture of faith and metaphysics, and insisting that "we know the nature of God and Christ only in their worth for us."[4] His most forthright statement is:

> *If Christ, by what he has done and suffered for my salvation, is my Lord, and if, by trusting to the power of what he has done for me, I honor him as my God, then that is a value-judgment of a direct kind. It is not a judgment that belongs to the sphere of disinterested scientific knowledge, like the formula of Chalcedon. Every recognition of a religious sort is a direct judgment of value.*[5]

Wilhelm Herrmann and Martin Kähler were two other nineteenth-century German theologians whose thought was moving along similar lines[6] and who may be considered forerunners of the explicitly "existentialist" Christology of the twentieth century.

Bultmann's clearest and most provocative statement of an existentialist Christology is to be found in his essay "The Christological Confession of the World Council of Churches,"[7] published in 1951, that is to say, three years after the formation of the council. Bultmann had been asked by a conference of liberal Swiss theologians to comment on the statement adopted at Amsterdam that "the World Council of Churches is composed of churches which acknowledge Jesus Christ as God and Savior."

About the use of the term *Savior* he sees no special problem. The term is perhaps indefinite and nowadays has an archaic ring to it, but it is a functional term and refers to what Christ does in the Christian community. The difficult question arises when one speaks of acknowledging Jesus Christ as God—and Bultmann notes that in the Christological confession under consideration it is this strong formulation of Christ as God that is put forward, not Christ as Son of God or Word of God or any other less direct formulation. This difficult question is whether the assertion that Christ Jesus is God speaks of his nature or of his significance. Is it a metaphysical assertion or a soteriological one? Or is it both? "Does the pronouncement have soteriological or cosmological character or both?"[8]

Bultmann's first step is to consider what grounds the New Testament offers for calling Jesus Christ "God." He finds that this way of speaking is hardly to be found in the sacred authors. "Neither in the Synoptic Gospels nor in the Pauline Epistles is Jesus called God; nor do we find him so called in the Acts of the Apostles or in the Apocalypse."[9] There are a few ambiguous passages in the deutero-Pauline literature, but Bultmann's conclusion is that "the only passage in which Jesus is undoubtedly designated or, more exactly, addressed as God is John 20:28, that is, at the end of the story of Thomas, where Thomas makes the confession, 'My Lord and my God!'"[10] To be sure, Bultmann acknowledges that some of the other titles applied to Jesus in the New Testament (and he tends to stress the Hellenistic rather than the Old Testament provenance of these terms) do elevate Jesus into the divine sphere, perhaps as a cultic deity or world ruler, but not so as to put him on a level with God.

It is worth noting that some other New Testament scholars reach conclusions less negative than Bultmann's on this issue. Raymond E. Brown, for instance, claims that "in three clear instances and in five instances that have a certain probability, Jesus is called 'God' in the New Testament."[11] The three allegedly clear instances include Thomas's confession, cited by Bultmann, together with Heb. 1:8 (in which a psalm is addressed to Jesus, "Thy throne, O God, is for ever") and John 1:1 ("The Word was God"). However, Brown claims that it is the neglect of some of the more marginal but probable instances that makes Bultmann's treatment of the question exaggeratedly negative. So whereas Bultmann says, "It is only with the Apostolic Fathers that free unambiguous reference to Jesus Christ as 'our God' begins,"[12] Brown is more cautious in observing that "the use of *theos* of Jesus which is attested in the early second century was a continuation of a usage which had begun in New Testament times."[13]

Even accepting Brown's more moderate position, one would still have to say that God as a direct appellation of Jesus is rare in the New Testament. What may be of greater importance here is that the clearest instance, the utterance of Thomas, is strongly confessional and existential. Furthermore, we find Brown asserting that most of the other instances he cites come from a liturgical background.[14]

If then we agree that Jesus Christ is rarely called explicitly God in the New Testament, and that when and if this does happen the context is confessional or liturgical rather than dogmatic, we are prepared for Bultmann's statement of his "existentialist" Christology. The question is whether these exalted ways of speaking of Jesus are descriptions of him in the sense of objectifying statements about his being, or whether they express his significance for the believer. To quote Bultmann: "Do they speak of his *physis* or of the *Christus pro me*? How far is a Christological pronouncement about him also a pronouncement about me? Does he help me because he is God's Son, or is he the Son of God because he helps me?"[15] Bultmann answers these questions in a strongly existentialist sense. Christ is God in the sense that in him I encounter God's word or God's act. So he can write,

> *The formula, "Christ is God," is false in every sense in which God can be understood as an entity which can be objectivized, whether it is understood in an Arian or Nicene, an orthodox or a liberal sense. It is correct, if "God" is understood here as the event of God's acting.*[16]

In this passage Bultmann would seem to be imposing a veto on any dogmatic, speculative, or metaphysical Christology—in his view these are all "objectifying," and that is always with him a bad word. In another essay he seems to allow the possibility of holding beliefs about the nature of Jesus Christ, although these would be very secondary in importance. He writes: "To have faith in Christ does not mean to hold particular opinions about his nature, although one can certainly have such opinions."[17] But although this might seem to suggest that speculative Christology is permissible, we read a little farther on: "What is meant by Christology?" and we get the answer: "It is not the theoretical explanation of experiential piety; it is not speculation and teaching about the divine nature of Christ. It is proclamation, it is summons."[18]

It is important to notice, however, that Bultmann is not trying to flee from the problem of how the divine and the human come together in Jesus. He rejects the Chalcedonian formula as objectification and, moreover, as impossible for our modern thought. But he equally rejects the suppression of the problem of Christ's person by the liberals who humanized him, and he thinks that the "Amsterdam people" (as he contemptuously calls them) are essentially no different from the liberals, because they too have suppressed the problem, although in the opposite direction. But Bultmann himself wants to maintain the paradox of the eschatological event—the event of the man Jesus of Nazareth, which is also the event of God's acting. The use of the word *event* here is important. "Christ's lordship, his deity, is always only an event at any given time."[19] That is to say, Christ's deity is not an eternal property of his person, nor is the confession of it an eternal dogmatic truth. Confession of his deity is a confession of his significance in the moment of encounter—the eschatological moment, in Bultmann's sense of the phrase. This also explains why Bultmann always held that Jesus' personality is unimportant and that discipleship does not consist in personal attachment or devotion to him. Jesus is the vehicle of the Word, first in his own preaching but then, more important, in the kerygma in which he became the preached, and for which his own preaching was only a preparation. It is in the hearing and proclaiming of the kerygma that God speaks and acts and the event of Christ's lordship takes place.

There is much that is attractive in Bultmann's Christology. It stays close to faith and does not wander into airy speculation and scholastic distinctions. In this regard we can see it as standing solidly in the Lutheran tradition, and it would be as fair to call it Lutheran as existentialist. It belongs, too, in the prophetic tradition and visualizes discipleship in primarily ethical terms, as obedience to the Word that meets us and makes its demand for love through Jesus Christ. We might say that it is a Christology stripped down to the most basic essentials, demythologized and deontologized.

Yet one must also raise several critical questions.

1. On what ground does one recognize the ultimacy of Jesus Christ or acknowledge that the kerygma brings us to face the Word of God? Bultmann may well be right in making commitment to the reality that meets us in Christ, the beginning point for Christology, but how easily we commit ourselves to that which is not ultimate, although we represent it as such. How does one guard against idolatry in such a commitment, save by reflection at the ontological level? Bultmann is very much afraid of "objectifying," of digressing from the existential

relation of faith into a possibly idle and uncommitted speculation. But surely there can be ontological reflection that does not degenerate into this. If one has decided that something is ultimate (a "Word of God"), then in view of the grave danger of idolatry or superstition or fanaticism, one must think out the question of what constitutes this ultimacy. Therefore one cannot avoid the question about Christ's relation to God. Bultmann may well set aside Chalcedon (though he does so in much too dismissive a fashion), but there is still a principle of incarnation that needs to be thought out insofar as he holds that a divine reality (God or God's word or act) impinges on us through a human reality (Jesus Christ or his Word or the kerygma in which he is proclaimed).

2. The question must also be asked whether a word can bear all the weight that Bultmann places upon it. We have seen that the personality of Jesus is of no importance—it is entirely absorbed into the Word. Preaching is the center of everything. Jesus himself preaches the Word. Whether one could say that he *is the Word* seems doubtful. He appears instead as the bearer of the Word, although this is the description that was traditionally applied to the Blessed Virgin. But then he becomes the one who is preached and is taken up into the kerygma. The risen Christ is identified with the word of preaching, which ever and again renews the eschatological moment. It has all become verbal. God has become a word, and God's act is the act of speaking. We have to ask at this point whether Christianity has been too narrowly confined to the speaking and hearing of language. This may arise from the fact that Bultmann seems to have no place for liturgy and worship, only for preaching. Even the sacraments are simply *verbum visibile*. But is not this a truncated version of Christianity, which thinks of it as a word to be heard and understood and obeyed, not as a wider reality that seeks to embrace and transform the whole human nature?

3. Following on this, one must ask whether the reduction of Jesus Christ to the bearer of a word does justice to his person or to that tradition of Christian spirituality that has prized incorporation into Christ, devotion to Christ, mystical communion with Christ, and so on. Bultmann, like many other German Protestant theologians before him, has no sympathy for mysticism. Equally, he is impatient of pietism—and rightly so, when this becomes a mere sentimental attachment to Jesus. But there is an important tradition of Catholic sacra-

mental spirituality that cannot be so lightly set aside. One can understand the protest of the Jesuit L. Malevez:

> *We are no longer confronted either by the ontological reality or the spiritual presence of the ever-living Christ. All that concerns us is the message of which he is the instrument. . . . How can the Christian reader of Bultmann help exclaiming in his surprise, "They have taken away my Lord, and I do not know where they have laid him"?*[20]

4. A related point concerns the possibility of growing and deepening in the Christian life. Like Kierkegaard, Bultmann denies that faith is a permanent possession. It needs to be renewed from one situation to another. In a sense this is surely correct. Yet Bultmann's view of the matter seems far too episodic. Christ's lordship, we are told, is only an event of the moment. No doubt there may be many moments, but presumably most of a person's life is lived in the intervals between those moments of high decision. Incidentally, Bultmann teaches the same episodic view of the believer's relation to God.[21] But surely one must make allowance for continuity as well as discontinuity, for what is called the "practice of the presence" of God or Christ, for steady growth in discipleship.

5. Finally, although Bultmann has no use for pietism and mysticism, he seems to suffer himself from what is the worst defect of pietism—its individualism. The *pro me* features prominently in Bultmann, and one cannot find in his works the *pro nobis*. Let us recall the sentence already quoted: "Does he help me because he is God's Son, or is he the Son of God because he helps me?" Bultmann may be right in thinking that soteriology affords the right way into the question of Christ's person, but what is required is a much broader and firmer·base than individual experience of salvation. It is enormously presumptuous to imply that Christ is the Son of God because he helps *me*—even where the "me" is Rudolf Bultmann! It is not enough to substitute for this even the collective Christian experience of salvation. One is brought back to the question of whether an existentialist (or functional or soteriological) approach to Christology does not demand to be onto-

logically deepened or, to put it in another way, whether consideration of *what Christ does* for us must not lead into the question of *who Christ is.*

Bultmann is the outstanding example of a theologian who has expounded an existentialist Christology, but he does this mainly on the grounds of his New Testament scholarship. It may be useful therefore to consider the views of two systematic theologians who have also followed the existentialist path in Christology: Friedrich Gogarten and Fritz Buri.

Gogarten's Christology is in many ways very close to Bultmann's, but he relates it more definitely to the development of Western thought. What characterizes the modern age is the supersession of metaphysics by history.

> *This historical approach is the expression of a profound change which has taken place since the beginning of the modern age in the relation of man to the world and to himself. This change means nothing more and nothing less than that by it the world has for man become his own world.*[22]

In the ancient world and the medieval world there was an unchanging metaphysical framework that formed, as it were, the stage on which history took place. Everything was already determined, and there was no place for human responsibility and creativity. But now the situation is reversed. Human beings make history. Metaphysical systems themselves are swallowed up in history and are seen to be products of history. So the problem for modern theologians is to take Christology out of its traditional metaphysical setting and express it in historical terms.

Like Bultmann, Gogarten dissociates himself from nineteenth-century liberalism. He is not concerned with reconstructing the "historical Jesus." Rather, it is a question of reading the existential significance of Jesus' history in such a way that it illuminates our own history and presents a possibility of existence. In that sense he can declare that "the word of Jesus is the word of God."[23] But, more clearly than Bultmann, Gogarten understands that to say this is to speak of an intimate relation between God and the Father. Moreover, he claims that this has a finality about it that distinguishes Jesus from the line of Hebrew prophets, who also spoke the Word of God. This relation is not for us expressible in outmoded metaphysical terms, although Gogarten is more respectful to the early councils than Bultmann is. Jesus' special relation to God consists in the fact that he was the first human being to accept full responsibility before God, and so the first also to be delivered from the idolizing of the powers of the world.[24] Gogarten, of course, was deeply impressed by Paul's teaching in Galatians that the Christian has come of age and been delivered by Christ from the tutelage of law and subordination to worldly powers. He brought the old world to an end and inaugurated the Kingdom of God in which human beings can be free, responsible co-workers with God. This is also associated by Gogarten with the idea of secularization. Secularization is in fact historicization, coming to grips with human responsibility before God in time.

It will be seen, then, that Gogarten does to some extent provide the sketch of an ontology of history, so that his existentialist Christology does begin to take up some of the questions left unanswered by Bultmann. But there are considerable obscurities in Gogarten's theology. Is liberation for historical responsibility in the world really the existential significance of Jesus? And even if Jesus conceived that responsibility as a responsibility before God, is that how it is being understood today? Here we strike on the ambiguities of a so-called secular Christianity, although Gogarten himself is not unaware of them. He writes in one place: "The difference between modern historical thought and Jesus' understanding of history is that virtually nothing remains of responsibility before God."[25] Again, when everything has been historicized and all metaphysical systems (including, one must suppose, theism) have been recognized as products of history, are we not plunged into a thoroughgoing relativism that threatens Gogarten's own positions? He might not be too worried about the undermining of theism, for, like Bultmann, he thinks of God as a call to existential responsibility rather than an object of thought. But what about the claim for Jesus' finality and the difference between him and the prophets who came before him? Must not Jesus be seen in a much more relative way, as an inaugurator who was important for his own time but whose significance will increasingly diminish as human beings "come of age" and take over their own responsibility, no longer understood as a responsibility before God?

With Fritz Buri there is something different again. Perhaps it should be said that here Buri is considered in his existentialist phase, for both before and after that phase his theology has had a somewhat different character. In some ways he is more thoroughly existentialist than Bultmann. He does not agree with the criticisms of those who have complained about the lack of an ontology in Bultmann, and says: "Bultmann has good reason for foregoing an ontology of faith. The analogical thinking that he hinted at cannot be carried through in the form of an ontology or metaphysic but is only manifested in the actualization of faithful existence."[26] Buri says this because, like Bultmann, he thinks that any ontology must involve an illegitimate objectifying of that which is nonobjectifiable and unconditioned, namely, personhood, responsibility, the voice that calls to responsibility (God). He seems also more existentialist than Bultmann in denying Jesus the decisive place as act or Word of God that Bultmann assigns to him. For Buri, "there is no difference in principle between philosophy of existence and theology of existence."[27] An authentic responsible existence is achievable apart from Christ. Nevertheless, Christ remains as a still-powerful symbol of such an existence, and Christian theology still has the task of unpacking in existential terms that symbol and the several doctrines derived from it.

> *There must be an enormous depth and inexhaustible fullness of possibilities of understanding and realization of human life in the eschatological christology of the New Testament, that through all changes, additions, deviations and distortions, it has been understood continually as the revelation of the redeeming grace of God. On theological, existential and ethical grounds, Christ Jesus is of immense significance for a christology of existence . . . he represents the prototype of a christology of existence. Therefore, the christology of existence conceives its task to be to transfer Jesus Christ from the historical past into the historicality of present existence by means of the transforming application of his self-understanding of existence.*[28]

But is there not an inconsistency in Buri at this point? Unlike Bultmann, he sought to demolish the difference between Christian faith and philosophy of existence. But in the passage just quoted, the claims made for Jesus Christ are surely such that he cannot be just an optional symbol of authentic existence.

There is no doubt about the strengths of existentialist Christology. They go back to the New Testament and have kept reappearing in the history of theology, especially Lutheran theology in the past four centuries. But I hope that I have made apparent some of the weak points also. A purely existentialist Christology is neither adequate nor self-consistent, and that is why I have advocated an existential-ontological approach.[29]

NOTES

This essay originally appeared as "Existentialist Christology" in *Christological Perspectives*, ed. Robert F. Berkey and Sarah A. Edwards (New York: The Pilgrim Press, 1982), 228–37. Used by permission.

1. Graham Stanton, "Incarnational Christology in the New Testament," in *Incarnation and Myth*, ed. M. Goulder (London: SCM Press, 1979), 155.

2. "The Large Catechism," in *The Book of Concord*, trans. and ed. Theodore G. Tappert (Philadelphia: Fortress Press, 1959), "The First Commandment," sec. 3.

3. Philipp Melanchthon, *Loci Communes* (1521), Plitt-Kolder ed. (Erlangen, 1890); my translation.

4. Albrecht Ritschl, *The Christian Doctrine of Justification and Reconciliation*, trans. H. R. Mackintosh and A. B. Macaulay (Edinburgh: T. & T. Clark, 1900), 212.

5. Ibid., 398.

6. Wilhelm Herrmann, *The Communion of the Christian with God*, trans. J. S. Stanyon and R. W. Stewart (London: Williams & Norgate, 1909); Martin Kähler, *The So-Called Historical Jesus and the Historic Biblical Christ*, trans. C. E. Braaten (Philadelphia: Fortress Press, 1964).

7. In Rudolf Bultmann, *Essays: Philosophical and Theological*, trans. J. C. Greig (London: SCM Press, 1955), 273–90.

8. Ibid., 275.

9. Ibid.

10. Ibid., 276.

11. Raymond E. Brown, *Jesus, God and Man* (New York: Macmillan, 1967), 28.

12. Bultmann, *Essays*, 276.

13. Brown, *Jesus*, 29.

14. Ibid., 36.

15. Bultmann, *Essays*, 280.

16. Ibid., 287.

17. Rudolf Bultmann, *Faith and Understanding*, trans. L. P. Smith (London: SCM Press, 1966), 276–77.

18. Ibid., 277.

19. Bultmann, *Essays*, 286.

20. L. Malevez, *The Christian Message and Myth*, trans. Olive Wyon (London: SCM Press, 1958), 124, 144.

21. Cf. John Macquarrie, *Thinking About God* (London: SCM Press; New York: Harper & Row, 1975), 179–90.

22. Friedrich Gogarten, *Demythologizing and History*, trans. N. H. Smith (London: SCM Press, 1955), 25–26.

23. Ibid., 69.

24. Friedrich Gogarten, *Christ the Crisis*, trans. R. A. Wilson (London: SCM Press, 1970), 196.

25. Ibid., 157.

26. Fritz Buri, *How Can We Still Speak Responsibly of God?* trans. C. D. Hardwick and H. H. Oliver (Philadelphia: Fortress Press, 1968), 37.

27. Fritz Buri, *Theology of Existence*, trans. H. H. Oliver and G. Onder (Greenwood, SC: Attic Press, 1966), 21.

28. Ibid., 83.

29. Cf. John Macquarrie, *Principles of Christian Theology*, 2d ed. (New York: Charles Scribner's Sons, 1977), 272ff.

CHAPTER TWENTY

CHRISTOLOGY IN DIALOGUE
WITH PROCESS THEOLOGY

LESLIE A. MURAY

Theologians who have developed Christologies using the conceptuality of process thought, like all theologians who have written about the meaning of Christ, have attempted to answer Jesus' question, "But who do you say that I am?" (Mark 8:29). Process Christologies share the characteristic feature of all such writing of being indissolubly linked to soteriology, of being profoundly shaped by the understanding of that from which we are to be "saved." And while rejecting the incoherence of the Hellenistic, supernaturalistic premises of Chalcedon, process Christologies seem haunted in some way by the existential insights behind the "one person, two natures" formula—namely, that what is salvific needs to be more than we are, i.e., divine, yet in contact with us and sharing our condition.

The first section of this essay delineates the major tenets of process thought. The second section explores the Christology of John B. Cobb, Jr., one of the major options among contemporary process Christologies.[1] I advance my own constructive proposals in the final section, moving the discussion "beyond dialogue," to borrow from the title of one of Cobb's books, "toward a mutual transformation" of Christology and process theology.[2]

PROCESS THOUGHT

Typically, process thought is defined in one of three ways: (1) as any worldview that sees reality as dynamic, relational, and creative, and that is based on the findings of modern science; (2) as the "Chicago School," after theologians at the University of Chicago Divinity School whose work in the earlier part of this century was characterized by the use of the sociohistorical method that viewed civilizations and religions as creative responses to felt social needs and challenges, shifting in later decades to more philosophical and metaphysical interests; and (3) as synonymous with the philosophies of Alfred North Whitehead (1861– 1947) and Charles Hartshorne (1897–   ). While I shall rely on theologians heavily influenced by the conceptuality of Whitehead and Hartshorne, I will also advocate a reappropriation of the sociohistorical method of the earlier Chicago School.

Perhaps the best way to approach process thought is to contrast it with the thread that links nearly all the history of Western philosophy. Substantialism is the notion that the underlying substance of a thing is what makes it what it is, that whatever changes it may undergo, its underlying substance remains unchanged. In contrast, the basic paradigm for the process understanding of reality is a momentary experience—a throbbing, dynamic "energy event." What appear to be solid objects are myriads of these energy events (there is no substance, just the momentary event) interrelated and interdependent, extended in space and time, with varying degrees of complexity of organization. To explain the model of a momentary experience in process thought, I will use the only experience we know from "the inside," our experience as human beings—although it should be kept in mind that, as with any metaphysical scheme that seeks to be consistent, coherent, and adequate, whatever we say about human beings we need to be able to say about anything actual, at no matter how rudimentary a level.

In process thought, a momentary, self-creative subject constitutes itself as it appropriates, internalizes, "prehends" data from the past (which includes the sociopoliticoeconomic systems, the cultures and subcultures, the families, and the nonhuman natural environment of which we are parts and which are parts of us; in fact, the past includes the past of the entire universe), and responds to the possibilities of the future.

The momentary-experiencing self-creative subject is internally related to the objective data of the past; as the immediacy of the momentary subjective experiencing "perishes," it becomes an objective datum in the becoming of other momentary-experiencing subjects. Profoundly shaped by the past, each momentary experience is nevertheless free as to *how* it appropriates data from the past and *how* it actualizes the possibilities of the future.

In the profoundly ecological vision of process thought, God is not an exception to metaphysical categories, but their chief exemplification. God is the supreme instance of the relatedness and creativity characteristic of all things, the web of relatedness that nurtures and empowers all creativity. As such, God experiences all creaturely experiences eminently and preserves them in the divine life everlastingly. And it is based on that divine experience of creaturely experience that God "lures" all creatures, persuasively and not coercively without foreknowing the details of creaturely decision, with novel possibilities relevant to what they have been and what they are becoming to realize their creative freedom in their fundamental interdependence with one another.

COBB'S CHRISTOLOGY

One of the more prominent and distinct options among process Christologies is that of John B. Cobb, Jr. His is one of the few contemporary Christologies "from above." According to Cobb, the task of theology, including the construction of an adequate contemporary Christology, is to think self-consciously as Christians about contemporary problems of importance.[3]

The starting point of Cobb's Christology is to identify the divine Logos with the active side of the Whiteheadian God that lures all momentary experiences to creative novelty and transformation, to their self-realization. Christ, more of an image than a concept, is the incarnate Logos, is present in all things as creative transformation. Thus, the presence of Christ is not restricted to Jesus. Nevertheless, there is distinctiveness to the presence of Christ in Jesus in overcoming the typical tension between the "I" and the lures of the Logos. As Cobb states:

> *The degree and the kind of Christ's presence varies. The fullest form of that presence is that in which he coconstitutes with the personal past the very selfhood of a person. That would be the paradigm of incarnation. In that case Christ would not simply be present in a person but would be that person. The distinctive structure of Jesus'*

> *existence was characterized by personal identity with the immanent Logos. Hence it is a matter of literal truth to affirm the identity of Jesus with Christ. In all things Christ is present. Jesus was Christ.*[4]

The symbol of Christ, as well as the various Christian concepts of God, is indissolubly linked to Jesus, a fully human carpenter from Nazareth who, in realizing in his creative freedom the ideal aims and lures presented by the Logos in every moment, is the incarnation of the divine in a special and distinctive way.[5]

Cobb has revised his Christology in responding to the challenges he has felt most keenly. Before doing so, however, he sets the context of his response by defining Christ not for all times and all places, but how today we might most appropriately identify that symbol: the power that works toward "the indivisible salvation of the world,"[6] "the life that struggles against the death- dealing powers that threaten us and the way that leads through the chaos of personal and global life to just, participatory, and sustainable society in which personal wholeness is possible."[7] As I have claimed is the case with all Christologies, Cobb's Christology is shaped by soteriological concerns.

The first of the challenges that have led Cobb to revise his Christology is presented by other religious traditions. Using Judaism and Buddhism as examples, to oversimplify his argument, in each case he urges such openness to the insights of the other, as well as sensitivity to differences, as to enable mutual transformation, which itself is the work of Christ.[8]

The second challenge is posed by Latin American liberation theology, which identifies Christ with the poor and oppressed and the work of Christ with the struggle for liberation. This is a contrast to the identification of Christ with the creative transformation of thought, personal experience, and cultural forms. More specifically, liberation theology questions whether Cobb's Christology is inherently elitist, whether the identification of Christ as creative transformation can be reconciled with locating Christ in the poor and the oppressed. Cobb maintains that this can be accomplished by seeing the Trinity itself incarnate in Jesus, instead of just the second person, the Son.[9] This revision, reminiscent of the Augustinian notion of the coinherence of the three persons of the Trinity—the idea that you cannot mention one person of the Trinity without simultaneously mentioning the other two—enables Cobb to locate Christ in *both* the suffering of the oppressed and creative transformation. The one who suffers with all the suffering is also the one in whom all things cohere, the truth, and "as the Word is present in all things as the way and the life, so all things are present in the truth, and the truth is present in all things."[10]

The final and deepest challenge to Cobb's Christology, and to the task of Christology itself, comes from feminism. Because the enterprise of Christology is inextricably linked to Jesus and the apostolic witness to him, feminists question whether a male savior can save women. Put differently, the patriarchal character of the inherited tradition is not an incidental but an essential (and irredeemable) part of Christianity. Some feminists see its central symbol of the cross as the epitome of suffering and love at odds with the self-affirmation vital to the salvation of women.[11]

To incorporate feminist insights, Cobb appropriates the use of the word *Wisdom* by Christian feminists influenced by biblical studies. Wisdom is capable of encompassing the way, the truth, and the life together, is biblically grounded, and is free of predominantly masculine connotations.[12] Consequently, "Sophia," the divine Wisdom, replaces the Logos in Cobb's Christology: "Christ names Sophia as she embodies herself in the world and receives the world into herself" and "Jesus is the incarnation of Sophia, the Divine Wisdom."[13]

I mostly agree with the thrust of Cobb's Christology, and my differences will be apparent in my own constructive proposals; therefore, at the risk of splitting hairs, I will raise only one substantive issue. Making some important points about the incarnation, Cobb claims that the presence of the light and life in Jesus should not have been interpreted as a metaphysical break radically distinguishing Jesus from other human beings, even though it gave expression to the insight that this light and life were incarnate in him in a special way.[14] He states, nevertheless, that "it does not suggest simply a fuller presence or effectiveness, a difference of degree, as is often proposed."[15] Rather, "it suggests—in some important sense—a qualitative or structural difference."[16]

Cobb's point is well taken. His concern is soteriological: while making clear that for Jesus to be salvific he has to be human—that is to say, there can be no ontological difference between Jesus and us—Cobb is asserting that Jesus also has to be "more" than we are, namely divine (shades of Chalcedon). I remain unconvinced that there can be a point of contact with humans, that Jesus can be fully human—something necessary if we are to be made whole—if the difference between him and us is one of kind rather than degree.

CONSTRUCTIVE PROPOSALS

First, if God is the supreme instance of the relational matrix that fosters creativity, Christ names the presence of the supreme instance of relatedness and creativity and is in turn incarnate in Jesus of Nazareth. One of numerous images in Christian Scripture, if I may be loose and impressionistic in my exegesis, provides an illustration: Jesus' encounter with the woman caught in adultery, accepting and forgiving her, thus enabling her to respond to a newness of life, turning upside down the accepted values of his hearers. I see this account as paradigmatic of Jesus' ability to take more and more of his world into himself, being creatively transformed and creatively transforming others in the process, being empowered and empowering others to respond creatively to previously unimaginable possibilities of the future—all signs of the presence of God's reign.

Second, if, as I have tried to maintain, there is an indissoluble link between Christology and soteriology, what we need to be saved from fundamentally shapes the form of any Christology. Thus, if Christ is the presence of the supreme instance of the relational matrix of creativity, Christ overcomes distortions in our relatedness that obstruct creativity. In other words, if our relationships, human and nonhuman, including our sociopoliticoeconomic systems, are constitutive of who we are and fundamentally shape our creativity, some relationships and some forms of relatedness enhance creativity and others obstruct it. This is particularly evident in oppressive and exploitative relations. The divine wisdom incarnate in Christ is God's solidarity with the suffering through which God empowers the struggle for liberation from the destructive forms of relatedness that obstruct creativity.

Third, to carry further the implications of the relational matrix of creativity for a process Christology, we need to be increasingly aware of how, as Bernard M. Loomer has written, "Christ owed . . . his character as a Christological figure . . . to those people whom he came to serve,"[17] and how "Christ's relations to his fellows and theirs to him were constitutive of his very being."[18] In a brilliant, groundbreaking, and significant recent work on Christology influenced by process thought and grounded in feminist insight, *Journeys by Heart: A Christology of Erotic Power*, Rita Nakashima Brock extends Loomer's claims considerably.[19] Seeking to liberate Christianity from its patriarchal captivity, she names erotic power the power of interrelatedness, a power born in us, as healing, wholemaking, empowering, and liberating; it is original grace.[20] Divine erotic power, the incarnate life-giving power of the universe, is the Heart of the Universe.[21] The divine dimension of human existence, of Heart, is the presence of erotic power.[22]

Brock's Christology is centered not in Jesus but in the Christa/ Community, the healing and wholemaking center of Christianity, because "what is truly Christological, that is, truly revealing of divine incarnation and salvific power in human life, must reside in connectedness and not in single individuals."[23] This implies that "if Jesus is reported to have been capable of profound love and concern for others, he was first loved and respected by the concrete persons of his life," and that "if he was liberated, he was involved in a community of mutual liberation."[24] Exploration of the presence of Christ in postpatriarchal, nonhierarchical, participatory, ecologically sustainable communities such as the Christa/Community is one of the most promising areas for future developments of Christologies influenced by a process conceptuality and illumined by feminist insights such as Brock's.

Fourth, I am in wholehearted agreement with Cobb's dual insistence that while Christ is present in all things, Christ and Jesus are nevertheless indissolubly linked. Perhaps paradoxically, I maintain that we would have a better sense of the contemporary presence and work of Christ if we engaged in an intentional retrieval of the historical Jesus and the earliest traditions about him. Such a move can help us to be self-conscious about seeing traditions as living, dynamic, creative responses to the challenges of the present as they appropriate and reappropriate, interpret and reinterpret the past in the process of reconstituting themselves. This process of retrieval and reconstruction has the liberative potential of uncovering problematic and oppressive features of the inherited tradition—patriarchism, classism, racism, anti-Judaism, anthropocentrism. An attempt at the kind of historical reconstruction I am proposing has not only intrinsic merit but can be helpful in retrieving the Jewish roots of Christianity, which is vital given the long, tragic history of relations between Christians and Jews. From a process perspective, historical retrieval can enable us to actualize nonpatriarchal, nonhierarchical, nonanthropocentric, liberating possibilities unseen and unrealized in the past.

Finally, I would advocate process theology's appropriation of an earlier phase of its own tradition, the sociohistorical method of the early Chicago School. In speaking of Christianity's constant appropriation and reappropriation of its part as creative responses to the felt needs and challenges of the present, I was using the language of the early Chicago School. What makes the Chicago School's sociohistorical method distinctive is its singular focus on social movements and forces and their relationship to doctrine—which Shailer Mathews, the preeminent representative of the school, described as a form of "transcendentalized politics."[25]

The strength of process theology lies in its relation to the history of ideas. In appropriating the sociohistorical method, process thought should not relinquish this strength nor its focus on metaphysics and the criteria of consistency, coherence, and adequacy for adjudicating truth claims. An appropriation of the sociohistorical method can, however, enable process theology to account more adequately for the relation between social movements and ideas, including the development of Christologies; to account more adequately for the political consequences of all theologies; to explore the link between its own social location and its theological constructions; to have a sense of connectedness to actual historical movements; and to be firmly rooted in history yet at the same time affirm the primacy of a creative response to the needs of the present.

My constructive proposals are multifaceted and would involve process theologians working collegially on many fronts at the same time. I hope these proposals will contribute to the mutual creative transformation of Christology and process theology to dynamic, ever-growing, inclusive, holistic, practical, and efficacious visions for participation in the "indivisible salvation of the world."

NOTES

1. Some of the major works in the historical development of process Christologies are Lionel S. Thornton, *The Incarnate Lord* (London: Longmans, Green, 1928); W. Norman Pittenger, *The Word Incarnate* (New York: Harper & Bros., 1959) and *Christology Reconsidered* (London: SCM Press, 1970); Henry Nelson Wieman, *The Source of Human Good* (Carbondale: Southern Illinois University Press, 1946), 39–44, and Wieman's posthumously published *Science Serving Faith*, ed. Creighton Peden and Charles Willig (Atlanta: Scholars Press, 1987); Daniel Day Williams, *The Spirit and the Forms of Love* (Washington, DC: University Press of America, 1981), 155–91, and *What Present-Day Theologians Are Thinking* (New York: Harper & Row, 1967), 154–82; Bernard M. Loomer, "Empirical Theology within Process Thought," in *The Future of Empirical Theology*, ed. Bernard E. Meland (Chicago: University of Chicago Press, 1969), 161–64; David R. Griffin, *A Process Christology* (Philadelphia: Westminster Press, 1973); Russell Pregeant, *Christology Beyond Dogma: Matthew's Christ in Process Hermeneutic* (Philadelphia: Fortress Press, 1978); Marjorie Hewitt Suchocki, *God-Christ-Church: A Practical Guide to Process Theology*, new rev. ed. (New York: Crossroad, 1989) 87–137; Clark M. Williamson, *Has God Rejected His People? Anti-Judaism in the Christian Church* (Nashville: Abingdon, 1982); Delwin Brown, *To Set at Liberty: Christian Faith and Human Freedom* (Maryknoll, NY: Orbis Books, 1981), 88–105; Bernard J. Lee, S. M., *The Galilean Jewishness of Jesus: Retrieving the Jewish Origins of Christianity* (Mahwah, NJ: Paulist Press, 1988); James E. Will, *A Christology of Peace* (Louisville: Westminster/John Knox Press, 1989).

One of the major alternatives to the Christology of John B. Cobb, Jr., that we shall consider is the "minimalist" Christology of Schubert M. Ogden. All of Ogden's works seek to integrate the insights of existentialism and process thought. See his *Christ Without Myth: A Study Based on the Theology of Rudolf Bultmann* (Dallas: SMU Press, 1979); "Bultmann's Demythologizing and Hartshorne's Dipolar Theism," in *Process and Divinity: Philosophical Essays Presented to Charles Hartshorne* (La Salle, IL: Open Court Publishing, 1964); *The Reality of God and Other Essays* (New York: Harper & Row, 1966). For his responses to liberation theology, see *Faith and Freedom: Toward a Theology of Liberation*, rev. enlarged ed. (Nashville: Abingdon Press, 1989), and *The Point of Christology* (San Francisco: Harper & Row, 1982). For a summary of his views on theological method and a range of other issues, see *On Theology* (San Francisco: Harper & Row, 1986).

2. John B. Cobb, Jr., *Beyond Dialogue: Toward a Mutual Transformation of Christianity and Buddhism* (Philadelphia: Fortress Press, 1982).

3. John B. Cobb, Jr., "Theology as Thoughtful Response to the Divine Call," in *The Vocation of the Theologian*, ed. Theodore W. Jennings, Jr. (Philadelphia: Fortress Press, 1985), 105.

4. John B. Cobb, Jr., *Christ in a Pluralistic Age* (Philadelphia: Westminster Press, 1975), 142.

5. John B. Cobb, Jr., "Christ Beyond Creative Transformation," in *Encountering Jesus: A Debate on Christology*, ed. Stephen T. David (Atlanta: John Knox Press, 1988), 144.

6. John B. Cobb, Jr., *Process Theology as Political Theology* (Philadelphia: Westminster Press, 1982). The phrase is taken from Dorothy Solle.

7. Cobb, "Christ Beyond Creative Transformation," 143.

8. Ibid., 147–50.

9. Ibid., 150–53.

10. Ibid., 153.

11. Ibid., 154–57.

12. Ibid., 157.

13. Ibid.

14. Ibid., 144–45.

15. Ibid., 145.

16. Ibid.

17. Loomer, "Empirical Theology within Process Thought," 162.

18. Ibid., 163.

19. New York: Crossroad Publishing Co., 1988.

20. Ibid., 25–26.

21. Ibid., 45.

22. Ibid., 46.

23. Ibid., 52.

24. Ibid., 66.

25. Shailer Mathews, *The Atonement and the Social Process* (New York: Macmillan, 1930), 92, 94.

CHAPTER TWENTY-ONE

CHRISTOLOGY AND THE
AFRICAN-AMERICAN PILGRIMAGE

THOMAS HOYT, JR.

Christology is foundational for the theological enterprise. It is concerned with the questions, Who is Jesus? What did Jesus accomplish? How did the Jesus of history become the Christ of faith? Who is Jesus Christ for us today? These questions confronted the early church and continue to confront us in every moment. African Americans have discussed all of these matters, but with faith stances conditioned by their special cultural and conversion experiences.

Jesus Christ in the experience of African Americans is Friend, Liberator, Reconciler, Savior, Lord, Prophet, Teacher, Healer, Way Maker, Bridge over Troubled Water, Lily of the Valley, Bright and Morning Star. It is no accident that Jesus Christ is described by titles, images, and phrases that correspond to the nature of African-American experiences in their sojourn within the American context. The nature of that sojourn evoked need for a God and consequently a Christ who provided and supplied what was necessary for salvation.

While the common belief is that one's understanding of the revelation of Jesus ultimately determines one's understanding of God and the meaning of human existence, the African-American experience has served as a catalyst for raising questions of the scriptural texts. These questions are indispensable for grasping the relevance of the Jesus Christ of the first century for the people of the twentieth century. Of course, one must be careful that the Jesus of the first century does not become identical with the Christ that people of the twentieth century have made in their own image. Yet it is axiological that any Christology that fails to speak to the needs of a particular age will not live.

The views of some African-American theologians who have published on the subject of African-American views of Christ will be the basis of this discussion and will provide building blocks for future investigation.

The question of whether Jesus was Black in a literal, ontological, or generic sense has been cogently argued by Albert Cleage, James Cone, and J. Deotis Roberts, Sr., respectively. We will be concerned here with two scholars' interpretations of Jesus Christ. Consequently, this discussion will revolve around not only who Jesus the Christ is for African-American theologians, but what this Christ does for the salvation of an oppressed people. Such concerns will be consistent with the general purpose and history of Christological debate. A brief review of the American experience of African Americans suggests how that experience has helped condition the explication of the Jesus Christ event.

THE AFRICAN-AMERICAN EXPERIENCE

According to Olin Moyd, African Americans have experienced five stages of history. Dr. Roberts lists them as:

> (1) the Formative period, from the Civil War through Reconstruction; (2) the Maturation period, from Reconstruction to the beginning of the Great Migration (1914); (3) the Expansion-Renaissance period, from the Great Migration to the beginning of World War II; (4) the Passive Protest period, from World War II to 1955; and (5) the Radical Reassertion period, from 1955 to the present.[1]

Roberts then divides Moyd's fifth stage into four of his own: (1) from 1954 to 1965 we may call the Civil Rights/Integration period; (2) from 1966 to 1972 was the Black Consciousness/Black Power period; (3) the Reformist period, began in 1973 and ended roughly in 1977; (4) the present period is one of Political Response to Neoracism.[2]

In each of these periods interpretations of Jesus Christ have corresponded to the times and experiences of the people. These have been discussed at length by various scholars.[3] The fact that the African-American experience in the United States since emancipation has not been amenable to the development of a positive self-image is so well known that only a brief reminder of its contours is needed: political disenfranchisement; military segregation and humiliation; restrictions in and exclusions from jobs and denials of promotion; restrictions in and exclusions from housing; segregation and discrimination in health care, medical services, and social welfare; frequent injustice in the courts; and exclusions from schools, churches, and voluntary, occupational, and professional associations. The restrictions and exclusions of the caste system have been at once so rigorous and so comprehensive that multitudes of African Americans have sought as a goal the best possible survival, rather than higher mountains to climb.

SLAVE RELIGION: JESUS AS LIBERATOR

Even before African-American theologians began to write that Jesus was liberator, the slaves through their songs, sermons, and prayers had so proclaimed. Ideas and records of the piety of slaves indicate that the Exodus and the resurrection are biblical supports from which African-American theologians have constructed a doctrine of God and a Christology, both of which have eschatological significance in terms of a praxis of liberation.

The experience of slavery shaped a theological faith that was concrete in helping African Americans deal with their realities. For example, God was described as the Father, loving, beneficent, forgiving, and gracious. God was also just and would deal justly with the disobedient, whether master or slave. Referring to the experience of Israel in the Old Testament, African-American slaves saw God moving them toward a destiny. All they were waiting for was their Moses. They preached and sang with the assurance that as God delivered Israel, so would God deliver them. God and deliverance are inseparable theological themes.

Other illustrations were used to celebrate God's deliverance, especially Daniel in the den of lions and the Hebrew children in the fiery furnace. God and deliverance would come as Ezekiel's "wheel in the middle of a wheel" or as Daniel's "stone hewed out of the mountain." God's deliverance would come on earth before it was done in heaven. Jesus was depicted by slaves as the elder brother. He was Savior, yes, but he was also a co-sufferer. He was accessible and ever present. Even now, when in trouble, African Americans whisper or cry aloud, "Help me, Jesus!" Because of the many similarities between the abuse that

Jesus suffered and that of the African-American man and woman, they could sing and preach about Jesus, being assured of divine companionship. Sin was not a philosophical abstract, nor was it limited to the negative moralisms emphasized in sermons preached by whites to slaves: "Don't drink," "Don't gamble," "Don't commit adultery," "Don't steal." These admonitions meant nothing to the slaves; they not only saw their masters doing these acts and more, they saw the evil of the system as a far more despicable wickedness than anything they were doing.

Slaves often affirmed in their faith the existence of heaven, for if life on earth was a foretaste of the hell to come, surely heaven must be the essence of extreme bliss. Because God was all that God is, and Jesus was all that Jesus is, how could God's abode not be all that is described in the Revelation? Slaves took seriously the idea that Jesus was going to prepare a place for them and would come back to receive them. All that they were denied on earth would be multiplied in heaven.

> *I've got shoes, you got shoes, all of God's children got shoes. When we get to Heaven, gonna put on our shoes and walk all over God's heaven.*

Heaven, however, had a dual implication for the African-American liberation of past days. It referred not only to life beyond this life, but also to a state *in* this life. Because of the risk involved in overtly preaching liberation, slaves learned how to sing liberation in the very presence of their masters, using the image of Jesus as a code.

> *Steal away, steal away, steal away to Jesus,*
> *Steal away, steal away home,*
> *I ain't got long to stay here*
> *(We've got a secret meeting tonight).*

Jesus, in the thinking of these theologians in the period of slavery, is characterized by those like Jarena Lee, who gave impetus to an "egalitarian Christology." In Jarena Lee's argument supporting the right of women to preach, she stated:

The Saviour died for women as well as for men. If the man may preach, because the Saviour died for him, why not the woman? Seeing he died for her also. Is he not a whole Saviour, instead of half one? as those who hold it wrong for a woman to preach, would seem to make it appear.[4]

Jesus as Savior is thus perceived as consequential for breaking down walls regarding vocational choices based on gender.

Jesus the Christ was seen as divine cosufferer. When African Americans could not find anyone to depend upon in this earthly arena, Jesus was the one who bore their pain. Black women, who have suffered the triple jeopardy of race, sex, and class, have been referred to by William Eichelberger as God's updated form of revelation to Western society. He says:

It is my feeling that God is now manifesting Himself, and has been for over 450 years, in the form of the Black American Woman, as mother, as wife, as nourisher, sustainer and preserver of life, the Suffering Servant who is despised and rejected by men, a personality of sorrow who is acquainted with grief. The Black Woman has borne our griefs and carried our sorrows. She has been wounded because of American white society's transgressions and bruised by white iniquities. It appears that she may be the instrumentality through whom God will make us whole.[5]

This significant statement not only conceives of the divine reality in other than male terms, albeit in traditional terminology, but it points out that African-American women's suffering is not unlike that of Jesus, who is their cosufferer. After reviewing slave narratives and confessions from persons like Sojourner Truth, Jacquelyn Grant said: "In the experiences of Black people, Jesus was 'all things.' Chief among these, however, was the belief in Jesus as the divine co-sufferer, who empowers them in situations of oppression."[6]

Let it be affirmed that the Christological emphases of the slave religion have dominated African-American theology to this day. We need only look at the work of two primary African-American theologians: James Cone and J. Deotis Roberts, Sr. The tension in their views of biblical faith and interpretations of the experience of African Americans informs their view of Jesus the Christ.

JAMES CONE

Professor Cone's view of biblical faith and the African-American experience is clearly articulated in his several books. Chief among them are *Black Theology and Black Power*,[7] *The Spirituals and the Blues: An Interpretation*,[8] *A Black Theology of Liberation*,[9] and *God of the Oppressed*.[10] The latter especially is a testament to the steadfast faith of African Americans in Jesus Christ, to their recognition of Christ as liberator and their ability to realize their liberation through faith in the power of his resurrection.

An authentic African-American Christology makes sense of the African-American experience:

> *We do not begin our theology with a reflection on divine revelation as if the God of our faith is separate from the suffering of our people. We do not believe that revelation is a deposit of fixed doctrines or an objective word of God that is then applied to the human situation. On the contrary, we contend that there is no truth outside or beyond the concrete historical events in which persons are engaged as agents. Truth is found in the histories, cultures, and religions of our peoples. Our focus of social and religio-cultural analyses separates our theological enterprise from the progressive and abstract theologies of Europe and North America. It also illuminates the reason why orthopraxis in contrast to orthodoxy has become for many of us the criterion of theology.*[11]

The issues of God, Jesus Christ, experience, and liberation are joined in Cone's statement:

> *The appearance of Black Theology on the American scene is due exclusively to the failure of white religionists to relate the gospel of Jesus to the pain of being Black in a racist society. . . . Therefore,*

> *Black Theology is one of liberation because it is a theology which*
> *arises from an identification with the oppressed Blacks of America,*
> *seeking to interpret the gospel in light of the Black condition. It be-*
> *lieves that the liberation of Black people is God's liberation.* [12]

Because Professor Cone took seriously the influence of slave reli-gion's view of God as liberator from oppression, he began to articulate a gospel of freedom based on the action of God within the Jewish community as told in the biblical story of the Exodus.

The Exodus story is the decisive event in Israel's history because of what it revealed. First, God is on the side of the weak and oppressed; second, God is able to break the bonds of the oppressor through God's power. Realizing the presence of God, the Israelites were willing to enter into a compact with Yahweh in order to solidify a permanent relationship. This covenant was based on what Yahweh had done, was doing, and would do in relationship with a people who had experienced oppression but who now experienced relative freedom with a chance to spread that freedom to all nations (Exod. 19:4–6).

Cone thinks that the Exodus-Sinai tradition, coupled with the theme of God's power in liberation that evolves from this tradition, unlocks the Old Testament in a thematic or systematic approach.

When Cone moves from the Exodus-Sinai tradition to other tradi-tions in the Old Testament, he handles them in interesting ways. God's liberating presence was with Israel even during those periods of disobe-dience. In periods of apostasy and unfaithfulness, from the wilderness to the promised land, God was liberating God's people.

In the prophetic tradition, the Exodus-Sinai tradition is remem-bered and invoked in relationship to a disobedient people. Amos, Hosea, Isaiah, Jeremiah, and Micah all called upon Israel to treat the poor, weak, and oppressed as if they were of the covenant in order to offset the coming judgment of the Almighty God. Cone saw the same emphasis in the David-Zion tradition. The prophet Isaiah of Jerusalem appealed to David's reign as the significant act of deliverance. Even here, "Yahweh is the God of justice who sides with the weak against the strong." [13] It is significant that in this one instance Cone concedes that there are other acts of deliverance besides the Exodus-Sinai event that could just as well unlock the door of the Old Testament.

In the poetry tradition, Cone sees the Davidic tradition undergirding the Psalms. However, in the wisdom literature, where his process of selectivity breaks down, he says: "Where the sages seem to be unaware of Israel's saving history, God's concern for the poor is nonetheless emphasized."[14] God still protects the weak, the poor, and orphans.[15]

Cone clearly makes God's alliance with the poor and oppressed his major theological foundation.

> *If theological speech is based on the traditions of the Old Testament, then it must heed their unanimous testimony to Yahweh's commitment to justice for the poor and weak. Accordingly it cannot avoid taking sides in politics, and the side that theology must take is disclosed in the side that Yahweh has already taken. Any other side, whether it be with the oppressors or the side of neutrality (which is nothing but a camouflaged identification with the rulers), is unbiblical. If theology does not side with the poor, then it cannot speak for Yahweh who is the God of the poor.*[16]

Moving to the New Testament, Cone considers liberation "the central motif of the gospel and one of the most creative elements of Black religion."[17] Jesus as liberator is seen especially in the cross and resurrection. Cone sees the cross and resurrection as a transforming event that started with Jesus' liberating ministry to a particular oppressed group and led to a liberating ministry for all the oppressed.[18]

While the cross made a statement about God's willingness to suffer in order to liberate humanity, the resurrection revealed that Jesus' liberating ministry had repercussions beyond first-century Jews. The resurrection also had implications for the universal freedom from oppression. Cone contends: "The resurrection is God's conquest of oppression and injustice, disclosing that the divine freedom revealed in Israel's history is now available to all."[19] This affirmation had special significance for those African Americans suffering oppression in the American context.

In seeking to do theology out of the context of the African-American experience, Cone goes to the spirituals and the blues as one of the roots of African-American life. African-American theologians use the spirituals of the slaves to understand Christology. Jesus' suffering is portrayed in some spirituals as a paradigm of the slaves' own suffering: "Were you there when they crucified my Lord?" Professor Cone explains: "Slaves knew the significance of the pain and shame of Jesus' death on the cross [and] they found themselves by his side."[20] The reciprocity between the salvific past and the redemptive present allowed them to transcend spatiotemporal limitations and placed them at the foot of the cross. They had no sense of contradiction in singing about Jesus' mother in the image of the Exodus:

Oh Mary, don't you weep, don't you moan,
Oh Mary, don't you weep, don't you moan,
Pharaoh's army got drownded,
Oh Mary, don't you weep.

The slaves in that spiritual relate the awesome events of the Exodus and the resurrection; the archetype of liberation and the prototype of the ultimate liberated person; the God of liberation and the Child of that God who was their sibling in suffering. The Exodus, for many slaves, was the sign of the inevitability of the resurrection. Developing this insight, African-American theologians claim that the resurrection has brought to eschatological fruition the promise enshrined in the covenant of Sinai.

The knowledge of Christ in the power of his resurrection justified the slaves' hope for a better life to come. Because of the resurrection, Cone contends, we can know that "death is not the goal of history. It was this truth that enabled Black slaves to survive humanely in a situation of extreme cruelty."[21]

Christ in the resurrection not only gave slaves power to endure the imminent cruelty of slavery, but also the power to overcome the fear of freedom. If there is no power to overcome, people will ask as the Israelites asked Moses when they found themselves between Pharaoh's army and the sea: "Is it because there are no graves in Egypt that you have taken us away to die in the wilderness? What have you done to us, bringing us out of Egypt?" (Exod. 14:11, RSV). "The fear of freedom and the risks contained in it are ever present realities in the fight for liberation," writes Cone. Those seeking liberation must trust that it is God's will for them to be liberated. Otherwise, "the oppressed will get tired and also become afraid of the risks of freedom."[22] The resurrection of Christ helps the community continue freedom's quest. Christ and the Exodus are inextricably connected.

Cone understands sin as connected with passivity and apathy on the part of one who refuses to stand up for freedom:

> *Sin then for Black people is the loss of identity. It is saying Yes to the White absurdity—accepting the world as it is by letting White people define Black existence. To be in sin is to be contented with White solutions for the "black problem" and not rebelling against every infringement of White being on Black being.*[23]

Some would think that by emphasizing sin as mere passivity, Cone has thereby minimized sin as pride, rebellion against God, the creature striving to become the Creator. Aren't both the oppressed and the oppressor in need of the grace of God?

Although Cone alludes to the universality of sin and Grace, he does not find this theme particularly relevant to political realities. He feels that African Americans need to be radicalized, that whites need to repent, and that traditional talk about sin does not satisfy.

The late bishop Joseph Johnson thinks that there is enough empirical data to sustain Cone's definition of sin in a time of rebellion. He eloquently says:

> *The tragedy of Cone's interpretation of whiteness, the personification of all that is evil and degrading in the world, is not due to the fact that it is not informed by the most profound insights of the Christian faith concerning human nature; but rather because so many facts can be used to support his contentions. The extermination of the Indians by whites; three-hundred years of second class citizenship for Blacks; the lynchings; the segregation, the discrimination and exploitation of Blacks; the murder of four Black children in a Baptist Church in Alabama, the tragic slaughter of three civil rights workers in Mississippi, the murder of Martin Luther King, Jr., the massacre at*

Attica Prison; the tragedy of Angela Davis; the extermination of the Black Panther Party in Chicago; the destruction of the Black male image under the guise of integration; the ghettoization of Blacks in the major urban centers; the flights of whites to suburbia; and the ruthless destruction of human life in Vietnam are some of the facts which may be used to support the position of James Cone.[24]

The bishop seems to feel, and rightly so, that the low self-image of an oppressed people raises basic questions about the idea that pride is synonymous with sin. Pride is sin only when one elevates one's own race as being superior; or when one fails to recognize one's Creator; or, in Christian terms, when one refuses to acknowledge Jesus Christ as Savior.

It is dangerous to talk about oppression and rebellion without also talking about sin and grace as a universal quality and condition of humankind. Just because God is participating in the fight for justice and supports the weak and helpless does not mean that African Americans do not need to be forgiven and walk in faith. This does not mean that Cone is unaware of this. He even says that prayer is the beginning of the practice of liberation.[25]

LIBERATION AND RECONCILIATION

J. Deotis Roberts defined African-American theology as "reflection upon the Christian experience in Black."[26] For Roberts, African-American theology, considered in a Christian perspective, must be rooted in biblical faith; must be informed by the African-American experience; must be revolutionary or political; will be situational or existential; will be ethical; and must be apologetic.[27] Further, African-American theology attempts to give constructive statements of what it really means to be a peculiar people, an elect nation, the chosen of God.[28] In amplifying his definition of African-American theology, Roberts ties it to freedom: "Liberation is revolutionary—it points to what ought to be. . . . Therefore, Black Theology is a Methodology of Liberation."[29] In other words, African-American theology is liberation that is also reconciling. The Exodus event and the ministry of Jesus are fundamental for understanding the liberating and reconciling aspects of Roberts' theology:

*The exodus provides a central category for interpreting not only the
Old Testament but the work of Jesus. . . . The exodus was an event
in which people experienced unexpected deliverance from bondage . . .
and meant the opening up of an until-then impossible future for those
who had been oppressed.*[30]

Just as the Exodus opened up possibilities for liberation and
reconciliation, it also served as a paradigm for interpreting the work of
Jesus. Jesus Christ, through the cross and resurrection, depicted suffering as divine reconciliation. For Roberts the Jesus of history par-
ticularized the gospel message, while the Christ of faith universalized
it. Jesus's concern was to liberate the oppressed, while the concern of
the Christ is for the reconciliation of all people to each other and to
God. If Jesus meant freedom and the Christ meant reconciliation, how
can these realities be explained? The cross of Christ provides an answer.

The cross revealed an identity with the liberation of the oppressed.
It represents unmerited suffering by Jesus in order that God's reconciliation might be effected for humanity. Thus for Roberts, "Christ is
Reconciler and the ministry of the cross is reconciliation."[31] This
Christological interpretation entails many consequences, one of which
is that the followers of the Reconciler are themselves called to be agents
of reconciliation.

Roberts thinks that we are in need of a deeper understanding of
the doctrine of resurrection—the symbol of victory over sin, evil, and
death. Faith in the risen Lord will lead to such understanding. He
cautions against a kind of "Jesusology" that may permit us to give up on
social justice in this life. Although Jesus reconciled us to God and our
task is reconciliation to each other, a liberating experience of reconciliation suggests that there can be no ethics without eschatology and no
eschatology without ethics.[32]

*My {Roberts'} program combines liberation and reconciliation. Many
feel that I am neither fish nor fowl. Some have observed that it is too
soon to talk of reconciliation. Others rule reconciliation out altogether. Still others insist that only whites should be concerned about
reconciliation and they are the oppressors. These are mainly reactions
from Blacks. Many Whites overlook liberation altogether and em-*

brace reconciliation as their only concern. They seek a kind of "cheap grace" approach to race relations.[33]

Liberation is the goal and reconciliation is the way, but if African-American theology is to be consistent to its goal, both must be taken together. Just ends must use just means. This was Martin Luther King, Jr.'s view in the civil rights movement, and it seems part of Roberts' methodology as well. He thereby avoids the "we-they" approach taken by such African-American theologians as Albert Cleage and James Cone.[34] He contends that one can be pro-African American without being anti-white.

Roberts' approach prevents the type of revolution that concedes guerilla warfare, genocide, or mutual suicide as the only options to the racial struggle. One must remember that he is speaking in terms of the American context and not that of Central America or South Africa:[35]

Christ the Liberator is also Christ the Reconciler. God was in Christ setting us free and God was in Christ reconciling the world unto himself. We are called forth as agents of reconciliation. . . . Reconciliation is a "costly game."[36]

On the road to reconciliation one must go through liberation, which itself entails confrontation and, consequentially, suffering.

When Roberts insists that suffering and reconciliation go together, he surely reflects Martin Luther King's concept of "redemptive suffering" in which suffering must somehow be transformed into moral and spiritual victory. It means *using* suffering rather than being used by it. While recognizing suffering as a part of the African-American experience, Roberts does not glorify it nor identify it as the plan of God. Either one of the latter directions would be dangerous.

CONCLUSION

The impact of the faith of the slaves has led African-American theologians to relate Jesus, the liberator, to Yahweh of the Exodus. Both reveal divine judgment on slavery and victimization. Thus, the faith of African-American theologians joins the Exodus and the cross/

resurrection. The Exodus is the paradigm of God as a God of liberation and foreshadows God's incarnation of the definitive revelation of the election of the oppressed—Jesus the co-sufferer, the Word of liberation made flesh.

Both James Cone and J. Deotis Roberts affirm the indispensable affirmation that the Jesus of history is identical with the Christ of faith. To those scholars who contend that almost nothing can be known of the historical Jesus, Cone issues a rebuttal:

> *The historical Jesus is indispensable for a knowledge of the Risen Christ. If it can be shown that the New Testament contains no reliable historical information about Jesus of Nazareth or that the Kerygma (early Christian preaching) bears no relation to the historical Jesus, then Christian theology is an impossible enterprise.*[37]

In a credo, Roberts summarizes whom he sees Jesus the Christ to be:

> *For me the Jesus of history is the Christ of Faith. The Incarnation is the Atonement. Jesus is concerned about this life as well as the next. He saves us body, mind, and spirit. Salvation is an experience of wholeness. Jesus is the Saviour of each people and every people. The particularism and the universalism of the gospel merge in His saving mission. He is prophet, priest, and king. As the Black Messiah he liberates us. We overcome our identity crisis through the symbol of the Black messiah. In His presence we cry out, "My lord and my God." As the universal word, He reconciles us with all humans. The Black messiah liberates; the universal Christ reconciles. The one who sets us free brings us together.*[38]

While we admit that Cone's view of Jesus the Christ as liberator and Roberts' view of Jesus Christ as liberator and reconciler further the quest for African-American Christology, the critique of the late bishop Joseph Johnson, Jr., is of utmost importance. He believes that an adequate Christology must be biblically based; must stress a Black Messiah patterned after the "portrait of Jesus of Nazareth which is presented to us in the four Gospels and especially in the Synoptic gospels"; and must have both a particularistic and universalistic quality about it, announcing the sinfulness of men and women and God's redeeming grace for them.[39]

NOTES

1. J. Deotis Roberts, *Roots of a Black Future: Family and Church* (Philadelphia: Westminster Press, 1980), 64.

2. Ibid., 71.

3. See James H. Cone and Gayraud S. Wilmore, eds., *Black Theology: A Documentary History, 1966–1979* (Maryknoll, NY: Orbis Books, 1979); E. Eric Lincoln, *Race, Religion, and the Continuing American Dilemma* (New York: Hill and Wang, 1984); Cain Felder, ed., *Stony the Road We Trod: African-American Biblical Interpretation* (Minneapolis: Fortress Press, 1991).

4. Quoted in Jacquelyn Grant, *White Women's Christ and Black Women's Jesus: Feminist Christology and Womanist Response* (Atlanta: Scholars Press, 1989), 219. The original source is Jarena Lee, *Religious Experiences and Journal of Mrs. Jarena Lee* (Philadelphia, 1849), 15–16.

5. William Eichelberger, "Reflections on the Person and Personality of the Black Messiah," *The Black Church* 2 (Spring 1974): 54.

6. Grant, *White Women's Christ*, 212

7. New York: Seabury Press, 1969.

8. New York: Seabury Press, 1969.

9. Philadelphia: Lippincott, 1970.

10. New York: Seabury Press, 1975.

11. James Cone, *For My People: Black Theology and the Black Church* (Maryknoll, NY: Orbis Books, 1974), 148.

12. Cone, *Black Theology of Liberation*, 23.

13. Cone, *God of the Oppressed*, 69.

14. Ibid., 70.

15. See my article, "The Biblical Tradition of the Poor and Martin Luther King, Jr.," in *The Interdenominational Theological Center* 4, no. 2 (Spring 1977): 12–32.

16. Cone, *God of the Oppressed*, 71.

17. Cone, *My Soul Looks Back*, 61.

18. Cone, *God of the Oppressed*, 135.

19. Ibid.

20. Cone, *Spirituals and the Blues*, 53.

21. Cone, *God of the Oppressed*, 161.

22. Ibid.

23. Cone, *Black Theology of Liberation*, 196.

24. Joseph Johnson, Jr., *Proclamation Theology* (Shreveport, LA: Fourth Episcopal District Press, 1977), 226.

25. Ibid., 144.

26. James J. Gardiner and J. Deotis Roberts, Jr., eds., *Quest for a Black Theology* (Philadelphia: The Pilgrim Press, 1971), ix.

27. Ibid., 65.

28. J. Deotis Roberts, Jr., *Liberation and Reconciliation* (Philadelphia: Westminster Press, 1973), 14–25, 33ff., 50. For a further study of Roberts' position on African-American theology, see his following works: *A Black Political Theology* (Philadelphia: Westminster Press, 1974), 19, 26, 50ff.; and "Black Theology in the Making," *Review and Expositor* 70, no. 3 (Summer 1973): 321–30.

29. Roberts, *Liberation*, 27.

30. Ibid., 29.

31. Roberts, *Black Political Theology*, 153.

32. Ibid., 178; *Liberation*, 26.

33. Roberts, "Black Theology in the Making," 325.

34. Ibid., 324.

35. One should note particularly the sanguine words of Peter Paris in this regard. See *The Social Teaching of the Black Churches* (Philadelphia: Fortress Press, 1985), 127.

The response of the black churches to the black theology movement, of which James H. Cone was the chief systematician and progenitor, has been similar in all respects to their response to black power and the NCNC (National Committee of Negro Churchmen). As they had rejected Marcus Garvey's African Orthodox Church because of the place of prominence it gave to race consciousness and its propositions that God is black (and, accordingly, its demands that the churches be purged of pictures of white Madonnas and the baby Jesus), so also they rejected black theology. Further, the black churches could never condone the tendency of the black power movement to set forth violence as a veiled threat, a practice that black theology justified under the principle of self-defense.

36. Roberts, "Black Theology in the Making," 327. See also Roberts, *Black Political Theology*, 218–19.

37. Cone, *God of the Oppressed*, 115.

38. Roberts, "Black Theology in the Making," 329.

39. Johnson, *Proclamation Theology*, 152.

CHAPTER TWENTY-TWO

CHRISTOLOGY IN DIALOGUE
WITH FEMINIST IDEOLOGY—
BODIES AND BOUNDARIES

ELEANOR MCLAUGHLIN

The most pleased of the lot was the other lion, who kept running about everywhere pretending to be very busy but really in order to say to everyone he met, "Did you hear what he said? *Us lions.* That means him and me. *Us lions.*"

C. S. Lewis, *The Lion, the Witch and the Wardrobe*

The Holy Scriptures and theological tradition are clear that the Deity transcends human sexuality, but they also accord a privileged status, interpreted through the Cross, to the masculine metaphors and terms of address.

Irenaeus Fellowship of Bishops (Episcopal Church, USA)

When God is male, the male is God.

Mary Daly, *Beyond God the Father*

Religion is potent. It has been the most potent ideology the world has known for undermining the integrity of women as first class members of humanity.

Daphne Hampson, "Is There a Place for Feminists in a Christian Church?"

SETTING THE PROBLEM

Women yearn for the experience of the newly freed lions of Narnia, to hear the icon of God say, "*Us women.*" The gender of the Son of God as a Christological problem is a relatively new question and a controversial one, even among feminists.[1] In the ordinary practice and preaching of the churches, the assumption remains strong, especially in the liberal churches, that there is no problem for women in traditional Christology or the language of worship because Jesus, although a man, saves by virtue of "his" humanity. During the debate among Episcopalians over the ordination of women, Richard Norris argued forcefully against those who did not believe it possible for women to be priests, that the maleness of Jesus symbolizes no important theological principle.[2] A recent survey of the history of Christological doctrine, John Macquarrie's *Jesus Christ in Modern Thought* (1990) makes no mention at all of the gender issues raised by feminists, dismissing the soteriological significance of Jesus' maleness in one brief aside: "Sexuality is an essential constitutive element in every human being, and Jesus was a man in the secondary sense that he was of the male sex. But I do not think that any theological importance attaches to this. Being human was essential to Jesus as the Christ; being male was, as far as I can see, contingent."[3]

In contrast to the liberal dismissal of Jesus' gender as a theological issue, for the more conservative churches the maleness of Jesus Christ, far from being a stumbling block, is a necessary symbol of the very essence of the Christian God and gospel. Grounded in an essentialist understanding of both human sexuality and the realist symbolic character of God-language and ritual, the Anglican theologian, E. L. Mascall argues that "the maleness of Jesus cannot be separated from the masculine imagery of revelation. He is the express image of the Father." Hence, "the priesthood of Christ is in no merely biological sense, but in some profound and mysterious sense that lies behind and provides the ground of the biological differentiation, a male function."[4] Indeed, that the being and ministry of Jesus Christ relate in some *real* way to sexual differentiation is celebrated each time the Marriage Office from the *Book of Common Prayer* is read: "Our Lord Jesus Christ adorned this manner of life by his presence and first miracle at a wedding in Cana of Galilee. It signifies to us the mystery of the union between Christ and his Church."[5] Jesus Christ is the Bridegroom, an image not only gendered but sexual. As Thomas Howard, a much-quoted American layman and a recent pilgrim from Canterbury to Rome, puts it, " Jews and Christians worship the God who has gone to vast and prolonged pains to disclose himself to us as he not she, as King and not Queen, and for Christians as Father not Mother, and who sent his Son not his daughter in his final unveiling of himself for our eyes."[6]

Not only conservatives but many women in the pew join academic theologians in an impatient rejection of the feminist complaint that women cannot find a "savior" in this God-Man Jesus, so shaped are we all by the teaching that Jesus Christ is the Representative Man, the Second Adam, the Man for Others, *Ecce Homo*, and therefore beyond or inclusive of all sexuality. It is accordingly difficult to carry on this conversation about the gender of Jesus in a culture that does not recognize that generic humanity has at least since Aristotle been constructed as normatively male, including women only as "defective and misbegotten." Our historicized mindset cannot imagine an alternative to the "obvious" maleness of the Jesus of Nazareth; our devotions celebrate this maleness as we sing, "Unto us a Child is born, to us a Son is given," and whether believer or secularized postmodern, we intuitively reject any alternative. We see evidence of this unconscious anger in the public revulsion that greeted Edwina Sandys' sculpture *Christa*, an icon of Jesus as crucified woman exhibited at the Cathedral of St. John the Divine. Resistance to any modification of the male imaging of Jesus and God can be seen in the continued discomfort and, in some quarters, hostility to women exercising priesthood in the Episcopal church and the rejection of women in priesthood by the majority of Orthodox and Roman Catholic Christians the world over.

DIFFICULTIES FOR FEMINISTS
IN TRADITIONAL CHRISTOLOGIES

What hermeneutical moves are required to meet the intuitively presented problem of classical Christology? If, as Athanasius puts it, God became man that men might become God, where is woman in the economy of salvation?

Daphne Hampson in *Theology and Feminism* presents one of the most far-reaching and persuasive accounts of the problem of Jesus for women. In her view, shifting historical perceptions since the Enlightenment preclude the inclusion of women in the humanity of Jesus Christ. Even though the fathers of the early church may have intended "*et homo factus est*" inclusively, in our post-Enlightenment world the philosophical realism of Plato that grounded the participation of men and women in the human has been lost.[7] Hampson is a true modern in her rigorous nominalism—man and woman are socially constructed as a mutually exclusive binarity, and each therefore represents only its like.[8] I would add that even before Thomas Aquinas argued, with the help of Aristotle, that woman is not perfectly human but a defective male, "humanity" has throughout Western history been constructed as normatively masculine, rational, spiritual, subject not object, capable of autonomous agency, transcendence, presider over persons and things—made in the image of God, who is also initiator and never birthgiver. Thus, "humanity" is gendered male, whether in a contemporary psychological index of personality traits,[9] or in the Nicene Creed of the fourth century: *Therefore, the male gender of Jesus as representative perfect humanity has and still does undergird the exclusivity of this androcentric cultural construction of humanity and is* not *historically contingent.* As soon as this reality is seen—that the so-called generic humanity, whether of the first century or of the twentieth century, is gendered male—Jesus the Christ loses his capacity to stand for women. That the maleness of Jesus' saving humanity has been emphasized since the Protestant Reformation is nicely illustrated by Leo Steinberg in *The Sexuality of Christ in Renaissance Art and in Modern Oblivion*.[10] Steinberg shows how the sacred humanity of Jesus, represented in the early and medieval church by the woman and her child, is from the late fifteenth century increasingly represented by the graphic energy of the erect phallus, gently veiled by the winding cloth of the about-to-be-resurrected God-Man. Recognizing the androcentricity of Jesus Christ as icon of God, representative of *some* and not of *others*, Hampson writes, "Once I grasped the centrality of symbolism to the religion and grasped its effect, it was time for me to leave."[11]

A second problem imbedded in the very foundation of traditional Christology follows from its androcentricity, i.e., the structural inequality of patriarchal assumptions. Hampson's realization that Jesus cannot embody an ethic of equality between the sexes and perhaps even other differentiated members of the species fuels her outrage that the religion of her birth is fundamentally immoral in its bias against one-half of humanity.[12] Central to my own concern in this investigation is the recognition that Jesus Christ as *symbol* of God for us, man for others, provides an ideological foundation for a series of exclusions and injustices. Perhaps women, designated in this century by Karl Barth as *B*, not *A*, represent the master paradigm of hierarchical discrimination. More likely, historical and hermeneutical work can show intimate relationships varying over time among a set of exclusions and subordinations—heretics, Jews, infidels, people of various non-European colors or unaccepted eating or sexual practices—of which the male/female is one of the more universal of these unequally empowered dualities. [13]

For many Christians and most modern unbelievers, the question of salvation and participation in the representative humanity of Jesus Christ as *the* way into the heart of God is not a burning issue. Hence, many feminist theologians seem to ignore the specifically *religious* resistances of ordinary churchwomen to making connections between the male Savior to whom they pray and the complicity of that male God symbol in the repressive institutions that weary their daily lives. [14] Feminist critique uncovers this ideologizing of structural injustice by showing the maleness of Jesus to be an icon of women's daily experience of sexist oppression. One thinks of the gendered character of obedience, self-sacrifice, the privileging of husbands' careers and lives in the choices of young working women and old, caretaking women, and the cultural protection given to male priests who abuse women and children. The words of Mary Daly, here paraphrased, underline the connections where God is Father and Son, all fathers are god, and sons are preferred. [15] Most of the members of a parish women's spirituality group in which I participate neither read Mary Daly nor make the connections between their pain and the gender of their Savior.

The interplay of the gendered Jesus with other oppressions is powerfully expressed by Celie in *The Color Purple*: "Ain't no way to read the bible and not think God white, she say. Then she sigh. When I found out I thought God was white, and a man, I lost interest." [16] How African-American womanist theologians are re-viewing this white, male Jesus/God is an exciting and important re-vision of Christology for white women to learn from. The role of Jesus' sonship and obedience to God in the marking of obediential hierarchical structures throughout Western history is also imprinted for women by the icon of the Son's mother, Mary: "*Fiat mihi* . . . be it unto me according to Thy will." Christian feminists are conducting an interesting conversation about the possibilities of Mary as a model for women. Protestant women are curious, but cannot imagine the Virgin Mary as an object of worship or model for home or work life. In the aftermath of Vatican II, the powerful Mary of the Assumption, co-mediatrix, virtually a member of the Godhead, was dethroned and the Mother subsumed into the functionally male church. Catholic feminists either react angrily against the nineteenth-century domesticated Mary of asexual purity and obedience, or turn to the Magnificat and the experience of the base communities of liberation for a Mary who "puts down the mighty from their seat." Few look to recover the Godlike mother and queen of medieval Christians as a modifier of the maleness of the Incarnation.[17] In the system of the oppressor, the Other, Mary, bears the repressed energies of intimacy, irrational forgiveness, the longed-for and feared Mother excluded from the Male-God icon. She may be as incomplete as the Sky-Boy Infant-God whom she suckles. Seen together, perhaps something more could be found.

The most carefully worked out connections between the gender of Jesus and the ecclesial structures that exclude women and focus male *dominium* for the culture are those made in recent Catholic thought between the male Jesus as high priest and the priesthood and magisterium of the church. The *Vatican Declaration on the Question of the Admission of Women to the Ministerial Priesthood* (1976) may be read in the historical context of the 1974 ordination of eleven Episcopal women in Philadelphia. Events often precipitate theological reflection. In the Vatican document the argument against the suggestion that women could be ordained to the priesthood is explicitly lodged in the maleness of the high priest Jesus Christ, whose human representative at the altar acts *in persona Christi*. With this definition of priestly ministry, the authors state, "When Christ's role in the Eucharist is to be expressed sacramentally, there would not be this 'natural resemblance' which must exist between Christ and his minister if the role of Christ were not taken by a man. In such a case it would be difficult to see in the minister the image of Christ. For Christ himself was and remains a man."[18] This text is exciting in that it uncovers the naked androcentricity of the entire Christian economy insofar as creation is understood as a sacrament, formed and imprinted with the very image of the Creator and a place of meeting between creature and Creator/ Redeemer. What is said here of the ordained, the priest, discloses the symbolic exclusion of women from the possibility of imaging Jesus Christ for reason of his maleness and women's *otherness*. In the woman, the Redeemer cannot be seen. How can the maleness of Jesus Christ function so essentially in his high priesthood and not in the very antetype of that priesthood on the cross, where he hangs as priest and victim, the unique means of salvation? If woman cannot participate in Christ's priesthood, she cannot participate in the saving event of the cross. The button worn by advocates of women priests is unanswerable in its logic: "What cannot be ordained cannot be baptized." Christians of the various branches of the Reformation escape this problem only by depriviliging in favor of the Word, the role of body—God's body and human body—priestly sacrifice, and sacramental participation as the ordinary way to be a part of the economy of salvation. For those Protestants who have thus de-emphasized a sacramental view of creation, reducing Christology to ethics, the willingness of women to listen to men, including the man Jesus, is the last thread holding the garment together. And it has begun to unravel.

SOME FEMINIST MOVES TOWARD
A USABLE CHRISTOLOGY

Many feminist theologians cope with this crisis in Christology by trying not to think about it. That is, many insist with their brothers that Jesus' sex doesn't really matter. For example, Patricia Wilson-Kastner faces the problem bravely and then shies off into the discourse of love, saying that Jesus' flesh embodies God as love and counting on us not to "exalt the concrete details of Jesus' life in an exclusive way."[19] History, like the stones, cries out, the Detail is exalted!

Jürgen Moltmann and Elisabeth Moltmann-Wendel represent the liberal de-emphasis upon the theological significance of Jesus' maleness, which, however, retains a classic centrality for the cross and redemptive suffering. Their Jesus is more than ethical model and teacher. Moltmann would argue that the cross, the suffering of God, is the primary symbol of salvation, within which gender pales before the wondrous scandal of a God who stands with us in our pain. Moltmann-Wendel warns that women can no longer look to the cross symbol without some wariness about the way "sacrifice" has been constructed as a virtue and required unjustly of women. She asks, "Will feminist theology become a theology without the cross?"[20] She muses that a "cup-a-soup sexuality: an all-too-easy agreement of bodies in an exchange of affirmations" seems to loom in feminist thought when it lets go of cross, pain, suffering, and associated maleness.[21] Ultimately, although she listens to the feminist critique of the "male system," and preference for the female images of deity by which birth replaces death[22] in what I would name the *liminal* space of transformation, Elisabeth Moltmann-Wendel spends more energy critiquing feminist alternatives than offering her own. She finally settles for the cross as a symbol of paradox, tree of life as well as gallows, which can free women as well as men from the partiality and reductionism of male experience.[23] This might work for some, but it avoids the question of the body on the cross as well as the cultural construction of exclusion and oppression that that male body privileges.

The insistence that Jesus' maleness is at least not primary could be said to be the position of Rosemary Radford Ruether, a member of the "radical middle" in feminist discourse who finds a canon within the Canon to correct and defy the reductive masculinity not only of religious traditions but of all known cultures and ethical systems. She is free of illusions about Enlightenment anthropology with its preachments of equality, finding more hope for a radical reconstruction of human institutions in the tradition of the Hebrew prophets, which she sees embodied and universalized in the Gospels.[24] But in taking this broadly defined Liberation Theology stance, she may succumb to Hampson's accusation that little of traditional soteriology remains. The *religious* work and person of Jesus as Savior does not seem to be Ruether's primary concern. She can set aside Jesus' maleness as having "theologically speaking . . . no ultimate significance." The prophetic Christ, met in the interaction of the Exodus tradition, in the Gospels, and in the ongoing Christian community, has been emptied of the male *Savior* Jesus for the sake of the pressing task of creating a just and peaceful world.[25]

Theologians have long responded to the problem for women of Jesus' maleness by giving precedence to his ministry and message over the saving work of Christ incarnate on the cross, resurrected. From Elizabeth Cady Stanton to Elisabeth Schüssler-Fiorenza, there has been a chorus of re-readers of the Synoptic narrative who see Jesus as a male feminist. In the earliest evidences of Christian community, read in the silences and between the lines of the biblical texts, Schüssler-Fiorenza finds a Jesus movement in which women took leading, perhaps even

equal, roles with men.[26] Pastoral and encouraging though this hermeneutic may be, it does not finally address the core problem of those
Christian women who need a god-person in their lives, not just an
ethic, and who do not find in the churches the "woman-friendly" Jesus
movement of the first century.

Behind these hermeneutical moves of feminist Christology lies the
tendency of contemporary historical scholarship, which includes biblical scholarship, to give up the search for the historical Jesus. The body
can't be found in the texts any more than in the tomb. Thus "He" easily
becomes for the more academic of us, an "it." If history cannot be very
important these days, then the move of feminist theology right out of
classical Christology becomes more attractive. Hence a modern Christology, such as that of Macquarrie, doesn't bother to address feminist
questions. Is it because he suspects they cannot successfully be addressed? As if agreeing, some feminists would leave Jesus in his maleness and turn to pneumatology, finding a feminine person in the
Godhead in the various "spirit" traditions: the *Shechinah* of God's
presence to God's people; the Wisdom tradition, which lies in Hebrew
scripture behind and within sapiential spirituality, sometimes identified with Jesus but more often with Mary; and the Holy Spirit as
female, a more powerful option in the orthodox tradition, although in
one Western fresco, a buxom female Spirit is set between two bearded
men in Trinitarian coherence. In addition to the often female representations of Sophia/Wisdom/Spirit traditions within the Godhead, there
is the long history of pneumatic and millennial heresies in which
women seem to have been prominent and female god-naming not
infrequent. One thinks of the second-century Montanist experience of
Christ's return as a woman; Mother Ann Lee, in whom Shakers saw a
female Incarnation; or Mary Baker Eddy's Mother-Father God.[27] Yet,
all too often, while maleness is deauthorized, embodiment is lost in
these ever-contemporary spirit epiphanies of the female Holy.

A more popular way out of classical Christology lies in the movement represented by Carol Christ's classic paper, "Why Women Need
the Goddess."[28] Included in this group of responses to the maleness of
the Incarnation are those who find in Mary, Virgin and Mother, an
alternative female icon of the Holy. Mary, so firmly part of universal
Christian devotion from the fourth through the sixteenth century, may

be an important body in a reborn Christology, but that cannot be argued for here. Let us be reminded that Mary functioned as a female mediatrix for theologians as well as the people, and that men as well as women participated in the saving rule and nurture of Mary, Queen of Heaven, Mother of God.[29]

The abandonment of the Western Christian tradition with its Christological centerpiece (what Mary Daly calls "Christolatry"),[30] for an exploration of the possibilities of Middle Eastern, neolithic, and Celtic goddesses has become a widespread and growing force in women's spiritualities.[31] As a student of medieval heresy, I might surmise, with the Dominican and Franciscan preachers of the thirteenth century, that when the church's altars fail to nourish, other tables will be found.[32] No Christian can fail to register the challenge to classical Christology present in this growing interest in Western female deities. What does it mean? A hunger for the affirmation of women's religious experience, for images of the Holy in which a woman may find her woman-self substantiated, for places and practices of sacrality that specifically embrace women's bodies and women's ways? A longing for stories of the Sacred in which women lead and rule, for narratives that are open, where "canon" may still be made out of daily encounters with the "god-ess" in oneself. We need ways of being with the Sacred that bind women to each other in community, sisterhood, and mutuality, without hierarchy or followership. As a priest working with traditional Christian women, I hear a curiosity about and attraction to the "goddess" that cannot be dismissed.

AN ALTERNATIVE FEMINIST CHRISTOLOGY:
RECLAIMING THE BODY

Before arguing for this revised Christology, I will suggest some of the ways in which I differ from, or would modify, some of the principal contemporary feminist Christologies. In the course of this, the components will emerge that I find necessary for a Christology in which women find themselves *subjects*, in God's image, whole and holy.

The Anglican theologian John Macquarrie points to the two authoritative sources for knowledge of Jesus Christ: "testimony of the past and experience of the present."[33] "The significance of Jesus Christ was not seen all at once."[34] Who Jesus *was* is inseparable from who Jesus *is* in the Christ event of the church's faith. Jesus Christ is the Word preached,[35] the sacraments celebrated and the Christian life lived. Macquarrie affirms that Jesus Christ is both historical fact and trans-historical symbol,[36] and that Christological titles are not limited to a particular culture, even that of the writers of the New Testament.[37] It would seem that this mainstream theologian presses for a Jesus Christ who is *not* the same today and yesterday, requiring modifications of the tradition similar to those of many feminist Christians, although in his otherwise exhaustive book he strangely ignores gender questions. I also seek a Christology adequate to contemporary experience and therefore responsive to the feminist difficulties with Jesus' maleness, but, like Macquarrie, I seek a revisionist Christology. In particular, I look for a Christology that is not simply intellectually adequate but a revision of the Christ symbol with which women and men can worship. A usable Christology must be prayable, for human beings were made to worship.

Macquarrie, citing James Dunn, offers an "irreducible minimum without which Christianity loses any distinctive definition."[38] This would involve affirmation of the historical Jew Jesus, fully (but not ordinarily) human, experienced as an exalted being, agent of God, supreme Lord, Son of God. This is a high Christology to which I invite conversation partners; unlike Hampson,[39] I am unwilling to put out of the discussions about Jesus those who don't fit any one of a dozen definitions of "really Christian." I am willing to play on a field without foul lines—it enriches the conversation.

With Carter Heyward, who stated herself to be "hooked on Jesus,"[40] this Jesus narrative and the symbols that ritualize the narrative seem central to me and much of Western religiously shaped culture. For this reason, I am not tempted to move outside the Christ event and the biblical narratives as the foundation-paradigms in which the self and the Holy are sought. Despite the unquestioned spiritual creativity that has been let loose by the rediscovery of the various ancient goddess religions, I have serious difficulties with this alternative to a revised Christology. For *women*, a historical sacred narrative does better than a mythological one because it presents the opportunity to deal with *embodiment* as an aspect of the Sacred. Another problem presented by goddess spirituality is the ease with which it commits the sin that it purports to address: the exclusion of one-half of the human race from an immediate experience of the Holy as Other and Like. We need all forms of creation to be found in God, the "chalice and the blade."

A third problem raised by goddess spirituality lies in the realm of the ethical. I have yet to see the goddess rites so understood and celebrated as to form a sense of right and good by which daily choice may be made and human institutions shaped. I miss in the goddess spiritualities a well-worked-out understanding of sin and its remedy. There is also the fundamental problem that the goddesses, not unlike Mary, may be as fully a product of patriarchy as their consorts and sons. Finally, creating cult and theology from scratch, with so few texts and traditions extant, seems more difficult than working with a fully fledged religious tradition that shapes our culture and unconscious even more dangerously if we ignore it. These caveats notwithstanding, the goddesses stand to correct, to supplant, to nurture, to give birth to much new life in the Christological debates among feminists. The place of the erotic in the Holy and the encounter of the Holy in our bodied experiences of loving, feeding, birthing, desiring, ecstatic consummating union are urgent questions that goddess spirituality helps us to address. The need for a Christology that embraces earth and all earth creatures, a less anthropocentric discourse could also be the result of these conversations between *thealogy* and Christology.

Is a certain unexamined commitment to Enlightenment epistemologies an aspect of many feminist Christologies, particularly Daphne Hampson's, which I find problematic?[41] The heart of the feminist theological enterprise is not the achievement of equality between men and women.[42] Too often equality in our culture means an African American or Hispanic man or woman or dominant culture woman entering the social system under the ground rules of the white male tradition. The admittedly dangerous invitation to explore what *woman* made in God's image might mean on women's terms courts essentialism but views equality as just one among many values. The discovery of woman-self, woman-voice, and woman-in-relation must take priority over, even stand in criticism of, a male-defined autonomous subjectivity or a spurious equality that defines woman in terms of male constructions of the human.

Many feminist Christian women ground their Christologies implicitly on Gal. 3:28, that eschatalogical vision of the baptized community beyond distinctions, where "there is neither Jew nor Greek, there is neither slave nor free, there is neither male nor female, for you are all one in Christ Jesus." Following the groundbreaking work of Elaine Pagels, many search for a way of being beyond sexuality in the extracanonical Gnostic texts where androgynous spiritualities dissolving sexual dualism offer attractive models for nonhierarchical Christian community.[43] Indeed there are many analogies between some feminist, New Age spiritualities and the Gnostic sensibilities of the early Christian centuries. I don't find this direction useful: it was, and remains, predominantly anti-incarnational, anti-body, dualist, anti-sensual, and profoundly individualistic. The Gnostic journey is personal and does not ground a spirituality for community, except in the sense of like-minded adepts. The Gnostic Christ has no body. That is too easy a way to be rid of the phallic signifier.

Many feminist Christologies share the strong bias of the liberal Protestant theological tradition since Schleiermacher in seeking to dismantle high Christological dogma in favor of a renewed sense of the full humanity of Jesus.[44] Such Christology "from below" has the advantage of taking seriously the New Testament narratives, full of Jesus as healer, liberator, friend of sinners, outcasts, and women. Combined with the history of religions, this preference for the historical Jesus can question Christianity's claims of a *unique* revelation of God in him and thus enable mutually enriching conversations with other religious communities. A Christology from below also accords with the feminist call for the priority of experience over extrinsic authority as the place of meeting with the Holy. Additionally, the tendency to let go of preexistence, miracles—up to and including the resurrection—and other instances of providential interruptions of natural causality is more in keeping with modern Enlightenment models of reality. I am willing to be anti-Enlightenment and entertain a second naiveté in the presence of this powerful religious symbol, Jesus Christ. Without denying that Jesus of Nazareth is an actual historical human figure, I affirm that the symbolic reality of Jesus that carries the specifically religious experience of the Holy is as important to me as what little the historians can say about that "heretical Jew, Jesus." Religious experience is mediated symbolically. And of Jesus there is no history free of the interpretation of religious symbol, whether in words or ritual gestures, song or sculpture or sacred building. Macquarrie reminds us that the "life of Jesus" has no more "reality" than the abstractions of Byzantine theology or the Pantocrator staring at us from the middle of a dazzling mosaic.[45] The only novelty in my approach may be an insistence on the Godness of Jesus Christ while seeking to uncover through his sacred humanity the lost Woman-God. I do believe that without the Godness there is no way to deconstruct, uncenter, uncover the maleness so that the woman-ness of God/Jesus can be seen and shared. If Jesus is not something more than a first-century Jewish rabbi, this enterprise is more trouble than it is worth.

Yet the historical particularity may not be lost from a feminist Christology, as so often happens when, with relief, women leave the male Jesus of childhood piety for the Christ of mature theological reflection.[46] Origen also played that intellectually elitist game, leaving the Jesus healer and savior for the unsophisticated while the spiritual "knower" could look to union with the Logos. Here our African-American sisters are extraordinarily helpful as they witness to the power of the historical Jesus, Jesus the liberator, who in his particularity is Black to stand with and redeem the particularity of Black suffering.[47] It is significant for this feminist enterprise that the discussion of or depiction of a Black or Chinese Jesus has caused no significant outcry. James Cone and womanist theologians such as Jacquelyn Grant have been able to contend for a Jesus who, though male, is experienced as Black. This stands in sharp contrast to the outrage that has greeted *Christa*, the sculpture of Jesus as woman crucified. The icon was described by opponents as "reprehensible and desecrating . . . totally changing the symbol."[48] This response is a reminder of the power of body, and of Jesus' historically particular male body. At last, with the now culturally presented opportunity to inscribe the Word made flesh in a Black body or a woman's body, we can again feel the power of the first-century scandal and stumbling block that was Jesus in our world. For first-century Jews and Greeks, God in any body was a scandal, a "clothing" of the universal in the particular. A feminist Christology must emphasize such embodiment, female embodiment, with all the outrage that the kenosis of male privilege arouses.

In keeping with the Enlightenment and liberal roots of the women's movement, too many feminist Christologies have simply avoided all such body talk, with its sexual penumbra. Suchocki's process Christology laments the reduction of "God" to maleness in the face of the Old Testament portrayal of a god beyond sexuality—and she would keep this godly absence of "strictly human features."[49] Such an approach does not meet the demands of women (and many men) that the desiccating dualisms of traditional Christianity be dismantled so that the sacred might once again be found in all embodied experience of life. These Christological reflections, by locating in the incarnate God the place where the Creator/creature dualism is shattered, also propose a violation of the gender binarity, male/female. Such a breaking of the boundaries opens to us a re-vision of the Holy in which relationality, sexuality, feeling, and the feminine join mind and word at the center of our God symbols.

Carter Heyward has written most powerfully of this need.[50] A re-visioned Christology must recover the unitive energies of the erotic. Such a spirituality of desire was known to the mystics from Plato's myth of yearning wholeness in the *Symposium*, Saint Bernard's confidence that in the desiring is the tasting of God and the impassioned union of the mystical marriage of the soul with Jesus. Whether the eros of *Braut-mystik* or the spiritual birth-giving by which the Christian is "pregnant" with God as Holy Child within (celebrated by Meister Eckhart, Catherine of Siena, and Birgitta of Sweden), these embodied devotions of late medieval mystical piety represent an experience of Jesus as mother, wife, sister, lover, and infant beneath our heart that give authorization to our task.[51] It is to this tradition of embodied spirituality that we look to overcome the body-fearing encratism of the New Testament texts on God's love and friendship.

Feminist Christologies have been caught up in the questions of Chalcedon, arguing with a fourth-century dilemma, of how to reconcile within the metaphysic of a dualist late-Platonic and Stoic worldview the apparent paradox of a human being experienced as God.[52] In contrast to this fourth-century consciousness, it is not divinity/humanity but the male/female binarity that bedevils the cultural place in which we stand. Therefore we have to argue what seems apparently as nonsensical as the Chalcedonian paradox of full divinity and humanity in one person: how is Jesus Christ a person whom we can experience as either man or woman. This discourse may not be carried out principally in word symbols but in ritual symbols, in some richer combination of "thick symbols" than is usual for theologians today. Only thus can this become a Christology, a way of imaging Jesus Christ, that can be *prayed and ritualized* by the people of God. Evagrius Ponticus from a fourth-century desert reminds us that the theologian is "one whose prayer is true."[53]

SOME PIECES OF THE BODY OF CHRIST, TREASURES OLD AND NEW

I offer here a suggestion of possible hermeneutical moves and point to some places in the Western Christian tradition where one might find conversation partners for exploring the religious questions raised by the contemporary experiences of women (and some men). I write as one still confident that the gospel accounts of Jesus are primal and life-giving *story*. With Judy Chicago I must affirm, "Our heritage is our power."[54]

We have seen and acknowledged the serious problem for many contemporary Christians of the indisputable historical "fact" that Jesus of Nazareth, worshiped as Christ and Lord, is/was an actual male person. Further, this male Christ, symbolized religiously, has been used to subordinate, dehumanize, and render women invisible and voiceless. Feminist Christologies maneuver to avoid this "fact," notably with a Bultmannian existentialist and demythologizing focus on the Christ event of contemporary experience. For the reasons adduced above, I argue that *feminist* Christology may not so lightly dismiss the "body." Without returning to the "primal naiveté" of a premodern consciousness, I propose we *remythologize* and *resymbolize*, with the help of the pre-Reformation spiritual tradition, to discover a Jesus who is for humanity, very God, very Man, and very Woman, or perhaps, never simply God or only man. This reconstruction is essential if Christianity is to break through androcentrism to the Gospel. It will have a destabilizing impact on the culture at large by deauthorizing the traditional Christologies that have limited and demeaned women, Jews, African Americans, and others who do not fall within the norms of white, male, Western Christian civilization. The feminist requirement that women be genuinely included in Jesus' humanity could be seen as a faithful response to the evangelical promise, "God so loved the world." The way I have made this discovery about Jesus Christ flows out of experience, through the tradition, to a literary-critical paradigm shift, and back into experience.

The experience with which I begin is my own dimly heard call from childhood to be an Anglican priest. The tradition is that now widely seen and appreciated strain of pre-Reformation piety through which Jesus (and sometimes God, Father, and Spirit) is addressed, prayed to, and sacramentally experienced as woman, true body (and woman *culturally represents* body),[55] as lover, child, nursing infant, and, in the vicarity of his mother, queen and female Savior. The literary critical paradigm is that of the transvestite—the taboo, transgressive, Third One who dismantles the binarities, male/female, law/gospel, insider/outsider, friend/enemy, God/world. Finally, the returning experience is the history of women priests in the American Episcopal church, whose being as God-persons and whose ways of presiding and ministering are deconstructing androcentric images and theologies. We are changing, as opponents promised we would, the ways in which God/Jesus/woman-self are experienced—bursting out of the categories and truly changing the gods.

The Experience. As the Episcopal church, led by the secular women's movement of the late 1960s and 1970s, began to consider the possibility that women could be called by God and the community to holy orders, this cradle Episcopalian, then a young professor of medieval history at Wellesley College, began to feel long-repressed stirrings. I could not, however, *imagine* a woman priest, for there were no words or icons that gave permission to *see* that new thing under the sun. My Harvard thesis adviser, who knew of my searchings, told me of an obscure French scholarly article on a little-known medieval devotion to "Jesus our mother."[56] The first article in English on this topic was thus written out of my personal dilemma, the tension between my sense of myself as a woman and a call to priesthood, which I understood quite traditionally and, with psychological accuracy, as an office in which one stood symbolically *in persona Christi.*[57] To discover that Jesus can be *prayed to* as a woman and *represented by* a woman, indeed as a mother like me, was an *empowerment* to action on behalf of structural and theological change in the church and recognition of my own vocation. I argued for the priesthood of women not in the liberal or Enlightenment language of "rights" but rather as a matter of theology—can Jesus Christ be represented by a woman-priest, does Jesus represent women? Can I, woman, made in God's image, see myself in God incarnate and speak with the authoritative subjectivity of the New Adam, naming the world, offering with Christ the sacrifice of praise and thanksgiving?

The Tradition. The address to Jesus as a woman, primarily as mother, begins early in the tradition and becomes more frequent from the twelfth century onward as devotion to the sacred humanity of Jesus and his mother flourishes.[58] The only gospel mother-naming, the Synoptic mother-hen metaphor, is a self-referent, significantly in the context of recalling Jerusalem's history of "killing the prophets and stoning those who are sent to you. How often would I have gathered your children together as a hen gathers her brood under her wings, and you would not!" (Matt. 23:37). This language may not be dismissed as mere literary trope, for tradition reminds us that Christianity's "sacred texts are chronicles of experience, armouries of metaphor, and purveyors of an interpretive tradition."[59] No longer may we give authority to naive distinctions between metaphysical or even historical propositions about God contrasted to the language of prayer or poetry, as if the propositional language of the theologian or the evidence of the historical method told the truth about the "Really Real" more surely than the figurative and affective language of the poet. A rediscovery of the truth-telling status of metaphorical language, known by the prescholastics, is part of the methodology of the renewed theology Christian feminists seek.

Female Jesus-naming throughout the tradition comes up as the bearer of particular theological motifs and in the literature of devotion rather than that of "school" theology. Clement of Alexandria, writing in *Christ the Educator*, experiences in both God the Father and Jesus Logos "care-banishing breasts" affording "the milk of love given by the Word who is father and mother, teacher and nurse."[60] The nurture and teaching of the embodied Logos known in the human Jesus, church, and sacraments contrasts to the spiritualizing flight from embodiment of the Gnostics whom Clement opposed. When spiritualizing threatens to erase the reality of incarnation, Jesus is seen woman-wise. Hence the devotion and defense of Mary, *Theotokos*, to face down Docetism by defenders of Jesus' humanity in what became orthodox Christology. To recover the female face of God is to be faithful to Catholic Christianity.

Carolyn Bynum shows how twelfth-century Cistercian abbots—anxious about the tensions raised between the gospel imperative of maternal charity, caretaking and sacrificial, and the good order of legal structures in their exercise of abbatial authority—used female namings for God and Jesus and themselves as abbots and mothers to their monastic charges.[61] Might it not be that Saint Anselm—reflecting with theological rigor upon the incarnation and the atonement and shaped by feudal theories of harsh justice and honor and by the early death of his mother and his own struggles for survival with an unyielding king—when he prayed found "Great Lord our elder brother" seated next to "Great Lady, our best of mothers,"[62] rule and mercy become one. Could his address to "Christ my mother" whose gentleness comforts the frightened and whose sweet smell revives the despairing, whose "warmth gives life to the dead," be the female Body of community that nurtures, clothed in male rule? The text "Therefore you are fathers by your effect/and mothers by your affection" referring to both Saint Paul and Jesus assumes sexual stereotypes and also transgresses the categories by constructing Paul and Jesus as women.[63] This is not androgyny; each is each, fully; Jesus and Paul are both mothers and men.

The now-familiar *Revelations* of Dame Julian of Norwich, whose Mother Jesus-naming is theologically contextualized, can also be read as texts of disclosure. This "gendered" Jesus, Jesus as woman, is no gesture of Jungian complementarity or androgynous nonperson, but a topsy-turvy and upsetting text with its litany of "Mother Jesus, He." Categories and boundaries are sundered as the entire universe is seen in a hazelnut; all the while no anger is seen in God[64] in the face of the church's clear teaching upon the reality of divine judgment and Dame Julian's own experience of the pain of sin. But Julian never allows herself to fall into categories heretic or orthodox. She sits in her anchorhold, cloistered and alone yet in sight of the bustle of Norwich. These are private visions, written down by the first Englishwoman theologian for the sake of a Christian public. From the single broken body of this Man/Mother streams the water and blood that give birth to and nourish community, Mother Church. Even more astounding, "our beloved *Mother*, Jesus, feeds us with *himself*."[65] The terrible pain and outward, physical sight of crucifixion is Julian's joy. She sees physically, "in actual vision, in imaginative understanding, and in spiritual sight."[66] The intertwining of inside and outside, physical and spiritual, both/and, not either/or, is texted by Jesus' motherhood, always coupled with the male pronoun. "And of his goodness he opens the eye of our understanding so that we can *see*."[67] The meaning of these "shewings" she sums up in the last chapter: "You would know our Lord's meaning in this thing? Know it well. Love was his meaning. Who showed it you? Love. What did he show you? Love."[68] Somehow, this meaning can be *seen* only in "God all-wise our kindly Mother," who is also "in this uniting together . . . our real, true husband."[69] Mother Jesus, He. This paradox is the clue and birth-giver to the meaning, Love, bodied in a point of time on the cross yet shared throughout eternity.

That Dame Julian's Mother Jesus was seen in the body of the Crucified One needs to be understood in the larger framework of late medieval devotion to the Passion of Jesus Christ. It is on the cross, and in the sacred humanity, which the historian's eye sees as male, that Jesus as lover and mother, priest and victim, is met in prayer and sacrament.[70] There are explicit links between devotion to the Five Wounds and Passion of Christ and the later development of the cult of the Sacred Heart of Jesus and the experience of Jesus as the one who embraces as lover, gives birth from womb/heart (to the world and the individual soul), and nurtures with the blood/water from the wounded side/ breasts of his body at Calvary and on the church's altars. So writes Marguerite d'Oingt: "Ah, who has seen a woman give birth thus! / And when the hour of birth came, they placed / You on the bed of the Cross. . . . And it is not astonishing your veins ruptured, as you gave birth in one single day, to the whole world!"[71] Carolyn Bynum's work on eucharistic devotion, especially among late medieval women, extends our understanding of how this female/male Jesus shaped real women's lives through ritual and spiritual practice. Bynum suggests that the identification of late medieval women with the nurturing materiality of Jesus, Body and Sacrament, gave women a literal sensibility of their identity with the humanity of the Son of God that men, "signifying divinity," could not access.[72]

A final text to remind us of this aquifer of hitherto untapped waters, *The Acts of the Martyrs of Lyon and Vienne*, takes us back to the early church, 177 C.E. Among those who suffered in the arena that day was a woman named Blandina. "Blandina was hung on a post and exposed as bait for the wild animals that were let loose on her. She seemed to hang there in the form of a cross, and by her fervent prayer she aroused intense enthusiasm in those who were undergoing their ordeal, for in their torment with their physical eyes they saw in the person of their *sister him* who was crucified for them, that he might convince all who believe in him that all who suffer for Christ's glory will have eternal fellowship in the living God."[73] The Passion of the Man that disclosed the motherhood of God, here revealed in the occasion of the sacrificing woman, the suffering Body of God is exactly what the Vatican Declaration insists is impossible! In each case, it is not just that Jesus, to be proclaimed and seen, must be embodied, and that that body is seen historically as male. But here the symbolic construction of Jesus/God's body is disclosed by Blandina's woman-body: "They saw in the person of their *sister him* who was crucified." To *see* the woman as a revealer of God, the God who is incarnate, in the flesh, she must be seen as neither essentially male nor essentially female but as both, and therefore as a Third One who opens the eyes of the beholder to something more than the expected: a torn and dying fanatic named Jesus or Blandina.

The appropriation of patristic or medieval constructions of devotion to the motherhood of God, Jesus, and Mary cannot be simple or straightforward. The milk and blood plucked from the female pelican and expressed from the breasts of the virgin mother, the experience of spiritual pregnancy, birth, and lactation, courtship, marriage, and consummation between Jesus and the soul, may have been occasions of empowerment and genuine experiences of woman-as-subject for the religious women who report these "shewings" of God infleshed and thus feminized. Contemporary women, Christian or not, will see the antisexual and body-destroying asceticism that too often accompanied this piety as part of our problem, not a way toward the empowerment of woman as subject.

These texts are therefore useful only to the point of deconstructing the "simply male," abstract, disembodied imagery and argument of the tradition. For example, Clarissa Atkinson, in her eye-opening book *The Oldest Vocation, Christian Motherhood in the Middle Ages* (1991) contextualizes the medieval devotion to Jesus, our Mother.[74] Motherhood in its twelfth- to fourteenth-century meanings, both experienced and idealized, involved the inevitability of suffering and the devaluing of all merely human relationships, not only with husbands but also with the "worldly goods" of children. Hence it is appropriate to find God to be a mother as well as a son suffering in self-offering upon the cross. What may be useful for us is not the historically intended meanings of late medieval images of the suffering mother/God—Pieta or Crucified One—but the way in which gender, and its symbolic freight, whether divine or human, was *fluid, unfixed, and flowing in and out of the social constructions of sex and gender roles of the culture.* Whatever the symbolized sex of God suffering on the cross was, he/she did not simply valorize the patriarchal social order. There is saving freedom for us in these gender-bending images, constructed out of the experience of celibate men in same-sex communities and celibate women amidst communities of women.

THE TRANSGRESSIVE PARADIGM, JESUS AS TRANSVESTITE

While teaching a course on women saints before the Reformation, I became fascinated with the phenomenon of transvestite holy women. Pelagia the Harlot, Mary of Egypt, Christina of Markyate, and Joan of Arc were some of the cross-dressed women whose texts I used. What aroused my interest was the fact that women seeking God in male clothes, often in response to God, behaving in what society constructs as masculine fashion, seemed more spiritually powerful than the holy men around them. This cross-dressing was more than a practical arrangement for survival in a man's world. When Perpetua gains a male body there is more to it than modesty, to protect her spiritual combat from the male gaze of the arena crowds. When a holy woman such as Gregory of Nyssa's sister Macrina or Jerome's Paula can no longer be spoken of by her "natural designation for one who went beyond the nature of a woman,"[75] can such a woman not be called a "Third Thing," one whose power to evangelize and change the world around her is by virtue of her indubitable womanness clothed in the mantle of male public strength?

Marjorie Garber's seriously playful study *Vested Interests, Cross-Dressing and Cultural Anxiety* can provide an exciting and disruptively illuminating hermeneutic not only for these cross-dressed texts of sainthood but also for our task at hand, a Christology beyond andro-centricity that preserves embodiment. Garber believes her interest in cross-dressing to be "an undertheorized recognition of the necessary critique of binary thinking."[76] One of the most creative contributions of this work lies in her exploration of what cross-dressing *is* in its social-dynamic function. The transvestite (not to be confused with transsexual or homosexual) reveals the cultural construction of gender categories,[77] making clear by the very ambiguity of the presentation that gender to a significant extent is symbolic and lies in the eyes of the beholder, who responds to a set of cultural clues. This is one of the reasons why Saint Joan was finally burned. Her insistence on wearing cross-gender as well as cross-class garb (male and knightly) was deemed an *unnatural* viola-tion of biological and social essentialist definitions of woman. Yet when she was recognized and canonized as a saint, her male garb became a symbol of divine vocation!

Transvestites *blur* and make ambiguous that which the culture believes it needs to see as clear and fixed—like the deacon in brocaded dalmatic who turns out to be a woman (dressed as a man dressed as a woman) when she starts to sing the gospel! Or Jesus, acting trans-vestically as he takes a drink from the religiously outcast Samaritan woman or kneels like a slave girl to wash his disciples' feet. Cross-dressing is to indulge in socially taboo behavior.

Garber takes great pains to clarify the insight that the cross-dresser is not a subject to be "seen through," such as the Hasty Pudding chorus girl who is actually a privileged Harvard undergraduate. The cross-dresser is not a "term" in itself but rather a "disruptive act of putting in question" essences and dualities.[78] What energizes the cross-dresser and destabilizes the onlooker is the rush of adrenalin that the transvestic person or behavior incurs as the categories crumble. The transvestite is a gender-bender, a person who opens our eyes to "the permanent crisis of category at the very heart of human culture."[79] As when an electron moves from one orbit to the next, energy is released and change can take place. We are anxious in the transvestite's presence, for we do not know what to expect. Fluidity replaces stability when gender is unclear. Does the transvestite woman saint participate in or reveal in some significant way the gender ambiguity of the Word made flesh?

How can this hermeneutical paradigm be useful to the construction of a feminist Christology? For almost two decades I have asked myself how I, a woman, can see myself as made in the image of a male God, a God whose human face is seen in the man Jesus? I was excited to discover that the tradition before the Protestant Reformation was widely sown with culturally constructed feminine images for Jesus and his mother, incarnated splendidly in many powerful and socially potent holy women, revered by the culture as saints. But these female namings for the Holy were often limited to mother images, images of abused and bleeding bodies, images of suffering, which in our culture has lost its redemptive value. Listening to women's painful memories of mothering, destructive self-sacrifice, demands a hermeneutic of suspicion for these medieval texts.

Too frequently the female faces of the Holy seem at first to be a feminine sacred constructed by men for male needs. The work of "unearthing" the female from an androcentric Christian culture is full of ambiguity. One has to ask, is Dame Julian's Mother Jesus but one more instance of the male construction of a male god with breasts, another way for the male to "have it all"? Does she point to a world like that confidently described by Saint Thomas, where for all useful activity men serve best, excepting the work of generation, and even that birthing can be accomplished by the Son of God?

The paradigm of cross-dressing deconstructs gender essentialism and thus has a hermeneutical potential—not only for re-reading and unloosing the energies of these texts by getting us beyond the question of historical "fact" to recognize their transgressive and disruptive symbolic potency in the past, but even more so for our eyes and ears. This paradigm might well unlock the Jesus women need for our time.

Luce Irigaray writes of this Jesus:

How could "God" reveal himself in all his magnificence and waste his substance on/in so weak and vile a creature as woman? . . . It means that love conquers everything that has already been said. And that one man, at least, has understood woman so well that he died in the most awful suffering. That most female of men, the Son.[80]

By this I would not suggest that Jesus is a "feminine" or androgynous man, but that, yes, Jesus, who was and is as both historical fact and symbol a man, is like a cross-dresser, one not able to be categorized. He is a rabbi who drinks and eats with the unclean. He is a preacher of the coming of God's Kingdom to Israel who proposes that the uninvited stranger and unkosher outsider will sit at the feast. He acknowledges his mother and brothers but unravels their family claims and acknowledges sisters and brothers without biological, ethnic, or religious boundaries. And that most awesome of the binarities, death, was, according to the narrative, also rent open like the temple veil, not by a ghost, but by a bodied one who ate and drank and walked through closed doors. We could go on throughout the gospel narratives, using Garber's outrageous hermeneutical lens to see in Jesus the King who died, the man whose life displays "women's ways" of love, sacrifice, and forgiveness, but who is never enclosed by the world's categories. The answer to Pilate's question, "What is truth?" lay outside the city walls. And perhaps, as we allow ourselves to be *offended* by the Cross-dressing, we will be able to take seriously the statement by Athanasius that "what is not taken up, is not redeemed," and let Jesus address us as one of her own.

Garber's transvestic phrase "Third Thing" is a conundrum through which we can to re-vision the Jesus of orthodox Christology, the Child of God, a scandal and a stumbling block, the only true God who was also true Man, no ordinary God, he. Embodied, fleshy, as only a woman in this culture can symbolize, he was a Third Thing, a destroyer of the dualities, in language of orthodox Christology, who broke the crystal wall between the heavens and the earth.

Today, in the churches and the culture, gender, not the divine/human dichotomy, is the paradigm of crisis, that is, a holy opportunity. Responding to this opportunity, this Christology invites a re-vision of Jesus Christ understood and prayed to with these transvestic sensibilities; he is the Trickster who peels us open to new depths of humanity, divinity, femaleness, maleness. There is no telling what boundaries and categories could be dismantled as male gender hegemony is disrobed. That is what the gospel is about, the piercing of categories—in the womb/by the dart of love. A *merely male* Jesus has been and continues to be a violation of the scandal and transgression that is the gospel.

Experience. The woman-priest stands at the altar, no matter what her theology of ordination, *in persona Christi*. She symbolizes body by her very womanness, and when as a priest she handles, "makes," God's Body, she stands for the crucified Jesus of the tradition giving birth to transformed and redeemed creation. To appreciate how repulsive this acted-out Christology is in an androcentric and misogynist church and society, look at the extraordinary *resistance* in the Anglican communion and the increasingly frantic opposition to any hint of allowing women to be priests in both Roman Catholicism and the Orthodox churches. The "woman dressed as a man dressed as a woman"[81] is a cross-dresser, "shaking the foundations" with the transgressive energy of a taboo gesture, a woman's body in a sacred space, mediating, as a representative Person, God. She flies in the face of culture and classical Christology, according to which only a man can be a representative person, whether Christ or priest.

It is very likely that with time, the experience of congregations who gather in sacramental celebration with such women will know Jesus differently. Women are in the arena, and like Blandina, their woman-ways of bodied being evoke the experience in those around them of "seeing with their physical eyes . . . in her, Him who was crucified for them." When the icons we use to mediate the Holy are women, we will see Jesus to be a her, like us. We will be like the lion who leaped with excited confirmation when Aslan said "*us lions.*" It will be a long time before that blurring of boundaries that is a promised sign of the reign of God will be greeted with ease and relief. We are still resistant to the Other, the threat that a Black Jesus or a Mother or Lover Jesus presents to normative male, white humanity, with its transcendent distinctions, anti-eroticism, and carefully delineated gender privilege. Children will have to be raised differently, fathered as intimately as they are mothered. All this does not happen in church, nor in a revisioned Christology. But supported by Christians called to break repressive convention, the Blandinas and Pelagias and Saint Joans of the tradition and women in whom the sacred is met in our dailiness will enable the world to *see* and to *sense* experience topsy-turvy, evangelically. The dualities will be broken—profane and holy, law and love, death and life—just as they were in the garden. Jesus, "dressed" in flesh, that most female of symbols, and God in man-flesh yet behaving like a woman—this "transvestite" Jesus makes a human space where no one is out of place because the notions of place and gender have been transformed. Yes human, yes god, yes woman, yes man, yes black, yes red, yes white, yes yellow, yes friend, yes stranger—yes, yes, yes.

NOTES

1. Daphne Hampson, *Theology and Feminism* (Oxford: Basil Blackwell, 1990), 71. Hampson remarks that as a Christian feminist, she had no interest in the gender of Christ, female symbols of the Holy, or "inclusive language."

2. "The Ordination of Women and the 'Maleness' of Christ," *Anglican Theological Review*, supp. series 6 (June 1976): 69–80.

3. John Macquarrie, *Jesus Christ in Modern Thought* (Philadelphia: Trinity Press International, 1990), 359–60.

4. E. L. Mascall, quoted in *Why Not? Priesthood and the Ministry of Women*, ed. Michael Bruce and G. E. Duffield (Appleford: Marcham Manor Press, 1972), 111–12.

5. *Book of Common Prayer* (New York: Seabury Press, 1953), 423.

6. From a speech by Bishop Graham Leonard to the General Synod of the Church of England, 8 November 1978 (Church Literature Association for the Church Union), cited in Hampson, *Theology*, 66.

7. Hampson, *Theology*, 56.

8. Ibid., 52.

9. See I. K. Braverman, D. M. Braverman, F. E. Clarkson, P. S. Rosenkrantz, and S. R. Vogel, "Sex Role Stereotypes and Clinical Judgments of Mental Health, *Journal of Consulting and Clinical Psychology* 34 (1970): 1–7, in which a study of responses to a questionnaire on the characteristics of a mentally healthy *person* were compared to those of a *man* and *woman*. The results were statistically identical for man and person, with opposite traits for woman.

10. Leo Steinberg, *The Sexuality of Christ in Renaissance Art and in Modern Oblivion* (New York: Random House, 1983). Steinberg's thesis that the "humanity" of Jesus came into prominence in the Renaissance and was symbolized by a new artistic focus

on the Son's phallus is only half right. The sacred humanity of Jesus became increasingly important in Christian devotion from the eleventh century and was iconically represented by the Mother with Child, devotion to the Jesus of the Passion, and the Five Wounds, and in eucharistic devotions, all of which were female or feminine in tenor. The shift in mentalities associated with the Renaissance and Protestant reformations is accompanied by a reaction against a sacramental and iconic worldview and representations of the female Holy. See Eleanor McLaughlin, "Male and Female in Christian Tradition: Was there a Reformation in the Sixteenth Century?" in *Male and Female, Christian Approaches to Sexuality*, ed. Ruth Tiffany Barnhouse and Urban Holmes (New York: Seabury, 1976), 39–52.

11. Hampson, *Theology*, 71.

12. Ibid., 53.

13. See Marjorie Garber, *Vested Interests: Cross-Dressing and Cultural Anxiety* (New York: Routledge, Chapman and Hall, 1992), 210–33, 267–352, for an example-filled (not simply theoretical) discussion of the interplay between gender, race, homosexuality, Jewishness, and non-European ethnicity.

14. Hampson, *Theology*, 170–71, is a helpful exception in discussing the challenge to prayer and religious experience of rethinking Christology. There are many fine collections of feminist liturgy and ritual, but the Christological implications of the new language are not always clear. If one believes *lex orandi, lex credendi est*, this is a problem.

15. Mary Daly, *Beyond God the Father: Toward a Philosophy of Women's Liberation* (Boston: Beacon Press, 1973), 19.

16. Alice Walker, *The Color Purple* (New York: Washington Square Press, 1982), 177.

17. See John deSatge, *Down to Earth: The New Protestant Vision of the Virgin Mary* (Washington, DC: Consortium Books, 1976), 124–29, for a traditional perspective; Marina Warner, *Alone of All Her Sex: The Myth and the Cult of the Virgin Mary* (New York: Vintage Books, 1976) is an exhaustive survey of the cult that finds little of use to women today; Andrew M. Greeley, *The Mary Myth: On the Femininity of God* (New York: Seabury, 1977), is suggestive, although better for men than women; China Galland, *Longing for Darkness: Tara and the Black Madonna* (New York: Penguin, 1990), is a highly personal and interreligious reflection on Mary among the mother goddesses.

18. See *Inter insigniores*, in Leonard Swidler and Arlene Swidler, *Women Priests: A Catholic Commentary on the Vatican Declaration* (New York: Paulist Press, 1977), 43–44, in which the authors, in contrast to Macquarrie, identify the symbolic Christ expressed sacramentally by the priest with the historical Christ, "himself was and remains a man."

19. Patricia Wilson-Kastner, *Faith, Feminism and the Christ* (Philadelphia: Fortress Press, 1983), 90.

20. Elisabeth Moltmann-Wendel and Jürgen Moltmann, *God—His and Hers* (New York: Crossroad, 1991), 78.

21. Ibid., 82.

22. Ibid.

23. Ibid., 91.

24. In Daphne Hampson and Rosemary Radford Ruether, "Is There a Place for Feminists in a Christian Church?" in *New Blackfriars*, January 1987, 11.

25. Rosemary Radford Ruether, *Sexism and God-Talk: Toward a Feminist Theology* (Boston: Beacon Press, 1983), 137–38.

26. Elisabeth Schüssler-Fiorenza, *In Memory of Her: A Feminist Theological Reconstruction of Christian Origins* (New York: Crossroad, 1983).

27. Virginia Ramey Mollenkott, *The Divine Feminine: The Biblical Imagery of God as Female* (New York: Crossroad, 1984), 36–43; Ruether, *Sexism*, 131–34.

28. In Carol P. Christ and Judith Plaskow, *Womanspirit Rising: A Feminist Reader in Religion* (San Francisco: Harper, 1979), 273–87.

29. Henry Adams, *Mont Saint Michel and Chartres* (Boston: Houghton Mifflin, 1933), 178–228, 249–81; Evelyn Underhill, *The Miracles of Our Lady St. Mary* (New York: E. P. Dutton, 1906). Mary legends reveal Mary's place in medieval Christian views of Providence.

30. Mary Daly and Jane Caputi, *Webster's First New Intergalactic Wickedary of the English Language* (Boston: Beacon Press, 1987), 189–90.

31. Monica Sjoo and Barbara Mor, *The Great Cosmic Mother: Rediscovering the Religion of the Earth* (San Francisco: Harper, 1987); Mary Condren, *The Serpent and the Goddess: Women, Religion, and Power in Celtic Ireland* (San Francisco: Harper, 1989).

32. Eleanor McLaughlin, "Women and Medieval Heresy: A Problem in the History of Spirituality," *Concilium, Revue Internationale de Theologie* 111 (1976): 73–90.

33. Macquarrie, *Jesus Christ*, 6.

34. Ibid., 12.

35. Ibid., 19–20.

36. Ibid., 302.

37. Ibid., 316, citing affirmatively Jon Sobrino, *Christology at the Crossroads: A Latin-American Approach*, trans. John Drury (Maryknoll, NY: Orbis Books, 1978), 379.

38. Ibid., 9; J. D. G. Dunn, *Unity and Diversity in the New Testament* (Philadelphia: Westminster Press, 1977), 376.

39. Hampson, *Theology*, 65; she dismisses Ruether as a humanist, not a Christian.

40. Carter Heyward, *The Redemption of God: A Theology of Mutual Relation* (Lanham, MD: United Press of America, 1982), 196.

41. Hampson, *Theology*, 61; she seems to make too sharp a distinction between historical "fact" and symbol, as if the historical "fact" of the maleness of Jesus does not function as a symbol, giving priority to historical "fact" as "true" in a way that symbol is not.

42. Ibid., 50. Hampson defines feminism as an extension of Enlightenment equality to women.

43. Elaine Pagels, *The Gnostic Gospels* (New York: Random House, 1979).

44. Heyward, *Redemption*, 185–86.

45. Macquarrie, *Jesus Christ*, 16, citing Martin Kähler, *The So-Called Historical Jesus and Historic Biblical Christ*, trans. and ed. Carl E. Braaten (Philadelphia: Fortress Press, 1964), 66.

46. Jacquelyn Grant, *White Women's Christ and Black Women's Jesus: Feminist Christology and Womanist Response* (Atlanta: Scholars Press, 1989), 144: "The maleness of Jesus is superseded by the Christness of Jesus."

47. Ibid., 215–16: "The identification is so real that Jesus Christ in fact becomes Black."

48. *New York Times*, 27 April 1984: "Bishop Dennis said he did not object to 'enhancing' symbols of Jesus by casting them in differing skin colors or ethnic characteristics. But he said the statue went too far by 'totally changing the symbol.'"

49. Marjorie Hewitt Suchocki, *God Christ Church: A Practical Guide to Process Theology* (New York: Crossroad, 1982), 104.

50. Carter Heyward, *Touching Our Strength: The Erotic as Power and the Love of God* (San Francisco: Harper & Row, 1989); Paul Avis, *Eros and the Sacred* (Harrisburg, PA: Morehouse, 1990); Alexander C. Irwin, *Eros Toward the World: Paul Tillich and the Theology of the Erotic* (Minneapolis: Fortress Press, 1991).

51. Avis, *Eros*, 128–37.

52. Irenaeus Fellowship of Bishops, *A Theological Critique of the Human Sexuality and Environment Sections of the Standing Commission on Human Affairs Report to the 70th General Convention of the Episcopal Church*, 5. The (unsigned) Episcopal authors attack the work of Sallie McFague and Carter Heyward as holding a too intimate connection between Creator and creation, teaching an embodied divinity that fails to honor the dualities between fallen world and good God.

53. Cited in Kenneth Leech, *True Prayer* (San Francisco: Harper & Row, 1980), 9.

54. Cited in Hampson, *Theology*, 33.

55. See for example, how the "body" of lay Christians is always represented as the female Bride of Christ, the Church, subordinate and obedient to her Bridegroom; how the female body is used in advertising to represent and arouse the response of male desire; how the earth has "breast" and the wind, "voice."

56. Andre Cabassut, *Revue d'ascetique et de mystique* 25 (1949): 234–45. I am indebted to Prof. Giles Constable, then at Harvard University, for this reference.

57. Eleanor McLaughlin, "Christ My Mother: Feminine Naming and Metaphor in Medieval Spirituality," *Nashotah Review* 15, no. 3 (Fall 1975): 228–48.

58. Caroline Bynum, "'. . . and Woman His Humanity': Female Imagery in the Religious Writing of the Later Middle Ages," in *Fragmentation and Redemption: Essays on Gender and the Human Body in Medieval Religion* (New York: Urzone, 1991), 151–71.

59. Janet Martin Soskice, *Metaphor and Religious Language* (Oxford: Clarendon, 1987), 160.

60. Clement of Alexandria, *Christ the Educator: The Fathers of the Church*, vol. 23 (New York: Fathers of the Church, 1954), I:43, I:42, 40–41. It may be because in "that other world," the "human person [is] freed from the lust that in life had made it either male or female" (I:10), that God the Father may be seen as equipped with breasts, and "it is more than evident that the Blood of Christ is milk" (I:40).

61. Caroline Walker Bynum, "Jesus as Mother and Abbot as Mother: Some Themes in Twelfth-Century Cistercian Writing," *Jesus as Mother Studies in the Spirituality of the High Middle Ages* (Berkeley and Los Angeles: University of California Press, 1982), 110–69.

62. *The Prayers and Meditations of Saint Anselm*, trans. and ed. Sister Benedicta Ward (Harmondsworth: Penguin, 1973), 124.

63. Ibid., 154–56.

64. Julian of Norwich, *Revelations of Divine Love*, ed. Clifton Wolters (Harmondsworth: Penguin, 1973), chap. 13, p. 84.

65. Ibid., chap. 60, p. 170.

66. Ibid., chaps. 9, 10, p. 76.

67. Ibid., chap. 52, p. 152.

68. Ibid., chap. 86, p. 211.

69. Ibid., chap. 58, p. 165.

70. "He openeth them as doth the mother her arms to embrace her beloved child. . . . And thou, dear Lord, goest spiritually toward us and to thy darlings with the same embrace as the mother to her children": *Ureisan of Ure Louerde*, ed. W. Meredith Thompson (London: Early English Text Society, 1958), 241, cited in John Bugge, *Virginitas: An Essay on the History of a Medieval Ideal* (The Hague: Martinus Nijhoff, 1975), 100. Bugge speaks of the "disquieting phenomenon" of the shift in the metaphorical sexuality of Christ from male to female. What he finds disquieting, I find central to the transvestic quality of incarnation.

71. McLaughlin, "Christ My Mother," 235, citing A. Duraffour, P. Gardette, and P. Durdilly, *Les Oeuvres de Marguerite d'Oingt* (Paris, 1965), 33–36.

72. Bynum, ". . . and Woman His Humanity," 179: "Religious women . . .

understood that 'man . . . signifies the divinity of the Son of God and woman his humanity.' And they understood that both equations were metaphorical. But, given the ultimate dichotomy of God and creation, the first was only metaphorical. Man was not divinity. The second was in some sense, however, literally true."

73. Herbert Musurillo, *The Acts of the Christian Martyrs* (Oxford: Clarendon, 1972), 75.

74. Atkinson is interested in what devotional materials can tell us about the social construction of human motherhood. I am particularly interested in developing theologically her identification of the shift from the valorizing of virginity in the Catholic centuries to the Protestant sacralizing of the heterosexual, patriarchal family. It is my thesis that the masculinization of God accompanies and perhaps contributes to this shift.

75. Gregory of Nyssa, *Life of St. Macrina: The Fathers of the Church*, vol. 58 (New York: Fathers of the Church, 1974), 163.

76. Garber, *Vested Interests*, 10–11.

77. Ibid., 9.

78. Ibid., 12.

79. Ibid., 16.

80. Luce Irigaray, *Speculum of the Other Woman* (Ithaca, NY: Cornell University Press, 1985), 199 (emphasis added).

81. Eleanor McLaughlin, "The Gendered Priest and the Passions and Parts of God," Johnson Lectures, Seabury Western Theological School, October 1987. Unpublished.

CHAPTER TWENTY-THREE

LIBERATING JESUS:
A DIALOGUE BETWEEN SOUTH AND NORTH

JOHN PARR

INTRODUCTION

Latin American theology of liberation has proved to be both creative and controversial since it first appeared just over twenty years ago. Its exponents have often advertised their enterprise as a new way of doing theology, a deliberate attempt to reinterpret the major texts and themes of Christian faith from within the struggle for a more just society. Its opponents have branded it as nothing more than a watered-down version of traditional Christianity, passing off sociopolitical liberation as if it were what the Bible meant by salvation. It is ironic that in addition to the interest shown by the wider church, this self-styled "theology of the streets" should now be receiving so much attention from the classroom. This is perhaps a measure of the success of its leading thinkers, writers, and publishers in reaching a wider audience. At a time when the center of gravity of the world church is moving rapidly from North to South, it is fitting that one of the more vibrant forms of Third World theology should be so much in the limelight.

In its early days, liberation theology tended to overwork the biblical theme of exodus. This is hardly surprising; such was the affinity between the oppressed in Latin America and the Hebrew slaves in Egypt that the ancient motif of liberation resonated strongly with the longings of the poor for freedom and justice. With its power to inspire hope and encourage militant faith, the Exodus became the paradigm event in an emerging understanding of salvation. But if published works are anything to go by, liberation theology has devoted more attention to the figure of Jesus in recent years. In tracing the main lines of liberation Christology, this chapter shows how its image of Jesus is the fruit of a conversation between South and North—Third World theologians and First World biblical scholarship—rooted in and nourished by the involvement of sections of the Latin American church in the liberation struggles of the past thirty years.

Liberation Christology might be seen as plotted along three axes. First, it takes its bearings from the Jesus of the Gospels rather than the Christ of dogma. The liberationists believe that God has been revealed in the entire sweep of what they see as the partisan humanity of Jesus, and not merely in his birth, death, and resurrection. This leads them to set about liberating Jesus from the abstractions of dogma, believing that a Christology based on developed church teaching runs the risk of distancing Jesus from historical struggles. A dogmatic Christology can be more readily used by those with political power as an ideological weapon. Pointed at the faithful in order to encourage them to be passive in the face of oppression, the Christ of the status quo silences protest and effectively sanctions injustice in the name of the Gospel. By contrast, liberation theology presents Jesus "from the underside of history" (to borrow a phrase from Gutiérrez). As we will see, this Jesus challenges the way power is used, whether by church or state.

Second, the figure of the liberating Jesus is drawn in relation to the active faith of particular Christian communities and seeks to interpret the gospel of Jesus Christ for them. In this sense, it is akin to the various New Testament theologies of Jesus. Its wellsprings lie in the popular reading of the Gospels in the base communities, where Jesus is "seen and loved as liberator" (Leonardo Boff). The Latin American poor feel a strong affinity with the "poor Christ"; they believe that his ministry was directed toward liberating the poor of his day from the oppression that weighed them down. Liberation Christology attempts to articulate the intuitive understandings of Jesus found among those who have taken up what the Conference of Latin American Bishops at Puebla (1979) called "the preferential option for the poor." We shall see that in their interpretive task, liberation theologians recognize the hermeneutical role of praxis, the life of discipleship. They make it clear that it is only by following Jesus *now* that we can understand the significance of what he said and did *then*.

Third, liberation Christology is set against a South-North axis.

Third World theologians evidently have drawn on First World biblical scholarship. Writers such as Leonardo Boff and Jon Sobrino have consciously re-read European and North American studies of Jesus. They have liberated Jesus from the power of northern academic theologians to define his image and have thereby fashioned a Christology with Latin American characteristics. Their reconstruction of Jesus is the result of reading the Gospels through the eyes of the poor and the writings of the scholars. What they have produced is a good example of the way liberation theology uses scholarship in the service of the mission of the church. We shall see how these three axes help to orientate the liberationists' picture of Jesus.

JESUS AND THE KINGDOM OF GOD

In common with studies of the historical Jesus since Weiss, liberation theology underlines the centrality of Jesus' proclamation of the coming Kingdom of God. In announcing God's rule, Jesus was of course using the language of power. He believed that in his ministry, the liberating power of God was confronting the destructive forces of evil, which threatened to return the world to chaos and disorder. In Latin America, the powers that hold sway in the world of the poor are those of oppression, injustice, and death. Unlike the forces of affluence, skepticism, and doubt in the First World, these Latin American powers do not make it harder for the poor to believe in the existence of God. But they do question the propriety of telling those deprived of their dignity and worth that the God whom Jesus addressed as *Abba* is also *their* Father. What kind of power does the God and Father of Jesus Christ exercise? The liberationists find their answer in the way the Gospels flesh out Jesus' ministry of the Kingdom of God.

In liberation Christology, Jesus' use of the language of "the Kingdom of God" has become an organizing principle for interpreting the Gospels. In common with the First World theologians they draw on, the liberationists understand the phrase as referring to God's saving power rather than a territorial realm. They agree that the kingdom reaches its goal in the renewal of the entire created order and not merely the enriching of individual spiritual experience. They concur that Jesus proclaimed the kingdom in what he did as well as said. In his ministry,

Israel's deeply rooted hopes were beginning to take shape, although salvation would only be fully realized in the future. For the liberationists, then, Jesus' proclamation of "the Kingdom of God" interpreted his own ministry in terms of the saving power of God directed toward an all-embracing communion with God and among persons.

The desire to plot their Christology along the axes of the Gospels' presentation of Jesus' ministry, contemporary discipleship, and North-South scholarly conversation leads liberation theologians to search for the basis of Jesus' work as liberator. They find it not in the ontological categories of incarnation or sonship but in the personal freedom he revealed in the way he lived. The social divisions, limited moral obligations, and religious observance imposed by contemporary interpreters of the Jewish law had no claim on him. Instead we see what Leonardo Boff calls Jesus' "novel and liberative praxis," a life based on the values of justice, mercy, and love rather than legal absolutes.[1] Boff's portrayal of Jesus sketches out his attractiveness to Christians in search of a role model for the praxis of liberation. Jesus united love of God and neighbor; he sought communion with oppressed and marginalized individuals and groups; he respected individual liberty and was ready to listen as well as speak, to persuade rather than coerce, to use everyday speech in preference to theological jargon. He could tolerate differences and mix with his opponents; he enjoined love for enemies rather than vengeance; he was not afraid to stand in places of conflict; he renounced power in order to serve and benefit all; he was willing to be misunderstood, defamed, isolated, persecuted, worn out for the sake of others. In Boff's words, "Jesus was completely empty of self in order to be full of others and God." This was the heart of his liberating work and the substance of the faith that inspired his gospel.

Because Jesus looked to the eventual renewal of the entire created order, what he said and did in Israel touched life at all levels—individual, social, religious, economic, political. Whereas First World scholars are often content to spiritualize Jesus' message or leave their understanding of the breadth of his vision in general terms, liberation theologians are much more specific in the way they discuss the significance of Jesus' eschatological ministry. They do not allow us to overlook the political significance of familiar features of the Gospels. In associating with tax collectors and sinners, Jesus worked with those at the margins of society. In challenging Pharisees and Sadducees, he confronted those who exercised power from the center of Israel's life. In all this, the liberationists do not lose sight of Jesus' concern for the individual, or for what we in the First World often see as spiritual issues. But they point out the broader implications of his ministry to needy individuals. For example, his willingness to accept sinners not only released them from guilt but also drew those who had been ostracized by the social power of religion back into the wider family of Israel (see Mark 6:34; Luke 19:9). Opening up a person's relationship with God could not be separated from restoring his or her place in society. In Sobrino's words, "Jesus' attitude . . . wells up from the innermost depths of his being, from the reality of the one he calls Father. And how can he be Father if he does not create a community of brothers and sisters?"[2]

Reading the Gospels from a situation marked by the struggle against injustice, it is hardly surprising that liberation theology fastens onto the conflictive dimensions of Jesus' ministry. Liberation theologians point out that Jesus' good news of the kingdom was in fact bad news for those who used their power to oppress—the rich, the religious leaders, the politicians. By turning their backs on the kingdom and its vision of total communion, the ruling classes and their allies showed that they were in the grip of sin. In the name of God's Kingdom, Jesus challenged this and called for repentance, a willingness to embrace the kingdom and its demands. Two comments are worth making on this interpretation of Jesus' fight against evil. First, the liberationists place more emphasis on Jesus' encounter with collective rather than individual sin. However, they do not restrict the sin of oppression to the powerful; they recognize that everyone has the potential to be an oppressor. But their concern to deal in historical categories leads them to identify concrete forms of sin, both in their own society and in that of Jesus. From a situation in which the oppression of one group by another is the most obvious threat to human solidarity, it is not surprising that their reading of the Gospels should identify the same dimension of human sinfulness in the world of Jesus.

Second, by equating repentance with the concrete demands of the kingdom, liberation theology explores the tensions inherent in the language of the Kingdom of God from a fresh perspective. First World theologians are well aware that Jesus understood the Kingdom of God as both gift and task, both present and future. Yet they often appear to confine their discussion of these tensions to the areas of thought and ideas. The Third World theologians' insistence on plotting Christology along the axis of contemporary discipleship leads them to view Jesus' proclamation from the perspective he himself adopted. He called others to enter into his own relation to the Kingdom of God. He saw the kingdom as God's gift in the sense that it created space for human beings to act, to repent by implementing the vision and values of God's rule. He did not expect his hearers to wait passively for the kingdom to arrive, but to allow their lives to be directed by the saving power of God, breaking into history in the events focused on his own ministry. Therefore, the coming kingdom began to be realized by those who identified with Jesus' liberating praxis. The life of discipleship gave shape to the coming Kingdom of God; liberating grace entered into human experience as the tasks of fashioning history were taken up. In Sobrino's words, the *thought* tension between divine gifts and human task dissolves in the life of discipleship, where the thought tension between present and future is experienced as undying hope.[3]

Those who are more used to identifying the revelation of God's saving power solely with Jesus' death and resurrection might wonder how successful his ministry actually was in bringing about salvation. The liberationists stress that he did manage to achieve a degree of genuine liberation by healing the sick, reintegrating lepers into society, overcoming age-old prejudices toward Samaritans and Gentiles, accepting women into the group that accompanied him, eating meals with sinners as well as friends, healing the possessed who embodied social divisions within themselves, and so on. Although his achievement was partial and provisional (as an anticipation of the fullness of the kingdom that was yet to come), it was nonetheless real and brought genuine hope to those who could otherwise expect no share in the coming new age.

We can see, then, how liberation Christology constructs its model of Jesus along the three axes of the Gospels, the base communities, and South-North biblical scholarship. Liberated for God and others, the liberating Jesus takes on the character of one who fights for justice in the name of God. His life is an inspiration for those who long for a better life in this world. Now as then, divine resources are available for the fight against evil. Whoever heeds Jesus' call to discipleship today can hope to experience something of the salvation that broke into human history two thousand years ago in Palestine.

JESUS AND THE POOR

We have seen how sensitive liberation Christology is to the depiction of Jesus' concern for the marginalized in the Gospels. Many Third World Christians, struggling against the debilitating and dehumanizing power of poverty, find hope in the liberating Jesus and his message of good news for the poor. His own bias toward the poor lies at the heart of the "preferential option for the poor" taken up by those parts of the Latin American church that have given birth to liberation theology. The liberationists are quick to point out that Christians who identify with the aspirations of the poor can help the wider church to be more faithful in its witness to the God who became poor in Jesus Christ. Because the divine option for the poor is preferential and not exclusive, the church must address its gospel to privileged and poverty-stricken alike. By reading the Gospel from the vantage point of those oppressed by poverty, all Christians can come to appreciate the richness of the saving work of the liberating Jesus.

Liberation theology draws its picture of Jesus' relation to the poor along the three axes we have already identified. Ernesto Cardenal's collections of *campesino* Bible studies from Nicaragua show how easily the stories of Jesus' birth and ministry resonate with the experiences and aspirations of those who long to be free from poverty.[4] Here we can see how readily members of a base community identify with "the poor Christ," a term that encapsulates the meaning of faith in the liberating Jesus. Not only does it suggest his nearness to the world of today's poor, it also makes the theological point that in the Incarnation, God has become poor. Furthermore, the term says something about the nature of Christian discipleship; those who come to God through Jesus cannot afford to ignore the way of Jesus in his poverty.

Dialogue with First World theology is responsible for further defining the image of the poor Christ. Gustavo Gutiérrez's work on poverty in the Bible has proved to be foundational for the Christology of liberation.[5] Drawing on contemporary European studies, he identified two strands in the Old Testament. Here poverty is both a scandalous condition, which law codes sought to prevent and prophets unequivocally condemned, and a spiritual attitude of faith and trust in God: openness to God's will rather than indifference toward possessions. While material and spiritual poverty cannot be equated, neither can they be totally separated. Gutiérrez maintains that spiritual poverty is more likely to be found among the materially poor, whose capacity for God is less likely to be weighed down by this world's goods. Jesus' attitude to the poor is worked out in the reading of the relevant parts of the Gospels against the teaching of the Old Testament. Some gospel passages that deal with poverty are more important than others to the liberationists, in the sense that they require a more detailed exegetical attention. The first beatitude (Matt. 5:3//Luke 6:20) and the eschatological parable of the sheep and goats (Matt. 25:31–46) are in this category and function as primary texts for this dimension of liberation Christology. The meaning of other passages, such as the Magnificat (Luke 1:46–55) and the account of Jesus' sermon at Nazareth (Luke 4:16–30), is more self-evident. In these supplementary texts we find unequivocal statements about the nature of the salvation Jesus brings: it consists of justice and liberation for the poor, oppressed, and marginalized. These apparently less ambiguous statements from the Gospels are woven together with the double strand of material and spiritual poverty from the Old Testament to provide the backdrop against which the primary texts are set.

Gutiérrez places the Matthean and Lucan versions of the first beatitude on this biblical canvas. He emphasizes that Jesus is first and foremost making a theological rather than an anthropological statement. Jesus' primary concern is with the God who blesses, rather than those who are blessed. Luke's "blessed are the poor" expresses his general attitude toward the outcast, whom he wishes to include in the coming new order. Here Jesus picks up the prophetic protest against material poverty, in the name of the Kingdom of God. Matthew's "blessed are the poor in spirit" introduces his outline of the righteousness Jesus looks for in his followers (Matt. 5:17). Here Jesus calls for the religious virtue of total dependence on God. Gutiérrez offers a synthesis of these two versions of Jesus' words, taking his cue from the Vatican II document *Lumen Gentium*. Jesus' self-giving is said to reveal the true meaning of Christian poverty (see Phil. 2:5–11). To be poor in spirit means being totally available to God, whose attitude to material poverty is sounded in Jesus' blessing of the poor. The first beatitude is therefore a call to solidarity with the poor and a protest against the conditions in which they are forced to live.

Along with the first beatitude, the words of the Son of Man on the day of judgment—"as you did it to one of the least of my brethren, you did it to me" (Matt. 25:40)—are of central importance in liberation theology. Gutiérrez's work on this text stands well within mainstream First World exegesis. He takes its obvious meaning to be the way the majority of exegetes read it, identifying the Son of Man not merely with the disadvantaged members of the Christian community (as in Origen and Luther), but with any who are needy. Not only, then, does Jesus declare God's blessing on the poor and needy, he also identifies himself with them to the extent that they represent him.

Gutiérrez's understanding of this text is fed by a number of other streams. The Hebrew scriptures emphasize that love is only found in concrete actions, such as helping the needy. In the New Testament, God is Love and known through love (1 John 4:7–8, 20). Without love the actions of Christians are empty (1 Cor. 13); true faith shows itself in deeds (James 2:20; 1 John 3:17–18). In parables such as that of the good Samaritan, Jesus underlines the primacy of love and communion among persons. The New Testament makes it clear that God cannot be constrained by holy places; the Divine is found in people, who become the temple of the Holy Spirit (1 Cor. 3:16–17; 6:19),[6] and especially in the marginalized. Recent Roman Catholic social teaching has highlighted the pervasive biblical themes that love of God is inseparable from love of neighbor: God is reached through human mediation. Congar refers to the neighbor as a sacrament, so that any act of love toward another human person is an act of love toward God.

When they are watered by these biblical and ecclesial streams, the words of the Son of Man—like the first beatitude—are flooded with anthropological and theological meaning. Those who heard Jesus' call to solidarity with the poor can expect to meet their Lord in the least of his Latin American brothers and sisters—the poor, oppressed, and marginalized. This suggests that the preferential option for the poor is not simply an ethical imperative but an authentic spiritual experience, an encounter with the God who has become poor in Jesus Christ.

Gutiérrez's reading of texts that are foundational for the liberationists' understanding of Jesus' attitude to the poor calls for some comment. He offers a creative reinterpretation of the first beatitude and the words of the Son of Man in which he acknowledges the distance between his own world and that of Jesus. Whatever Matthew may have understood by poverty of spirit in the circumstances of his own day, that same availability to the Lord shows itself today as solidarity with the poor. Luke may have assured the poor in his church that their situation was incompatible with the reign of God; Gutiérrez invests the same theological conviction in the contemporary protest against poverty and injustice in Latin American society. The fact that the words of the Son of Man are only found in Matthew's gospel, and that they are part of the evangelist's distinctive understanding of discipleship as performing the words of Jesus (see Matt. 7:24–27; 28:20), does not seem to trouble Gutiérrez. What is important is that the judge identifies with those who are otherwise reckoned to be of no account. In Gutiérrez's world, there can be no doubt as to the identify of "the least"; they are the poor, who incarnate the Son of Man such that response to them is the measure of response to Jesus.

In using these primary texts as sources for Jesus' attitude toward the poor, Gutiérrez is not fundamentally concerned with the historical question of what Jesus himself may or may not have said, or with the nuances of Matthean and Lucan redaction.[7] This is not to say that his interpretation is tendentious and two-dimensional, configured only by the axes of the Gospels and the goals of the base communities. There is ample evidence of the way biblical scholarship from outside Latin America is used to check and confirm the intuitions of grassroots gospel study. As a result, the credibility of this image of the liberating Jesus is not limited to those who are drawn to him as the "poor Christ." Gutiérrez sets out what he believes Jesus and the evangelists would say, were they asked to direct and encourage Christian witness in the face of the grinding poverty in Latin America. In all this, Jesus' solidarity with the poor has an inspirational rather than a prescriptive role. Gutiérrez and the other liberation theologians see Jesus calling today's disciples to translate the impulses of his own concern for the poor, as the evangelists have transmitted them, into words and deeds that are appropriate to the concrete circumstances they face.

JESUS AND POLITICS

By drawing attention to the liberationists' emphases on Jesus' associations with the marginalized and his challenge to the powerful, we have already hinted at the political dimensions of liberation Christology. Among Latin American Christians dedicated to building a new social order, the issue of the so-called "political messiahship" of Jesus has proved to be particularly pressing. In their reflections on this aspect of Jesus' work, liberation theologians make use of the now-familiar three axes. Where the Gospels are read in the base communities, the political significance of Jesus' words and deeds is not lost. One of Cardenal's Bible-study transcriptions includes the revealing remark from a participant that when Jesus announced an end to oppression in his sermon in Nazareth, "he said it in church."[8] Politics and religion are inextricably linked, then as now. This is also true for First World as well as Third World students of the Gospels. The past forty years have seen a good deal of interest among European scholars in the political dimensions of Jesus' ministry, and liberation theologians have availed themselves of the literature that has stemmed from the pioneering work of Brandon.[9]

The liberationists are at pains to stress that Jesus was not a professional politician. He made no attempt to free Israel from Roman rule or to bring down the structures that were responsible for oppressing the poor. His message was essentially religious and pastoral: he revealed the true nature of God and the vocation and destiny of human persons; he preached the values of freedom and justice; he held out the promise of God's new order. Yet the implications of his ministry were clearly political. His readiness to use the symbolic language of the Kingdom of God inevitably resonated with the deeply rooted aspirations of an occupied people for the salvation of their nation. By giving pride of place in the coming kingdom to the poor and outcast, he could not help but make an impression on the political fabric of Israel's life. In the words and deeds of the liberating Jesus, the threads of religion and politics were inextricably intertwined.

Liberation theology explores the political dimensions of Jesus' ministry from three perspectives: his relationship with the Zealot movement; his conflict with those in authority; and his arrest, trial, and execution. Sobrino draws attention to an often-overlooked feature of the Gospels: in contrast to his treatment of the Pharisees and Sadducees, Jesus never criticized the Zealots. The temptation stories suggest that he felt the attraction of political power as a means of bringing about the Kingdom of God. His execution as "King of the Jews" may indicate some overlap between his cause and that of the Zealots, at least in the minds of his opponents. But however close Jesus and the Zealots may have been, Sobrino is not blind to the differences between them. For Jesus, God's Kingdom was his gift, not the fruit of armed insurrection; its embrace was much wider than Zealot nationalism could allow; its enemies were to be met with love, not violence. However attractive a Zealot-style Jesus might be for Christians committed to political change in Latin America, liberation theologians do not challenge the consensus of the European scholarship they draw on. Both Jesus and the Zealots longed for Israel's salvation, but the liberationists can only insist that the two movements offered alternative strategies.[10]

Jesus' conflict with power groups in Israel is a much more promising resource for the political messiahship of Jesus. Those who live and work in a secular society in which religion has been effectively marginalized may be able to separate the religious and political dimensions of reality. Perhaps they can well imagine Jesus operating as a religious figure independently of sociopolitical structures. However, the liberationists are all too aware of the power of organized religion to shape and direct public as well as private life in their own countries. This makes them particularly sensitive to the political power of those religious officials and institutions we encounter in the Gospels. Segundo has no doubt that it is the political key that most effectively unlocks the full significance of Jesus' words and deeds. Once we recognize that the Sadducees and Pharisees, and not the Roman officials, effectively determined the sociopolitical structure within Israelite society, the fact that Jesus was not a political agitator or revolutionary in the modern sense is immaterial. What at first may appear to be nothing more than a challenge to religious authority becomes political in Jesus' words and deeds.

Pixley's class-based analysis of the confrontation between Jesus and Jerusalem makes further use of the political key and strengthens our perception of the broader impact of Jesus' public ministry. Pixley points out that although Palestine was under Roman rule, its basic class structure had remained intact for the best part of six centuries. Roles and relationships were effectively controlled by Mosaic rather than Roman law. Rome allowed the temple priesthood to maintain its position as the dominant class so long as it kept the peace and ensured that Roman taxes were collected. The "Jesus movement," with its Galilean roots and egalitarian emphasis, effectively denied the class structure that supported the priestly caste. The movement's principal enemies were the beneficiaries of the class system and those whose religious ideology underpinned it—the priests in Jerusalem and the Pharisees in the villages. The final journey to Jerusalem gave Jesus the opportunity to confront the power center of the prevailing order. By acting against the temple and announcing its destruction, he signaled his opposition to the dominant class system in Palestine. The political dimension of his ministry could hardly be more plain. [12]

Liberation theologians also find evidence of the political messiahship of Jesus in the way his ministry ended. We have already noted that the prime movers behind his arrest—the Sanhedrin—were a religious group who wielded political power. Gutiérrez does not deny that in their eyes Jesus was guilty. He had, after all, challenged the basis and legitimacy of their position in the name of a higher authority. He was a threat to every level of public order—religious, social, economic, political. To allow him to persist with his challenge to Israel's religious authorities would be to put the peace of Jerusalem at risk. The fact that Jesus was taken before Pilate the Roman governor, on the way to being crucified as King of the Jews, sets the seal on this political reading of the gospel narratives. Evidence that he was a political agitator may well be lacking, but there can be little doubt that his ministry should be located within the political processes at work in Israel.

Although they interpret Jesus' ministry with the help of a political key, the liberationists do not force the Gospels into a political mold in order to fashion a liberating figure who demands direct political action from his followers today. They are careful to emphasize that Jesus' concern for the political realities of his own world has an inspirational rather than a prescriptive value. His political messiahship neither offers a blueprint for, nor imposes a ban on, particular courses of action today. Liberation Christology encourages Christians to be involved in political struggles but cautions them against drawing straight lines between the Gospels and the present. The followers of Jesus must express their political interests in ways appropriate to the historical situations in which they find themselves, just as Jesus did.

JESUS' PASSION AND RESURRECTION

It should come as no surprise to learn that the liberationists root their discussion of the Passion and resurrection of Jesus in the evangelists' narratives rather than the doctrinal formulations of the catholic church. To be more specific, they locate the cross of Jesus in the space defined by the now familiar axes of gospel story, base community praxis, and conversation with First World scholarship, and wonder what kind of shadow it casts over a landscape dominated by suffering, death, and martyrdom. The ubiquitous Latin American crucifix carries a dead Christ, passively resigned to accepting what came his way as the will of God. But much of the suffering of today's poor can be laid at the feet of injustice and oppression rather than God. Religious images of resignation and passivity may anesthetize the pain of the poor, but they give free reign to those who are responsible for human anguish. The alternative to passive acceptance of the status quo is active struggle for a better order; many of those who belong to the base communities are committed to this. But those who prefer resistance over resignation have to reckon with the death squads. This means that liberation theologians are forced to view Jesus' passion and resurrection through the lens of oppression and injustice, imprisonment and torture, repression and abandonment.[13] What kind of image do they see?

Liberation theologians are unwilling to isolate what happened at the end of Jesus' life from the events that led up to it. Their sensitivity to the forces that operate in their own societies is matched by their concern to recover the historical impulses behind the evangelists' Passion narratives. They are aware that this is no easy task, not least because the Gospels are shot through with later theological reflection that can so easily obscure the human story of Jesus' passion. Today's readers do not share the evangelists' theological and apologetic interests. Devices such as the quotations from the Hebrew scriptures around which the Passion narratives are constructed may once have nourished faith in a suffering and dying Messiah who was subsequently raised to God's right hand. But they are now more likely to give the impression that Jesus was caught up in a suprahistorical drama in which the human actors were stripped of all responsibility for their actions. Such a theological account of Jesus' passion can do little to encourage the historical struggles of his Latin American followers. What is more, the processes of softening the harsh, human side of Jesus' passion are already well under way in the New Testament. Witness Luke's and John's versions of Jesus' last words as he died: his cry of God-forsakenness, which echoes in every place of suffering and torment, becomes a prayer of faith or a shout of triumph (Luke 23:46; John 19:30; cf. Mark 15:34//Matt. 27:46). Elsewhere in the New Testament, historical narrative gives way to theological formula: the scandal of the abandoned Son of God is hidden behind the one whom God set forth as the sacrifice that deals with the sins of the world.

The main task of liberation Christology in relation to Jesus' death and resurrection is to find ways of inserting one Passion story into another, of bringing together the suffering of Jesus and the struggles of the poor against oppression and injustice. The work of sifting through the theologically motivated gospel accounts in order to extract whatever historical fragments remain has yielded a valuable residue. The liberationists claim that in one sense, Jesus' death was unremarkable. He died for the same reasons as the prophets who came before him; according to Segundo, Jesus reincarnated their fate. Like them, he challenged those who stalked the corridors of power and called into question the values of the defenders of the established order. He needed no special supernatural insight, only a cursory knowledge of the story of his own people told in Scripture, to anticipate what lay ahead should he persist in his course of action. The history of Israel simply repeated itself in the events of his own life.

We have already drawn attention to the conflict between Jesus and the Sanhedrin, who were instrumental in having him arrested and dispatched to execution. Sobrino and Boff fasten onto the contrasting ideologies of Jesus and the Jewish leaders. Each had a different view of God: Jesus confronted the "God of religion," whose presence was mediated by the temple and its privileged priestly caste, with the "God of liberation," whose concern extended to those whom the powerful alienated and oppressed. But this ideological struggle was more than a battle of ideas. Following Moltmann, Sobrino sees it as the trial of God. His language is perhaps extravagant, but it allows Sobrino to grasp the issues at stake in the showdown with the Sanhedrin. Jesus accused his opponents of using religious ideology to cover a sinful situation, manipulating the Deity to further their own ends. He challenged them to reject the false God who wielded oppressive power in favor of the true God of liberation. That he was accused of blasphemy indicates that his ideology was unacceptable to the Jewish leaders.

Although Jesus stood alone before the Jewish authorities, Boff and Sobrino remind us that he was not an isolated figure. Boff is aware that his popularity with the crowds, particularly the Galilean pilgrims who had flocked to Jerusalem for the Passover festival, made him a particular threat to the precarious peace of Jerusalem and with it the place of the Sanhedrin in the political order. Sobrino takes this further in his discussion of Jesus before Pilate. According to John 19:12, the governor was presented with a clear alternative—Jesus or Caesar. Jesus represented the rule of God, Caesar the Roman Empire. The God of Jesus was pitted against the political gods of the Roman occupation forces. Before the Sanhedrin and Pilate, theological conflict was inseparable from political struggle, and the outcome was inevitable. There is an air of plausibility about this reconstruction of Jesus' unremarkable rejection and death. Liberation theologians know firsthand what happens to those who plead the cause of the poor in God's name. By challenging the religious and political ideologies that promote injustice, and even putting God on trial once again, they reincarnate the fate of Jesus.

Because Jesus did not simply die but was executed, the liberationists insist that the meaning of the cross is given by all that preceded it. His death was of a piece with his life; the values he incarnated in his ministry provoked the conflict that ultimately brought about his end. His praxis was rooted in his experience of God as Father, the one who searches out, waits for, and rejoices over the lost. Boff sees Jesus as "the believer par excellence," whose life was based on nothing other than God. Jesus was therefore free to live totally for others; and Boff stresses that his entire life, not merely what happened at the end, was redemptive. His death was simply the culmination of all that had preceded it. Throughout his ministry, he revealed the true nature of divine power as the love that liberates people by opening them up for communion with God and each other. Jesus' true greatness is seen in his determination to stand by his cause in the face of opposition and condemnation, and his refusal to give way to resignation even when he felt abandoned on the cross. Boff believes that Jesus' liberation is in some sense complete in his death, even without the resurrection. By standing firm, Jesus demonstrated that he was able to trust himself and his cause to God, with a hope that had already begun to overcome death. The liberating power of Jesus revealed in the Gospel is undiminished, even in death.

Liberation theology sees Jesus' passion, then, as a consequence of his profound solidarity with the oppressed. His active suffering discloses the saving power of God as the love that enters the world of the poor and takes up their hopes for a better life. Inspired once again by Moltmann, Sobrino is struck by the paradox of solidarity and abandonment in the cross. God's identification with human suffering is revealed in the one whom God abandons on the cross. Handing over Jesus to the power of concrete, human sin demonstrates God's loving solidarity with humanity and willingness to be affected by the suffering of God's children. The influence of Matt. 25:40 is apparent throughout Sobrino's reflections on this aspect of the Passion. The Son of Man is identified with the least of his brothers and sisters; God is found where least expected. Again Sobrino uses extravagant language to drive his point home when he writes of the "real cross of the poor" as the "privileged mediation of God."

The contextual influence on this reconstruction of Jesus' passion should be obvious. The Latin American theologians are intent on liberating the death of Jesus from a dogmatic and ahistorical interpretation that can only foster resignation in the face of the suffering caused by oppression and injustice. By reading Jesus' execution as part of the story of his life, they allow the cross to become a symbol of active discipleship and hope. Jesus went to the cross because he was determined to hold on to the values of God's Kingdom and stand up to the powers that opposed his vision of God's rule. His struggle against oppression is an inspiration to those who today are weighed down by injustice. His cross issues a call to follow his example by challenging the powers that pass themselves off as God. Not only does the story of his passion show what human beings do to one another when they turn their backs on God, it also demonstrates how life is redeemed through sacrificial love for others. Jesus' passion reveals the presence of God, as much in the power of his death to gather up God's loving solidarity with humankind as in the Godforsakenness he experienced in his last hour. By highlighting the paradox of the cross in terms of power and weakness, salvation and undeserved suffering, solidarity and abandonment, the liberationists succeed in inserting the Passion story that lies at the heart of the Gospel into the one that is still being written in the lives of the poor and oppressed. This allows them to proclaim the suffering Jesus as the source of liberating power to a continent that has experienced more than enough sorrow, resignation, and death.

In their desire to sever the connections between Jesus' passion and an attitude of passive resignation, liberation theologians emphasize the sufficiency of the cross as the symbol of salvation. They are prepared to speak about the liberating power of Jesus, even without the resurrection. But this does not diminish the fundamental importance of Easter in liberation theology. In common with the First World theologians whose work they draw on, the liberationists underline the elements of revelation, vindication, and hope in the resurrection of Jesus. The New Testament defines God as the one who raised Jesus Christ from the dead (e.g., Rom. 4:24). God proved faithful to the crucified Jesus and so revealed God's power as the love that enters into solidarity with the oppressed, overcoming evil from within. The very language of resurrection points to divine activity. In the Easter event God confirmed Jesus' life and ministry, and especially his cross. As a result of what Boff calls "the explosion of the resurrection," the first disciples came to realize that the whole of Jesus' life had been suffused with a liberative meaning. The resurrection stories express the Easter hope in narrative form: Jesus pardoned those who denied and deserted him, and they in turn embarked on a mission to announce the good news of Jesus Christ to all the world.

All this is familiar to those who are accustomed to First World biblical scholarship. However, the liberationists do not merely read the writings of European and North American theologians—they *re-read* them, giving them a new location within the struggles of the Latin American Christian communities they serve. We have seen the effect of this re-reading on their treatment of Jesus' passion, and it is no less evident in the way they interpret his resurrection. For example, First World scholars unfailingly point out that the language of resurrection belongs to the apocalyptic mentality of the adventist strands in the Judaism of Jesus' day. What these scholars often miss is the key element of justice in Jewish apocalyptic. The revelation of God's Kingdom will usher in a new order that will end the injustice under which God's people have suffered. Sobrino takes seriously the apocalyptic horizon of early Christian preaching. The resurrection of Jesus means that the new order of justice is defined by Jesus' preaching, praxis, and passion. Easter makes it possible to hope for justice, even in the face of all that denies it.

The liberationists' treatment of the historicity of the resurrection is another example of re-reading. Boff and Sobrino reveal their easy familiarity with the assumptions and arguments of twentieth-century New Testament scholarship. They concur that the Easter event is shrouded in mystery, and that the stories of the appearance of the risen Christ may well owe more to post-Easter faith than to what actually took place. It is enough for Boff that the gospel texts testify to the faith and hope of the earliest Christian communities. As such, their meaning can be grasped by the faith and hope they inspire in those who read them today. Sobrino takes this approach further, by borrowing Molt-mann's understanding of history. In his *Theology of Hope*, Moltmann argued that an event is historical inasmuch as it points to something as yet unfulfilled and at the same time creates the opportunity for human beings to act in history. On this understanding, Sobrino maintains that the resurrection of Jesus is historical in two respects. First, as the beginning of the general resurrection, it points ahead of itself. The saving power of Jesus' resurrection has yet to be seen in all its fullness, but Easter is nevertheless the promise of an all-embracing new order of justice. Second, the resurrection of Jesus has set in motion a historical process, of which the mission of the church is the primary witness. The resurrection has therefore opened up a space into which human beings are drawn as they respond to the story of Jesus and begin to change the world.

Boff and Sobrino would agree, then, that the meaning of Easter can only be grasped from the perspective of Christian discipleship. Faith, understood as the praxis that transforms the world in the direction of God's justice, provides the link between what is narrated in the Gospels and the present. It is worth noting the different ways in which Boff and Sobrino relate the resurrection of Jesus to discipleship. Without underestimating the presence of the risen Lord, Boff stresses the inspirational and exemplary power of Easter. The resurrection of the one who was crucified proves that living and dying for justice and truth are not without meaning. Jesus' resurrection is an inspiring example of the victory of life over death, and a powerful symbol that drives the human struggle for liberation. Without denying its inspirational and exemplary power, Sobrino sees the resurrection more as the inauguration of a historical movement in which human persons are called to participate. The life of discipleship—to be specific, the preferential option for the poor—is part of the process of transformation that began with Jesus and will reach its fulfillment at the general resurrection of the dead.

What comes across strongly in this Latin American understanding of Jesus' passion and resurrection is the hermeneutical value of Christian discipleship. As perhaps the dominant axis against which the image of the crucified and risen Christ is set, it represents the struggled for life in the midst of death that is characteristic of the Latin American scene. Justice will never be established as long as the oppressed are further bound by the chains of resignation. But even the faintest glow from the sparks of struggle can begin to shed light on the power of the liberating Jesus. The crucified and risen one is the example par excellence of faith, the embodiment of love, and the ground of hope. The liberationists are right to draw attention to these virtues; without them oppression and injustice, imprisonment and torture, repression and abandonment will reign forever.

DOES THE LIBERATING JESUS SAVE US FROM SIN?

The liberationists tend to play down traditional formulaic understandings of the death of Christ in favor of a more historical approach to his passion. We may wonder about the effect of this on their understanding of Jesus' saving work in relation to sin. Some First World theologians have noted the absence from liberation theology of leading themes such as Christ the sin-bearer and the atoning power of his death. Liberation theology replaces the theocentric focus of traditional Christian soteriology with an emphasis on the part played by human beings (both within and beyond the church) in effecting the saving purposes of God. Some of their evangelical Latin American critics accuse liberation theologians of diminishing the personal aspects of sin as an affront to God in favor of its social and interpersonal dimensions.[14] In what sense, then, does liberation theology see Jesus as the one who saves his people from their sins (Matt. 1:21)?

Boff is uneasy with notions of vicarious sacrificial atonement found in the New Testament because they give the impression that the redemptive work of Jesus is concentrated in the last hours of his life. He wishes to underline the saving power of the whole of Jesus' life, not least because of the resonance between the gospel story of his hopes and struggles and the experiences of those who work for justice and freedom today. If Jesus is Savior only in his death, his solidarity with the oppressed is merely accidental. Why should today's poor feel any affinity with him? Traditional theological models of the atonement, such as expiatory sacrifice, ransom, and vicarious satisfaction place the Passion of Jesus beyond the reach of contemporary reality, largely because they fail to answer the questions put to the Gospel by those involved in the liberation struggle. Here we reach the nub of the issue between traditional theology and liberation soteriology.

Bultmann pointed out that biblical interpretation proceeds on the basis of a life-relation between the subject matter of the text and the concerns of its readers. Much European and North American Protestant theology is indebted to the question, "What must I do to be saved?" (Acts 16:30). By contrast, liberation theology arises out of the question, "How does the process of liberation, to which many Christians are committed, relate to the salvation offered by Jesus Christ?" These questions are themselves based on different conceptions of the human predicament—of what it is that human beings need to be saved from. Generally speaking, First World Protestantism has a more individualistic understanding of humanity: sin is more readily seen in terms of personal moral failure, and salvation is sheer divine gift, passively received in faith. By contrast, liberation theology, in both Roman Catholic and Protestant forms, combines a more active understanding of the human vocation with a corporate sense of sin.[15] The different character of these basic soteriological questions, including the anthropologies they carry, dictates the choice between theological formula and gospel narrative.

It is worth outlining the way liberation theologians envisage the saving work of Jesus in relation to sin in order to show how the basic Latin American soteriological question helps to form the impression of Jesus as Savior. Gutiérrez's *A Theology of Liberation* is perhaps the most sustained exposition of liberation soteriology.[16] He reads the Bible as a single text, organizing its various themes—creation, exodus, justice, eschatology, Jesus—around the principal semantic axis of salvation. This central Christian mystery is understood as communion with God and among human persons; it cannot be contained in the church or confined to whatever may happen beyond death. God's work in creation and salvation is universal, and drives history forward. Humankind, made in the image of God, is called to cooperate with God to establish communion, and the human vocation finds expression in the struggle for freedom at all levels—political (in the fight against oppression), historical (as agents committed to the transformation of history), and spiritual (communion with God is essential if liberation is to be complete). Salvation is found in all attempts to order society according to the true knowledge of God, which is the practice of justice (Jer. 22:15–16). But as the gift of God, salvation will only reach its fullness in the Parousia of the Lord. However much God's reign takes root in liberation projects, it can never be unequivocally identified with any particular human endeavor.

For Gutiérrez, then, sin is an obstacle to salvation in that it represents a turning aside from communion, a breach of friendship with God and other people. From a Protestant perspective, Bonino sees sin as humankind's failure to take up the work entrusted by God in creation, namely the responsibility to create history and culture, to transform the world within the matrix of human relationships and in partnership with God.[17] Not surprisingly, Gutiérrez and Bonino are unhappy with abstract notions of sin. Gutiérrez prefers the term "structural sin," which includes but transcends the total influence of individual moral failings on the ordering of society. In a continent over-whelmed by poverty, the death-dealing power of sin is felt most keenly in oppression and injustice, which certainly rupture communion with the God of Jesus Christ and among God's children. The struggle for liberation is therefore a struggle against these historical manifestations of sin.

According to Gutiérrez, the saving work of Jesus embraced the historical, political, and spiritual levels of liberation found in the Old Testament, as he sought to introduce people into his own communion with God and one another. He went to the cross, says Sobrino, laden with concrete historical sin, which he conquered from within. His resurrection enabled him to transcend the constraints of his earthly ministry without eliminating its essential character.[18] Gutiérrez sees Jesus giving a universal scope to the promises of this-worldly salvation found in the Hebrew scriptures. Christ's gift of filiation and friendship, which overcomes the power of sin, is now available to all through the gift of the Spirit. Those who receive it in faith are converted and become brothers and sisters who are ready to embark upon the continu-ing struggle against concrete sin. According to Bonino, this is the fruit of the forgiveness of sins, which brings the freedom to take up the work that God has entrusted to humankind in creation.

A vision such as this of Christ's victory over sin can readily find a place among those who work for justice. They will be encouraged both by its confidence in the decisive victory of Jesus over sin and by its insistence on the continuing demand to fight against the historical manifestations of sin in oppression and injustice. On this understand-ing, the liberating work of Christ is not yet finished, but the fruits of his victory are available through the presence of the crucified and risen Lord in the gift of God's Spirit. Because it has been fashioned from within the struggle for liberation, this vision of Christ's saving work has much to offer to the political process, not least as a useful critique of any tendency to promote an attenuated view of what it is to be human or what it means to be free.

It could be argued that any attempt to articulate the significance of Jesus' role as Savior from sin depends on the way we envisage the human predicament that we believe his work remedies. Latin America is dominated by sorrow, suffering, and death. Historically, the cross of

Jesus has been associated with a resigned attitude in the face of what are now understood as concrete manifestations of sin. Such a religiously informed response to the power of sin can do little to break its grip. If liberation soteriology is to proclaim the victory of Christ over the power of sin at work in the public domain, it must move beyond those theological formulas and theories that speak most powerfully to the wounded conscience. Of course, there is more to sin than that which leads to social breakdown, oppression, and injustice. But for those who are involved in the liberation struggle, what is called "structural sin" is its most pressing instance and demands the most immediate theological attention.

In the Scriptures, sin is both personal moral failure and oppressive structural power. Given the intention of liberation theology to work from within political struggles, it is perhaps inevitable that one end of the biblical range should receive more attention than the other. Two things have occurred to me in reflecting on this Latin American understanding of Jesus as Savior. First, liberation theology has much in common with Saint Paul's understanding of sin. In the letter to the Romans, he writes of sin as a power that works against the divine purpose, not only by holding humankind in the realm of the flesh but also by using the law to divide humanity into Jew and Gentile. In Gutiérrez's terminology, Paul sees sin as an oppressive power that damaged communion with God and among persons. Second, liberation theology's determination to begin with the story of Jesus asks us to consider whether the soteriological formulas of the New Testament were informed by all that led up to the cross. Why should the death of Christ reveal God's love for humankind if it is unrelated to the life whose end it marked? Could it be that the familiar expressions embedded in liturgy and taken up by doctrine are in fact shorthand statements whose referents in Jesus' career have been lost by Christian theology? The liberationists issue an important corrective to those traditional theologies of the cross that attenuate—and therefore fail to do justice to—the universal scope of God's saving work in Christ. By rooting its reflections in the story of his struggle against the concrete power of sin, liberation theology opens our eyes to the possibilities of appropriating the fruits of Christ's victory where the brokenness of creation is most acutely felt.

CONCLUSION

We may wonder which of the three axes along which liberation Christology is plotted is dominant—the Jesus of the Gospels, the active faith of the base communities, or the conversation with First World biblical and theological scholarship. My guess is that the second—the life and witness of the base communities—has the controlling interest. Liberation theology is a good example of the way in which the practical commitments of theologians inform their work.[19] We have seen that the liberationists' decision to fashion a Christology on the basis of the Gospels is hardly arbitrary. Narrative is more easily accessible than dogma to those who have taken up the preferential option for the poor and who are therefore caught up in a historical struggle against the forces of oppression and injustice. What is also clear is that however much they draw on theological resources from outside Latin America, the liberationists are concerned to use them as the basis of a Christology that makes sense in relation to the struggles for justice.

Liberation Christology reveals the hermeneutical importance of active faith, expressed in the preferential option for the poor. To borrow a phrase from Theo Witvliet, this form of Christian discipleship provides "cognitive access" to the mystery of the liberating Jesus.[20] In Boff's words, praxis "fires the logical mechanisms of the cognitive process." The liberationists are therefore sensitized to aspects of the Christian gospel that other approaches miss, simply because of their involvement in the struggles of the poor. Practical interests open up some key areas of investigation and close down others; the preference for the language of solidarity over sacrifice in relation to the death of Jesus is an example. With this in mind, it is refreshing to discover that liberation theologians are open about their inability to offer anything other than a partial interpretation of the Christian mystery. Here, of course, they speak for all theologians. If it is impossible to throw off the influence of our theoretical and practical interests, we can only hope to pursue the truth of Jesus Christ in dialogue with others who see things differently. The fact that the liberationists' writings repeatedly make reference to biblical and theological studies that emanate from other practical options is a hopeful sign for the future of liberation theology.

As it continues to develop, liberation Christology would certainly benefit from conversation with some of the more recent approaches to the study of the Gospels, many of which have entered the wider world of biblical scholarship only since the major texts of liberation theology were first published. It would be interesting to see what liberation Christology might make of the work of Ben Meyer, John Riches, and E. P. Sanders on the Jewish matrix of Jesus' ministry. I wonder how the Latin American image of the liberating Jesus would fare alongside the figure who was devoted to the restoration of Israel in the face of the cultural impact of Hellenization.[21] Unlike its South African counterpart, Latin American liberation theology appears to make little use of the materialist approaches to the Gospels developed by Belo, whose work has become popular among those inclined toward liberation theology in Europe and North America.[22] A notable exception is Pixley, whose *God's Kingdom* looks forward to the greater availability of knowledge about the material base of daily life in Palestine. Research into the socioeconomic dimensions of early Christianity could add further substance to the liberationists' sense of Jesus' solidarity with the oppressed.[23] Gutiérrez has recently acknowledged that the Latin American liberation struggle is beginning to wake up to the intolerable situations in which women are forced to live. If Fiorenza's continuing call for the development of a more critical reading of the Gospels is heard, we can expect further clarification of the liberating power of Jesus for oppressed women.[24]

As a form of theological discourse, liberation theology is driven by the mission of the church, and the scholarly community is the servant of that mission. As the preferential option for the poor rises to new challenges in the encounter with other forms of oppression, we can expect the conversation with First World theology to continue. As it does, the newly emerging voices in biblical and theological studies will further enrich the image of the one whom the poor know and love as the liberating Jesus.

NOTES

1. L. Boff, "Christ's Liberation via Oppression: An Attempt at Theological Construction from the Standpoint of Latin America," in *Frontiers of Theology in Latin America*, ed. R. Gibellini (Maryknoll, NY: Orbis Books, 1979; London: SCM Press, 1980), 100–132.

2. J. Sobrino, *Christology at the Crossroads: A Latin-American Approach*, trans. John Drury (Maryknoll, NY: Orbis Books, 1978; London: SCM Press, 1978), 46.

3. J. Sobrino, *Jesus in Latin America* (Maryknoll, NY: Orbis Books, 1987), 95.

4. E. Cardenal, *The Gospel in Solentiname*, 4 vols. (Maryknoll, NY: Orbis Books, 1976–84).

5. G. Gutiérrez, *A Theology of Liberation: History, Politics and Salvation* (Maryknoll, NY: Orbis Books, 1973; rev. ed. 1988; London: SCM Press, 1974, 1988), chap. 13.

6. Strictly speaking, we can only say that humankind is potentially the temple of God; Saint Paul uses the image to refer to believers.

7. See J. Segundo, *Jesus of Nazareth Yesterday and Today*. Vol. 2, *The Historical Jesus of the Synoptics* (Maryknoll, NY: Orbis Books, 1985), chap. 7, for a discussion of these issues.

8. Cardenal, *Gospel in Solentiname*, 1:132.

9. See, for example, S. G. F. Brandon, *Jesus and the Zealots* (Manchester: Manchester University Press, 1967); M. Hengel, *Was Jesus a Revolutionist?* (Philadelphia: Fortress Press, 1971); O. Cullmann, *Jesus and the Revolutionaries* (New York: Harper & Row, 1970); A. Richardson, *The Political Christ* (London: SCM Press, 1973); E. Bammel and C. F. D. Moule, eds., *Jesus and the Politics of His Day* (Cambridge: Cambridge University Press, 1984).

10. Sobrino, *Christology*, 211ff.; Gutiérrez, *Theology*, rev. ed., 131f.

11. Segundo, *Jesus of Nazareth*, appendix 2.

12. G. Pixley, *God's Kingdom* (Maryknoll, NY: Orbis Books, 1981), chap. 5.

13. L. Boff, *Passion of Christ, Passion of the World: The Facts, Their Interpretation and Their Meaning Yesterday and Today* (Maryknoll, NY: Orbis Books, 1987), chap. 1; see also his *Jesus Christ Liberator: A Critical Christology of Our Time* (Maryknoll, NY: Orbis Books, 1978; London: SPCK, 1980), chap. 6; Sobrino, *Christology*, chap. 6, and *Jesus*, chap. 4; Segundo, *Jesus of Nazareth*, chap. 1.

14. C. Braaten, "The Christian Doctrine of Salvation," and D. Bloesch, "Soteriology in Contemporary Christian Thought," in *Interpretation* 35, no. 2 (April 1981); G. Cook, *The Expectation of the Poor: Latin American Basic Ecclesial Communities in Protestant Perspective* (Maryknoll, NY: Orbis Books, 1985), 150–53.

15. R. Bultmann, "Is Exegesis Without Presuppositions Possible?" reprinted in *Rudolf Bultmann: New Testament and Mythology and Other Basic Writings*, ed. S. Ogden (Philadelphia: Fortress Press, 1984; London: SCM Press, 1985), 145–54; Gutiérrez sets out liberation theology's questions in *Theology*, rev. ed., 72–83.

16. See especially Gutiérrez, *Theology*, rev. ed., chap. 9 and pp. 130–35.

17. J. Miguez Bonino, *Doing Theology in a Revolutionary Situation* (Philadelphia: Fortress Press, 1975), and *Room To Be People: An Interpretation of the Message of the Bible for Today's World* (Philadelphia: Fortress Press, 1979).

18. Sobrino, *Jesus*, 34–35.

19. C. Boff, *Theology and Praxis: Epistemological Foundations* (Maryknoll, NY: Orbis Books, 1987), part 3; Gutiérrez, *The Power of the Poor in History: Selected Writings*, chap. 7; cf. G. Turner, "Preunderstanding and New Testament Interpretation," *Scottish Journal of Theology* 28, no. 3 (1975): 227–42.

20. T. Witvliet, *A Place in the Sun: An Introduction to Liberation Theology in the Third World* (London: SCM press, 1985), 137.

21. B. Meyer, *The Aims of Jesus* (London: SCM Press, 1979); J. Riches, *Jesus and the Transformation of Judaism* (London: Darton, Longman and Todd, 1980); E. P. Sanders, *Jesus and Judaism* (London: SCM Press, 1985). S. Freyne's recent study of the significance of Galilee in the ministry of Jesus, *Galilee, Jesus and the Gospels: Literary Approaches and Historical Investigations* (Dublin: Gill and Macmillan, 1988), is referred to in Gutiérrez's most recent work, *The God of Life* (Maryknoll, NY: Orbis Books, 1991), chap. 6.

22. F. Belo, *A Materialist Reading of the Gospel of Mark* (Maryknoll, NY: Orbis Books, 1981); M. Clévenot, *Materialist Approaches to the Bible* (Maryknoll, NY: Orbis Books, 1985); C. Myers, *Binding the Strong Man: A Political Reading of Mark's Story of Jesus* (Maryknoll, NY: Orbis Books, 1988); C. Rowland and M. Corner, *Liberating Exegesis: The Challenge of Liberation Theology to Biblical Studies* (London: SPCK, 1990); I. Mosala, *Biblical Hermeneutics and Black Theology in South Africa* (Grand Rapids: Eerdmans, 1989).

23. M. Crosby, *House of Disciples: Church, Economics and Justice in Matthew* (Maryknoll, NY: Orbis Books, 1988); P. Esler, *Community and Gospel and Luke-Acts: The Social and Political Motivations of Lucan Theology* (Cambridge: Cambridge University Press, 1987); H. Moxnes, *The Economy of the Kingdom: Social Conflict and Economic Relations in Luke's Gospel* (Philadelphia: Fortress Press, 1988).

24. E. Schüssler-Fiorenza, "The Politics of Otherness: Biblical Interpretation as a Critical Praxis for Liberation," in *Expanding the View: Gustavo Gutiérrez and the Future of Liberation Theology*, ed. M. Ellis and O. Maduro (Maryknoll, NY: Orbis Books, 1990), chap. 11. See also in the same volume Gutiérrez's essay "Expanding the View," 7 and 9, for his comments on the need to address the oppression of women.

CHAPTER TWENTY-FOUR

CHRISTOLOGY AND INTERFAITH DIALOGUE: THE PROBLEM OF UNIQUENESS

KARL-JOSEF KUSCHEL

TRANSLATED BY KENNETH BREWER

A book with the provocative title *The Myth of God Incarnate*, edited by British theologian John Hick, appeared in England in 1977.[1] Unfortunately, it scarcely found any notice in Germany and did not arouse any concern in the theological guild.[2] At the same time, its thrust was of fundamental theological significance. The book not only asked in the narrower Christological sense if the belief in the incarnation of Jesus Christ belongs at all to the center of Christianity. It also asked more fundamentally if the doctrine of the preexistence and incarnation has not always led to proclaiming Jesus Christ as the only Savior of the world. Thus Hick sought to demonstrate the superiority of Christianity over other religions.

CHRISTOLOGY—INCAPABLE OF INTERRELIGIOUS DIALOGUE?

The question of the status of the doctrines of preexistence and incarnation is anything but the special question of a "professor's theology for theology professors." It touches on a problem of ecumenical significance: the ability of Christianity to relate to the billions of human beings comprising the non-Christian world. Here lies the actual strategical goal of the myth-of-God-incarnate debate. This was recently clarified by the second volume, *The Myth of Christian Uniqueness*, published in 1987. In this volume an entire theological group has emerged under the programmatic banner of a "pluralistic theology of religions" (along with John Hick are, above all, Paul F. Knitter, G. Kaufman, and

R. Panikkar). This volume has now made clear what was at issue from the very beginning. It advocated a fundamental critique of traditional Christology that consistently justifies the "superiority" of Christianity over the other world religions in categories such as "the unique definitiveness, absoluteness and normativity" of Christ and, as a consequence, makes dialogue with the non-Christian religions essentially impossible.[3]

Have not the Christian churches in recent times begun to revise their relationship to the non-Christian religions? Do not worlds lie between the World Missionary Conference in Edinburgh in 1910 (where participants still anticipated a speedy Christianization of the whole of humankind) and subsequent activities of the Ecumenical Councils of the Churches in the decades following World War II? The Delegations Conference was held in Kandy (Ceylon) in 1967; the Central Committee Meeting in Addis Ababa in 1971; the Full Assembly in Nairobi in 1975; and the Consultation of Chiang Mai (Thailand) in 1977. All these assemblies finally led to "Guidelines on the Dialogue with People of Different Religions and Ideologies" (1979), which stood under the key words *community* and *dialogue*, although the World Council has not been able to this day to say a clear word about the salvation of non-Christians.

On this point the Roman Catholic church was bolder. The Second Vatican Council clarified tough dogmatic positions by saying that the grace of God is active "invisibly" in the hearts "of all people of good will" (*Gaudium et Spes*, 22) and conceded the possibility of salvation of non-Christians: "Those also can attain to everlasting salvation who through no fault of their own do not know the gospel of Christ or His Church, yet sincerely seek God and, moved by grace, strive by their deeds to do His will as it is known to them through the dictates of conscience" (*Lumen Gentium*, 19). One particular "explanation" of the council, "On the Relationship of the Church to the Non-Christian Religions," reads: "The Catholic Church rejects nothing which is true and holy in these religions."

Do not such statements also bring certain consequences for Christology arising from this new attitude? How can one respect the other religions in the dialogue, accepting their truth and holiness, even conceding the possibility of salvation for their followers, and at the same time insist on the uniqueness of the redemptive role of Jesus Christ? This is exactly what the representatives of the pluralistic theology of religions now contest. As John Hick puts it, "once it is granted that salvation is in fact taking place not only within Christianity but also within the other great traditions, it seems arbitrary and unrealistic to go on insisting that the Christ-event is the sole and exclusive source of human salvation."[4]

THE ALTERNATIVE: INCARNATION IN PLURAL

What theological alternative can make it possible to do justice to the challenge of religious pluralism and to reject every form of Christian superiority? Certainly, the sketches within the pluralistic theology of religions group have their own individual profiles. Here common argumentive ground structures emerge that one can reconstruct tersely.

Already an epistemological consequence is to be derived from the insight of the fundamental historical relativity of all events and knowledge. If one takes earnestly the fact of an all-determining "historical consciousness" (E. Troeltsch), then one must—according to Paul Knitter—"grant in all honesty, that under human conditions there can be no final word about truth, nor can there be only one way to know it, a word and a way which would be valid for all times and all peoples."[5] Consequently, there is "no firm place for the truth."[6]

The reality of God is always greater than a single person can comprehend or express. The Divine can only be understood ultimately as an unspeakable, incomprehensible, eternally unattainable mystery. For the interfaith dialogue, this means that "no religion and no revelation can be the unique, final, exclusive or inclusive word of God. Such a final word would limit God and take his mystery from him."[7]

The various religions are nothing other than different manifestations of the transcendent ground of the Eternal One. Whether Zeus, Yahweh, Allah, or Krishna, they are all manifestations of the Eternal One who always lies in front of every name, but who also is simultaneously manifest in many different ways. One must depart from an exclusive conception of revelation and incarnation in view of the plurality of religions. Incarnations of divine spirit or word have taken place continually. "Incarnation in this sense," says John Hick, "has occurred and is occurring in many different ways and degrees in many different persons."[8]

If no religion, no revelation, and no redeemer can fully represent the mystery of God, it follows that Christianity also has to understand itself as a part of the multifaceted religions. A literal Copernican revolution is demanded from the Christian church. Christianity and its Christ are no longer the sun in the center, around which the other world religions circle as planets. *God* is in the center. Around that eternal God Christianity and all other religions of humankind revolve. A pluralistic Christology follows from this pluralistic theology.

This pluralistic Christology contests neither the universality nor the uniqueness of Jesus Christ, which remain nevertheless both concrete and empirical. Jesus of Nazareth is unique, as every person in his or her own way is unique. And Jesus Christ is universal because Christians throughout the world believe in him. Therefore, it is valid to say that Jesus Christ may be for Christians the special revelation or the incarnation of God. But outside Jesus Christ there are other, just as valid, comprehensive revelations of God. As John Hick maintains: "We want to say of Jesus that he was *totus deus*, 'wholly God,' in the sense that his *agapé* was genuinely the *Agapé* of God at work on earth, but not that he was *totum dei*, 'the whole of God,' in the sense that the divine *Agapé* was expressed without remainder in each or even in the sum of his actions."[9] Or as Paul Knitter argues: "In the way that Jesus is *one* window through which we can . . . look on the universe of the divine mystery, there can certainly also be still *other* windows."[10]

It follows, therefore, that the Christological definitions of the ancient church councils must also be relativized historically: the expressions of the councils of Nicea (325) and Constantinople (381) concerning the preexistence ("from the Father, born before all time"), divinity ("God from God"), agency of creation ("through him all things were made"), significance of salvation ("descended for us all") and incarnation ("and took on flesh") of the Son of God. These affirmations are only one form of expressing the significance of Jesus, dependent upon the Greco-Roman culture from which they originated. Their mythological character must first be recognized and then interpreted.[11] A serious change from the Jewish-flavored New Testament to the Hellenistic-oriented early church must also be taken into account. The title "Son of God," borrowed from Judaism, had little metaphysical significance for Jesus in the New Testament, but was a symbolic, metaphorical paraphrase of significance for Jewish Christians. After a century of debate (Nicea to Chalcedon) the church had no inhibitions about attributing to Jesus an identical essence with God (Nicea) joined with a fully human nature (Chalcedon). What was poetry in the New Testament was now transformed into prose; what had been symbols was transferred into ontological-metaphysical systems; what appeared as a "living picture" was now replaced by "rigid and literally understood dogmas."[12] This was fatal for the relationship of Christians to non-Christian religions, as John Hick sums it up: "For understood literally . . . God-incarnate language implies that God can be adequately known and responded to *only* through Jesus; and the whole religious life of mankind, beyond the stream of Judaic-Christian faith, is thus by implication excluded as lying outside the sphere of salvation."[13]

COMPELLING ALTERNATIVES?

One must admit that the arguments of the pluralistic theology of religions are impressive because of the fatal consequences of the Christian claim of superiority; because of the way the fact of religious pluralism is taken earnestly in the one world in which we live; and because of the capacity for tolerance and Christian self-denial. Indeed, one can ask: Is not a disarming of dogmatic Christology long overdue for the sake of Christianity's capacity for dialogue with the other world religions? To be sure, the left wing of dogmatic Christology actually has often been not only fatally anti-Semitic, according to Rosemary Ruether, but also an advocate of fanatical Christian exclusiveness and of the arrogant claim to superiority. Must one not cross the theological Rubicon after both the model of intolerant exclusiveness (salvation *only* in Christ) and that of gracious inclusiveness (acknowledgment of the possibility of salvation in other religions as a result of Christ's work of salvation) have worn out their plausibility? Is not every dogmatic claim for Christ and Christianity as exploitative for all other religions, as is a sexism that makes specific male experience the universal norm for the whole of humanity?[14] Consequently, does only the rejection of the superiority and finality of Christ or of Christianity remain, and with that the acknowledgment of the complete equality and validity of other ways of salvation?

We must take seriously this challenge of the Anglo-Saxon pluralistic theology of religions. And this we can do only if we encounter its rational structure with serious theological *Sachkritik* (content criticism). Any such pluralistic theology must be evaluated on the basis of the Christian character of the criteria that are used. Christology might play a key role therein. The decisive questions therefore must be: Will the pluralistic theology do justice to the fundamental Christian witnesses and to the authoritative interpretations of the church? On the other hand, does the belief in the uniqueness and finality of Christ lead *inevitably* to an intolerant exclusiveness of Christianity over against other religions?

This question can only to be answered on the basis of the New Testament and the ancient church councils themselves; that is, from the framework of a critical contextual exegesis and hermeneutic of dogmas. In this case, unfortunately, there is no well-formulated biblical theology of interreligious dialogue written from the position of the latest exegetical research. Therefore, a provisional attempt should be made to examine its Christological theses in two test cases: the hymn of the letter to the Colossians and the faith confession of the council of Nicea.[15]

COLOSSIANS 1:15–20

15   *He is the image of the invisible God, the firstborn over all creation;*

16   *for in him all things were created, in heaven and on earth, visible and invisible, whether thrones or dominions or principalities or authorities—all things were created through him and for him.*

17   *He is before all things, and in him all things hold together.*

18   *He is the head of the body, the church; he is the beginning, the first-born from the dead, that in everything he might be preeminent.*

19   *For in him all the fullness of God was pleased to dwell,*

20 *and through him to reconcile to himself all things, whether on earth or in heaven, making peace by the blood of his cross.*

Whoever isolates this text, which its author had previously found and edited as a hymn (visible above all in vv. 18 and 20), certainly might find in it a powerful expression of Christian superiority. Can one as a Christian hold to anything higher than the claim that Christ was previously the mediator of God at the protocreation and everything "in heaven and on earth" is not only *made* through him and for him, but everything also *holds together in him*. Past, present, and future—the entire creation was formed, imbued, and held together by the power and might of Christ. He and only he appears to matter, nothing else!

Projecting this text or other biblical texts onto the present conversation with the non-Christian religions results in the conclusion that if everything has been made through Christ and for Christ, then the religions of the world are also part of God's creation. Thus, it follows that all non-Christian religions are to be relativized by the lordship of Christ, indeed to be condemned as "heresy."[16] Their position is completely governed by the one who has "in everything the preeminence." Following on this, a Christian exclusivism, triumphalism, and claim of superiority may seem to be well established. What then?

But if one does not isolate this text in an unhistorical manner but considers its individual biographical, political, and sociological context, another picture comes to light. Although the context suggests the situational conditioning of a timeless content that could be discarded with sufficient historical distance, it can also be seen as constitutive for the abiding sense of this confession to Christ.

In order to understand the context, one should know first that this letter, whether Pauline or not, went to a city in Asia Minor that at that time belonged to the Roman province of Asia. Today this place is called Konas and lies in southwest Turkey. Then it was an insignificant center of wool processing: "The few Christians of Colossae earned their money in the cloth industry. One could be a weaver, a dyer or a shepherd in Colossae. Dyed woollen material was produced above everything else."[17] Moreover, according to the Annals of Tacitus, the region around this city must have been destroyed by an earthquake in 61 C.E. It had obviously been rebuilt when this letter was received. One of the key phrases of the text that speaks of the menacing "elemental powers of the world" would have echoed the crumbling, shaking ground for the original readers. Thus, this community's faith in Christ had a catastrophe immediately behind it.

The apostle Paul is portrayed here not as a triumphal preacher, but as a political prisoner who sits in jail because of his conviction: "Remember my fetters" (4:18). He is a prisoner who not only finds himself in a situation of "suffering" (1:24), but knows that the recipients of his letter are also threatened. "Paul" must have thought about a competing mission during his absence from the community; only in this way will his allusion to a "difficult struggle" (2:1) for them be understandable. Over and above all this, "Paul" must write against competing philosophies and religious practices. Therefore, he alludes to the "elemental spirits of the universe" and to the problem of religious food regulations and observance of days, of angel worship, visions, and religious asceticism (2:16–23). Finally, "Paul" must contend with moral neglect in the community; he writes about lewdness, shamelessness, evil desire, and greed; about anger, rage, filthy talk, dirty jokes, and lies (3:5–8).

If one reads the Christ hymn in this context, its expressions about Christ may scarcely raise triumphal feelings, obsession with exclusivism, or desires for superiority. Conversely, what lies in Col. 1:15–20 for us is nothing other than the song of trust and hope of a man, literally with chains on his hands, who from the perspective of a caged bird seeks to justify his faith in Christ in this earthquake-prone corner of the Roman Empire. The song is not superioristic; rather, it's "crazy." Can one claim anything crazier than that God(!) wanted to dwell "with all his fullness" in the once-crucified Nazarene? Can one in a situation of constant natural disasters express anything bolder than the "pre-eminence over all creation" of a man who himself ended up on the gallows? Can one formulate something more politically dangerous than the allusion to the thrones and lordships, powers and forces, if one did not know who at that time exercised lordship over the world, who controlled all powers and forces, namely, the Roman military power who had enforced the *pax romana* with force of weapons in all regions of its empire? We do not know exactly why "Paul" was thrown into prison, but this song would have sufficed.

In this hymn from an insignificant and powerless community who were once Gentiles, three points were mentioned:

1. God is truly invisible, hidden to all, yet not simply a dark

puzzle, an unfathomable mystery. God has become clear in the picture of the Christ who was resurrected from the dead, exalted, and, in this way, "first born." Indeed, the hymn receives its entire power from the conviction that Christ is the reliable, normative picture of God.

2. If Christ is the picture of the invisible God, then trust in creation is justified in defiance of all empires. Despite everything, creation is not delivered over to cosmic potencies and fatalistic powers; despite all of the catastrophic experiences, creation is not arbitrary with regard to its origin, not chaotic with regard to its course, and not blind with regard to its goal—it is held together by Christ, i.e., by reconciliation, peace, and love. In this hymn the definitiveness of the Christ event is indisputable.

3. The belief in the "new people" (3:10), who are in Christ, was substantiated with this song. With this aim in view the author makes clear that the Christ event is no coincidence of history, but a "mystery which for ages and generations" has been hidden by God (1:26). In this hymn, God is indeed not surprised by history. God is Lord of history, before whose eyes everything already appears that is still hidden from earthly eyes. From the beginning, therefore, the Christ event stood "before the eyes" of God, so that the entire creation could be designed toward this event. Creation and redemption belong together in Christ. The finality of the Christ event results therefore from belief in the creative power and historical might of the one God.

Therefore, the song is directed to the "new and unheard of Christ-mystery." What does this new element consist of? It is the possibility of faith in the true God that was opened by God in Christ to both Jew and Gentile, made possible by a completely surprising, gracious turning of God to those who do not even belong to the chosen people. Such privilege of salvation, however, no longer plays a role in Christ. God has broken through all of the old, established religious systems and reveals the possibility of true faith. This faith is made concrete in the freedom from all (Jewish) commands and prohibitions and all possible (Gentile) philosophies and practices.

Therefore, this new people will be "sincerely compassionate," "kind, humble, gentle, patient" (3:12).

Put on then . . . compassion . . . forbearing one another and, if one has a complaint against another, forgiving each other; as the Lord has forgiven you, so you also must forgive. And above all these put on love, which binds everything together in perfect harmony. And let the peace of Christ rule in your hearts. (3:12–15)

To those who make Christ the norm of their picture of God and humanity, religious and social origins no longer play a role. To put it another way, for this author normativity of the Christ event establishes the "new way of being human." Were it otherwise, one could live and justify anything in the name of God.

With this it is clear that the uniqueness, the finality of the Christ event is redefined. It is an expression of the belief that God was revealed in Christ. Neither an exclusivity nor an arrogant superiority are claimed for Christ in this letter. Not arrogance, but thankfulness and humility would be the qualities of a person who is taken up by the spirit of this song.

The self-obligation of the love and peace of Christ includes for the Colossians the prophetic protest and resistance against every kind of false doctrine, superstition, and idolatry. The freedom of the "new person" certainly does not consist of "cheap tolerance," but in the testing of the spirit, namely, whether everything that is offered in philosophies and false doctrines in the supermarket of religious options (whether from that time or today) also corresponds to the spirit of Christ and does not lead again to slavery. Christ's uniqueness does not mean superiority but rather otherness and distinctiveness.

THE CHRISTOLOGY OF NICEA

What then of the decisions of the councils concerning Christ? The difficulties with their statements run through the Christian church itself. Since the Enlightenment, criticisms of this fourth-century Christology have ranged from its unintelligibility and complexity to its remoteness from life and Scripture. And yet this Christology in the end has held a high status through the liturgy of the Christian church.

The hermeneutics of Catholic dogma start out today from the position that Nicea's statements about Christ must be explained from historical situations of confrontation. They must be understood from the worldview of middle-Platonism, which prevailed at that time and was marked by a strong separation of God and the world. The so-called world soul was thought of as a divine principle that makes a connection between the divine and the earthly, the above and below. The "first god," who is fundamentally unreachable and unknowable by human-kind, could in this way remain pure being, - active in the transitory world only by means of the "second god," the "world soul." The transcendence of God was thereby safeguarded. This God participated only indirectly with the world.

This three-layered middle-Platonic worldview became a problem for Christian theology and the church. Then an Alexandrian priest named Arius considered it his calling to explain the relation of God, world, and Christ with its help. He was of the opinion that God is ultimately unknowable not only for humanity but also for the Logos, Jesus Christ, so that the "Son" does not know the "Father" in depth. Why not? Because the Son is also a creature! However, for Arius, the Son did not exist from eternity as a creature because God alone was eternal, unbegotten, uncreated, indivisible, and unchangeable. There was therefore a time when the Son was not. God was not always the Father of this Son. For Arius it followed that Father and Son are themselves in essence foreign and dissimilar from one another; God is a self-existent, mysterious monad, lonesome and remote from the world.

The reaction of the council of Nicea must be understood from this background. It is above all concerned with justifying anew a central element of the New Testament message. Nicea expressly did not want to go beyond Scripture with its confession of Christ, but understood its creed as a contribution to the interpretation of Scripture. Therefore, it is not in the end clothed in the form of a dogmatic treatise, but in the form of a confession.

For Nicea the problem was focused upon the matter that a central idea of the New Testament should be adhered to, namely, that God was revealed not partially but definitively and unconditionally in Jesus Christ. In view of the metaphysical presuppositions of the time and of such a challenging philosophical-theological system as that of Arius, there was only one alternative: either Jesus Christ belongs to the substance of the created world or he belongs totally to the uncreated order. Thus he is "God of God," "Light of Light," "very God of very God." The choice of this (admittedly unbiblical) terminology was therefore necessary in order to preserve the biblical ideas of revelation and redemption under the new philosophical presuppositions.

To put it another way, whatever one says today about the political context of the councils and about the historical relativity of the categories of Hellenistic ontology; whatever one has to make clear about the epochal paradigm change[18] between the world of the New Testament and that of the ancient church[19]—through all discontinuity, a continuity of content is given between the Christ hymn of the Colossians' letter and the faith confession of Nicea. Each time it concerns the decisive statement of faith that the person, cause and fate of Jesus Christ belongs definitely to the notion of the eternal essence of God. Already in the New Testament Christological statements are directed toward the uncommonly bold ideas that Jesus of Nazareth was not merely "in the thought of God" from eternity, but also that the "event of Jesus Christ" (always to be understood as a unity of preaching, death, and resurrection) provides decisive consequences for determining the essence of God. The ancient church councils have adequately interpreted the New Testament kerygma in this decisive statement of faith, so that one can say:

> *In Jesus Christ it has been made manifest once and for all and conclusively who God is and who the human being is. In Jesus Christ it has been made manifest in time and in history that God is as Jesus Christ proclaimed him to be . . . from all eternity the love which gives itself away. . . . The Father is the origin and source of the Son. The Son possesses, however, the same divine essence given by the Father. Therefore, he is of one essence with the Father. He came from there not as something created from nothing, not made, but begotten, without a timeless beginning in the eternal now of the eternity of God.[20]*

Were it otherwise, the Christ event would not be definitive and normative and there would be, next to and outside of Christ, other just as comprehensive incarnations or revelations of God. God would ultimately remain an impenetrable puzzle whose credibility would be at stake. Were it otherwise, had the Son not really known and revealed the

Father, God would be seen in this way today and in another way tomorrow. Were it otherwise, Jesus Christ would be only one window to this ultimately inexpressible mystery, and the foundation of the "new being" would also ultimately be unsecured. For the sake of the reliability and credibility of God, the expression is indisputable that God's "whole fullness" dwells in Christ, that Jesus Christ is the essence of God. Josef Ratzinger has paraphrased these basic ideas in view of the council of Nicea as follows:

> The philosophical vocabulary "same essence" adds nothing to the New Testament, but the defense of its literalness against all allegorisms is in the decisive position of its witnesses. It therefore means that God's Word does not deceive us. Jesus is not only designated as the Son of God, he is it. God does not remain hidden forever under the cloud of metaphors which are more concealing than revealing. He really touches humanity and lets himself really be touched by humanity in him, who is the Son. When the New Testament speaks of the Son, it breaks through the god images in the history of religion and shows us the reality—the truth, upon which we can stand, live and die.[21]

CONSEQUENCES FOR A CHRISTOLOGY IN CONVERSATION WITH THE WORLD RELIGIONS

A theology of religion for which God is ultimately a mystery to humankind manifests itself culturally in ever different ways. The New Testament understanding of God's mystery in particular is not to be confused with the modern epistemological understanding of mystery. Especially in the New Testament, God is not an unrecognizable, unclear mystery withdrawn from all understanding and comprehension. Such a conception would do justice neither to the person and preaching of Jesus (Abba—form of address); nor to the theology of the Synoptics (reign of God in the parables; Mark 4:11//); nor to that of John, according to whom "no one" has ever seen God but "the Son," who is "at the side of the Father" (John 1:18). It's true that God's depths are also unfathomable for Paul; at the same time, however, the apostle leaves no doubt that God has made the mystery evident in Jesus Christ, who therefore can be called the "mystery of the hidden wisdom of God"

(1 Cor. 2:7). The same is also valid for the deutero-Pauline writings (cf. Eph. 1:8f.; Col. 2:2f). According to the New Testament, Christians who trust themselves to Jesus Christ may therefore trust that God does not intend to be an impenetrable puzzle, that rather God's mystery has been made evident, believable, and credible in Christ.

The pluralistic theology of religion is correct in its critique of the cultural, political, and social consequences of the Christian claim to absoluteness and superiority. Conversely, the connection of the superiority of Christianity as a politically effective organization is not founded upon the original statements of the New Testament concerning the definitiveness of the Christ event. The universal-cosmic statements from the New Testament and from church tradition that were sung in songs and preserved in confessions about Christ as the mediator of creation and the Son of God can and must be interpreted in a non-absolutist and nonsuperior way as testimonies of faith by those who intend to trust in the reliability of God for their life and death. To substantiate a superiority of the Christian over the non-Christian with these bold, indeed daring, and consequently vulnerable statements of faith would mean betraying what one seeks to advocate as the spirit of Christ. An intolerant exclusivism, absolutism, and triumphalism that seeks to characterize the theological uniqueness and superiority of its own religion at the expense of others ends every dialogue before it has begun.

Dialogue among religions does not replace the Christian witness or the church's preaching, which come from self-commitment to the truth of the Christian revelation. Dialogue among the religions does not presuppose the suspension of the question of truth, as if the goal of dialogue between the religions were the finding of a truth that would not have been there before. The claim that there could be no "final word" and no "solid place" for truth under human conditions is unbiblical and secular and suppresses the decisive dimensions of faith. It cannot be, therefore, a question of a dialogue that disregards truth, but a dialogue *in* the truth and *for* the truth, a truth that one hopes always to understand more deeply and comprehensively in the dialogue. Therefore, the capacity for dialogue presupposes a commitment to truth.

The reality of the "new person" that was made possible through the activity of God in Christ is decisive for the determining of the specifically Christian element. The signature of the "new person" is unconditional trust upon "God," on the one hand, and the qualities of peace, love, and reconciliation on the other. All religious alternatives are to be put under this one general criterium: do they encourage the promotion of the "new person" or hinder its development? It is thereby not concerned about a demand upon all non-Christians, nor about the suggestion that all non-Christians should first join the real, existing churches in their desire for salvation, but about this question of the "new person." Wherever the promotion of this "new person" occurs, there the spirit of Christ reigns. Wherever goodness, humility, meekness, and patience are lived, wherever forgiveness, love, and peace reign, there Christ will be concrete, whether latent or manifest. And who would contest empirically that a Jew from Jewish tradition, a Muslim from Muslim spirit, a Hindu from Hindu thinking, and a Buddhist from Buddhist conviction can also make something of this "new person" visible and audible? Therefore, it is fundamentally valid to say that the relationship of Christianity and non-Christian religions can be founded rightly only upon a biblically grounded Christological pneumatology. As Pope John Paul II correctly said in his most recent encyclical on the question of mission:

> *The dialogue comes out of the deepest respect, above all, for what the Spirit, who blows where it wills, has done in humanity. The Church intends to discover in Him " 'he seed corn of the Word" and the "rays of truth, which enlighten all people"—seed corn and rays which are found in the persons and in the religious traditions of humankind. Dialogue founded on hope and love will bring fruit in the Spirit. The other religions represent a positive challenge for the Church; they prompt it both to discover and to recognize the signs of the present Christ and the work of the Spirit, as well as to deepen its own identity and to testify to the entirety of revelation.*[22]

Not the "cheap tolerance" of "anything goes," but prophetic resistance and protest is fitting against practices in all religions where this faith or this spirit has been made impossible: through all possible forms of superstition, idolatry, moral brutalization, fabrication of miracle and violation of human rights. This resistance and prophetic pro-test, however, presupposes for Christians the finality and definitiveness of the Christ event. Wherever in Christianity itself the reality of the "new person" has been or will be betrayed (beginning with anti-Judaism, through heretic and witch burning, to violent fanaticism, discrimination, and violations of human rights), Christians must listen to the protests of others.

The affirmation of Christ without claim to absoluteness, finality without exclusivism, definitiveness without superiority is theologically justifiable on the basis of the New Testament and the ancient church councils—understood in the framework of a contextual exegesis and hermeneutic of dogmas. The great religions of the world can be under-stood from the perspective of believing Christians as a positive chal-lenge presented by God to Christians to establish deeper and live more credibly their own faith witness. The final and definitive position of the non-Christian religions in God's plan for humankind is God's matter alone. Here the statement is valid that Paul made in his reflection about the future of the Jewish people who do not follow Christ: "O the depth of the riches and wisdom and knowledge of God! How unsearchable are his judgments and how inscrutable his ways! For 'who has known the mind of the Lord, or who has been his counselor?' Or 'who has given a gift to him that he might be repaid?' For from him and through him and to him are all things. To him be the glory for ever. Amen" (Rom. 11:33–36).

NOTES

This essay originally appeared as "Christologie und interreligiöser Dialog" in *Stimmen der Zeit* (June 1991). Used by permission.

1. John Hick, ed., *The Myth of God Incarnate* (Philadelphia: Westminster Press, 1977). Hereafter, this book is referred to as *Myth I*.

2. The exceptions are: K. Kremkau, ed., *Christus allein—allein das Christentum?* Vorträge der Vierten theologischen Konferenz zwischen Vertretern der evangelischen Kirche in Deutschland und der Kirche von England (Frankfurt: Lembec, 1979) (Beiheft zur Ökumenischen Rundschau Nr. 36); I. U. Dalferth, "Der Mythos vom inkarnierten Gott und das Thema der Christologie," *Zeitschrift für Theologie und Kirche*

84 (1987): 320–44; R. Bernhardt, *Der Absolutheitsanspruch des Christentums: Von der Aufklärung bis zur pluralistischen Religionstheologie* (Gütersloh: Gütersloher Verlagshaus, 1970), 199–225.

3. John Hick and Paul Knitter, eds., *The Myth of Christian Uniqueness* (Maryknoll, NY: Orbis Books, 1987). Hereafter, this book will be referred to as *Myth II*.

4. Hick, *Myth II*, 22.

5. Paul F. Knitter, "Nochmals die Absolutheitsfrage. Gründe für eine Pluralistische Theologie der Religionen," *Evangelische Theologie* 49 (1989): 508.

6. Ibid.

7. Ibid., 509.

8. Hick, *Myth II*, 32.

9. John Hick, *God and the Universe of Faiths: Essays in the Philosophy of Religion* (London: Macmillan, 1973), 159.

10. Knitter, "Nochmals die Absolutheitsfrage," 510.

11. Hick, *Myth I*, 176.

12. Ibid., 175–88.

13. Ibid., 179.

14. Rosemary Ruether, "Feminism and Jewish-Christian Dialogue: Particularism and Universalism in the Search for Religious Truth," in *Myth II*, 137–48.

15. On the problem of preexistence Christology in recent systematic-theological as well as exegetical-historical perspective, cf. Karl-Josef Kuschel, *Geboren vor aller Zeit? Der Streit um Christi Ursprung* (Munich: Piper, 1990); on the Colossians Hymn, cf. 421–37; and on Nicea, cf. 645–54.

16. This is how it is explained in the latest document of the Evangelical Church in Germany, *Christliches Bekenntnis und biblischer Auftrag angesichts des Islam: Ein Wort der Konferenz bekennender Gemeinschaften in evangelischen Krichen Deutschlands und der Arbeitsgemeinschaft evangelikaler Missionen* (1984).

17. L. Schottroff, "Der Christushymnus im Kolosserbrief. Bibelarbeit zu Koll, 15–23," in *Die Erde gehört Gott: Texte zur Bibelarbeit von Frauen*, ed. D. Sölle and L. Schottroff (Reinbec bei Hamburg: Rowohlt, 1985), 120.

18. Hans Küng, "Paradigm Change in Theology and Science: A Fundamental Historical-Theological Clarification," in *Theology for the Third Millennium: An Ecumenical View* (New York: Doubleday, 1988), 123–69; also, *Global Responsibility: In Search of a New World Ethic* (London: SCM Press, 1991), 108–38.

19. "The step from the Bible to Nicea and with that to the classical dogmatic and Christology [is] an epochal and—in essence—not a simply explicit step" (B. Welte). It is to the merit of the Catholic philosopher of religion B. Welte to have already called attention to the "paradigm change" between the world of the New Testament and the world of the ancient church in "Die Krise der dogmatischen Christusaussagen," in *Die Frage nach Jesus*, ed. A. Paus (Graz-Wien-Köln: Verli Styria,

1973), 151–79; also, "Die Lehrformel von Nikaia und die abendländische Metaphysik," in *Zur Frühgeschichte der Christologie*, ed. B. Welte (Freiburg im Breisgau: Herder 1970), 100–117.

20. W. Kasper, *Katholische Erwachsenenkathechismus* (Kevelar: Butzon Bercker, 1985), 79.

21. J. Ratzinger, *Schauen auf den Durchbohrten: Versuche zu einer spirituellen Christologies* (Einsiedeln: Johannes Verlag, 1984), 32f.

22. John Paul II, "'Redemptoris Missio': Enzyklika über die fortdauernde Gültigkeit des missionarischen Auftrags," in *L'Osservatore Romano vom 1. Februar 1991* (citation #56).

NOTES ON CONTRIBUTORS

Mahmoud Ayoub is professor of Islamic studies at Temple University and adjunct professor at Hartford Seminary.

Robert F. Berkey is professor of religion at Mount Holyoke College.

Otto Betz is professor of New Testament at the University of Tübingen.

Kenneth Cragg is honorary assistant bishop of the Diocese of Oxford and formerly was Anglican bishop of North Africa.

James D. G. Dunn is professor of New Testament in the Department of Theology at the University of Durham.

Sarah A. Edwards is adjunct professor of biblical studies at Hartford Seminary.

John Dykstra Eusden is Nathan Jackson Professor of Religion emeritus and visiting professor of environmental studies at Williams College.

Reginald H. Fuller is professor emeritus of New Testament at Virginia Theological Seminary.

Thomas Hoyt, Jr., is professor of New Testament at Hartford Seminary and director of the Black Ministries Certificate Program.

Howard Clark Kee is professor emeritus of the New Testament at Boston University and senior research fellow at the University of Pennsylvania.

David A. Kerr is professor of Islamic studies at Hartford Seminary and director of the Duncan Black Macdonald Center for the Study of Muslim-Christian Relations.

Hans Küng is professor of ecumenical theology and director of the Institute for Ecumenical Research at the University of Tübingen.

Karl-Josef Kuschel is lecturer in ecumenical theology at the University of Tübingen.

Harvey K. McArthur is professor emeritus of biblical studies and former acting president at Hartford Seminary.

Eleanor McLaughlin is an Episcopal priest and has taught at Wellesley College and Andover Newton Theological Seminary. Most recently she has served as dean of the College Chapel at Mount Holyoke.

John Macquarrie is Lady Margaret Professor of Divinity emeritus at Oxford University.

Paul S. Minear is Winkley Professor of Biblical Theology emeritus at Yale University.

Leslie A. Muray is professor of religion at Lansing Community College.

Elaine H. Pagels is professor of religion at Princeton University.

John Parr is a tutor in biblical studies and chaplain at Ridley Hall, Cambridge, England.

Pheme Perkins is a professor of theology at Boston College.

Thomas Schmeller is professor of New Testament at the University of Munich.

Alan F. Segal is professor of religion at Barnard College, Columbia University.

SUGGESTED READING

Beker, J. Christian. *Paul the Apostle.* Philadelphia: Fortress Press, 1980.

Bornkamm, Günther. *Jesus of Nazareth,* trans. Irene and Fraser McLuskey with James M. Robinson. San Francisco: Harper & Bros., 1959.

Brown, Raymond E. *The Birth of the Messiah.* Garden City, NY: Doubleday, 1977.

———. *The Gospel According to John.* Garden City, NY: Doubleday, Anchor Bible, vol. 29, 1966, and vol. 29A, 1970.

Bultmann, Rudolf. *History of the Synoptic Tradition,* trans. John Marsh. New York: Harper & Row, 1976.

———. *Theology of the New Testament,* trans. Kendrick Grobel. New York: Charles Scribner's Sons, 1951.

Cobb, John B., Jr. *Christ in a Pluralistic Age.* Philadelphia: Westminster Press, 1975.

Conzelmann, Hans. *An Outline of the Theology of the New Testament,* trans. John Bowden. New York: Harper & Row, 1969.

Cragg, Kenneth. *Jesus and the Muslim: An Exploration.* London: George Allen and Unwin, 1985.

Crossan, John D. *The Historical Jesus: The Life of a Mediterranean Jewish Peasant.* San Francisco: Harper, 1991.

Dahl, Nils. *Jesus the Christ,* ed. Donald Juel. Minneapolis: Fortress Press, 1991.

Davies, W. D. *Paul and Rabbinic Judaism.* 1948; New York: Harper & Brothers, 1967.

de Jonge, Marinus. *Christology in Context.* Philadelphia: Westminster Press, 1988.

Dunn, James D. G. *Christology in the Making.* Philadelphia: Westminster Press, 1989; London: SCM Press, 1990.

Fitzmyer, Joseph A. *The Gospel According to Luke.* Garden City, NY: Doubleday, Anchor Bible, vol. 28, 1981, and vol. 28A, 1985.

Fuller, Reginald H. *The Foundations of New Testament Christology,* New York: Charles Scribner's Sons, 1965.

Fuller, Reginald H., and Pheme Perkins. *Who Is This Christ?* Philadelphia: Fortress Press, 1983.

Hahn, Ferdinand. *The Titles of Jesus in Christology,* trans. Harold Knight and George Ogg. New York: World, 1969.

Hengel, Martin. *Judaism and Hellenism,* trans. John Bowden. Philadelphia: Fortress Press, 1974.

Jeremias, Joachim. *New Testament Theology*, trans. John Bowden. New York: Charles Scribner's Sons, 1971.

Kähler, Martin. *The So-Called Historical Jesus and the Historic Biblical Christ*, trans. and ed. Carl E. Braaten. Philadelphia: Fortress Press, 1964.

Keck, Leander E., and L. Louis Martyn, eds. *Studies in Luke-Acts*. Nashville: Abingdon Press, 1966.

Kingsbury, Jack Dean. *The Christology of Mark's Gospel*. Philadelphia: Fortress Press, 1983.

Knox, John. *The Death of Christ*. New York and Nashville: Abingdon Press, 1958.

Kümmel, Werner George. *The Theology of the New Testament*, trans. John E. Steely. Nashville: Abingdon Press, 1973.

Küng, Hans. *Judaism*, trans. John Bowden. New York: Crossroad, 1992.

———. *On Being a Christian*, trans. Edward Quinn. Garden City, NY: Doubleday, 1976.

Macquarrie, John. *Jesus Christ in Modern Thought*. London: SCM Press, 1990.

Matera, Frank F. *Passion Narratives and Gospel Theologies*. Mahwah, NJ: Paulist Press, 1986.

McArthur, Harvey K. *Understanding the Sermon on the Mount*. New York: Harper & Bros., 1960.

Meier, John. *A Marginal Jew: Rethinking the Historical Jesus*. New York: Doubleday, 1991.

Moule, C. F. D. *The Origin of Christology*. Cambridge: Cambridge University Press, 1977.

Neusner, Jacob. *Messiah in Context: Israel's History and Destiny in Formative Judaism*. Philadelphia: Fortress, 1984.

Ogden, Schubert. *The Point of Christology*. San Francisco: Harper & Row, 1982.

Pagels, Elaine. *The Gnostic Gospels*. New York: Random House, Vintage Books, 1989.

Perrin, Norman. *Rediscovering the Teaching of Jesus*. New York: Harper & Row, 1967.

Schillebeeckx, Edward. *Jesus: An Experiment in Christology*, trans. Hubert Hoskins. New York: Crossroad, 1979.

Schnackenburg, Rudolf. *New Testament Theology Today*, trans. David Askew and Geoffrey Chapman. New York: Herder & Herder, 1963.

Segundo, Juan Luis. *The Historical Jesus of the Synoptics*, trans. John Drury. Maryknoll, NY: Orbis Books, 1985.

Sobrino, Jon. *Christology at the Crossroads: A Latin-American Approach*, trans. John Drury. Maryknoll, NY: Orbis Books, 1978.

Speight, R. Marston. *God Is One: The Way of Islam*. New York: Friendship Press, 1989.

Von Rad, Gerhard. *Old Testament Theology*, trans. D. M. G. Stalker. New York: Harper & Row, vol. 1, 1962, and vol. 2, 1965.

no one had ever heard of a man playing any different position on defense from what he played on offense; if he was a halfback on offense that's what he played on defense, and that ended it. But in that year . . . I became impressed with the senselessness of my left halfback, a very fast but light man, battering himself to pieces helping to repel the heavy onslaughts while my fullback—a big, strong, husky fellow stood away back practically doing nothing for nearly all the time that opponents had the ball. So I put the little fellow at fullback's place and rested him up whenever we lost the ball, and had my fullback come up close and help back up the line.[13]

Heisman's plan proved to be so popular that other teams were soon doing basically the same thing. This maneuver would ultimately demand that the quarterback, usually the lightest man on the team, be the deepest man back on defense, such a station carrying the designation of "safety man."

In February, 1893, Heisman suddenly accepted a position as director of athletics at Buchtel College (now the University of Akron), located less than fifty miles south of Cleveland. Athletics had not been faring well at the Akron school, and when news of Heisman's coaching success at Oberlin spread to the Buchtel campus, the students, with the administration's approval, hired the young coach as their "physical director," with duties to consist mainly of coaching the football and baseball teams. It was the promise of an annual salary that convinced Heisman to take the job. At Oberlin he had received no regular pay, having gotten only token remuneration by random passing of the hat at games, while at Buchtel he was to be paid the munificent sum of $750 a year.

Heisman's spirited arrival on campus, as such an event would prove to be throughout his coaching career, had an immediate impact on the students' morale: "The coming of Mr. Heisman made the year 1893 a most significant one. The first thing to be done was the building of a baseball cage, toward the construction of which the boys had promised to raise four hundred dollars. . . . To hasten the work, the men of the College, under Heisman's direction, put on the shingles."[14] As a result, the money was subsequently raised and the job completed.

But Coach Heisman did not find his task of building an athletic program at Buchtel an easy one. Years later, he commented on the problem of his coaching days at the Akron school: "Athletics, as I remember matters, was a very difficult thing at Buchtel at that time." With only a little over a hundred male students, most of whom were working their way through college, Buchtel had difficulty in attracting a sufficient number of athletes to even field a team. "Under the circumstances," said Heisman, "I fancy we really did well enough."[15]

In spite of his contractual agreement with Buchtel in 1893, Heisman somehow managed to maintain his athletic ties with Oberlin that same year. He himself has revealed that in 1893 he coached the Oberlin football team on its westward trip, in which both Chicago and Illinois were defeated. Because of his previous year's success and familiarity with the players, it could have been that Oberlin obtained special permission to use him in a coaching capacity.

Oberlin's successful westward trip was a pivotal event in Heisman's young career, in that the extremely rough play the team encountered in these two games started him to thinking of ways to open up game strategy and help alleviate the brutal elements of the mass momentum offense, which was so prominent in the early 1890s. The infamous wedge formation that had originated at Harvard in 1892 and evolved into Penn's flying interference offense quickly found its way to the Midwest. But Heisman's coaching experiences would soon lead him to conclude that "the human frame is unequal to the wedge."[16] As we have seen, he had fashioned his own version of the wedge his first year at Oberlin, but after a few games he began to dwell more and more on ways to protect his players from their opponents' increasingly vicious onslaughts. One of his original methods was to fight fire with fire. For example, just before the 1893 game with Chicago, he gave the players his mandatory pep talk: "Don't stall around to see what they have. Jump in on them at the whistle. Bam! Like that. Don't let them get set. Charge, charge, charge. Start charging at the kickoff and keep it up."[17]

However, as the toll on his players continued to rise, Heisman began to realize that, in general, "counterattacks were as menacing to life and limb as the mass offensives."[18] In one of his most vivid accounts, he drew on Oberlin's 1893 westward trip to describe the physical mayhem that could result from the mass momentum offense:

Surely few coaches have had a more impressive array of mass play casualties than I had at Oberlin in 1893. Even such men as I was able to impress into service were bandaged almost beyond recognition. Football was a serious occupation. A team played at least twice a week and maybe more. It used up men.

On Saturday my Oberlin men overcame Alonzo Stagg's mighty Chicago squad, 33 to 12, and were reduced to crutches, canes, splints and yards of plaster thereby. On the following Monday we staggered off the field at Champaign, Ill., the very groggy victors over [the] University of Illinois team, 34 to 24.

On the trip home, Heisman noted that there was hardly any one of his players who "did not have his head bandaged and his face court-plastered."[19]

Although Heisman was recounting this story many years later, he realized at the time that something had to be done to eliminate the game's brutality or football would soon sound its own death knell. A visiting Frenchman who had viewed the Harvard–Penn game in 1893 provided a graphic contemporary description of the game's extreme roughness in an essay on American manners. He concluded that American football is a "fearful game":

The roughness with which the opposing players seize the bearer of the ball is impossible to imagine. He is grasped by the middle of the body, by the head, by the legs, by the feet. He rolls over and his assailants roll with him. As they fight for the ball, the two sides come to the rescue, and fall into a heap of twenty-two bodies tumbling on top of one another, like an inextricable knot of serpents with human heads. This heap writhes on the ground and tugs at itself. One sees faces, hair, backs, or legs appearing in a monstrous and agitated melee. Then this murderous knot unravels itself and the ball, thrown by the most agile, bounds away and is again followed with the same fury.

Often, after one of those frenzied entanglements, one of the combatants remains on the field motionless, incapable of rising, so hard has he been hit.[20]

By this time, too, a chorus of domestic criticism directed toward such irresponsible violence was rising in an even more acrimonious vein, as we shall see.

Heisman's record at Buchtel, while not as sensational as his previous year's accomplishment at Oberlin had been, did result in his winning five out of seven football games, in which his opponents were outscored 276–82. He also produced the state's best college baseball team. His innovations continued, too, with most of these designed to correct recognizable defects in game procedures. One of them led to the first use of the center snap, at least as Heisman would later recall the event:

As far as I know, I was the first coach to change the method of passing the ball from center to quarter. At the time we were following the current mode. The center would place one end of the ball on the ground. On the other end he'd place his hand. He'd press down smartly and, at the same time, draw his hand back. The result was that the ball would, when released, snap off the ground and backward. It was up to the quarterback to grab it.

At Buchtel, Heisman recalled in this same article that his quarterback was too tall to receive the ball this way. He suggested that the center "throw the ball up to him." It worked and "within the season all the colleges were using this method of transferring the ball."[21]

Following the invention of the scrimmage line in 1880, the direct relationship between the center and the quarterback compelled teams to start utilizing some kind of signal system to get a play off and running. Heisman has told us of one way tried by the early teams:

The quarterback usually asked for the ball by scratching the hard-working center's leg, which was quite all right as long as the leg scratching was done by your own quarterback.

I was the victim of a foul scratch while playing center for Penn. . . . Instead of passing the ball with my foot I was following the example of our regular center, and putting it into play with one hand. Thus intent I did not notice the hand of my long-armed opponent center circle my leg. But I felt his scratch—and passed the ball. That pass cost us five yards.[22]

Actually, Heisman's earliest experience with signals, as he tells us in this same article (p.13), had been that of the spoken code method employed by the club teams at Brown. This system consisted of a series of short sentences uttered by the quarterback, each one alerting the players to the type play they were expected to execute. For example, "Line up, Brown" meant left tackle through right tackle; "Charge hard now" meant left end around right; "Hit 'em hard, bullies" meant left half around his own end; and so on.

It was during the latter part of his years at Penn, though, that things began to get a little more sophisticated. According to Heisman:

> Cornell was perhaps the first of the colleges to deviate from this spoken code, Glenn Warner tells me. The Cornell quarterback might chatter his head off but the actual signals were his gestures and the movements of his legs. . . .
>
> Elwood O. Wagenhurst, captain of Princeton in 1887, came to Penn three years later as head coach and almost at once he concocted the first considerable variation in the favored signal system of that time. It was simple too, sending none of us to the hospital with brain fever. All that we had to do was to note carefully the first word of every sentence uttered by the quarterback.
>
> If that first word ended with "Y," our right half was to carry the ball around left end—if he could. If that first word concluded with a "K," it was up to our left to lay down his life, if necessary, for Alma Mater.[23]

Although the Buchtel faculty tolerated football, faculty opposition to it was growing, mainly because of the increasing number of serious injuries, even deaths, that were occurring wherever football was being played. To many, Heisman's professional style of coaching, with its strong emphasis on playing to win as opposed to the amateur notion of participating in a sport purely for the physical good to be gained from it, did not sit well. In fact, the faculty even wrote Heisman a letter to this effect, and it probably led to his departure after the 1894 baseball season.[24]

From such contrasting attitudes toward athletics—his own and those of academia—a conflict emanated that Heisman (as well as many other coaches) would confront from time to time for the rest of his career: a conflict involving the role of athletics and its proper relationship to the academic mission. By his own convictions, as we have seen, Heisman always placed academics far ahead of athletics. But he was never hesitant to remind the critics of sports that football played an important educational role in developing a young man's moral character as well as contributing to his healthy mental outlook. Many of Heisman's ideas about this relationship, which were in the formative stage at this time, would find full expression in his 1922 book, *Principles of Football*. With his greatest success on the gridiron behind him by the time of its publication, Heisman had formulated a coaching philosophy that was uniquely his own.

Even though Heisman left Buchtel before the 1894 football season to return to Oberlin, some Buchtel players recruited him as player-coach in 1894 for a game with Ohio State. It was to be played as part of a football tournament involving several other Ohio schools at the state fairgrounds in Columbus. As Buchtel's only game of the 1894 season (actually the game was played September 1 before the school year got underway), it afforded Heisman's critics considerable insight into his contention that disciplined training and inspirational leadership were equally important in building the proper winning attitude in football players and that they were stronger men for having had these experiences. Heisman, of course, recognized that the match with Ohio State was an opportunity not only to put his team on public display, but to showcase his coaching tactics as well. So to prepare for what was tantamount to an exhibition game, he drove his players through a rigorous training program at a summer camp near Akron. The outcome of the game has been reconstructed from a letter Heisman wrote to a Buchtel official in later years: "After playing two twenty-minute halves in burning heat, and the score deadlocked at six points apiece, the teams took a ten-minute rest and then started a 'sudden death' overtime period." Heisman, who was playing quarterback, drove his team to Ohio State's four-yard line. Following a short, inspirational talk, he directed a play in which the fullback, who had been given the ball, was literally pulled across the goal line. According to Heisman, "We all went through together, just like the water of a mill dam when the dam goes out."[25] Questionable tactics notwithstanding, Buchtel had won, 12–6, the only time in its football history that the school would defeat Ohio State.

Other than his satisfying role in helping win this game, there was another, more intimate, reason for John Heisman to maintain his ties with Buchtel. It was there that he became involved in his first serious romance. According to his nephew, W. Lee Heisman, the young coach had courted a Buchtel coed from Wisconsin named Edith Maora Cole, but when she discovered she had a tubercular condition, they had decided not to marry. (In those days, tuberculosis was considered an incurable disease.) Although they drifted apart when Heisman's coaching pursuits took him south in 1895, they would eventually marry in the 1920s, following Heisman's divorce from his first wife in 1919.[26] As one singularly devoted to the things of a man's world, Heisman, like most men of his day, assumed a somewhat Victorian attitude toward the opposite sex and affairs of the heart. Consequently, we know very little of his intimate relationships with or personal attitudes toward the women with whom he came in contact.

In spite of the growing criticism of football and those like Heisman who were either daring or foolhardy enough to coach it, an appreciative audience for the game was now springing up everywhere it appeared. One of the reasons for this reception was the expanding urbanization of that day, which had created, in effect, a captive audience hungry for the emotional outlet that sports afforded. Accordingly, as the popularity of professional baseball and intercollegiate sports increased, the daily newspapers of large cities were beginning to devote more space to sporting activities to satisfy the demanding tastes of an ever-expanding audience. Not only were the results of significant sporting events being reported, but those who covered these events were beginning to express their own opinions about the participants, coaches, and personalities involved in such activities, recognizing that their readers might also have personal preferences for the background or human interest side of sports. For example, a reporter for the *Akron Beacon* in 1893 assessed Heisman's brief tenure at Buchtel as follows: "J. W. Heisman, the coach, has met with great success. He is an all-round athlete, and has that requisite of a successful coach—firmness. He has certainly done wonders in putting the team in shape." (Quotation is from Heisman's privately printed pamphlet, c. 1900, to promote his coaching qualifications. See below, note 27.) In other words, those who reported athletic events had begun to take on something of an editorial posture, reminding readers of the reasons for athletic success (and failure) and as a result helping to mold their attitudes toward sports. The day of the daily sports columnist who would play a key role in creating the cult of athletic hero worship was near at hand.

As far as his relationship with the press was concerned, the charismatic Heisman and the American newspaper were made for each other. In working to establish his coaching persona, he quickly grew sensitive to the power of the press to make or break the public image of an athletic team and also, by extension, its coach. As his career developed, Heisman himself would take on the role of a sports commentator. Prime examples of his unique ability in this area were the pieces he wrote for Atlanta newspapers and school publications while coaching at Georgia Tech and ultimately the personal reminiscences of his career published in *Collier's* weekly during the late 1920s. Even though he was not always on the best of terms with reporters in later years, Heisman continued to be a popular personality who attracted the press everywhere he coached. Even after he returned to Oberlin in 1894 and compiled a rather mediocre 4–3–1 record (two of the losses were in close games with Michigan and Penn State), news coverage about the young coach was still generous and commendatory. *The Oberlin News* commented in 1894: "Much praise is due to Heisman. He has made Oberlin football a synonym for good football." *The Oberlin College Review* had even higher praise, flatly stating: "We have the best coach in the West."[27] By the time Heisman left Oberlin in 1895 at the age of twenty-five, he had laid the foundation for his public image as a football coach. In this respect he had blazed a trail for other media-minded coaches to follow—notably Knute Rockne.

THE EASTERN GAME (1892–1894)

But what had been going on in the East during the three years after Heisman had departed Penn and the eastern gridiron wars? In 1892, the Yale Bulldogs continued to dominate the larger football scene, extending their unbeaten, untied, and unscored-on string to twenty-seven straight games. (The string had begun with a last game win over Princeton in 1890.) Sparked by the indomitable Frank Hinkey at end and coached by former Yale back Billy Bull, the Yale Blue, at 13–0, was declared national champion.

Harvard, with only a 6–0 loss to Yale, was runner-up in 1892. (The loss occurred in the infamous flying wedge game.) The Harvard Crimson featured the outstanding play of Marshall "Ma" Newell at tackle and William Henry Lewis at center. Newell was the first of only four men to make the All-America team four times (the others were Yale's Pudge Heffelfinger and Frank Hinkey and Penn's Truxton Hare), while Lewis, who had formerly played at Amherst, was the first black All-American.

In 1892, Heisman's alma mater was also in the thick of things, as new coach George Woodruff brought Penn to the fore with only a loss to Yale marring its record. Beating Princeton for the first time was a real boon, but a major reason for Penn's success was Woodruff's offensive strategy and effective use of the quick kick, as discussed earlier. Due to the lax eligibility rules of that day, he also had a number of graduate and professional school students playing for him, which naturally rankled a number of his opponents who lacked such experienced players.

In 1893, Yale's unbeaten shutout string reached thirty-five games, but the unscored-on record ended in the 14–6 win over Penn. However, Princeton (11–0) was named national champion when it hung a 6–0 shutout on Yale to end the Bulldogs' unbeaten streak.

With the flying wedge and V attack outlawed for the season of 1894, mass interference formations took over, and, as we have seen, Woodruff's Penn Quakers led the way here, compiling a 12–0 record. Nevertheless, Yale (16–0) won the national championship. This was also the year that playing time was cut to two thirty-five-minute halves, and a linesman was added to the crew of officials to keep track of time.

THE RISE OF MIDWESTERN FOOTBALL IN THE 1890s

During Heisman's three years at Oberlin and Buchtel, America was in the process of becoming a country where economic progress was something of a religion and urbanization its prophet and prime motivator in an increasingly materialistic culture. It was an era that separated a newer, more confident America from an older, more conservative and culturally isolated America. Growing cities like Cleveland and Akron, where Heisman periodically lived and coached during this time, epitomized what was happening in a sociocultural sense to the America of the 1890s. Through expansive industrialization the larger midwestern cities were attracting thousands of people from the outlying rural areas, as well as multitudes of immigrants from European countries to the job opportunities that these industrial centers had to offer. Cleveland, a veritable melting pot of foreign nationals, had

profited from the industrializing efforts of prototypical go-getters like Rockefeller and politician Mark Hanna, so that by the 1890s this city had established
itself as a leading steel, oil, railway, and manufacturing center. During this
same time, Akron, with the advent of the automobile just around the corner
and the attendant growth of the rubber industry, was on the verge of becoming a thriving boomtown as the country's tire-manufacturing center.

But it was the colossus of the Midwest, Chicago, that projected more
dynamically than any other place at this time both the raw power that had
energized the region and all the cultural inconsistencies and contradictions
of the American experience. Although the railroad and telegraph had spanned
the land by this time and brought the country closer together in a communications sense (these advances would help spread the cause of sports through
access to mass travel and quicker circulation of media information through
on-site reporting), an ingrained provincialism kept the economic concerns of
rural America far removed from the capitalistic priorities of industrialized
urban society. And even while the United States was challenging England
for first place in the world manufacturing marketplace, a persistent and
pervasive hierarchy of social sectionalism divided the "haves" and the "have-
nots." Whereas Chicago investors had made fortunes in wheat, meat packing,
iron, and the railroad, it had been Civil War profiteering and the influx of
immigrant labor that helped them maintain that wealth. Naturally, in such
a milieu, corruption, political and otherwise, was bound to thrive. If Chicago
was something of a living microcosm for all this, as Carl Sandburg would
soon express so vividly in his poetry, it was also the cultural center of the
Midwest, no matter how crude the city might have appeared on the surface.

Perhaps the World's Columbian Exposition held in Chicago in 1893, when
Heisman was coaching at Buchtel, represented better than anything else the
marvelous heights that the city had risen to, in both a cultural and a materialistic sense. To commemorate the four hundredth anniversary of Columbus'
discovery of the New World, Chicago had carved a symbolic testimonial to
progress out of six hundred acres of waterfront swampland—a paradoxical
and miraculous feat. The exposition served as a showcase not only for the
achievements of Chicago itself but for those of the age.

That Chicago was a fitting location for a fair of international scope was
attested to by the fact that in the year the Exposition opened, the city had
gained a population exceeding one million, over two-thirds of which were
foreign-born. In this kind of environment the acquisitive nature of capitalism
was being continually tempered by the challenge of the adjacent frontier
lands awaiting development. Contradictory forces continued to flourish, such
as the vested interests of capital versus those of labor, the advantages of the
wealthy over the squalor of the impoverished, and the attractions of high
culture as contrasted with the low-life elements of the city. In keeping with
these dichotomies, the view from the fair's giant ferris wheel included that
of the University of Chicago's new campus. There, the city's inherent conflict

between culture and vulgarism would find a fitting parallel in the clash between academics and athletics, particularly in the aggrandizing game of football as it was taking form at the university during the 1890s under the leadership of its dynamic, progressive president William Rainey Harper and its innovative new coach Amos Alonzo Stagg—one of John Heisman's truly great contemporaries.

A former Yale football player under advisory coach Walter Camp in the 1880s and one of Camp's first All-America picks at end, Stagg came to Chicago in 1892 after a short coaching stint at Springfield College (1890–1891).[28] Football was to be a unique sport at the brand new Chicago institution in that, unlike other schools, the University of Chicago and football would grow up together. For a football coach, Stagg's situation was unique, too, in that he held faculty rank as "director of physical culture." He had been specifically hired by Rainey to put Chicago on the gridiron map.

But Stagg found rough going in the beginning of his tenure due to the problems most coaches of that day (and many since) encountered: lack of funding, facilities, and equipment, as well as lack of faculty support. Although John D. Rockefeller had bequeathed a large sum of money to help the University get started, apparently none of it found its way to the athletic department. Stagg himself wrote about the problem of faculty opposition during those early years under President Harper:

For all his advanced views on physical training and his keen sense of advertising values, Dr. Harper shared the prevailing faculty fear of over-stressing competitive athletics as a public show.
"It is not the function of the university to provide at great cost spectacular entertainment for enormous crowds of people," he read into the constitution, so to speak, of the school.[29]

Nevertheless, Stagg's unflagging faith in the future of football was as strong as his own Christian faith and the city of Chicago's staunch belief in its own destiny. Thus it was not long before he was consistently turning out winning teams that attracted a loyal following. Indeed, the University of Chicago Maroon supporters soon found themselves with plenty to cheer about, as in over forty years of coaching at Chicago, Stagg would see four of his Maroon teams go undefeated and twelve of them lose only one game in a season. Stagg's best team was the 1905 undefeated squad that beat strong Michigan and Wisconsin teams and was declared national champion.

Also during the 1890s, Stagg appeared to be contributing more than anyone else to the strategic development of football, including his pioneering contemporaries, John Heisman and Glenn Warner. If there was controversy later on as to who first introduced a particular innovation, the reason for dispute was simply, as Stagg himself put it, that "credit often went astray in the '90s for new plays, due to the inadequate reporting and the lack of contact between the sport of one region with that of another."[30] It was an era when pioneering coaches of kindred spirit and a real feel for the game could come up with similar innovative techniques within a season or two of each other (perhaps even a few weeks) and never know who had been first.

For example, while Heisman was experimenting with his version of the mass momentum formations in the early 1890s, Stagg was doing the same thing at Springfield. He would ultimately receive credit for originating the first of such formations, the "ends back" formation, which in stationing linemen in the backfield looked ahead to formations such as Glenn Warner's double wingback attack. Heisman himself later admitted his debt to Stagg: "The business of pulling linemen back and giving them the ball was not at all new. . . . As early as 1891 Stagg, in his first year as a coach, utilized his ends as runners with the ball at Springfield. He ran them like halfbacks and I copied his theory and carried it along for years."[31] At about the same time, Stagg came up with a criss-cross play featuring deceptive handoffs, including a hidden-ball maneuver. Also during this period he invented a tactic he called the "Whoa Back" play, which was the forerunner of the fullback spinner play, only in this formation the quarterback was the one who spun around to make or take a handoff. Other mass interference formations considered to have originated with Stagg were the fanciful "turtle-back" in 1891 and the "tackles back" in 1894.

Stagg's innovations continued unabated over the decade. In 1894 he implemented a backward or lateral pass on the kickoff, and supposedly the center snap, which, as previously noted, Heisman claims to have invented at Buchtel in 1893. By 1896, Stagg was directing his punter to take a direct snap from center. Stagg's version of the on-side kickoff appeared in 1894, as did his modification of the quarterback's stance in the basic T-formation from that of a squatting position to one of a semistanding stance to receive the center snap as today's quarterbacks do.

As some of the Maroons' early games were played indoors in the old Chicago Coliseum, Stagg introduced the offensive huddle in 1896 to combat the noise level. This was long before the huddle would become an outdoor fixture, although Glenn Warner used it against John Heisman's Auburn team the same year. (See p. 52.) It was also the year he implemented his version of the quick kick, and a year later Chicago tried one of the first place kicks from scrimmage instead of a drop kick, although Penn claimed to have used it first that same year.

During this time Stagg's fertile mind was also busy originating defensive innovations. In 1890 he was utilizing a 7–2–2 defense when most teams were still relying on a nine-man line, and by 1898 he was pulling his center back to function as a linebacker to assist the regular defensive backs. Numerous other later contributions that Stagg made to the game were mostly in the area of offensive strategy, which will be described later. Many of his contributions had nothing to do with football strategy but rather with college

sports traditions, such as the idea of awarding players letters (school em-
blems) as rewards for athletic achievement. Hence the term *letterman* that
applies to a player who has played a sufficient amount of time to earn his
letter.

The main point to consider here concerning the development of football
in the 1890s is that its uncertain status continually invited innovation to give
the game needed stability. In this vein, Stagg and Heisman were two seminal
minds who were clearly in the right places at the right time, regardless of
who received credit for being first at any one thing. Both men believed in
the power of inspirational leadership in coaching, although they had somewhat different approaches to what leadership was all about. Stagg, who had
studied for the ministry at Yale, decided early on against a career in the
pulpit, feeling that he could minister more effectively to young men as a
football coach. In fact, when he took on the head coaching position at Chicago, he declared that "it will give me such a fine chance to do Christian
work among the boys who are sure to have the most influence. Win the
athletes of any college for Christ, and you will have the strongest working
element attainable in college life."[32] Appropriately enough, he proudly expressed in his 1927 autobiography that all his coaching years up to that time
had been a form of ministering for Jesus Christ.

While John Heisman never professed Stagg's evangelical faith, he was no
less dedicated to teaching his players about the worth of their commitment
to an ideal. In fact, if Heisman had a personal religion (his formal church
allegiance was Episcopalian), it was expressed in his belief that the strong
inner desire of an individual to work toward a goal was the key to success
at whatever task one undertook. For as we have seen, his personal formula
for success was inherited from the go-getter philosophy of the American
industrialist and businessman. That there was something akin to a religious
experience concerning the varsity athlete's dedication to all-round individual
excellence had always been an essential part of traditional college athletics
with roots in England's Victorian concept of the "muscular Christian." But
by the 1890s, with the advent of professional coaches like Heisman and Stagg
and the competitive standards they established, this experience had developed
into an idealized socialization process in American intercollegiate athletics,
of which the varsity athlete was the exemplar. Although considerable social
change has impacted on college athletics over the years, the code of character
building and religious identification through sports involvement is still very
much with us today, expressing itself through such active organizations as
the Fellowship of Christian Athletes and Athletes in Action.

With such a dedicated and highly respected coach as Amos Alonzo Stagg
continually refining and actively promoting the game, football quickly became a natural attraction to sports fans not only in the Chicago area but also
throughout the Midwest. By 1895, the game had such a large following in
the region that a number of schools came together to form one of college

football's first leagues—what was then called the Western Conference, whose seven charter members were actually the nucleus of an organization that would soon become popularly known as the Big Ten. Officially recognized as the Intercollegiate Conference of Faculty Representatives, this organization attempted to establish a semblance of order and ethical standards throughout its membership by agreeing to a uniform set of rules governing play and eligibility. By acting collectively, the Western Conference pioneered the first effective system for controlling athletic standards. Chicago was one of its first powers, along with Michigan and Wisconsin, winner of the first conference championship in 1896.

If there were any who doubted the ability of midwestern teams to compete on an even par with the eastern powers, all doubts would have been erased had they been among the ten thousand people who witnessed the Penn–Chicago game in Philadelphia on October 29, 1898. Having gone undefeated the previous season and riding the crest of nine straight victories prior to the Chicago game, the Quakers were considered the best in the land at the time. But the determined Stagg had his team fully prepared for Coach George Woodruff's team and at halftime the Maroons led the mighty Quakers, 6–5. Nevertheless, the more experienced Penn team came back in the second half to win, 23–11, much to the relief of the hometown fans. Even so, eastern gridiron observers had been impressed with the level of competition that Coach Stagg's team had demonstrated. Clearly, with a degree of parity now beginning to set in, football was on the verge of becoming a national sport.

SOUTHERN FOOTBALL IN THE 1890s

By the mid-1890s, football was also establishing itself in other parts of the country other than the East and Midwest. Organizational efforts were especially evident among the southern schools during these years. While flagship institutions like the University of Virginia and the University of North Carolina had gotten an earlier start, the schools in the deep South, particularly in the Gulf states, didn't get football programs underway until the 1890s, and then in a very limited way. What was essential to the growth of the game in this region was recruitment of the so-called missionary coaches through whom the Midwest had so ably profited, particularly in their practical ability to teach promising candidates the basic playing skills of the game. According to some reports, the first game in the region was played in 1890 between Vanderbilt and the University of Nashville, which Vandy won, 46–0. Harry Thornton, one of Heisman's teammates at Penn, became the first full-time coach in the South when Vanderbilt paid him $400 a year for his services.

Even though the noble militaristic side of football appealed strongly to the southern desire to identify itself with a winning cause, especially after the bitter defeat of the Civil War, it would be years before the South would be capable of successfully competing with the teams of the East and Midwest. In 1890, for example, the University of Virginia had suffered a humiliating 115–0 defeat at the hands of Princeton, even though the Virginia Cavaliers were supposedly in the vanguard of southern football at this time.

By the fall of 1892, schools in the states of Tennessee, Mississippi, and Louisiana had also started playing football. But because an athletics governing body for the region was still several years away, player eligibility was difficult to control, as it had been in all areas of the country. Too often, faculty, coaches, and even nonstudents or tramp athletes called ringers, who sold their services, wound up playing. Since high school football in the South was virtually unheard of at this time except in Virginia and Tennessee, most football candidates' introduction to the game did not come until college. Like elsewhere, the style of play favored brute force over speed and quickness, with the flying wedge holding forth at those schools that had learned about it. Like elsewhere, too, injuries were rampant, and at many schools only those students who had secured parental permission could play football.

Practically from the start, southern schools that fielded teams began to point toward a big-game finale with a rival institution on Thanksgiving Day, as northern schools had been doing. So it soon became their practice to schedule games with a number of prep schools and athletic clubs in October as preliminary warm-ups for the tougher games along the way toward the big, climactic November match. Some of the South's biggest rivalries grew out of this practice as, for example, the Auburn–Georgia game, which for a number of years was played on Thanksgiving Day in Atlanta. Even extending beyond the "Turkey Day" tradition, rivalries of all sorts would soon start springing up, matchups that were considered to be social as well as athletic events. As football historian John McCallum has put it: "Down in Southeast territory, college football long ago became a geographical, historical, or social event—sometimes all three. The fans down there have always had somebody they especially love to see whomped. There are all kinds of rivalries: intra-state, border, crosstown and personal—all commonly classed as 'natural' rivalries."[33] During John Heisman's twenty-five years coaching at three southern schools—Auburn, Clemson, and Georgia Tech (1895–1919)—football took on one of its major distinguishing characteristics as a sport: a strong sense of place and deep pride as expressed through the gridiron fortunes of a particular school.

By the close of the 1920s, when the South had finally put itself on the national football map, one game played during this time vividly exemplified what football had come to mean to this part of the country. The year was 1929, and the event was the dedication of Sanford Stadium at Athens, Georgia, where Yale had come down to play the University of Georgia. By this time, intersectional games were common and they sparked considerable national interest. In this matchup, the southern exposure proved a little too much for the Yale team and its great back Albie Booth, as the Yale Blue wilted in the heat and lost, 15–0. Amid all the celebrating that followed, no one caught the spirit of the occasion more aptly than did *New York Sun* reporter George Trevor: "Football provides an escape valve for that adventurous urge; that martial ardor, which despite an outward appearance of languor is the heritage of every son of Dixie. Northerners may have originated the American version of rugby, but the game is in the blood down here in the Deep South, and they play it for blood."[34]

That football was in the southern blood was made evident on December 22, 1894, when Dr. William L. Dudley, a Vanderbilt dean, met in Atlanta with university representatives from Alabama, Auburn, Georgia, Georgia Tech, North Carolina, and Sewanee (the University of the South) to found a new athletic conference. Because a number of abuses had infiltrated college athletics in the South, chairman Dudley's avowed purpose in establishing an association of schools that participated in organized sports was "to develop, regulate, and purify intercollegiate athletics . . . in the South."[35] The new conference, of which these schools became the charter members, was called the Southern Intercollegiate Athletic Association (SIAA). It would eventually become so large and unwieldy that in 1920 it broke up into the Southern Conference, which in turn fragmented into the Southeastern (1932) and Atlantic Coast (1953) conferences, comprised of the region's largest schools.

With the establishment of the SIAA, nearly all the major southern colleges started playing football. This paved the way for the arrival of professional or paid coaches as well as more stringent interinstitutional control of player eligibility. Accordingly, concerns in this latter problematic area during Auburn's 1894 football season precipitated the search for a knowledgeable coach who could project an authoritative image to enforce strict standards.

HEISMAN'S AUBURN YEARS (1895–1899)

The fact that John Heisman had done rather well in coaching against a number of reputable Midwest teams during his time at Oberlin and Buchtel undoubtedly caught the eye of the people at the Agricultural and Mechanical College of Alabama (now Auburn) when the school became a charter member of the SIAA. In seeking him out as the Auburn coach, they reasoned that someone with proven credentials in coaching the game of football was exactly what was needed if they were to compete successfully against the caliber of teams in the league. (In three years of participating in football the Auburn record stood at a mediocre 6–6–1.) But how and why John Heisman finally decided to come to this school located some fifty miles east of Montgomery in an attractive but somewhat isolated village called Auburn is a story in itself.

Although he had grown up in a relatively small town, Titusville was not the usual tranquil American town, for reasons discussed in chapter 1. Having gone on to live in growing metropolitan areas such as Providence, Philadelphia, Cleveland, and Akron, John Heisman, during this early phase of his career, had been assimilating a variety of cosmopolitan experiences in addition to the go-getter influence of his youth. As a bona fide city man of urbane manners and interests, he undoubtedly thought of himself as a man of the world.

In spite of his basically urban background, the real reason for Heisman's decision to coach at Auburn was probably the challenge it presented him to "spread the gospel" of football in what was then virgin territory. Having been in the vanguard of football's key developmental years in the East as a player and then as a coach during the game's spread to the Midwest, the young, idealistic Heisman undoubtedly welcomed the opportunity that the South presented him to further the cause of his game, particularly at an athletically ambitious school like Auburn.

As an early land-grant college created by the Morrill Act of 1862, the school had a great deal to prove about itself—particularly, it needed to create an identity. Originally known as the East Alabama Male College, a Methodist liberal arts school dating from the 1850s, the college fell on hard times after the Civil War and deeded its property to the state of Alabama in 1872 for the establishment of a land-grant institution. The provisions of the Morrill Act stipulated that the curriculum of land-grant schools must consist mainly of agricultural and mechanical studies. Military tactics also had a significant place, with the traditional liberal arts playing more of a secondary role. Because of its emphasis on the practical side of education, such an institution of higher learning was made to order for this part of the South at the time, with its need to catch up with the more industrialized areas of the country.

But in spite of federal support, Auburn's early days were a time of financial struggle, characterized by occasional clashes between the faculty members who professed the agricultural and mechanical side of the curriculum and those who supported the traditional liberal arts as being essential to the proper mission of a university. To some, such a conflict would be never ending, but by 1885 the school's financial difficulties were alleviated to a large extent when the state legislature allocated funds to support agricultural research. Fortunately, it was a time when southern legislators were beginning to consider scientific education more seriously, and because of this attitude the school began to receive more support over the years. Today Auburn is widely known for its contributions to research and development in both agriculture and technology, but in John Heisman's day it was a school much like himself, still searching to establish an appropriate identity. Over a five-year coaching tenure at Auburn, Heisman's achievements on the football field would go a long way in helping to establish the school's long-standing athletic reputation as well as a name for himself. A concomitant result was a strong sense of community identity for the school. By 1899, Heisman's last year there, the institution's name had been changed from the Agricultural and Mechanical College of Alabama to Alabama Polytechnic Institute, but the place name eventually grew so popular that in 1960 the state legislature approved the name of Auburn University.

Prior to Heisman's arrival, the football team had gone through four coaches, each lasting no longer than a year. (There had been two appointments in the year 1893 alone.) The first, Dr. George Petrie, a history professor who had volunteered to coach the team in his spare time, had the distinction of also being the first coach of the oldest football rivalry in this part of the country, the Auburn–Georgia series, whose initial match was played in Atlanta in 1892 and won by Auburn, 10–0.

With a Princeton man (F. M. Hall) at the helm in 1894, though, Auburn thought it might have come up with the right person for the job of football mentor, but the only bright spot during the season was a record-setting 94–0 win over Georgia Tech. (At the time, the rules allowed the scoring team to get the ball right back on the ensuing kickoff, thus affording Auburn the opportunity to dominate possession in this match.) Over a four-game schedule, losses were to Vanderbilt, 20–4, and most disappointingly, to Georgia, 10–8, and Alabama, 18–0. This latter defeat was the first after two previous victories. The loss was particularly bitter because of two ringers the officials allowed to play even after Auburn had challenged their eligibility. These ringers went on to figure prominently in the game's final score, and helped fire up a heated rivalry that has lasted to this day. The upshot of the 1894 season, though, was that Auburn was now in the market for a new coach, one well versed in all the intricacies of the game. This qualification was particularly necessary due to the game's ever-changing rules and the attendant skills that players needed to keep abreast of to perform successfully. Thus, a man of John Heisman's proven capabilities appeared to be the answer to Auburn's immediate coaching needs.

Displaying his usual bold determination and infectious enthusiasm, Heisman boldly started out in 1895 to build a competitive football team at Auburn. Uncharacteristically, though, his first match ended up in a close 9–6 loss to Vanderbilt on a muddy field in Nashville. More prophetic of Heisman's future coaching style was his origination and use of a hidden-ball play in this game. With Vanderbilt leading 9–0 in the second half, Heisman relates that the Auburn team lined up in a revolving wedge, containing their quarterback, Reynolds Tichenor, with the ball:

The moment the milling started, Tichenor stuffed the ball under the front of his jersey. The mass around him disintegrated, the players scurrying to wide and varied parts of the field and with them went the Vanderbilt men who had industriously been trying to break up the wedge. Only Tichenor remained and he, apparently, was out of the play. He was on one knee, busy at tying his shoe lace.

But when the Vanderbilt team was as widely spread as his own, Tichenor arose and nonchalantly catfooted down the field for a deceitful touchdown.[36]

The play was soon to be outlawed, but the story of its origin at Auburn is worth retelling. In a bull session with some of his players, Heisman casually remarked, "You know, boys, I had a kid ask me once if it was against the rules to hide the ball. I don't see anything against it, but I honestly don't see how you could work a trick like that." This started everyone to thinking, and "once it was established that the ball could be easily and quickly concealed [under a jersey], they set up a formation to cover up the trick and draw opponents away from Tichenor so he could get free."[37] Auburn had a chance to win the Vanderbilt game when the Tigers moved the ball to the 2-yard line with two minutes to play. But the referee called the game "on account of darkness," even though a contemporary account reported that the sun had not yet set. Heisman's irate reaction was the first of many run-ins he would have with southern officials.

Later that season, the hidden-ball play is supposed to have also worked against Georgia, but there is no official record of its use. At any rate, Glenn "Pop" Warner, who was the Georgia coach, carried the same play with him to his next coaching appointment at Cornell, where in 1898 he was mistakenly credited with having invented it.[38] Heisman was obsessed, it seems, with inventing ways to hide the football. Even when he was at Georgia Tech, one of his players, Al Loeb, reported that Heisman "had players wear leather patches in the shape of footballs on the front of their jerseys, and opponents mistook them for the real thing and tackled the wrong guys."[39]

Auburn's 1895 season consisted of only three scheduled games, but with wins over rivals Alabama, 48–0, and Georgia, 16–6, Heisman's first season had ended auspiciously. Student reaction to Heisman's first year as head coach was positively reported in the school newspaper, *The Orange and Blue*: "As long as Heisman wishes to sign an Auburn contract, he may do it. Before he had been here a week, he had gained the love, admiration and confidence of every member of the faculty as well as the boys." (Quotation is from Heisman's promotional pamphlet.) The reason Heisman was so well liked was due to more than just his winning ways on the gridiron. He quickly became a respected member of the Auburn community, teaching classes in oratory (always a forte of his) and even trying his hand at acting in local play productions, an activity he would become increasingly involved in during his free time.

Earlier that year an event of monumental import for the future of football had occurred in Atlanta while Heisman was watching two other teams play. One of the first coaches to "scout" an opponent, Heisman was taking in the North Carolina–Georgia game when he witnessed the first use of the forward pass. Although such a play was then illegal, he immediately realized the impact that this innovation could have on opening up the game. With time running out and neither side having scored, the Carolina team found itself backed up to the goal line and its fullback preparing to punt. Heisman recounted the outcome:

But instead of punting straight into the leaping bodies of these on-rushing Georgians [the fullback] ran a few mincing steps to the right. Raising the ball to his shoulder he tossed it.

Luck was with the boy. The ball was caught by a North Carolinian.

Now as we today know forward passes it was not much. It traveled a few yards, and laterally as well as forward. It may have appeared to the spectators that it had been knocked from that fullback's hands.

At any rate that lad who caught it ran 70 yards for a touchdown!

Georgia was stunned, not quite realizing what had happened there beneath North Carolina's goal. But Glenn Warner, then coaching Georgia, had not missed a moment of it. And neither had I. I had been standing not more than eight yards from North Carolina's fullback.

I had seen the first forward pass in football. It was illegal, of course. Already Warner was storming at the referee. But the referee had not seen the North Carolina lad, goaded to desperation, toss the ball. And he refused to recall the ball. A touchdown had been made and a touchdown it remained.[40]

Heisman had long realized that the closed style of play created by the mass momentum tactics was "killing the game as well as the players," as he noted in his article about the illegal forward pass. From that time on, his crusade to get the Rules Committee to adopt the forward pass became a personal obsession. But it would not be until 1906 that his efforts came to fruition. Walter Camp, as an influential member of the committee, maintained a strongly conservative position. As a result, he was fearful of what the adoption of the forward pass would do to the basic nature of the game. In the long run, only the stubborn persistence of a man like John Heisman would ultimately turn his head.

It didn't take long for football to spread and entrench itself in the Deep South. During most of the 1890s, Virginia and North Carolina were the premier teams of the entire South, but by the middle of the decade the signs of change were in the air. In 1895, Virginia had barely defeated Vanderbilt, 6–4, for the SIAA championship. But in 1896, North Carolina was finally beaten (24–16) by a team from the Deep South—Glenn Warner's Georgia Bulldogs. At Auburn, Heisman's second year was upbeat, with convincing wins over Mercer (46–0), Georgia Tech (40–0), and Sewanee (38–6). Only a narrow 12–6 loss to Georgia kept the Tigers from an undefeated four-game schedule.

It was also in the Georgia game that Heisman met his match as far as the introduction of innovative play by a coaching opponent was concerned. Glenn Warner, who as a player had learned his football at Cornell and whose coaching career would be as far-ranging as Heisman's, went on to become one of the creative geniuses of the game. (His many significant contributions to football will be discussed later.) In the game with Auburn, played on Thanksgiving Day in Atlanta before a crowd of eight thousand spectators, Warner had his players prepare their plays out of a huddle, the first time such a procedure had ever taken place on an outdoor football field. This innovation proved to be so confusing to the Auburn players that they had a difficult time setting their defense, and it had a great deal to do with their defeat in this game. Ever the student of the game and willing to try anything new, Heisman must have learned a lot from this experience. In fact, before his tenure at Auburn was over, he had devised his own unique system for starting up a play from scrimmage:

At Alabama Poly I had my quarterback use the word "hike" when he was ready to receive the ball, and the word became popular for that office. It served us variously. For example, our opponents, hearing the quarterback's "hike," would charge, but presently we adopted a trick of trapping them by not putting the ball into play at the sound "hike" but waiting a couple of seconds. Naturally we won many off-side penalties.

Feeling that this procedure was an example of bad sportsmanship, Heisman wrote Walter Camp about it, and a rule was adopted forbidding a team to intentionally draw an opponent offside.[41]

With the limited material Heisman initially found at Auburn, he felt compelled to come up with as much deception as he could (hence, the hidden-ball play). Another deceptive play Heisman used at Auburn, one that would have wide-ranging impact, he claimed to have literally dreamed up. "I dreamed many plays, but this was the only dream of mine that ever worked," he declared:

The dream was too vivid to ignore. So we tried it on the scrubs. The quarterback simply gave the ball to, say, the right end while the latter was on the dead run. The right halfback and fullback galloped in front of the left halfback, who stood still until the right end passed him.

Then he took the ball from the right end and went through center with the quarterback preceding him. They found nobody there. My dream had produced a touchdown in its first trial. That play, virtually the forerunner of all delayed bucks, served me for fifteen years and with it my teams gained thousands of yards.[42]

But it was Heisman's unique brand of inspirational leadership that got the most results, commanding his players to give their all on the field of play. Edwin Pope has observed how Heisman "railed and snorted in practice, imploring players to do their all for God, Country, Auburn, and Heisman. Before each game he made squadsmen take a nonshirk, nonflinch oath."[43] In 1897, with Auburn reputed to have its lightest team and its first six-game schedule, Heisman knew he had to muster all the resources at his command.

The first two games of the season resulted in relatively easy wins over Mercer (26–0) and the University of Nashville (14–4), but the match with the University of the South at Sewanee, Tennessee, proved to be an altogether different matter. Having split two previous games with Auburn,

Sewanee was on the verge of becoming a recognized southern football power. While Vanderbilt was considered Sewanee's natural rival, a rivalry of sorts had also been developing between Auburn and the Sewanee Purple. In twelve games played between 1893 and 1931, Auburn always found the Purple a tough foe, with the Tigers managing only four wins, while two games ended in ties in this series. This rivalry can be attributed to the controversial incidents that seemed to always occur when these two teams played each other. In 1893, a tying Sewanee touchdown was allowed to stand after fans had interfered with Auburn players so that the Purple could score. Officials awarded Sewanee a 2-point conversion for a 16–14 win over Auburn, whose players had left the field in protest. The 1897 game, although it ended as a 0–0 tie, was not without its share of controversy, once again due to questionable officiating. When the regular officials for the game failed to show up (a common occurrence in those days), the Sewanee coach and an injured Auburn player agreed to officiate, with the natural result that each man exhibited undue favoritism toward his own team. By the second half there had been so much disagreement over questionable decisions that the match had to be called early "on account of darkness." Considering the state of flux in which the game of football found itself during the 1880s–1890s and the rate at which rule changes were implemented, it is not surprising that up-to-date, well-informed officials were so hard to come by at this time. By 1894, the crew of officials consisted of an umpire, referee, and linesman. They were usually men who had played the game, but who found it difficult to keep abreast of the latest rules developments. Although this was a problem that undoubtedly irked Heisman no little, it was one that would loom even larger in his final years at Auburn.

But there were other concerns of greater consequence to the future of football. On the day after the Auburn–Sewanee game—October 31, 1897—a tragedy occurred on the gridiron that came close to putting an end to football in the South. In the second half of the Georgia–Virginia game, played in Atlanta, the Georgia fullback, Richard Von Gammon, suffered severe injuries and died the following morning. After a hard-driving smash into the Virginia line, Von Gammon fell unconscious during the ensuing pileup of players. Doctors on hand diagnosed his case as a severe concussion, and although he was rushed to the hospital Von Gammon never recovered consciousness. Virginia went on to win the game, 17–4. When word of the Georgia player's death got out, a huge cry against football was raised all over the South. Most schools, including Auburn, cancelled the remaining games on their schedules. John Heisman's worst fears about the future of football, due primarily to its failure to open up the game, seemed about to come true.

The fate of football, at least in Georgia, appeared to lie in the hands of the state legislature, which after considerable debate voted to abolish the game as a collegiate sport. The governor vetoed the bill, however. What helped sway his mind was a letter to the trustees of the university from the mother of the deceased student. Because of her son's deep love of the game, Mrs. Von Gammon expressed her desire that football not be abolished. Rather, she felt that if schools—particularly the University of Georgia—would continue playing the game, it would be a kind of memorial to her son.

Although repercussions from Von Gammon's untimely death were still in the air by the time the 1898 season rolled around, most southern schools were gearing up to field teams as usual. For Auburn the three games that had been cancelled after the Georgia player's death were carried over to make up the 1898 schedule. The games had all been set for November, so Heisman and his players had a lot of time to prepare for them. Their efforts paid off, too, as they defeated Georgia Tech, 29–4, and their big rival of the time, Georgia, 18–17. The Tigers lost to a powerful North Carolina Tar Heel team, 24–0, as the Tar Heels went on to win the Southern championship that year.

The victory over Georgia was not without controversy, however, as once again shoddy officiating figured in the game's outcome. (By now, Heisman had to conclude that poor officiating was getting to be as much of a problem as brutal playing tactics.) This time, though, the judgment of the officials favored Auburn. After falling behind at the half, 13–4, Heisman directed his big fullback, George Mitcham, to start pounding at the line, a strategy that soon resulted in three touchdowns and the score in Auburn's favor, 18–13. Nevertheless, Georgia came back to score a touchdown, only to miss the extra-point try. Although the Georgia players tried to convince the officials that Auburn had been offside on the play, they were overruled. With the score at 18–17 and eight minutes still left in the game, the Georgia team walked off the field in protest.

Heisman had to make the most of this game's fortuitous outcome because the next year he was involved in two games in which officiating figured more prominently against him than ever before. One of these games, the last of the season with Sewanee, may have actually helped him make up his mind to secure another coaching position. In 1898, the Sewanee Purple was a team on the rise, defeating its big rival and the dominant power of the region, Vanderbilt, 19–4. That same year, the ambitious Vanderbilt team ventured north to engage in one of the Deep South's first intersectional clashes, only to lose to the University of Cincinnati, 10–0. While Sewanee was on the verge of making a strong impact in the southern region, a national football reputation for the South still lay some years in the future.

The season of 1899, John Heisman's last at Auburn, promised to be his best. He had finally built a team of veteran players who obviously responded to his flair for no-nonsense, aggressive leadership. The Auburn attack in 1899 featured a cadre of hard-running backs led by Captain Arthur Feagin, Franklin Bivings, and Ed Huguley. Heisman, in fact, began the tradition of great running backs at Auburn. That year also brought significant changes in football's scoring system: touchdowns were now worth 5 points instead of 4; extra points after touchdowns became 1 point instead of 2; but field goals, which were still nearly always drop-kicked, were still worth 5 points. Clearly, though, the running game was about to catch up with the kicking game.

Playing a five-game schedule, Auburn blew out its first three opponents: Georgia Tech, 63–0; the Montgomery Athletic Club, 41–0; and Clemson, 34–0. (This game may have alerted Clemson, another athletically ambitious school, that John Heisman would be a good choice as their next coach.) But what happened in the next two games undoubtedly convinced Heisman that southern officials were out to get both him and his Auburn team and that it might be time to depart from the Alabama school.

Typically, the Georgia game, played in Atlanta on November 18, turned out to be another hard-fought contest. But with only thirty seconds left in the game and Auburn leading, 11–6, the umpire, Mr. Rowbotham, called the match "on account of darkness," a major reason many games were never finished in those days. However, not only did Rowbotham call the match, he also declared that because the game had not been completed, the final score should stand at 0–0. An incensed Heisman, feeling that he had again been victimized by an official, protested the outcome to the SIAA. It was not until a year later that the executive committee of the Association ruled in Auburn's favor, with the final score reverting back to 11–6. This reversal was unusual for the time, because an official's final decision was usually never questioned. But there was even more controversy to come in the next game, the outcome of which was to be debated long after it was played.

The Auburn game with Sewanee would decide who played North Carolina for the Southern championship. Because Sewanee's Purple from the mountains of Tennessee were unbeaten at the time, there was much ballyhoo over this match to be played Thanksgiving Day in Montgomery. One of the reasons for the hoopla was Sewanee had fielded the South's first notable football power in 1899. Not only were the Purple unscored on in ten consecutive contests, they had recently returned from a road trip on which they had defeated five big schools in six days (Texas, Texas A&M, Tulane, LSU, and Ole Miss).

But by the day of the Auburn game, either Sewanee's luck had run out or its players were just plain worn out from so much traveling, for Heisman's team was soon running circles around them. At one point, after Auburn had advanced the ball to Sewanee's 10-yard line, the Purple took over on downs and punted, but Auburn was not to be denied. After three straight plays, the ball wound up on Sewanee's 10-yard line, from which point Auburn scored. But the referee called the play back, indicating that the whistle had blown before the touchdown was made. Undaunted, Auburn came right back for a touchdown, the first score against Sewanee that year.

Things looked bad for Sewanee when minutes later the speedy Ed Huguley broke loose for a 50-yard touchdown. Once again the referee ruled against the score, this time without even an explanation. After Sewanee got the ball, they launched their first determined drive, which resulted in a score.

Auburn countered with another big run by Huguley, who later scored, but the point after was missed, making the score 10–5, Auburn's favor. Fuzzy Woodruff described how the game ended:

Darkness was beginning to fall. Simpkins' powerful toe sent the ball to Auburn's 5-yard line and Auburn fumbled. Sewanee recovered, and it looked like a game of football.

Three times the Sewanee backs hit the Auburn line, and in all three trials they didn't advance the ball a foot. The ball went over and Auburn heaved a sigh of relief.

On the first play, the ball was given to Huguley. Ed fumbled but Dan Martin of Auburn fell on the ball.

Again enter the referee.

For some reason, never explained until this good day, he gave the ball to Sewanee on Auburn's 1-yard line. Simpkins went over for the touchdown and kicked goal. The score was 11–10, and Sewanee had won the game.[44]

Something of a charmed team that year, Sewanee went on in the very next game to win its first Southern championship, defeating North Carolina in Atlanta, 5–0. Needless to say, Sewanee's success did little to pacify John Heisman, who was thoroughly outraged at the questionable work of the officials, particularly after having endured the absurd ruling that altered the score of the Georgia game played earlier. Little wonder, then, that the pros and cons of Sewanee's fortunate win over Auburn continued to be debated by football fans for a long time afterwards. The vagaries leading to the game's outcome even compelled Heisman to state his case in a lengthy letter to the sporting editor of a Birmingham newspaper on December 4, 1899: "I think we completely outplayed Sewanee from start to finish, both offensively and defensively; and it was only the outrageous work of the officials that made it possible for Sewanee to score at all. I think the work of both officials was, by all odds, the worst I ever saw, and I don't mind proclaiming it from the housetops." Heisman went on to point out that he had no intention of lodging a protest, although umpire William P. Taylor, a boys' school headmaster, had willfully made a series of poor decisions that countered whatever chances Auburn had of winning the game. (Heisman characteristically labeled the man's actions as "meddling interposition.") Heisman appeared to be more concerned about the umpire's decisions contributing to "bad blood" between the two schools, rather than about making an official protest, as the close of his letter indicated.[45]

The very next day Taylor came back with an embittered rebuttal in a lengthy letter of his own. His argument appeared to stem from the unfounded contention that the Auburn team was poorly coached and had been resorting to unfair tactics on the playing field. To Taylor, Heisman was not a coach, but a "would-be actor of character parts." He wrote:

The plain truth of the matter is that Coach Heisman has proved a failure in producing winning teams at Auburn; he wishes to retain his position as football coach and hopes to be retained also as professor of elocution and oratory. Is it not most likely that he must keep in Auburn's good graces by ascribing his defeats to the officials?[46]

Clearly, Heisman's letter had struck a sensitive nerve in Taylor, and he was striking back any way he could, lashing out in particular at the man's professional abilities as both a coach and an actor—one of the earliest attempts, it would appear, to discredit a sporting figure by referring to him as an entertainer. Nevertheless, Taylor's diatribe served mainly to undermine his own weak argument, particularly when he naively remarked that the public cared little for the finer technical points of the game and that Heisman was guilty of corrupting his athletes.

What Taylor had done now, of course, was to pour more oil on the fire, and Heisman, drawing on his best debating skills, came right back at him in another letter on December 8:

What on earth has my capacity or incapacity as an actor to do with Mr. Taylor's rank football decisions on Thursday last? I charge him with transgressing his powers as umpire in ordering play to be resumed, and he answers, "You are a very bad actor." I state that it is the referee's business to judge of fair catches, and his reply is that the Auburn team was poorly coached. . . . Have I then proved such an ignominious failure as a coach? I suppose I ought to begin to worry. Singular, though, that I have coached for eight years in succession, and the last five of them at Auburn. People don't usually re-engage failures. Strange that I have never failed to get two or three offers each year, and already have them for next season.[47]

And so, John Heisman, with clearly the stronger case in this overdrawn matter, had the last word. With the 1899 season now history, it was time to turn his attention to other, more important concerns. Like that mentioned in his letter of securing another coaching position, something that had been in the back of his mind for some time. But now, after the public debate with umpire Taylor, the goal of proving himself elsewhere had become an even more pressing matter. If he had an honorable way out of his Auburn commitment, it was primarily because the school was unable to meet his demands for a higher salary.

Actually, Heisman had come to feel very much at home at Auburn. Evidence is he enjoyed a good relationship with the administration and faculty as well as his players. In later life, thinking back on his Auburn years, he observed: "I never had a team at Auburn that I did not love, nor did I have one quarrel with any player during the whole five years. . . . There is not one man who ever played with me during those five years that is not still my very warm friend."[48] But Heisman had been compelled to supplement his income by teaching classes in elocution and oratory and by acting in stock productions during the summer in Atlanta and other area locations. How he got into acting should make an interesting story in itself, but this surprising side of the man appears to have been kept pretty much to himself. Perhaps teaching elocution aroused in him a natural inclination toward histrionic expression, for such patterns cropped up frequently in his speech and writings. And although he was somewhat reserved by nature, there was a decided theatrical bent to his public posture.

The comments of one of Heisman's Auburn players, Walter R. Shafer, who was a fullback on the 1895 team, provide a clue to Heisman's motivation for a higher salary. As though to counter any future attacks on his coaching qualifications by someone like the "meddling" William Taylor, Heisman had a personal brochure printed while he was at Clemson. In it he cited numerous references by his former players and positive comments of the press concerning his growing reputation as a successful coach. Shafer's remarks in this document appear to substantiate the fact that Heisman's eventual move to Clemson was financially motivated: "Mr. J. W. Heisman is a thoroughly cultured gentleman in every sense of the word. As a football coach his work is incessant, careful, painstaking and, above all, honest. . . . That my old team is unable to employ him is a source of sincere regret; our inability, financially, and that alone being the cause."[49]

But there was another, perhaps more personal reason for Heisman's decision to cast his lot with Clemson. An "Auburn connection" was already there in the person of Walter Merritt Riggs, a professor of engineering who had been at Auburn before Heisman's arrival in 1895. While at Auburn, Riggs had been introduced to football and had immediately fallen in love with the game. Upon his arrival at Clemson in 1895, it was at Riggs's urging that Clemson fielded its first football team the following year. In fact, Riggs, who would go on to become president of the college, was himself the school's first coach, leading the team to wins over Furman and Wofford, while losing to South Carolina by a close score in what was to become one of the South's longest-standing rivalries. Riggs even brought with him Auburn's nickname of "Tigers" and the school's colors of orange and dark blue. Others who coached during the years before Heisman arrived were also Auburn men, but together with Riggs they had a combined record of only nine wins against eight losses. So when Auburn defeated Clemson, 34–0, in 1899, the ambitious Riggs, who headed the Clemson Athletic Association, realized that if his athletically minded school was ever to field a first-rate football team, then John Heisman would be the man to get the job done. A significant reason for the ready acceptance of football by many southern schools was that

academicians like Riggs were staunchly in favor of participation in football
as a true test of manhood, and ambitious coaches like Heisman supported
this outlook.

THE NATIONAL GAME (1895–1899)

While Heisman was at Auburn, his alma mater, the University of Pennsylvania, continued to win big under the redoubtable George Woodruff,
fashioning a 14–0 season in 1895 on the way to a national championship. In
the process, the Quakers had edged out another tough Yale team that had
only two ties to mar its record. Actually, Penn was into its great winning
streak at this time, one that after thirty-four games would finally be broken
in 1896 by Lafayette, 6–4. That year Princeton survived a scoreless tie against
this same strong Lafayette team to win the national crown. But in 1897,
Penn, with what many think was its greatest team, rolled to a 15–0 season
and the national championship. This was also the year that the Quakers were
supposed to have made the first-ever field goal from a place kick. The fact
that the ball was now more of a prolate spheroid in shape helped make for
a better goal-kicking game.

By 1898, Woodruff had his Penn team working on another string of victories, this one ending at thirty-one, when Harvard beat the Quakers for the
national title. The Crimson would repeat in 1899 as they began to make the
most of their day in the sun. In the Midwest, Michigan (11–0) won its first
Western Conference crown, while a Chicago back named Clarence Hersh-
berger became the first man who was not from the East to make Walter
Camp's All-America team. In selecting his dream team, Camp was now
finding it increasingly difficult to ignore the accomplishments of players from
other parts of the country.

The 1880s and 1890s had seen the first heroic figures emerge from the
game, mostly in the East. Much of the public adulation of these players
resulted from the newspapers' glorified descriptions of their achievements on
the playing field as well as the increasing popularity of Camp's annual All-
America selections. As we have seen, Camp had a wealth of material to
choose from in the East, particularly in a day when linemen could steal the
show running with the ball as Pudge Heffelfinger, Frank Hinkey, Ma Newell,
and Truxton Hare often did. There was even a brother troupe during this
era—the six Poes who played at Princeton between 1889 and 1900. Of the
three who were All-Americans—Arthur, Edgar, and John—Arthur was the
most outstanding because of his ability at both running and kicking.

Although during this period the game was still primitive in a number of
respects, kicking was given top priority, and some great kickers came forth
to meet the challenge. One of the greatest was Princeton's Alex Moffat (1882–
1884), who as a drop-kicker made thirty-two field goals in fifteen games,
including six in one match against Penn in 1882. To John Heisman such

players were "giants," in that they played at a time when "individual genius stood out more prominently . . . because the mass play was the customary ground-gainer."[50] His admiration extended to Alex Moffatt, of course:

Here was a youth with wings on his heels. He could stop dead from a hard run and in that same moment boot the ball, frequently 65 yards. No trouble at all. No fiddling for stance or shifting of feet. Either of Alex's feet could send the ball 50, 60, 70 yards. Against Harvard in 1883 he drop-kicked four field goals—two with the right foot and two with the left.[51]

Toward the end of the 1890s, another giant appeared in the unlikely person of an Australian playing for Wisconsin in the Western Conference. Primarily because of his prodigious drop-kicking and punting ability, Pat O'Dea led the Badgers to two consecutive conference championships in 1896 and 1897. Having perfected the spiral punt, he averaged an astounding sixty to eighty yards a kick on most attempts. Consistent and accurate, his dropkicks were almost always good from up to fifty yards out. Surely, here was one player from another part of the country that Walter Camp could not readily ignore, and when the Badgers came east in 1899 to face Yale, Camp got a firsthand look as O'Dea put on another eye-popping display of his kicking prowess.

Harvard closed out the 1890s by winning the national championship with a 10–0–1 record, as only Yale had held the Crimson to a 0–0 tie. Also in 1899, there were signs of things to come upon Glenn Warner's arrival at a small Indian school in Pennsylvania called Carlisle. He displayed his naturally innovative side in the 45–0 win over Columbia by having his linemen position themselves in a three-point crouching stance. The standing pugilistic posture of linemen would soon be a thing of the past.

HEISMAN'S CLEMSON YEARS (1900–1903)

So it was that 1900 saw the coach that many called the best in the South come to Clemson for an undisclosed salary, which was probably in the range of $1,000 annually when the usual baseball coaching responsibilities are taken into consideration. (Before the day of specialization, as we have seen in Heisman's other coaching tenures, a football coach's duties usually included every sport in its season.)

Although he was earning more money than he ever had before, Heisman must have thought himself in a world even more isolated than Auburn had been when he first arrived in the Clemson community. Located in a rural area near Greenville in the northwest part of South Carolina, Clemson, like Auburn, was a land-grant institution with one notable difference from the Alabama school. Its student body was strictly military in makeup, a situation that was to play into Heisman's hands, for it undoubtedly accounted for Clemson's fierce competitive spirit, the quality that Heisman found so essential to building a successful football team. (With some modifications, Clemson would remain primarily a military school until 1955.)

The school itself had opened its doors in 1893 to 446 students. But as the pet project of then Governor "Pitchfork Ben" Tillman and philanthropist Thomas G. Clemson, the school was born out of controversy, mainly about the kind of role it should play in comparison to the other state-supported school, the flagship University of South Carolina at Columbia. Tillman and his supporters ultimately won out over the opposing forces, contending that Clemson was founded to "give practical education at such a slight cost that any boy in South Carolina, if only he be diligent, shall be able to attain it."[52] The day of practical education had arrived in the South, and naturally South Carolina was as ready for it as Alabama had been with the establishment of its own land-grant college.

Just as he had at Auburn, John Heisman found the student athletes at Clemson much to his liking—green but eager and receptive to his rugged training methods and strict disciplinary measures. It was this mutual relationship that became the chief ingredient in accomplishing what southern football authority Fuzzy Woodruff described as "the sudden and sensational rise of Clemson from a little school whose football teams had never been heard of before, to become a football machine of the very first power."[53]

As he had done elsewhere, Heisman quickly established his coaching presence at Clemson. Indeed the very first game played in 1900, a 64–0 pasting of Davidson, started Clemson on its first undefeated, untied football season, a feat that would not be equaled at Clemson until 1947 by Coach Frank Howard. But even though Heisman's team went on that year to shut out Wofford (21–0), South Carolina (51–0), and Alabama (35–0) and to down Virginia Polytechnic Institute (VPI), 12–5, it was the big win over Georgia that made everyone sit up and take notice. The game was played November 10 in Athens, and after Heisman turned loose his fleet-footed runners with their deceptive line bucks and power-primed end runs, the Bulldogs ultimately found themselves on the short end of a devastating 39–5 score. The convincing win demonstrated that Heisman had brought with him his natural propensity for innovation as well as his genius for strategy, which often bordered on trickery. Winning football had finally arrived at Clemson, and local supporters were obviously ready for it.

Heisman's achievement in capturing an SIAA championship in his first year at Clemson was best summed up by the press. After the South Carolina game, the *Columbia State* reported: "The greatness of Clemson's game lay in the play of scientific football. Never before have so many new formations been put into play." The *Atlanta Journal* was even more lavish with its praise: "Clemson has the strongest team in the South. Heisman has taught them to play like lightening. In one year Clemson has risen to sublime heights in football." (Quotes are from Heisman's privately printed pamphlet.) True to Walter Riggs's expectations, John Heisman had gotten the job done, but in much quicker fashion than Riggs had ever dreamed he would. The results should not have been too surprising, though, because everywhere he had gone in his young career, Heisman had established his formidable coaching presence in the very first year.

In 1901, though, there was something of a falling off, with a tie and a loss over a five-game schedule. But following the opening game stalemate with Tennessee (6–6), Clemson amassed the greatest point total in its football history against Guilford, 122–0, even though the game was called after thirty minutes of play for obvious reasons. The Clemson Tigers continued to flex their muscles in convincing wins over Georgia (29–5) and perennial power, North Carolina (22–10), with their only loss that year to troublesome VPI, 17–11. But having compiled a scintillating 9–1–1 record after two years, Heisman realized that his veteran players were primed for the 1902 season, one that would turn out to be another one of his better efforts. After a close opening victory over N.C. State (11–5), his team pounded Georgia Tech, 44–5, a defeat so embarrassing that it must have started the Atlanta school to thinking it needed a coach on the order of a John Heisman.

Then the inspired strategy that Heisman pulled off in the Furman game, which was played at nearby Greenville, proved once again that he had not lost his touch for improvising. Fond of employing the lateral pass in practically any situation, Heisman appeared to have hit on the ultimate lateral tactic in this game. The moment he spied an oak tree that "stood on the 50-yard line well inside the boundary," he had a "beautiful idea" for a play, which, after he explained it to his players, came off as follows:

We had worked the ball nearly to mid-field. The oak was on our right and slightly ahead of us. We started what appeared to be a short end run toward the tree. Maxwell, our quarterback, slipped the ball to Pollitzer, left half, and Pollitzer darted off in a curving end run just inside of the oak, thereby drawing Furman's left and secondary defense down to that threatened area.

But Sitton, my left end, had sped off past Pollitzer and behind and past the tree. And there he was, alone, uncovered. Polly, safe behind strong interference, flipped the ball laterally to Sitton, who ran 40 yards for a touchdown.[54]

Relying on this play twice more that afternoon, Clemson won the game, 28–0.

Heisman's ingenuity for devising deceptive plays was apparently limitless, and he made a practice, it seems, of trying out something different in virtually every game at this time. Many opposing coaches, aware that the man made use of everything in the book, had to conclude, often too late, that he also pulled off a lot of things that were not in the book. However, a later Clemson coach, C. R. "Bob" Williams, who had coached against Heisman while at South Carolina, said that it was fruitless to scout any of Heisman's games because he rarely used the same trick over again.

Sometimes, though, the Heisman brand of deception might even take place off-field, as in the case of a comic episode that could possibly have contributed to the lopsided Georgia Tech defeat mentioned above. The story has gone down as another version of the classic situation of country bumpkin winning out over city slicker. When the train with the Clemson contingent had arrived in Atlanta the day before the game, the Tech supporters made it a special point to entertain their opponents in royal fashion. Marveling at the ease with which they were able to get the Clemson players to sneak out that night, the Tech boosters seized the opportunity to keep them out late, drinking and carousing, thus setting the stage for a sure gambling bet on Tech to win. Considering the disastrous results of the game, though, the Tech supporters had to wonder at the hardiness of the Clemson men in winning so handily after enduring a night of debauchery. That is, until they discovered that Coach Heisman had sent a bunch of country boys ahead to Atlanta with the team's equipment the night before the game while keeping his varsity players at Lula, Georgia, a small town some miles from Atlanta.

Perhaps looking ahead to both Georgia and Auburn was the reason Clemson was upset by South Carolina that year, 12–6, their only loss, and a painful one. The defeat obviously taught Heisman a lesson in game preparation, though, for his team went on to a second SIAA championship by shutting out their remaining foes: Georgia, 36–0 (clearly, Clemson had the Bulldogs' number in those days); Auburn, 16–0; and Tennessee, 11–0.

The Auburn game had to have been the one Heisman was more concerned about prior to the South Carolina game, for it would mark the first time he had faced his old school since his departure. Played at Auburn, the emotional aura of this setting alone could have presented some real problems for Heisman. Although Auburn put up a good battle, Heisman's predilection for trick plays was evident throughout the game as he employed the double pass (that day's term for the reverse play) on several occasions and the quarterback on-side kick a number of times, resulting in three touchdowns and an extra point. In shutting out Auburn, Clemson had held them to just thirty yards. Obviously, Heisman's soft spot for Auburn did not extend to competition on the football field.

It was in the Tennessee game, the last of the season, that a feat occurred which, according to Heisman, turned out to be the longest punt ever executed, a 109-yard boot by Tennessee's Toots Douglas on a field then 110 yards in length. In recording the event, Heisman noted that the game was played in a full-scale blizzard:

Toots was a great natural punter to begin with. But on this memorable day his powerful kicking foot gave the ball to the winds and the combination broke all records.

Johnny Maxwell, Clemson's safety man, was fifty yards behind our line. His face filled with amusement and snow, Johnny watched the ball fly high and wide above his head. And then he joined the chase. It fell to earth I know not where but presently it halted on our one-yard line, where Johnny fell on it and on him twenty-one of his playmates. Clemson won with two touchdowns but the talk that night was all of Toots Douglas' 109-yard wallop.[55]

The unexpected loss to South Carolina earlier that season resulted in an unfortunate encounter between the students and supporters of both schools, one that could have ended in tragedy had cooler heads not prevailed. The game was played at the State Fairgrounds in Columbia during Fair Week, a tradition that would continue until 1960. But the outcome of this game revealed the staunchly partisan posture that southern football supporters had taken by this time concerning their favorite teams.

Favored to beat the Gamecocks for the fifth straight time, Clemson found itself the victim of a major upset by game's end, 12–6. The worst was yet to be, however, when that night following a South Carolina victory parade, the Clemson cadets and Carolina students confronted each other in a potential brawl involving firearms. Violence was finally averted when police, faculty, and a joint committee of students negotiated a settlement.[56] The emotional aura of this incident had run so high, however, that Carolina athletic officials were moved to break off football relations with Clemson, and the series between the two schools was not resumed until 1909. Clearly, Southerners had begun to take their football seriously.

As to Heisman's reaction to all this furor we have no information, probably because the incident did not directly involve his players. Concerning his attitude toward how barbarous the field of play itself had become, though, he undoubtedly took a dim view of any situation that would provoke the students and supporters of opposing teams into a kind of open war among themselves. One thing he surely realized at this time, though, was that intrastate football rivalries in the South had become a serious business.

The year 1903, Heisman's last at Clemson, was a momentous one in his personal life for several reasons. His team had now developed into an annual contender for the SIAA championship, one openly feared by the other schools in the league as well as others outside it; in October, following his first serious courtship since his Buchtel days, he was married; and in the first game of the season his team hung such a devastating defeat on Georgia Tech that football supporters in Atlanta started a campaign to obtain the Clemson coach as their own.

The surprising thing about the outcome of the Georgia Tech game is that this was the year that the Techs thought they at last had a real chance to win. They heard that Vedder Sitton, the star back for Clemson (and a future major league baseball player), had been injured and would not play. This news was highly encouraging to the Tech ranks because Sitton had been the player chiefly responsible for their humiliating defeat of the previous year. Now once again there was heavy betting on Tech to win the match. But the ever-resourceful Heisman came up with a dependable substitute for his incapacitated back, and even though the game was played on a muddy field, the Tigers came through with a resounding 73–0 victory. Disgruntled Tech supporters now knew beyond a shadow of a doubt whom they wanted as their next coach, as the drive to recruit Heisman doubled in intensity.

In its next game Clemson once again took the measure of Georgia, this time by a score of 29–0. Along with the Georgia Tech backers, there were probably many Bulldog supporters wondering what it would take to secure the coaching services of the redoubtable Heisman who, in less than ten years in the South, had built such a strong reputation for himself.

But there were areas other than coaching in which John Heisman had been active since arriving in the South. It was during his Clemson years that he met, courted, and married Evelyn McCollum Cox, an attractive widow who was one of the featured actresses in a summer stock company with which Heisman had become associated and in which he occasionally took part in plays that were staged in the area. Concerning Heisman's sideline as an actor, Al Thomy has commented:

> As he was born to the game of football, [Heisman] also was born to the theater. Many coaches have acted. Knute Rockne was adept in playing parts. But Heisman was a professional actor and a lawyer and a coach, a deadly combination. . . .
>
> He was proud of his acting. But a writer-friend, commenting on this facet of his personality, put it succinctly. "John Heisman," wrote Fuzzy Woodruff, "is a great coach and a terrible thespian."[57]

Although Heisman's ability as an actor was subject to question and even ridicule, his real-life side at this time was evidently appealing enough to Evelyn Cox for their relationship to be consummated in marriage on October 24, 1903, one day after the groom's thirty-fourth birthday. Like the wives of most coaches, though, the new Mrs. Heisman soon realized that her new role would be primarily that of a "football widow." Heisman now found himself a father, too, for a twelve-year-old stepson came with the marriage.

The remaining games of the 1903 season saw Clemson defeat N.C. State, 24–0; lose to North Carolina, 11–6; shut out Davidson, 24–0—the team's fourth whitewash effort of the season; and vie with a strong Cumberland team for the SIAA championship.

Played in Montgomery on Thanksgiving Day, the match with Cumberland, a small college located at Lebanon, Tennessee, that had earlier defeated powerful Vanderbilt, turned out to be a thriller when Clemson made a great second-half comeback. During the first half, Clemson was never really in the game due mainly to the formidable line play of the Bridges brothers— giants in their day at 6 feet 4 inches—and a big center named "Red" Smith, who was all over the field backing up the Cumberland line on defense. Clemson had been outweighed before, but certainly not like this. As one reporter who witnessed the game put it: "The Clemson players seemed mere dwarfs as they lined up for the kickoff. To the crowd on the sidelines it didn't seem that Heisman's charges could possibly do more than give a gallant account of themselves in a losing battle."[58]

And as expected, by the end of the first half Cumberland, having forced the Tigers into a defensive game, found itself ahead by a comfortable 11–0 score. So by now the main question on the minds of most onlookers was just how large the final Cumberland point total was going to be. But the never-say-die Heisman evidently charged up his players with another of his patented pep talks. For at the start of the second half, Maxwell, the Clemson quarterback, took the kickoff behind his goal and following perfect interference, ran the length of the field for a touchdown. After the goal was kicked, the score stood at 11–6, and Clemson was back in the game.

By this time, too, the brothers Bridges were tiring, and toward the end, with darkness descending, Heisman saw his chance to exploit a weakness in the Cumberland defense: run the ball where the ubiquitous Red Smith wasn't. So the next time Sitton started out on one of his slashing end runs, at the last second he tossed the ball back to the fullback who charged straight ahead over center (where Smith would have been except that he was zeroing in on the elusive Sitton) and went all the way for a tying touchdown. All that now remained between Clemson and the SIAA championship was an extra point. But the kick was missed, and the game ended in an 11–11 tie. Fittingly, the next monumental meeting between Heisman and a Cumberland team would be Georgia Tech's classic runaway game in 1916.

With feelers now starting to come his way from Atlanta, this disappointing outcome must have prompted Heisman to seriously consider whether or not to cast his lot with Georgia Tech. Although he had been coaching now for nearly ten years in the South and had even captured two SIAA championships at Clemson, Heisman was now looking to locate where he could achieve even more recognition. He had built his reputation on taking the most unlikely material and molding it into a smooth-running football machine. Accordingly, the stamina and dedication of his players were established facts. Game reports, in fact, revealed that Heisman took only a half dozen substitutes with him on road trips, and one of his players, J. A. "Pee Wee" Forsythe, a tackle, probably held the endurance record for his day for playing every minute of every Clemson game during 1901–1903. If he could produce championship teams with inferior material, what was he capable of doing with superior players?

Perhaps over the long run, then, the thinness in the ranks of his country-boy players had been the thing that was holding Heisman back from true greatness. What he really needed was more players coming out of high school who were already knowledgeable of the game's finer points instead of the green candidates he had been training from scratch. One of Heisman's classic stories concerning the naïveté of his players occurred at Auburn when one of his country boys reported for football and admitted he had never seen a football game before:

"That's all right," I said after sizing him up and recognizing the possibilities he represented. "When you come upon something you don't understand, just ask me." Presently he came to me and said: "Mr. Heisman, I've been hearing the fellows talking about the first half and the second half and what's puzzling me is, how many halves do you have in this game anyway?"[59]

With Virginia and Tennessee as model states, football had helped build up the high-school sports system in the South, and finally it was beginning to spread. Heisman could possibly have realized that moving to a metropolitan area like Atlanta would be a step in the right direction as far as recruiting more quality material was concerned.

Then, too, at this point in his young coaching career, Heisman knew he was at a crossroads. College football, in spite of its problems, was becoming an integral force in the American sporting scene, and because of his intense love of the game, he undoubtedly wanted to be where he could do the most good in helping promote it. In seeing to it that he was sought out for the right place at the right time, Heisman was his own best press agent. As sportswriter Joe Williams noted, Heisman was never "suffocatingly modest,"[60] and whenever he put pen to paper, he was not only extolling the accomplishments of the school where he was coaching but those of John Heisman as well. For example, in 1903, he identified the qualifications of a winning coach—knowledge of the game, teaching ability, inspirational leadership, maintenance of physical conditioning, and knowing the capability of his players:

In the light of these required qualifications, it is small wonder that successful coaches—i.e., those who can consistently turn out winning teams year after year no matter what the obstacles and conditions—are few and far between, and when found it is equally small wonder that they command salaries practically without limit.

At Clemson we have a style of football play radically different from any other on earth. Its notoriety and the fear and admiration of it have spread throughout the length and breadth of the entire Southern world of football and even further.... Three wonderfully successful seasons of "Heisman Football" have served to establish the system as Clemson's traditional policy of play.[61]

With "Heisman Football" now a marketable product, its progenitor's intent was to promote his commodity in true go-getter fashion—that is, to use its salability to enhance his own professional reputation. The promotional pamphlet Heisman had put together earlier was clearly in this vein, and one of the more noteworthy endorsements it contained was that of Walter Riggs, president of the Clemson Athletic Association and then vice-president of the SIAA. He expressed the following sentiments about the inventor of Heisman Football:

In my opinion [John Heisman] is the best football coach in the South or, indeed, in the whole country. His strategy is of the highest order, and as a predictor of opponent's [sic] movements and an ingenious deviser of modes of defense he is a wonder. His systems of play are classic, far above anything encountered in the South. Rapid and varied movements, ability to keep opponents always guessing, and a desire on the part of his men to risk all to win—these qualities have made his coaching well-nigh phenomenal. As a disciplinarian I have never seen his equal; he commands and receives, with cheerful compliance, absolute obedience. We hope that no college will be able to take him from us.[62]

But Riggs's hope that his charismatic coach would stay on at Clemson was to no avail, as Georgia Tech ultimately succeeded in luring Heisman to Atlanta for the then princely sum of $2,000 per year plus 30 percent of the net gate receipts for both baseball and football. (Heisman's salary during his final year at Clemson was reputed to be $1,800.) Heisman's contention that "successful coaches . . . command salaries practically without limit" had been put to the test in his negotiations with Tech, as the sterling 19–3–2 record he had compiled at Clemson as well as the one-sided defeats his teams had administered to the Tech team provided sufficient leverage to secure the lucrative contract.

There were other positive points Heisman must have considered in moving to Tech. Having played many of his matches in Atlanta since his Auburn days, he was well-enough acquainted with the city to realize that urban life afforded numerous cultural advantages. Also the fact that he now had a family—a wife along with a stepson—to support made taking any available opportunity to supplement his income more mandatory. His wife also had family ties with Cherokee County, Georgia, north of Atlanta. In a sense, then, the move was a kind of homecoming for Evelyn Heisman. So the chance to associate with still another athletically ambitious school, but one in a fast-growing metropolitan area, had to be naturally appealing to Heisman. And for someone of his cosmopolitan bent, the city was the natural place to be, the place where momentous things were happening during this time in the country's history.

Nevertheless, it had not been easy for Georgia Tech to recruit Heisman. In fact, had it not been for the campaign efforts of a Tech alumnus and current faculty member named Frank Turner, Heisman might have stayed on at Clemson or taken another more financially rewarding position, which was really what he was after at this point in his career. In fact, Lyman Hall, the president of Georgia Tech, had not made the coaching job seem altogether enticing in his meeting and correspondence with Heisman, for in his letter of November 12, 1903 offering the job, he was somewhat noncommittal and even careless enough to misspell the prospective coach's name.

Clearly it was time for someone with the drive of a Frank Turner to step in and take action, and according to Georgia Tech historian Robert Wallace that is precisely what happened. After convincing the faculty and student body that Tech should get into big-time athletics, Turner spearheaded a fund drive to recruit Heisman as their head football coach:

The success of the fund drive helped Turner convince Heisman to leave Clemson for Tech after President Hall's lukewarm letter had failed to excite the coach about the school's coaching vacancy. Before the contract was signed, Turner—who eventually became the first graduate manager of athletics—had to make a couple of trips to South Carolina to talk to Heisman and convince him that the floundering athletic program was a challenge he couldn't resist.[63]

Turner's dogged efforts paid off, even though Heisman, ever the one for dramatics, did not wire his acceptance until the day after President Hall's specified deadline of November 25, 1903. Upon hearing the news, Tech students were so elated that during their Thanksgiving Day game with South Carolina they strung up an intimidating banner proclaiming, "TECH GETS HEISMAN FOR 1904." The Heisman era at Georgia Tech had gotten off on a typically theatrical note even before the star of the show had come on stage.

THE NATIONAL SCENE (1900–1903)

As it had been throughout the 1890s, the overall mood of the country at the turn of the century was one compounded of boundless energy and supreme confidence. The brief but decisive Spanish-American War of 1898 had turned in America's favor, producing a cadre of honored military heroes and the undeniable feeling among most Americans that the American way was the best way; indeed to many, America's way was God's way. That America was divinely blessed was attested to by the country's soaring economic progress resulting from the expansion and productivity of business and industry during the last quarter of the nineteenth century as well as the numerous technological advances of the day—in particular, the revolutionary inventions that were transforming the life-styles of the American people.

Although it still had a long way to go as a practical tool, the telephone was becoming fairly well entrenched by the start of the new century, a significant step toward drawing the country closer together. The capability of controlling electrical energy now made it possible to expand opportunities and services in the areas of home life, entertainment, business and industry, and even sporting events, primarily through more efficient power sources. The motor car was also becoming an adjunct to American social life, and in Heisman's last year at Clemson, the first continental crossing of the United States by automobile was accomplished. In the same year came the incorporation of the Ford Motor Company, whose mass production methods would transform the country both socially and economically. That same year also saw the most world-shaking achievement of all—the first flight of the Wright brothers and the birth of air travel, the repercussions of which are still being felt today.

It was a fabulous time to be alive, provided one had the wherewithal to maintain a comfortable level of living. Whatever the ills of society at large—and there were many—the American political philosophy referred to as Progressivism existed to make things right. Or so most everyone thought. Although the predominantly agrarian South of Heisman's day had its share of economic and social problems, its isolation made it seem fairly immune to many of the problematic issues that had affected urban areas—dire poverty, mounting labor concerns, the influx of immigrants, and the suffrage question, to name some of the more pervasive. But in a country of over sixty million people of which seven million were black (most of whom resided in the South), it would not be until the second half of the century that the nation's social conscience would fully awaken. In this earlier time, America was a country where social responsibility was held in check by a simplistic philosophy of life that emphasized the intrinsic worth of the individual and one's special capabilities for achieving success, no matter what the circumstances of one's background. It was thought that every American had the potential to realize the rewards of the American Dream. Therefore, anyone could get ahead in life if he but tried.

Having become part of the ideology of the American public school system, this socialization process was most dramatically exemplified in intercollegiate athletics and the coaching philosophies of men like Amos Alonzo Stagg and John Heisman. They saw individual success in sports as the measure of a man's worth off the field as well as on. Even black athletes had begun to prove the supposed validity of this outlook during the 1890s through their limited but quality performances on eastern football teams. Denied participation on the segregated southern college teams, some outstanding players migrated to the North to realize their full potential. As noted earlier, one of them was William Henry Lewis, who went to Amherst and later Harvard, where he was named the center on Walter Camp's All-America teams in 1892 and 1893. (In the early 1900s Lewis was an assistant football coach at Harvard, probably the first black man in the history of intercollegiate athletics to fill such a position.) Soon after the establishment of black institutions in the South with their industrial training missions, these schools started fielding their own teams. But from a national perspective the day of the black athlete would not come into its own until the 1960s. The black athletes of this later day would succeed to a degree that people around the turn of the century would never have dreamed possible.

That sports were becoming a social force in American life was affirmed by Vice-President Theodore Roosevelt (soon to be president upon the assassination of William McKinley in 1901), in word as well as deed. Athletically active himself, Roosevelt saw the college athletic field as a necessary training ground for the youth of this country who would become its future leaders. The outspoken enemy of any negative force, foreign or domestic, that sought to undermine the American way, Roosevelt stood up for the virtues of what he termed the "strenuous life," which he made public in a notable speech in 1899. Its summation was highly prophetic:

The twentieth century looms before us big with the fate of many nations. If we stand idly by, if we seek merely swollen, slothful ease, and ignoble peace, if we shrink from the hard contests where men must win at hazard of their lives and at the risk of all they hold dear, then the bolder and stronger peoples will pass us by and will win for themselves the domination of the world. Let us therefore boldly face the life of strife, resolute to do our duty well and manfully. . . . Above all, let us shrink from no strife, moral or physical, within or without the nation, provided we are certain that the strife is justified; for it is only through strife, through hard and dangerous endeavor, that we shall ultimately win the goal of true national greatness.[64]

It was a social philosophy that could easily have emanated from the football field, which had greatly inspired Roosevelt, a Harvard man, in the choice of many of his metaphors. It was the kind of philosophy, too, that John Heisman certainly subscribed to. Even though the game of football was in serious trouble during the 1890s and the early part of the twentieth century, both Heisman and Roosevelt, as proponents of the "strenuous life," would eventually play significant roles in saving the game from itself. During the early years of the new century, Heisman, as one of football's most active promoters, would build toward his greatest success as a football coach and become an "ardent admirer and supporter of Teddy Roosevelt and the Bull Moose party."[65] Roosevelt, as a supporter of football and of Heisman's push to make the forward pass an integral part of the game, was naturally sensitive to whatever changes the game needed to open it up and free itself from the inherent brutality that had characterized intercollegiate football from its inception.

THE NATIONAL GAME (1900–1903)

Since 1893, which had been the roughest year in intercollegiate competition up to that time, various rule changes had been implemented to lessen the game's rougher aspects, as we have seen. But other important steps toward eliminating mass interference plays occurred in 1896, when rules were introduced that commanded five men to be on the line of scrimmage and that an offensive player could not take more than one step without coming to a full stop before the ball was put in play. Another rule in the same vein was established in 1902, stipulating that seven men had to be on the offensive line between the 25-yard lines; and in 1903, any back who first handled the ball could run forward with it as long as he was five yards from the center. This change supplanted the old rule dictating that a quarterback could not run with the ball until another player touched it. In spite of all these rule changes, though, the game was still terribly rough by any standard, and football's survival was in jeopardy in the years just ahead.

That college football was still growing in popularity around the turn of the century, though, was confirmed by the ever-increasing attendance at popular matchups. Played as the last game of the year for the first time, the Yale–Harvard game of 1900 determined the national championship (won by Yale, as usual) and attracted over twenty thousand spectators. It was only natural, then, that by 1903, Harvard dedicated a significant monument to its own overall gridiron success—the largest reinforced steel and concrete stadium in the world at the time. Seating close to sixty thousand, the Harvard Stadium was America's first football coliseum, presaging the day of big-time college football that would take the nation by storm in just a few years. By 1914, both Yale and Princeton had their own stadiums, but the Yale Bowl outdid them all at this time with its seating capacity of seventy-five thousand.

It was estimated that by 1896 approximately five thousand school and college football games were being played across the country on Thanksgiving Day, not only attesting to football's growing popularity but revealing that such events had been elevated to glamorous social spectacles that could be attended by males and females alike. The epitome of the Thanksgiving Day game as social event was the game played in New York City, usually between Princeton and Yale, with area socialites in prominent attendance among the forty thousand spectators at the Polo Grounds. Big-game football weekends provided women with a grand opportunity to show off the fashionable finery of the day and to be around men in a socially acceptable sphere of activity. The popular conception of the sophisticated, independent woman known as the Gibson Girl was rapidly becoming a fact of life at this time. (John Heisman himself had dared to marry an actress, the kind of woman who a generation before would have been socially unacceptable, and in many circles still was.) Also with college alumni rolls swelling across the nation, many schools recognized that athletic events like big-game football rivalries represented a way not only to keep in touch with alumni but to gain their financial support. The times were ripe for football's expansion, and as a significant social attraction, the game had begun to vie with vaudeville and the theater as a popular source of entertainment. With a ready-made audience awaiting, the main thing college football coaches had to do now to hold their followers' interest and support was produce a winner. Under this kind of pressure, increased professionalization of the game was inevitable.

While Heisman was enjoying his success at Clemson there were some big winners coming to the fore in the Midwest. In 1900, physician Dr. Henry Williams left Penn, where he had been a devotee of George Woodruff, and went to Minnesota, where he devised the tackle-back formation and won the Western Conference title with an unbeaten record that included two ties.

Just two years later in 1902, Nebraska wound up unbeaten, untied, and unscored on in ten games, while Amos Alonzo Stagg was experimenting with the unbalanced line at Chicago with great success.

But during the period 1901–1905, the coach at the University of Michigan named Fielding Yost overshadowed the accomplishments of practically everyone else. Having coached successfully at Kansas before arriving at Michigan, Yost had performed as a tramp athlete when he "transferred" from West Virginia to Lafayette in 1896 to play against the Penn dynasty. In one of that day's biggest upsets, Lafayette defeated the Quakers, 6–4. At Michigan, in the first five years of the 1900s, Yost produced a dynasty of teams that compiled an astounding 55–0–1 record, scoring 2,821 points to only 40 for their opposition. Because the 1901–1905 teams averaged more than 560 points a season they earned the apt epithet of "point a minute." Yost's 1901 and 1902 teams would be the first from outside the East to win national championships. Stressing speed over brawn to wear down an opponent (heretofore brute force had been a trademark of Midwestern teams), Yost, an intense, straitlaced man, picked up the nickname "Hurry Up" by training his men to start up a play even before the opposing team had recovered from the previous play. Made to order for this kind of attack was a powerful, fleet-footed All-American halfback named Willie Heston, who in his four years of play scored an astounding ninety-three touchdowns, still a national record.

Although the official records reveal that the January 1, 1916 contest between Brown and Washington State was the first game to be played in the Rose Bowl series, Yost's great 1901 Michigan team had been invited to Pasadena to play Stanford on January 1, 1902, in what was actually the prototypical game for the Rose Bowl. Sponsored by the Tournament of Roses Association and played before over eight thousand spectators, this game undoubtedly provided the group with the seminal idea for an annual affair, in spite of Stanford's embarrassing 49–0 loss to the team from the Midwest. (The game turned out to be so one-sided that it was called at the request of Stanford with ten minutes still left to be played.)

In 1903, Princeton was recognized as national champion, but Minnesota had helped out Princeton's cause by tying Michigan, 6–6, thus ending the Wolverines' twenty-nine-game winning streak. This was also the game that started these two teams playing for the Little Brown Jug, one of the more popular traditions that grew out of this era of increased rivalries in college football. However, the precedent for one of football's greatest traditions— the post-season bowl game—was the most significant introduced during this period. Although it took some years for the concept to catch on, the early years of the Rose Bowl saw only the strong teams of the East and Midwest receiving invitations to play. As football powers, the teams of the Far West, Southwest, and South were yet to have their day in the sun. As far as John Heisman was concerned, though, his move to Georgia Tech presented him a ripe opportunity to see to it that the South would have its day—although not as soon as he would have liked.

NOTES

1. See Gene Griessman, "The Coach," in *The Heisman: A Symbol of Excellence* by John T. Brady (New York: Atheneum, 1984), 21.

2. "Who's He and Why?" (Heisman profile in Georgia Tech student magazine) *The Yellow Jacket* (March 1913): 418–21.

3. See J. H. Nichols, "50 Years of Football," *Oberlin Alumni Magazine* (1941).

4. David P. Simpson, "Historical Sketches of Athletics at Oberlin," *Oberlin Alumni Magazine* 10, no. 6 (March 1914): 161–62.

5. John Durant and Les Etter, *Highlights of College Football* (New York: Hastings House, 1970), 72. Yale and Princeton produced most of these "missionary" coaches, but Harvard and Penn turned out their share, too. That the East was still showing the way in training innovations was evidenced by the contributions of Harvard's captain Arthur Cumnock in 1890, which included the startup of spring practice, stressing calisthenics for warming up, the use of a tackle dummy, and the invention of the nose guard, as ineffectual as it may have been.

6. Quoted in Nichols, "50 Years of Football."

7. John W. Heisman, "The Thundering Herd," *Collier's*, October 13, 1928, 13.

8. Ibid., 59.

9. John W. Heisman, "Between Halves," *Collier's*, November 17, 1928, 18.

10. Heisman, "The Thundering Herd," 13.

11. John W. Heisman, "Look Sharp Now!" *Collier's*, November 3, 1928, 19.

12. John W. Heisman, "Signals," *Collier's*, October 6, 1928, 31.

13. John W. Heisman, "Inventions in Football," *The Baseball Magazine* 1, no. 6 (October 1908): 40–42.

14. A. I. Spanton, ed. *Fifty Years of Buchtel, 1870–1920* (Akron, Ohio: Buchtel Alumni Association, 1922), 244.

15. Ibid., 247.

16. Heisman, "The Thundering Herd," 13.

17. Heisman, "Hold 'em!" *Collier's*, October 27, 1928, 50.

18. Ibid.

19. Heisman, "The Thundering Herd," 13.

20. See Charles J. P. Bourget, "Poet Beyond the Sea," in *This Was America*, ed. Oscar Handlin (New York: Harper and Row, 1964), 370–83.

21. John W. Heisman, "Fast and Loose," *Collier's*, October 20, 1928, 54.

22. Heisman, "Signals," 31.

23. Ibid., 13, 31.

24. The letter, dated February 23, 1894, read in part: "The main object should not be to win in the contests in which the clubs may participate, but to minister to the physical development of those engaged in the exercise." We can well imagine Heisman's indignation at receiving what amounted to a pointed criticism of himself and his coaching methods. See Spanton, *Fifty Years of Buchtel*, 246.

25. George W. Knepper, *New Lamps for Old* (Akron, Ohio: University of Akron

Centennial, 1970), 71. Centennial publication on the one-hundredth anniversary of the University of Akron.

26. See Griessman, "The Coach," 27.

27. Heisman would eventually make use of such laudatory comments in a promotional pamphlet he had printed to publicize his qualifications as a coach: "Announcement of Mr. John W. Heisman, Football and Baseball Coach," seven-page pamphlet, privately printed, from the early 1900s. That Oberlin still thinks highly of its first football coach is attested to by the establishment in 1978 of the John Heisman Club, an organization of alumni and supporters whose aim is to keep both the academic and athletic programs as strong as possible through the recruitment of scholar athletes.

28. This would place Stagg at Springfield during the same time that another inventive spirit was on hand, Dr. James Naismith of the local YMCA, who came up with basketball as an indoor sport to be played during the winter months. It would go on to rival, but not outdo, football as a popular intercollegiate sport.

29. Quoted in Allison Danzig, *Oh, How They Played the Game* (New York: Macmillan, 1971), 29.

30. Ibid., 37.

31. Heisman, "The Thundering Herd," 13.

32. Richard J. Storr, *Harper's University: The Beginnings* (Chicago: University of Chicago Press, 1966), 179.

33. John McCallum, *Southeastern Conference Football* (New York: Scribners, 1980), 4.

34. Bob Gutkowski, ed., *The College Game* (Indianapolis: Bobbs-Merrill, 1974), 60.

35. McCallum, *Southeastern Conference Football*, 31.

36. John W. Heisman, "Rules Rush In," *Collier's*, 10 November 1928, 42.

37. Edwin Pope, *Football's Greatest Coaches* (Atlanta, Ga.: Tupper and Love, 1956), 122–23.

38. Although he was unsure of the dates that Warner used the hidden-ball trick at Carlisle, Heisman recorded his own use of it in an apologetic manner in later years:

> The hidden-ball trick which the Carlisle Indians played successfully on Harvard about 1898 or 1899 first originated with me, I believe; though I take no great pride in the matter as I used the play but one year, coming to the conclusion that it was a play open to question from the standpoint of pure and clean sportsmanship. (Heisman, "Inventions in Football," 41.) [Actually, Warner used the play as late as 1903 against Harvard.]

39. See Al Thomy, *The Ramblin' Wreck: A Story of Georgia Tech Football* (Huntsville, Ala.: Strode Publishers, 1973), 42.

40. John W. Heisman, "Fast and Loose," *Collier's*, October 20, 1928, 14.

41. Heisman, "Signals," 31.

42. Heisman, "The Thundering Herd," 60.

43. Pope, *Football's Greatest Coaches*, 122.

44. L. F. "Fuzzy" Woodruff, *History of Southern Football*, vol. 1 (Atlanta, Ga.: Georgia Southern, 1928), 100–101.

45. Heisman's letter appeared in the *Birmingham Age-Herald*, December 4, 1899.

46. Taylor's reply appeared in the *Birmingham Age-Herald*, December 5, 1899.

47. Heisman rebutted in the *Birmingham Age-Herald*, December 8, 1899.

48. Griessman, "The Coach," 24.

49. "Announcement of Mr. John W. Heisman," privately printed pamphlet.

50. Heisman, "The Thundering Herd," 13.

51. Heisman, "Fast and Loose," 15.

52. Wright Bryan, *Clemson: An Informal History of the University, 1889–1979* (Columbia, S.C.: R. L. Bryan Co., 1979), 38.

53. Woodruff, *History of Southern Football*, Vol I, 103.

54. Heisman, "The Thundering Herd," 59.

55. John W. Heisman, "Hero Stuff," *Collier's*, November 2, 1929, 18.

56. For a full account of this incident, see Bryan, *Clemson: An Informal History*, 76–77.

57. Thomy, *The Ramblin' Wreck*, 35.

58. Woodruff, *History of Southern Football*, Vol I, 152.

59. Heisman, "The Thundering Herd," 60.

60. Joe Williams, "Heisman Knew Football," *New York World-Telegram*, October 1936.

61. Quoted in Joe Sherman, *Clemson Tigers: A History of Clemson Football* (Columbia, S.C.: R. L. Bryan Co., 1976), 8–9.

62. This quote, dated July 2, 1902, is from Heisman's privately printed pamphlet cited at note 49, above.

63. Robert B. Wallace, *Dress Her in White and Gold: A Biography of Georgia Tech* (Atlanta: Georgia Tech Foundation, 1969), 51.

64. Quoted in Oliver Jensen, ed., *The Nineties* (New York: American Heritage, 1967), 84.

65. "Who's He and Why?" 418–21.

3

Heisman and the Coming of the Forward Pass (1904–1911)

Heisman's worth was never better displayed than when he left a college. He departed from Auburn and pretty soon Auburn's football glory went glimmering. He departed from Clemson in 1903 and from the minute of his departure Clemson dwindled as a football power. He came to Georgia Tech the next year and Tech promptly arose from a team of tertiary importance in a football way, to a football power that must be reckoned with and finally to a position of undisputed domination in the Southern section.

> —L. F. "Fuzzy" Woodruff,
> *History of Southern Football* (1928)

The addition of Tech's first full-time football coach, John Heisman, the erudite, creative, colorful genius of the sport, was probably the move that made more impression on the outside world than any other appointment in the history of the school.

> —Robert B. Wallace, Jr.,
> *Dress Her in White and Gold: A Biography of Georgia Tech* (1969)

HEISMAN AT GEORGIA TECH (1904–1905)

Although his Auburn and Clemson teams had played numerous times there, John Heisman probably never gave a passing thought to the notion that one day he would actually be living in Atlanta. Affording a variety of cultural attractions, Atlanta also presented a great many acting opportunities for both himself and his wife. And because of his own natural desire to write, he realized that such a cosmopolitan city could provide numerous opportunities for publishing. So it was that in February, 1904, Heisman and his new bride moved into a house on Ponce de Leon Avenue in one of the city's more respectable neighborhoods near the Tech campus. Evelyn's son, Carlisle Cox, came with them, of course, and although the boy had disapproved of his mother's marriage in the beginning, the new father, or "Cousin Jack" as he was referred to by his young charge, soon won the boy over.

The Atlanta that John Heisman and his family settled in at this time was a city that had literally risen from the ashes of the Civil War, as only forty years before, General Sherman's troops had left the city in smoking ruins. By 1900, however, the population had grown to ninety thousand, and by the time of Heisman's departure some twenty years later, Atlanta's population would have nearly doubled in size. With the expansion of the railroad system throughout the South, Atlanta, by virtue of its strategic location, was destined to become a major railroad hub as well as a financial center and distribution point for the Southeast. And, naturally, its centrality as a railroad city was one reason a large number of college football games were scheduled there during this time.

Work had recently begun on another dynamic symbol of the new South, the Candler Building at the corner of Peachtree and Houston streets. When it was completed in 1906 its seventeen stories of skyscraper opulence were a graphic advertisement for Atlanta's resurgence as a city. Asa G. Candler, for whom the building was named, was something of a symbol himself. Having acquired the rights to a soft-drink formula, he had established the Coca-Cola Company in 1892, through which he soon parlayed his modest investment into a fabulous fortune. In promoting the soft drink that would become a national habit, another go-getter of the day had made his mark, and the name Candler soon became part of the Atlanta heritage.

At the time of Heisman's arrival, the history of the school known popularly as Georgia Tech had been a brief one. Established in 1885 by legislative act, the Georgia School of Technology had had a difficult time coming into being, due mainly to the University of Georgia's desire to have the proposed technological school made an integral part of its own campus in Athens. Like the states of Alabama and South Carolina, Georgia placed a high premium on technological education as a key factor in helping build the new South. Nathaniel Harris, a Macon attorney, had actually won a seat in the state legislature campaigning for the establishment of a state-supported technological school. Because of his diligent work toward this end during the early 1880s, it is Harris who deserves most of the credit for the eventual establishment of Georgia Tech. The University of Georgia, with its well-entrenched departments of physics, chemistry, and agriculture, believed it had a natural right to absorb the new school into its own operations. And although various cities and towns throughout the state put in their bids for the school, Athens had more reason to fight against having a state-supported school established in another area, especially in the fast-growing city of

Atlanta, which would create more competition for legislative funding support. Nonetheless, by 1887, Atlanta had won out as the locale for the school, and nine acres of land in what was then the outskirts of the city were acquired for the startup of the Georgia School of Technology. The matriculation of its first class commenced in October, 1888. (Not until 1948 was the name changed to the Georgia Institute of Technology.) Although in the beginning it was organized and administered as a branch of the University of Georgia, the school soon evolved into an increasingly autonomous entity deserving a separate identity and separate funding. Indeed, by the time of Heisman's arrival in 1904, political relations with Athens had become steadily more competitive as the upstart Atlanta school had grown in size and reputation. It was a situation that helped fire the natural athletic rivalry between the two schools, particularly on the gridiron. But Georgia failed to beat Georgia Tech in six tries following Heisman's appointment, and it was not until 1910 that the Bulldogs recorded their first win over a Tech team. During John Heisman's tenure as coach the Atlanta school would put itself on the map, both as a school and as a football power.

Actually, had it not been for the energy and determination of one man, football might have taken a long time to catch on at Georgia Tech. In 1893, Captain Leonard Wood, a medical officer at nearby Fort McPherson, had enrolled in a course at the Atlanta school—not necessarily to broaden himself but rather for the express purpose of playing football. The 1892 team, the school's first, had lost all its games, so Wood figured he was the man destined to set the true course for Tech football. Having earned an M.D. degree at Harvard in 1884, he was familiar with the eastern style of play, while as a professional military man he had served successfully in the West as an Indian fighter. Apparently, the rugged military flavor of football appealed to the action-oriented nature of Leonard Wood.

As Tech's first football captain and its first unofficial coach, Wood challenged the University of Georgia to a match in 1893. To his everlasting fame among Tech supporters, he produced a decisive 28–6 win over the Athens team. However, Wood's military career soon sent him on to other ventures—the irrepressible Wood eventually became a founder of Teddy Roosevelt's Rough Riders, Army Chief of Staff, and even a presidential candidate in 1920—and Tech's football program foundered. Before Heisman's arrival, in fact, Tech had compiled a dismally poor record of only eight wins in forty-five games after eleven years of competition. Only the unbeaten 1901 team with its 4–0–1 season had enjoyed any success.

Realizing that to build a winning football team at Georgia Tech would be no easy task, John Heisman went right to work in his usual no-nonsense manner to create a winning environment. As the school lacked a playing field, he first set his sights on securing one, recognizing, of course, that the clause in his contract giving him 30 percent of the gate would not amount to very much without a home field to play on. Even after obtaining a seven-year lease on a parcel of land from a local real estate company, Heisman did not see his plan to construct an athletic complex for both football and baseball taking shape until the winter of 1905. To clear the leased land of stumps and undergrowth, he had the city put to work a large group of convicts, while the Tech students themselves were sufficiently inspired to build a wooden grandstand along the steep bank that flanked the field as well as a fence to enclose the entire area. The low-lying field, which was then referred to as the Flats, formed part of what was to become the present-day Bobby Dodd Stadium. By the time the 1905 baseball season opened, Tech athletes found themselves with a brand-new diamond and gridiron awaiting play.

Heisman's baseball teams at Tech were as well-coached as his football teams; the 1906 team, led by pitcher Ed LaFitte, who would wind up in the Majors, won the Southern championship with a 14–3 record. Tech would also capture the 1909 baseball championship.

As he had done in all his previous appointments, Heisman made his presence known among both students and players right from the start. He was now a bona fide professional coach, highly motivated to achieve the goal of competitive excellence in his own inimitable way. In holding to his football conditioning theories, he put his men through fast-paced practices, even requiring them to run extra laps that a manager was appointed to keep a record of. One of his later players recalled:

> There was nothing easy about a Heisman practice. At the time there was a 40-foot hill right behind the athletic offices, and there were two trenches, about waist high. We'd run up one trench, make a circle, and come down the other one until we were exhausted.
> Heisman demanded few calisthenics. Mostly it was running up and down that hill and scrimmages, about two hours of scrimmaging and dummy drills.[1]

He also enforced strict training rules that some of his players later said were actually a reflection of the man's own peculiar prejudices. They were ordered to take only cold showers after practice with warm showers permitted only after a game. As far as the training table was concerned, Heisman forbade the consumption of pastry, coffee, pork, veal, cabbage, hot bread, nuts, and apples mainly because, as his players recalled, these things disagreed with Heisman himself, and, of course, he considered his players as extensions of himself. The water allowance on the practice field was strictly rationed, and meat, usually roast beef, was served practically raw on the assumption that such half-cooked fare would make his men tougher. One of Georgia Tech's early football players, who ironically was on Turner's committee that actively sought out Heisman as the school's first full-time coach, later observed: "I never really liked him too much. He was too rough and too demanding. But, being realistic about it, the football process was new, and I imagine it needed a coach like Heisman."[2]

In terms of on-field success, this latter surmise proved correct, as Heisman's regimented coaching style paid off with an 8–1–1 record chalked up by his first Tech team in 1904. Highlights of the season included wins over the University of Florida (77–0), just then starting out playing the game; Tennessee (2–0); Georgia (23–6); and Cumberland (18–0). But the match with Heisman's previous school, Clemson, ended in an 11–11 tie while his other southern school, Auburn, with new coach Mike Donahue at the helm, shut him out, 12–0.

The Tennessee contest on October 22 of that year was a grueling affair in which Heisman's disciplined training was the determining factor. After a scoreless first half, Tech drove to the Volunteer 3-yard line, where it gave up the ball on downs. After two futile shots at the line, Tennessee dropped back to punt, but the kick was blocked and recovered by the Volunteers behind the goal for a Tech safety, the only points of the game.

Since Tech had never beaten Auburn, supporters had hoped that Heisman would come up with a victory his first time out. But not only did Tech lose, the game marked the first time in Heisman's football career that a team of his did not make a single first down. One questionable feature of this game that gave the Tech team problems was Donahue's "hike" play, in which a big lineman, as the ball carrier, was dragged or pushed along by a backfield man for whatever first-down yardage was needed. (This tactic would soon be declared illegal.) In spite of Heisman's nearly miraculous success in beginning anew at a different school, the Auburn match revealed that there was a human side to the man's coaching. In effect, there was still plenty of work ahead to get Georgia Tech up to the competitive level of schools like Auburn and Clemson, whose gridiron reputation Heisman had played such a big role in building. Tech supporters in the meantime would learn to cultivate a degree of patience in awaiting their team's day in the sun.

Another bizarre incident involving a Heisman team occurred that year in the game against Georgia, which was played in Atlanta's Piedmont Park. (All of Tech's 1904 home games were scheduled there while Heisman planned for his new campus athletic complex.) At one point in the game, the Georgia punter dropped back behind his goal line to punt, but his kick struck the goalpost and the ball bounded back over the fence behind him. As there was then no rule to cover the situation, the ensuing confusion was not resolved until, following a wild melee, a Tech player leaped over the fence and retrieved the ball for a touchdown!

But if John Heisman had been the reigning master of southern football during his tenures at Auburn and Clemson, he would soon be overshadowed by the accomplishments of two new professional coaches who arrived on the southern scene in 1904: Vanderbilt's Dan McGugin, who had been a lineman at Michigan under Fielding Yost; and Auburn's Mike Donahue, a Yale man.

The two coaches had distinctly contrasting styles of play. Donahue instituted a conservative, eastern approach to the game while McGugin, in line with his midwestern background, took a more open tact, particularly on offense. Along with Heisman, both coaches would help put southern football on the map.

These two coaches and their schools, as well as his old nemesis Sewanee, would give Heisman his biggest headaches during his Tech tenure. Although he would lose only twenty-nine games in sixteen years at Tech, ten of these losses would be to Auburn's Donahue while Tech would lose three of the five games it played against Vanderbilt and McGugin. And in spite of Heisman's overall success at Tech (102 wins from 1904 to 1919), it was soon clear that Auburn's Donahue had Heisman's number, as over the stretch of 1906–1914, Tech won only one match with the Auburn Tigers, losing eight in a row, while three matches with Vanderbilt during this time (1906, 1907, and 1910) resulted in lopsided losses. (Actually, Vanderbilt was the dominant team in the South at this time, regularly winning the SIAA championship.) During these years, five of eight matches would be lost to Sewanee. Thus, eighteen out of Tech's twenty-nine losses would be to just three schools. The losses to Vanderbilt Heisman could readily attribute to the quality players produced by Tennessee's superior secondary/preparatory school system, but the reason for his lack of success against his former school Auburn must have weighed heavily on his mind.

Nevertheless, without either Auburn or Vanderbilt on the 1905 schedule, Heisman's Tech team, which was apparently inspired, too, by at last beginning play on its new home field, turned in an undefeated season of 6–0–1 but conceded the SIAA championship to powerful Vanderbilt. A satisfying 17–10 win over Clemson came early in the season, this after the Tigers, in a brilliant goal-line stand, held Tech for three downs within inches of the goal. (This was the first game in which Chip Robert appeared. Weighing less than 150 pounds, the fleet-footed halfback would become one of Tech's all-time greats.) Other big wins came over Alabama (12–5); Cumberland (15–0), now starting to wane as a southern power; Tennessee (45–0), and Georgia (46–0). The only blemish on the 1905 record was an 18–18 tie with Sewanee, but considering Heisman's poor luck with the Purple a tie had to be something of a moral victory.

The Alabama game turned out to be one of Heisman's most rewarding victories of his early years at Tech. In spite of the brilliant play of Auxford Burks, the Crimson Tide's great back, Tech hung on to win, 12–5. The overworked Burks, who appeared to bear the entire brunt of Alabama's offense, collapsed during the second half and had to be carried off the field. In the Cumberland match, the Tennesseans ran the ball up and down the field throughout the game but made numerous mistakes on which Heisman readily capitalized. One of Heisman's prime dictums, of course, was to make the most of an opponent's errors, and this game served him well in this respect. The decisive victory over Tennessee was the result of plain old-fashioned, pile-driving football. But the game with that other perennially troublesome Tennessee school, Sewanee, saw an entirely different approach that exemplified the exciting possibilities of open-style football. After Tech scored first, the Purple tied it up on a 50-yard run, but Heisman's team took the lead again after a long drive. The score was tied at the half, 12–12, when Sewanee scored on another long run, this one for forty-five yards. Sewanee grabbed the lead for the first time in the second half on a drive of its own, only to have Tech come up with a scoring run of fifty yards to ensure the final 18–18 tie. For the first time, Georgia Tech had made a good showing against this always tough opponent. The lopsided win over Georgia was highlighted by two sensational runs by Tech players, one of ninety-five yards and the other the entire length of the field.

In spite of their success, Tech players knew that a lot of hard work lay ahead under their demanding new coach if they were to develop into the kind of team he envisioned. Although from a national perspective football had considerable public image problems by this time, Heisman had never lost his enthusiasm for the game. Indeed, if anything, his dedication to football had waxed even stronger as its problems proliferated.

THE NATIONAL GAME (1904–1905)

Although certain rule changes were enacted in 1904 to help alleviate the game's brutal aspects, they actually had little impact overall. To counter mass momentum play, the entire field was now covered with five-yard squares to govern the ruling that the first man to receive the ball from the center had to be five yards behind the line before running forward. Six men were now stationed on the line, and the field goal was reduced in value from 5 to 4 points. Significantly enough, this marked the first time that a touchdown was worth more than a field goal.

In spite of its critics, football continued to grow in popularity. Penn, with its 12–0, unscored-on record, was considered the national champion. The team was coached by Dr. Carl Williams, who succeeded George Woodruff in 1902 and who had been one of Heisman's star backs at Oberlin. This team featured the stellar defensive play of its All-American captain, Bob Torrey, whose playing style heralded the arrival of the roving center. In the Midwest, Michigan continued its winning ways under Fielding Yost with an 11–0 record. The Michigan Wolverines fielded a huge—for that time—line, anchored by Adolf "Germany" Schulz, a 245-pound All-American center, while the backfield showcased Willie Heston, a not-necessarily fast but lighting-quick runner, who as a senior brought his touchdown total for his career to an incredible ninety-three.

Meanwhile at Chicago, Amos Alonzo Stagg was still experimenting with various training and strategic innovations that other coaches would soon adopt, such as devising a charging sled for linemen to use in practice and initiating the backfield shift and the quarterback "keeper" play. Minnesota, under Dr. Henry Williams, turned in a perfect 13–0 season and was considered by many to be the national champion, while Nebraska's twenty-seven-game winning streak came to an end at the hands of Colorado, 6–0. As regional pride helped rivalries increase in intensity, the popularity of the game increased as well.

The year 1905 saw the Chicago–Michigan game that was played in Chicago determine the national champion and attract the largest crowd (25,791) to see a football game in the Midwest up to that time. Still a recognized power, even without the great Willie Heston, Michigan lost on a safety, 2–0, in an exciting, fiercely contested match that even found Walter Camp in attendance. His presence was further testimony to the fact that midwestern football had arrived. Back east, though, the Harvard–Yale game, won by the Yale Bulldogs, 6–0, attracted forty-three thousand fans, the largest football crowd anywhere up to that time.

THE FORWARD PASS WARS (1904–1906)

Rumblings from various quarters over the apparent disregard for player safety continued, however. Although the innovative Glenn Warner introduced the use of fiber-constructed shoulder and thigh pads during this time, deaths and injuries continued to mount. (Heisman also claimed to have invented "thigh protectors" at this same time, as discussed in note 38 of Chapter 1.) In 1904, twenty-one players had been reported killed and over two hundred injured, and a year later twenty-three deaths were recorded along with an astronomical number of debilitating injuries. For all the changes enacted since the 1890s by the Intercollegiate Rules Committee to help rid the game of its inherent brutality, playing football continued to be a barbaric experience in which a player risked life and limb on the field of competition.

Ironically, at a time when football was enduring its most severe criticism, its popular image was at a high peak, as attested to by the reception of Gilbert Patten's stories about super athlete Frank Merriwell and his exploits at Yale, and a veritable deluge of other fiction series for juveniles in which college athletics were prominent. Magazine stories for adults and popular plays of the contemporary New York stage such as George Ade's *The College Widow* (1904) and Rida Johnson Young's *Brown of Harvard* (1906), whose central action revolved around football, also extended the game's popularity. And, of course, game attendance was building unabated.

Nevertheless, since 1893, the most serious attacks on football had been generated by muckraker journalism, which kept appearing in reputable journals like *Nation*, *Harper's*, and *McClure's*, as well as respected newspapers such as the *New York Times*. One of the most vociferous voices during this time was that of Edward L. Godkin, who soundly denounced football because, in his view, "it undermined scholarship, scared away potential students, and attracted depraved elements of society."[3] By 1905, the sound and fury had reached such a pitch that a University of Chicago professor was moved to attack football as "a social obsession—a boy-killing, education-prostituting, gladiatorial sport. It teaches virility and courage, but so does war. I do not know what should take its place, but the new game should not require the services of a physician, the maintenance of a hospital, and the celebration of funerals."[4] For some schools the "new game" was rugby, which California and Stanford wound up substituting for football during the years 1906–1914. (These two perennially athletically minded schools would eventually relent and produce powerful football teams in the 1920s.) During this same time Columbia discontinued football as did Northwestern, although for only two years. Some members of the Western Conference (Big Ten) conceded by cutting their schedules in half. Clearly, the antifootball movement was becoming national in scope.

But it was Henry Beech Needham's two-part condemnation of football serialized in *McClure's* in 1905 that spurred President Theodore Roosevelt into taking remedial action. Roosevelt, an avowed supporter of intercollegiate football, summoned representatives from Harvard, Yale, and Princeton to meet with him in October 1905 to discuss how to eliminate the game's rough elements. As a Harvard man himself, Roosevelt was undoubtedly fearful that the school's president, Charles W. Eliot, a confirmed opponent of the game, would take steps to abolish it and do away with one of the President's prized systems for nurturing manhood. While Eliot's public stand denounced football as not only brutal but overly commercial, Roosevelt's attitude toward the abuses that had corrupted the worth of college football was always constructively expressed, as in his Harvard Union address, delivered on February 23, 1907, a year after the legalization of the forward pass. Because preparatory schools had been "able to keep football clean," Roosevelt contended that colleges should be able to follow suit in order to justify the continuation of this "manly sport":

We cannot afford to turn out of college men who shrink from physical effort or from a little physical pain. In any republic courage is a prime necessity for the average citizen if he is to be a good citizen, and he needs physical courage no less than moral courage. . . . Athletics are good, especially in their rougher forms, because they tend to develop such courage. They are good also because they encourage a true democratic spirit.[5]

Even though the upshot of his White House meeting did little more than inform the public that there really were some concerned individuals interested in reforming football's unethical side, Roosevelt's remedial posture would help inspire concerned coaches like John Heisman and set the stage for important later meetings on a national scale. These meetings would be designed to review the rules and enact new ones, with the intent to do away with football's overly brutal elements. Despite the problems football was facing, many educators were beginning to accept football as an integral part of campus life by this time, choosing

to compromise their views or even to revel in the new prominence their institutions enjoyed each fall. Emerging from the gray decades of the late 1800s into an era of larger student bodies and increased public interest in higher education, it was easy to conclude that football was somehow responsible, if only partially so. And despite the outraged cries of a few, one could agree with a certain validity (as some still do) that the sport contributed much to college life.[6]

As a result, two opposing camps concerning the future of football had formed: those who sought ways to keep football a part of college life and those who would do away with it altogether. One person who was influential enough to help resolve the game's problems was Walter Camp, whose long-time membership on the Intercollegiate Rules Committee had ensured his role as caretaker of the game's healthy development and expansion. Having attended President Roosevelt's White House meeting, he had expressed his sincere interest in developing a cleaner game. As one observer put it, however, Camp was an "able diplomat [who] deftly steered football around the shoals of public criticism and intercollegiate squabbles without hampering its phe-nomenal growth."[7] In short, Camp's relationship with the game he had nourished from its beginnings had become increasingly conservative as he grew older. He was therefore opposed to any radical rule changes, in par-ticular the proposal of what some referred to as the "dream-like" forward pass, although in some quarters its adoption was gaining momentum.

Ever since the day in Atlanta in 1895 when Auburn coach John Heisman had witnessed the startling results of an illegal forward pass and immediately realized its merits and possibilities in helping to open up the game, he had been its champion. But it was not until 1903, while he was still at Clemson, that he started actively campaigning for adoption of the forward pass, se-curing the support of many worthy contemporaries. Among those who sup-ported Heisman's radical proposal were Navy coach Paul Dashiell, former Penn standout John Bell, Amos Alonzo Stagg, and then Clemson coach Eddie Cochems. In advocating adoption of the forward pass, Heisman wrote di-rectly to the keeper of the rules, Walter Camp himself. As Heisman reflected:

Remembering the desperate fling of that tired boy from North Carolina I wrote to Walter Camp, chairman of the Rules Committee. Here was a way to open up the game we loved too much to see proscribed. The forward pass would scatter the mob. With the forward pass speed would supplant bull strength. Lighter, faster men would succeed the beefy giants whose crushing weight maimed or killed their opponents.

But after writing, Heisman disclosed that he "got no reply from Mr. Camp." So in spite of "a great hue and cry," the old mass plays resulted in longer "casualty lists," prompting another letter to Camp, but

again he was silent. However, he must have been pondering it because, in 1905, at a meeting of the Rules Committee he spread before the members the forward pass plan with his own excellent restrictions thereof.

The forward pass had been legalized. American football had come over the line which divides the modern game from the old. Whether it was my contribution to football or Camp's is, perhaps, immaterial. Football had been saved from itself.[8]

However, general acceptance of the forward pass did not come about as readily or promptly as Heisman would have us believe. (Not until 1906 was the forward pass finally legalized, and then only after long and arduous debate in a series of significant meetings.) In fact, had it not been for the mounting public pressure brought to bear on the college football establishment to come up with ways to open up the game, the forward pass as a part of football strategy might have been delayed indefinitely. Camp and his followers, who were at first simply too protective and conservative to wholeheartedly endorse anything as radical as the forward pass, eventually yielded to the inevitable.

Accordingly, the meetings that followed Teddy Roosevelt's original entreaty served to keep the key issues before a concerned public who, by now, fully expected some kind of remedial action to be taken. The most auspicious of these gatherings was the national convention of football-playing schools held in New York on December 28, 1905 (the meeting to which Heisman was referring above).[9] With delegates from nearly seventy schools all over the country attending—some determined to abolish the game, others to save it through reform—agreement was finally reached to form a new committee charged to negotiate with Walter Camp's existing Rules Committee and develop necessary resolutions. After considerable behind-the-scenes maneuvering, a master committee (The Intercollegiate Athletic Association) was ultimately organized, which by 1910 would evolve into the National Collegiate Athletic Association (NCAA). Relatively weak in its beginnings, this organization would grow in power over the years as an autocratic interpreter of the rules, particularly as member institutions began to subscribe to more parochial interpretations in lieu of their previous collective outlooks.

The major charges of the original committee were to develop and enforce rules of play and eligibility and to oversee their general administration. A concurrent development of the 1905 convention was the acknowledgment that the academic authorities, whether they liked it or not, were responsible for the integrity of their respective programs. (Unfortunately, this charge would result in a lack of collective purpose and continuing abuses, as each institution sought to either ignore their problems or resolve them as school authorities saw fit.) Since each geographical section of the country had representation on the committee, delegates were asked to submit their personal recommendations for bringing about the desired results. The suggestions of the Washington and Jefferson College delegation are typical of those presented at large: that rules be enacted to encourage the development of playing skills that would help create a more open game, such as requiring ten yards in three downs and adopting some variation of the forward pass; that rough and brutal playing be eliminated by penalizing a guilty player through his dismissal from the game for the rest of the half; and that eligibility rules hold the duration of a player's career to four years and bar professional athletes from play.[10]

While a series of meetings over the next several months were scheduled to discuss the implications of such recommendations and produce rule changes that would help improve the game, the delegates usually wound up in fierce debate and lack of consensus over what was needed to achieve this end. Nevertheless, by the spring of 1906, the committee finally came forth with some significant revisions. Linemen could no longer drop back on offense, since at least six men had to be on the line. There would now be four officials (a referee, two umpires, and a linesman) on the field to help control the game's progress; playing time was reduced to sixty minutes; hurdling and mass momentum plays were strictly prohibited; a neutral zone was established between opposing lines; and a team on the offense would have to gain ten yards in three downs to retain possession of the ball.

Most significantly, the controversial forward pass was legalized, but with the following restrictions (for which Walter Camp was primarily responsible): If an attempted pass fell incomplete on first and second down, a 15-yard penalty would result, and if incomplete on third down, the passing team would lose possession regardless of who recovered the ball. Even passes that had been touched but not caught could be recovered by either side. Also, the ball had to be thrown to only an end or a back from at least five yards behind the line of scrimmage, and it had to cross the line five yards to the right or left of the spot where the ball was put in play.

In spite of these revolutionary changes, the season of 1906 would see teams use the forward pass sparingly, if at all. For most teams, there was simply too much risk involved to even attempt a pass, so teams usually relied on it only as a last resort. Nevertheless, there were sporadic reports of success with this newly acquired offensive weapon, particularly in the Midwest where coaches were more prone to innovate. As to who was the first to use the forward pass, claims vary. Wesleyan University completed a pass against Yale on October 3, 1906 for an 18-yard gain, while Marietta College of Ohio passed for 47 yards and a touchdown against Ohio University about the same time. (As early as December, 1905, prior to the legalization of the forward pass, two Kansas colleges, Fairmont and Washburn, played a game in which they experimented with the uses of the forward pass.)

However, it would appear that the most valid claim to the first official use

of the forward pass is that of St. Louis University, which successfully completed a pass in early September 1906 against Carroll College of Waukesha,
Wisconsin. The St. Louis coach, Eddie Cochems, was, along with Heisman,
among the few who had long recognized the potential of the forward pass
and had been preparing for its advent. In Cochems' own words:

> Of course we developed the pass first, at St. Louis University. I first conceived
> the idea immediately on getting the official football guide of 1906. . . . In 1905, as
> coach at Clemson College, John Heisman (whose place I took when he went to Georgia
> Tech) and I talked over the possibility of having the Rules Committee permit the
> use of the forward pass. . . .
> I took the team [St. Louis] to Lake Beulah, north of Chicago, in July, 1906, for
> the sole purpose of studying and developing the pass.[11]

That Cochems was ahead of his time in realizing what could be done with
this new offensive weapon was attested to by a contemporary sportswriter.
Ed Wray of the *St. Louis Post-Dispatch* described the reaction of a referee who
worked one of Cochems' games in 1906:

> The St. Louis style of pass differs entirely from that in use in the East. There the
> ball is thrown high in the air and the runner who is to catch it is protected by several
> of his teammates forming an interference for him. The St. Louis players shoot the
> ball hard and accurately to the man who is to receive it and the latter is not protected.
> With the high pass, protection is necessary. . . . The fast throw by St. Louis enables
> the receiving player to dodge the opposing players, and it struck me as being all but
> perfect.[12]

At 11–0, St. Louis was even in the running for the national championship
in 1906, but yielded the title to a more reputable school, Princeton, which
finished its season at 9–0–1.

Although the forward pass was now legal, it would not be until some years
later that its full potential would be universally acknowledged—most dramatically in the 1913 Notre Dame–Army game. In the meantime, most
coaches, particularly those in the East, were reluctant to employ this new-
fangled device, apparently fearful that it would either backfire on them or
that it would turn the game into an aerial circus, undermining what they
considered to be the true nature of football.

HEISMAN, THE FORWARD PASS, AND THE QUICK SHIFT (1906)

Although John Heisman had to be highly pleased with the news of the
forward pass's acceptance, the date of his first use of it is open to conjecture.
But use it he did in the very first year it was legalized. In fact, in the 1906
game with Auburn in Atlanta, the forward pass figured in yet another of
those controversial plays that seemed to dog Heisman everywhere he went.

Called on to punt during the first half, Tech kicker W. S. "Lobster" Brown sliced the ball off his foot directly up in the air. It came down into the hands of a Tech player who, in a moment of inspired improvisation, threw a touchdown pass to halfback Chip Robert. With nothing in the rules against it, the referee allowed the play to stand. Later, Robert scooped up a blocked Auburn punt and ran it in for a touchdown. The final score was 11–0, marking the first time ever that Georgia Tech had defeated Auburn.

But even with the forward pass at his disposal, Heisman produced a rather lackluster 5–3–1 season in 1906. Other wins were over Davidson (4–0), thanks to Lobster Brown's 40-yard field goal, and Georgia (17–0), while the match with surprising Maryville of Tennessee resulted in a 6–6 tie. Losses were to Sewanee, as usual (16–0); to Clemson (10–0), a Thanksgiving Day game in which the Tigers finally tried their first forward pass; and to powerful Vanderbilt (37–6). The Georgia win featured the stellar play of Chip Robert, particularly his timely pass receptions that set up two touchdowns.

The game with the Vanderbilt Commodores was played on a stormy day, alternately raining and snowing, and the only bright spot in the embarrassing loss occurred when Chip Robert recovered a muffed punt attempt behind Vandy's goal line for Tech's only score. In planning to kick the coveted extra point, Heisman pulled off a ruse that was yet another example of his knack for skirting the rules. He sent a substitute into the game who was wearing a raincoat to keep the football he was carrying dry. When Vanderbilt protested, Heisman countered the referee: "All that the rules say is that the game be played with the prolate spheroid specified in the rules. Well, here's a prolate spheroid, the twin of the one we've just made a touchdown with. How about it?" Finding nothing in the book to refute Heisman's contention, the referee allowed the punt to be kicked with the fresh ball. But today, as Heisman indicated, "the referee decides when a new ball shall be taken into the game, and not the coach."[13]

Although Tech never came close to winning the game, its supporters, having wagered large sums of money on its team to at least score in the match, wound up winning in a big monetary way, this being a time when open gambling on sporting events was not under close surveillance as it is today. Accordingly, the 1906 game with Clemson saw Tech supporters at a fever pitch of gambling frenzy. Taking any odds the Clemson backers offered, Atlanta wagerers were sure they would be in complete command of this match. But (according to Fuzzy Woodruff) Tech's 10–0 defeat "came close to bankrupting Atlanta."[14]

After having tied Sewanee the previous year, Tech reverted to its old ways in the loss to the Purple. Nevertheless, the game was notable for the first appearance of Heisman's soon to be notorious "jump shift," which he would use in ensuing years with considerable success. A contemporary reporter, as Woodruff notes, questioned the legality of the innovation "that was later to revolutionize football attack and defense in the South":

"That's a neat trick of Heisman's," says the chronicler, "in making a fake move just before the ball is snapped."

He then explained that as he saw the play, Heisman caused his team to shift in order to have the other team charge too soon and be penalized for being offside.[15]

According to Heisman, though, the "quick shift," as he referred to it, occurs "when a team, after seemingly assuming a settled position or formation, rapidly shifts one or more of its men to new positions, and then shoots the ball into play immediately after those men have come to a stop in their shifting movement." The most important advantage of the quick shift formation, according to Heisman, it that it affords a team

a great variety of differing formations while the ball, coming back so soon after the strange formation has been assumed, allows opponents no time in which to "size-up" that it is different from the others; or, if some of the defensive players should be quick enough to note the change, they have no time to notify their comrades thereof nor to confer with each other as to the best way to meet it.[16]

Ironically, years later, the venerable Amos Alonzo Stagg, who himself had been a pioneer of such tactics, criticized Heisman's quick shift tactics as a reintroduction of the momentum principle that gave his team an unfair advantage and "violated the spirit of the rules."[17] Nevertheless, during the 1920s many teams would come up with variations of the shift formations developed at both Georgia Tech and Minnesota, as we shall see. Heisman would continue to experiment with his shift offensive during the time that his pet project—the forward pass—had been finally approved, with both developments attesting to his perennial obsession with innovation.

THE FORWARD PASS AND THE NATIONAL GAME (1906)

The upshot of that first year of the forward pass was that while its adoption did help open up the game, it had little impact on bringing about a decrease in the injury and death tolls. Clearly, there were still a number of strategic problems to be dealt with in football. But from a tactical point of view, the coming of the forward pass functioned as an on-field equalizer in that it afforded small schools more of an opportunity to compete on equal footing with larger schools. For example, during the first years of its use of the forward pass, St. Louis University won all its games, scoring 402 points to 11 for its opponents, even defeating Midwest power Iowa, 39–0. In the South, schools on the order of Davidson clearly benefited from the new rule when, for example, it beat Georgia, 15–0, by effectively employing a short pass over the middle of the line. Surprisingly, high schools began implementing the forward pass as soon as the rule appeared, and as a result it was not long before players skilled in the special proficiencies that the new rule required began filtering into the college ranks.

Other than Heisman and Cochems, others who were quick to make the most of the forward pass and its strategic possibilities were, as expected, Amos Alonzo Stagg and Glenn Warner. At Chicago, the ever-inventive Stagg, who always seemed to be ahead of his time, began to experiment with what today would be known as a play-action pass. In such a play the quarterback had the options of faking to a back running toward the line and then throwing to an end, or pitching to a halfback who could then roll out to pass to an end or halfback, or throwing directly to either an end in close or to an end flanked wide. With a coach like Stagg the natural opportunities the new rule afforded were unlimited.

Warner's inventiveness also extended to areas other than that of utilizing the forward pass. As noted, John Heisman had already experienced a sampling of this man's creative tactics in the 1895 Auburn–Georgia game. But when Warner took on the challenge of coaching at a small Indian school called Carlisle in 1899, his talent for innovation began to assert itself in earnest.

As an agricultural and mechanical college situated on a former Army installation in Pennsylvania, the school had been set up to teach trade skills to the disenfranchised American Indian. When football was introduced as a varsity sport, eligible students, of whom there were only about 250 on the undergraduate level, took to it with unexcelled enthusiasm. Their zeal for the game inspired Warner to schedule road games against some of the toughest opponents in the country. This was the main reason he was continually compelled to come up with new approaches to playing style and game strategy. For example, in 1899 he instructed his linemen to use a crouching start. This resulted not only in a quicker play start but better blocking leverage. Anticipating Heisman's quick shift, Warner also implemented a modified shift formation by having his linemen move a step or two either to the right or the left before the ball was snapped.

In 1903, Warner even resurrected the old hidden-ball trick that Heisman had concocted. During the game against Harvard with the Crimson ahead, 6–0, Carlisle took the second half kickoff and after withdrawing into a wedge near their goal line, one of the players stuffed the ball under the back of a teammate's jersey. Using their helmets as improvised "footballs," the Carlisle players proceeded to divert the Harvard defense while the designated ball carrier ran the length of the field to score unmolested. (The touchdown wasn't declared official until a teammate rushed up, pulled the ball out of the jersey, and touched it to the ground, a required ritual in those days.) Such Heisman-like deception was not enough to help the Carlisle cause, though, as Harvard went on to win the close contest, 12–11.

The fact of the matter is, Carlisle played everybody tough in those days without much recourse to deception. After going on to coach three years at Cornell, his alma mater, Warner returned to Carlisle in 1907 and turned out one of his best teams, a team that in eleven games lost only to Princeton to warrant high national ranking. Warner's Carlisle teams were characterized by a competitive ardor that grew out of the Indians' strong sense of pride in their race and the opportunity that football offered to compete with the white man on an equal footing. The Indians' ability to beat white men at their own game was never more dramatically projected than through the stirring efforts of Warner's Carlisle football teams in their heyday. And no team of their day made more effective use of the forward pass than did Carlisle, as a number of outstanding teams discovered. Villanova, Penn, Harvard, Minnesota, and Chicago were all victims of Warner's deployment of the pass in 1907.

At this time, too, the Carlisle coach must have been looking ahead to the advent of the single-wingback formation, one of his major contributions to the game. Capitalizing on a rule that allowed an offensive man to be stationed outside and behind an end, provided there were six men on the line, Warner came up with a new kind of power attack that provided additional interference for the ball carrier. But more glory days lay ahead for the Carlisle Indians, mainly because of the future exploits of a player who made his first appearance in 1907, a player many would acclaim as the greatest all-around football player ever: Jim Thorpe.

RINGERS ON THE SOUTHERN SCENE (1907–1908)

In the meantime, Heisman, now fully acclimated to his Atlanta environs, had high hopes for his 1907 team. But, as so often happens in the fortunes of football, Heisman's expectations were not to be realized. In this, his fourth season, Tech supporters had been confidently looking to a possible Southern championship, especially after two warmup opponents were demolished by the combined score of 123–0. But a close 6–4 win over Tennessee revealed that against frontline competition Tech's Yellow Jackets had some serious problems in getting their attack on course. In fact, Tech's victory had really resulted from a lucky break. At one point in the first half, a Tech back fumbled and Tennessee recovered near its goal line. Dropping back behind his own goal to punt, the Tennessee kicker's foot missed the ball completely and a Tech player jumped on the loose ball for the only touchdown of the game. The Vols managed to kick a 4-point field goal in the second half, but by then it was too late to pull the game out.

Next came Heisman's growing nemesis, Auburn, and this time the Tech team was not to be so lucky. Although the overall quality of Heisman's players was superior to that of Donahue's, the Auburn team had always presented something of a psychological problem to Tech, and this meeting proved to be no exception. Actually, in preparing for this match Heisman's game plan was complicated by another concern: a natural tendency to look past Auburn to the game with big rival Georgia the very next week.

Tied at the half, 6–6, the Auburn game could easily have ended with that score intact, except that toward the end of the contest, Tech elected to throw a desperation pass from midfield. It was intercepted and returned for a touchdown, making the final score 12–6, in favor of Auburn. It must have been difficult for Heisman to realize how the revolutionary innovation for which he had campaigned so long and hard could work against him so tellingly in this painful loss. But being the natural competitor that he was, it is likely that Heisman would have readily acknowledged that, in relying on the forward pass, a coach had to live or die by whatever breaks or misfortunes came his way.

The year 1907 was declared the "Ringer Season" in many quarters, and the events leading up to the Georgia match the following Saturday show the term was aptly coined. Mainly due to Vanderbilt's growing domination, a number of Southern schools desirous of competing on a more equal footing with the Commodores had taken to recruiting tramp athletes or ringers, as they were referred to then. Heisman's own pet term for the tramp athlete was "boilermaker." These were football players who traveled the college circuit offering their talents to any school that would have them for a price. (Other eligibility concerns at this time had to do with controlling the participation of freshmen, graduate, special or transfer students, and even alumni.) In promoting the Georgia game, the Atlanta papers had set the stage for a battle royal by openly charging the Bulldogs of professionalism due to their alleged recruitment of ringers. Although local reporters had demanded an official announcement of the starting lineup from Georgia authorities so that the players' eligibility could be verified, the actual lineup was not revealed until just before the opening kickoff, when a Georgia official furnished the referee with a list of starters. Thus the scene was set for a grudge match with repercussions transcending the game's outcome.

Yellow Jacket fortunes appeared bleak at the very start when Chip Robert, Tech's multitalented halfback, dislocated his shoulder on the runback of the kickoff and was forced to leave the game. Following this blow, the match settled into a defensive struggle with each side waiting for the other to make a mistake. It finally came when overly aggressive Georgia players tackled a Tech man who had signaled for the fair catch of a punt. The ensuing penalty resulted in a free kick from placement, for 4 points. Then after a 45-yard touchdown pass in the second half, Heisman's team took a commanding 10–0 lead. Georgia managed to score after a Tech kick was blocked, making the final score 10–6. Ringers or no, Heisman had won four straight over his big intrastate rival, and Bulldog morale was now at a very low ebb indeed.

In addition to the pressures on its players stemming from charges of professionalism, Georgia's poor team play in this game was supposedly related to gambling. According to Fuzzy Woodruff, the Georgia supporters, having wagered thousands of dollars, had promised the Bulldog player who scored the first touchdown a large sum of money. Consequently, "individual jealousies" destroyed Georgia's teamwork.[18]

The aftermath of this game was a large-scale investigation of players' credentials who had suddenly and inexplicably shown up on southern campuses. Georgia, Alabama, Sewanee, and even Georgia Tech were among the schools open to suspicion of having used ringers in their games. With alumni numbers growing each year, many of these "professional" players had been recruited by overzealous boosters eager for their teams to compete on a more competitive basis, particularly with powerful Vanderbilt. Due to a steady stream of seasoned players coming in from Tennessee's prep schools, Vanderbilt, with little or no recruiting problems, had achieved the role of the team to beat each year in the SIAA. The Nashville team was also beginning to establish itself as a national power.

In 1906, Coach McGugin had taken the Commodores north to play his alma mater, powerful Michigan, and lost by the surprisingly close score of 10–4. That same season, Vanderbilt took on Glenn Warner's Carlisle Indians, the great barnstorming team with a reputation for winning on the road. But this time Vanderbilt shocked the football world by setting up a strong defense and winning, 4–0. With only one loss at 8–1, the Commodores finished in the running for the national championship, the first southern team to do so. With Vandy in the vanguard, southern football was starting to make a name for itself.

As far as charges of professionalism at Georgia Tech were concerned, though, Heisman appears to have run a program that, like those of other schools, took advantage of the lax recruiting regulations of that day. If institutions were expected to monitor their own programs, then abuses were bound to occur. But because of his strong views on the worth of an education to the student athlete, Heisman would not have taken kindly to the tramp athlete who was out primarily to play football rather than attend class. His own outlook on the problem of recruiting, which was summed up in an article he later wrote in 1928, sided with the players, justifying the system as a means to an end:

> There are many lusty boys who could not get college training unless they traded their athletic cunning for jobs which defray the expense of tuition, board and lodging. And there have been a surprising number of these poor but strong youths who have by their postgraduate contributions to society justified their education. Society would have been the poorer had college athletics been purer.[19]

Ironically, as Heisman analyzed the situation, the problems of his own day appear to be not that much different from our own, particularly with regard to overzealous alumni and boosters eager to keep their school among the front-runners at any cost. Nevertheless, the fact that Georgia Tech was aboveboard in its recruiting practices was attested to in an article Heisman wrote in 1912 on the difficulties he encountered inducing athletes to come to the Atlanta school:

Many a time when I have been told by an athletic boy that he would like to come to Tech if we could only give him such or such financial assistance, and I have had to tell him that we could not and did not do that at Tech, he has bobbed up serenely at some other Southern college; after telling me in the most positive manner that he could not go to any college unless given financial aid. Well, that difficulty we shall never be able to overcome at Tech, for we couldn't do it if we would, and we wouldn't do it if we could.[20]

The problems, temptations, and pressures that recruiting presented to Heisman at Georgia Tech would continue until his departure following the 1919 season. In fact, they would pursue him throughout his coaching career.

After the resounding 54–0 defeat at the hands of Vanderbilt in 1907, Heisman must have been convinced that nothing less than a whole team of "boilermakers" would have succeeded against this increasingly formidable foe. Once again the forward pass had been a big factor in Tech's downfall. Other than problems with opponents who recruited ringers, it appeared that Heisman was now facing a potentially more problematic concern in trying to come up with a way to defend against the innovation he had ardently campaigned for as a way to improve the game.

Heisman most assuredly would prefer posterity to forget about the two other 1907 games in what would be his most mediocre (4–4) season at Tech: an 18–0 loss to Sewanee and a 6–5 squeaker defeat at the hands of Clemson. For the most part of ten years giant-killing Sewanee had been rampaging southern football fields, so Heisman had become reconciled to the Purple's winning ways. But to lose to Clemson in so close a match must have been a bitter pill to swallow.

One of the big surprises of the 1908 season—Louisiana State University's 10–2 win over Auburn—served notice that professionalism was a bigger problem in the South than most people had realized. Grantland Rice, beginning to make a name for himself at this time as a sports reporter for the *Nashville Tennesseean*, published a documented story charging the LSU football staff with using seven players who had been paid specifically to play football. LSU officials denied the charge, but Rice stuck to his guns, declaring that he could prove his contention. Although no investigation came about, LSU, which at 10–0 considered itself a contender for the Southern championship, had now lost its credibility, and Auburn went on to claim the crown that year. In just two years, in 1910, the National Collegiate Athletic Association would appear, and steps toward the regulation of player eligibility would begin in earnest. It would be some years, though, before this organization would become a powerful force in controlling the eligibility process.

Georgia Tech's 1908 season started off with easy wins over the usual "breather" opponents—the military prep and normal schools. Then in an extremely rough contest, Tech defeated Mississippi A&M (later, Mississippi State), 23–0. In this game Chip Robert was ejected for "unduly vigorous" play, as the euphemistic style of that day's sportswriters described his behavior. In another October match that featured Heisman's increasingly successful adaptation to the pass, Tech came from behind to defeat Alabama, 11–6. However, three straight losses followed to undermine the Yellow Jackets' title chances that year: to Tennessee (6–5), Auburn (44–0), and Sewanee (6–0). Tech had started off strong against Auburn, but once Coach Donahue's defensive strategy asserted itself, the Tech offense and defense both collapsed, particularly after Auburn halfback L. W. Hardage ran the second-half kickoff back 108 yards for a touchdown.

Nevertheless, the 1908 season closed out on a positive note for Heisman, with wins over Mercer (16–6) and Clemson (30–6). Not only was Tech's 6–3 record an improvement over the preceding season, it also boded well for the 1909 season and the elusive hunt for the Southern championship. On a grim note, the death of a VMI player in a game with Roanoke College that fall once again reminded the football world that, in spite of recent rule changes designed to open up tactics, the brutality of the game remained an ever-present problem.

THE COMING OF THE HAUGHTON SYSTEM (1908)

That football's changing style of play and coaching techniques, as well as the fact that it had ceased to be a student-controlled activity, had begun to reflect an instinctive corporate nature was borne out in 1908, with the appointment of Percy Haughton as head coach at Harvard. Haughton wasted no time in implementing an executive management style of coaching that soon came to be known as the Haughton System. It was a system, in fact, in which the coach was in complete control. Recognizing the game's expanding areas of specialization, Haughton was the first coach to hire assistants who functioned primarily as backfield, line, kicking, and even scouting specialists. As an innovator who took what he needed from other systems to mold his own, Haughton was an iron disciplinarian and perfectionist who sought to promote a winning psychology predicated on the strictest possible training schedule and diligent attention to the game's fundamentals.

In demanding the undivided allegiance of both his coaches and players, Haughton's game strategy was designed to wear down an opponent over the early stages of a match so his team could be in an advantageous position to ensure winning toward the end. Also, with no huddle to detract from his quick striking offense (similar to the way Heisman's Georgia Tech teams functioned at this time), Haughton advocated punting early during a series of downs to force a break. If it came, then his team was directed to revert immediately to a power or surprise play, depending on the on-field situation. Prophetically, the field goal played a prominent part in his system, although he viewed the forward pass as essentially a means to an end, the kind of play that would hopefully set up a scoring opportunity. In his strategic plan, a strong defense was as essential as a powerful offense, because continual pressure on an opponent's kicker could result in an offensive break. He scouted future opponents for both their strengths and weaknesses (again like Heisman) and developed defensive signals tailored to each opponent, which the center could call by numbers and signs.

The Haughton System resulted in Harvard's Golden Era (1908–1916), during which the Crimson won seventy-one games (including a streak of thirty-three without a loss), lost only seven, and tied five. Best of all, for Harvard supporters during this period, Haughton's teams lost only once to Yale. While his first team went undefeated, as did others later, Haughton rated his 1914 team with its unbeaten but twice-tied record 7–0–2 as his best because of its fighting, never-say-die spirit. To Haughton, football was a metaphor for war, a game essentially militaristic in nature in which the coach was the field general and the players his troops. (In a few short years, many gridiron warriors as well as Haughton himself would have the opportunity to translate their football experiences into the grim reality of the World War I battlefield.)

Like Heisman, Haughton had championed the intrinsic worth of the forward pass and was adamantly opposed to the original restrictions Walter Camp had placed on it. In the winter of 1909–1910, after the deaths of still more players had put football on the spot once again, Haughton competed outright with Camp for leadership of the new Rules Committee of the NCAA. He did this mainly by proposing changes to eliminate the existing restrictions on the forward pass, to adopt a fourth down, and to protect the pass receiver, who was then subject to defensive interference without penalty. Haughton also maintained that a player who had to leave a game ought to be allowed to return if healthy enough. Clearly, Percy Haughton proved himself a dynamic force in affecting football's future, both on the field and off.

Because John Heisman's coaching style also advocated military-style discipline, authoritarian rule of the coach, strategic innovation, and a winning philosophy derived from absolute player loyalty, he probably came closer to practicing the professional standards of Percy Haughton than any other coach of that day. Throughout their careers, too, both coaches maintained an aloofness from their players which stemmed from their strict attitude toward team discipline. Although Heisman's relationship with his players did not exactly command their love and affection, Haughton's was so demanding, particularly during practice, that some of his players confessed to actually hating the man. In action and deed Percy Haughton was truly the go-getter type from American business and industry made over into a football coach.

It was also in 1908 that Jim Thorpe's career moved into high gear, and for some time thereafter the back that many would hail as the greatest football player ever to suit up for a game helped keep the name of Carlisle in the limelight. (After the 1908 and 1909 seasons he left school, but he returned for the 1911 and 1912 campaigns.) At about 180 pounds, Thorpe was built for the game in a way most backs of his day were not. His style of play incorporated speed, elusiveness, and extraordinary strength. He was also very versatile, excelling in punting, drop kicking, passing, blocking, and tackling. In short, Jim Thorpe was a football coach's dream come true, and those coaches who saw or heard of his exploits on the gridiron, including John Heisman, must have fairly drooled at the thought of having him as a player. In another of the *Collier's* pieces written in 1929, Heisman reminisced on Thorpe's greatness as a player: "Jim was so good that he liked to amuse himself and his mates by telling an end or a tackle to get set because . . . he was coming that way in a moment. And he'd do it."[21] Although Thorpe never played for Heisman, the Tech coach would be fortunate enough to recruit one of Carlisle's most talented athletes during the Yellow Jackets' highly successful seasons of 1917 and 1918. Joe Guyon, whose contributions to the accomplishments of the Georgia Tech team will be recounted later, had already played several seasons at Carlisle when he transferred to Tech. But in those days there were no strict rules governing the eligibility of transfer athletes, as has been pointed out.

HEISMAN AND THE 1909 SEASON

By this time, John Heisman, at 39, had become a well-known and respected figure in the Atlanta area. Popular with the press and with area business leaders, he had forged an identity for his Tech teams that commanded strong allegiance from both the campus and Atlanta communities. In fact, a number of civic leaders were lending their full support to Heisman in his quest to build Georgia Tech into a national gridiron power. Among these were industrial and business captains George Adair, Lowry Arnold, Frank Holland, Robert T. Jones (father of Bobby Jones, the great golfer of the 1920s), Billy Oldknow, Joe Rhodes, and Marion Swann—all influential names in the building of Atlanta's modern image. They typified the new wave of successful industry and business men who made it a special point to become directly involved in community affairs.

Heisman himself was taking an active part in the community; in 1908 he was appointed athletic director of the Atlanta Athletic Club. Organizations like this, supported by private membership, were common to large cities throughout the South around the turn of the century, and many of them fielded athletic teams that competed with those of area colleges. Heisman's directorship of the Atlanta club not only substantiated his positive image in the community, it also provided him with another income source, evidently a perennial concern of this opportunistic son of Titusville, Pennsylvania's oil boom era. (This experience also prepared him for a role he would fill in his final years—athletic director of the Downtown Athletic Club of New York

City.) If there was a way to pick up some extra money, Heisman seemed always prepared to take advantage of any situation that came his way. Shortly, he would be dabbling in real estate.

As a coach, of course, Heisman had established a strong personal image among his players on the practice field. Normally attired in high turtleneck sweater and baseball cap with his ever-ready megaphone in hand, he struck a commanding figure as he drove his players through their drills. At 170 pounds, he had gained some weight since his playing days, but his 5 feet 10 inch frame didn't display an ounce of flab. To complement his militaristic physical bearing, Heisman's stridently demanding voice seemed to come from all directions at once. In 1913, during the heart of his Tech tenure, a student wrote in the school magazine a rather down-to-earth profile of his imperious locker-room and practice field manner. After complaining about his squad's slowness in suiting up and the team manager's oversights, Heisman urged his players to take the field:

> They are out with a whoop, and, from then on until well after dark, Tech Flats resound with the bark of the quarterback, the thud of falling bodies, and [the] stentorian tones of Coach Heisman. It is a rush from start to finish, hard, sweaty, grinding work with a relentless taskmaster, ever calling for better and more sustained effort. It all seems a mere jumble of motion and command, but at the end of the week Tech watches with pride the smooth piece of machinery that trots out on the gridiron, the result of weeks of preparation.[22]

Heisman's genius for turning out a "smooth piece of machinery" from raw, untried material endeared him to those supporters who looked upon him as a true symbol of Georgia Tech athletics and the formulation of a winning tradition. But because of his autocratic coaching posture not many of his players really took to him personally. They respected him, but that was about as far as the relationship between Heisman and most of his players went. This, of course, was the way he preferred to keep the relationship. Over the years, though, his attitude toward his players would deteriorate to the point of arrogance toward some and favoritism toward others, particularly during his final years at Rice and the waning of his coaching prowess. His later years at Tech were a time when his coaching system was at its peak, bringing his players' abilities to a national championship level.

The 1909 season loomed as another promising one for Tech's football fortunes, but once again, losses to Sewanee and Auburn burst Heisman's bubble. In fact, Sewanee, with its undefeated and untied record, would capture the Southern championship that year, overcoming the perennially tough obstacles of Vanderbilt and Auburn. An early 59–0 whipping of South Carolina had Tech supporters dreaming of a championship season, but in the very next game, Sewanee took advantage of Tech fumbling to deflate any hopes Tech fans might have had, 15–0. Later, the 8–0 defeat by Auburn sealed the Yellow Jackets' doom. It was another typical contest with the Tigers, with Tech playing as though it already knew defeat was eminent. Heisman must have been talking to himself by now about what he had to do to win over Sewanee and Auburn.

On the bright side of this 7–2 season, Tech won its last three games: Georgia (12–6), Mercer (35–0), and Clemson (29–3). Tennessee had been beaten in an earlier game, 29–0. The Georgia match saw Heisman up to his old tricks, this time at the very outset. Echoes of the hidden-ball play Pop Warner perpetrated against Harvard in 1903 were heard after a Tech player was tackled and the Bulldogs discovered that the man had been carrying his helmet to simulate a football while the real ball carrier had gone on to score. Even the officials had been fooled, and, as though to pacify their ruffled dignity as much as to help resolve the matter, they called the ball back to the point of the headgear tackle, penalizing Tech with a loss of down. Although football was moving away from such deceptive practices as variations on the old hidden-ball trick, Heisman evidently had difficulty resisting an occasional sly experiment of his own.

John Heisman's perennial obsession with football's rules and how they might be interpreted, modified, or even circumvented in order to win got him into some strange onfield predicaments at times, a number of which have been previously cited. But in 1928, he based one of his *Collier's* articles on such unexpected situations, some of which actually resulted in rule changes. Once, for example, when his Alabama Polytechnic (Auburn) team was playing Georgia Tech in the 1890s, a Tech punt that had traveled straight up in the air came down and was recovered by Tech following a mad scramble. But instead of awarding the ball to Auburn because Tech had failed to gain the necessary first-down yardage, the referee ruled a "free fumble" and thus granted Tech a first down. Heisman reacted indignantly:

"Free fumble," I roared. "Why, man, there hasn't been any such term since Noah played the game. There's nothing in the rules today about a free fumble. Tech kicked and Tech recovered. Also Tech had five yards to gain and hasn't made it. Poly touched the ball several times during the scramble, but we never had possession. It was never in our control. Therefore they've had it for the full number of downs and they haven't made their distance. Give us the ball."

Nevertheless, the referee ruled in Georgia Tech's favor. Heisman wasn't through, though. After writing to the Rules Committee, he saw his contention become part of the rules: "That when a fumbled ball is recovered by the team which fumbled, it counts as a down. Unless, of course, the required distance to first down is made in the excitement."[23]

Although his deceptive practices had been something of a trademark, Heisman went on in this piece to discuss how the rules had succeeded in banishing "hocus-pocus"—uniforms with leather handles (for pulling), feet-first hurdling by running backs, the hidden-ball variations and even disguised players hiding on the sidelines—from football. He concluded by defending the rulemakers for their efforts:

I hear it said that the Rules Committee is forever doing its utmost to kill the game—smother it with rules. That criticism is unintelligent. These critics have it that the game is being ruled colorless, that the machine age in which we are living is making the game mechanical and that it develops no great heroes as it did in the days of Hinkey, Heffelfinger, Hare, Heston, DeWitt, Thorpe and Mahan. That, of course, is nonsense. The Rules Committee has compelled the development of team play.[24]

But 1909–1910 was still a far cry from Heisman's 1928 viewpoint, when, for all intents and purposes, football had been transformed into the modern game by the rulemakers.

A real boost to Heisman's coaching morale at this time came in the first appearance of Al Loeb at center, a player who would become one of the all-time Georgia Tech greats. Severely nearsighted and outweighed by all opponents he faced at his position, Loeb was a dramatic example of the rare player who excelled not so much through athletic ability as by an indomitable fighting spirit. He would figure prominently in Tech's next three seasons and, as a spirited little man, develop into one of Heisman's all-time favorite players.

THE NATIONAL GAME (1909–1910): MORE RULE CHANGES

Among the eastern teams, the 1909 Yale Bulldogs compiled a 10–0 record and once again captured the national championship. With All-American Ted Coy at fullback (six Yale players were named to that year's All-America team) and Coach Howard Jones, a stickler for the fundamentals of blocking and tackling, at the helm, the Bulldogs proved their championship caliber by going through the season unscored on.

In other areas of the country, Minnesota, on its way to the Western Conference title, enhanced its success with a flamboyant tactic soon to be nicknamed the "flea flicker" (a forward pass off a lateral). Notre Dame, inspired for the first time by the stirring strains of its great fight song, the "Victory March," defeated Michigan at last and went 7–0–1. Other undefeated season records were posted by Arkansas (7–0), Washington (7–0), Missouri (6–0–1), Harvard (8–1–0), and Penn State (5–0–1), as college football continued to infiltrate all areas of the country.

In the same year, there was another important change in scoring rules: The field goal was now valued at 3 points and has remained so ever since. But 1909 was also the year when matters of a more serious nature came to a head. In spite of the forward pass and relevant rule changes designed to lessen brutality, a total of eight college players were killed that fall, and the high injury count continued. As a result, the public outcry against football had begun to swell again.

Subsequently, early in 1910, the organization officially known for the first time as the National Collegiate Athletic Association held a series of meetings to produce yet another set of rules aimed at remedying football's propensity toward brutality and violence. This time, modification of the rules governing the forward pass loomed as the most formidable problem to deal with. Even though there were still those who wanted the forward pass abolished, stronger voices, such as that of Percy Haughton, advocated retaining this still-relatively-new tactic. Haughton wrote to fellow supporter Amos Alonzo Stagg that unless the forward pass was retained, football would die. And of course retention of the pass still had the unflagging support of John Heisman and his camp.

In early January, 1910, Walter Camp had written to Heisman concerning some suggested changes in the rules governing offensive formations, particularly those running out of a shift, the formation Heisman had helped pioneer. Camp's major recommendations to Heisman were to station the offensive backs at longer intervals behind the line and to make the required distance for a first down fifteen yards in three downs. At a meeting of SIAA representatives in Atlanta, Heisman had his players perform practical demonstrations of the changes Camp had proposed. However, he and his fellow members discovered in this experiment that backs would now be more disposed to running the ends than before, since their more distant stations behind the line made it easier to gain yardage that way. By now it was obvious to Heisman that Camp was looking for more conservative alternatives to the forward pass to open up the game. At any rate, Heisman soon wrote Camp a detailed letter of the results of his demonstrations, concluding that he and his representatives could see no real worth in Camp's suggestions.

To Heisman's way of thinking there were better ways to open up the game than to spread out offensive formations, and the forward pass was certainly one way that offered unlimited possibilities. So before the NCAA met that spring in New York, SIAA representatives, under Heisman's direction, came up with fourteen suggested modifications and rule changes of their own, of which the following were the most significant:

1. Remove practically all the penalties restricting offensive use of the forward pass.

2. Penalize a defensive player who interferes with an offensive player trying to catch a forward pass.

3. Require seven men to be on the line and all three of the backs (outside the quarterback) to be five yards apart.

4. Divide the game into quarters of even length with a rest period between each quarter.

5. Strictly enforce the penalty for piling on.

Other recommendations mainly had to do with safety factors such as the addition of a "new official to the game called Official Physician, who . . . shall have the power arbitrarily to stop the game at any time . . . in order to investigate the condition of any player." There were also several suggestions designed to monitor the health of players prior to participation, during practice, and during a game. The strangest of all the SIAA recommendations had to do with a new scoring system that would award a point for each 5-yard advance within the 25-yard line.[25]

While this last suggestion failed to gain any national support, the proposals as to the number of players on the line of scrimmage, dividing the game into quarters, and restricting piling on won a sufficient number of converts. But it was not until the May 13, 1910, NCAA meeting that the last of the important rule changes helping transform football into its modern prototype were announced.

Prior to this date, the following changes proposed by the SIAA and other representatives had already been adopted: A game was now to be played with four fifteen-minute quarters; a seven-man offensive line was mandated; interlocking interference was outlawed (as was the flying tackle); pushing or pulling of a ball carrier by his teammates was prohibited; and an on-side kick now had to travel at least twenty yards.

Curiously, though, nothing much had been done to change the rules governing the forward pass until the May 13 meeting when, much to the satisfaction of Heisman and others who saw the forward pass as the real solution to football's problems, some realistic rule changes were finally announced. Not only would there now be no penalty for an incomplete pass, the ball was to be brought back to the original line of scrimmage where play would be resumed. While the ball carrier would now be allowed to cross the line of scrimmage at any point, a pass could be thrown in any direction across the line. However, restrictions were also set forth, requiring that the ball be thrown from at least five yards behind the line and that a pass could not be completed for longer than twenty yards down field. But as the SIAA contingent and Percy Haughton had desired, defensive players were forbidden to make contact with a pass receiver before a reception. In line with Haughton's thinking, too, one other change would lead to a more open substitution system—a player who left the game in one quarter was permitted to return at the start of the next.

Innovative coaches across the country were quick to take advantage of the new rules. Now that a back could run in any direction after he received the ball from center, Amos Alonzo Stagg expanded on the possibilities of the quarterback option play in which the quarterback could either hand the ball off to another back, keep the ball and run with it, or throw a forward pass. The mandate for a seven-man line had both Harry Williams at Minnesota and John Heisman experimenting with the further possibilities of shift formations in which offensive players would move into new positions just before the ball was snapped, holding their stances long enough to satisfy the rule governing motion prior to the snap of the ball. Use of the shift was a successful tactic for any team who could perfect the required timing, since its success depended on hitting a point of attack before the defense could rise to the occasion. Heisman has described the similarities and differences between his and Williams's shifts: "Fundamentally the shifts were alike, but my backs at Georgia Tech took wholly different positions. The Tech backs lined up, upon the shift signal, in Indian file and at right angles to the rush line."[26] Not to be outdone in the move toward more advantageous blocking, Pop Warner concocted the Z-formation, which was actually another step toward the final unveiling of his single-wing attack.

Clearly, football had developed around the periodic introduction of rules designed to refine the game's rough spots and the reaction of enterprising coaches in developing innovations to extend the game's strategic possibilities within the rules' restrictions. Coaches like Stagg, Warner, Williams, and Heisman were among the most successful because they could always come up with imaginative ways to extend these possibilities.

THE NATIONAL SCENE (1910)

But if football was making progress in both refining and defining itself as a national game, there were important developments in other sociocultural areas that were evidence of not only progress but also tradition-breaking changes in the world of 1910—changes that in their way would contribute to making society more receptive to sports. Although the world moved at a much slower pace then, there were definite signs that life in America was on the verge of dramatic social transformation, primarily due to revolutionary technological breakthroughs. With more than two hundred thousand motor vehicles on the road at the beginning of the year, the automobile industry was on its way to becoming one of the nation's largest. (Heisman himself is reputed to have purchased one of the first cars in Atlanta, a Maxwell. It was said that Heisman had considerable difficulty in learning how to correlate its brakes and clutch.) Concomitantly, the success of the automobile industry led to commercial developments in other areas, such as a tremendous increase in the production of crude oil, the manufacture of rubber tires, and the proliferation of concrete roads. Even so, the railroad, with its three hundred thousand miles of track, still offered the most efficient mode of mass travel at this time and would continue to do so well into the century.

The nation at large was still undergoing its inevitable urbanization process, with Heisman's Atlanta becoming a prime example of this trend. The United States was now a country of some 90 million people, eight million of whom had immigrated to the country since 1900. But the more provincial United States still had a long way to go to overtake the British Empire as a world industrial and military power. Nevertheless, with the Germans and Japanese flexing their muscles for all the world to see, the unthinkable reality of a catastrophic world war lay just ahead, an event that would catapult America headlong into the status of a world power, whether it wanted to be or not.

As successor to Teddy Roosevelt, who as president had been mainly concerned with creating a conducive climate for the development of business and industry, William Howard Taft was naturally inclined toward maintaining the country's conservative values. In fact, among Taft's proudest achievements was being the first president to perform the ritual of throwing out a baseball to signify the beginning of the baseball season.

At this time, baseball was by far the most popular team sport, with sixteen professional teams playing to some seven million fans in 1910. (Football's day as a professional sport lay far in the future, although the college game was gaining momentum year by year.) Always the opportunist, John Heisman capitalized on the popularity of professional baseball by functioning as the president of the Atlanta Baseball Association from 1910 through 1914. Heisman, of course, was eminently qualified for the position, not only because of his management abilities, but also because he had turned out successful baseball teams everywhere he had coached, some of championship caliber. Football would always remain his first love, however, and as much as he liked the game of baseball it would only be of peripheral interest to him throughout his life.

As sports increased in popularity, the newspapers began allotting more space to them. This was particularly true with baseball, which, due to the expansion of the major leagues, was developing a strong following in the big cities of the Northeast and Midwest. Also of special interest during that day were the heavyweight boxing matches, which the papers treated with a great deal of ballyhoo. One in particular, the bout between Jack Johnson and Jim Jeffries, was promoted as the fight to decide the superiority of the "Great White Hope" (Jeffries) over the black man (Johnson). Staged in Reno, Nevada, on July 4, 1910, the fight disappointed supporters of the white cause when Johnson won in fifteen rounds of a scheduled forty-five-round match. The press, in its zeal to publicize the outcome of this event, played an unwitting role in precipitating racial violence in certain parts of the country. Even Atlanta, with its large black population, felt the shock tremors of this momentous sporting event.

By this time, newspapers were beginning to realize the power of sports as a social force. Sportswriters like Grantland Rice, who had demonstrated a flair for the investigative in exposing football professionalism at LSU in 1908, were becoming increasingly aware of their power to alert the public to problem areas. With an ever-expanding, ready-made audience awaiting, the sportswriter would come into his own by the 1920s. The versatile John Heisman, with two newspapers at his disposal in Atlanta (the *Constitution* and the *Journal*), would even try his hand at writing sports pieces. In addition, he turned out periodic articles for Tech's student magazine (*The Yellow Jacket*),

but most of his sports publications were clearly of the inspirationally pos-
turing type, written mainly to encourage both student and local support of
Tech's athletic teams. In 1922, he would publish his well-received *Principles
of Football*, a highly personalized explanation of his approach to coaching the
game. His later pieces for *Collier's*, written in the late 1920s when he was
out of coaching altogether, gave him free rein to say just about anything he
wanted. Heisman's mind was a veritable compendium of football history and
knowledge, and he had begun working on a history of the game just before
he died in 1936. Had he lived to complete the book, it likely would have
stood out as the definitive study of the origin and development of American
football up until that time.

While vaudeville and the legitimate theater still provided the major sources
of mass entertainment in 1910, the Hollywood movie was beginning to make
inroads, attracting nationwide audiences of ten million people a week who
willingly paid to sit in a darkened room and experience the novelty of viewing
dreamlike figures moving around on a luminescent screen. Although the
motion picture was still in an embryonic state as far as technical achievements
and treatment of subject matter were concerned, sporting events became a
popular attraction right from the beginning, particularly newsreel footage of
sensational events like the Johnson–Jeffries fight. In a few short years, sports
would provide the subject matter for a significant number of Hollywood's
fantasized film stories. Sports also had an impact on entertainment modes
closer to home, such as the piano (every parlor had one) and the windup
phonograph, with an increased circulation of popular college fight songs
(Georgia Tech's, like Notre Dame's, was among the most popular) and sports-
related songs like "Take Me Out to the Ballgame" in sheet music and phonograph record form. As expressed through the forms of popular culture,
sports were becoming an integral and acceptable part of American social life.

Another popular "sport" of the time was that of looking to the skies to
follow the development of the airplane. Since its inauspicious appearance in
1903, the airplane was developing into more that just a novelty. With the
advent of World War I just a few years away, air power would become a
new, powerful force in planning military tactics. But in 1910 people were
looking to the skies for yet another reason. It was the year of the return of
Halley's Comet. And in spite of the prophets of doom who looked upon its
coming as a harbinger of worldwide destruction, its arrival presaged a world
that between 1910 and its next appearance in 1985 would change drastically,
particularly in sociological and technological ways. The quarter-century of
John Heisman's life that remained (1911–1936) would also witness considerable change. Naturally, the increasingly popular game he coached would
undergo further changes indicative of the times that would produce them.

Although there were coaches who complained of the major rule changes
introduced in 1910, it was soon apparent, particularly from the spectator's
point of view, that the game would be much improved because of them.

Indeed, the popularity of football, which in spite of its image problems had never really waned, began to take on even more momentum as a spectator sport during this year. Alumni and other supporters began to demand the renovation and expansion of existing stadiums and the construction of new, gigantic facilities around the country. And because of the rule changes affecting the style of play, the game as we know it today was coming into its own as a socially acceptable sport around this time.

HEISMAN AND THE 1910 SEASON

From a coaching perspective, John Heisman was well prepared to take full advantage of the rule changes of 1910. After four games, with the Yellow Jackets at 4–0 and having scored 159 points to their opponents' 0, he had his players and followers burning with enthusiasm. But, unfortunately, three straight devastating losses ensued: 16–0 to Auburn, 23–0 to Vanderbilt, and 11–6 to Georgia, the first time a Heisman-coached team had lost to the Athens school.

In the Auburn game, played in the rain on a muddy field, miscues were highly instrumental in the outcome as the opportunistic Tigers converted key Tech fumbles into touchdowns. In the next match, Tech's misfortunes continued as Vanderbilt, destined to be SIAA champions once again at 7–0–1, shut out the Yellow Jackets. But losing to the powerful Commodores was not a great embarrassment at this time, as earlier that year they had enhanced the cause of southern football by holding Yale to a 0–0 tie in New Haven.

But then came the demoralizing loss to Georgia, which was largely attributable to the spectacular play of a running back who would become one of the Bulldogs' all-time greats and one of Tech's most formidable foes—Bob McWhorter. In fact, during the course of McWhorter's four-year career, Tech would not win one game against the Bulldogs. The 1910 game, witnessed by one of the largest crowds ever to congregate at Atlanta's Ponce de Leon Field, was rated even by area gamblers. Although Tech led at the half by 6–0, the Bulldogs, behind the hard, shifty running of McWhorter, came back in the second half to win, 11–6. The only bright spot for Heisman the rest of that disappointing 5–3 season was the expected season-ending victory over Clemson—this time, 34–0. Ever since his first season at Tech in 1904, Heisman's teams had been averaging no better than six wins per season. He knew he had to find ways to improve if Tech was ever to capture the coveted SIAA championship.

THE NATIONAL GAME (1910)

Nationally, Harvard was still making an impact, yielding only one touchdown all year and, with a 0–0 tie with Yale, going undefeated (8–0–1).

Another team in the East that enjoyed a successful season was Navy, which, except for a tie with Rutgers, was also unbeaten. In the Midwest, both Illinois and Pittsburgh, with undefeated seasons, were coming to the fore as powers to be reckoned with. In the West, Washington at 7–0 was still enjoying its unbeaten status under second-year coach Gil Dobie. (In fact, during his spectacular nine-year reign at Washington, Dobie's teams would remain unbeaten, an all-time record.) Regional pride had become a decisive factor in inspiring many schools to field teams that would soon be capable of competing with those of any other region in the country.

HEISMAN AND HIS "COLLEGE SPIRIT" GOSPEL (1911)

For Heisman, the disappointing letdown of the 1910 season was not easy to dismiss, and before the 1911 campaign got underway he took steps to avoid another lackluster season. He signed Pete Hauser, who had been an All-America fullback at Carlisle, as assistant coach, apparently hoping that Carlisle's winning ways would rub off on the Tech players. Heisman was also trying every ploy he could to instill in Tech's student body an inveterate interest in football, not only for moral support but to find a plan to help recruit more skilled, able-bodied players. As it was everywhere he had been, Heisman's coaching system depended on involving everyone he could in his recruiting plans, particularly those students who knew of talented athletes who could become candidates for the football team.

Accordingly, Heisman believed that the most important factor needed to generate success in athletics was plain, old-fashioned college spirit. It was an attitude that had originated in the 1890s with the eastern colleges who saw in football a way to bring the college community together. To remind students of the necessity to get behind their teams and be a part of the Tech community, Heisman helped establish the Tech Spirit Club, complete with membership buttons. It was actually a project designed to set a more positive tone for the 1911 season, since a serious dearth of experienced football material would follow graduation that spring. But writing in *The Yellow Jacket* in October of that year, Heisman maintained his positive outlook and reprimanded those slackers who were not taking the school spirit challenge seriously enough:

Fellows, college spirit makes fighting spirit on the football field. . . . If you can't play you can go down a couple of times a week at least and watch the practice and help swell the cheering. Learn the Tech yells, so that you know how to join in at the games. If for any reason you can't play yourself see if you can't get out some promising looking fellow who can. Take an interest in what the football men are doing. If they are eating or drinking things they should not, take the bull by the horns and go right up and tell them so. If reasoning with them doesn't do any good come and tell me about it. Yes, it's your business and your duty. That's the least you can do for the success of the team, seeing that you can't or don't come out and play yourself. If you are going to have the real, right college spirit this year you want to be man enough to take your stand and do your share to frown down on anything and everything that will work against the success of the team.[27]

Imagine a football coach of today resorting to such seemingly antiquated tactics to instill school spirit in students, and they in turn trying to keep a school's players from breaking training rules according to these suggestions. Yet in Heisman's day such cajolery was not too far-fetched, for as intercollegiate athletics grew less student centered, efforts to maintain involvement in the school community automatically devolved on athletic coaches. This responsibility also had the support of college authorities, since it relieved them of such pressures. Even today, many coaches feel compelled to get the student body behind their teams by using the most old-fashioned methods available—fiery speeches, pep rallies, and various promotional stunts. In athletics some things never go out of style, and in appealing directly to students, the Heisman method is still a viable means to encourage support to produce a winner.

Even with the 1911 season two-thirds over and Tech having lost yet another game to Auburn (11–6), the irrepressible Heisman issued still another call for players in *The Yellow Jacket*, this time a "Third and Last Call." Almost as though the season were just getting underway and he were out to recruit new material, Heisman presented his usual sales pitch on why a man should come out for football: First, for his "physical welfare"; next, for his "development of character"; and finally, to show his "college spirit."[28]

The season itself had started out in its usual promising fashion with convincing wins over Howard (28–0) and Tennessee (24–0). But then came a frustrating 0–0 tie with Alabama in a game that the Yellow Jackets were favored to win. It was one of those games in which neither team could do much once they were within sight of the goal. After the frustrating match was over, Heisman rationalized the tie by singling out the play of Alabama back Hargrove Vandergraaf as superior to everyone else. Never, he said, had he "seen a player so thoroughly imbued with the true spirit of football." Ironically, the spirit he had desired to see in his own players was more fully embodied in the play of an opponent, and he made sure they knew about it. Hardly one to give praise where it was due, particularly to his own players, Heisman was more prone to be critical than lavish with his praise; praising the play of an opponent was a way of alerting his players to their own weaknesses.[29]

In this same piece in *The Yellow Jacket*, Heisman went on to reveal why he was loathe to praise his players—he feared that telling them how good they were would spoil them. So he admonished the team's supporters to refrain from praising any player: "When a man is satisfied with himself in anything he will never improve further; he has reached the limit of his game and development. Don't you help him to become satisfied with himself."

After the next game against Auburn, Heisman probably concluded that never in his lifetime would he ever beat the Tigers. Even after gaining 246 yards from scrimmage to Auburn's meager 41 and amassing fourteen first downs to Auburn's three, Tech lost, 11–6. To make matters worse, Auburn's win was accomplished with Coach Donahue ill and his team having to rely on a makeshift lineup due to the illness of several key players. But two long scoring plays had done in Tech: a 102-yard return of an intercepted pass and a 75-yard punt return. With perennially tough Sewanee as his next opponent, Heisman surely figured that the fates were conspiring against him.

Nevertheless, Heisman's faith in college spirit was redeemed when the Yellow Jackets actually came through with a rare win over Sewanee by the convincing score of 23–0. The highlight of the game came when Tech's Homer Cook returned a punt forty-five yards for a touchdown. Supporters were so ecstatic over the victory that they predicted a new age for Georgia Tech football. But the new age was short-lived, as on the heels of the glorious Sewanee victory came another defeat at the hands of Georgia and the indomitable Bob McWhorter. With the ball at midfield in the closing moments and the game looking as though it would end in a scoreless tie, McWhorter suddenly burst off tackle and went all the way for the winning touchdown and a final score of 5–0. After the two disheartening losses to Auburn and Georgia, a 32–0 win over Clemson seemed anticlimactic as Heisman chalked up another 6–2–1 season.

The 1911 season marked the first appearance of a substitute lineman for Tech named William A. Alexander. Although he had served as captain of the scrub team, he seemed a most unlikely candidate for any kind of leadership role, due mainly to his extremely reticent nature. Nevertheless, he would ultimately spend a total of forty-four years at Tech—six as a student and player, eight as a math instructor and aide to Heisman, twenty-five as head coach after succeeding Heisman in 1920, and five as athletic director. Always at Heisman's elbow as an assistant coach, he obviously learned a great deal from his mentor. But as the first alumnus to coach at a southern school, his style was "a drastic change from the coaching of Heisman," according to one of Alexander's early players. "Aleck made you like the game of football, and it ceased to be a punishing grind. And instead of fiery orations by the eloquent Heisman, we were treated to low-key talks that relaxed our tensions before we went on the field."[30] Alexander, who coached from 1920 until 1945, when Bobby Dodd took over, led the Yellow Jackets to all four major bowls of the day, a feat that Georgia Tech was the first team to accomplish.

The 1911 season was hardly over when the relentless Heisman turned his attention to another source of gridiron talent—Tech's class games. These were intramural contests played between the various classes to determine a school champion in football. In addition to fostering school spirit, Heisman's underlying motive for promoting the worth of class games was to uncover additional football talent. In another of his articles in *The Yellow Jacket*, he praised this system, calling it

> one of the biggest stepping stones toward ultimately making the Varsity that you can find; in proof of which you can look over our Varsity of this year and ask yourself the question where in the world would we have been this fall if a very large number of our Varsity players had not been largely developed by the class ball they played last winter?[31]

Always the opportunist, Heisman had turned to a proven source to help build his team for the 1912 season.

THE NATIONAL GAME (1911)

From a national perspective, the 1911 team of the year was Princeton, which went 8–0–2. The Tigers' coach, Bill Roper, was another unique study in the varied coaching styles that the increasingly professional side of the game was now attracting. An intensely emotional man, Roper fired up his players through spirited oratory that made them want to go out and "die" for Old Nassau. John Heisman naturally adulated this man's coaching manner because if any coach epitomized college spirit, it was Bill Roper.

Navy enjoyed an impressive 6–0–3 year, proving that the service academies could compete with the best. But the major event of the 1911 season was the return of Jim Thorpe after a two-year layoff. Demonstrating his worth in his inimitably dramatic fashion, he helped Carlisle beat Harvard with a 48-yard field goal, 18–15. At 11–1–0, Carlisle probably had the best team in the country but not, unfortunately, the prestige of Princeton. Elsewhere, Penn State (8–0–1) went undefeated while Washington (7–0) continued its winning ways.

At this point in his Georgia Tech tenure, John Heisman had seen the game of football weather severe storms of public protest and periods of doubt concerning its future role as an acceptable varsity sport. The major forces behind the trend toward football's long-term acceptability, of course, were its development into more of an open-ended game due to the adoption of the forward pass and the introduction of new tactical formations that lent themselves to a more wide-open style of play. Although the growing popularity of football since his arrival at Georgia Tech assured Heisman that the game had a bright future, one thing still concerned the ambitious coach more than anything else: his failure to lead Tech to the Southern championship. But the best days of the Heisman regime in Atlanta lay just ahead, an era that would result in an even-bigger prize than southern laurels—the first-ever national championship for a southern team.

NOTES

1. The player quoted was Bill Fincher, in Al Thomy, *The Ramblin' Wreck: A Story of Georgia Tech Football* (Huntsville, Ala.: Strode Publishers, 1973), 107.

2. Ibid., 32.

3. See John Hammond Moore, "Football's Ugly Decades, 1893–1913," *The Smithsonian Journal of History* 2 (Fall 1967): 49–68.

4. Ibid. 59.

5. Quoted by Allison Danzig in *Oh, How They Played the Game* (New York: Macmillan, 1971), 152–54.

6. Moore, "Football's Ugly Decades," 67.

7. John S. Watterson, "Inventing Modern Football," *American Heritage* 39, no. 6 (September/October 1988): 103–13.

8. John W. Heisman, "Fast and Loose," *Collier's*, October 20, 1918, 14–15.

9. It was Chancellor Henry MacCracken of New York University, with the support of Palmer Pierce of West Point, who convened the conference at the Murray Hill Hotel. It was attended by national representatives from the major football-playing schools of the day. Dr. Henry Williams of Minnesota, with the cooperation of Paul Dashiell of Navy, led the section on the forward pass.

10. For a detailed analysis of these suggestions, see David Scarborough, "Intercollegiate Athletics at Washington and Jefferson College: The Building of a Tradition" (Ph.D. diss., University of Pittsburgh, 1979), 36–37.

11. Quoted in Danzig, *Oh, How They Played*, 178.

12. Ibid., 182–83.

13. John W. Heisman, "Rules Rush In," *Collier's*, November 10, 1928, 12.

14. L. F. "Fuzzy" Woodruff, *History of Southern Football*, vol. 1 (Atlanta, Ga.: Georgia Southern, 1928), 196.

15. Ibid., 189.

16. John W. Heisman, *Principles of Football* (St. Louis: Sports Publishing Bureau, 1922), 267–73.

17. Quoted in Danzig, *Oh, How They Played*, 36.

18. See Woodruff, *History of Southern Football*, Vol. 1, 206.

19. John W. Heisman, "Their Weight in Gold," *Collier's*, November 24, 1928, 28.

20. John W. Heisman, "Our Athletic Outlook," *The Yellow Jacket* (October 1912): 77–78.

21. John W. Heisman, "Hero Stuff," *Collier's*, November 2, 1929, 73. Heisman once confessed to coveting a dream backfield composed of Thorpe, Willie Heston, and Red Grange.

22. "Who's He and Why?" *The Yellow Jacket* (March 1913): 418.

23. John W. Heisman, "Rules Rush In," *Collier's*, November 10, 1928, 12.

24. Ibid., 42.

25. John W. Heisman, "Suggestions As to Football Rule Changes for 1910," 2-page pamphlet (undated).

26. John W. Heisman, "The Thundering Herd," *Collier's*, October 13, 1928, 60.

27. John W. Heisman, "More About College Spirit," *The Yellow Jacket* (October 1911): 21.

28. John W. Heisman, "Are You Coming Out for Football? If Not, Why Not?" *The Yellow Jacket* (November 1911): 12.

29. John W. Heisman, "Our Football Team and Others," *The Yellow Jacket* (November 1912): 179–83.

30. Quoted in Thomy, *The Ramblin' Wreck*, 88.

31. John W. Heisman, "All Aboard for the Class Games," *The Yellow Jacket* (December 1911): 16.

4

Heisman and the Shaping of the Modern Game (1912–1919)

Armed with a marvelous invention, the forward pass, and chastened by President Theodore Roosevelt's stern admonitions . . . , football was no longer a simple campus diversion. . . . Football had moved from the province of the students to the hearts and pocketbooks of the old grads, who now made it a point to see that the old school kept up with other schools. Rivalries were born.

—Furman Bisher,
"Saturday's Child" in *The College Game* (1974)

In that intercollegiate sport and other extracurricular activities satisfied needs that were at least as important as involvement in intellectual activity or study to prepare for a professional career, athletic departments and student services became official concerns of educators. This triumph of anti-intellectual forces resulted in the creation of an operational structure that made possible the tremendous expansion of intercollegiate sport after 1920.

—Guy Lewis,
"Enterprise on the Campus: Developments in Intercollegiate Sport and Higher Education, 1875–1939" (1972)

SIGNIFICANT CHANGES IN THE GAME (1912)

The year 1912 can be considered a major point of demarcation in the development of American football—a time when the style of play began to look very nearly like that we know today. The major rule changes of that year were chiefly responsible for this transition. To the delight of John Heisman and other proponents of the forward pass, the rule restricting a pass to twenty yards had been abolished. The field was now one-hundred yards in length, with a ten-yard end zone at each end of the field. Accordingly, a forward pass caught in the end zone by the offense was to be ruled a touchdown instead of a touchback. To enhance the passing game the ball was trimmed down to afford a better grip. A touchdown was now worth 6 points, and the introduction of four downs in which to gain ten yards was instrumental in modifying offensive strategy. It had been forty-three years since that wild, primeval contest between Princeton and Rutgers was played, but as far as its on-field look was concerned, football was now fairly well set to project its modern image.

HEISMAN AND THE 1912 SEASON

Despite the new rule changes and the lifting of the restrictive limitations on the forward pass, Heisman looked toward the 1912 season with a degree of caution. The main reason for this outlook was the lack of suitable replacements for players who had graduated. But lack of experience and lack of talent were nothing compared to lack of grit, so he kept warning his players against yielding to what he called the quitter attitude: "Absolutely nothing can be done with a 'quitter,' and if there are too many of that kind on a team, you might as well say 'Good night,' and give it up for another year."[1]

Having built better-than-average football teams out of inferior material for years, Heisman was not about to tolerate a defeatist attitude among his players and supporters. In fact, a dominant factor of the coaching philosophy of John Heisman was that a positive outlook could be gleaned even from adversity:

Let's not get discouraged. Remember, I have had to face this proposition for years, and am quite undaunted by it. All I ask is that everyone of you look at the situation the same way I do, with complete realization of what a task we have before us, but yet with courage and determination to weather the storm, if such a thing is within the bounds of the possible.[2]

In order to keep his players properly motivated and updated on his football philosophy, Heisman, by this time, had begun to formulate a list of dos and don'ts about game play that he either posted in the locker room or periodically circulated among his players. Essentially, these pithy comments represented ways to avoid the psychological pitfalls Heisman had learned about the game at this point in his career. In his *Principles of Football* (1922) he enumerated them as "Heisman's Football Axioms." Following are some of his more characteristic and memorable maxims:

- Don't try to play without your head.
- Don't look toward where the play is going.

- Don't fumble; you might better have died when you were a little boy.
- Don't see how light you can hit, but how hard.
- Don't lose the game.
- Don't wait for opponents to come to you. Take the battle to them.
- Use your brain on both offense and defense all the time.
- Use your opponent up and yourself as well, till the game is won.
- You can't play superior football without brains.
- You can't fight like a man with less than 100 per cent loyalty and college spirit.
- You can't be a great player if you have the swell head.
- Never come on the field without your brains.[3]

Judging from their common theme, this sampling clearly demonstrates the high premium John Heisman placed on his players' intelligence as a contributing factor to successfully playing the game of football.

During the winter of 1912–1913, Heisman's football concerns were temporarily put on the back burner when he assumed coaching responsibilities for yet another sport at Tech. As basketball had been growing in popularity since its invention in the 1890s and Georgia Tech now had a "first-class basketball court," he issued a call for players to try out for a varsity team that fall; that is, for those students "who are not engaged with football." Class basketball had been played sporadically at Tech since the early part of the century, and in 1908–1909 the first varsity team took to the court, ingloriously losing five of six games. Clearly, the game of basketball was not taken very seriously at Tech until Heisman issued his call for the 1912–1913 season, when a more dedicated attitude to the sport became apparent. To instill fresh enthusiasm for basketball, he even referred to this campaign as "our first year at the game," concluding that "there is no reason that I can discern why we should not make a first-rate showing even in our first year."[4]

Even in taking up a fledgling sport he knew very little about, Heisman was able to project his natural flair for positive thinking. But the final record of this team, with wins over only Mercer and Clemson in eight games, was just slightly better than in 1908–1909. Not until the 1913–1914 season would Tech record its first winning basketball season, a 6–2 campaign highlighted by a win over Auburn, with losses only to Georgia.

The first football game of the 1912 season—October 5 against The Citadel at Charleston, South Carolina—proved to Heisman and his team just how potent a weapon the forward pass could be in the hands of an opponent that knew how to make the most of it. After "fifteen hours on a slow train," the stiff and cramped players found themselves more ready for bed than exploring the town on their arrival in Charleston. But the next morning they got their tour of the area, the highlight, according to Heisman, being Fort Sumter, where he led his contingent on a "brushup of our history." The scholarly side of John Heisman naturally came to the fore when his players had an opportunity to expand their intellectual horizons.

But in the football game that afternoon, his players soon learned something else of more immediate concern: The Citadel football team was no pushover. According to Heisman, one reason their opponent played them with such fierce intensity is that Tech came into the game highly rated. The newspapers by this time were well into their role of comparing the worth of opposing teams to help promote a game. As Heisman later reported:

> The papers said we were always four touchdowns better than Clemson, and Clemson was two better than Citadel, and so they feared we were going to be real rude about the way we would project our heads against their stomachs whenever we had the ball. . . .
>
> Their forward pass game was the best we have ever seen, and it was not until we were in the third quarter that our boys finally learned how to smother them up on this play, and then we made them fail on about eight out of ten.[5]

So in spite of The Citadel's "scintillating passing attack," as one reporter described it, Tech went on to win the game, 20–6. Pleased with the outcome, Heisman allowed his players to attend a local dance that night in their honor. But to keep them mindful of the real purpose of the trip, he called a team meeting punctually at the 10:00 P.M. curfew hour: "At the hotel . . . we all went up into one of the larger rooms, and we had a little 'pink tea.' Just what transpired there is not for everybody to know, but the result of it you all saw when we played Alabama on the 12th."[6]

In this latter game, Heisman turned the tables by installing a devastating passing attack of his own, and won, 20–3. With Homer Cook effectively demonstrating what he could do with the pass, Tech completely dominated the second half. But the key player of the game, according to Heisman, was little Al Loeb, whose fighting spirit he revered. Heisman later reminisced about Loeb's role in this game. The Tech team, out on the field first, watched in awe as the huge Alabama squad appeared. But Al Loeb was unimpressed:

> "Huh," he scoffed. "Well, fellows, we've seen them. Can't help seeing them. But they're going to FEEL us. Yessir. We gotta make them feel us the first time we meet. And they gotta feel as if somebody had slapped them with the grand stand. Understand? We gotta get mad. Listen; I'm so mad right now after seeing the drove of beef that I'd—Oh, hell, tell them to start this game so I'll have something soft to bite."[7]

According to Heisman, Loeb's speech inspired his teammates, and they went on to win, 20–3. The inspirational example of Al Loeb was enhanced by the fact that he played the entire game with two broken bones in his hand.

On the occasion of a big win, Heisman once again took the opportunity to remind the team's followers just what it takes to build a winning combination in modern football:

Playing old-style football perhaps [Alabama] would have beaten us. But what business has a team of featherweights like ours playing old-time football? None whatever. We have to play open formations with an extremely varied attack, and be pretty good at the forward pass game. I think we have shown that we can adapt ourselves to the times and to conditions.[8]

The essence of Heisman's football philosophy is contained in this last sentence, stressing that to be successful at football you have to adapt to change. Because the game had been evolving so rapidly, the most successful teams, Heisman would contend, were those who had sufficiently adapted to meet the challenges of the new rules.

Next came the University of Florida in a game played in Jacksonville, and after the Gators tied the game on a long pass, Tech went on to win it in the second half, 14–7. Once again the season's hopes were high, but then came a three-game stretch against formidable foes Auburn, Sewanee, and Georgia with the usual results. Against the Tigers of Auburn, Tech confronted a battering offensive attack in the 27–7 loss that featured an 80-yard run in the second half by Auburn's Kirk Newell. The game with Sewanee was much closer, but the Purple capitalized on a Tech miscue when one of its players scooped up a fumble and returned it for the only score of the game to win, 7–0.

Even though the Bulldogs' lineup still featured the incomparable Bob McWhorter, this was the year that Tech followers figured it could beat Georgia. Their reasoning was based on comparative scores of the teams' respective games against Alabama, Tech having decisively defeated the Tuscaloosa team while Georgia had barely eked out a last-second win. But once again McWhorter proved himself too tough to stop, and Tech went down, 20–0. Three games had resulted in three losses, and Heisman's championship hopes, as well as those of Tech's followers, were dashed again.

Heisman must have been convinced by now that the talent he had to choose from was decidedly inferior to that of his more competitive opponents, as Vanderbilt again captured the Southern championship. Since 1904, the Commodores and Sewanee had dominated the region, but now Auburn was coming to the fore. Even after Tech's expected Thanksgiving victory over Clemson (23–0), Heisman was probably wondering what else he had to do to attract the kind of talent he needed to compete successfully against the kingpins of the conference.

THE NATIONAL GAME (1912)

The national team of the year was undefeated Harvard (9–0), which under Percy Haughton was into the school's longest unbeaten streak. (Over a thirty-three game stretch the Crimson would win thirty games and tie three.) Many of these wins were achieved through the dropkicking skills of the fabulous

Charley Brickley, whose accuracy was unequaled within the 40-yard line. Other top teams of the year were Wisconsin (7–0), winner of the Western Conference, Notre Dame (7–0), Penn State (7–0), and Carlisle (12–1–1). Vanderbilt again made a strong pitch for the improved quality of southern football with a close 9–3 loss to Harvard, the only defeat on its schedule. At this time Heisman could well be envious of the Tennessee school and its coach, whose winning ways kept attracting high quality talent.

Penn State attributed a great deal of its success to copying the offensive style of Carlisle, as in 1912 Pop Warner produced a system that would have tremendous impact on offensive play—the single-wingback formation. Generating a power attack behind well-timed blocking, the single-wing had evolved from Warner's Z-formation. Now the key to a successful offense called for a versatile halfback who could do the things Jim Thorpe was so good at—running, kicking, and passing. Shortly, the sportswriters would be referring to such a player as a "triple-threat tailback." Many schools would soon be switching over to this kind of attack as their coaches became convinced of its potential, particularly when Warner first unveiled his new system and trounced Army, 27–6.

HEISMAN AND THE 1913 SEASON

During the off-season, Heisman attempted to impress on his football players the necessity of staying in shape. In the January 1913 issue of *The Yellow Jacket* he wrote a rather lengthy and didactic piece on the roles of sacrifice and perseverance in an athlete's quest for success in both athletics and academics. According to Heisman, the way to succeed in both areas was essentially the same:

> Even if your ambition for athletic excellence be the stronger of the two, don't lose sight of the fact that at an engineering institution you have positively got to be a student before you can be an athlete; that no matter how talented you may be in an athletic way it will count for nothing and you will never get a chance to flash your gem "of purest ray serene," unless and until you have done some flashing (and not flushing) in the classroom.[9]

In addition to keeping his football players up to par, both academically and physically, Heisman had other concerns during the off-season. There was the brand new basketball team, whose entire eight-game schedule was to be played during the month of February. In describing the team's progress prior to the season, Heisman took a more realistic approach than he had the previous year: "Basketball teams cannot be made from the ground up in a single season any more than can football teams, and we will all have to be patient."[10] This turned out to be a prophetic observation, as the team won only two games.

However, Heisman was highly pleased with the way the class games in football and basketball had come off. In picking an All-Class football team, he even singled out certain players for special praise in *The Yellow Jacket* with the hope, of course, that these men would be coming out for the varsity in the fall.

By spring he had once again turned his attention to baseball, presenting a progress report in the May issue of *The Yellow Jacket*. Having won two previous baseball championships at Tech (1906 and 1909), Heisman always displayed more than just an incidental interest in the promise of a new season. (Also, in serving as president of the Atlanta Baseball Association, he kept an eye open for any talent that might be worthy of the professional ranks.) Praising the physical condition of the Tech baseball diamond, he used the opportunity to express pride in the entire athletic complex, the project he had initiated upon his arrival in 1904. Urging the students to help keep the area free of rocks and debris, Heisman made it clear that he was depending on their support to make it "the very finest field in the entire South."[11]

He was especially proud of another part of the sports complex—the newly proposed track—that would provide an excellent showcase for Georgia Tech's growing emphasis on all athletics. Heisman wrote glowingly: "It is going to be an "A" No. 1 track. Nothing in the South will come anywhere near touching it. Think of its proportions!"[12] An ulterior motive on Heisman's part, of course, was that the new track would not only help attract quality athletes but motivate his football players who didn't participate in other spring sports to take part in track and field activities and help keep themselves in shape.

That September Heisman presented his outlook for the football season. He was unusually optimistic, due mainly to the incoming athletes who had been recruited according to the college spirit system he had implemented the previous year. It was a system that would soon result in the best teams of his career. Accordingly, Heisman was quite lavish in bestowing praise on those who had helped out: "Our athletic outlook for this year is, in my honest opinion, brighter than it has ever been before in the history of athletics at Tech. . . . And for this state of affairs we have no one to thank but ourselves. . . . Never have I seen every man at a college put shoulder to the wheel the way nearly all have done at Tech during the past eight months to bring about this better state of affairs."

But lest anyone happen to get a big head from such praise, Heisman went on to remind his followers that they still had a lot of hard work ahead in helping build a solid football team: "Fellows, it takes cooperation and work to get material, and after that it takes more cooperation and much more work to weld it and make it win." It was a message directed to Tech supporters as well as players, for to Heisman's way of thinking they were *all* on the same team.

Just how seriously Heisman took his leadership role in alerting Tech supporters to their special involvement in helping mold a first-rate team is reflected in the emotionally strong words he expressed toward the end of his article. To Heisman, his athletes had taken a solemn pledge to uphold the honor of their school:

> And . . . every man who secretly does break [this] pledge is, and should be regarded, as a *traitor* and an enemy to Tech and to her best interests. And when I say that I mean that any Tech man who at any time sees or hears of an athlete breaking the training pledge he has signed it is his patriotic and true *duty* to let the athletic authorities know what he knows, in order that the whole barrel may not be spoiled by that one rotten apple. When you keep silent under such circumstances you are "aiding and abetting a felony" against your college laws, against your Alma Mater's very life.[13]

The results of the 1913 campaign, in which Tech won seven of nine games, underscored the effectiveness of Heisman's recruiting system. But in losing once again to both Auburn and Georgia, he was again prompted in another of his pieces in *The Yellow Jacket* to rationalize the losses as the result of Tech's inferior material and injuries to key players. Undaunted, though, he emphasized the need not to let up in pointing toward the next season. Appropriately, with the world situation being what it was at that time, Heisman chose a prophetic image to get across his main point:

> I am here to tell every Tech man that [our opponents] are not going to be content to stand in 1914 just where they stood this fall with regard to material. They are going to work their heads off to get on, *on*—ever on and forward, ever building for the future. It's like the battleship-building race between England and Germany. These two nations are never content with what ships they *have*; they both realize they must continue building and getting *more, more,* if they wish to at all hold their own with rival nations.

Heisman closed out his "sermon" in an emotionally charged manner that clearly revealed his special feel for football as something more than a mere game. Rather, to him the game of football offered both participants and supporters a challenging experience through which they could learn to cope with the exigencies of life itself. Thus Heisman reminded both his players and supporters of their concomitant roles: "Don't fumble! Don't get discouraged! Put drive in your offense! Organize, cooperate! Fight like wildcats on defense! Every man hustle for material! This is the game of football; this is the battle of life."[14]

Georgia Tech's 7–2 record in 1913 earned it a third-place ranking after SIAA champion Auburn and runner-up Georgia. The Tigers (8–0), introducing their battle cry "War Eagle!" went on to dominate the region after this season by winning twenty-two of their next twenty-three games—twenty-one by shutouts. In so doing, Coach Mike Donahue fashioned one of Auburn's greatest eras on the gridiron. As a championship contender for the first time, the Yellow Jackets had defeated a surprisingly tough Florida team, 13–3, and followed up this victory with its most convincing win ever over Sewanee, 33–0. Highlighted by Homer Cook's 80-yard touchdown run in the opening minutes, the Sewanee game started fans contemplating a championship season at last. But then came shutout losses to Auburn (20–0) and Georgia (14–0), which, of course, eliminated Tech from the championship picture.

Nevertheless, there were a few bright moments in the loss to Auburn. During the first half, the Yellow Jackets had held Donahue's team to a scoreless tie, but then the championship-bound Tigers poured it on in the second half. In the Georgia contest, Bob McWhorter once again proved too hot for Tech to handle as he scored both Bulldog touchdowns. For the Yellow Jackets the only pleasant thing to recall about this game was that it would be the last time they would have to face McWhorter. However, the 32–0 Thanksgiving Day win over Clemson enabled the Yellow Jackets to finish third in the conference and salvage some degree of satisfaction.

Although it resulted in a loss, the Georgia game that year did help bring about an important rule change in 1914 concerning the neutral zone between opposing lines: "the neutral zone may not be encroached upon *until* the ball is put in play." Before this rule came into effect, many teams had been shifting players through the neutral zone prior to starting a play. In the 1913 Georgia–Georgia Tech game, for example, the Bulldogs had some of their linemen doing this with advantageous results. According to Heisman, "Before our linemen could get back into position Georgia would put the ball in play, catch us out of position and charge all over us." Heisman then wrote a letter to Walter Camp, who saw to it that a rule was enacted banning all players from the neutral zone *until* the ball is put in play.[15]

During that season, too, an incident occurred that underscored the increasingly irascible nature of John Heisman at this time in his life. Sports editor Morgan Blake of the *Atlanta Journal* had drawn a favorable comparison between Tech's quarterback and a star player for Vanderbilt. Unbelievably, Heisman took offense at the former Nashville newsman and admonished him: "You must be careful not to make so many Nashville references. Remember, you are in Atlanta now!" Although football schools had grown fiercely proud of the regions they represented, Heisman's comment was certainly uncalled for.

In his forties by now, there were growing signs that he was not getting along with his wife as well as he did when they had first arrived in Atlanta. This situation was probably due to his increased involvement in numerous public relations roles as well as his time-consuming athletic endeavors. Never one to cultivate intimate friendships, though, Heisman at this time seemed more attracted to solitary pursuits in his spare time. As *The Yellow Jacket* reporter put it in his profile of Heisman cited earlier: "His particular pleasures

are playing the phonograph . . . playing chess, and reading on biology, anthropology, archaeology, and kindred sciences. He hopes some day to have
both the time and money to poke both his nose and walking-stick among the
famous ruins of the world."[16]

If any athletic coach fitted the description of an intellectual, it was certainly
John Heisman, though he was never one to exhibit a narrowly specialized
interest in a scholarly subject. Clearly, he commanded a wide range of pursuits, and throughout his life his versatility and diversity of interests continued to amaze all those with whom he came in contact. Heisman's versatility
extended to the athletic field where his natural ability to motivate his players
inspired one of his star performers, Al Loeb, to call him an outright "genius.
He could take minimums and make them into maximums. . . . He did that
with me."[17] Along with a handful of other coaches of his day, Heisman
helped bring an air of respectability to the game of football, not only due to
his understanding of the game as a builder of manhood but because of his
scholarly manner as well.

THE NATIONAL GAME (1913)

From a national perspective, football had now achieved such popularity
that by October 1913 it was competing with the World Series for attention.
With big-game matchups growing more prominent, even more spectacular
intersectional pairings would soon be in the offing. Percy Haughton's Harvard team, led by All-American halfback Eddie Mahan and fullback Charley
Brickley, went undefeated again (9–0) and won the national title. When the
incomparable Brickley kicked five field goals in the Yale game, a mass mania
developed around the art of drop kicking, as children as well as prep school
and college players all over the country attempted to emulate Brickley's heroic
feats. With the mass-circulated magazines and the newspaper sports pages
becoming highly sensitized to their audience's growing reverence of sports
heroes, Charley Brickley was a natural subject for feature story emphasis.

This was also the year that future power Ohio State was admitted to the
prospering Western Conference, but Chicago, at 7–0, was the champion of
the region. Still as inventive as ever, Coach Alonzo Stagg came up with the
first instance of the Statue of Liberty play, resulting in a near score against
Minnesota. Originally referred to as the Cherry Picker, the play received its
ultimate name from the way an offensive back held the ball up as though to
pass while another back retrieved it and took off on a run. The tactical vision
of a coach like Stagg was still proving that the play possibilities of football
were limitless.

The most startling achievement of 1913, though, was produced by a then
little-known college in Indiana called Notre Dame. When it went east and
defeated Army, 35–13, for the Cadets' only loss that year, the little Catholic
school demonstrated the devastating potential of the forward pass, which

even by this time was still a little-used weapon. Notre Dame would finish up the season undefeated at 7–0. The story has been frequently told of how quarterback Gus Dorais and end Knute Rockne practiced during the summer previous to the game by hooking up on a well-timed passing combination and then during the game that fall springing the results on unsuspecting West Point. Although the Irish led at the half by just 14–13, the combination of Dorais and Rockne picked up the pace in the second half to win easily. By the end of the game, Dorais had completed fourteen of seventeen passes for 243 yards, an astounding statistic for that day. To be sure, the modern day of the forward pass had now arrived. Rockne, who was to go on to even greater fame as a coach, later concluded that the Notre Dame win of 1913 was the first real demonstration of the advantages that the open style of play had over the traditional closed style.

John Heisman, an unsung hero in overseeing the triumph of the forward pass, undoubtedly envisioned what the shocking Notre Dame victory meant for college football. The age of giant stadiums, boosterism, and bowl game mania was now imminent with the demonstrable success of the forward pass and a more open style of play. In just a few years, the 1920s would showcase big-time football as a highly glamorous sporting spectacle that would attract millions through the turnstiles every fall. It is an ongoing social phenomenon that has changed very little since that time.

HEISMAN AND THE 1914 SEASON

In the spring of 1914, Heisman once again turned his attention to baseball, and with the turnout of "well over 100 applicants for places" he was highly optimistic about the team's prospects. But his review of the season's results in June revealed that the campaign had not lived up to expectations: "Candor compels the statement that the team was one of the most erratic in its performances I have ever seen." Clearly more concerned about what the football season held for Tech that fall, he again issued an appeal for athletes according to the recruiting system he had implemented.[18]

The 1914 football season at Tech, while not particularly noteworthy in terms of its 6–2 record, is notable because this was the year the Yellow Jackets started out on their fabulous thirty-three-game unbeaten streak, one that would peak with Heisman's 1917 national championship team. During this period his concerted recruiting tactics would finally begin to pay off as Tech assembled one of its greatest aggregations of football players ever.

Heisman's characteristic emphasis on defense resulted in four shutout wins in 1914—South Carolina (20–0), Mercer (105–0), Sewanee (20–0), and Georgia (7–0). Of these, the most treasured victories, of course, were those over Sewanee and Georgia. The Georgia win was the first in five years over the Bulldogs, as Heisman at last appeared to be gaining the upper hand over this old foe. But the lopsided win over Mercer served to underscore Heisman's propensity for running up the score whenever he had the opportunity. It was also a harbinger of things to come, since the classic runaway game with Cumberland was just two years away.

Other big wins that year were over VMI (28–7) and Clemson (26–6). Defeats were administered by a surprising Alabama team (13–0) and, as usual, by Auburn (14–0). But the Tigers would be the last team to beat the Yellow Jackets until Pitt would win in the sixth game of the 1918 season. The 1914 game with Auburn was fairly close throughout, but Tech fumbled at three critical moments, one resulting in a first-half touchdown. Not until the final quarter did the Tigers score their second touchdown, but by then it was too late for the Yellow Jackets to pull the game out. Incidentally, this was the game in which the South got its first view of players with numbered jerseys, a practice that received instant approval, particularly from the sportswriters. At first, numerals were worn only on the back of jerseys, and it was not until 1937 that they were required on both front and back. (Washington and Jefferson College, one of Heisman's future coaching assignments, is reported to have first worn numerals as early as 1908.) In spite of Auburn's claim, Tennessee with its 9–0 record was awarded the SIAA championship.

THE NATIONAL GAME (1914)

In 1914 American optimism was at a high point with the official opening of the Panama Canal, an achievement that ranks among the greatest engineering feats of all time. Ten years in coming, the Canal exemplified what could be accomplished through large-scale collective methods, a system of construction that would become one of the hallmarks of twentieth-century technology. Even the advent of dire political events in eastern Europe, which would eventually plunge the world into an unprecedented global conflict, could not diminish the feeling of intense nationalism that spread throughout the country following the canal's opening. Likewise, the sports world was caught up in patriotic fervor, and the game of football, as an example of goal-oriented collective techniques in its own right, was destined to increase in popularity during this time.

Fittingly enough, a military school was the team of the year, as Army turned out its first all-victorious team (9–0). Mindful of what had happened in the previous year's game with Notre Dame, the Cadets dismantled the Irish this time around, 20–7. Players on this team, along with All-American center John McEwan, who would go on to greater fame, were future Tennessee coach Bob Neyland and future military leaders James Van Fleet and Omar Bradley. If the game of football could be interpreted as a metaphor for war, as many did, it was certainly proving its worth at this time as a training ground for men of military bent.

In 1914, Coach Bob Zuppke was serving his second year of a record twenty-nine-year tenure at Illinois, leading his team to an undefeated season (7–0).

Pioneering the backfield I-formation, Zuppke was a highly enthusiastic coach who leaned toward a lot of razzle-dazzle in his attack, particularly precision-like lateral passes that appeared as though they should have been stopped long before they resulted in long yardage gains. Other specialties of Zuppke were the screen pass and the hook and lateral, in which a pass receiver curled back to make a pass reception and then passed off to a trailing player. In ten years he would showcase a halfback named Red Grange who would create his own kind of razzle-dazzle.

By this year, too, football in the Southwest (an area that would figure auspiciously in John Heisman's future) had begun to make an impression as the University of Texas Longhorns came up with eight wins and no losses. That the day of the giant stadium had finally arrived was celebrated on the occasion of the first game to be played in the seventy-five thousand-seat Yale Bowl. Embarrassingly enough the game resulted in a 36–0 defeat of the Blue by Percy Haughton's Harvard Crimson, who at 7–0–2 were again undefeated. (Characteristic of college football over the years is the fact that it has never been a respecter of any sentimental favorite to win a game commemorating a special occasion.)

Although John Heisman had been experimenting with an offensive shift for a number of years, other coaches around the country were more influential at this time in bringing this tactic to national attention. Foremost were Dr. Henry Williams at Minnesota, Alonzo Stagg at Chicago, and Jesse Harper at Notre Dame. One of Harper's players, Knute Rockne, would refine the Notre Dame shift to his own specifications when he became coach of the Irish in 1918.

While most students of the game would credit Williams as the originator of the shift, a strong case can be made for Stagg, who was said to have been experimenting with some form of the shift as early as 1903 or 1904. Regardless, the Minnesota version of the shift was apparently the most efficient to be implemented in its prototypical form, and its success influenced a number of other schools to take up this system of attack. Split-second timing among the movement of the linemen was the key to the success of Williams's system. The result was a confused defense being out-manned at the point of attack, particularly during an era before the Rules Committee ordered a one-second stop by all members of the offense prior to the snap of the ball.

By the time Notre Dame took up the shift under Jesse Harper (around 1913–1914 and later under his pupil Rockne), the emphasis was on the backfield shifting from the T-formation to a box formation. In such a move, the defense could never be sure if a run or a pass was in the offing. While Heisman credited Williams for his innovations in this area of the game, Rockne would identify Stagg as the real father of the shift because of his influential experimentation in the early part of the century. Regardless of which coach should receive credit, it was the utilization of an offensive shift, as well as the forward pass, that added an exciting new open dimension to football. This development paved the way for a multitude of formations to follow and the national acceptance of the game as a highly appealing spectator sport.

HEISMAN AND THE 1915 SEASON

The year 1915 would turn out to be Heisman's most successful football campaign since his arrival at Tech. But in turning his attention to baseball prospects that spring in one of his articles in *The Yellow Jacket*, he dwelled at some length on the unpleasant subject of why coaches now had to cut players unsuited for varsity play. It would be a "fine thing," he wrote, if a coach could work indefinitely with every player who came out.

> But that is not the province of the salaried varsity coach. He is paid, not to teach everybody in a college how to play ball, but to take vigorous hold of a few of those who have already reached a certain stage of proficiency and do the very best he can with this limited few in a very limited time by molding them into the strongest varsity, or *first*, team that he can.[19]

That college football had now reached a high level of professionalism was attested to by the motivation of the salaried varsity coach, to use Heisman's term, in selecting his players; coaches tried to mold the strongest varsity team or winning combination they could, developing recruiting and training systems like that utilized by Heisman in the selection of candidates for his football team. Such highly competitive systems can be taken as an indication of the growing pressure to win that all salaried coaches were starting to feel at this time.

By this time in his coaching career, though, Heisman had seen enough players come and go that he had developed his own strict personal standards regarding the qualities that constituted a good athlete and a successful football player. In his 1922 book, *Principles of Football*, the rational side of Heisman came up with the following valuations of football players' "natural quali-fications"[20]: Athletic talent (25 percent), aggressiveness (20 percent), men-tality (20 percent), speed (20 percent), and weight (15 percent). At this point in his coaching career, Heisman was at last able to recruit more players who had the desired qualities in the right percentage amounts. As a result, he was getting closer to turning out the strongest varsity he had yet produced.

That the quality of players at Tech had reached a high level was confirmed by the turnout for the 1915 team. Even though the number of candidates was not as great as in previous seasons, Heisman had determined that his system would work more efficiently with fewer players as long as they were of high quality. He observed in the October 1915 issue of *The Yellow Jacket* "that we shall this year keep the squad down to about 60 in an endeavor to concentrate the coaching on a smaller number of promising men rather than diffuse it over a large class."[21]

Also because the 1915 schedule, according to Heisman, was "a hard one, quite the toughest Tech [has] ever faced," and because there were "more good teams in the South . . . than ever before," he took steps to beef up his coaching staff. In addition to his immediate assistant Bill Alexander, he hired a coach to handle the scrub team. He also appointed a line coach, who had been an assistant at the University of Michigan and "had much experience from one end of the line to the other. . . . [He] will, I feel confident, prove a most capable director of the linemen.[22] By this time the corporate nature of football had begun to dictate specialized coaching assignments. As Percy Haughton had done at Harvard, so Heisman was taking the initiative to respond to this fast-developing aspect of the game, actually another sign of its growing professionalization. However, his characteristic optimism about the upcoming season was tempered by his usual note of caution as he warned students and supporters alike against the overconfidence that had preceded the shocking loss to Alabama in the previous season.

But with the anticipated completion of Tech's expanded athletic complex, Heisman had good cause to be enthusiastic about the Yellow Jackets' fortunes. In the article cited above, he boldly proclaimed the project as "the best athletic field in the entire south," one that would greatly enhance Tech's future athletic endeavors. In 1913, Atlanta businessman John W. Grant had donated $50,000 for the expansion of the stands that the students had originally designed and constructed upon Heisman's arrival in 1904. Grant stipulated that the new stadium be named the Hugh Inman Grant field in memory of his deceased son, and in ensuing years, the original stadium site, which originally seated fifty-six hundred, was periodically added on to until by 1925, it had a capacity of thirty thousand. (Today the stadium has been expanded to more than twice this capacity and renamed in honor of a later Tech coach, Bobby Dodd.)

Because of Grant's philanthropy the momentum for establishing giant stadiums in the South was put in motion, and the next several years saw the erection and expansion of football facilities throughout the region. In 1915, though, the act of donating private money for the improvement of an athletic complex was practically unheard of. So Heisman was highly moved by Grant's generosity: "I am certain that I echo the sentiment that pervades the heart of every Tech man, past, present and future, when I say that we are duly appreciative of Mr. Grant's benefactions, and that we will ever try to prove ourselves worthy of such a superb gift as Grant Field."[23]

As was still customary, Heisman had scheduled three October tuneup games, and the runaway matches with Mercer (52–0) and Transylvania (67–0) went according to plans. But the contest with Davidson turned out to be entirely different, for by the end of the first half Tech found itself on the short end of a 7–0 score. Everett Strupper, freshman safety man for Tech, had fumbled a first-quarter punt, and a Davidson player had scooped up the ball and run it in for a touchdown. Strupper would go on to become one of

Tech's greatest running backs, but his miscue was sufficient for Heisman to lash out at his players during halftime, inciting them to come back in the second half and win handily, 27–7.

On October 23, even the social distractions of New Orleans didn't seem to phase Strupper and fullback Tommy Spence as they led the Yellow Jackets to an easy 36–7 win over Louisiana State University (LSU). But Coach Heisman was not to be so fortunate during this game: After becoming involved in another of his patented arguments with the officials, he was escorted off the field by the police, much to the amusement of the partisan fans.

In the next game against the University of North Carolina, Strupper came into his own, running for two touchdowns as Tech defeated the Carolina Tar Heels, 23–3. The Yellow Jackets' rock-ribbed defense held Carolina to only one first down throughout the game. Even so, Heisman must have had an eye on the upcoming game with Alabama, which had become something of a vengeance match because of Tech's upset loss the previous year.

Once again, Everett Strupper came through, leading the Yellow Jackets to a convincing 21–7 victory. But it was Alabama that came up with the most sensational play of the day when the Tide's one-man gang, Bully Vandergraaf, started out on an end run with the entire Tech defense in hot pursuit. Stopping suddenly in his tracks, Vandergraaf fired the ball back across the field to a player who, with no defenders around him, dashed sixty yards for Alabama's only score of the day. Because of its natural tendency toward wide-open play, the pass, whether forward or lateral, was proving itself a formidable, if sometimes unpredictable, weapon.

With Heisman and his supporters now thinking toward possibly winning the Southern championship, Tech went into the Georgia game a heavy favorite. The fact that the game was played in a deluge undoubtedly had something to do with the disappointing 0–0 outcome. The fleet Yellow Jacket backs, having great difficulty with their footing, were kept bottled up; and, of course, in that day a passing game under such conditions was out of the question. But for the Bulldogs the situation proved ideal, as they set up a stubborn defense and turned loose a pile-driving fullback who at one point in the game had been the brunt of attack in moving the ball down to Tech's 10-yard line. At that point Heisman pulled one of his greatest defensive moves. He sent Canty Alexander, a defensive lineman, into the game to take the place of a tiring lineman the Georgia backs had been running all over. Known for his ferocious defensive manner in goal-line situations, Alexander wasted little time in proving his worth and the wisdom of Heisman's judgment as he personally stopped Georgia's line bucks four straight times.[24] It was a one-man defensive show, and instead of a defeat, Tech walked off the field with a tie and its undefeated string, now standing at nine games, still intact. Better yet, its shot at the Southern championship was still alive.

In the final game of that momentous season, which was played in Atlanta on Thanksgiving Day, Tech came away with a 7–0 win over Auburn, only the second time in the series that the Yellow Jackets had defeated the Tigers. Once again, Everett Strupper was the offensive star as he dashed for a 25-yard touchdown in the first half, a score that held up for the remainder of the game. The Tigers' most serious bid was halted on the 6-inch line.

With its 7–0–1 record, Heisman's 1915 team expected to be crowned SIAA champions. But Vanderbilt, although they had been beaten by Virginia, also entered a claim to the title. As a result no decision was ever made, which unfortunately was usually the case in those days when conference officials could not come up with a clear-cut winner. Heisman now realized that if he were ever to produce a championship team at Tech, then he had to put together a powerhouse that would decisively defeat all comers to win the championship outright. Accordingly, at this point in his coaching career John Heisman was building what would be his strongest team in his quest for a championship.

THE NATIONAL GAME (1915)

At the national level, Cornell claimed the championship by posting its first perfect season (9–0). Led by All-American quarterback Charley Barrett, the Big Red helped its cause in the year's biggest game by defeating All-American Eddie Mahan and his Harvard team, 10–0, and at the same time ending the Crimson's thirty-three-game unbeaten string.

With its football program now enduring its worst days, Pop Warner departed Carlisle this year and went to the University of Pittsburgh, where he turned in a surprising undefeated season (8–0) his first year. Compiling a string of thirty-one wins, Warner's Pitt teams never lost during the first three years of his tenure.

In other areas of the country, Nebraska, laying the foundation for an illustrious gridiron reputation, produced an all-victorious season (8–0) and extended its record since 1911 to 35–2–3. In the process the Huskers won the Missouri Valley Conference six straight times. But it was in this year's Notre Dame match that Nebraska won national recognition for the first time. Sparked by all-conference halfback Guy Chamberlain, the Huskers came back after trailing at the half, 13–7, to defeat the Irish, 20–19.

The University of Oklahoma also began to attract attention during this time, mainly due to its proficient passing attack, which was the main factor in producing a 10–0 season in 1915. Pioneering the option pass/run, the Sooners were unique for their day in that they averaged thirty passes a game.

The year 1915 was significant for football in the southwestern area, too, as the Southwest Conference was founded. It was composed of charter members Arkansas, Baylor, LSU (soon replaced by Rice, one of Heisman's future coaching stations), Oklahoma (replaced by Southern Methodist University), Oklahoma A&M (replaced by Texas Christian University), Southwestern (which soon dropped out), Texas, and Texas A&M. By this point in its forty-five-year history, college football had entrenched itself in every section of the country.

Other important developments saw the Rose Bowl, the prototype of all the annual bowl games, officially come into being, with Brown selected to face Washington State. Ironically, the Washington State Cougars were picked to play in this bowl game over Coach Gil Dobie's Washington Huskies, who at 7–0 had extended their amazing unbeaten streak. Although Brown featured the play of halfback Fritz Pollard, one of the first great black players, and future coach Wallace Wade, the Cougars won 14–0 before seven thousand fans in the rain. This was also the year when wearing numbered jerseys became standard practice. Signifying the growing need for an official to oversee downfield decisions and to keep a precise account of the time, the field judge became a permanent fixture in game officiating this year.

This era was propitious for the emergence of the black football player. Up until this time black athletes had a difficult time in gaining acceptance on the field of competition at predominantly white institutions. Following the sporadic success of football players like William Henry Lewis at Amherst and Harvard and halfback George Jewett, who played for Michigan in 1890, other black players began to find their way northward. By 1900, in fact, blacks playing at northern schools were no longer a novelty. Nevertheless, racial incidents persisted. Indeed, some schools, particularly those in the South, would not play a team that fielded black players, although there were seldom more than two on a squad. (Observe how Heisman's 1923 Washington and Jefferson team, which was scheduled to play a southern school, reacted to this problem, in chapter 5.)   To ensure increased opportunity and greater recognition and representation for their players, a number of black schools banded together in 1912 to form their own intercollegiate conference.

Due to inadequate training and poor facilities at racially segregated high schools, most black players came to college woefully lacking in game fundamentals. But the natural abilities and competitive instincts of athletes like Fritz Pollard and Princeton's Paul Robeson were exceptional enough to transcend the boundaries of race and belie the views of white supremacists.

Pollard, the first black running back named to Walter Camp's All-America team (1916), was a study in contrasts to Robeson. Whereas Pollard was small in stature and not much given to studious pursuits, Robeson entered Princeton (which traditionally had maintained all-white athletic programs) on an academic scholarship. A superb physical specimen, Robeson exhibited astonishing versatility as not only an end in football but also as a basketball star and world-class performer in track and field. He would go on to earn a Phi Beta Kappa key, perform as a leading operatic singer and actor, and become a controversial figure in the civil rights movement. The trail-blazing examples of Pollard and Robeson, each in his own way, would inspire many young blacks to follow in their footsteps even though the trail would prove a treacherous one, full of pitfalls for those daring enough to try to better their lot over the next several decades.

HEISMAN AND THE 1916 SEASON

With "some forty men [on hand] who possess undoubted football talent and who have been more or less well grounded in the theory of the game,"[25] Heisman approached the 1916 season with more than his usual share of optimism. Yet in beating perenially weak sister Mercer, 61–0, in the first game of the season, Heisman's charges, in spite of the lopsided score, never came close to the stride they would hit in the following week's game on October 7 against Cumberland. In that game, when the dust finally settled on Grant Field, the Yellow Jackets had rolled up the biggest point total in football history.

The game itself has been referred to as the funniest, strangest, most bizarre, if not the most mismatched football game ever played. According to Heisman in a 1928 *Collier's* article, his players had an ulterior motive in doing what they did:

"If you boys don't lick Cumberland by 50 points," said Bill Alexander, my assistant coach, "you ought to be whipped."

"If we score 100 will you set 'em up for the gang, Alex?" cried Strupper, one of our halfbacks.

"I'll set 'em up for the varsity scrubs and the frosh if you make it 200," grinned Alex.

Alex then left on a scouting trip. He must have felt faint when he read the newspapers. The score was Georgia Tech 222, Cumberland 0.[26]

The final score represented thirty-two touchdowns (the inspired Everett Strupper scored eight of them) and eighteen consecutive extra points in the first half alone (kicked by Jim Preas)—all are national records that still stand. While Georgia Tech recorded twenty first downs, Cumberland, unable to move the ball when it had possession, failed to register a single first down. Its biggest rushing gains were two 5-yard runs, while it managed to complete two of fifteen passes for fourteen yards (six of these were intercepted, five for touchdowns.) Not having to, Tech, of course, threw no passes and piled up a total of 501 rushing yards to −42 for Cumberland.

Once-proud Cumberland, in the process of disbanding football due to financial problems but eager to collect a $500 guarantee, showed up in Atlanta with a hastily recruited group of players, who were obviously not anticipating playing one of the strongest teams in the South. And as it turned out, the game was a total mismatch from beginning to end. By the end of the first quarter the Yellow Jackets found themselves ahead by 63–0, and the score was 126–0 at the half. At this juncture, the Cumberland players were un-doubtedly ready to throw in the towel, for as Heisman humorously recalled the situation:

As you may suspect, Cumberland lost considerable interest in proceedings after Tech had scored her first hundred points and was inclined to let matters take whatever course they might. Among those enjoying it least were the Cumberland backs. All any one of them had to do to be subjected to a thorough going over was to receive the ball; and presently none of the Cumberland men appeared to care where the ball was—as long as it wasn't near them.

Once a Cumberland halfback found himself possessed of it. Instantly he was tackled so hard that he and the ball separated. It rolled toward the other halfback. One of Cumberland's ends yelled: "Fall on it, Pete, fall on it."

Pete looked at the fellow with infinite scorn. "Fall on it yourself—I didn't fumble it."[27]

Despite the overwhelming score at this point, though, Heisman was in no mood to show mercy as he told his charges during halftime: "Men, we're in front, but you never know what those Cumberland players have up their sleeves. So, in the second half, go out and hit 'em clean and hit 'em hard. Don't let up."[28]

Nevertheless, they did let up but just barely, adding another 96 points to their already momentous total, even though the final two quarters were cut to twelve and a half minutes each. In the third quarter when Strupper scored his seventh touchdown of the day for a 154–0 lead, Tech became the highest-scoring college football team of all time, surpassing Michigan's 153 point total against a practice opponent during Fielding Yost's tenure. By the end of the third quarter the score stood at 180–0, at which point the game should have been called, but the Yellow Jackets went on to pile up 42 more mean-ingless points. Naturally, most of the records set that day have stood the test of time: biggest score, greatest number of touchdowns and points after, highest score for a single quarter and half, most points kicked after touchdown by one player (Jim Preas established this record in the first half as three players divided the point-after chores in the second half, making twelve out of fourteen attempts), and greatest number of players scoring (twelve). Never having to punt, Tech gained over five-hundred yards in both punt and kickoff returns, with total all-purpose yards totaling 1,179.

Since the game was considered just another warmup contest that schools of that day were accustomed to scheduling, the Atlanta newspapers thought so little of the one-sided game that they devoted no more than a column of space to it. But later on, Heisman claimed he had a special reason for giving no quarter and instructing his players to amass all those points. He had a bone to pick with all the sportswriters who relied too much on football's statistics to make useless comparisons in publicizing teams and determining national rankings. So according to Heisman, the joke was on them. As he commented in the 1917 Tech yearbook,

The writer has often contended that this habit on the part of sport writers of totaling up, from week's end to week's end, the number of points each team had amassed in its various games, and comparing them one with another, was a useless thing, for it means nothing whatever in the way of determining which is the better of an evenly grouped set of college teams. . . .

Accordingly, in the Cumberland game the Jackets set all their sails to make a record run, and for the first time in our football career we turned loose all we had in the way of scoring stuff, and the result was a world's record of 222 points rolled up in 45 minutes of play. [The last quarter was called with five minutes to play.][29]

According to Gene Griessman there was actually another reason for Heisman's running up the score—a grudge. In a letter one of Heisman's players wrote:

The reason for the high score was a grudge that existed between [Heisman] and Dan McGugin, who was the football coach at Vanderbilt. The year before, Vanderbilt played a rather weak schedule and ran up some high scores on weak teams. By this, he gained a lot of publicity and it got under coach's skin.[30]

Heisman also insisted that the opening game with Mercer, won by the Yellow Jackets, 61–0, was an experiment in which he wanted to see how much scoring his team could produce by running only through the middle of the line.

All experiments were off, though, when Heisman and his charges played the Davidson Wildcats on the following Saturday. As usual when they took on Tech, the Davidson players seemed to be at their inspired best, and at the half the score stood as a surprising scoreless tie. In the second half, though, Jim Senter, Everett Strupper, and Tommy Spence finally got on track, and the Yellow Jackets pulled out a hard-fought 9–0 win.

Another tough game was in store when Tech hosted North Carolina the following week. In this one, the "S" boys were not so fortunate. Strupper, who had scored on a 60-yard run to help lead the Yellow Jackets to a 10–0 advantage, was injured and had to leave the game. Next the hard-driving Senter broke his leg, and after Spence, an all-southern back, hurt his neck, Heisman realized that the depth of his team would be put to the test. At this point, the Tar Heels generated a successful drive to make the score 10–6. Then another drive stalled at the Tech 10-yard line, but a poor Yellow Jacket punt gave the ball right back to Carolina on the 15-yard line. A couple of plays later, the Tar Heels had a first down on the 5-yard line, but instead of running, the quarterback tried a pass, which fell incomplete. At that time, an incomplete pass over the goal line reverted back to the other team's possession. But for some reason the official became confused and awarded the ball to Carolina, only to see an irate Heisman charge out onto the field to straighten the matter out. Tech had won another game, but just barely.

Close matches had become the order of the day, and when Washington and Lee came to Atlanta on October 28, Tech found itself in another dogfight. The W&L Generals were one of the South's tougher teams, and defeat seemed likely early in the game as Tech's stage fright allowed W&L to penetrate to the 10-yard line. At this point, Heisman called on his old reliable, Canty Alexander, to stop the attack, and once again the feisty tackle rose to the occasion to help throw back four successive plays. But after Strupper's punt was blocked, Tech had to hold again, only to see Strupper's next punt also blocked, giving W&L possession on the 20-yard line. Following a fake line buck and end run, the ball wound up on the 2-yard line, from where the Generals scored to take the lead, 7–0.

It was beginning to look as though it would not be Tech's day, and Heisman could sense it. Especially after the Yellow Jackets moved the ball to the 15-yard line, where they tried a field goal with a drop kick, only to see the ball hit the upright, fall to the cross bar, dribble along it, and finally fall off on the wrong side. But during halftime, the Heisman "school spirit" magic apparently took hold again as the Tech men came back strong defensively, mustering enough offense to allow Strupper to pass for the tying score, and the game ended in a 7–7 tie. It was the second tie in his undefeated streak, but Heisman's men had shown they could hold up against the onslaught of a team considered by many to be their superior.

As though a premonition of things to come, Tech closed out the 1916 season with four convincing wins. After hammering Tulane, 45–0, the Yellow Jackets went against an Alabama team that at first appeared to have figured out how to stop Heisman's jump shift cold: move the defense with the offensive shift and wait for the play to develop. In spite of this maneuver, though, the Tech men had enough offense to win out in the end, 13–0.

Now the championship of the South depended on the outcome of the Tech–Georgia game, which was to be played on November 18 in Athens. Although both teams were unbeaten, Tech was the betting favorite. Because Georgia had scouted the Alabama game, Heisman fully expected the Bulldogs to come up with a similar defensive system to halt his jump shift. In order to counter their strategy, the wily coach directed his backs to move in the opposite direction from which the shift was normally meant to go. As a result, when the game was underway the Georgia defense became hopelessly confused, especially after it stopped shifting with the jump, only to see Tech return to its original system.

However, the turning point of the game came when Heisman sent in the ever-dependable Canty Alexander to shore up the defense after Georgia wound up with the ball on Tech's 5-yard line as the result of a poor punt. Playing his usual stubbornly determined role, Alexander managed to rally his teammates to hurl back the Bulldog attack four times in a row. After that, it was Katy bar the door, as Tommy Spence and Everett Strupper alternated in moving the ball down field for the first touchdown, eventually adding two more for a 21–0 victory.

With the Yellow Jackets blasting Auburn, 33–7, in their Thanksgiving Day classic, Georgia Tech finally won the SIAA championship uncontested. In accounting for its big win, the Yellow Jackets had put the game on ice in the second quarter by scoring three touchdowns. In going nineteen games without a loss, Tech had managed to beat Auburn two years in a row for the first time. But despite Tech's tremendous success in 1916 and the attendant jubilation of Heisman and his supporters over winning the Southern championship, the best was yet to come.

THE NATIONAL GAME (1916)

The national teams of the year were Pitt and Army, both undefeated, but Helms awarded Pitt (8–0) the championship. Pitt's Pop Warner, who by this time was tiring of the single-wingback with which he had enjoyed so much success, was starting to experiment with his inevitable variation—the double-wingback. The result was an offense characterized by a plethora of fakes and reverses that could be run to either side of the line, as well as increased passing possibilities because of the number of receivers available.

Led by All-American halfback Elmer Oliphant, unbeaten Army (9–0) defeated Notre Dame, 30–10. An all-round athlete, Oliphant came to West Point from Purdue where he had been a four-sport man. At West Point he also participated in boxing, swimming, and hockey, in addition to football. His six touchdowns and 45 points scored that year against Villanova still stand as West Point records.

One of the year's biggest upsets was engineered by up-and-coming Illinois coach Bob Zuppke as he concocted a way to stop the Minnesota shift and beat the Gophers, 14–9, to hand them their only loss of the season.

Yale, under its new coach Tad Jones, won all its games except the one against Brown as Fritz Pollard scored three times in the second half to down the Blue, 21–6. This was also the year of the Harvard game when Jones delivered his famous pep talk that started off: "You are now going out to play football against Harvard. Never again in your whole life will you do anything so important."[31] His words worked their magic as Yale beat the Crimson for the first time in seven years, 6–3.

With halfback Chic Harley at the helm, Ohio State went undefeated for the first time (7–0). He single-handedly beat Illinois (7–6) and Wisconsin (14–13) as he scored touchdowns and then kicked extra points to win both games for the Buckeyes.

This was the year, too, that the Pacific Coast Conference got underway with charter members California, Oregon, Oregon State, and Washington signing up. Stanford and Washington State would join the following year;

Idaho and Southern Cal in 1922; Montana in 1924; and UCLA in 1929. With another game in the revived Rose Bowl series to be played, football was now fairly well established in the West. In this year's match between Oregon and Penn, the Ducks of Oregon came out on top, 14–0. Future sports luminaries playing for Penn were quarterback Bert Bell, who would become commissioner of the National Football League, and tackle Lou Little, who would return to the Rose Bowl as coach of the Columbia Lions in 1934 and defeat Stanford in an upset, 7–0.

That some peculiar aspects of football's rules still needed overhauling in 1916 was attested to by an incident that decided the outcome of the Georgia–Auburn game. Played in Columbus, Georgia, where this matchup would continue to be scheduled until 1959, the close game was won by the Tigers, 3–0, when they kicked a 45-yard field goal that had been teed-up on a helmet! Although Georgia questioned the legality of the play, it was allowed to stand by the officials as just one more unexpected development the Rules Committee would have to look into.

HEISMAN AND THE 1917 SEASON

In climax to the unsettled European conditions of the past several years, in 1917 the United States was thrust into the war it had been trying to avoid but could no longer. The sinking of the British ocean liner *Lusitania* in May 1915 had brought the United States and Germany to the brink of war, but when German submarines sank three U.S. ships President Woodrow Wilson asked Congress in April 1917 to declare war. By May the conscription of men between the ages of twenty-one and thirty was underway. The impact on college football was immediate.

Ironically, preparation in the South for the 1917 season was more widespread than it had ever been before. Football was still growing in popularity year by year, and with many of the football-playing schools committed to enhancing their images, they were now putting more money into coach's salaries and athletic-support equipment. But dissension was dividing the member schools of the SIAA. It resulted from a quarrel over a proposed ruling that would require all athletes, mainly freshmen, to be in residence for a year before they could play. Most northern schools had made interinstitutional agreements restricting freshman eligibility, but in the South it was still a problem. To restrict the eligibility of freshmen would definitely hurt the smaller schools, for with fewer players to choose from they needed their freshmen athletes to help field a complete team.

But it was the call to arms that had begun to dominate everyone's thoughts, and particularly Georgia Tech football players' plans. Should they answer the call or stay in school? Since patriotic fervor characterized the reaction of most of these men, it wasn't long before nearby Camp Gordon was brimming over with former football players applying for officer candidate school. The game of football was thought by some to be a training ground for war, and those gladiators who had performed admirably on the gridiron were considered to be prime contenders for battle. Harvard coach Percy Haughton, who would serve as an Army officer, later wrote: "Football is a miniature war game played under somewhat more civilized rules of conduct, in which the team becomes the military force of the school or university it represents. Most of the combat principles of the Field Service Regulations of the U.S. Army are applicable to the modern game of football."[32] But those who marched off to war would quickly realize that the horrors of the battlefield itself greatly overshadowed the ephemeral skirmishes of the football field. An early casualty of the war was Georgia Tech's own Tommy Spence, who had trained as an aviator and was killed in Europe. As Tech's first athlete to die in combat, Spence's tragic death helped drive home the grim reality of the war.

However, Heisman had his own viewpoints about how a young man in college should cope with the temptation to volunteer, contending that a student could best serve his country by staying in school and awaiting his call. To back up his stand, the erudite coach quoted the duke of Wellington's famous line—the battle of Waterloo had been won on the playing fields of Eton and Harrow. Nevertheless, there were those who were critical of Heisman, charging that he was purposely trying to keep his players from joining the armed forces. These same critics were undoubtedly also aware of Heisman's Germanic origins. But Bill Fincher, one of the players on this 1917 team, called the basis for these charges "absurd" and "a lot of hogwash." Fincher went on to say: "I never heard Heisman say a word against volunteering. Fact is, after the 1917 season only three players did not go into service. I was rejected because I had only one eye. Another guy had a physical disability, and [Indian Joe] Guyon, oddly enough, was said to be an alien."[33]

Nevertheless, by the fall of 1917, Heisman had assembled a group of young men that for many years would be considered the greatest football team the South had ever produced. It won all nine of its games, seven of them by shutouts, scoring 491 points to the opposition's 17. In fact, over Tech's last five games for that year, the team averaged an astounding 72 points a game. What's more, not only did Georgia Tech win another SIAA championship, the team was declared national champion, the first southern team to claim the honor.

Much of Heisman's success that year can be attributed to the backfield he put together, consisting of quarterback Al Hill, halfbacks Everett Strupper (who had certainly proven his worth in previous campaigns), Indian Joe Guyon (a transfer from Carlisle), and fullback Judy Harlan. A strong case could be made for this group as the greatest backfield a southern school has ever assembled. The line was one of the best ever, too, with Cy Bell and Ray Ulrich at the ends, Bill "Big Six" Carpenter and Bill Fincher at tackles, Dan Whelchel and Ham Dowling at guards, and Pup Phillips at center. Of these players, Strupper and Carpenter were the first players from the Deep South to be named to a national All-America team in 1917. (With America at war in 1917, Walter Camp himself did not select his All-America team; and in 1918, he chose an All-Service team made up of players from military training camps.)

One of Heisman's favorite players, Bill Carpenter, performed with a sense of dedication that was hard to match. As Heisman wrote: "On three of Georgia Tech's greatest teams Bill Carpenter—Big Six—played right tackle in the manner that makes coaches believe that life is good. Even the coaches of the teams we walloped were given to saying that it was worth a beating to watch Bill."[34] Heisman then told how Carpenter was advised to quit football after suffering an internal injury during the 1916 season that resulted in the removal of one of his kidneys. So intent was he on playing the 1917 season, however, that he countered the opinions of his doctor, the Georgia Tech president, and even the governor of the state, who happened to be chairman of the board of trustees to whom Carpenter had made his last appeal to play. Upon hearing his case and realizing just how dedicated Carpenter was, the governor relented and allowed him to play, wishing "God and good luck" to be with him.

Surely one of the most colorful players Heisman ever coached was Indian Joe Guyon. An assistant coach for the Yellow Jacket team during this era was a personable fellow named Charley "Wahoo" Guyon, whom Heisman had hired from Carlisle. As a result, his brother Joe, who had been a star running back at Carlisle for several years, showed up on campus in 1917 ready to perform for the Yellow Jackets. And a formidable performer Guyon proved to be, as his play over the next two seasons attest. (He would go on to become one of the pioneer players in professional football.)

But Indian Joe was as notable for his wacky behavior as he was for his outstanding athletic performances. Teammate Judy Harlan in his later years offered some insights into Guyon's eccentric personality: "Once in a while the Indian would come out in Joe, such as the nights Heisman gave us a white football and had us working out under the lights. That's when Guyon would give out with the blood-curdling war whoops." And according to Harlan, Guyon was not above using a few old Indian tricks, either. Like the time in 1917 when he knocked out a W&L player by wearing an old horse collar shaped into a shoulder pad but reinforced with a little steel.[35]

A major reason for Heisman's 1917 success was that he now possessed the perfect material for executing the jump shift that he had been experimenting with for about a decade. Although some of today's football fans may think the I-formation and T-formation are of recent development, these later formations are really derivatives of a system like Heisman used during the 1917 season. As Al Thomy describes the 1917 Yellow Jacket attack,

First the Jackets lined up in the I, with Harlan, Guyon, and Strupper in a straight line behind Hill. Center Phillips stood erect, hands on hips, looking over his shoulder.

When he saw teammates in line, he bent over the ball, and that was the signal to shift to the T.

The shift barely preceded the snap of the ball—usually a direct snap to Strupper who went to his left or right behind the interference of three backs and two guards, a five-man convoy.[36]

According to New York sportswriter George Trevor, the Tech attack was something awesome to behold: "At the shift signal, the phalanx deployed with the startling suddenness of a Jeb Stuart cavalry raid."[37] But Heisman himself admitted to having difficulty in coming up with the proper signal system to get a shift play off and running:

At first the quarterback would set the shift . . . in motion by barking "Now" or "Shift" whereat all those required to "shift" would move with the rhythmic hop, step or skip to their new positions in so many synchronized counts. Then, at a new command, the ball would be snapped. To start my own shift we used "Now" but presently we found our opponents committing sabotage on our nice machinery by calling "Now" at frequent and disconcerting intervals.

Inasmuch as that situation demanded quick remedy I substituted a sight signal. My center would stand erect. All the other players would watch his head. The instant he started to bend forward, the shift would start. It worked beautifully and I am quite sure that many of our opponents never did unravel the mystery.[38]

The first to feel the sting of the Yellow Jacket attack in 1917 was not one team but two, as Tech took on both Wake Forest and Furman on the same day. There is no explanation as to why Heisman found himself having to face two teams on the same date, except that there must have been some kind of scheduling conflict and the Tech coach felt bound to honor his commitments. Or Heisman could actually have felt confident enough to take on these two teams on the same day, as talented as his players were. At any rate, Wake Forest fell 33–0 in the opening contest, and then Furman, against whom Heisman used only second-string players (with the exception of his quarterback Al Hill) went down, 25–0. Undefeated now in twenty-one straight contests, the 1917 Yellow Jackets were off and running toward regional honors. But it was the October 6 match, when Penn was scheduled to come south for the first time, that focused the national spotlight on Atlanta.

Until this time, southern teams had not fared well against northern opponents. Dan McGugin's Vanderbilt Commodores had given a good account of themselves in losing close matches to Michigan in 1906, 1907, and 1911. They had also come up with ties against Navy in 1907 and Yale in 1910. But only Virginia had turned in a win against a major northern school by pummeling Yale in 1915, 10–0.

Now it was Georgia Tech's turn to face a northern team, and ironically enough that team represented Coach Heisman's alma mater—a nationally ranked team that was heavily favored, mainly because it boasted four players of All-America caliber. These included quarterback Bert Bell and a pile-driving fullback named Howard Berry. It soon became obvious, however, that the Yellow Jackets had not paid much attention to the newspapers' predictions, as on the game's first play Everett Strupper streaked sixty-eight yards around left end for a touchdown. To the delight of ten thousand fans Heisman's jump shift was clicking on all cylinders that day, and by the half his men led, 20–0. In the meantime Penn's main offensive weapon, Berry, was stopped cold. By the end of the game Strupper had scored twice, Hill three times, and Judy Harlan, in his first varsity action, had intercepted a Bert Bell pass and had run it back seventy yards for a score. With Fincher making good on five extra points, the Yellow Jackets enjoyed a satisfying 41–0 victory. What's more, Heisman's team now found itself basking in the national limelight for the first time. After all the years of SIAA championship anticipation, on that memorable afternoon in Atlanta Tech supporters now had real cause to celebrate national aspirations.

It was in this same Penn game that Tech inherited its most colorful nickname. With the devastating defeat of the Quakers and the resultant national attention, Morgan Blake of the *Atlanta Journal* wrote of the "Golden Tornado attack" that had so handily beaten the northern visitors. The Golden Tornado tag soon gained favor with both the students and the public, and it didn't begin to fade from popularity until after the advent of Bobby Dodd's 1952 Sugar Bowl team.[39]

But Heisman knew only too well that a letdown could easily follow a big win, especially when the next opponent was a team that had always given the Yellow Jackets a rough time—Davidson. Accordingly, with their sensational back Buck Flowers running wild, the Wildcats of Davidson got off to a good start and even led for a while. But they soon fell to the Yellow Jackets' superior manpower as Tech went on to win, 32–10. Nevertheless, Davidson's point total was the highest that would be scored on Tech in a game that year.

After this test the flood gates were opened as the Yellow Jackets, led by Al Hill, overwhelmed one of the previous year's toughest teams, 63–0. Next, Vanderbilt suffered the worst football defeat in its history, 83–0. In this game the Tech backfield was so difficult to contain that it never failed to gain, and Bill Fincher kicked eleven out of eleven extra point attempts. As most onlookers found it hard to believe that a Dan McGugin team could be beaten so thoroughly, they had to concede that John Heisman had indeed put together a team of national championship caliber, a team that could defeat any it played.

When the once-heralded Carlisle team came to Atlanta on November 10, any doubt about Tech's potential as a national power was erased as the Yellow Jackets demolished the Indians, 98–0. The score could have been even higher except that the game had to be called in the final quarter when Carlisle ran out of substitutes. It was thought that the outcome of this game helped to close the doors of the proud Indian school, which during its brief career had so many grand and glorious accomplishments on the gridiron. But the times were now changing at too rapid a pace for a school like Carlisle to keep up with its more fortunate competitors.

Having earlier shut out Tulane, 48–0, Heisman's best team to date was looking to capture another Southern championship as Tech prepared to meet traditional foe Auburn. With Everett Strupper and Indian Joe Guyon well in command, the game, like all played that memorable season, wasn't even close. The Yellow Jackets won, 68–7, as Auburn endured one of its worst defeats ever.

Georgia Tech, of course, won the 1917 Southern championship, but in the previous week the Auburn Tigers had played a key role in helping the Yellow Jackets gain legitimate recognition for their first national championship. In a widely heralded matchup played in Montgomery, Alabama, Auburn had held national champion contender Ohio State and All-American Chic Harley to a 0–0 tie. Naturally, when Tech beat Auburn by 61 points the press had to recognize the Yellow Jackets as national champions, although Heisman had challenged Pop Warner's Pitt Panthers to a post-season match to determine the championship. Such contests were not readily organized in those days, and consequently the Pitt–Tech game wound up being scheduled for the regular 1918 season.

In addition to the national championship there were other honors for the Yellow Jackets in 1917: Besides Everett Strupper and Bill Carpenter being chosen for the first-team All-America, Joe Guyon and Al Hill were chosen for the second team, and six of Heisman's players were named to the all-southern team. Among them, of course, were Hill and Strupper who between them had scored forty-two touchdowns, and Bill Fincher who had kicked forty-nine extra points. To be sure, John Heisman had fashioned a scoring machine the likes of which would rarely be seen again, in the South or anywhere. Nevertheless, his own personal assessment of this team's success had more to do with his overall philosophy of football than it did with singling out various individuals for praise. As he wrote in the 1917 Georgia Tech yearbook:

In a system of play it's unfair to single out men too much for praise. To be sure we had our stars, as teams always must have; but the best part of a good football team's work is that it teaches a man his place in the scheme of things. It teaches him to subordinate himself to the rules that apply to all. It teaches him to give help to others by showing him how others will help him. . . .

The lesson is not only for this Fall's football, but for all of life and for all time to come—and for all of you. Ponder it.[40]

Once again, Heisman took the opportunity to express his understanding of success in football as an object lesson about success in life.

THE NATIONAL GAME (1917)

On the national scene, another successful team, in addition to Pitt (9–0) and Ohio State (8–0–1), was Texas A&M, who under first-year coach Dana X. Bible also went undefeated (8–0). Bible would enjoy many more successful years ahead. It being a war year, the Rose Bowl saw fit to fill its New Year's date with two military teams: the Army team from Fort Lewis against the Marines from Mare Island. The game was won by the Marines, 19–7.

With the Meuse–Argonne campaign in France having gotten underway right at the start of the 1918 football season, the city of Atlanta was naturally more interested in casualty lists than in football scores. (Something like 120,000 Americans would be killed in combat, many of them southern boys representing every state in the South.) A number of southern schools did not even field teams this year, including Alabama, Georgia, LSU, North Carolina, Tennessee, and Virginia; those teams that did play had abbreviated schedules. In the East, Cornell and Yale were conspicuously absent from area football schedules, and symbolically, the Army–Navy match was cancelled. Because of the lack of competition, other areas of the country, like the Southwest and the Pacific Coast, decided not to award a championship.

Writing at a point not far removed from these times, Fuzzy Woodruff, in his inimitable style, made some interesting comments about the football situation during the war years, not only in the South but across the country:

> Football is a game that demands mass support and feminine adulation to produce its color. There was nobody much who cared about seeing football games in the fall of 1918, and the fair sex was far more interested in men who wore Sam Browne belts than men who wore a letter on their sweaters.
>
> Then too, the football coach had disappeared. It was war time. Luxuries such as football coaches couldn't be afforded. Some of the coaches were hired by the government to stick around as athletic instructors but the salaries paid were meagre and the support given was decidedly limited.

Woodruff went on to show how schedule making had deteriorated as a result of all the colleges that had dropped football. In this void, military installations, practically all of which fielded football teams made up of former college stars, came to the rescue. "They would play anybody, anywhere, any time, and financial considerations didn't amount to anything."[41]

HEISMAN AND THE 1918 SEASON

Many coaches may have disappeared from the college scene at the time, as Woodruff points out (even Walter Camp had accepted an appointment as physical fitness director for the Navy Department), but John Heisman was still around, alive and well, and looking to play another season. In his late forties now, he was among the older active coaches, but there were continuing signs that things were not as amicable as they had been between the coach and his wife of fifteen years. So with his own private domestic war to wage, Heisman looked to the football campaign as a kind of buffer to ward off his problems at home. As a confirmed "football widow," though, Evelyn Heisman surely knew by now what her husband's real love was. Her loneliness was compounded by the fact that her son, Carlisle, was now gone. He had attended Georgia Tech, even played football under his stepfather, and although a scrub played sufficiently well to win his letter. (Clearly not taking the game as seriously as his illustrious coach, he labeled himself "The Eternal Scrub.") Joining up at the right time, Carlisle Cox went on to a distinguished military career.

With most football players, including his own, now gone into the service, Heisman had a hard time coming up with a competitive schedule. Joe Guyon was the sole holdover from the backfield that had demolished all their opponents of a year earlier. But on October 5, against traditional foe Clemson, Heisman unveiled another talented back in freshman Red Barron, whose running ability amazed the game crowd in a 28–0 win. Then the following week Tech overwhelmed Furman, 118–0. One of the main reasons for the lopsided score was halfback Buck Flowers, the same Davidson player who had given the Yellow Jackets such a tough time in the past but who had transferred to the Atlanta school. Since the SIAA had "no eligibility rules or disbarments for a football career" at the time, his eligibility was never questioned.[42] With Guyon, Barron, and Flowers in the lineup on November 9, Heisman and his team celebrated the signing of the Armistice two days early by lambasting N.C. State, 128–0.

When news of the Armistice was finally received, there was widespread, tumultuous celebration in Atlanta and throughout the country, as well as a deep feeling of relief that the conflict was over. No less a celebrant was John Heisman who, with the threat of the draft soon to be removed, looked to a return to prewar normalcy. But first there were other pressing matters to be taken care of, and after big wins over two Army camp teams, Tech approached its big game with Pitt, having averaged 84 unanswered points in its last five games. Signs looked good for a win over its northern foe.

But when Heisman took his Yellow Jackets to Pittsburgh's Forbes Field on November 23 to play Pop Warner's Panthers, he did not know at the time that he would be going up against the team of the year. The Panthers had a huge line in front of two All-American players in fullback Tank McLaren and halfback Tom Davies. All Tech had going for it were its three talented backs and its thirty-three-game unbeaten string. But these were not nearly enough as Pitt dominated the game from start to finish. Davies, who seemed to be all over the field that day, ran fifty yards for one touchdown, returned one punt fifty yards for another, then ran back another sixty yards for a score, and, to add insult to injury, threw two touchdown passes as Pitt won, 32–0. It was one of the blackest days in Heisman's coaching career, and now he could only wish that his

1917 team had played Pitt. While Joe Guyon had shown up well in a losing cause, Pop Warner called Red Barron, whose finest days still lay ahead, the "best half-back I've ever seen on Forbes Field."[43]

Even though the thirty-three-game unbeaten streak was now broken, Heisman still had a wagon-load of glowing statistics to savor. From late in 1914 through the fifth game of the 1918 campaign, his teams had scored 1,599 points for a 48.5 average per game, while holding opponents to a total of only 67 points, a mere 2.0 average per game. Twenty-one of the thirty-three games were shutouts, and no team had scored more than one touchdown in any game against the Yellow Jackets during that era. Truly, John Heisman had fashioned one of football's greatest dynasties.

After the loss to Pitt, Tech's immediate obligation was to beat Auburn on Thanksgiving and win another SIAA championship. And beat the Tigers they did, 41–0. Indian Joe Guyon closed out his career gloriously, scoring twice, once on a 25-yard pass from Flowers and then on a line plunge. The wet field conditions did not seem to bother the Yellow Jackets as they scored in every quarter to build up their final point total.

THE NATIONAL GAME (1918)

Although named national champion in 1918, Pitt saw its own winning streak, extending over a four-year period, come to an end. It came in a game with a service team, the Cleveland Naval Reserve, which, as expected, was made up of a considerable number of ex-college players. Former Georgia Tech back Judy Harlan was instrumental in the outcome of this game, as Al Thomy relates:

> Harlan managed a bit of personal revenge when he served in the Navy at Cleveland during the 1918 season.
> "We beat Pittsburgh 10–9," he says, "it was their only loss of the season. [Richard] Ducote kicked the winning field goal, and I intercepted a pass and returned it to midfield in the fourth quarter. I felt at least I had evened up some of the losses we had at Tech."[44]

Years later Tech would finally beat Pitt in the Sugar Bowl and Gator Bowl.

Because of the war, northern schools had begun to use freshman players for the first time, in contrast to the South where freshmen had always been eligible. Although playing abbreviated schedules, Michigan and Navy (under second-year coach Gil Dobie) turned out top teams. Other successful teams were Texas (9–0) and Virginia Tech (7–0). But for the future of football, from a national point of view, the most momentous, although unheralded, event of the year was the appointment of Knute Rockne as head coach of Notre Dame. As his career was soon to prove, he established himself as the model football coach whose success during his relatively brief tenure would become legendary.

Actually, a great deal of Rockne's coaching success can be attributed to the man's vibrant personality, which extended beyond the bounds of the football field. Whereas John Heisman could be crusty, even venomous in his dealings with players and public alike, Rockne conveyed a personable, human side that immediately won people over. Inclined to scholarship like Heisman (Rockne had been a chemistry professor who could quote the classics), the new Irish coach was more of a psychologist when it came to dealing with his players. Whereas Heisman had a manner that could rub a player the wrong way (as when he once publicly denounced Red Barron, who would earn a reputation as one of the South's greatest running backs, as a "flaming jackass" because of a defensive lapse), Rockne could be firm and yet understanding of any on- or off-field personal problems his players might be experiencing.

His handling of the talented but emotionally troubled George Gipp is a case in point. As a talented football player who could do everything the game demanded exceptionally well—run, pass, drop kick, and punt—Gipp required very little coaching. Yet he was somewhat lazy, even electing to forgo practice sessions occasionally, a problem that Rockne managed to handle quite tactfully. As a result, he got some superb performances out of the problematic Gipp. "A reputation as a martinet is invaluable to a coach," Rockne once said and then added, "providing he doesn't work at it too hard." For all his success as a coach, it would appear in retrospect that John Heisman did work consciously hard at being a disciplinarian. When Knute Rockne got his highly successful program underway at Notre Dame, Heisman, being the astute observer of the game that he was, undoubtedly marveled at and envied the tremendous success the man enjoyed, recognizing in him the necessary qualities a coach should possess in getting the most out of his players. At heart, the basic difference between the two coaches was in their personalities, for in their understanding of the game they had a lot in common.

After a 3–1–2 first year, Rockne would go on over his tragically shortened career to an amazing 105–12–5 record, a .881 percentage, which included five undefeated seasons. But his greatest contribution to the game itself was endowing it with more of a national image by helping to move it away from the control of the Eastern establishment. Naturally, the great teams he produced and with which he confronted any challenge from coast to coast were the major factor in this transition. Because of the thousands who had never seen the Notre Dame campus but became deep-dyed Irish fans anyway, college football took on even more of a popular image, a game not just reserved for the students and alumni but for the general public as well.

Due to the fact that the abbreviated schedules of that year had given the Rose Bowl organizers a limited picture of the strength of eastern teams, two service teams were again invited to play, this time the Great Lakes Navy team versus the Mare Island Marines. Led by a plucky back named George

Halas, the Navy team won, 17–0. Halas, who was named the outstanding player of the game, would go on to found the professional Chicago Bears. He, in fact, would become one of the early pioneers of professional football in the 1920s, a decade that saw a number of midwestern cities establish franchises, only to see many of them fold in the same year they were founded. It was an uncertain, highly experimental era for a professional sport that no one could have dreamed at the time would have such a glorious and prosperous future. Many of the early professional teams, which attracted college players like Jim Thorpe, Joe Guyon, and Pete Henry, originated as promotional ventures for the companies that supported them as, for example, the Decatur, Illinois, Staleys. Hired as the athletic director of the Staley Starch Company, George Halas, at twenty-two, began his professional sports career as player-coach of the Staleys.

THE NATIONAL SCENE (1919)

The year 1919, which was to be Heisman's last at Georgia Tech, was one of great prosperity in the South as it was in most areas of the land. In spite of the optimistic tenor that had pervaded the country at the close of the war, though, there were signs, both social and political, that America would never again be the same country it had been prior to the war. In January, one of Heisman's personal heroes, Theodore Roosevelt, died, and with him passed the spirit of an era. Following the Bolshevik Revolution of 1917, the threat of a Communist takeover generated periodic outbursts of Red hysteria around the country. While a death-dealing influenza epidemic had been raging throughout the country since 1918, sufficiently widespread to test the latest advances in medicine, there also sprang up rampant inflation, labor disputes, and occasional race riots, revealing that all was not well in the land, both economically and socially. Even continued technological advances, mainly in communications and transportation (the first nonstop trans-Atlantic flight was accomplished in 1919), were greeted with an air of suspicion in some quarters, an obvious reaction to the disenchantment with science that had grown out of the war itself. Other social developments like the Suffrage movement, which had been evolving since 1913, and Prohibition, which would result in the Eighteenth Amendment being finally ratified in 1919, would realize their fullest impact in the 1920s. But a social transformation had been set in motion, and America would never again have the complacent feeling and insular contentment it had enjoyed before the world-shaking events that occurred between 1914 and 1918.

The college campuses of 1919 were booming, as veterans returned to take up where they had left off. With many former football players back, too, the gridiron sport was poised to enjoy one of its most popular seasons. To meet spectator demands, Georgia Tech immediately realized it could use a stadium that would seat at least twenty-five thousand fans. On a wider front the practice of building stadiums or expanding those in existence was soon spreading all over the South, as most campuses of significant size looked for sufficient funding or perhaps even a philanthropist on the order of Atlanta's John W. Grant to help build a showpiece stadium. The day of football as a form of mass entertainment staged on a grand scale was fast approaching.

HEISMAN AND THE 1919 SEASON

As for Tech's football prospects for 1919, Heisman greeted Judy Harlan (back from military service), Ham Dowling, Bill Fincher, and Pup Phillips from the great 1917 team, and the backs Red Barron and Buck Flowers from the 1918 team. Thus he naturally felt he had the nucleus for another fine team. Nevertheless, something seemed to be missing in Heisman's usual enthusiasm, and once the season got underway, an uncharacteristic lack of intensity began to show. He began to spend more and more time away from the team, depending on assistant coach Alexander to take charge in his absence. Were the marital problems he was experiencing at home starting to weigh on his mind? Or was his atypical attitude due to the fact that after nearly sixteen years of coaching at Tech he was ready for a change?

At any rate, something that had occurred that spring may have had a lot to do with his dispirited frame of mind. It also pointed out what could result from the fierce rivalries that intercollegiate athletics had spawned by this time. The University of Georgia, which had not fielded a football team during the war years of 1917–1918, was ready to renew its gridiron series with Tech when a parade following a baseball game between the two schools in May 1919 aroused feelings of animosity that had been building for some time. Except for the years dominated by the great Bob McWhorter, Heisman's teams had pretty much had their own way with the Bulldogs, having built up a 7–4–1 advantage over the years, so the competition between the two schools remained intense. Furthermore, as Al Thomy points out:

Georgia men were somewhat resentful that Tech continued to field teams during the war years and, in fact, did win the national championship in 1917, not to mention the claiming of back-to-back Southern championships. Heisman made no apologies. He argued that wars should not stop the wheels of everyday life, and he denied discouraging his players from volunteering for service.

Judy Harlan backed up his coach's stand, saying that he volunteered in 1918 along with "just about the whole team" and Heisman said nothing to discourage him.[45]

It was during the student-sponsored victory parade in Athens that all these bad feelings came to a head. There was a series of comic exhibits in the parade that insinuated that Tech men had been slackers during the war years.

Tech officials, including athletic director Dr. J. B. Crenshaw, were outraged, and Crenshaw immediately took steps to break off all athletic relations with the University of Georgia. Heisman reacted as Thomy described, but the bitter feeling between the two schools would last for years, and the football series was not resumed until 1925. Such rivalries were not uncommon now in the South or, for that matter, in other areas of the country. During these years football's biggest intrastate rivalries began to develop, particularly between a state's two largest schools as, for example, LSU–Tulane, Texas–Texas A&M, and Indiana–Purdue. The growing obsession for winning was behind it all, of course, and great care was taken so that schedules could be arranged to accommodate a number of setup games at a season's beginning, leaving the important games for the end of the season, particularly the Big Game with an intrastate rival, usually scheduled as the final game of the season.

After opening up in 1919 against a service team it whipped 48–0, Georgia Tech went through its series of noncontenders, scoring three more shutouts in the process (Furman, 74–0; Wake Forest, 14–0; and Clemson, 28–0). On October 18 came the Yellow Jackets' first real test, against Vanderbilt in Atlanta. The Commodores had a superlative lineman in Josh Cody, but Tech still had its super back Buck Flowers, who scored three touchdowns that day on two punt returns and a long run, leading Tech to a surprisingly easy 20–0 win. It began to look as though Heisman had fashioned yet another powerhouse.

But then came another trip to Pittsburgh and another loss to the Pitt Panthers, this time by a closer score, 16–6. The outcome could have been worse, though, if Tech had not held Pitt on the 6-inch line in a remarkable goal-line stand. The following week, the Yellow Jackets got back in gear by overwhelming their old nemesis Davidson, 33–0, as Buck Flowers ran wild against his old teammates. But then on November 8 Tech was beaten by a southern opponent for the first time since 1914. The victor was Washington and Lee, which managed to kick a last-quarter field goal to win, 3–0.

Having lost two of his last three games, Heisman was thought by some to have lost his coaching touch as well. The players themselves must have sensed by now that some personal problem was eating at their coach, mainly due to his intermittent absences from the practice field. Even when he did show up, he seemed pressured into trying out plays that were so radically new they undermined team cohesiveness. Judy Harlan, in fact, felt that Tech lost the W&L game "because Heisman changed the offense completely during the week of the game and we didn't have a chance to learn it."[46]

Yet as the records reveal, John Heisman had one more surprising maneuver to introduce before he departed Atlanta. It occurred in the next-to-last game of the season, against Georgetown, when the first modern quick-kick in intercollegiate football is reported to have been officially pulled off. The Georgetown Hoyas, who had beaten Navy the week before, came into the game as openly confident as any team could be, and during the early stages of the game they had the Yellow Jackets backed up against their own goal line. Nevertheless, on an obvious punting down, Tech shifted into running formation with Buck Flowers prepared to receive the ball from center. Instead of running with it, he promptly drop-kicked a spiral that seemed to gather more energy as it soared over the surprised Hoya defenders. In fact, the ball did not come to rest until it had landed and rolled dead some eighty-five yards away! The play so completely shocked the Georgetown team that momentum fell Tech's way the rest of the day, resulting in a 27–0 win. The surprise element of the quick-kick would make it a forceful defensive weapon for many years to come, especially for those teams that employed the single-wingback formation.

In later years Flowers credited assistant coach Bill Alexander as having originally proposed the idea of the quick-kick. Flowers, who had honed his basic kicking skills during the two years he was at Davidson, soon caught Alexander's eye when he arrived on campus and, in addition to his running ability, demonstrated an uncanny knack for getting off a punt faster than anyone the assistant coach had ever seen. Everett Strupper, himself one of Tech's all-time backs, described Flowers' all-round abilities as follows:

He was a player without a weakness. . . . A specialist at the difficult business of kicking off, a punter of unequaled precision and consistency, a deadly drop-kicker within 35 yards, an amazing blocker for his inches and poundage, one of the hardest tacklers who ever hit me, a crack passer and an even better pass receiver, a master of knifing thrusts for a few necessary yards, a wizard in the open.[47]

The fact, too, that the quick-kick became a long-standing tradition during Alexander's coaching tenure underscores how instrumental he must have been in its development.

The win over Georgetown was to be Heisman's last at Tech. In spite of being favored by 2–1 odds over Auburn, the Yellow Jackets lost a tough game, 14–7, on Thanksgiving Day, and mistakes played a big part in the outcome. After staking his team to a 7–0 lead on a 42-yard pass play, Judy Harlan went back to punt from behind his own goal line in the second quarter. Sensing that his kick might be blocked by an on-charging Auburn lineman, Harlan deliberately stepped out of bounds to give Auburn a safety, which at this point in the game looked better than the touchdown that might have resulted. But, ironically enough, in the third quarter the Tigers scored on a 35-yard blocked punt play to take an 8–7 lead. The clincher and final insult came in the fourth period when Fatty Warren, the huge Auburn lineman, picked up a fumbled punt and lumbered forty-five yards for a score. Although undefeated W&L put in a claim for the championship, Auburn was declared 1919 champion. For Heisman the game with Auburn, played before the largest crowd ever to see a football game in the South up to that time (fifteen thousand), was a devastating loss, and it must have helped him make up his mind about something that had been bothering him for some time now.

Heisman and his wife had performed in summer stock together many times in the past, but their last act together was to outdo anything they had ever done before. Chip Robert, the former Tech athlete who had played under Heisman and who was now a key member of the school's athletic board, must have realized something was amiss when he received a Sunday morning telephone call from Heisman soon after the close of the football season. The call started out simply enough as an invitation to lunch, but then Heisman indicated he had something else to tell Robert and the members of the board, something about his continuing relationship with Georgia Tech. Sensing the seriousness in Heisman's tone of voice, Robert contacted the other members, who included noted Atlantans George Adair and Lowry Arnold, all of whom had been highly supportive of Heisman and his football program.

Lunch at the Heisman home went pleasantly enough, but soon afterwards Coach Heisman pulled off one of the most dramatic moments of his life when he arose from his chair to announce that he and his wife were in the process of getting a divorce. "There are no hard feelings, however," Heisman continued, "and I have agreed that wherever Mrs. Heisman wishes to live, I will live in another place. This will prevent any social embarrassment. If she decides to stay in Atlanta, I leave."[48]

After the initial shock had subsided, the board members, upon request, helped make an equitable division of some stocks and bonds between the two. Upon learning of Mrs. Heisman's decision to stay in Atlanta, they suddenly realized that they had lost their beloved coach and hastily departed, preparing to announce the startling news to the press.

If the University of Pennsylvania had made any overtures to Heisman to become its new head football coach at this time, a good job had been done in keeping the negotiations a secret. Nevertheless, something of this kind must have been going on behind the scenes, because early in 1920 John Heisman was in Philadelphia making plans to coach the Quakers that fall. The opportunity to coach in the East, particularly at his alma mater, was naturally very appealing to Heisman. Although football had begun to take on more of a national image, the East was still recognized as the hotbed of intercollegiate football. To coach at Penn presented Heisman a golden opportunity to add more laurels to his already illustrious career. His situation also pointed out the growing competition that existed among schools to recruit the services of a proven coach.

THE NATIONAL GAME (1919)

At Harvard, though, Percy Haughton had forsaken the gridiron to apply his management techniques to the world of business, and ex-Crimson player